A GOOD LIFE

LEO HICKMAN

Contents

What is ethical living?

There is a paradox that is beginning to make many of us stop and think: why, when we've never been healthier or wealthier, are we not feeling better about our lives? After all, we should be the happiest generation ever: we work fewer hours than ever before; we have more disposable income; we are better educated; we have access to cheap and plentiful food supplies; we are spared many mundane chores by technology; we have the cushion of a vast social welfare system to catch us when we fall; we have the freedom and means to travel on a whim; we are living longer and we reside in a mature, stable democracy. In theory, we have never had it so good.

So why is it that 'happiness' levels, as recorded by a number of western governments, have not risen in the past 50 years, despite massive increases in personal and state wealth? Why are more and more of us beginning to ask what the cost of the perceived 'advances' in our lives is to our communities, to the environment and to people in less 'developed' nations? In essence, the larger philosophical question that some of us seem to be asking is whether we're really sure that, as a society, we're moving in the right direction.

Ethical living is an attempt to address this paradox. It is not a movement with a strict manifesto or a set of rules. Rather, its aim is simply to promote a mindset that espouses a better awareness and sense of conscience about one's actions. It is about longterm versus shortterm thinking. It is about moving from the 'me' to the 'we' culture. Look up the word 'ethical' in a dictionary and you are likely to find 'following the right course of action' listed as a definition. You will also find a list of synonyms: just, honest, fair, decent, principled, right-minded and honourable. But in the context of this book, 'ethical' means, above all, taking personal responsibility. This, in turn, means considering the 'sustainability' of everything you do – making sure that your actions do not have a negative influence on you or, more importantly, the wider world.

Environmentalists often explain sustainability by referring to our 'ecological footprint' – the amount of land, water and other natural resources required to support our lifestyle. In its *Living Planet Report 2004*, the environmental campaign group WWF said that in 2001 humanity's ecological footprint exceeded global biocapacity by 21 per cent. In other words, we are now using natural resources faster than they can be replenished – something that has been occurring since the 1980s. Furthermore, this figure is an average for the world's population as a whole; the west is consuming resources at a far greater rate. In fact, if the whole world lived as Americans do – per capita, the people with the largest impact – we would need six Earths to meet the demand for natural resources.

This may sound like a theoretical fancy, but much of the world is fast catching up with the west in terms of consumption habits. In recent years, a significant rise in the world's 'consumer class' has been detected. These are people who earn the equivalent of $7,000 or more a year (roughly the official poverty line in the west) and therefore can afford the consumer goods we in the west take for granted, such as televisions, telephones, computers and domestic appliances. More than a quarter of the world's population – 1.7 billion people – now fall into this category. And about a fifth of the world's consumer class live in India and China – the same number as in the US, UK and Germany combined.

As more and more people around the world, rightly or wrongly, aspire to and obtain western lifestyles, the pressure on natural resources will become even more intense. Therefore, a major tenet of ethical living is to attempt, wherever possible, to reduce one's own demand for resources – be it driving less, changing wasteful shopping habits, eating more locally and seasonally produced food, or turning the thermostat on the central heating down. Simply, it is a call to consume a fairer and more proportionate slice of the pie.

But ethical living isn't just about environmental concerns – although they are an extremely significant component of this book's message. Ethical living also attempts to focus on our emotional wellbeing, principally through our relationships with others. This can mean familial, personal and workplace relationships, but it also means wider, more abstract relationships: for example, how best to nurture community relations, or how to look at a product in a shop and relate to the person who produced it.

Professor Lord Layard, an emeritus professor of economics at the London School of Economics, has identified seven key factors that most affect our emotional wellbeing (or 'happiness', as he says). Coming from an economist, you might expect these to include

economic indicators long favoured by governments around the world, such as gross domestic product (GDP, the total value of goods and services produced by a nation over a given period, usually one year), but Layard's factors are of a much more human scale. They are: an adequate income, mental health, satisfying and secure work, a secure and loving private life, a safe community, freedom, and 'moral values' (by which he largely means good citizenship). These, he says, do more to promote wellbeing than money alone ever could – a point he has urged policy-makers to heed. Research has often shown that once people reach an 'adequate' income, additional wealth rarely has any further positive effect on happiness. Instead, it seems that contentment is, in large part, determined by the success of the relationships we make at home, at work and in the community. The more we work to strengthen bonds with one another, understand and alleviate each other's problems and consider everyone's needs, the happier we all become. The message is hardly new — the world's religions have all, in their own ways, urged similar sentiments for centuries — but it is one worth repeating in the increasingly self-serving and stratified society found in the UK today.

Others also agree that we need to assess the quality and success of our lives using indicators that don't simply look to financial and material wealth. The New Economics Foundation (NEF) — an economic, social, and environmental thinktank — also dismisses the usefulness of traditional indicators such as GDP. Instead it proposes a new indicator, the measure of domestic progress (MDP). It aims to reflect progress in quality of life as well as progress towards a sustainable economy by factoring in the social and environmental costs of economic growth, as well as the benefits of unpaid work such as household labour, that are excluded from GDP. Other factors include the cost of crime, the breakdown of families and the loss of farmland to urban development. NEF figures suggest that while GDP per capita in the UK rose by 80 per cent over the past 30 years, MDP fell throughout the 1980s, rose in the late 1990s, but has yet to recapture its 1976 peak. Another sign, therefore, that all is not well.

In short, ethical living is a call for us to counter this trend by leading more considerate, thoughtful lives. As this book shows, it often begins by taking a step back from our everyday actions and reflecting on their longterm legacy. But running through the book are some other recurrent themes:

- **Shopping/acting locally**
- **Rethinking the food you eat**
- **Reducing your energy demands**
- **Considering the impact of travel**
- **Donating your time and money**
- **Alleviating social injustice**
- **Encouraging companies to be more accountable for their actions**
- **Nurturing community spirit**
- **Reducing the impact of toxic chemicals**

A daunting list perhaps, but the good news is that you will not be alone in attempting to tackle it: there is a growing number of like-minded people in the UK and across the world. Research consistently shows that more and more people are adopting the principles of ethical living. For example, according to the *Ethical Consumerism Report 2003*, the total value of ethical consumption in the UK in 2003 was £24.7 billion, a 16.3 per cent rise on the previous year. This total included money spent on ethical banking products, sales of ethical goods and services such as fair trade and organic foods and eco-holidays, as well as the economic value of 'ethical invisibles' such as money spent on public transport for environmental reasons and avoiding 'unethical brands'.

Likewise, in 2004, a *Guardian*/Toyota survey found that two-thirds of respondents saw themselves as 'green' or 'ethical' consumers. Two-fifths said they bought organic or fairly traded food and over half said ethics influenced their choice of purchases ranging from pensions to cars. Fewer than a third believed their personal convenience should take priority over the wellbeing of their community.

Of course, there's often a marked difference between people seeing themselves as being ethically minded and their actual behaviour — something campaigners refer to as the 'action gap'. This book attempts to close this gap by first explaining in detail some of the problems and injustices our habits and lifestyles are causing and then presenting practical solutions to reducing their impact, from eating less meat and lowering car emissions to domestic cleaning advice and ways to volunteer. (Each chapter concludes with a directory containing many companies, services and organisations that can help you make the transition.) But it also aims to instill the belief that rather than being passive automatons pushing trolleys mindlessly around the supermarket, we can actually wield incredible power as shoppers and force positive change. It strives to empower and radicalise readers who still hold firm to apathy's mantra, 'but what difference can I make?'

For once, a book that can guarantee it is a 'good' read.

The 'Best Buys' in the directories at the end of each chapter are compiled by *Ethical Consumer* magazine. Since 1989 it has published more than 300 buyers' guides and over 100 of the guides' Best Buy conclusions have been updated and reproduced in summary form for this book.

To decide if a company should deserve its Best Buy rating, *Ethical Consumer* judges the performance of a company against 16 different ethical criteria. In researching a category, it draws on information in the public domain, as well as from campaign groups such as Greenpeace and Oxfam.

The ethical criteria used for rating companies have changed over time but currently they are: environmental reporting; pollution; nuclear power; 'other' environment (includes involvement in unsustainable forestry practices, habitat destruction and damaging sectors, such as automobile and cement production); oppressive regimes; workers' rights; supplier code of conduct; irresponsible marketing; armaments; animal testing; factory farming; 'other' animal rights (includes ownership of a slaughterhouse and involvement in supplying products requiring the killing of animals); genetic engineering; boycott call; political activity; and 'alert' (includes excessive directors' pay, tax havens and human rights abuses). *Ethical Consumer* ratings also usually include an assessment of the individual product's environmental and social impact.

In September 2004, each category was re-checked by *Ethical Consumer* researchers for inclusion in this book. Best Buys may occasionally recommend some 'problem' companies when they are the least bad in a sector. Best Buys may also occasionally omit some very good companies when there are too many smaller ethical suppliers to list, or when a company was formed since the report was first published.

More information about the rationale behind specific Best Buy categories in this book will, in most cases, appear in the corresponding *Ethical Consumer* buyers' guide. Each buyers' guide also has an accompanying research supplement that explains in further detail the reasons for each element of a company's ethical rating. A range of buyers' guides, an index of all published reports and research supplements, and a detailed explanation of the rating system can be found at www.ethicalconsumer.org.

Ethical Consumer is published by the Ethical Consumer Research Association (ECRA), a not-for-profit workers' co-operative. It costs £21 per year to subscribe to the magazine, which helps to support the organisation's work of promoting change by informing and empowering consumers. To subscribe contact:

Ethical Consumer
ECRA, Unit 21, 41 Old Birley Street,
Manchester M15 5RF
0161 226 2929
www.ethicalconsumer.org

A GOOD LIFE

Food and Drink

Introduction

Looks delicious, doesn't it? A classic cooked breakfast with all the trimmings – sausage, bacon, eggs, buttered toast, tomatoes, beans, mushrooms, all washed down with some coffee and orange juice. And if somehow you're still feeling peckish, how about a poached kipper, bowl of cereal or croissant?

Not exactly an everyday meal, but it's one that illustrates much about what's wrong with the food we eat – and not just in terms of putting on the pounds. Examine each part of the meal separately and there's a story to be told: the North African migrant workers who picked the heavily sprayed tomato in a Spanish field for a pittance; the cows fed GM maize then intensively milked to make the butter; the illegal traces of antibiotics hidden within the battery-farmed egg; the high levels of salt and sugar in the breakfast cereal that's aggressively marketed at children; the artificial 'smoky' flavourings, preservatives and water injected into the bacon to increase profit margins; the greenhouse gases emitted as a result of air-freighting the orange juice from a plantation abroad; the loss of biodiversity caused by growing wheat on an industrial scale for the bread; the coffee farmer in Africa put out of business by giant food companies using their muscle to artificially depress bean prices to keep their shareholders happy; the pressure put on the local landfill site by excessive food packaging; the kipper made from herring stocks, already exhausted by overfishing, polluted with dioxins and PCBs from the North Sea; the hydrogenated fat used to bulk up the croissant. Bon appetit.

In our consumption-led world, food is still the only commodity that we truly must have. We could do without the CDs, the clothes, the new cars, the holidays, but we wouldn't last long without food. Demand is ceaseless. Supply is ceaseless. It's a fact that has led to a world in which farming subsidies make up about half the entire EU budget, 40 per cent of haulage on our roads is food related, and supermarkets and agribusiness giants are now among the world's largest and most powerful companies.

The driving force behind this behemoth is, of course, profit. Not necessarily anything bad in that, but where belts may be tightened and corners cut to increase profit flow in other businesses, with the food industry this invariably leads to problems – for the consumer, the producer and the environment. For example, little, if any, good has ever arisen out of the use of harsh pesticides on crops, artificial additives, sugar, salt and fat being placed in food, or flying vegetables across the globe, except shareholder glee or consumer 'convenience'.

Our choice about what we eat is one of the most important, and most frequent, ethical decisions we can make. It's also a daily choice that arguably has the potential to make the most difference – if approached with consideration – to you, your family and the environment.

So, every time you sit down to eat, ask yourself five key questions:

- How was this food produced?
- How did it get to be on my plate?
- What did it 'cost' me?
- Why did I buy it?
- Is there an alternative?

How was this food produced?

Industry obscuration and poor labelling laws make this a difficult question to answer fully, but it's one that we must nevertheless try asking ourselves. The fact that a survey in 2002 of inner-city school children aged eight to nine in Scotland found that a third of them didn't know that eggs are produced by chickens should help answer why.

The production of food has become so industrialised that many of us have little idea about how food is grown, reared or processed. The steak in a plastic tray wrapped in film on your supermarket shelf tells little of the story about how it was likely to have been 'made' – the diet of antibiotics and pesticide-laden hay fed to the cattle who often spend the entire winter indoors, the mass slaughtering facilities they will pass through, and the multi-billion-pound system of farming grants and EU subsidies that keeps this unsustainable cycle in motion. Even after a decade of food scares, particularly centred on intensive farming practices, a large percentage of us still remain relatively ignorant about the precise nature of how our food is produced.

The wholesale use of pesticides on farms is a good example of where we're going wrong. Pesticides are the 'miracle' of modern farming – they allow higher yields to feed an ever-increasing global population. And it is big business, with over 2.5 million tonnes of pesticides, worth over $30 billion, sprayed on the world's farms each year. Here in the UK, our farmers are the largest users of pesticides in Europe, pouring twice the average amount onto crops, according to the Organisation for Economic Co-operation and Development.

Even though the warning signs have long been plentiful, the true price of pesticide use is only slowly starting to register with the wider public. The World Health Organisation (WHO) estimates that worldwide 220,000 deaths a year are directly caused by pesticide poisoning. In the US, the Smithsonian Migratory Bird Centre says that across the nation pesticides, directly or indirectly, kill 67 million birds a year. And in the UK, when pesticide residues are found in human breastmilk, it understandably makes headlines.

Perhaps we shouldn't be shocked by this legacy. After all, some fertilisers are a by-product of nerve gas development during the second world war.

Industry regulators claim that pesticides are safe to use on farms. But while individual pesticides may be passed as safe as long as they are used within strictly controlled levels, little is known about the so-called 'cocktail effect' (see page 106) – their cumulative reaction with other

chemicals, such as artificial food additives – when inside the body. The truth is that we are the lab rats (rightly, perhaps, as we are the ones making and using these toxic chemicals) and it will be future generations who will truly know the test results.

Future generations may also look back aghast at the current scale and methods of meat production. The UN Food and Agriculture Organisation (UNFAO) reports that, globally, about 51 billion animals were slaughtered in 2003, with 837 million chickens killed in the UK alone (1,592 a minute). That's roughly 10 animals a year for every person on the planet. No wonder that 70 per cent of the world's agricultural land – 80 per cent in the UK – and one third of the world's grain crop, is used to rear livestock. Factor in the 50,000–100,000 litres of water needed to produce one kilo of meat (compared with 900 litres to produce one kilo of wheat) and it is to our shame that we in the west put such pressure on natural resources by being by far the largest consumers of meat with our typically high-protein diet. To put this into even harsher perspective, it takes 24 acres (9.7 hectares) of land to sustain an American, nine acres (3.6 hectares) an Italian and just under an acre (0.4 hectares) for an Indian.

But this is only half the story of how our food is made. A large percentage of that virgin produce from our farms is packed off to a factory where, behind closed doors, it is processed into convenience foods, such as readymeals, takeaways and snacks. This part of the food industry grew by 400 per cent in the 1990s. And convenience foods have become increasingly alluring to consumers in developing nations: a third of the world's obese people –

a strong indicator of heavy consumption of highly processed foods – are now found in the developing world. This is due to the high – many say addictive – levels of salt, sugar and saturated (animal) fat found in most convenience foods. On top of this, a panoply of artificial additives, such as flavourings, colourings and preservatives, are often added to processed foods, again causing a host of reported side-effects. Children are especially vulnerable, with many suffering allergic reactions, hypertension and asthma attacks.

As uncomfortable as it is to confront the truth about how the food we eat is produced, as more and more revelations surface about methods used, it is essential that we do face up to it if we are to move away from such an unsustainable system.

How did it get to be on my plate?
The term 'food miles' has become something of a green movement catchphrase in recent years – and rightly so. Its intention is to raise awareness that 45 per cent of our food in the UK is imported from abroad – much of it transported many thousands of miles for our convenience, often by plane with all the greenhouse gas emissions this entails. Over half, 56 per cent, of the organic produce we buy is also imported.

In only a generation we have lost touch with the fact that fruit and vegetables grow seasonally, such is the year-round omnipresence of strawberries, asparagus and peas on our supermarket shelves – produce that was once savoured as a summer treat.

The problem of food miles-related pollution is clear:

It takes **50,000–100,000 litres** of water to produce one kg of meat but just **900 litres** to produce one kg of wheat

a kiwi fruit flown from New Zealand to Britain leads to five times its own weight in greenhouse gas emissions. But other, less obvious problems also exist. The more we truck, ship and fly our food before it reaches our plate, the more it loses its vital nutrients and the more we need to treat it with toxic chemicals such as fungicides to keep it 'fresh'. Food miles also increasingly tie the food we eat to the oil economy, a situation that could prove catastrophic should oil supplies become threatened. And the more a food is transported, the more it needs to be protected with packaging, which is rarely recycled and ends up costing the consumer more. One sixth of what we pay in the UK for food goes on packaging – a staggering £470 per household per year.

But it's not just imported food that is guilty of clocking up the miles. The extremely centralised distribution network of UK supermarkets means that while we may live a few miles from where the food we buy is grown or reared, before it appears on a supermarket shelf near us, it may have travelled hundreds of miles being packaged, processed and re-distributed. According to a Friends of the Earth survey in 2002, supermarkets now classify 'local' food as that grown in the UK.

What did it 'cost' me?

Sounds like an easy one to answer at first. Whatever it says on the label, surely? Perhaps, but many campaigners are now starting to raise awareness about the hidden costs of much of our food – obesity and other health concerns, price-inflating cartels, subsidies and monopolies, the cost of cleaning up pesticide pollution, wasteful and expensive packaging and, as just mentioned, the expenditure and pollution of excessive transportation.

A quick glance at the basic economics of contemporary farming reveals why the sums don't add up – except for the supermarkets, of course. Take a savoy cabbage. It costs 13p to grow one, but the farmer will earn only 11p when selling it to a wholesaler. The shortfall, in theory, is made up by farming subsidies. However, we will pay 47p for it at the supermarket. As subsidies are paid for via taxation, we are, in effect, paying for the cabbage twice.

Take another example – the cow. For each cow reared within the EU, the farmer receives about €2 a day in subsidies. Perversely, that's more than the daily income of 75 per cent of Africans.

But that's not the end of it. We, the taxpayer, will also have to pay for the land and waterways to be cleaned by organisations such as the Environment Agency, the public body with the responsibility of looking after the 'air, land and water' in England and Wales, due to pesticide run-off from farms. In fact, £120 million is spent annually removing pesticide residues from our drinking water; to put this in perspective, the whole UK pesticide market is worth £500 million.

And the farming community is often just as short-changed as the consumer, despite receiving £3 billion worth of subsidies a year. For every pound spent on food at supermarkets, just 9p makes it back to the farmer. Fifty years ago, this was nearer 50–60p.

30 per cent of cancers in the west are linked to dietary factors

More importantly, however, is the cost much of our food is placing on our health. With about 30 per cent of cancers in the west linked to dietary factors, it is clear the food we eat is literally killing us – especially when you consider that much of our diet is nutritionally poor and highly processed. In the US, 325,000 deaths a year are attributed to obesity – more than are caused by road accidents, illegal drugs, alcohol and firearms combined. Never have we been further away from the maxim, 'Eat yourself well.'

Why did I buy it?

Another seemingly simple question. How about because I'm hungry? Sadly, the days when we ate food solely because we required sustenance are long gone. Now there are an array of other influences on our decision-making, ranging from convenience and social pressure to targeted advertising and clever marketing tricks.

Take 'convenience'. In a world where the average mealtime in McDonald's is 11 minutes and where the average British family spends more time in the car than around the dining table, food that requires minimal preparation and cooking is king. The 'readymeal' is the answer to every time-poor, stressed-out worker, who has little time in the evening to bath their children, let alone prepare a meal from scratch.

Reminding that worker slumped in front of the TV at the end of a hard day that they must buy that readymeal, takeaway or snack are adverts – dozens of them – night after night. For example, McDonald's spends more than $1 billion a year globally on advertising, Coca-Cola $800 million. And working in tandem with this battering ram are the supermarkets with alluring loyalty reward cards and 'two-for-one' offers, together with the food manufacturers exploiting every labelling loophole in the book to disguise the true contents of their food within slick, inviting packaging.

Sadly, children are targeted just as assiduously as adults, but with 'pester power' a near-universal problem for parents, it's little comfort to know that 95 per cent of food advertising on children's primetime television (usually fronted by heroes such as football stars) is for products that are high in fat, salt and sugar.

Are we buying food because we want it, or because we are being told to? It's sometimes hard to know.

Is there an alternative?

Thankfully, yes. Putting more thought and effort into what you eat is a vital, if not inseparable, part of ethical living. This begins when we're shopping. The more we all choose to avoid goods produced in the way described above, the more the farmers, supermarkets and government will listen and be forced to alter their habits. In the first instance, this means choosing more fair-trade and organic products. But there are also more subtle ways to change the status quo: buy only locally grown, seasonal produce; boycott firms you know use unethical practices; support firms who are now trying to improve their practices; choose local shops over giant supermarket chains.

And there's a lot you can do at home: cut back on your meat intake; keep up to date with the methods and practices of a fast-evolving food industry; avoid foods that contain high levels of salt, sugar, fats and additives; investigate whether a local box scheme could supply your fruit and vegetables; grow your own produce in a window box or small patch; take children to visit an organic farm; explain to firms in writing why you no longer support them, copying in your MP.

Fruit and veg

The advice from health professionals is consistent and straightforward: eat five portions of fruit and vegetables a day – equal to 400g – to help yourself stay healthy. The truth is that, on average, we eat nearer three. This figure is even more depressing when we learn that we should actually be eating nine portions a day, according to nutrition researchers at Cambridge University. The reason we're not told this, it seems, is because there's a fear that we would ignore the advice if confronted by such a high total.

But as important as our low fruit and vegetable intake is the way in which we consume it. According to government figures released each year about typical food consumption in the UK, we are now eating fewer green vegetables and more fruit 'products', ie processed foods containing fruit. In 1975, for example, we ate over 341g of fresh green vegetables a week, whereas in 2002/03 the figure stood at just 231g. In comparison, in 1975 we ate just 228g of fruit 'products' a week. In 2002/03 that weekly figure had risen to 413g.

Thankfully, it's not an issue that is being ignored – fresh fruit and vegetables are now distributed free at most primary schools and 'Healthy Start' vouchers worth at least £2.80 a week are being introduced from 2005 to encourage low-income families to buy more fresh fruit and vegetables. (In 2002/03, the average household spend on fresh fruit and vegetables each week was £5.40. In contrast, £5.50 was spent on buns, cakes, biscuits, chocolate and soft drinks.)

But while encouragement and assistance from the state is welcome, much of the responsibility remains with us. So rule number one when it comes to eating fruit and vegetables is quite simple – just eat more of the stuff. You will be more healthy for it, you should require less medical help later in life (many studies now show consuming fresh fruit and vegetables reduces the risk of heart diseases and certain cancers) and you will be giving less money to the processed food industry (see page 48).

To eat ethically, it's not just a case of consuming more fruit and vegetables, but also asking other questions of the produce we eat: Who grew my apple, for example? Who picked it? Where and how was it transported? Was it sprayed with pesticides? Is it currently the right season for such produce?

Four key things – all of them interconnected and all driven overwhelmingly by market desire to 'satisfy' you, the consumer – should be in the forefront of your mind when buying fruit and vegetables:

● Pesticide residues
● Food miles
● Grower and picker rights
● Seasonality

Pesticide residues

Fruit and vegetables are always the first things greeting you as you step into a supermarket, aren't they? They all look so perfect and inviting – much more so than the washing powder or tins of beans. But too perfect? It seems that we're a picky bunch. The supermarkets say that we want our produce to be blemish-free, in plentiful supply and available all year round to fit in with our high-convenience, fast-paced life. To meet these demands, supermarkets put extreme pressure on their suppliers to supply perfectly formed produce, which in turn puts the pressure all the way down the food chain to deliver.

In the UK, this pressure is felt most acutely by farmers. To keep the supermarkets happy (there are no contracts here; usually just week-by-week, verbal 'deals' that the supermarkets can, and do, renege on at will) the farmer works hard to produce 'perfect' produce, or face much of it being rejected during the dreaded 'grade out' – the process by which supermarkets inspect, often with electronic scanning equipment, produce for quality of appearance and 'feel'.

To reduce the risk of blemishes and misshapen produce, farmers typically rely on a range of pesticides. To keep yields up, fertilisers are also used. Generations ago, farmers would have used 'natural methods' such as crop rotation, but since the second world war more and more farmers have relied on synthetic chemical pesticides and fertilisers. Ironically, this period is often labelled 'the green revolution' – the damaging effect of which was one of the main catalysts for the birth of the organic farming movement (see page 26). As the years have gone on, the more damaging these chemicals appear to be – to the farmers who handle them, to the environment to which they are applied, and to the consumers who eat them via their food.

Cumulative distance travelled by 20 items of fresh food in a shopping basket was a staggering **100,943 miles** – just under half the distance to the moon

And the evidence grows all the time: a study in 2003 by scientists at the University of Lancaster showed that organophosphorus pesticides – banned some 15–20 years ago – are still detectable in our blood today. ICI, which initially developed them as nerve agents during the second world war, had a surplus after the war and lobbied hard for them to be subsidised and given as agrochemicals to farmers. In 2001, the University of North Carolina conducted a study of over 700 women living near crops sprayed with certain pesticides and found they faced a 40–120 per cent increased risk of miscarriage or birth defects.

These findings were compounded in late 2003, when the supreme court in Florida awarded a US family $7 million in damages after their son was born with empty eye sockets in 1990. The judges accepted that the agrochemical Benlate was to blame after it was proved the boy's mother had walked past a field being sprayed with Benlate when seven weeks pregnant. It was the first time in legal history that a chemical company – in this instance, Du Pont – had been found guilty of causing birth defects. Benlate was used for years on farms and in gardens in the UK to control fungal infections until Du Pont took it off the market in 2001.

But it's not just humans that suffer, indirectly or directly, from pesticide and fertiliser use. Our natural waterways and drinking water sources are contaminated by run-off from fields. Nitrates, used as fertilisers, are a particular problem. The underground water that feeds our springs and rivers and provides a third of our drinking water is becoming seriously polluted with nitrates, causing a threat to wildlife and landing us with growing water bills as more needs to be spent on purification. Nitrates cause 'blue baby' syndrome and prevent the blood from carrying oxygen, so they must be removed from the water if it is to be safe to drink. In streams, rivers and lakes they continue acting as a fertiliser, causing algae to multiply rapidly: a problem known as eutrophication. Fish may be smothered when the oxygen is used up, and when the algae turn toxic, wildlife and farm animals may be poisoned. In 2003, water companies said that consumers, who were already paying £7 each a year to remove nitrates and pesticides, could expect the amount to rise to £25 or more over the next five years.

Pesticides are not, therefore, just bad for your health, they're also bad for your pocket. So, as a consumer, it is best practice to make every effort not only to exclude pesticide residues from your diet, but also to boycott the multi-billion-pound agrochemical industry that produces and markets them. The only realistic way to do this – other than growing your own and following government advice to 'top and tail' and wash everything – is to eat organically grown produce (see page 26).

Food miles

To illustrate how acute the problem of food miles has become, in 2003 the *Guardian* bought a basket of fresh food containing 20 items. It included pears from

Dilemma

Should I eat the NZ organic apple, the Kent non-organic apple, or the Fairtrade apple from South Africa?

The simple answer is all of them, but it depends where your priorities lie.

Friends of the Earth now annually highlights the plight of UK apple farmers saying that retailers need to start supporting homegrown apples more. If not, the accelerating loss of orchards will affect biodiversity on our farmed land, rural economies will suffer yet further and even more food miles will be burned. In its 2003 survey of the apple market, it found that just 38 per cent of apples sold in supermarkets were grown in the UK. It also found a poor range of varieties on offer with just 14 British varieties on sale in supermarkets. In contrast, 28 varieties were found on market stalls.

The survey also revealed that homegrown apples from market stalls (including farmers' markets) were actually cheaper than at supermarkets, despite the ever-present price wars. The average price of a kilo of Cox apples in the supermarkets was £1.18 whereas at the local market it was just £1.02.

Therefore, when in season, buy your apples from local market stalls, or direct from farmers where possible. Outside the British apple season (which runs from the end of July through, if cold stores are used, to the following April), if you must have an imported apple, your choice should be limited to either organic or Fairtrade (see page 60). Both have the major disadvantage of needing to be transported from afar. However, both are a better choice than imported non-organic apples that may have been sprayed up to 35 times with pesticides.

If only because of the lesser distance they need to travel, you should probably favour Fairtrade apples from South Africa, if you can find them, over the more available organic ones from New Zealand. Fairtrade apples have been available to buy in the UK since 2003. They are grown by South African farmers who are part of the Thandi Initiative. This was launched in 2002 by the Capespan Foundation as part of the South African government's land transformation programme. It encourages joint ownership and empowerment through 'capacity building' (improving local social capital) in the country's fruit industry. The Thandi Initiative also supplies Fairtrade seedless grapes, oranges and lemons. (NB. Fairtrade farmers around the world are encouraged to farm sensitively with regard to pesticides and the environment. Some are even certified organic.)

Argentina, garden peas from South Africa, tomatoes from Saudi Arabia and lettuce from Spain. The cumulative distance travelled by the contents of the basket was a staggering 100,943 miles – just under half the distance to the moon.

How did we reach this state of affairs? The simple answer is globalisation. In the search for better profits, supermarkets look far and wide for suppliers who will supply what they need to give to consumers, at the right price and time. If that means air-freighting green beans from Kenya rather than trucking them in from a farm in Suffolk, then so be it. The fact that air fuel isn't taxed (see page 156) only adds to the allure of air-freighting.

Of course, we, the consumers, are to blame, too. Our tastes have become more exotic – just think of the metropolitan trend for Thai curries in the 1990s that required an all-year supply of ingredients grown far from our shores, such as lemongrass, chillies and ginger. And so the supermarkets have battled to give us what we want. As a result, the choice we have is incredible, with more than 40,000 different products available to us at some larger stores.

But this choice comes with a big price tag – a huge increase in food transportation-related pollution. The food chain's contribution to the UK's annual greenhouse gas emissions is at least 20 per cent.

Spotlight

Variety is the spice of life

One fruit has come to symbolise the sad lack of variety we are now offered by the supermarket – the strawberry. Traditionally a treat in the early summer months, it is now available all year round thanks to cutting-edge growing technology, packaging and air-freighting.

But a single variety of strawberry – Elsanta – now dominates the market, boasting an incredible 80 per cent share. Despite the fact that it isn't rated at all for its flavour, it is popular with the supermarkets simply because it stores and travels well, an essential asset for all produce today.

It's a sad state of affairs. Strawberries have a strong heritage in the UK: the wild wood strawberry is one of our classic indigenous fruits. As explorers returned from their foreign travels in previous centuries so the number of varieties grew. Hundreds now exist, with weird and wonderful names – Keens' Imperial, Royal Sovereign, Honeoye, My Girl – but they're rarely eaten, or even seen by shoppers.

Even so, we shouldn't cast these varieties into the history books. Diversity is one of nature's most potent forms of self-defence and maintaining plentiful plant varieties is one of the best ways of

discovering new disease- and pest-resistant varieties. Even more importantly, keeping an abundance of plant varieties available to medical researchers could make all the difference in finding cures for human ailments such as cancer.

Scientists fear that the trend towards monoculture, in which one or two high-yield varieties dominate, will mean older types are lost. The practice of monoculture led to almost a million deaths during the Irish potato famine because the predominant strain of potato was blighted.

Hampering diversity is the Plant Varieties Act of 1997. Under this act, every new variety must be patented and then annually renewed – an expensive process that only large companies can afford. It is illegal for a hobby gardener who creates a new variety in their greenhouse to sell it on without such a patent.

For more information about how plant varieties are being saved, visit the Millennium Seed Bank Project at www.kew.org/msbp.

For information about the Plant Varieties Act 1997, visit www.defra.gov.uk/planth/pvs.

Air-freighting food from abroad is top of the list of concerns for those who campaign against food miles. How can it make sense, they say, that for every calorie of carrot flown in from South Africa, 66 calories of fuel will be expended? Or that for every 100 items of fruit consumed in any one day, only five will have been grown in the UK? Or that for every kilo of blueberries flown in from New Zealand, over 10kg of carbon dioxide (CO_2) will be emitted?

The answer, of course, is to buy local produce where possible – and local means local, not just 'British grown' as classified by the supermarkets. Because of the way supermarkets distribute food – everything passing through a centralised point, often more than once, to be packaged and then sent to stores – produce is largely moved around the UK by truck, with only a shameful one per cent of food moved by train. Where possible, buy your fruit and vegetables via local greengrocers, farmers' markets, farm shops or box schemes. These will be sourced from farms directly or via the wholesale markets that supply greengrocers and restaurants. The supermarkets now largely strike their own exclusive deals with 'preferred' growers, therefore the two worlds rarely cross over. It's a battle for our custom they seem to be winning hands down: supermarkets now account for 80 per cent of the nation's fruit and vegetable sales, whereas in the 1970s, 90 per cent of fresh produce in the UK was sold via greengrocers and market stalls.

If you are in a supermarket, though, look for produce that has travelled from within mainland Europe, rather than farther afield, as it has more than likely arrived by ship or truck, both of which are much less polluting than planes. Another, often overlooked reason to buy local food is that it will contain more nutrients. Spinach, for example, can lose up to 90 per cent of its vitamin C in the 24 hours after harvest.

Finally, one extra thing to consider when weighing up the pros and cons of food miles: in which country has the produce been grown? If part of ethical living is to shun companies that are acting in a negative way, then consider avoiding food grown in countries ruled by oppressive regimes, or that have been cited for committing human rights abuses, or who act aggressively towards others.

There's no broadbrush solution to this dilemma: for every person who is unsettled by, say, Israel's relationship with its neighbours, there'll be another who will support that country's stance – and buy its produce. (Interestingly, because the EU and Israel disagree whether the occupied territories should be eligible for preferential EU import tariffs, supermarkets now have to differentiate produce grown in 'Gaza' and 'Israel'.) But before deciding to boycott produce from any offending country, remember that your actions may simply punish the country's farmers and not its leaders. Therefore, only support a boycott if the farmers (or pickers) themselves are calling for it.

Grower and picker rights

'The supermarkets have pretty much got an arm-lock on you at the moment.'

These were the words of Tony Blair as he addressed farmers at Hartpury College, an agricultural college in Gloucestershire. The foot-and-mouth epidemic of 2001 was at its height. Here was a prime minister acknowledging, for the first time in public, that supermarkets hold a dominant and often crippling grip on their food suppliers.

Unsurprisingly, the supermarkets hit back. The response from Asda's spokesperson was typical of other supermarkets. 'We are too busy working for our customers to pay much attention to what Tony Blair said. If he wants to play politics and scrabble around looking for scapegoats then that is down to him. We were under the impression that it was the Ministry of Agriculture, and not the supermarkets, which set agri-policy in this country.'

And then there's the farmer, caught between the demands of giant supermarkets and government policy. Many British farmers struggle to earn a living wage: in 2003, the average income for farmers in the north-east of England, for example, fell beneath £10,000 a year.

But don't farmers in Europe do very well out of subsidies and grants? After all, half of the entire EU budget is spent on agricultural subsidies. And, as many campaigners point out, doesn't the current system, while artificially supporting farmers in the west, only suppress farmers in developing nations further still? An editorial in the *Guardian* in 2004 – sparked by news that some of the country's richest landowners receive hundreds of thousands of pounds a year in subsidies – illustrated the unjust system that underpins, yet grossly distorts, worldwide food production:

'Subsidies worked wonders in solving the post-war food shortages, but they have long outlived their usefulness. It is morally wrong and economically mad to pay farmers to produce unwanted surpluses that are dumped, thanks to export subsidies, at artificially low prices on the Third World, thereby putting their farmers out of business. Oxfam claims that UK subsidies (minus levies) in 2002 were £2.6 billion, which was more than the total income from farming. The madness reaches farcical proportions with sugar beet, a product that costs more than twice as much to produce in Europe as the cane sugar grown in tropical regions, but in which Europe has cornered the world market. Why? Could it be anything to do with the fact that sugar farmers receive £740 in subsidy for each hectare farmed and – wait for it – import restrictions keep EU prices three

Dilemma

Should I support a consumer boycott?

At any one time there will be dozens of consumer boycotts taking place around the world for a wide variety of reasons. Oil companies, supermarkets, DIY chains, fast-food giants, cruise-ship operators, airlines, fashion labels, entertainment corporations, soft-drink multinationals, banks — the list of sectors, firms and even countries targeted is long. They become the focus of a consumer boycott because, in the eyes of some, their practices are unethical; either they are damaging to the environment, oppressive to workers, cruel to animals, leading to a monopoly, supporting an unsavoury political regime — again, the list is long. The aim, of course, is to hit where it hurts the most: sales.

But do consumer boycotts work? And should they be supported? They can certainly work. Many groups have won spectacular successes against hugely powerful corporations. Two of the most memorable are Greenpeace's 1995 campaign against Shell sinking its Brent Spa oil platform in the North Sea, and the student boycott of Barclays Bank for its involvement in South Africa during apartheid. But consumer boycotts should never be supported blindly. It is essential that you research precisely why a boycott has been called, and who by. For example, organisations such as Cafod and Oxfam are concerned that boycotts of companies involved in workers' rights abuses could potentially put the workers' livelihoods at risk. These types of boycotts should, therefore, only be supported if the workers themselves are calling for it.

There is also little point supporting a boycott if you do not tell the firm why you are boycotting their products or services, otherwise they may remain ignorant of your actions, or put the decline in sales down to 'competitive market forces', as has been done in the past to deflect negative publicity. Boycotts should be just one of several techniques used to urge a firm to change its negative actions. You should also write to the company's directors, sign petitions, join non-violent protests, encourage shareholder revolts and lobby your MP to put down an Early Day Motion (see www.theyworkforyou.com and http://edm.ais.co.uk) or apply governmental pressure in support of your cause.

For more information about boycotts, including a list of current campaigns, visit www.ethicalconsumer.org. Also look at www.karmabanque.com.

times higher than world market levels? Globally, agriculture receives a startling $300 billion a year in subsidies. If they were abolished, everyone in the Organisation for Economic Co-operation and Development (OECD) would get the equivalent of a cashback of over $200 and the developing world would get the biggest economic boost it has ever had. In Britain, subsidies cost the taxpayer over £3 billion a year. The real solution is to abolish all agricultural subsidies. But until the world accepts its duty, they should at least be transparent and capped so the fat cats do not once again take the cream.'

It is this unethical system that has been the catalyst for the Fairtrade movement — a way for consumers to know that a guaranteed, fair price has been paid directly to the farmer, invariably in a developing nation (see page 60).

Hunting down the Fairtrade mark when shopping is a big step in helping to end the oppression on many of the world's farmers. Equally, to support British farmers, it is best, as ever, to buy as directly and as locally as possible, be it through farmers' markets, farm shops or box schemes.

One caveat: it is always worth remembering under what conditions your fruit and vegetables were picked. Increasingly, we are reading headlines about the 'gangmasters' who force migrant workers to labour in bad conditions, tragically illustrated by the death of 21 cockle-pickers in Morecambe Bay in 2004. While there's usually no way of knowing if your produce has passed through such a system, it pays to know about the practices of your local farmers. Following the tragedy, the Gangmasters Licensing Act was introduced to ensure that labour providers had to be licensed. However, abuses are still being reported.

But bad pay is also a huge issue, and one worth urging your MP to campaign against. In 2004 the Transport and General Workers' Union highlighted a case where migrant workers packing fruit for a supermarket were left with wages of just 78p a week after their gangmaster had deducted 'rent and transport costs'.

Seasonality

'Many consumers have simply given up buying pricey items such as plums, strawberries, peaches and apricots entirely because they are such a dismal let-down. The frisson of excitement that true seasonality provides, and the appetite-whetting response it should generate, are absent. Inspiration is shrivelled, for example, by the stultifying knowledge that whether it's March, July or November, you will always find grapes in the middle of gondola three, on aisle number two, and they will always be Thomson Seedless.'

From *Shopped: The Shocking Powers of British Supermarkets*, by Joanna Blythman (Fourth Estate, 2004).

We are often told by the supermarkets – and we believe them – that we are spoilt for choice when it comes to the range of fruit and vegetables available to us all year round. We've never had it so good, they say. But, as the food campaigner and writer Joanna Blythman illustrates above, it's an illusion that consumers are starting to wake up to.

Blythman has coined the term 'PGST', or Permanent Global Summertime, to describe the nature-defying way in which supermarkets are forever stocked with produce that was once savoured and cherished for just a few weeks or months a year when 'in season'. Because herbs can be flown in from Israel, or plums from South Africa, we have lost touch with the natural growing cycles of this country. We have forgotten what an apple fresh off the tree actually tastes like. Instead, while we may have access to all manner of fruit and vegetables at all times, by the time it reaches us

from the other side of the globe, it has lost much of its taste and nutrients.

Even though we now blithely accept that our food is flown in from Spain, Egypt, Thailand – name your place – it is also starting to affect how produce is grown here in the UK. Since 1999, over 2,000 hectares of Herefordshire, Kent and parts of Scotland have been given over to polytunnels. The steel-framed structures are erected each spring to protect vulnerable crops and are taken down again after the last crop in November. Up to 80 per cent of British summer fruit is now grown under plastic for up to six months of the year.

Polytunnel advocates say they enable food to be grown in the UK that would otherwise be flown in from abroad. Furthermore, produce can be grown with a reduced need for pesticides. Critics say they are ruining the look of the countryside. However, polytunnels are also further distancing us from the natural seasons and changing our perceptions of what should be available to eat through the year. In addition, they are further industrialising our farms. In 2004, S&A Produce, one of the UK's largest strawberry growers, had an application to build a village of 300 mobile homes in Herefordshire for its migrant pickers turned down following complaints from locals. The newspaper headlines highlighted the fact that most of the workers would be coming from eastern Europe but the real issue was the proposed scale of the farm, not untypical now in the UK. The company had submitted plans to cultivate 81 hectares (200 acres) producing 3,000 tonnes of fruit a year, grown entirely under plastic. The application also specified there would be 450 lorry movements through the nearby hamlet of Brierley Court near Leominster over the 150-day harvest period. (Strawberries, remember, naturally have only a two-month harvest season).

As consumers, we would all benefit from a return to eating seasonal, local food. It would cut back on the extravagant amounts of greenhouse gases emitted through air freight. It would help struggling local farmers. But above all, it would reintroduce us to more nutritional, tastier food as well as helping us to reconnect with the people that produce our food – and, most importantly, the food itself.

A calendar of British seasonal produce

January The winter months are the time to enjoy British root vegetables as well as local fruit that has been stored in cold, dry and dark conditions from the previous autumn's harvest. Being harvested this month are leeks, green cabbages, parsnips, turnips, sprouts, celeriac, Jerusalem artichokes, shallots, mushrooms and forced rhubarb. From cold store, you can buy British apples and pears, beetroot and potatoes. Main crop carrots are either stored in the ground or kept in cold store to be available from September till the end of May. Onions are available most of the year.

February Winter root crops are still going strong. This is the month for early winter cauliflower, leeks, turnips, spinach grown under cloches, swede, celeriac, chard, forced rhubarb, and carrots. Potatoes, apples and pears are available from store. The Brussels sprout season comes to an end. Mushrooms are available most of the year.

March New crops of vegetables planted the previous year come into season, including purple sprouting broccoli, more cauliflower, spring greens, radishes, parsley, early rhubarb, and leeks. Carrots are available both from the ground and from store but beetroot from store is finishing. Potatoes, apples and pears are available from store.

April Stored British crops start finishing in the middle of the month, but new crops are not in full flow. Mid-April to mid-June is the leanest time – the so-called 'hungry gap'. But new season's lettuce and watercress come in, along with some overwintered spinach, and more radishes and purple sprouting broccoli. Rhubarb is in too. Carrots and potatoes are still available from store but apples and pears are finishing.

May This is the leanest month, as winter crops finish and stores decline. But coming in are the first new potatoes and asparagus. Radishes are available. Carrots and potatoes are still in store but winter cauliflower and spinach come to an end. Rhubarb is available. (Incidentally, the very end of the month sees the first outdoor-reared, grass-fed spring lambs come into season.)

June By the middle of the month, there is a wealth of fruit and vegetables to choose from. New potatoes are more plentiful, asparagus continues. New carrots come in at the end of month as do soft fruits including blackcurrants, strawberries, gooseberries and cherries. Tomatoes are in, broccoli is beginning, and cauliflower comes at the back end of the month. Lettuce gets into full flow as do fennel, peppers, broad beans, Chinese leaves, and green beans grown in tunnels. Herbs are coming in.

July Another peak month, with strawberries, loganberries, redcurrants, blackcurrants, tayberries, summer cabbage, spring cabbage, new potatoes, courgettes, broad beans, fennel, the first outdoor French beans, tomatoes, watercress, new cauliflower, carrots, lettuce, cucumber and broccoli.

August Vegetables and soft fruits continue. Tree fruits come in at the end of the month. Lettuce, peppers, new potatoes, courgettes, leeks, sweetcorn, peas, aubergines, strawberries, loganberries, gooseberries, herbs, chard, courgettes, fennel, main crop carrots and broccoli are all in. Onions are being harvested and will be stored through the winter. The first apples and Victoria plums are picked at end of month, just as the season for venison from wild fallow and red deer begins.

September A good month for fruit, and summer vegetables are joined by the earliest of winter ones. Blackberries, early apples, damsons, early pears, plums, spinach, figs, onions, all of the cabbages, curly kale, cucumbers, lettuce, tomatoes, French beans, courgettes, red onions, peppers, aubergines, marrows, sweetcorn, leeks, red cabbage, beetroot and broccoli are in. Swedes come back and Brussels sprouts begin. Main crop potatoes are lifted in September and October and stored until the beginning of the next year's summer months.

October This is the main season for apples and pears. The first Bramleys are in season. Also available are sweetcorn, marrrow, mushrooms, beetroots, squash, watercress, onions and leeks. The Jerusalem artichoke season begins, while cauliflowers are at their peak, as are main crop potatoes and carrots, sprouts, and broccoli. Lettuce is running out by the middle of the month, and courgettes finish towards the end.

November Tender vegetable crops are disappearing as the frosts arrive, but still going are cabbage, cauliflower, potatoes, carrots, leeks, swede, parsnips, apples, pears, quinces, and sprouts.

December It's back to winter vegetables and stores, with Brussels sprouts, turnips, swede and parsnips available and potatoes, carrots, red cabbage, beetroot, apples and pears coming from store.

NB. Produce grown with artificial light and heat not included.

EXPLAINER Organic food

What exactly does 'organic' mean?

In 2003, sales of organic food topped £1 billion for the first time, making the UK the world's third largest market for organic produce after the US and Germany. But what is organic food?

Applied to many things and used widely, the term 'organic' literally means something relating to, or derived from, living organisms. However, in the case of food production it means something quite specific. In fact, a food manufacturer can break the law by misusing the term. As such — and a little confusingly — there are now 10 official organic certification bodies in the UK, each with subtly different methodologies and criteria for what, in their eyes, can claim to be 'organic'.

To provide a broad philosophical overview of what constitutes organic food production, the World Health Organisation and UN Food and Agriculture Organisation have jointly defined it as 'a holistic production management system which promotes and enhances agro-ecosystem health, including biodiversity, biological cycles, and soil biological activity. The primary goal of organic agriculture is to optimise the health and productivity of interdependent communities of soil life, plants, animals and people.'

Organic production, therefore, can be said to acknowledge a natural symbiosis that conventional agriculture, by and large, does not take into account. It is seen by proponents as offering a more sustainable method of production.

To achieve this, organic production severely restricts the use of artificial chemicals, fertilisers and pesticides routinely used in conventional farming. Genetically modified (GM) materials are also excluded. In the case of livestock husbandry, organic farming also prohibits the routine use of antibiotics and hormones.

In Britain, overall responsibility for regulating organic food production, as well as the different certifying bodies, lies with the UK Register of Organic Food Standards (UKROFS) which is under the control of the Department for the Environment, Food and Rural Affairs (Defra). UKROFS ensures that the term 'organic' is correctly applied to every stage of production — from growing or importing food, to processing it. But it is the

task of the certifying bodies to inspect farmers and manufacturers at least once a year to make sure they are following UKROFS rules, as well as meeting their own standards.

Critics of the organic movement often highlight the fact that there are hundreds of certification bodies around the world, each with subtly different criteria for judging what can and cannot be called organic. Since 1993, organic food produced within the EU has had to meet the criteria set down by the EU Organic Regulation. A limited number of countries outside the EU are recognised as having an equivalent system and their food may be freely imported and sold. For other countries the importer must demonstrate that the food has been produced to organic standards equivalent to the EU Organic Regulation.

The unifying authority for the global organic farming movement is the International Federation of Organic Agriculture Movements (IFOAM), based in Bonn, Germany.

How does organic farming differ from conventional farming?

UKROFS standards define the organic production system as one that is 'designed to produce optimum quantities of food of high nutritional quality by using management practices which aim to avoid the use of agrochemical inputs and which minimise damage to the environment and wildlife'. This system relies on crop rotation, cover crops and compost to keep the soil enriched. Between harvests, organic farmers will plough in their cover crops, typically clover or rye, to replenish nitrogen levels in the soil.

It is a system that is gaining more and more of a following. From just 900 organic producers a few years ago, there are now more than 4,000. About 40 farmers convert to organic farming in the UK each month.

Not all organic farms are exclusively organic. But where farmers raise both non-organic and organic livestock they must be physically, financially and operationally separate. Similarly, in terms of food processing and distribution, organic produce must be kept completely separate from non-organic produce. Few abattoirs, for example, are fully organic, but they will dedicate certain days to the slaughter of organic livestock.

Does organic mean pesticide-free?
The answer, in short, is no. However, rules are exceptionally strict for organic farmers. More than 450 pesticides have been passed for use on conventional farms by Defra in the UK, whereas only a handful have been authorised by IFOAM. In the UK, just two — soft soap and sulphur — can be used without prior permission.

How do I know with certainty that produce is organic?
Look for the 'UK' code, followed by a number, on the packaging. Each of the certifying bodies is assigned a number. Most of us recognise the Soil Association logo, as it is found on over 70 per cent of organic products in the UK, but produce that is certified by the Soil Association will also carry the code 'UK5'. For a full list of the other certifying bodies, with code numbers and contact details, see page 77.

Is organic farming better for animal welfare?
Yes. Animals are kept in more natural, free-range conditions. Compassion in World Farming, the farm animal welfare campaign group, supports organic methods because high standards of care are considered central. Livestock must be given high-quality, non-GM feed, be exercised, have access to pasturage, and be kept in appropriate stocking densities. This, in turn, is believed to encourage natural immunological defences, cutting out the need for the routine use of preventative drugs.

Are organic products better for your health?
A survey by the Soil Association in 2003 found that consumers were most likely to cite taste and health benefits as their reasons for trying organic fruit or vegetables. This may explain why three-quarters of babies in the UK are now fed organic food as part of their diet.

Taste is a matter for personal assessment, but there is a great deal of controversy over whether organic food is healthier — so much so that food labelling laws forbid health claims on packaging.

Although the Food Standards Agency, the food safety watchdog, supports organic food because it gives consumers more choice and minimises the use of pesticides, it does not support claims that organic products offer health benefits. The FSA maintains that 'the current scientific evidence does not show that organic food is any safer or more nutritious than conventionally produced food'. Similarly, a *Which?* report by the Consumers' Association in 2003 concluded that there was 'no consensus' on the health benefits of eating organically.

The main debate focuses on the comparative use of pesticides, additives and antibiotics. In 2001, government tests found pesticide residues in 1,148 samples of conventionally grown food. Only six organic samples contained residues. In 2002, a US study published in *Food Additives and Contaminants* reported that some organic food contained a third fewer pesticide contaminants than conventional food. It also found that when residues were present in organic food they were less likely to be multiple residues, and more likely to be at a lower concentration.

There is no firm evidence of suspected links between certain human health problems and the amount of antibiotics routinely fed to conventionally reared animals. But many consumers are reassured by the methods of organic production which ensure drugs are given only therapeutically and not preventatively. Growth hormones to control reproduction are prohibited, as is any animal treatment involving the use of organophosphates. If drugs do have to be used because an animal is in pain or its health is in danger, a 'withdrawal period' is enforced so that the animal cannot return to the herd or flock or be sent for slaughter.

Some studies suggest that organic produce has certain advantages. For example, a comparison of soups made with organic and non-organic vegetables in 2003 found the former to have significantly higher levels of

56 per cent of organic food sold in the UK is imported from abroad

salicylic acid, a natural anti-inflammatory ingredient found in aspirin (which has itself been positively linked to the prevention of bowel cancer and heart disease).

Where the organic sector does seem to agree with the FSA is that there is unlikely to be any difference between microbiological contamination (such as bacteria) in organic and non-organic systems. Similarly, heavy-industry emissions containing dioxins (see page 106) affect all agricultural systems equally.

So when a product says organic, is it 100 per cent organic?

Not necessarily. Because there is not yet an organic version of every ingredient required for food production, manufacturers are allowed to use specified non-organic ingredients. However, organic ingredients must make up at least 95 per cent of the product. If the percentage is lower than that, the term 'organic' can only be used on the ingredients list. The front label must also clearly state the total percentage of organic ingredients.

Isn't most of the organic food available in the UK grown abroad?

For people concerned about food miles (see page 18), this has long been a gripe about organic produce. But in recent years the percentage of imported produce has fallen considerably. Just a few years ago, as much as three-quarters of organic food was imported, whereas the percentage is now about half (56 per cent). This is still much too high for many. Like all imported food, organic produce grown abroad is legally required to have more protective packaging and extra treatment to keep it free from pests and diseases. Extra energy is expended, for example, steaming organic papayas and mangoes rather than fumigating them like their non-organic equivalent, or dipping organic bananas in hot water before they're shipped. Therefore, in the first instance buy locally grown organic produce.

Why is organic food so expensive?

The question of cost is one that is fiercely debated. A farmer choosing to go organic certainly has initial conversion costs, but is able to apply for grants to help with this process. For consumers it usually comes down to tests of comparative shopping baskets — one organic, one non-organic. Although a *Which?* report in 2003 found organic food to be up to 40 per cent more expensive, proponents insist this is not always the case. The only way to answer this is to price-test things yourself and, importantly, not only compare costs within supermarkets where organic produce is often cynically marked up as a 'premium product'. Organic produce via a local box scheme (see page 52), for example, can often compete in price with non-organic equivalents. More importantly, fans of organic produce say we should stop thinking about price the way supermarkets do. Instead, we should think about the true cost of non-organic produce: the cost of having to clean up pesticide run-off from our land and watercourses; the animal welfare concerns associated with conventional farming; and the legacy of routinely using antibiotics and growth promoters when rearing livestock. In other words, food should always be seen as an investment and not simply an expense.

Further reading
www.guardian.co.uk/food
www.soilassociation.org
www.fao.org/organicag
www.ifoam.org
www.defra.gov.uk/farm/organic/consumers
www.food.gov.uk/science/sciencetopics/organicfood
www.sustainweb.org
www.hdra.org.uk
www.pan-uk.org
www.pesticides.gov.uk

A life in the day of a potato

The British are the third largest consumers of potatoes in Europe behind the Portuguese and the Irish, eating, on average, 103kg – or 500 medium-sized potatoes – each a year. UK farmers grow about 80 varieties of potato – with just two, Maris Piper and Estima, accounting for a third of the annual harvest. But the non-organic varieties receive an average of 12 'applications' before they reach the plate, including…

Fertilisers: The main growing season starts between March and April, depending on the weather. Potatoes should ideally be planted in fresh ground on a seven-year rotation. Fertilisers will generally be applied to the growing field at this stage. All chemicals sprayed on crops and/or fields must be passed as safe by Defra. Each chemical has a maximum dose per hectare allowance as set out by the Food and Environment Protection Act 1985 (and amended by the Control of Pesticides Regulations 1986).

Herbicides: These will be applied early in the growing process to prevent weed contamination. They can include linuron, diquat and metribuzin. Most crops will be sprayed just once. Linuron and diquat have potential to cause ground water contamination; metribuzin is classified as 'moderately hazardous' by the WHO. (Various organisations, – WHO, the EC, WWF etc – rate the acute (short-term) toxicity of pesticides, and their ratings are based on toxicity tests with animals, usually rats, that are fed varying doses of a chemical to measure oral toxicity and/or skin irritation.)

Fungicides: As the plants grow, they become vulnerable to fungi, insects, molluscs and nematodes (microscopic parasitic worms). Fungicidal treatments include cymoxanil ('slightly hazardous' – WHO's toxicity rating), fentin hydroxide ('moderately hazardous' – WHO), ethoprofos ('extremely hazardous' – WHO) and mancozeb ('endocrine disrupter' – WWF). Insecticides include fosthiazate ('toxic' – EC classification). Nematicides include aldicarb ('extremely dangerous' – WHO, 'endocrine disrupter' – WWF), and 1,3-dichloropropene ('danger/poison, possible carcinogen' – US government's Environmental Protection Agency). Aldicarb was withdrawn from general use for EC review in September 2004, but for 'esssential uses', which includes potato crops, it was granted extended UK approval by Defra until December 31, 2007. Crops may be treated up to six times in a growing season.

Growth regulator: Towards July and August regulators are applied to limit the growth of surrounding weeds. These are not generally highly toxic as it is important not to kill the potato plants. However, one regulator, maleic hydrazide, can, under some conditions, break down into hydrazine ('possible carcinogen' – WHO's toxicity rating).

Desiccants: In September/October, sulphuric acid, a desiccant that has a maximum dosage level of 340 litres per hectare for potato crops in the UK, is often applied to the tops of the potato plants to kill the greenery and to make picking easier. Sulphuric acid's toxicity is rated as 'corrosive' by the EC and may cause ground water contamination.

Storage: Potatoes that are being used for processing are stored at higher temperatures than those that are being sold for eating. This prevents the carbohydrates turning to sugar and spoiling the look of foods such as chips.

Processing: The potato will now enter the food processing stage where, if it is to become a packet of crisps, for example, it may be treated and cooked with a wide range of artificial preservatives, colourings, flavourings and sweeteners.

Have we seen the back of GM foods?

In 1996, an innocuous-looking tomato arrived on our shores. Named the 'flavr savr', it contained antisene genes to delay the ripening process. It marked the start of the UK's battle over genetically modified (GM) food.

Shortly afterwards the first GM test fields were cultivated across the UK. Fears over contamination of conventional and organic crops from these fields led to protestors pulling up the plants. In 1999 more than 60 arrests were made after over 30 crop destructions, rallies and protests. The most high-profile crop destruction involved Lord Melchett, then head of Greenpeace, and 27 others. They were subsequently accused of ripping up and stealing £750 worth of genetically modified, herbicide-tolerant maize belonging to the biotechnology company AgrEvo.

The biotechnology industry has now invested billions in developing GM crops only to be met with similar resistance throughout Europe and many other parts of the world. Biotech firms have claimed GM technology will help to:

● Alleviate global food shortages and therefore prevent global hunger and disease.

● Eradicate weaknesses in crops as seen in the case of FuturaGene. Developed by US scientists, the gene increases plants' resistance to salty soils, cold weather and drought, allowing crops to grow in inhospitable soils.

● Reduce levels of allergens in a crop. For example, a soya bean is currently in development that will, the makers say, negate potential allergens that currently affect a wide number of people.

● Positively alter nutritional profiles to help combat poor diet and malnutrition. In the case of so-called 'Golden Rice', vitamin A was 'bred' into rice with the aim of alleviating malnutrition in the developing world.

● Increase crop yields on ever smaller plots of land, consequently leaving more land available for wildlife and free from intensive agriculture.

● Promote 'greener' farming. As some crops are inherently resistant to disease, they will not need to be sprayed with pesticides.

Exponents also claim that by resisting GM crops, which will aim to be cheaper than conventionally farmed crops, we will hamper the UK's ability to trade globally in the future. However, such claims have failed to convince the majority of UK consumers. In 2003 the government conducted a national GM survey. It concluded that at least four out of five people were against GM crops and that only two per cent would eat GM foods. The main concerns over GM crops include:

● Negative effects on human health. Opponents point to a lack of systematic testing to understand the potential health effects of GM entering the food chain.

● Giant biotech firms would have control over the global larder. Through patented processes, seeds and chemicals, they would have control over everything we eat.

● Potential contamination through pollen from GM to non-GM conventional, organic and wild crops and plants.

● Claims that GM is the answer to feeding a burgeoning population are simply not true. The UN says global population will stabilise by 2050 so no urgent increase in production of food is required. In any case, there are food surpluses all over the world that need to be better managed.

● 'Hidden' GM. For example, in some countries GM potatoes are used in starch production that ends up as animal feed. Current labelling laws do not require GM feed used to produce meat or eggs to be labelled meaning a consumer could buy GM products unknowingly.

● The threat of 'superweeds'. There are fears of transmission of pest resistance to weeds which could potentially kill other crops and require huge amounts of polluting herbicides and pesticides to control.

And there are plenty of instances of GM failing to live up to its developers' claims. In Argentina, GM soya was supposed to be the miracle solution after the country's economic collapse. About 150,000 small farmers were driven off the land as big growers dedicated more than 11 million hectares – mostly on environmentally fragile pampas areas – to growing Monsanto's GM soya. This created a monoculture – the agricultural equivalent of putting all your eggs in one basket. Recent research, reported by *New Scientist*, uncovered an environmental crisis in the country where soya has damaged soil bacteria and allowed herbicide-resistant weeds to grow out of control.

Rice has also been the focus of a high-profile biotech scandal. In the late 1990s, RiceTec Inc, a Texas-based company owned by Liechtenstein's royal family, was granted a controversial US patent for three basmati rice varieties (snappily registered as Rice Lines Bas 867, RT1117 and RT112, but trademarked as 'Texmati', 'Jasmati' and 'Kasmati'). Considering that the much-savoured basmati rice had been grown for centuries in the Greater Punjab region of south Asia, it rightly caused outcry. To protect its domestic farmers, the Indian Council of Agricultural Research was forced to spend huge sums securing DNA fingerprinting of other crop varieties and medicinal plants. But in the UK, the Ministry of Agriculture, Fisheries and Food (which in 2001 became the Department for Environment, Food and Rural Affairs, or Defra) concluded through DNA analysis that RiceTec's 'basmati' rice was actually closer to American long grain rice than the true basmati rice variety of the Punjab. (RiceTec has always marketed its basmati products as 'American basmati'.) A consumer boycott of RiceTech soon followed.

Consumer boycotts and protests have been enormously successful at halting the march of biotechnology. Between 2000 and 2001 there were 159 applications from biotech firms to start field trials in the UK in the hope they would lead to patents. But by 2004 only one crop, a herbicide-resistant pea, was put forward by the biotech firms for a trial licence. The failure by the firms to test further varieties of crops has been interpreted by industry watchers as despair at ever getting the technology accepted in the UK. The anti-GM movement celebrated when Bayer, the inventors of a GM maize crop 'Chardon LL', announced that it was withdrawing from the UK. This was just days after the government gave the go-ahead for it to be added to the national seed list; all new varieties of certain species of plants and seeds have to be approved under the Seeds (National Lists of Varieties) Regulations 2001 before they can be grown commercially.

However, GM technology is far from gone. Currently, most GM crops are largely confined to four countries – the US, Argentina, Canada and China. Pressure is increasing from the US and other GM markets that will inevitably force some trading countries to accept GM too.

The first signs of GM slowly creeping into resistant markets are already evident. When canned maize, the BT11 corn variety, manufactured by the Swiss firm Syngenta was approved by the EU in 2004 it marked the end of a five-year hiatus that had kept all new GM products out of Europe since 1998. It was approved despite the fact that 70 per cent of the European public do not want it. Many fear that it will open the floodgates to the dozens of products still awaiting EU approval. Monsanto said it was abandoning plans to introduce a GM herbicide-tolerant wheat to the world market due to resistance from Canadian and US growers, fearful of losing massive export markets to Europe and Japan. However, given that biotech firms such as Monsanto have now invested billions in research trying to develop GM wheat and other crops, it is unlikely that they will give up the technology entirely.

In fact, many biotech firms are now focusing on 'phase two' GM crops. As well as to increase farmers' yields or resist droughts, these new crops are being designed to be used as ingredients in medicine, to allow vitamins to be bred directly into plants, or to create allergen-free soya beans. It remains to be seen whether these will be the GM crops that finally win round sceptical consumers.

Meat

In contrast to our low intake of fresh fruit and vegetables, in the UK we have a huge appetite for meat. While five per cent of the population claim to be vegetarian, 860 million animals are reared in the UK for food every year. Eating a daily plate of 'meat and two vegetables' is still very much part of the national mindset. In fact, it sometimes seems as though the British Sunday roast is treated as a civil right. Even the horrors of BSE, foot-and-mouth disease, and the fact that 95 per cent of food poisoning incidents are attributable to meat haven't put us off our favourite protein source. According to the Consumer Analysis Group, the average European meat-eater can expect to consume 760 chickens, 20 pigs, 29 sheep, five cows and half a trawler net of fish in a lifetime.

However, eating large quantities of meat leaves us with considerable health, environmental and animal welfare problems:

● Meat is high in saturated fat and a major contributor to ailments such as coronary heart disease and obesity. In turn, obesity is linked to at least five per cent of cancers.

● Since the 1950s most of the meat we consume has been intensively reared. Animals have become little more than a unit cost on a spreadsheet and as a result attention to animal welfare has inevitably suffered.

● Intensively reared livestock is often kept for long periods – if not entirely – indoors in unhygienic, unnatural conditions. To prevent disease and to promote growth, animals are routinely fed antibiotics that then enter the food chain and, as a result, can cause antibiotic resistance in humans.

● Since 1950, worldwide production of meat has increased fivefold. But meat production on this scale is unsustainable. A growing global herd places increasing strain on precious water and soil resources, both of which are being depleted and polluted faster than ever before.

● Intensive livestock farming places a huge burden on the environment. Crops for animal feed are routinely grown using heavy doses of fertilisers, pesticides and even GM technology. Livestock herds account for 10 per cent of greenhouse gases and the 13 billion tonnes of farm waste produced per year lead to high levels of damaging chemicals such as ammonia nitrate, polluting land, water and air.

So why do we need to eat so much meat? After all, one billion people in the world manage to exist as vegetarians or vegans. Even health warnings fail to deter us – witness cyclical fads for high-protein diets. In general, we know that excessive meat consumption can have grave implications for our health. It's rich in refined carbohydrates and saturated fat, thereby significantly contributing to heart disease, diabetes and obesity in an era when 21 per cent of UK men and 24 per cent of UK women are clinically obese. But since rationing ended after the war and farming became increasingly industrialised, consumption of meat on a large scale has come to be a major symbol of social and economic affluence. It is proving to be a hard habit to break, but it's a habit that we must aim to reduce.

The hidden cost of meat

Fuelling our habit is the fact that meat costs less than ever before. In fact, this is the case for most of our food, not just meat. We now spend less than 10 per cent of our total income on food as opposed to the 35 per cent we paid in the 1930s. In 2002/03, the average weekly spend per household on meat (processed, frozen and fresh) was £7.90, with a further £1.60 on fish. Intensive production techniques have led to high yields which in turn have allowed the price of joints and cuts of meat to fall over the years. Pressure put on farmers by supermarkets, coupled with cheap imports, have kept prices consistently low.

On the surface this might seem welcome to consumers. Yet food crises such as BSE and foot and mouth have bluntly exposed some of the pitfalls of intensive livestock rearing: the lengthy transportation of live animals, the dangers of contaminated feed and the reality of the poor living conditions have left many of us questioning the true cost of cheap meat. In the case of BSE, the taxpayers' bill is around £4 billion and still counting. And in the case of 2001's foot-and-mouth outbreak, around £5 billion in lost tourism revenue.

After many years in the ascendant, excessive meat production is now proving to be unsustainable. In 2004, Compassion in World Farming (CIWF), an international farm animal welfare group campaigning for an end to factory farming and live animal exports, ranked excessive meat consumption as one of the top threats to the stability of humankind. Since 1950, per capita consumption of meat globally has more than doubled.

Our cheap meat culture, provided courtesy of intensive global production, is made possible by cheap energy and access to water – both key resources that are now being rapidly depleted. There is a stark contrast between traditional techniques of animal husbandry and the factory farming of animals today. Traditionally, ruminants – mammals, such as goats, sheep and cows, that chew the cud – were encouraged to forage for food in their natural habitats of hills and pastures. Poultry and pigs would then clear up behind. This is a largely sustainable process known, in conjunction with the growing of complementary crops, as mixed farming. However, intensive farming, where the farmer concentrates on rearing one type of animal, does the opposite. Intensively farmed livestock are mostly reared indoors (consuming half of the world's grain supplies in the process) and are raised on one third of the world's arable land (typically with the aid of polluting pesticides). As a result, the global herd (the number of livestock alive at any one time) continues to swell – already it includes one billion pigs, 1.3 billion cows, 1.8 billion sheep and goats and 15.4 billion chickens (three times as many as human beings). The agronomists David Pimental and Robert Goodland have calculated

The European meat-eater can expect, on average, to consume **760** chickens, **20** pigs, **29** sheep, **5** cows and half a trawler net of fish in a lifetime

Dilemma

Should meat substitutes be an option?

While some vegetarians are against the idea of 'cheat meats', many find meat substitutes can provide alternatives to everything from chicken nuggets to bacon rashers.

Quorn™

Over 20 million Europeans have eaten Quorn™, which has been on the market for almost 20 years. A completely synthetic product, it was developed in the 1960s amid fears that the world was about to run out of food. It is a fungal protein that it is set in a glucose solution and then fermented. But it has also proved to be controversial. In 2003 claims were made by a variety of US organisations that Quorn™ was a potential allergen. The Food Standards Agency (FSA) has listed Quorn™ as an allergen on its website but says intolerance to the product is 'much less frequent than to other foods, such as soya and dairy products'. However, the range of Quorn™ products has continued to expand, providing alternatives to just about every meat product, from imitation mince and chicken nuggets to 'Deli Rasher' slices for sandwiches.

Soya

Forming the basis for many meat substitutes, soya is low in fat and has been shown to be a good source of protein. Consequently, it is popular with vegans, who may find it hard to find alternative sources of protein in their diets. Epidemiological studies (primarily in Japan) suggest that consumption of soya may be beneficial in preventing certain cancers, including breast and prostate cancer. However, the ubiquity of GM soya in some parts of the world has led to concerns that many soya products could be contaminated. Intensive soya production in countries such as Brazil has also led to rainforest being cleared.

Tofu

Manufactured by a process similar to cheese-making but made from soya milk derived from a compressed soya bean, tofu absorbs flavours easily. It has been around in oriental cookery for centuries and is very versatile. See above for information on soya production.

TVP

The stalwart of cheat meat, the unappealingly titled Textured Vegetable Protein has been around for 30 years. Found in a wide variety of veggie-burgers, veggie-sausages and veggie-mince it is also available in basic form from some health shops and is very versatile – just add water to use in recipes. It is very low in fat and a good source of fibre. It is, however, a by-product of the soya oil industry.

that rearing a kilogram of beef requires around 100,000 litres of water. In contrast, 900 litres of water is needed to produce a kilo of wheat.

If meat consumption continues to grow, by 2050 livestock will require the equivalent amount of land and water as four billion people. Pitched against a growing global population – UN estimates suggest there could be as many as 9.3 billion people on the planet by 2050 – these levels of consumption look wildly unsustainable.

As a result, we will be faced with a choice: do we use the world's arable land and water supplies to grow crops for humans, or to 'grow' meat for humans? The answer surely is to start cutting down our meat consumption, and, if not choosing vegetarianism, to return to a pattern of food consumption that mirrors habits before industrial farming took hold when meat was reserved for Sundays and special occasions, rather than eaten every day of the week.

Animal welfare

As far back as 1964, the author Ruth Harrison offered the first insight into the world of intensive meat and dairy production with her book *Animal Machines*. It exposed the plight of calves, hens, broiler chickens and pigs, all crowded indoors under artificial lighting and pumped full of growth hormones in the nascent world of factory farming. As consumers, we've been slow to take note; it wasn't until 1997 that the EU even recognised livestock as 'sentient beings'. Rather, we have found it easier to disconnect ourselves from the realities of meat production. Local butchers, where meat hung on hooks over floors covered in sawdust, have been replaced by anodyne supermarket fridges. In 1985 there were 23,000 high street butchers, whereas in 2000 there were just 9,721. Under the strip lights of the supermarket fridge, meat lies neatly in trays, wrapped in plastic packaging often lined with preserving agents such as butylated hydroxyanisole (BHA) or tertiary-butylhydroquinone (TBHQ) – both 'reasonably anticipated to be a human carcinogen', according to the International Agency for Research on Cancer. The meat may even have undergone modified atmosphere processing or been washed in chlorine, but to the consumer it looks sanitised, far removed from the rearing shed or abattoir.

While many of us may have lost touch with the true derivation of meat, the demands of campaigners and members of the public concerned by food scares linked to meat, occasionally in tandem with producers, have led to advances in the living conditions for some farmed animals. In some areas of the UK producers are ahead of forthcoming EU legislation. For example, pig farmers in the UK no longer use tethers in sow stalls. Sow stalls are a confining structure, usually measuring 0.7m by 2.1m, where pregnant pigs are kept throughout a 16-week pregnancy. The stalls restrict their movement to such an extent that they cannot turn around, let alone exercise. A sow tether is a heavy collar and chain, also used to curtail movement during pregnancy. However, an EU ban forbidding the use of tethers does not come into effect until 2006 and sow stalls will not be outlawed until 2013.

Likewise, conventional battery cages for hens are also being phased out in favour of 'enriched cages'. An enriched cage gives battery hens extra floorspace – an increase from $450cm^2$ to $600cm^2$ (the size of a sheet of A4 paper). The stocking density of birds per cage is also reduced – from five to four. But for many campaigners the principal issue is whether birds should be reared in cages at all.

Ultimately, buying certified organic British meat is the best way of ensuring high standards of animal welfare. One of the few good stories that came out of the BSE crisis was the increasing demand for organic

Spotlight

Delicacies

Synonymous with glamour and wealth, some delicacies have a global market and fetch extremely high prices. But concerns about animal welfare and the environment should play heavily on the mind in the case of three of the world's most savoured foodstuffs. . .

Foie gras
Ninety per cent of all foie gras – goose liver – is consumed by the French. In fact demand for it is so high in France that domestic production cannot meet it. Hungary, now the world's biggest exporter, fulfils most of that demand and also sells huge quantities to Japan and Belgium. Foie gras literally translates as fat liver. Which is exactly what two-month-old geese and ducks get when they are force-fed huge amounts of food through tubes or pipes for two to three weeks. Once the birds' livers have expanded to up to 10 times their normal size the bird is killed. Through force-feeding they can also suffer from throat bruising, and occasionally suffocation. The EU acknowledges that foie gras production contravenes animal welfare regulations, but has not yet moved to make force-feeding illegal. It has, however, asked producers to find alternative methods of feeding birds, but has given them 15 years to do so.

Caviar
Wildlife campaign groups say Beluga sturgeon, the most famous source of caviar, is on the brink of extinction. When the Soviet Union collapsed in 1991, regulations surrounding the delicate ecosystem around the shores of the inland Caspian sea collapsed with it. This area provides 90 per cent of the world's caviar (sturgeon roe). Motivated by the lure of huge profits, rival groups have over-harvested the area, causing pollution and habitat loss. The sturgeon has a very slow reproduction rate and it remains to be seen if the wild stock will recover. →

beef, with provenance becoming increasingly important to the consumer. In fact, sales of organic beef since the crisis have risen by 53 per cent, with organic lamb sales rising by 212 per cent over the same period.

But it's worth bearing in mind that organic standards from elsewhere in the EU are not always as high as those in the UK. Danish free-range pigs, for example, can be classified as 'organic' by local organic certifying bodies because they are raised on organic feed. But because the pigs wear nose rings (used by some farmers to stop pigs from fighting and foraging too deeply and churning up land) they don't meet the standards of animal husbandry required for Soil Association accreditation (see page 26).

The organic meat industry has also been criticised in other areas. In the UK, the rise in demand for organic lamb and beef is largely being satisfied through imports, as most of the leading supermarkets keep prices lower and volume sales up by importing from abroad. For example, a survey by the Soil Association in 2004 found that less than one quarter of organic pork on sale in Asda was from UK farms. In Tesco half of the organic pork on sale and under half of beef was imported. Imports commonly come from Argentina, Denmark, Germany, Austria and New Zealand despite the fact that organic farmers in the UK could supply the current demand for organic meat. Therefore, where possible try to buy UK-reared organic produce (preferably locally reared).

Where organic meat holds a huge advantage over 'conventionally' reared meat is in the reduced use of antibiotics. In organic herds, a small number of strictly selected antibiotics are permitted for veterinary use, and only as a last resort. This contrasts sharply with intensive production where animals are raised in conditions described by Compassion in World Farming (CIWF) as 'crowded, unhealthy and likely to lead to the spread of infections', and so are routinely fed antibiotics to prevent disease and to promote growth. Although the practice of injecting or feeding farm animals with antibiotics dates back to the 1950s, the ramifications are 'still not well understood', according to a report by the American Society for Microbiology. There is concern that antibiotic-resistant bacteria entering the food chain are giving rise to so-called 'superbugs'. Researchers at St Bartholomew's hospital in London found that 11 per cent of stool samples from children contained bacteria, such as E coli, resistant to the broad-spectrum antibiotic chloramphenicol. As this is a drug rarely given to children, it suggested that these children had acquired resistance without ever having taken the antibiotics.

But besides organic certification, other animal welfare assurance schemes exist, too. For example, almost 2,000 non-organic producers now conform to welfare standards specified by the RSPCA under its Freedom Foods label (www.freedomfood.org.uk). The scheme oversees the rearing of 20 million animals, including laying hens, broiler chickens, dairy and beef cattle, sheep, pigs, turkeys, ducks and salmon. Other than through supermarkets, accredited producers can also sell straight to the customer online at www.farmgatedirect.com. Another scheme is the Red Tractor (www.littleredtractor.org.uk), a voluntary quality assurance label developed by the National Farmers' Union. However, CIWF has investigated the scheme and is highly critical. Its report can be found at www.redtractortruth.com.

Researching the exact provenance of any meat you eat is an important step to take. Even so, each type of meat presents its own points of concern, organic or otherwise:

Beef

In the late 1980s, beef made news when it was highlighted that hundreds of thousands of acres of rainforests were being destroyed to graze cattle for burgers. In 1996, a link between variant CJD in humans and BSE in cattle was finally confirmed. But the BSE-related bad news has continued. In May 2004, research from Derriford Hospital in Plymouth and the CJD Surveillance Unit suggested that 3,800 Britons could be harbouring CJD. Also in 2004, the FSA admitted to some slip-ups in the testing of beef products when a number of cows were allowed into the food chain

We eat 820 million chickens every year in the UK, **five times more** than we ate in the 1980s

without being tested – a mandatory requirement since 2001. However, only a few cases of BSE have been confirmed in herds that have recently been converted to organic farming practices and none in established organic herds. This has helped, in part, to inspire consumer confidence in organic beef.

Chicken

We eat 820 million chickens every year in the UK, five times more than we ate in the 1980s. Intensive poultry farming is the fastest growing form of intensive farming in the world. It is also one of the least humane, making the hapless chicken one of the most abused animals on the planet. Typically born into vast hatcheries, day-old chicks are stuffed into crates and taken to rearing sheds, each one holding 30,000–50,000 birds. Selectively bred to reach slaughter weight in just 41 days (twice the natural rate of growth) the broiler chicken – the name is a hybrid derived from 'roasting' and 'boiling' – can experience health problems including painful lameness caused by the bird's enforced inactivity, lack of hygiene in the shed and the fact that its unnatural weight is restricted to an area less than the size of a sheet of A4 paper.

At the time of slaughter the broiler can look forward to being hung upside down and shackled for as long as three minutes before it is lowered into an electrocution bath. For this reason, the animal welfare group People for the Ethical Treatment of Animals (Peta) is campaigning for chickens to be gassed instead of electrocuted as it claims this is the more humane option.

But still chicken manages to maintain a reputation for being a healthy meat. Many consumers remain ignorant of what happens to most chicken meat after the bird is slaughtered. Water and proteins are routinely added to chicken meat to increase its weight, and so its price. This practice is not illegal, though the Food Standards Authority is campaigning to get the EU to limit added water content to 15 per cent. In 2003 a joint investigation by the *Guardian* and BBC's *Panorama* unearthed Dutch and German additive suppliers and

protein manufacturers running a multi-million-pound scam that involved injecting chicken with beef protein (listed on labels as 'hydrolised protein'), which, due to the beef protein's ability to allow greater water retention, enabled them to inject more water than 'normal' into the meat to bulk it out, and thereby raise its price.

Chicken is now one of the major weapons in the supermarkets' ongoing price wars and is actually cheaper than it was 20 years ago. But this competitive market encourages some unscrupulous suppliers to continue to falsify labels and to inject water and proteins.

There are also growing concerns about the safety of chicken meat. Half of all supermarket chickens are believed to contain campylobacter, a bacteria that causes food poisoning. Cheap cuts of chicken should be avoided as they are easily tampered with. For example, in 2000 imported frozen chicken breasts from a Dutch company were found to contain 40 per cent water.

The terms 'free range', 'corn fed' and 'organic' are frequently used when selling chicken. But what do they really mean? The life of a free-range chicken should, in theory, be better than that of its conventional, intensively reared counterpart. For instance, birds must have access to open-air runs during half of their lifetime. The free-range stocking rate (the number of birds in an area) is limited to 400 per acre by the EU. Neither can free-range chickens be killed before they are 56 days old. In practice, though, many free-range birds have a far from ideal existence. Stocking rates are still high, and so the problems associated with oversized flocks, such as aggression, fighting and the spread of disease, can still exist in the free-range system. Access to the outside is usually through 'pop holes', which are often controlled by aggressive birds. Consequently, many birds will never venture outside.

Used on its own, the description 'corn fed' doesn't mean very much. According to Defra, corn-fed is not recognised as a term by the EU but is usually understood to mean that at least 50 per cent of a bird's feed is maize or corn. For this label to be meaningful, it really needs to be used in conjunction

Dilemma

Vegetarian, vegan or fruitarian?

In a 2003 survey by the Food Standards Agency, six per cent of 3,121 individuals polled in the UK said they lived in a household containing one 'completely' vegetarian resident, with 'completely' meaning that they did not eat meat or fish but did eat eggs and dairy produce. So how ethical does that make them?

Statistically, it should certainly make them healthier; research by the World Cancer Research Fund has shown that vegetarians have lower overall mortality rates, as well as a lower risk of heart disease, obesity and cancers. Given that in the UK many millions of animals are reared and killed for food each year, it also relieves them of any associated guilt. However, by drinking milk and eating eggs, 'lacto-ovo-vegetarians' (the most common kind) still have 'blood on their hands'. Conventional milk production is claimed by groups such as Peta to be intrinsically cruel. In order to lactate, cows obviously have to be pregnant. But their calves are removed almost immediately and male calves are often killed within a couple of weeks. Dairy cattle and poultry are also routinely fed with fishmeal. And if the vegetarian eats conventionally-produced cheese they may unwittingly be eating rennet – an ingredient in cheese that's extracted from the stomach lining of slaughtered calves.

Vegans, however, take a further ethical step. At the core of their philosophy is the belief that animals should be free to act in a completely natural state, follow their own instincts, eat whatever they want and feed their young. So no dairy products or eggs are permitted. Vegans do not prop up the meat industry in any way. This has traditionally left the vegan reliant on soya for protein, which also places less strain on the planet. It takes only 2,000 litres of water to produce one kilo of soya beans, as opposed to 100,000 litres to produce a kilo of meat. Even so, soya isn't guilt-free as rainforests in countries such as Brazil are cleared to make way for its production – a process that relies on pesticides just like many other crops.

Fruitarians go even further than vegans. They believe that only plant foods that can be harvested without killing the plant should be eaten. As the name suggests, raw fruit is the food of choice but grains and nuts are also eaten. 'Windfall fruitarians' take it to the extreme. Fruit cannot be picked or plucked from a tree. It must fall naturally. In terms of minimising our footprint on the earth and working with nature, this approach is extremely ethical. But just how practical it can ever be is another question...

For more information, contact the Vegetarian Society (www.vegsoc.org), the Vegan Society (www.vegansociety.com) and the Fruitarian Foundation (www.fruitarian.com).

with 'free range' or 'organic'.

Organic chickens have low stocking densities. For Soil Association accreditation, the number of chickens in a single unit must not exceed 1,000 (the number of chickens in intensive units can soar to 40,000). Crucially, organic chickens also feed outdoors, typically under giant moveable hangers so that they can be frequently moved to forage on fresh land. While sick birds can be treated appropriately, the routine use of antibiotic growth promoters is not permitted and chickens grow at a natural rate, being typically reared for 81 days.

So, when buying chicken, organic is always preferable – or at the very least choose free range, thereby ensuring the bird has had some access to outside space. It is also far better to buy a whole bird as opposed to cuts to limit the amount of handling and processing it may have been subjected to.

Pork

Unlike other intensively reared meats, pork has become more expensive in the past five years. In 1996, restrictions imposed after BSE on the sale of waste pig parts for animal bonemeal brought an end to a lucrative area of the pork trade. Unlike beef and lamb farmers, pig farmers don't receive any subsidies (nor, incidentally, do poultry farmers). Consequently, 2,000 pig farmers have gone out of business since 2001 and the number of breeding sows in the British pig herd has fallen from 800,000 to 500,000.

But while the UK pork industry may have suffered economically, standards of animal welfare have risen. For example, in the UK sow tethers have been illegal since 1996.

So does this mean that intensively produced pig meat is OK to buy? Not exactly. Compassion in World Farming's Supermarket Survey 2003/2004 showed that imported pork still makes up nearly half of all sales through some of the main supermarkets. In the EU, sow tethers and sow stalls are still permitted until 2006, but in the rest of the world there are no plans to phase them out.

Where possible it is best to buy organic pork – conventionally farmed pigs are still routinely injected or fed with up to 10 different types of antibiotics. In contrast, antibiotics are rarely given to organically reared pigs. If you are buying non-organic pork try to ensure that it has been reared outdoors. Ask the butcher or supermarket. Before considering imported pork, look for meat reared via more humane non-crate indoor systems, which is now more common. For instance, look for the RSPCA's Freedom Food label. In the CIWF survey, all the main supermarkets were found to offer lines of either outdoor- or non-crate-reared pork. But you need to study the label, or ask the staff, to be sure.

Lamb

Simply in terms of animal welfare, lambs have traditionally fared better than cows, chickens and pigs. There has never been much of a market for sheep milk in modern times so ewes have been left unhindered to suckle their young for longer. And sheep are also predominantly left to feed on grass in fields, meaning a healthier outdoor existence.

However, over the past few decades there has been a steady intensification of lamb rearing. In the 1990s, demand for year-round 'spring' lamb led supermarket buyers to instruct producers 'to alter the seasonal output'. This meant injecting ewes with fertility-boosting drugs, such as melatonin and the cheaper progesterone, a practice now widespread in intensive lamb farming. These drugs help to speed up ovulation, allowing the 'spring' lamb to be born around Christmas and ready to slaughter at Easter, when lamb is most in demand and so can be sold at premium prices.

Drugs also now enable ewes to produce up to three families of lambs every year, and selective breeding means that many of these will be multiple births. However, around four million lambs die each year from exposure, hypothermia, starvation and disease. Many ewes also die giving birth leaving around 35,000 orphaned lambs to be sent to market each year. Intensive farming also means lambs are weaned earlier, fed on milk substitutes and housed indoors, leading to problems such as sheep lice. Animal welfare concerns include docking lambs' tails, which routinely occurs without anaesthetic. Meanwhile, increasing flock sizes have led to environmental problems such as overgrazing in upland areas, which leads to loss of vegetation and soil erosion.

Live transportation is top of the list of campaigners' worries. The foot-and-mouth crisis in 2001 demonstrated how far sheep are transported around the UK on the hoof (alive) rather than on the hook (as carcasses). Between one million and one-and-a-half million lambs are still exported for slaughter abroad. Around 70,000 tonnes of lamb (half of which is produced in the UK) is exported to France and Belgium every year. One sixth of these exports will travel 'live'. This is despite the fact that the EU's Scientific Veterinary Committee has stressed that 'live transport should be avoided whenever possible...as the occurrence of poor welfare can be reduced considerably by slaughtering near the point of rearing and transporting meat'. A large proportion of the live exports will be slaughtered in local abattoirs and sold on at a premium as 'fresh, local lamb' to French and Belgian consumers. Perversely, as British lamb is exported to the continent, almost 80,000 tonnes of New Zealand lamb is imported to the UK each year.

As consumers, buying British lamb from as local a source as possible can help to sustain the home-grown lamb market and so reduce the need to transport lamb on the hoof in uncomfortable, crowded road transporters for hundreds of miles. It's also important to buy seasonally in a way that will support traditional spring lamb rearing and move away from intensified lamb production. Go for organic where lambs are reared naturally. Alternatively, lambs from hill and upland flocks – where harsh weather rules out births outside of the natural spring and summer lambing seasons – are likely to be born in springtime, and so are less likely to have been produced by ewes injected with fertility drugs.

Fish

There's a lot to consider when buying fish. Not only are there widespread concerns over the contamination of fish stocks – swordfish and tuna have been shown to contain very high traces of mercury – but global fish stocks are under extreme threat from overfishing. Some of the largest fish populations, including marlin, swordfish and tuna, have dropped by 90 per cent in the past 50 years, and the global cod catch has suffered a 70 per cent drop in the past 30 years. The United Nations Food and Agriculture Organisation (UNFAO) currently believes that of the world's commercially important marine fish stocks 25 per cent are under-exploited, 47 per cent are fully fished, 15 per cent are over-exploited, and 10 per cent are depleted or slowly recovering.

As the world's fishing fleets chase increasingly small amounts of fish, they are forced to go deeper and farther for their catch, leading to reliance on fishing techniques, such as drag-net trawling, that decimate the surrounding marine environment. Meanwhile, salmon and even cod are being reared intensively on fish farms or, in the case of prawns, through aquaculture. These intensive farming systems can produce large amounts of toxic waste, with harsh chemicals and fertilisers seeping into local water sources. So when buying all forms of seafood there are a number of questions to ask the fishmonger:

● Is the fish from sustainable stock as opposed to endangered stock? The blue tick mark of the Marine Stewardship Council (MSC, www.msc.org) indicates that fish are certified as being from well-managed, sustainable fisheries. Also take time to read the 'Fish to Avoid' and 'Fish to Eat' sections of the Marine Conservation Society website at www.fishonline.org, or buy its *Good Fish Guide* (£10, via the website, or call 01989 566017).
● Is it from natural waters, or has it been reared on a fish farm?

● Has it been caught in the most environmentally sensitive way possible? For example, line-caught rather than by environmentally degrading methods, such as bottom trawling?
● And for shellfish, is it possible that production has resulted in environmental and even social injustice?

Despite the warnings about our fish stocks, according to the FSA we are still not eating enough fish. The omega-3 fatty acids found in fish have substantial health benefits and help to lower the risk of heart disease. But given that much of our fish, particularly oily fish, contains traces of mercury, dioxins and PCBs (see page 106), you could be forgiven for being nervous about eating more of it.

So is fish safe to eat given current levels of contamination, especially when it's thought that a third of us already exceed the recommended maximum for ingesting contaminants? The FSA thinks so, saying in 2004 that, on current evidence, the positives outweigh the negatives, recommending that we eat two portions per week, one of which should be oily fish. However, what made headlines was the FSA's proviso that 'girls and women who may become pregnant at some point in their lives' should limit their consumption of oily fish to two portions a week. The same advice was issued to pregnant and breastfeeding women, who were also advised not to eat any shark, marlin and swordfish, and not to eat large amounts of tuna, due to concerns about traces of toxins.

Overfishing

According to a 2003 study in *Nature*, industrial fleets have fished out 90 per cent of large ocean predators, such as tuna, marlin and swordfish. This is due to the demands of a global fish market – over 40 per cent of fish is sold internationally. Environmental degradation is also playing its part. As the North Sea becomes warmer – a result of climate change – levels of certain planktons will dwindle. Plankton is the staple food of cod larvae. The lack of food for the larvae to eat, coupled with the further depletion of fish stocks by overfishing, mean that natural sea cod are in danger of extinction by 2020.

Fish quotas have been a feature of the fishing industry over the past 20 years. Designed to reduce access to fishing grounds to combat overfishing, and to allow stocks to replenish, they are seen by environmentalists as being increasingly important. But fish quotas also mean job losses in the fishing community. There are now just 12,000 fishermen in the UK, 33 per cent fewer than in 1995. Just under 1,000 boats are now in pursuit of the last remaining cod, haddock, sole and plaice stocks off Britain's coast. It is now estimated that the national fleet needs to be cut to 801 boats by 2013 if stocks are to be sustained. The Marine Stewardship Council puts it starkly: either we start fishing sustainably, or we stop fishing altogether.

But while fishing quotas may be saving European fish stocks, they are arguably only displacing the problem. For example, some EU countries, such as Spain and Portugal, have negotiated deals with other nations to fish their waters via 'transfer agreements'. This means that European fleets, using long-range, industrial-scale trawlers, are now plundering the seas off west Africa, a coast inhabited by some of the poorest people on earth. The answer, it seems, is that we must, as with meat, be increasingly wary about the provenance of the fish we eat.

Salmon

The problem of toxin contamination is acute in salmon because the fish has a high fat content and toxins accumulate in fatty tissue. Unsurprisingly, farmed salmon is more prone to contamination as it has an even higher fat content than wild varieties. However, over 40 per cent of the salmon in the ocean are now thought to have escaped from fish farms, raising concerns about contamination in all salmon.

In January 2004 the safety of UK-reared salmon was further questioned. After analysing two tonnes of wild and farmed salmon, Ronald Hites at Indiana University and Steven Schwager at Cornell University in New York declared that Atlantic salmon farmed in Scotland contained the highest levels of cancer-causing chemicals anywhere in the world. So contaminated was the fish that the scientists recommended people eat it no more than once every four months. The study, which appeared in the journal *Science*, prompted an immediate response from Sir

John Krebs, chairman of the FSA, who said the benefits of eating salmon outweighed the risks.

But the warning signs don't stop there. According to a 2001 study by Friends of the Earth Scotland, a typical salmon farm relies on more than 25 different chemical treatments, including antibiotics, disinfectants and antimicrobial drugs. Salmon can also be fed dyes, usually canthaxanthin or astaxanthin, to make them pink. Wild salmon normally turn a pale pink as they pick up the pigmentation of crustaceans and other sea life on which they feed. At salmon farms, breeders choose the colour they want the salmon to be using a 'salmofan', a fan of varyingly pink-hued cards that spreads out and describes how much dye is needed in the fish feed to achieve the desired colouring.

According to information published by the Veterinary Residues Committee for the year 2002, traces of a toxic antiparasitic chemical called malachite green were found in farmed trout and salmon reared in both the UK and the EU. The chemical was banned the same year by Defra, but figures showing how well farms have complied have yet to be released. Many experts believe that for some fish farmers, the temptation to use powerful antiparasitic drugs to protect fish from possible infections could be too much. Where possible, then, opt for line-caught salmon over farmed, unless it is certified organic.

Cod

We spent over £254 million on cod in 2003; along with haddock, salmon, plaice and prawns, cod accounts for 70 per cent of our fish consumption. Cod used to live for 40 years and grow to six feet in length. But in 2003, 90 per cent of the catch from the North Sea was less than two years old and had not yet had a chance to breed. Depleted cod stocks in the sea have led fish farms to expand into farming cod raised in submerged cages. For the consumer a more sustainable option is to buy less popular, unendangered trawler-caught fish – such as pollack – from an MSC-certified fishery, or haddock, for which the catch quota was raised, in places, by 53 per cent in 2004 due to restored stock levels. If you can't do without cod, then some environmentalists consider only Icelandic cod to be fished in a sustainable manner. However, bear in mind that Iceland has also reportedly proposed new legislation to allow the killing of whales to 'protect' its fish stocks.

Tuna

All commercially fished species of tuna are now endangered, according to the Marine Conservation Society. Southern blue fin is critically endangered, due to the completely unsustainable way it is fished across the oceans of the southern hemisphere. WWF has dubbed tuna 'the new foie gras', and its popularity across the Mediterranean and in Japan means it attracts premium prices.

Tuna fishing, especially yellow-fin fishing, commonly uses nets that can trap and kill dolphins. So is 'dolphin-friendly' tuna the answer? Not according to research carried out by the hydrodynamics expert Daniel Weihs at the Israel Institute of Technology. He concluded that dolphin calves are being caught up by the drag stream of fishing boats, separated from their mothers, and so die. This may explain why dolphin-friendly techniques have not yet led to a recovery in dolphin populations in the east Pacific. However, if you are going to eat tuna, pole-caught skipjack or yellow-fin fresh tuna is the best

option. A word about tinned tuna: don't assume that by consuming it you are eating an oily fish rich in omega-3 acids. The FSA says that only fresh tuna counts as an oily fish because during the canning process the tuna's fats are reduced to levels similar to those in white fish.

Prawns

Prawns have become much cheaper in the past decade but where do they come from? Three-quarters are caught by boats dragging huge nets across many of the world's estuaries and bays. Fishing for prawns destroys natural habitats and scoops up other marine species known as 'bycatch', which are often thrown back dead into the water. The remainder of the prawns we buy have been farmed by a method called aquaculture. Ninety per cent of prawn farms are found in Asia in developing areas. Unsurprisingly, aquaculture has grave implications for the environment. Harsh chemicals and fertilisers are routinely used and seep into local water supplies,

while waste from the process (some of it highly toxic) is dumped into the ocean. Aid agencies such as Save the Children Fund and Oxfam have also campaigned against large-scale prawn farming on the grounds of social injustice. They say that Asia's prawn fisheries routinely use child labour and many workers are very poorly paid. In addition, farmers are often encouraged to convert arable land to prawn fisheries, then, if the business goes bust, the land is irrevocably damaged. For these reasons, it's best to avoid warm-water prawns altogether, which are typically labelled as 'tiger prawns' and 'king prawns'. If you do have to buy them, look out for organic (almost exclusively from Ecuador) or Madagascan (currently working to make all its prawn fisheries sustainable) tiger prawns. Smaller prawns from the cold Atlantic (often labelled as Cold Atlantic prawns) are still trawled, but with technological advances the bycatch is greatly reduced. The most sustainably managed Atlantic fisheries are in Iceland.

Some of the largest fish populations have dropped by **90 per cent** in the past 50 years

What are we feeding our children?

As an indication of how little we tend to invest in the future, looking closely at what we feed our children is hard to beat. Even though damning evidence about our children's woeful diets is overwhelming and at times unrelenting, still the problem seems to worsen. Whereas malnutrition and famine are among the developing nations' principal concerns, conversely (and perversely, perhaps) in the west the problem is that our children are becoming ever heavier as they feast on poor-quality foods and snacks. With almost one third of all children in the UK now obese or overweight – a rise of 50 per cent since 1990 – many of them can look forward to an adulthood blighted by illnesses such as cancers, heart disease and diabetes. Unless current trends are reversed (we have the fastest-growing obesity rates in Europe) half of all British children could be obese by 2020. Hardly what you would call a good start in life.

For parents wishing to reverse this trend, four key areas of concern require attention: snacking, pester power, food labels and school meals.

Snacking

Children have long loved sweets and soft drinks, but instead of seeing them as treats, many children have now developed a habit of 'grazing' on snacks – eating them throughout the day between meals. In fact, 99 per cent of children between four and 11 now regularly buy and eat snacks, with 61 per cent of four- to five-year-olds actually buying their own snacks – some spending up to £1.50 a day. To put this into historical context, children now consume 30 times more soft drinks and 25 times more confectionery than they did 50 years ago. And as the majority of snacks contain high levels of salt, sugar, fat and/or artificial additives, snacking is often cited by health professionals as a major reason why our children's diets are so nutritionally poor and unhealthy. It's a point that's easy to understand when you learn that crisps are regularly eaten by 75 per cent of children, whereas just 68 per cent regularly eat any fresh fruit.

Pester power

That moment when a child pleads with their parent to buy a packet of sweets or drink at a supermarket checkout is often the culmination of a long-planned and carefully executed, multi-million-pound advertising campaign by a food company aggressively vying with its rivals for the hearts, minds and stomachs of our children. 'Best to catch 'em young' is evidently many food manufacturers' reasoning, given the lengths they go to to secure a child's custom.

In recent years a number of food companies have been embarrassed when details of their marketing campaigns have been made public. In 2004, following a campaign by the Parents Jury (a panel of 800 parents set up by the Food Commission to examine how food is marketed to children), the BBC began issuing nutritional standards when licensing its Tweenies, Fimbles, Bill & Ben and Teletubbies characters to food manufacturers. In 2003, the Food Commission calculated that if a 10-year-old wanted to earn a 'free' basketball through a Cadbury's vouchers-for-sports equipment offer, they would need to play the game for 90 hours to burn off the 38,463 calories from eating all the chocolate that would need to be bought. Cadbury's later changed the way the promotion worked following criticism.

In 2004, the *Guardian* obtained documents that revealed the wording of a detailed submission by advertising agency Leo Burnett to the Institute of Practitioners in Advertising in 2002. This was for an 'effectiveness award' and explained how its campaign for Kellogg's Real Fruit Winders 'entered the world of kids in a way never done before', and managed to 'not let mum in on the act'. In the same year, a headline-grabbing report into the nation's obesity problem said that MPs were 'appalled' by the Walkers campaign for Wotsits that 'deliberately sought to undermine parental control over children's nutrition'. Walkers Crisps advertising agency Abbott Mead Vickers also boasted in its submission for an effectiveness award

The average amount spent on snacks by children at school each day is 73p, more than **twice the amount** spent on each meal by the school's caterer

that its association with the football star Gary Lineker had produced sales of an extra 114 million packets of crisps over a two-year period. It's no wonder that there are growing calls for a ban on food companies advertising their products during children's TV programmes – a move that the government has signalled it will enforce.

Food labels

If all the children's foods that celebrities advertise on TV were well-balanced and nutritionally sound it would be applauded, but look on the label of most food targeted at children and you will see a list that includes a high proportion of salt, sugars, fats and additives – all of which, if consumed in high levels, are proved to be detrimental to longterm health. Paying close attention to all food labels is the only way for a parent to police what their child eats (unless, of course, they prepare and cook all food from scratch with fresh ingredients). But labelling laws don't make it easy for parents to decipher the true content of foods. For example, the Food Commission found in 2004 that a 330ml bottle of Coca-Cola contains 35g sugar, equivalent to one and a quarter packs of Rowntrees Fruit Gums. This information becomes more significant when compared with the RDA, the government's 'Recommended Daily Allowances', with the RDA of sugar for a 10-year-old being 60g. But this information isn't required to be printed on the label.

Artificial additives are another huge concern for parents. Some children are consuming up to 80 additives a day – 50 of which come from snack foods. Many parents and food campaigners have increasing doubts as to whether children should be consuming these additives, claiming some additives are responsible for hyperactivity and mood swings.

School meals

It's one thing controlling what a child eats at home, but when they're at school things become even harder. This isn't helped by the generally poor standard of food served at most schools. This is largely explained by simple economics. Whereas the average amount spent on snacks by children at school each day is 73p, less than half this amount is spent by the school's meal provider on the ingredients for the main meal at lunch (by comparison, 86p is spent on each prison meal). This inevitably means that to eke out any profit the private caterers granted contracts by local education authorities will use cheaper, poorer quality ingredients.

The presence of vending machines in some schools is also a problem. They provide children with easy access to snacks but also provide food manufacturers with a shop window to promote their wares to a wide-eyed, captive audience.

In addition, the route home from school provides a tempting opportunity for children to snack out of sight of their parents. In fact, 96 per cent of children now consume snacks on their way home from school, with 60 per cent of them eating a packet of crisps.

A better start

Eat with your children whenever possible and involve them in cooking from as young an age as possible.

Support the Food For Life campaign (www.foodforlifeuk.org, tel 0117 914 2446), which aims to improve the quality of food served in schools.

Reduce your child's exposure to pesticide residues. Wash and peel all fresh fruit and vegetables – even if it claims to be 'ready-washed' – and discard any outer leaves. Trim fat from meat and skin from poultry and fish: pesticide residues can collect in fat.

Vary their diet as much as possible, allowing snacks and soft drinks only as 'treats'.

Be wary of 'children's menus' at restaurants. They often offer cheap, processed foods, presuming it is what parents want their children to eat.

Be wary of products selling themselves as 'low-sugar' or 'sugar-free'. They may contain artificial sweeteners.

Try to replace readymeals, crisps and sweets with alternatives, such as vegetable sticks in dips, rice cakes and fresh fruit.

Monitor the hours your child watches TV. Manufacturers of processed foods aggressively market products between 4 and 6pm. Support Sustain's campaign to ban unhealthy food marketing to children (www.sustainweb.org, tel: 020 7837 1228), and complain to Ofcom, the communication industry's regulator (www.ofcom.org.uk, tel: 0845 456 3000).

Suspect the worst when ingredient listings use loose terms such as 'flavourings' or 'colourings'. Likewise, be wary of the word 'flavour'. The difference between snacks that are 'cheese flavour' and 'cheese flavoured' is that the latter actually has cheese in it.

Remember that labelling laws dictate that if a product doesn't actually have any fruit in it, its manufacturer cannot illustrate the packaging with pictures of fresh fruit. Especially relevant to yoghurts.

Watch out for high levels of salt in foods you would not normally associate with it, such as breakfast cereals. Look for the word 'sodium' as well as salt on labels. For more information, visit www.salt.gov.uk.

Likewise, look out for high levels of sugar, an ingredient that has many names, such as sucrose, fructose, maltose, dextrose and glucose.

Join the Parents Jury (www.parentsjury.org.uk, tel: 020 7837 2250). It campaigns against poor quality 'children's menus', confronts the way confectionery manufacturers lure children to buy sweets in exchange for 'free' sports equipment, and aims to prevent the stocking of supermarket checkouts with tempting eye-level sweets.

Lobbying for change can make a difference. Kraft, the world's second largest food company, recently announced it will start reducing its advertising aimed at children, reduce portion sizes and cut back on some of its most unhealthy products.

Avoid foods that contain additives, especially for children. Parents should particularly avoid the following: monosodium glutamate (E621); disodium 5'-ribonucleotide (E635); artificial sweeteners; sodium benzoate (E211); sulphur dioxide (E220); the colourings Quinoline Yellow (E104), Brilliant Blue (E133), Sunset Yellow (E110), Carmoisine (E122), Ponceau 4R (E124), and Indigo Carmine (E132).

If you are concerned your child is suffering from hyperactivity, contact the Hyperactive Children's Support Group (www.hacsg.org.uk). It offers information and advice about what effects food additives can have on children.

Urge your school governors and local education authority to ban advertising in schools via vending machines, scrap tuck shops that sell sweets and fizzy drinks, teach more cooking skills, and lobby hard for more to be spent on school meals. Urge your school to start an organic fruit-only tuck shop (see www. sustainweb.org/g5ap).

The rise of convenience foods

On April 6, 1954, a US firm called CA Swanson & Sons kick-started the convenience food industry by putting the world's first 'TV dinner' on the market. For the record, the meal consisted of roast turkey with stuffing, gravy, sweet potatoes and peas. It sold for 98 cents, came in an aluminium tray and took 30 minutes to cook. Conceived as an innovative, temporary answer to dealing with 236,000kg of surplus turkey following one Christmas, the concept became a runaway success. Americans, and soon much of the rest of the world, rapidly adopted the concept of quick, convenient meals and snacks. It's hard now to think of a world without them. The figures are staggering:

- In 2000, the readymeal market across the UK, France, Germany, Spain and Italy was worth £5.7 billion, a 19 per cent rise on 1996. The UK accounted for almost half of all sales.

- India's fast-food industry is growing at over 40 per cent a year, while a quarter of the country remains undernourished. In China, there are now 800 KFCs and 100 Pizza Huts.

- In the UK, we eat more than 10 billion bags of crisps a year, more than 150 packs per person per year and more than the rest of Europe put together.

- In 2002, Americans drank 189 billion fizzy drinks – that's 650 per person a year, or nearly two cans or bottles a day.

- More people in the world now recognise the golden arches of McDonald's than the Christian cross.

All convenience food is 'processed' in some way; totally, or partially, made in advance in a factory. The reason for its popularity is clear: it's the perfect partner to our new 'time-poor' social order, a world of working mothers, single households, and long hours spent at the office and commuting. Nothing is easier than popping a readymeal in the microwave or grabbing a fast-food takeaway on the way home.

But why are we constantly told that all this processed food is so bad for us? In simple health terms, it means we are consuming much more salt, sugar and fat (particularly saturated fat) than ever before – all of which have been repeatedly linked to obesity, high blood pressure, cardiovascular disease and certain cancers. Our bodies are just not designed to deal with these levels of salt, sugar and fat. Given that we were hunter-gatherers for 100,000 generations, farmers for 500 generations, but have now been consumers of processed, highly industrialised food for just two generations, it's little surprise that we haven't adjusted – if we ever will – to such an extreme, new diet. Just one meal at a fast-food outlet can contain more than 100 per cent of your RDA (recommended daily allowance) of salt, fat and sugar.

Obesity – or 'diabesity' as it's often called in the US due to its close link with diabetes – is the most visible side-effect of our love affair with convenience foods. In 1980, the average man in the UK weighed 73.7kg and woman 62.2kg. By 2000 that had increased to 81.6kg and 68.8kg respectively. In a world where nearly half of Britons eat their evening meal in front of the TV, it's right that our poor diet (ironic, given that we now eat, in terms of sheer volume, more than ever before) is being called a health 'time-bomb' and 'epidemic'.

There are other, less publicised, negative side-effects associated with eating such high levels of processed foods. What about all the artificial additives prevalent in processed foods? Why are they there? The answer is profit margins. Even though these additives contain no nutritional value they make food last longer, look better, taste more appealing, and, lastly, 'emulsify' ingredients that would not naturally sit well together (such as water and oil). In other words, they are there to disguise the fact that the raw ingredients are typically cheap and of poor quality. Not too many people would stomach 'mechanically recovered meat' if it wasn't treated first with additives. And even though many campaigners doubt the long-term safety of artificial sweeteners, the food manufacturers still use them because they serve the dual purpose of allowing them to make 'health' claims on packaging ('Low Sugar!') and cut costs (it costs 6p to sweeten a litre of soft drink with sugar, whereas it costs 2p to sweeten it with aspartame (E951) or 0.2p with saccharin (E954).

While each of the 540 food additives currently available to food manufacturers, including sweeteners, is cleared as 'safe' by UK food regulators, some campaigners, including Erik Millstone, reader in science policy at the University of Sussex and author of *Food Additives*, insist that doubts remain for about 200 of them. They feel that much more research needs to be done into some of these synthetic chemicals, in particular those that have been cited as carcinogens, endocrine disrupters (see page 106) or as inducing allergies and hyperactivity in children.

Worse still, there are growing concerns about the so-called 'cocktail effect' (see page 106): what all these chemicals are doing in combination once inside our bodies. It's an unsettling thought: in the west, it's calculated that we each eat between six and seven kilos of food additives each year and food regulators test additives only in isolation, not in combination.

Processed food is aggressively marketed. Billions are spent each year by the multinational food companies, convincing us to keep buying their products. And in this hugely competitive market the relative cost of food keeps dropping, so lowering our perceived value of food. Take the cost of the average shopping basket. Fifty years ago, the average European family spent half its income on feeding itself. In the west that figure now stands at 15 per cent and is even lower in the UK and US. Italians, for example, spend 10 per cent of their income on mobile phones versus 12 per cent on what they eat. Some will applaud this because it means more can afford to eat, but can cheap, poor quality food be claimed to be a sensible social investment?

Agricultural subsidies make processed food even cheaper. While most food types receive this kind of funding, a disproportionate amount of money is spent subsidising the key ingredients for processed foods, such as meat, sugar and wheat. Take away the subsidies and a cheap burger, cola and fries deal costing £1.36 would actually cost £4.10. And then there are the low-pay jobs – the so-called 'McJobs' – linked with fast-food chains and food-processing factories...

In short, convenience food has no redeeming features – cut it out of your diet as much as you can.

Slow Food: an antidote to fast food

It's no surprise that the sparks of a major rebellion against our fast-food obsession first ignited in a sleepy town in Italy. The idea for the Slow Food movement, now boasting over 80,000 members across the world, was first cooked up in 1986 in the famous wine centre of Barolo. Its manifesto is simple: 'a movement for the protection of the right to taste'.

The movement now organises the world's largest food festival, the Salone del Gusto (Hall of Taste), which takes place every two years in Turin. In addition, it also oversees the 'Ark of Taste' project: an attempt to identify and catalogue artisan products and regional dishes that are in danger of being lost to the onslaught of fast-food hegemony. For more information about the Slow Food movement, visit www.slowfood.com.

The supermarkets' 'supergrip'

Supermarkets have got us in their pockets. We purchase 80 per cent of our food from them and for every £8 spent by UK consumers, £1 goes to Tesco, the leader of the Big Four supermarkets. The other three are Asda, Sainsbury's and Morrisons. To sustain their allure and maintain the edge in the battle for the UK's £100 billion grocery market, they have a number of tricks up their sleeves...

Own-label goods

Are these as much of a bargain as they seem? Own-label ranges have become more sophisticated. No longer the simply packaged value ranges of the past, they are now cleverly packaged approximations of high-quality brands. In fact, 21 per cent of us are said to have picked up 'copycat' versions of our favourite brands by mistake. Supermarkets in the UK have one of the most advanced own-label programmes in the world. According to market analysts, own-label ranges make UK supermarkets substantially more profitable than their EU counterparts. And they fight hard to ensure that 50 per cent of our shopping baskets are filled with them. Which, in turn, guarantees bigger profit margins.

Whereas brands give consumers quality assurance, there may be some evidence that the quality of own-label ranges has been reduced. As own-label ranges are used in the permanent price war between the Big Four, according to Joanna Blythman in *Shopped: The Shocking Power of British Supermarkets*, some suppliers have complained that they are subject to constant price squeezes and forced to compromise on quality.

'Local' produce

In the absence of any standard, legal definition, supermarkets have largely chosen to interpret the word 'local' as meaning from the same country as opposed to the same county. 'Local' and 'regional' are often deployed in advertising campaigns to appeal to our growing demand for more information about the provenance of food. But in reality there is often only a passing connection behind the terms 'Welsh' lamb or 'Scottish' beef, as the animals may have been pastured in that area for only two weeks. The reason is simple: supermarkets now have hugely centralised operations. Even if produce originates from a field near your local superstore, the chances are that it's still been on a round trip of several hundred miles to be packed. In contrast, farmers' markets usually sell produce grown within a 30–40 mile radius.

Loss leaders

Literally the bread and butter of supermarkets, loss leaders are 'essential' items at knock-down prices aimed at repeatedly luring us in. Often sold at a price below the true cost of production, they're also known as KVIs or 'known value items': essentials such as bread and milk that we know the price of and so are placed at the front line of the supermarkets' fierce price war. Once we're in the store, the KVIs are the benchmark from which we form our impression of a store's overall pricing. Consequently, the retailer is able to take the opportunity to hike up the prices of other items where we are unable to make price comparisons, often healthy, fresh produce.

Loyalty cards

Now that 60 per cent of us have a loyalty card – with 11 million of us now holders of a Nectar combination reward card – points should definitely mean prizes. Although a closer look would suggest that prizes do not always go to the consumer – for example, 500 Nectar points, earned through a £250 spend, buys one McDonald's Medium Value Extra Meal or a movie rental from Blockbuster. You get the burger or video, but the supermarkets' data analysts and marketers get the benefit of all kinds of information about you, such as your shopping habits and projected spending patterns. Collecting those points also prompts us to consolidate our spending at that store, causing us to spend an extra 1–4 per cent. Meanwhile, all that information keeps building up a useful profile of which part of the 'market segment' you belong to (ie, your race, age, income level). And once calculated, the store can then work out how much it needs to keep stocking items you buy: 57 per cent of a store's profits come from just 30 per cent of customers. For more information about how supermarkets use loyalty cards to their gain, visit the Consumers Against Supermarket Privacy Invasion and Numbering (Caspian) website at www.nocards.org.

Buy one get one free

This 'fantastic' offer will be found in one of the supermarket's 'hot spot' positions, such as a gondola end, carefully positioned at eye level. But the 'buy one get one free' deal, or BOGOF as it's known in the trade, is not necessarily as good as it seems. Not unless you know how much the item in question costs in the first place, and you can be pretty sure it won't be as cheap as one of the KVIs. And when, on average, 35 per cent of what we put in the fridge gets thrown away, does it really make sense to double up?

'Farmer's friend' produce

You may have noticed that packaging, especially for meat products, is now emblazoned with the image of a smiling farmer. But is that farmer smiling through gritted teeth? In reality, UK farmers are at the mercy of the supermarket buyers, who are powerful enough to make or break a farmer's business. Just 100 supermarket buyers hold the key to the 250 million consumers in Europe. Farmers live under constant threat of being delisted for non-compliance with supermarkets' demands. As much as 35 per cent of fruit and vegetables are routinely rejected during the 'grade out' (see page 17) for failing to conform to the supermarkets' exacting cosmetic standards.

RFID Technology

Radio frequency identification tags, or 'RFIDs', are now touted as the successor to bar codes. These tiny electronic chips can be secured to packaging and, using

in-store scanners, monitored. Embedded in products, the chips provide a data chain by transmitting radio signals, that are, in turn, picked up by a scanner allowing both the consumer and the goods to be tracked. However, they raise serious consumer privacy issues. Early in 2003 the National Consumer Council identified RFIDs as a major concern as they allow consumers to be covertly monitored and tracked throughout a store. If chips are not deactivated at point of sale, the shopper's purchases could also in theory be scanned in subsequent stores, enabling sophisticated spending profiling. Tescos has already trialled RFIDs on razors (a favourite with shoplifters due to their size-to-price ratio), whereas Marks & Spencer has trialled the technology on the labels of its men's clothes range. For more information about the concerns many have about the use of RFIDs, visit www.spychips.com.

Breaking free from the supermarkets

Since 1969, when the first supermarket opened in the UK, we have steadily become dependent on them. Yet if each of us spent just one per cent of what we spend at the supermarkets with local retailers, farm shops and box schemes, it's estimated that an extra £52 million each year would find its way into the local economy. Beating a path away from the supermarket could also bring you closer to more local, fresh and seasonal produce. . .

Local shops

Between 1995 and 2000 we lost one fifth of our local shops and services and in the five years up to 2002, 50 specialist stores closed every week. Many of us have now realised that driving to an out-of-town superstore to pick up a pint of milk is not that convenient after all. A new movement is afoot to bring back more local shops and support existing ones in towns, high streets and village centres. Independent, local shops can be a natural hub for communities. As they are small, it suits them better to work with local suppliers and producers (as well as cutting down on food miles). A report produced on behalf of the Countryside Agency showed that local shops help the local economy by typically employing between two and 15 people (who can usually walk to work). Fruit and vegetables are usually sold loose, thereby cutting down on packaging, and the shops provide wider community functions as meeting places and information points.

Food co-operatives

Often, those on low incomes can't afford good quality, fresh food. This is being tackled by the establishment of food co-operatives within the community. Usually run by volunteers, the co-operatives buy fresh food wholesale from local suppliers and sell it back to the community for a minimum profit. The schemes work particularly well in urban areas, where higher demand reduces the wholesale price. Successful flagship schemes include the Glasgow Healthy Castlemill Co-operative which serves 3,000 people from local estates, charging them a one per cent mark-up, and the Birmingham Organic Roundabout, which supplies fresh food to around 3,000 households and sources from 36 organic farmers. For more information, contact Sustain (www.sustainweb. org, tel: 020 7837 1228), Co-operatives UK (www.cooponline.coop, tel: 0161 246 2900), or visit www.localfoodworks.org.

Farmers' markets

Since the first farmers' market was held in Bath in 1997, there are now at least 450 markets with a combined annual turnover of more than £160 million. It's a simple concept: farmers, growers or producers from a defined local area (usually a 30–40 mile radius, but this stretches up to 100 miles in urban or very remote rural areas) congregate at a set place and time to sell their own produce direct to the public. The farmer or producer typically gets to take home 80–90 per cent of the 'food pound' – compared with the 10 per cent or so they could expect to receive from the supermarket buyers. The consumer is also able to buy fresh, local produce direct from the seller – and drastically reduce any associated food miles. For a list of farmers' markets around the UK, see page 72.

Box schemes

The first UK box scheme started in 1991 at Northwood Farm, Christow, when the owners began delivering a weekly box of organic vegetables to locals from an eight-hectare holding. Now, 60,000 households across the UK are supplied by 400 box schemes, 300 of which are certified organic by the Soil Association. The best schemes use organic, locally grown, seasonal produce. Only about 30 per cent of the organic food we consume is produced in the UK, so many box schemes do still rely on some imported organic produce, especially during the so-called 'hungry gap' in late spring. But supporting organic box schemes helps the sector expand as well as giving business to local farmers. In Denmark, 95 per cent of all organic food is distributed this way. For a list of box schemes, see page 68.

Community-supported agriculture

Shorten the distance between the farm and the table by getting a stake in the farm that produces your food. Community-supported agriculture is an idea imported from the US, where there are more than 1,000 schemes with 77,000 members. Members pay growers for a share of the farm's harvest and in turn growers provide a weekly share of food from the farm of guaranteed quality and quantity. Research shows that the produce from these schemes is around one third cheaper than that found in supermarkets and the scheme also guarantees farmers a steady income. And because farmers grow specifically for the consumer's needs, CSA schemes can also promote diversity of food and crops. Growers are freed up from producing the crop that produces the highest yields or what the supermarkets demand. Consumers, meanwhile, get a chance to 'connect' with their food, especially if they take up the opportunity to get their hands dirty every now and again. For more information, visit www.cuco.org.uk.

Pick your own/farm shops

From May to October pick-your-own schemes offer the ultimate way to connect with produce by harvesting your own from local farms. The pick-your-own season traditionally starts with asparagus, followed by broad beans and strawberries through to soft fruits from the end of summer and into autumn. There are 1,500–2,000 registered farms (many certified organic) throughout the country so it's usually possible to find somewhere local. Overall, pick-your-own produce is cheaper than that found in supermarkets. It is also unpackaged, as you usually take your own container with you. And children find picking their own food fun.

Allotments

Make sure that your food is free from pesticides and additives, and reduce food miles by getting an allotment. Research by the Gardening for Health allotment programme in Bradford has also shown that, apart from learning gardening skills, participants learn food preparation and dietary skills as they incorporate their freshly grown produce into their diets. In the UK there are 300,000 allotments on 12,150 hectares yielding 215,000 tonnes of fresh produce. But the number of allotments is in decline (see page 116) so sign up now for one and help the UK to preserve this important public growing space. For more information, contact the National Society of Allotment and Leisure Gardeners (www.nsalg.org.uk, tel: 01536 266576).

Dairy

In 2001 a cow called Marissa broke milk records in the UK: at nine years old, she had produced more than 100,000 litres of milk from just seven calvings, averaging 35 litres a day for 10 years.

The lot of most dairy cows is not a happy one. New production methods have increased a dairy cow's average annual yield from 4,000 litres a few decades ago to 5,800 litres today. In order to lactate, cows obviously need to give birth to calves. But calves are generally used as a device to stimulate a cow's milk production: as the milk is destined for human consumption, the cow will almost never get to suckle her calf. Unable to produce milk, and therefore useless to the £6 billion dairy industry, male calves are usually killed within two weeks.

High yields are everything in modern farming and it's no different on dairy farms. Consequently, cows are given fertility drugs to increase pregnancy rates. Some are milked up to three times a day, and days are lengthened by the use of artificial lighting. The intensive nature of milking combined with large dairy herds held in cramped conditions leads to mastitis, dystocia, lameness and overstocking of udders. Up to 20 per cent of the UK dairy herd has a 'physiological abnormality causing them to be lame', according to the Farm Animal Welfare Council. But the condition of dairy herds can also have implications for human health: a cow's illness is routinely controlled by large doses of antibiotics, which can find their way into dairy products. As is the case with most foods, buying organic dairy products is the best way to ensure both higher standards of welfare for cattle and to avoid antibiotic residues in produce.

Since intensive farming methods became commonplace, a milking cow's life expectancy has gradually decreased and now lasts on average only three or four 'lactations'. In fact, only a quarter of all dairy cows live to more than seven years, and a quarter are culled before they are 39 months old. What's more, half of all dairy cows are now slaughtered for beef, inextricably linking the dairy and beef trades – often a reason given by vegans for avoiding dairy altogether.

When buying dairy products, always buy those produced within the EU, preferably the UK, as outside the EU milk yields can be boosted – up to 15 per cent – using a synthetic version of a cow's growth hormone called recombinant bovine somatotropin (rBST). Some campaigners, particularly in the US where it is used, believe that milk produced using rBST is linked to a rise in levels of the hormone IGF-1, which, the campaigners claim, is linked to breast and colon cancer, hypertension and diabetes in some consumers. On the other hand, respected health bodies, such as the UN Food and Agriculture Organisation and the World Health Organisation, have passed the use of rBST as safe. However, a precautionary approach seems sensible.

But beyond the issues of animal welfare and the intensification of farming methods, there are other areas of concern for the ethically minded consumer when it comes to consuming dairy products…

> As milk is destined for human consumption, the cow will almost never get to suckle her own calf

Since 1997 the income of most dairy farmers, including income from subsidies, has averaged at **£2.90 per hour**

Subsidies

Who gets the benefits of increasing yields? Not the farmers, it seems. It costs the UK dairy farmer about 18–23p on average to produce a litre of milk, yet since 2000 average 'farm-gate' prices have been about 16–20p per litre, leading to the fact that since 1997 the income of most dairy farmers has, including income from subsidies, averaged at £2.90 per hour. However, a litre of milk sells in the shops for about 43p.

A report by Sustain has shown that milk processing and exporting companies receive seven times more subsidies than dairy farmers. Common Agricultural Policy (CAP) subsidies also allow traders to export dairy products below cost onto the international market, often destroying the livelihoods of small-scale farms in developing nations, such as Jamaica and Kenya, where farmers cannot compete.

Subsidies have almost become synonymous with milk and dairy. Dairy farmers have received subsidies from the EU's CAP since the 1950s – introduced then to ensure a constant and secure food supply after the lean and insecure postwar years. By the 1980s, the dairy industry was over-producing on such a large scale that TV footage showed farmers pouring surplus milk down drains. Milk quotas were introduced for each farm in an effort to reduce production. However, as each farmer intensified production to increase revenue, standards of animal welfare inevitably declined. Many smaller dairy farmers went out of business, leaving large-scale industrialised farms to monopolise the industry. Meanwhile, quotas became precious commodities and until 2003, anybody could trade in milk quotas, which were bought and sold like company shares.

Food miles

Dairy products are likely to have clocked up a significant amount of food miles before they reach your fridge. Between 1961 and 1999, milk exports increased by 500 per cent. Perversely, in 2001 the UK exported 149,000 tonnes of milk (mostly to non-EU countries), but also imported 110,000 tonnes of fresh milk (mostly from the EU).

Once milk is turned into another dairy product the

food miles rise further. A German study that examined the environmental costs of producing a jar of strawberry yoghurt found that, although the milk and the jar that contained it were produced locally, the strawberries had been imported from Poland. The yoghurt was then processed on the other side of the country at a central processing depot. The yoghurt cultures used had been brought in from north Germany and sugar beet brought in from the east of the country. Meanwhile, corn and wheat flour (surprising ingredients for a yoghurt, perhaps) came from the Netherlands. Altogether, to produce the yoghurt, a hypothetical truck travelled over 1,000 kilometres using 400 litres of diesel.

Therefore, it makes sense to support small, local producers by buying from farmers' markets and local suppliers wherever possible.

Feed for dairy herds

What farmers feed their dairy herds has long been a contentious issue. One of the major concerns today is GM feed. Post BSE, feeding intensively reared cows on bonemeal made from ruminants is illegal and many farmers have subsequently found alternative cheap feed in the form of GM soya and maize. Six per cent of animal feed in the UK is now GM. Although the Dairy Industry Association still denies that British milk contains GM material, action groups point to the fact that many consumers are unaware that dairy herds are fed on GM soya and maize. Research by Greenpeace in 2004 suggested that the UK dairy industry could stop using imported GM cattle feed for an increased cost of just under 1p per litre of milk. It also suggested that supermarkets bear the extra cost as almost all of their own-brand milk comes from cows fed on GM feed imported from the US and Argentina. Campaigners such as Greenpeace and Farm (an organisation promoting the interests of UK farmers) would like to see farmers grow some of their own food – lupins, for example – as dairy herd feed. This would help to raise consumer confidence about the provenance of milk and prevent reliance on controversial GM technology, which is only used because it can produce cheaper feed.

Unsurprisingly, the better the cow's diet, the healthier the butter made from the milk. Researchers at Queens University, Belfast, found a diet rich in rapeseed yields healthier milk. This, in turn, produces a more naturally spreadable butter – a key demand of butter consumers. Dairy products also, said the researchers, contain lower levels of saturated fats – linked to heart disease and obesity – and higher levels of unsaturated fats, which may help decrease cholesterol levels in humans. Rapeseed is rich in unsaturated fats, which pass through the cow's digestive system into its milk. One of these fats, oleic acid, makes butter spread more easily when still chilled. Stocked by retailers including Marks & Spencer, this is a good alternative to spreads or margarines containing hydrogenated vegetable oils, and is a lower-fat alternative to conventional butter.

High-fat diets

The production of one fifth of regular, full-fat butter is subsidised. This raises the question: why are we taxed in order to put unwanted butter into our diets at a time when 22 per cent of Britons are obese and three-quarters are deemed overweight? The WHO's annual report in 2002 reported that 60 per cent of world deaths are 'clearly related to changes in dietary patterns and increased consumption of processed fatty, salty and sugary foods'. In contrast, the EU is still promoting the consumption of full-fat dairy products in a number of different ways:

● Subsidies for schools to buy full-fat milk, yoghurt and cheese and incentives to schools to set up 'milk bars', despite the fact that 10 per cent of six-year-olds are obese, rising to 17 per cent of 15-year-olds.
● Subsidies to bakers, ice-cream and chocolate makers to use butter – a quarter of EU butter enters our food in this way.
● Subsidies to school and hospital caterers to use butter instead of vegetable oils.

Dilemma

Why cow's milk? Why not donkey milk?

We grow up on milk, progressing from breastmilk or formula straight on to cows' milk. The 'Great British Pinta' occupies a special place in our national consciousness. It's become the ultimate nutritional hero, the 'liquid calcium' saviour of children's bones and teeth, the defender against osteoporosis, and is endorsed by celebrities and sporting heroes through TV advertising such as the 'White Stuff' campaign.

It's the 'stuff' of our childhood. And the dairy industry would like it to be the stuff of our adult life too. In 2002, the National Dairy Council launched a campaign to target the two-and-a-half million young adults and women who they claim do not get enough calcium in their diets and so are at risk of osteoporosis. The prescription? A three-a-day dairy plan, including a pint of milk. However, a study conducted over 15 years and published in the British Medical Journal found that 'reduced intake of dietary calcium does not seem to be a risk factor' and recommended that exercise may be the best protection. It has also been shown that although women in the US are among the highest consumers of calcium in the world, they also have one of the highest levels of osteoporosis in the world.

A substantial number of people are also lactose intolerant – allergic to the naturally occurring sugar in cow's milk (and, incidentally, goat's milk). As early as 1965 investigators at Johns Hopkins University in the US found that 15 per cent of white people and almost three-quarters of black people they tested were unable to digest lactose.

So why do we continue to drink cow's milk? Partly because the majority of us think it's necessary for a healthy diet. After all, children were given free milk at school every day for almost 25 years on nutritional grounds until Margaret 'Milk Snatcher' Thatcher took it away. Then there's the fact that the UK's dairy industry is heavily subsidised; its herds of primarily Holstein Friesians (the breed that produces the biggest milk yield) are pushed into producing a certain amount of milk to fulfil quotas. Meanwhile, Defra sponsors both the dairy industry and the marketing of milk through the Milk Development Council.

But without these influencing factors we might well be drinking ewe's milk or even donkey's milk. Both were commonly available in the UK until the 1900s, and some consider donkey milk to be better for infants as it contains more protein, and substantially less fat, than cow's milk. But how would contemporary marketeers try to sell us cartons of donkey milk? They would be faced with an insurmountable image problem. It's an example of how, as consumers, we are often unquestioning in accepting that a product is automatically the 'best' option for us.

The story of the egg

The first 'egg quality standard' was introduced during the war in 1941. Egg producers – at that time, small-scale farmers who reared hens on mixed farms – were policed by 'area egg officers' supervising efficient production to help feed the nation through the rationing years. Egg production in the early post-war years was a much more serious affair, forming the shape of today's multi-million-pound industry, which now 'lays' 8,940 million eggs a year.

In 1957 the British Lion symbol appeared for the first time. It was developed as the symbol of the British Egg Marketing Board, who bought up most of the UK's eggs, paying a pool price to producers and then selling them through retailers. The symbol is still found on 80 per cent of UK eggs. Since 1988 the symbol also denotes that the laying hen has been vaccinated against salmonella and a best-before date has also been added as part of the drive to make eggs safe for public consumption. It does not, however, suggest that the eggs are free range, which is sometimes an area of confusion for consumers.

The egg boom

The British Egg Marketing Board launched their famous 'go to work on an egg' slogan in the 1960s and sent egg sales soaring. They were marketed as the perfect convenience food (an idea used again in a 2001 advertising campaign): easy to cook yet packed with nutritional goodness. But behind the scenes the first large-scale battery farms were starting to emerge, using wire cages to house thousands of birds in one place.

Battery hens

Over the years, the living conditions of battery hens has caused considerable debate. Thousands of hens are kept four to a cage, where they are able to display little, if any, natural behaviour such as flapping their wings or scratching the ground. Kept under artificial light for 16 hours a day, one hen must lay over 300 eggs in a year.

In 1997, the Farm Animal Welfare Council, an independent advisory body established by the government in 1979, stated that confinement in a caged system leads to broken bones and extensive feather and foot damage. At 70 weeks, old 'spent' hens are typically sold to processors for as little as 2p and converted into a range of foods including babyfood, pies and soups. Under normal conditions, these hens would go through a non-laying moulting season then continue to lay during a five- to six-year lifespan.

The salmonella years

The plight of battery hens and the problems caused by intensive farming and high stocking densities was publicly highlighted in 1987. Edwina Currie, then minister for health, became forever associated with eggs when she claimed that most British eggs were infected with salmonella. Egg sales fell by 10 per cent and over 5,000 producers went out of business. Edwina Currie was sacked. However, in 1989 her claims were vindicated when a House of Commons select committee announced that there was indeed a link between eggs and salmonella. Two million chickens were slaughtered as a precaution.

Arguably, this was the first time that consumers became aware of the serious potential health cost attached to intensively farmed, cheap eggs. Following the salmonella scare a programme was set up to vaccinate laying hens against the most common form of the disease, salmonella enteritidis. Throughout the 1990s there was a steady decrease in the number of cases of human illness through the disease. In 2004 an FSA survey announced that the risk of salmonella had been halved through vaccination. Out of 28,518 eggs tested (from battery to organic) only one in every 290 boxes of six eggs was found to have any salmonella contamination.

Drug contamination

So are eggs safe to eat now? You should certainly avoid battery-farmed eggs, despite the success of salmonella vaccinations. Finding non-battery produced eggs is now much easier. As part of labelling laws introduced in 2004, producers are no longer permitted to use terms such as 'fresh' or 'farm fresh', but have to specify 'eggs from caged birds'. These eggs are produced in an inhumane way and the use of drugs through feed and the risk of contamination is high. The Veterinary Residues Committee (VRC) has pointed to unacceptably high levels of use of drugs in the poultry industry, mostly aimed at combating fast-spreading infections and parasites. A recent VRC survey found nearly one in 10 chickens tested breached limits for the drug nicarbazin. Inspectors believe that a mix-up at a feeding mill could have been partly to blame. In addition, if chicken coops are not cleaned out regularly, birds can end up ingesting more drugs than intended.

Similarly, in 2004 the Soil Association reported that up to three million eggs eaten each day in the UK were contaminated with another such drug, lasalocid, one that is banned in the EU for use with laying hens. Lasalocid has been linked to Sudden Adult Death Syndrome and cardiac arrhythmia, a disease that affects half a million people in the UK. The FSA responded by saying levels of lasalocid in eggs did not raise any immediate health concerns for consumers. It did add though that it was urging the industry to address this problem and was 'disappointed by the failure of industry to take effective action against bad practice'.

The end of battery hens?

Thankfully, the EU is finally calling time on battery-caged systems. In 2003, the EU Laying Hens Directive announced that battery cages would be phased out by 2006. This has proved to be something of a pyrrhic victory for campaigners as standard cages can be replaced by 'enriched' cages (see page 35). But does this really represent a better standard of welfare for hens – a bird whose natural habitat is the forest floor? The issue for many groups and consumers is that hens should not be kept in cages at all. It remains to be seen whether the UK government will follow Germany's lead and ban all cages.

Producers say it will cost them around £687 million to switch to enriched or free-range systems, bringing about the end of cheap eggs. They also warn of the threat of cheap, unregulated imports. However, half a dozen free-range eggs already cost around 50p more than eggs from caged hens and still make up a quarter of the egg market. There is also rapidly growing demand for British organic eggs (demand already outstrips supply) which make up two per cent of the market.

Alternative egg production

While free-range systems are preferable, they don't raise standards as much as many of us may imagine: flock sizes are still large – up to 1,000 birds per hectare – and birds are kept in at night. Many birds are still de-beaked in an effort to prevent feather plucking and cannibalism caused by cramped conditions. In theory, the birds must have access to the outdoors for at least eight hours a day. But when researchers from Oxford University monitored a commercial chicken farm in 2003, they found that just 15 per cent of the chickens even poked their heads outside. The rest were deterred by aggressive birds blocking the exit.

Free-range hens, like their battery cousins, are routinely fed yolk colourants in feed. These are usually citranaxanthin (E161) and beta-apo 8 carotenol (E160), which help egg yolks to score 8/9 on the Roche scale, the official egg yolk colouring chart. Both colourants are classified as safe additives, but their widespread use begs the question as to why producers feel the need to include extra additives to give yolks a fake colour.

Similarly, hens in 'barn egg' systems are also fed yolk colourants and antibiotics. In this system, birds are kept indoors in 'barns' and equipped with perches, nest boxes and facilities for dust bathing, which gives them some opportunity to display natural behaviours. But they are still subject to beak trimming and can live in colonies of up to 4,000 birds.

Ideally, it's best to buy organic eggs. Organic systems have lower stocking densities, prohibit beak trimming and birds are fed a natural vegetarian diet. Alternatively, buy eggs certified by the RSPCA's Freedom Food scheme (www.freedomfood.org.uk), which offers higher standards of animal welfare and has been particularly successful – 82 million Freedom Food eggs are now sold every month.

EXPLAINER Fair trade

FAIRTRADE Guarantees a **better deal** for Third World Producers

How did it all start?

The official Fairtrade mark was launched in 1994. In March 2004, the Fairtrade Foundation celebrated the 10th anniversary with an announcement that sales of fair-trade products in the UK had broken through the £100 million-a-year barrier.

It all started with just three companies, Clipper, Green & Black's and Cafédirect, offering the UK's first certifiably fair-trade products – tea, Maya Gold chocolate and coffee, respectively. Now British shoppers can choose from more than 250 products from more than 100 companies.

But what does fair trade mean?

Fair trade addresses social and economic justice. Whereas the organic movement has been driven primarily by concerns about the environment and the sustainability and potential health risks of industrialised agriculture, fair trade centres on the plight of the grower or farmer. It acknowledges that the lot of many growers and producers in the developing world is often a pretty miserable one. Overall, world trade has grown sixfold since the early 1990s, yet the price of commodities has scarcely risen in 20 years. It's a situation that has led some growers to trade at a loss, and work and live in poor conditions.

The aim of fair trade is to give power back to the workers rather than impose an unfair commercial system on them from afar. Disadvantaged producers gain access to more lucrative markets and growers, producers and consumers together send out the message that the dominant world trading system (see below) can be challenged. To do this, fair-trade buyers adhere to a set of principles:

● Pay producers a price that covers production. When markets are buoyant, the fair-trade price increases, but when international prices fall, the producer still receives an agreed price. This gives growers some financial security, allowing them to plan for the future.
● Encourage social premiums. Although the emphasis is always on trade rather than aid, fair trade is also about development. As a consumer, you may pay more for fair trade, but the surplus is channelled back into developing

some key aspect of the producer's life, perhaps through contributing to a local school.
● Promote democratic organisations. Smallholders and larger groups, such as plantation workers, are organised into cooperatives or other democratic groups and allowed to join unions to protect their rights.
● Prohibit child labour.
● Promote decent and fair working conditions, and recognise trade unions.
● Promote environmental sustainability. Fair trade encourages pesticide-free, sustainable farming methods.

During the 1990s, several organisations, including Christian Aid, Oxfam, Traidcraft and the World Development Movement, created the Fairtrade Foundation (www.fairtrade.org.uk). The foundation now awards the UK's Fairtrade mark, which guarantees a better deal for third world producers. The mark also guarantees that every person and organisation along the supply chain, including producers, processors, wholesalers and retailers, has conformed to the foundation's trading standards and will:

● Pay a price to producers that covers the costs of sustainable production and living.
● Pay a premium that producers can invest in development.
● Partially pay in advance, when producers ask for it.
● Sign contracts that allow for longterm planning and sustainable production practices.

The Fairtrade Foundation is the UK member of the Fairtrade Labelling Organisation (FLO), based in Germany. Nineteen other international fair-trade organisations also belong to the FLO. Details of their logos can be found at www.fairtrade.net.

What fair-trade products are available?

Since 2004, FLO standards have existed for coffee, tea, cocoa, sugar, honey, various fresh fruits and vegetables, dried fruit, fruit juices, rice, wine, nuts and oilseeds, cut flowers, ornamental plants, spices and herbs, cotton and sports balls.

Bananas are one of the movement's biggest success stories. As the UK's most popular fruit, overtaking apples in 1998, about seven billion bananas are shipped to the UK each year. Bananas make up approximately 28 per cent of all fruit sales in the UK, significantly contributing to supermarket profits – only petrol and lottery tickets generate higher sales and the profit from these items is negligible. Bananas are the subject of frequent price-cutting wars between supermarket chains, which invariably means growers' profits are squeezed. But even though competition is exceptionally fierce, a million fair-trade bananas are sold a week at Sainsbury's, thereby guaranteeing thousands of workers a fair wage.

Further standards are being developed all the time, but as the Fairtrade mark can be applied only to products containing commodities for which there are internationally agreed suppliers and prices, it is not yet available on clothing, textiles, craft goods or toiletries. However, fair-trade versions of these products can be found either through fair-trade shops, run by the British Association for Fair Trade Shops (www.bafts.org.uk), or Oxfam (www.oxfam.org.uk), which has run fair-trade projects for many years and sells its own branded textiles and crafts. Similarly, Traidcraft (www.traidcraft.org.uk), the UK's leading fair-trade organisation, sells more than 100 different fair-trade ranges, some bearing just the organisation's own logo, and others that have also been certified by the Fairtrade Foundation.

More recently, the concept of fair trade has started to move into the workplace and can form an important part of an organisation's green-purchasing strategy (see page 268). In March 2004, the Office of Government Commerce issued guidelines on how government procurement offices could source fair-trade foods. The Salvation Army, Youth Hostel Association and British Medical Association have now all made the switch to fair-trade tea and coffee.

Is conventional trade really that 'unfair'?

Over the past decade, growing numbers of consumers and charities such as Action Aid, Oxfam and Christian Aid have turned their attention to what they perceive to be gross inequalities in trade laws between the richest and poorest countries. Groups such as the Trade Justice Movement (www.tjm.org.uk) and campaigns such as Oxfam's Make Trade Fair (www.maketradefair.com) are committed to changing world trade rules in order to fight global poverty.

Through 'free-trade' agreements and systems created and enforced by the World Bank, the World Trade Organisation and the International Monetary Fund, the poorest nations are forced to open up their markets to rich nations, who simultaneously protect their own markets through subsidies and tariffs. For example, the richest countries spend an estimated $1 billion a day on agricultural subsidies, but often end up dumping surplus crops grown using the subsidies on world markets at a much reduced price, thereby greatly undermining producers in the poorest countries trying to sell their own produce.

In a 2002 report entitled *Rigged Rules and Double Standards*, Oxfam said that 'if Africa, East Asia, South Asia, and Latin America were each to increase their share of world exports by one per cent, the resulting gains in income could lift 128 million people out of poverty. In Africa alone, this would generate $70 billion – approximately five times what the continent receives in aid.'

And when the richest countries have the upper hand, the poorest countries have little voice and, consequently, even less power. The fair-trade movement articulates the plight of producers to consumers all over the world. In *The No-Nonsense Guide to Fair Trade*, David Ransom writes: 'One way or another, unfair free trade is now on trial. That involves discovering exactly how and by whom the things we consume are made, and examining the evidence. Conventional trade relies on our remaining blind to this kind of evidence. The greatest single virtue of fair trade is that it encourages us to take a closer look, to engage more critically with the intriguing, sometimes shameful, details of everyday life.'

Further reading
www.guardian.co.uk/fairtrade
www.fairtrade.org.uk
www.fairtrade.net
www.traidcraft.co.uk
www.bafts.org.uk
www.ifat.org
www.tjm.org.uk
www.maketradefair.com

The store cupboard

Rice

It is the world's most common crop, covering about one per cent of the Earth's land surface. It is also the primary food source for billions of people.

Rice cultivation causes one per cent of the total methyl bromide and five per cent of the methyl iodide emissions – both ozone depleters – into the atmosphere. And its cultivation largely relies on the widespread use of pesticides and fertilisers – of extra environmental concern due to the amount of surface water required to grow rice.

Organic rice is becoming more available. In 2003, the Spanish Ornithological Society planted its first certified crop of organic rice at their Riet Vell nature reserve in Spain's Ebro Delta in an attempt to attract birdlife back to the area following a period of high-intensity rice production. It is now available from the RSPCA. Fairtrade rice is also making its first tentative steps onto the market. But if neither of these is readily available choose brown rice over white, as it's nutritionally superior. White rice has been milled and its outer bran layer removed, losing about 2.5g of fibre and between two-thirds and a half of its vitamins and minerals, such as magnesium, riboflavin, niacin, selenium and zinc, per cup.

Bread

Considering how much of it we eat, we can hardly claim to be a nation of bread enthusiasts. About 80 per cent of bread sold in the UK is the sliced, plastic-wrapped product of the ubiquitous 'Chorleywood Bread Process' – a highly-industrialised method that, through the addition of extra fat, yeast, ascorbic acid, salt and sugar, reduces proving times from hours to a matter of minutes. It may cut down on time and money, but it also cuts down on taste and nutritional value.

Most bread is made from refined flour – removing most of the wheat's natural fibre, vitamins and minerals – and then 'fortified', that's to say, the vitamins are artificially added again. Why not just eat wholesome bread in the first place, and, by doing so, give custom to the country's artisan bakers? An astonishing 81 per cent of the UK's bread is made by just 12 companies – the two largest, Allied Bakeries and British Bakeries,

accounting for 55 per cent of sales. Supermarket in-store bakeries make up 17 per cent of sales, leaving just 2 per cent for the small bakeries, such as Greggs, and artisan bakers. As always, this monoculture means losing our long bread-making heritage that gave us varieties such as Bara Plac, Cornish saffron cake, Glasgow rolls, Hawkshead Wigs and the Huffkin.

Cooking oil

Ask most people what the healthiest cooking or salad oil is and the response will invariably be 'olive oil'. You wouldn't be wrong in thinking so, but, as one of the most subsidised food items produced in the EU, olive oil receives plenty of funding for positive, health-related PR. The fact is that, in terms of omega-3 content, a health-giving essential fatty acid, other oils fare much better, for example, flax and linseed (both contain 53 per cent omega-3), walnut (19 per cent), soybean (7 per cent) and rapeseed (9 per cent). In comparison, olive oil contains just one per cent omega-3.

There are environmental considerations when choosing oil. Olive oil has traditionally been a sustainable crop throughout southern Europe but intensification of its farming has led to soil erosion and reduced biodiversity. Other edible, less popularised oils to consider include hemp, safflower, walnut and poppy. However, most of the world's vegetable oil comes from soya beans, which have the triple negative associations with GM technology, high pesticide use and the widespread clearing of virgin rainforest in places such as Brazil. Palm oil is also linked to rainforest clearance. Oilseed rape is the only vegetable oil crop (also known as canola oil) grown in temperate climates and will therefore clock up fewer food miles. Groundnut oil is an important crop for farmers from poorer nations and is often traded via local co-operatives. Therefore, it is the nearest thing to a fair-trade oil – ask the retailer or manufacturer where it came from to be sure.

Canned foods

Steel cans have been used for packaging since 1810 and they are still one of the world's most popular ways for the longterm storage of food. But to stop the food tasting of tin and to prevent corrosion, manufacturers line the inside of many cans with Bisphenol A, which, as a suspected endocrine disrupter, has been the focus of campaigns by Friends of the Earth and WWF. In 2003, Friends of the Earth said that about 80 per cent of cans still contained the chemical despite protestations – a problem compounded by the fact that manufacturers are not required to declare its presence on labels. Think about using bottled produce instead and, in general, cut back on tinned products to reduce your intake of processed food. Recycle any cans you do use – the amount of steel retrieved from cans in Europe each year is said to be the equivalent of 132 Eiffel Towers, or 4,000 jumbo jets.

Sugar

Sugar may leave a sweet taste in the mouth, but its production sours the environment and, quite simply, makes us fat.

There are two principal sources of sugar: sugar cane – which accounts for 82 per cent of the world's production – and sugar beet, which is largely grown within Europe and sold under brand names such as Silver Spoon. Both raise major environmental concerns.

To grow sugar cane, nitrogen and phosphorus are applied to the ground to promote growth. As sugar cane requires plenty of water to grow (an extra five million litres of water per hectare can raise yields by three tonnes per hectare), coastal wetlands and mangrove areas are often popular areas to grow crops. But the run-off from agrochemicals is a major problem. In Queensland, Australia, run-off from sugar cane crops has damaged the Great Barrier Reef. Sugar cane crops are traditionally burnt prior to harvest to kill off pests and clear foliage, thereby causing air pollution.

Sugar beet is heavily sprayed with pesticides – up to 13 different pesticides in some cases in the UK. It requires a lot of energy and mechanisation to get it out of the ground and, crucially, is one of the most heavily subsidised crops in the EU (see page 21) – it is now one of the most over-supplied crops in the world.

Sugar, in all its many forms (brown, refined, syrup, molasses, dextrose, etc), is stripped of virtually all its natural nutrients when processed and is often referred to as 'empty' calories by nutritionists. It is also used excessively and extensively in processed foods (see page 48).

Other than excluding it from your diet as much as possible, the next best option is to buy organic or fair-trade sugars. Sugar growers in Costa Rica now provide that rarest of commodities – a product that is both organic and fair trade.

Drink

Over the past decade, it seems that what you drink has become an increasingly important signifier of your status and lifestyle. Whereas drinks such as wine, spirits, tea and even cola have traditionally 'said something' about the drinker, the recent boom in coffee bars, juice bars and bottled water suggest that we want our drinks to do much more than quench our thirst. But the next time you buy that juice or coffee on the way to work, consider the following. . .

Orange juice

By far the world's most popular fruit juice, orange juice makes us think of sunny, healthy living. But the truth is that the vast majority of the orange juice we drink is actually the product of a highly industrialised process that can harm the environment and even promote child labour. Its nutritional value is also questionable.

The US is the largest consumer of orange juice by far, drinking about half of all the world's juice – 20 litres per person a year, compared to 14 litres in the UK. Such is the appetite for orange juice in the US that it conceived and nurtured the Florida Department of Citrus. In the 1940s, it was decided that an alternative supply of oranges was necessary in case the Floridian crop ever suffered frost damage. The Brazilian orange industry was then created – now the largest in the world and a producer of a third of the world's oranges – 95 per cent of which are juiced. Florida is the second-largest producer, growing 15 per cent of the world's oranges.

Most orange juice is sold as a concentrate, which means it has been pasteurised then evaporated until its total water content is down to just 35 per cent. This allows its naturally short shelf life to be extended from a few days to many months. But the production methods involved in this process are extremely resource-intensive. A single glass of orange juice requires 22 glasses of water for processing and over 1,000 glasses of water for irrigation. And for every tonne of orange juice produced, 100kg of crude oil and diesel are required to pasteurise and concentrate the juice.

Orange farming relies heavily on the use of pesticides and fertilisers. In 1999, the UK Working Party on Pesticide Residues found pesticide residues in all 66 samples of oranges from a range of countries including Israel, Morocco, South Africa, Spain and Zimbabwe. The lack of diversity in orange varieties used is also a problem. Spain, for example, grows mainly navels and navelinas. The market can become flooded with the same varieties, farmers can then receive lower prices for their crops, and a monoculture of crops is promoted which can threaten biodiversity. The industry's links to child labour are also of major concern. In Brazil and Mexico it has been reported that thousands of children work as orange pickers. Because concentrated juice is rarely labelled with its country of origin, it's impossible to know which orange juice could be the product of child labour. These children can be paid as little as 21 cents an hour over a 14-hour day and are also closely exposed to highly toxic pesticides. Buying fair-trade orange juice, preferably organic, is the only way to avoid this.

Pay attention to the type of the orange juice you buy too. 'Made from concentrate' means that the juice has been concentrated and frozen abroad before being reconstituted in the UK with water, then pasteurised and possibly even supplemented with orange oils. 'Not From Concentrate' (also called NFC or 'Pure Squeezed') is juice that has been freshly squeezed and pasteurised abroad before being shipped to the UK. 'Freshly squeezed' means the oranges are shipped to the UK as fruit, then squeezed and delivered to stores within 24 hours.

But what you should be most wary of is 'orange juice drink', a product that is commonly marketed at children, most famously by Sunny Delight (or Sunny D as it is now known). By law, orange juice drink need only contain one per cent orange juice and typically includes added ingredients such as water, artificial sweeteners, colourings and flavourings. According to the Food Commission, some 'juice drinks' and squashes contain so little pure juice that if parents were trying to buy pure juices at the same price per litre, it could cost them up to £34.67 for a litre.

Similarly, it said that some children's juice products contained so little real juice that a child would have to down 100 cartons to consume one litre.

Coffee

The rapid growth of high-street coffee shops was one of the symbols of the 1990s. The idea of a female-friendly meeting place acting as an alternative to pubs and bars was popularised by the Central Perk café in the US sitcom *Friends*, but is illustrated by the explosion of international coffee retail brands such as Starbucks.

Behind the skinny lattes and moccachinos lies the humble coffee bean — and the farmers who grow it. Coffee, the world's second most valuable commodity after oil, is grown predominantly in a band of 50 or so countries located near the equator and provides a living for more than 20 million farmers. Including those involved in growing, processing, trading and retailing it, up to 100 million people worldwide earn their living out of coffee.

But those who actually farm the coffee see the smallest share of the profits. Most coffee farmers live in some of the poorest countries on earth, and their cut from their crops is getting ever smaller. It's estimated that since the 1980s, revenue from the coffee trade

has doubled to reach $60 billion a year. But whereas in the 1980s the coffee-producing countries would have kept 30 per cent of that revenue, now they keep only 10 per cent.

This is mostly due to the handful of companies dominating the world's coffee markets. In 2000, Nestlé, the world's largest food company, purchased 13 per cent of the world's coffee beans. Kraft and Sara Lee are among the other major players. Inevitably, this small band of buyers weild incredible influence and in recent years have forced coffee bean prices down to a 30-year low. The result is that the economic fate of coffee-producing nations is now largely in these companies' control. In Ethiopia, coffee accounts for 50 per cent of total export revenues. In Burundi, the figure is 80 per cent. Falling coffee prices are now affecting Honduras, Colombia, Guatemala, Costa Rica, El Salvador, Uganda, and Rwanda.

The environmental cost of coffee farming is hard to bear as well. Farmers in Vietnam and Brazil, who are among the world's largest coffee bean exporters, have relied heavily on intensive production methods and, as a result, large swaths of land have been effectively poisoned. Don't forget that harmful residues from pesticides can end up in your cup of coffee. (A note on instant coffee: because the process of making instant coffee strips away the bean's distinctive aroma, other additives, including volatile oils, are added to make it smell of fresh coffee.)

One of the principal success stories of the fair-trade movement has been the popularity of fair-trade coffee which is now widely available. In 2004, Oxfam said it was launching the UK's first fair-trade high-street coffee shops called Progreso (www.progreso.org.uk). By 2007, it expects to have opened 20 shops across the country.

Alcohol

If you're looking for an example of how good can flourish from bad, the story of the anti-freeze scandal in Austrian wine is hard to beat. In 1985, unscrupulous Austrian winemakers used an anti-freeze called diethylene glycol instead of a natural glucose on their grapes to cut cost. The resulting scandal decimated the country's wine industry but, in turn, led the country to adopt organic farming principles across a large proportion of its farms. Austria is now one of Europe's flagship organic wine producers.

But the tale highlights the fact that many of our alcoholic drinks contain additives. Current EU labelling laws do not force the wine and beer industries to adhere to the same nutritional labelling requirements as food producers. An ingredients listing on a bottle of wine would not make comforting reading. For example, some wines are labelled 'suitable for vegetarians'. This is because it will have been made without animal-derived fining agents such as isinglass, derived from fish swim-bladders.

There's no reason to assume that even organic wines are totally free from additives or pesticide residues. A recent survey of organic and standard wines from southern Italy found residues of various pesticides and fungicides in 61 per cent of organic and 87 per cent of conventional wines. A second study found that while lead contamination of wine – a result of heavy-industry emissions collecting on grapes – had fallen drastically from the 1950s to the present day, the levels were still high enough for variations in lead contamination to be used to authenticate the location of the vintners. For example, a recent study of Bulgarian wine found that varieties from a vineyard in a heavily polluted region contained more than double the maximum amount of lead allowed.

Beyond the issue of additives and pesticide residues, the consumption of alcohol throws up other ethical considerations. While much is made about the reported health-giving properties of red wine if drunk in moderation, there's no denying that alcoholism and alcohol-related social disorder plague the industry. The issue of corporate responsibility is one that the drinks industry evidently worries about, given that it funds the Portman Group, an organisation that exists to promote responsible drinking. Even so, the Portman Group has opposed measures such as lowering the permissible blood alcohol level for drivers as a drink-driving prevention strategy.

Spotlight

Dasani's watery grave

Few brands have fallen from grace so spectacularly as Coca-Cola's bottled water Dasani. In 2004, Coca-Cola had to withdraw all UK supplies of its newly launched Dasani brand after levels of bromate were found to be in excess of UK legal standards. Bromate is a chemical that is linked with increased cancer risk if taken in large quantities. Even though Coca-Cola stressed that there was no health risk from drinking it, and that the withdrawal was precautionary, the damage to the brand was deemed irreversible.

But Dasani had been a double disaster for Coca-Cola. When the brand was launched a few weeks earlier its image was hurt by the revelation that the contents of each bottle was merely processed tap water from the Thames that cost just 0.03p per 500ml compared with Dasani's 95p per 500ml. Over the course of the scandal, it was also revealed that around 40 per cent of all mineral water is just processed tap water too. Water inspectors for years have pointed out that UK tap water is at least as good as its mineral equivalent, especially if cooled in the refrigerator first – and that was before bromate was discovered in Dasani. In fact, in the UK, all known sources of spring water still contain traces of the endocrine-disrupting herbicide atrazine, even though its use was restricted for agricultural use in the early 1990s.

Yet our love affair with bottled water continues – in 1999 alone sales of bottled water leapt by 20 per cent in the UK. We now drink about 14 litres each a year on average. In 2000, a Friends of the Earth spokesman called bottled water 'environmental madness': 'It's absolutely absurd to be putting this very heavy bulky and yet supercheap product in bottles, which weigh almost as much as the product and carting them around the world. It uses enormous amounts of energy and that, in turn, fuels climate change. Yet it's climate change which is the biggest threat facing the world's water resources in the future. This is just craziness!'

Some alcoholic drinks firms have faced consumer boycotts. For example, Bacardi has been the subject of a boycott by the Cuba Solidarity Campaign who accused the company of supporting sanctions against Cuba while using images of Cuban heritage in its marketing campaigns.

Fizzy drinks

Fizzy drinks manufacturers are one of the most recognisable faces of globalisation and have been the focus of campaigners' ire for some time. PepsiCo and Coca-Cola are the world's leading producers of colas and many other familiar drink and snack brands (PepsiCo brands include Walkers crisps, Quaker oats and Tropicana juice; Coca-Cola brands include Sprite, Lilt, and Evian). Both have faced much criticism about the way they have managed to achieve such widespread global penetration of their brands. There are now even websites that monitor these, and other companies' actions, such as www.cokewatch.org and www.oligopolywatch.com.

Campaigners often complain about manufacturers' tactics for achieving global domination, such as forcing retailers to stock only their own brands on shelves and store fridges. They also face criticism for aggressively

marketing goods – particularly at children – that contain high levels of sugar, caffeine, and artificial additives. In 2004, legal filings in US courts even claimed that Coca-Cola and its Colombian bottlers had hired rightwing death squads to intimidate unions at the plants. They claimed nine union organisers had been killed in the past decade. The company's chairman and chief executive (the fact that these two roles are filled by one person has also been a subject of criticism) responded by saying the charges 'are false and outrageous'. Other criticism has centred on allegations that the company's bottling plants in India are depleting water supplies in local communities and causing pollution with discharged materials.

It is not surprising, therefore, that self-certified ethical alternatives have sprung up in recent years such as Qibla-Cola (www.qibla-cola.com) and Mecca-Cola (www.mecca-cola.com). While not independently authenticated as fair trade, such brands claim to reinvest profits into the communities and charities in the regions they operate in, as well as being founded on the principles of fair-trade and ethical business practice. The best option, though, if only in the interests of health, is to cut back on fizzy drink consumption as much as possible.

Directory

BOX SCHEMES

Box schemes vary hugely, from the bigger companies who offer everything from bread through to meat and washing-up liquid, to smaller firms or co-ops offering just boxes of local organic fruit and veg. Either way, try to find the one that is nearest to you and has a commitment to reducing food miles wherever possible

National

Abel and Cole
8-15 MGI Estate, Milkwood Road,
London SE24 0JF
☎ 0845 262 6262
www.abel-cole.co.uk

Fresh Food Company
The Orchard, 50 Wormholt Road,
London W12 0LS
☎ 020 8749 8778
www.freshfood.co.uk

Farmaround Organic
45 Race Course Road, Richmond,
North Yorkshire DL 10 4TG
☎ 020 7627 8066
www.farmaround.co.uk

The Organic Farmer's Market
Dart's Farm, Clyst St George,
Exeter, Devon, EX3 0QH
☎ 01392 875678
www.theorganicfarmersmarket.co.uk

Westcountry Organics
Tedburn St Mary, Exeter,
Devon EX6 6ET
☎ 0164 724724
www.westcountryorganics.co.uk

Mrs Tee's Wild Mushrooms
Gorse Meadow, Sway Road,
Lymington, Hampshire SO41 8LR
☎ 01590 673354
www.wildmushrooms.co.uk

London/South-east

Ashurst Organics
The Orchard, Ashurst Farm,
Ashurst Lane, Plumpton,
East Sussex BN7 3AP
☎ 01273 891219

Everybody Organic
6 Hill Rise, Potters Bar,
Herts EN6 2RR
☎ 01707 651243
www.everybodyorganic.com

FieldFare Organic & Natural
The Barns, Springfield Farm,
Nash Lee Lane, Wendover,
Bucks HP22 6BG
☎ 0845 601 3240
www.fieldfare-organics.com

Growing Communities
The Old Fire Station, 61 Leswin Road,
Stoke Newington, London N16 7NY
☎ 020 7502 7588
www.growingcommunities.org

Just Organic
113 Wilberforce Road,
London N4 2SP
☎ 020 7704 2566

The Organic Delivery Company
72 Rivington Street,
London EC2A 3AY
☎ 020 7739 8181
www.organicdelivery.co.uk

Perry Court Farm
Bilting, Ashford, Kent TN25 4ES
☎ 01233 812302
www.perrycourt.com

Real Farm Foods
Wantage, Oxon OX12 9LJ
☎ 0808 006 7426
www.realfarmfoods.com

Sunshine Organics
2 Knowle Cottages, Knowle Lane,
Cranleigh, Surrey, GU6 8JL
☎ 01483 268014
www.sunshine-organics.co.uk

Wayside Organics
Wayside, Oving, Chichester,
West Sussex
☎ 01243 779716

Midlands

Fern Verrow Vegetables
St Margarets, Herefordshire
☎ 01981 510288

FoodLife Doorstep Deliveries
68 Buckingham Rd, Cheadle Hulme,
Cheadle, Stockport SK8 5NA
☎ 0161 486 1173

Hopwood Organic Farm
Bickenhill Lane, Catherine-de-Barnes,
Solihull, West Midlands B92 0DE
☎ 0121 711 7787
www.hopwoodorganic.co.uk

North

Arthur Street Trading Co.
Unit 2, 23 Arthur Street,
Hull HU3 6BH
☎ 01482 576374
www.arthursorganics.com

Cheshire Organics
5 Booths Hill Road, Lymm,
Cheshire WA13 0DJ
☎ 01925 758575

Growing with Grace
Clapham Nursery, Clapham,
Lancaster LA2 8ER
☎ 01524 251723
www.growingwithgrace.co.uk

Growing with Nature
Bradshaw Lane Nursery, Pilling,
Preston, Lancashire, PR3 6AX
☎ 01253 790046

Goosemoor Organic Produce
Warfield Lane, Cowthorpe, Wetherby,
North Yorkshire, LS22 5EU
☎ 01423 358887
www.goosemoor.org.uk

Howbarrow Organic Farm
Cartmel, Grange-over-Sands, Cumbria,
LA11 7SS
☎ 01539 536330
www.howbarroworganic.demon.co.uk

North East Organic Growers
Earth Balance, West Sleekburn Farm,
Bomarsund, Bedlington NE22 7AD
☎ 01670 821070
www.neog.co.uk

South-west

Cusgarne Organic Box Scheme
Cusgarne Wollas, Cusgarne, Truro,
Cornwall TR4 8RL
☎ 01872 865922

Linscombe Farm
New Buildings, Sandford, Crediton,
Devon, EX17 4PS
☎ 01363 84291

Peppers by Post
Sea Spring Farm, West Bexington,
Dorchester. Dorset DT2 9DD
☎ 01308 897892
www.peppersbypost.biz

Riverford Organic Vegetables
Wash Barn, Buckfastleigh,
Devon, TQ11 0LD
☎ 0845 600 2311
www.riverford.co.uk

Stoneage Organics
Stoneage Farm, Cothelstone,
Taunton TA4 3ED
☎ 01823 432488
www.stoneageorganics.co.uk

Sunnyfields Organic
Jacobs Gutter Lane, Totton,
Southampton, SO40 9FX
☎ 023 8087 1408
www.sunnyfields.co.uk

South

Coleshill Organics
59 Coleshill, Swindon,
Wiltshire SN6 7PT
☎ 01793 861070
www.coleshillorganics.co.uk

Organic Trail
10 St Pauls Court, Stony Stratford,
Milton Keynes, Buckinghamshire,
MK11 1LJ
☎ 01908 568952
www.organictrail.co.uk

Tolhurst Organic Produce
2 West Lodge, Hardwick Estate,
Whitchurch, Pangbourne, Berkshire,
RG8 7RA
☎ 01189 843428

Warborne Organic Vegetables
Warborne Lane, Boldre, Lymington,
Hampshire SO41 5QD
☎ 01590 688488

West/Wales

Green Cuisine
Unit 2, Taff Workshops, Tresillian
Terrace, Cardiff CF10 5DE
☎ 029 2039 4321

Organics to Go
Werndolau, Gelli Aur, Golden Grove,
Carmarthen, SA32 8NE
☎ 0800 458 2524

Slipstream Organics
34a Langdon Rd, Leckhampton,
Cheltenham, Gloucestershire,
GL53 7NZ
☎ 01242 227273
www.slipstream-organics.co.uk

East

Abbey Farm Organics
Abbey Farm, Abbey Road, Flitcham,
Kings Lynn, Norfolk PE31 6BT
☎ 01485 609094

Greens Organic
Millway Farm, Millway Lane,
Palgrave, Diss IP22 1SN
www.greensorganic.co.uk

Woodlands Farm
Woodlands Farm, Kirton House, Kirton,
Boston, Lincolnshire PE20 1JD
☎ 01205 724778
www.woodlandsfarm.co.uk

Scotland

Grow Wild
Unit 8, Block 3, Whiteside Industrial
Estate, Bathgate, West Lothian
EH48 2RX
☎ 0845 226 3393
www.growwild.co.uk

Lembas
Lorieneen, Bridge of Muchalls,
Stonehaven, Kincardineshire
AB39 3RU
☎ 01569 731746

Northern Ireland

Helen's Bay Organic Gardens
13 Seaview Terrace, Holywood,
Co. Down BT18 9DT
☎ 028 9185 3122
www.helensbayorganicgardens.com

WHOLEFOOD AND ORGANIC SHOPS

Central, East and North

Beano Wholefoods
36 New Briggate, Leeds, LS1 6NU
☎ 0113 243 5737
www.beanowholefoods.co.uk

Botton Village Store
Camphill Village Trust, Danby, Whitby,
Yorks YO21 2NJ
☎ 01287 661273
www.camphill.org.uk/botton.htm

Chorlton Wholefoods
64 Beech Road, Manchester M21 9EG
☎ 0161 881 6399

Cooks Delight
360–4 High Street, Berkhamsted,
HP41 1HU
☎ 01442 863584
www.cooksdelight.co.uk

Define Food and Wine
Chester Road, Sandiway,
Cheshire CW8 2NH
☎ 01606 882101

Down to Earth Organic
96A Earlsdon Street, Coventry,
CV5 6EJ
☎ 02476 677500

Food Therapy
11 Northgate, Halifax HX1 1UR
☎ 01422 350826

Growing with Grace
Clapham Nursery, Clapham,
Lancaster LA2 8ER
☎ 01524 251723
www.growingwithgrace.co.uk

The Health Warehouse
15 Post House Wind, Darlington
DL3 7LU
☎ 01325 468570

Lembas Ltd
Unit 5, The Old Tannery, Whiting Street,
Sheffield S8 9QR
☎ 0845 458 1585
www.lembas.co.uk

Mossley Organic and Fine Foods
11–13 Arundel Street, Mossley,
Manchester OL5 0NY
☎ 01457 837743
www.mossleyorganicandfinefoods.co.uk

**The Naturally Good Food
Delivery Service**
Stable Yard, Coatsbach Hall, Main
Street, Coatsbach, Leicestershire
LE17 4HX
☎ 01455 556878
www.goodfooddelivery.co.uk

On the Eighth Day Co-operative
111 Oxford Road, Manchester
M1 7DU
☎ 0161 273 4878
www.eighth-day.co.uk

ORG
79 Great George Street, Leeds
LS1 3BR
☎ 0113 234 7000
www.org-organics.org.uk

Organicfair
43 St James Street, Chester CH1 3EY
☎ 01244 400158
www.organicfair.co.uk

Out of this World (branches)
Gosforth Shopping Centre, High Street,
Newcastle upon Tyne NE3 1JZ
☎ 0191 213 0421
Villa Street, Beeston,
Nottingham NG9 2NY
☎ 0115 943 1311

Rainbow Wholefoods
Old Fire Station Stables, Labour In Vain
Yard, Guildhall Hill, Norwich NR2 1JD
☎ 01603 630484
www.rainbowwholefoods.co.uk

Sage Wholefoods
148 Alcester Road, Mosely,
Birmingham B13 8HS
☎ 0121 449 6909
www.sagewholefoods.com

Unicorn Grocery
89 Albany Road, Chorlton,
Manchester M21 0BN
☎ 0161 861 0010
www.unicorn-grocery.co.uk

Wild Carrot
5 Bridge St, Buxton,
Derbyshire SK17 6BS
☎ 01298 22843
www.wildcarrot.freeserve.co.uk

Wyedean Wholefoods (branches)
13 Market St, Cinderford GL14 2RT
2 Hare Lane, Gloucester GL1 2BB
28 High Street, Chepstow NP16 5LJ
☎ 01594 826639

Scotland

Damhead Organic Food
32A Damhead, Old Pentland Rd,
Lothianburn, Edinburgh EH10 7EA
☎ 0131 448 2091
www.damhead.co.uk

Grassroots
20 Woodlands Road, Charing Cross,
Glasgow G3 6UR
☎ 0141 353 3278
www.grassrootsorganic.com

**New Leaf Vegetarian
and Organic Wholefoods**
20 Argyle Place, Marchmont,
Edinburgh EH9 1JJ
☎ 0131 228 8840
www.edinburghbuddhistcentre.org.uk

Phoenix Community Stores
The Park, Findhorn Bay, Forres,
Moray IV36 3TZ
☎ 01309 690110

Real Foods
37 Broughton St, Edinburgh EH1 3SU
☎ 0131 557 1911

Sunrise Wholefoods
49 Kings Street, Castle Douglas,
Dumfries & Galloway DG7 1AE
☎ 01556 504455

London

As Nature Intended
201 Chiswick High Road,
London W4 2DR
☎ 020 8742 8838
www.asnatureintended.uk.com

Bumblebee
30, 32 & 33 Brecknock Rd,
London N7 0DD
☎ 020 7607 1936
www.bumblebee.co.uk

Bushwacker Whole Foods
132 King Street, London W6 0QU
☎ 020 8748 2061

Farm W5
19 The Green, London W5 5DA
☎ 020 8566 1965
www.farmw5.co.uk

Fresh and Wild (branches)
210 Westbourne Grove,
London W11 2RH
☎ 020 7229 1063
69–75 Brewer Street,
London W1F 9US
☎ 020 7434 3179
49 Parkway, London NW1 7PN
☎ 020 7428 7575
305–311 Lavender Hill,
London SW11 1LN
☎ 020 7585 1488
32–40 Stoke Newington Church Street,
London N16 0LU
☎ 020 7254 2332
194 Old Street, London EC1V 9FR
☎ 020 7250 1708
www.freshandwild.com

Greenwich Organic Foods
86 Royal Hill, Greenwich,
London SE10 8RT
☎ 020 8488 6764
www.greenwichorganics.co.uk

Here Chelsea Farmers' Market
125 Sydney Street, London SW3 6NR
☎ 020 7351 4321
www.herestores.com

Just Natural
304 Park Road, London N8 8LA
☎ 020 8340 1720

Kelly's Organic Foods
46 Northcote Road,
London SW11 1NZ
☎ 020 7207 3967

Oliver's Wholefood Store
5 Station Approach, Kew Gardens,
Richmond, London TW9 3QB
☎ 020 8948 3990

The Organic Grocer
17 Clifton Road, London W9 1SY
☎ 020 7286 1400

Planet Organic (branches)
42 Westbourne Grove,
London W2 5SH
☎ 020 7727 2227
22 Torrington Place, London WC1 7JE
☎ 020 7436 1929
25 Effie Road, Fulham, London SW6 1EL
☎ 020 7731 7222
www.planetorganic.com

Portobello Wholefoods
266 Portobello Road,
London W10 5TY
☎ 020 8968 9133

South-east

Body and Soul
1 Parade Court, Ockham Road South,
East Horsley KT24 6QR
☎ 01483 282868
www.organic-gmfree.co.uk

Le Grand Fromage
8 East Street, Shoreham-by-Sea,
West Sussex BN43 5ZE
☎ 01273 440337
www.legrandfromage.co.uk

Healthy Stuff
11 Liston Court, High St, Marlow,
Bucks SL7 1ER
☎ 01628 473684
www.healthy-stuff.co.uk

Infinity Food Shop and Bakery
25 North Road, Brighton BN1 1YA
☎ 01273 603563
www.infinityfoods.co.uk

The Seasons (Forest Row)
10–11 Hartfield Road, Forest Row,
East Sussex, RH18 5DN
☎ 01342 824673

South-west

Bath Organic Farms
6 Brookside House, High Street,
Weston, Bath, Somerset BA1 4BY
☎ 01225 421507
www.bathorganicfarms.com

Better Food Company
The Bristol Proving House,
Sevier Street, Bristol BS2 9QS
☎ 0117 935 1725
www.betterfood.co.uk

Carley's of Cornwall
34–6 St Austell Street, Truro TR1 1SE
☎ 01872 277686
www.carleys.co.uk

Field Fayre
18–19 Broad Street, Ross-on-Wye,
Herefordshire HR9 7EA
☎ 01989 566683
www.field-fayre.co.uk

Garlands Organic
6 Reading Road, Pangbourne,
Berks RG8 7LY
☎ 0118 984 4770
www.makessense.co.uk/garlands

Godshill Organics
Yard Parlour, Newport Road, Godshill,
Isle of Wight PO38 3LY
☎ 01983 840723

The Green House
2A Lower Pannier Market, Crediton,
Devon EX17 2BL
☎ 01363 775580

Hay Wholefoods and Delicatessen
41 Lion Street, Hay-on-Wye, Hereford,
HR3 5AA
☎ 01497 820708

Norwood Farm
Bath Road, Norton St Philip,
Bath BA3 6LP
☎ 01373 834356

Marshford Organic Produce
Churchill Way, Northam, North Devon,
EX39 1NS, or 11 Butcher's Row,
Barnstaple EX31 3BB
☎ 01237 477160
www.marshford.co.uk

The Natural Grocery Store
150–6 Bath Road,
Cheltenham GL53 7NG
☎ 01242 243737

The Organic Shop
The Square, Stow-on-the-Wold,
Gloucestershire GL54 1AB
☎ 01451 831004

Spencer's of Wells
4 Tucker Street, Wells,
Somerset BA5 2DZ
☎ 01749 672357
www.spencersofwells.co.uk

Wales

Beanfreaks
3 St Mary Street, Cardiff CF10 2AT
(also branches in Newport, Cwmbran,
and Bridgend)
☎ 02920 251671
www.swissherbalremedies.com

The Treehouse
14 Baker Street, Aberystwyth,
West Wales SY23 2BJ
☎ 01970 615791
www.aber-treehouse.com

Rhug
The Rhug Estate Office, Corwen,
Denbyshire, LL21 0EH
☎ 01490 413000
www.rhugorganic.com

Northern Ireland

Life Tree
37 Spencer Road, Derry,
Co. Londonderry BT47 6AA
☎ 028 7134 2865

FARM SHOPS

National

Farm Gate Direct *(accredited by
RSPCA Freedom Food scheme)*
Freedom Food, Wilberforce Way,
Southwater, Horsham, West Sussex
RH13 9RS
☎ 0870 754 0014
www.farmgatedirect.com

South-west

Daylesford Organic Farm Shop
Daylesford, near Kingham,
Gloucestershire, GL55 0YG
☎ 01608 731700
www.daylesfordorganic.com

Owls Barn Organic Farm Shop
Derritt Lane, Sopley, Christchurch,
Dorset BH23 7AZ
☎ 01425 672239
www.owlsbarn.com

Trading Post
The Old Filling Station, Lopenhead,
South Petherton, Somerset TA13 5JH
☎ 01460 241666

South-east

Boathouse Organic Farm Shop
The Orchards, Uckfield Rd, Lewes,
Sussex BN8 5RX
☎ 01273 814188

Cranleigh Organic Farm Shop
Lower Barrihurst Farm, Dunsfold Rd,
Cranleigh, Surrey GU6 8LG
☎ 01483 272896

Holly Park Organics
Hollypark North Lane, Guestling Thorn,
East Sussex, TN35 4LX
☎ 01424 812229

Old Plaw Hatch Farm
Plaw Hatch Lane, Sharpthorne,
West Sussex RH19 4JL
☎ 01342 810201

Swan Inn Farm Shop
Hungerford, Berks RG17 9DX
☎ 01488 668326
www.theswaninn-organics.co.uk

Tablehurst Farm
London Road, Forest Row,
East Sussex RH18 5DP
☎ 01342 823173

Wingham Country Market
The Depot, Shatterling, Canterbury,
Kent CT3 1JW
☎ 01227 720567

East

The Prospects Trust
Snakehall Farm, 50 Swaffham Road,
Reach, Cambs CB5 0HZ
☎ 01638 741551

Central/North

Brocksbushes Farm
Stocksfield, Northumberland NE43 7UB
☎ 01434 633100
www.brocksbushes.co.uk

Church Farm Organics
Church Lane, Thurstaston,
Wirral CH61 0HW
☎ 0151 648 7838
www.churchfarm.org.uk

Elmhurst Farm Shop
Bow Lane, Withybrook, Coventry,
West Midlands CV7 9LQ
☎ 01788 832233

Kites Nest Farm
Broadway, Worcestershire WR12 7JT
☎ 01386 853320

Larchfield Community
Stokesley Road, Hemlington,
Middlesbrough, Cleveland TS8 9DY
☎ 01642 593688

Manor Farm
Long Whatton, Loughborough
LE12 5DF
☎ 01509 646413
www.manororganicfarm.co.uk

Meanwood Valley Urban Farm
Sugarwell Road, Meanwood,
Leeds LS7 2QG
☎ 0113 262 9759

The Organic Farm Shop
Standfield Hall Farm, Westgate Carr
Road, Pickering YO18 8LX
☎ 01751 472249
www.theorganicfarmshop.com

The Organic Stores
Brooklyn Farm, Sealand Road,
Chester CH5 2LQ
☎ 01244 881209

Sturts Farm
Three Cross Roads, West Moors,
Ferndown, BH22 0NF
☎ 01202 894292

Scotland

Henderson's Shop
92 Hanover Street,
Edinburgh EH2 1DR
☎ 0131 225 6694
www.hendersonsofedinburgh.co.uk

Jamesfield Farm Shop
Jamesfield Farm,
Newburgh KY14 6EW
☎ 01738 850498
www.jamesfieldfarm.com

Saulmore Farm Shop
Connel nr Oban, Argyll, PA37 1PU
☎ 01631 710247
www.saulmore.com

Loch Arthur
Camphill Village Trust, Beeswing,
Dumfries DG2 8JQ
☎ 01387 760296
www.locharthur.org.uk

Pillars of Hercules Organic Farm
Falkland, Fife KY15 7AD
☎ 01337 857749
www.pillars.co.uk

Wales

The Organic Farm Shop
186 Prendergast,
Haverfordwest SA61 2PQ
☎ 01437 765040

Northern Ireland

Ballylagan Organic Farm Shop
12 Ballylagan Road, Straid, Ballyclare,
Co. Antrim BT39 9NF
☎ 028 9332 2867
www.ballylagan.com

FARMERS' MARKETS

Finding them:

*National Farmers' Retail and
Markets Association (FARMA)*
PO Box 575, Southampton SO15 7BZ
www.farmersmarkets.net

London Farmers' Markets
☎ 020 7704 9659
www.lfm.org.uk

*Scottish Association of
Farmers Markets*
www.scottishfarmersmarkets.co.uk

Growing Communities
☎ 020 7502 7588
www.growingcommunities.org

A selection of the best:

London

Blackheath
Blackheath rail station car park,
2 Blackheath Village, SE3
Sun 10am–2pm

Islington
Essex Road, opposite Islington Green,
London N1
Sun 10am–2pm

Notting Hill
Car park off Kensington Place, behind
Waterstones, corner of Kensington
Church Street, London W8
Sat 9am–1pm

Marylebone
Cramer St car park off Marylebone
High Street, London W1
Sun 10am–2pm

Peckham
Peckham Square, Peckham High
Street, opposite Peckham Library
SE15
Sun 9.30am–1.30pm

Stoke Newington
The Old Fire Station,
61 Leswin Road, N16
Sat 10am–2.30pm
www.growingcommunities.org

Wimbledon
Wimbledon Park First School,
Havana Road, SW19
Sat 9am–1pm

South-east/East

Canterbury
The Goods Shed, Station Road West,
Canterbury, Kent
Every day, except Mondays
☎ 01227 459153

Rolvenden
Parish Church St Mary The Virgin and
Village Hall, Rolvenden, Kent
Thur 10am–noon
www.rolvendenfarmersmarket.co.uk

Lewes
Cliffe Pedestrian Precinct, Lewes,
East Sussex
1st Sat mthly 9am–1pm
www.farmersmarkets.net

Haywards Heath
Haywards Road West car park,
Haywards Heath, West Sussex
3rd Thur mthly 9am–2pm
www.farmersmarkets.net

Needham Market
Alder Carr Farm,
Needham Market, Suffolk
3rd Sat mthly 9am–1pm
www.farmersmarkets.net

Birmingham New Street
Victoria Square
1st and 3rd Wed mthly, 9am–5pm
www.farmersmarkets.net

Hexham
Market Place, Hexham,
Northumberland
2nd and 4th Sat mthly 9am–1.30pm
www.farmersmarkets.net

Hinckley
The Market Place, Hinckley
3rd Thurs mthly 9am–2pm
www.farmersmarkets.net

Lichfield
Market Square, Lichfield
1st Thurs mthly 9am–3pm

Liverpool
Chavasse Park, South John Street,
Liverpool City Centre
3rd Sat mthly 9am–2pm

Manchester
Fountain side of Piccadilly Gardens,
next to Queen Victoria Statue,
City Centre, Manchester
2nd Fri & Sat mthly 11am–5pm
& 10am–4pm
www.manchester.gov.uk/markets

Orton
Market Hall, Orton Village, Cumbria
2nd Sat mthly, 9.30am–2.30pm
www.ortonfarmers.co.uk

Stratford-upon-Avon
Rother Street Market, Stratford
1st and 3rd Sat mthly 9am–2pm
www.sketts.co.uk

York
Parliament Street,
York City Centre, Yorkshire
days vary
www.farmersmarkets.net

Bristol
Corn Street, Bristol
Wed 9.30am–2.30pm

Crediton
Market Square, Crediton, Devon
1st Sat mthly 10am–1pm

Newport
St Thomas' Square, Newport,
Isle of Wight
Fri 9am–3pm

Taunton
High Street, Taunton, Somerset
Thurs 9am–3pm

Winchester
Middle Brook Street and Middle Brook
Street car park, Winchester, Hampshire
days vary
www.hampshirefarmersmarkets.co.uk

Aberystwyth
North Parade, Aberystwyth
3rd Sat mthly 10am–3pm

Belfast
St George's Market,
Oxford Street, Belfast
1st and 3rd Sat 8am–1pm

Cardiff
Fitzhammon Embankment,
Riverside, Cardiff
Sun 10am–2pm
www.riversidemarket.org.uk

Edinburgh
Castle Terrace, Edinburgh
1st and 3rd Sat mthly 9am–2pm
www.scottishfarmersmarkets.co.uk

Glasgow
Mansfield Park, Partick, Glasgow
2nd and 4th Sat mthly 10am–3pm

Haverfordwest
Riverside Quay, Haverfordwest,
Pembrokeshire
Fri ftnightly 9am–3pm

FAIR TRADE

**British Association
of Fair Trade Shops**
☎ 020 7739 4197
www.bafts.org.uk

Ethical Shopper
☎ 0845 456 2429
www.ethicalshopper.co.uk

Fairtrade Foundation
☎ 020 7405 5942
www.fairtrade.org.uk

FAIR TRADE BRANDS

Brian Wogan
Bourbon House, 2 Clement Street,
Bristol BS2 9EQ
☎ 0117 955 3564
www.wogan-coffee.co.uk
(organic and fairtrade coffees)

Cafédirect/Teadirect
City Cloisters, Suite B2, 196 Old St,
London EC1V 9FR
☎ 020 7490 9520
www.cafedirect.co.uk
(coffee, tea, drinking chocolate)

Chocaid
www.chocaid.com
(chocolate)

ClipperTea
Beaminster Business Park,
Broadwindsor Road, Beaminster,
Dorset DT8 3PR
☎ 01308 863344
www.clipper-teas.com
(tea, coffee and drinking chocolate)

Day Chocolate Company
4 Gainsford St, London SE1 2NE
☎ 020 7378 6550
www.divinechocolate.com
www.dubble.co.uk
(Divine and Dubble Chocolate)

Equal Exchange
10a Queensferry Street, Edinburgh
EH2 4PG
☎ 0131 220 3484
www.equalexchange.co.uk
(coffee, tea, honey, chocolate-coated
brazil nuts, cane sugar)

Fruit Passion
www.fruit-passion.com
(fruit juices)

73

Green & Black's
2 Valentine Place, London SE1 8QH
☎ 020 7633 5900
www.greenandblacks.com
(chocolate and ice cream)

Hampstead Tea & Coffee Company
PO Box 2448, London NW11 7DR
☎ 020 8731 9833
www.hampsteadtea.com
(tea and coffee)

Oxfam
☎ 01865 312334
www.oxfam.org.uk/shop
(coffees, teas, nuts and chocolate)

Percol Food Brands Group
9/10 Calico House, Plantation Wharf,
Battersea SW11 3TN
☎ 020 7978 5300
www.percol.co.uk
(coffee, tea)

Suma
Lacy Way, Lowfields Business Park,
Elland, West Yorkshire HX5 9DB
☎ 01422 313840
www.suma.co.uk
(tea, coffee and chocolate)

Tea and Coffee Plant
180 Portobello Rd, London W11 2EB
☎ 020 7221 8137
www.coffee.uk.com
(tea and coffee)

Traidcraft
☎ 0870 443 1017
www.traidcraft.co.uk
(chocolate, honey, biscuits,
Geobars, jams, rice, sugar)

Union Coffee Roasters
Unit 2, 7a South Crescent,
London E16 4TL
☎ 020 7474 8990
www.unionroasters.com
(coffee)

MEAT AND POULTRY

**The following meat producers
offer national deliveries: there
are also dozens of wonderful
butchers around the country
offering local, organic meat.
Ask around in your area.**

National

Blackface
Weatherall Foods Limited, Crochmore
House, Irongray, Dumfries, DG2 9SF,
Scotland
☎ 01387 730326
www.blackface.co.uk

Bowlees Organic Farm
Wolsingham, Weardale,
Co. Durham, DL13 3JF
☎ 01388 528305
www.bowleesorganicfarm.com

Bumpylane Rare Breeds
Shortlands Farm, Druidston,
Haverfordwest,
Pembrokeshire SA62 3NE
☎ 01437 781234
www.bumpylane.co.uk

Cambrian Organics
Horeb, Llandysul SA44 4JG
☎ 01559 363151
www.cambrianorganics.com

Eastbrook Farms Organic Meat
Bishopstone, Swindon,
Wiltshire SN6 8PL
☎ 01793 790460
www.helenbrowningorganics.co.uk

Eversfield Manor
Bratton, Clovelly, Okehampton,
Devon EX20 4JF
☎ 01837 871400
www.eversfieldmanor.co.uk

Graig Farm Organics
Dolau, Llandrindod Wells, LD1 5TL
☎ 01597 851655
www.graigfarm.co.uk

Growing Concern Organic Farm
Home Farm, Woodhouse Lane,
Nanpanton, Loughborough, LE11 3YG
☎ 01509 239228
www.growingconcern.co.uk

Heritage Prime
Shedbush Farm, Muddy Ford Lane,
Stanton Street, Gabriel, Bridport,
Dorset DT6 6DR
☎ 01297 489304
www.heritageprime.co.uk

Higher Hacknell Organic Meat
Burrington, Umberleigh,
Devon EX37 9LX
☎ 01769 560909
www.higherhacknell.co.uk

Highlander Organics
14 Bittacy Hill, London NW7 1LB
☎ 020 8346 1055
www.highlanderorganics.co.uk

Kelly Turkeys
Springate Farm, Bicknacre Road,
Danbury, Essex CM3 4EP
☎ 01245 223581
www.kellyturkeys.com

Lower Hurst Farm
Hartington, Nr Buxton, SK17 0HJ
☎ 01298 84900
www.lowerhurstfarm.co.uk

Northumbrian Quality Meats
Monkridge Hill Farm, West Woodburn,
Hexham NE48 2TU
☎ 01434 270184
www.northumbrian-organic-meat.co.uk

Real Farm Foods
Wantage, Oxon OX12 9LJ
☎ 0808 006 7426
www.realfarmfoods.com

Pampered Pigs
2, The Green, Tolpuddle,
Dorset DT2 7EX
☎ 01305 848107
www.organic-pork.co.uk

Providence Farm Organic Meats
Crosspark Cross, Holsworthy,
Devon EX22 6JW
☎ 01409 254421
www.providencefarm.co.uk

The Real Meat Company
Warminster, Wilts BA12 0HR
☎ 01985 840562
www.realmeat.co.uk

Save the Bacon
Castle Ashby Road, Yardley, Hastings,
Northamptonshire NN7 1EL
☎ 01604 696859
www.savethebacon.com

Sheepdrove Organic Farm
Warren Farm, Lambourn,
Berks RG17 7UU
☎ 01488 71659
www.sheepdrove.com

Somerset Organics
Gilcombe Farm, Bruton,
Somerset BA10 0QE
☎ 01749 813710
www.somersetorganics.co.uk

Swaddles Organic
Swaddles Green Farm, Hare Lane,
Buckland St Mary, Chard,
Somerset TA20 3JR
☎ 0845 456 1768/ 01460 234387
www.swaddles.co.uk

Well Hung Meat
Tordean Farm, Dean Prior,
Buckfastleigh TQ11 0LY
☎ 0845 230 3131
www.wellhungmeat.com

Welsh Hook Meat Centre
Woodfield, Haverfordwest SA62 4BW
☎ 01437 768876
www.welsh-organic-meat.co.uk

Wild Beef
Hillhead Farm, Chagford,
Devon TQ13 8DY
☎ 01647 433433

South-east

The Game Larder
24 The Parade, Claygate,
Surrey KT10 0NU
☎ 01372 462879

FISH

The following fishmongers offer home deliveries nationwide

National

Cornish Fish Direct
The Pilchard Works, Newlyn,
Penzance, Cornwall
☎ 01736 332112
www.cornishfish.com

Fowey Fish
37 Fore Street, Fowey, Cornwall
☎ 01726 832422
www.foweyfish.com

Hawkshead Organic Farmed Fish
The Boat House, Ridding Wood,
Hawkshead, Ambleside,
Cumbria LA22 0QF
☎ 01539 436541
www.organicfish.com

Kinvara Organic Smoked Salmon
Kinvara, Co. Galway
☎ 00 353 91 637489
www.kinvarasmokedsalmon.com

Loch Fyne Oysters
Clachan, Cairndow, Argyll PA26 8BL
☎ 01499 600264
www.loch-fyne.com

Organic Salmon Company
The Shed, Withermarsh Green, Stoke
by Nayland, Colchester,
Essex CO6 4TD
☎ 01206 337447

Purely Organic
Deverill Trout Farm, Longbridge
Deverill, Warminster BA12 7DZ
☎ 01985 841093
www.purelyorganic.co.uk

CHEESE

National

Daisy and Co
Tree Tops Farm, North Brewham,
Bruton, Somerset BA10 0JS
☎ 01749 850254
www.daisyandco.co.uk

Godminster Farm
Bruton, Somerset BA10 0NE
☎ 01749 813733
www.godminster.co.uk

High Weald Dairy
Tremains Farm, Horsted Keynes,
Haywards Heath,
West Sussex RH17 7EA
☎ 01825 791636
www.highwealddairy.co.uk

Neal's Yard Dairy
Caperthy, Arthurstone Lane, Dorstone,
nr Hay on Wye HR3 6AX
☎ 01981 500395
www.nealsyarddairy.co.uk

Paxton and Whitfield
6 Fosseway Business Park, Moreton in
Marsh, Gloucestershire GL56 9NQ
☎ 01608 652090
www.paxtonandwhitfield.co.uk

Raven's Oak Dairy
Burland Farm, Burland,
Nantwich CW5 8ND
☎ 01270 524624
www.ravensoakdairy.co.uk

Specialist Cheesemakers Association
17 Clerkenwell Green,
London EC1R 0DP
☎ 020 7253 2114
www.specialistcheesemakers.co.uk

Midlands/North

The Cheese Shop
116 Northgate Street,
Chester CH1 2HT
☎ 01244 346240
www.chestercheeseshop.com

Leagram Organic Dairy
High Head Farm Building, Green Lane,
Chipping, nr Preston,
Lancashire PR3 2TQ
☎ 01995 61532
www.cheese-experience.com

Staffordshire Organic Cheese
Newhouse Farm, Acton, Newcastle
Under Lyme, Staffordshire ST5 4EE
☎ 01782 680366

Ireland

Sheridan's Cheesemongers
☎ 00 353 9 156 4829 (Galway)
☎ 00 353 1 679 3143 (Dublin)
www.sheridanscheesemongers.com

Scotland

I J Mellis
Edinburgh and Glasgow
☎ 0131 661 9955
www.ijmellischeesemonger.com

Wales

Caws Cenarth Cheese
Glyneithinog Farm, Pontseli, Boncath,
Dyfed SA37 0LH
☎ 01239 710432
www.cawscenarth.co.uk

Llanboidy Cheesemakers
Cilowen Uchaf, Login,
Whitland SA34 0TJ
☎ 01994 448303
www.llanboidycheese.co.uk

DRINK

London and South-east

**Broughton Pastures Organic
Fruit Wine**
The Old Silk Mill, Brook Street,
Tring HP23 5EF
☎ 01442 823993

Davenport Vineyards
Limney Farm, Castle Hill, Rotherfield,
East Sussex TN6 3RR
☎ 01892 852380
www.davenportvineyards.co.uk

Hidden Spring Vineyard
and Organic Orchard
Vines Cross Road, Horam, Heathfield,
East Sussex TN21 0HF
☎ 01435 812640
www.hiddenspring.co.uk

Sedlescombe Organic Vineyard
Cripps Corner, Robertsbridge, East
Sussex TN32 5SA
☎ 0800 980 2884
www.englishorganicwine.co.uk

The Tea and Coffee Plant
180 Portobello Road,
London W11 2EB
☎ 020 7221 8137
www.coffee.uk.com

South-west

Avalon Vineyard
The Drove, East Pennard, Shepton
Mallet, Somerset BA4 6UA
☎ 01749 860393
www.pennardorganicwines.co.uk

Central/North

Belvoir Fruit Farms
Belvoir, Grantham,
Lincolnshire NG32 1PB
☎ 01476 870286
www.belvoircordials.co.uk

Chevelswarde Organic Growers
Chevel House, The Belt, South
Kilworth, Lutterworth, LE17 6DX
☎ 01858 575309
www.chevel.freeserve.co.uk

Dunkertons Cider Company
Pembridge, Leominster,
Herefordshire HR6 9ED
☎ 01544 388653
www.dunkertons.co.uk

Weston's Cider
The Bounds, Much Marcle,
Herefordshire HR8 2NQ
☎ 01531 660233
www.westons-cider.co.uk

East

Crone's
Fairview, Fersfield Road, Kenninghall,
Norfolk NR16 2DP
☎ 01379 687687
www.crones.co.uk

SPECIALIST RETAILERS AND WINE CLUBS

The Beer Shop
14 Pitfield Street, London N1 6EY
☎ 020 7739 3701
www.pitfieldbeershop.co.uk

Beers Unlimited
500 London Road, Westcliff-on-Sea,
Essex SS0 9LD
☎ 01702 345474
www.beersunlimited.co.uk

Henry Doubleday Research
Association Wineclub
☎ 0113 244 0002
www.hdra.org.uk/wineclub

The Pure Wine Company
Ocean House, 51 Alcantara Crescent,
Ocean Village, Southampton,
Hampshire SO14 3HR
☎ 023 8023 8214
www.purewine.co.uk

Ravensbourne Wine
Unit 602, Bell House, 49 Greenwich
High Rd, London SE10 8JL
☎ 020 8692 9655
www.ravensbournewine.co.uk

Unicorn Grocery
89 Albany Road, Chorlton,
Manchester M21 0BN
☎ 0161 861 0010
www.unicorn-grocery.co.uk

Vinceremos
74 Kirkgate, Leeds LS2 7DJ
☎ 0113 244 0002
www.vinceremos.co.uk

Vintage Roots
Farley Farms, Bridge Farm, Reading
Road, Arborfield, Berkshire RG2 9HT
☎ 0800 980 4992
www.vintageroots.co.uk

The Wine Basket
144 Dundas St, Edinburgh EH3 5DQ
☎ 0131 557 2530

York Beer and Wine Shop
28 Sandringham St, Fishergate,
York YO10 4BA
☎ 01904 647136
www.yorkbeerandwineshop.co.uk

TREATS

**The following companies offer
luxury goods ranging from
chocolate and pastries to
bread and ice cream**

Artisan Bread
Unit 16/17 John Wilson Business
Park, Whitstable, Kent, CT5 3QZ
☎ 01227 771881
www.artisanbread.ltd.uk

The Celtic Bakers
42b Waterloo Rd, Cricklewood, London
NW2 7UH
☎ 020 8452 4390
www.thecelticbakers.co.uk

The Chocolate Society
36 Elizabeth Street,
London SW1W 9NZ
☎ 01423 322230
www.chocolate.co.uk

Doves Farm Foods
Salisbury Road, Hungerford,
Berkshire RG17 0RF
☎ 01488 684880
www.dovesfarm.co.uk

Flour Power City
Unit 5b Juno Way, Elizabeth Industrial
Estate, Surrey Quays,
London SE14 5RW
☎ 020 8691 2288
www.flourpowercity.com

Green & Black's
2 Valentine Place, London SE1 8QH
☎ 020 7633 5900
www.greenandblacks.com

Hobbs House Bakery
Unit 6, Chipping Edge Industrial Estate,
Hatters Lane, Chipping Sodbury,
Bristol, BS37 6AA
☎ 01454 321629
www.hobbshousebakery.co.uk

Montezuma's Chocolates
29 East Street, Chichester PO19 1HS,
15 Duke Street, Brighton BN1 1AH
☎ 01243 537385/ 01273 324979
www.montezumas.co.uk

The Old Post Office Bakery
76 Landor Rd, Clapham North,
London SW9 9PH
☎ 020 7326 4408
www.oldpostofficebakery.co.uk

The Organic Pudding Company
Lower Pertwood Farm, Hindon,
Salisbury SP3 6TA
☎ 01747 820719
www.wildpuddings.com

Paul's/Soyfoods
66 Snow Hill, Melton Mowbray,
LE13 1PD
☎ 01664 560572
www.soyfoods.co.uk

Rocombe Farm Organic Ice Cream
Old Newton Road, Heathfield, Newton
Abbot, Devon TQ12 6RA
☎ 01626 834545
www.rocombefarm.co.uk

St John Bread and Wine
94–6 Commercial St, London E1 6LZ
☎ 020 7247 8172
www.stjohnbreadandwine.com

September Organic Dairy
Unit 5 Whitehill Park, Weobley,
Herefordshire HR4 8QE
☎ 01544 312910
www.september-organic.co.uk

The Village Bakery
Melmerby, Penrith, Cumbria CA10 1HE
☎ 01768 881811
www.village-bakery.com

ORGANIC BABY FOOD

Baby Organix
Christchurch, Dorset
☎ 0800 393511
www.babyorganix.co.uk

Hipp Organic
165 Main Street, New Greenham Park,
Newbury, Berks RG19 6HN
☎ 0845 050 1351
www.hipp.co.uk

Pots for Tots
Unit WHE 112, The Wandsworth
Business Village, 3–9 Broomhill Road,
London SW18 4JQ
☎ 0845 450 0875
www.potsfortots.co.uk

Peter Rabbit Organics
Buxton Foods Limited, 12 Harley
Street, London W1G 9PG
☎ 020 7637 5505
www.stamp-collection.co.uk/rabbit

Truuuly Scrumptious Organic
Baby Food
Charmborough Farm, Charlton Road,
Holcombe, Radstock BA3 5EX
☎ 01761 239300
www.bathorganicbabyfood.co.uk

ORGANIC CERTIFYING BODIES

**The following organisations
are responsible for certifying
organic produce in the UK.
Look for their UK code on
produce and contact them
to find your nearest stockist**

Ascisco Limited (UK15)
☎ 0117 914 2406

CMi Certification (UK10)
☎ 01993 885 651
www.cmi-plc.com

Demeter (UK6)
☎ 01453 759501
www.anth.org.uk/biodynamic

Food Certification (Scotland) (UK8)
☎ 0870 286 2860
www.foodcertificationscotland.co.uk

The Irish Organic Farmers
and Growers (UK7)
☎ 00 353 506 32563
www.vic.ie/iofga.htm

Organic Farmers and Growers (UK2)
☎ 01743 440512
www.organicfarmers.uk.com

The Organic Food Federation (UK4)
☎ 01760 720444
www.orgfoodfed.com

Organic Trust (UK9)
☎ 00 353 185 30271
http://ireland.iol.ie/~organic/trust.html

Quality Welsh Food Certification
(UK13)
☎ 01970 636688
www.wfsagri.net

The Scottish Organic Producers
Association (UK3)
☎ 0131 335 6606
www.sopa.org.uk

SGS United Kingdom (UK14)
☎ 0117 914 2406
www.sgs.co.uk

The Soil Association (UK5)
☎ 0117 914 2400
www.soilassociation.org

CAMPAIGNS

**There are many organisations
campaigning to change our
food system for the better. All
need your support.**

Baby Milk Action
www.babymilkaction.org

Child Poverty Action Group
www.cpag.org.uk

Compassion in World Farming
www.ciwf.org.uk

Eat Better
www.eat-better.org

Eat The View
www.eat-the-view.org.uk

Ethical Consumer
www.ethicalconsumer.org

Five Year Freeze
www.fiveyearfreeze.org

Food Commission
www.foodcomm.org.uk

Friends of the Earth
www.foe.co.uk

Greenpeace
www.greenpeace.org.uk

Health Education Trust
www.healthedtrust.com

Local Food Works
www.localfoodworks.org

Soil Association
www.soilassociation.org.uk

Sustain
www.sustainweb.org

The Caroline Walker Trust
www.cwt.org.uk

The Parents Jury
www.parentsjury.org

CONTACTING SUPERMARKETS

**If you don't agree with the
practices of the supermarkets,
let their customer service
departments know why...**

ASDA
☎ 0500 177 755
www.asda.co.uk

Morrisons
☎ 01924 870000
www.morereasons.co.uk

Safeway
☎ 01924 875 355
www.safeway.co.uk

Sainsbury's
☎ 0800 636 262
www.sainsburys.co.uk

Tesco
☎ 0800 50 55 55
www.tesco.co.uk

Waitrose
☎ 0800 188 884
www.waitrose.com

For a detailed explanation about these best buys, see page 9

Unless different for each product, company details are listed in first entry only.

Baby food

Baby Organix
☎ 0800 393511
www.babyorganix.co.uk

Hipp Organics
☎ 0845 050 1351
www.hipp.co.uk

Baby milk

Hipp Organics

Drinks

Beer/lager

Black Isle Brewery
☎ 01463 811871
www.blackislebrewery.com
brands: Blond, Red Kite Ale, Scotch Ale, Thornbush Porter, Wheat Beer, Yellow Hammer Bitter

Broughton Ales
☎ 01899 830345
www.broughton-ales.co.uk
brands: Border Gold, Waitrose Organic Ale, Angel Organic Lager

Freedom
☎ 020 8748 0903
www.freedombrew.co.uk

Fuller's
☎ 020 8996 2000
www.fullers.co.uk
brand: Honey Dew

Marble Brewery
☎ 0161 819 2694
www.marblebeers.co.uk
brands: N/4 Bitter, Cloudy Marble, Manchester Bitter, Uncut Amber, Old Lag, Chocolate Heavy

Organic Brewhouse
☎ 01326 241555
brands: Black Rock Stout, Halzephron Gold, Lizard Point, Serpentine Dark Ale, Wolf Rock

Pitfield Brewery
☎ 020 7739 3701
www.pitfieldbeershop.co.uk
brands: Organic Lager, Original Bitter, Shoreditch Stout, East Kent Goldings, Eco Warrier, Hoxton Best Bitter, Black Eagle

Samuel Smith
☎ 01937 832 225
brands: Organic Lager, Organic Pale Ale

St Peter's
☎ 01986 782322
www.stpetersbrewery.co.uk
brands: Organic Ale, Organic Best Bitter

Wine

Vinceremos
☎ 0113 244 0002
www.vinceremos.co.uk

Vintage Roots
☎ 0800 980 4992
www.vintageroots.co.uk

Bottled water

Ben Shaws
☎ 01484 427427
www.benshaws.com,
brands: Fountain Head, Pennine Hills

Highland Spring
☎ 01764 660500
www.highlandspring.com

Llanllyr Source
☎ 01570 470788
www.llanllyrwater.com

Coffee

Cafédirect
☎ 020 7490 9520
www.cafedirect.co.uk

Equal Exchange
☎ 0131 220 3484
www.equalexchange.co.uk

Traidcraft
☎ 0870 443 1017
www.traidcraft.co.uk

Tea

Cafédirect

Clipper
☎ 0800 169 3552
www.clipper-teas.com

Equal Exchange

Traidcraft

Fruit juice

Biona
☎ 020 7924 2300

Botton Village
☎ 01287 661273
www.camphill.org.uk/botton.htm

James White
☎ 01473 890111
www.jameswhite.co.uk

Organico
☎ 0118 951 0518
www.organico.co.uk
brands: Vitalia

Store cupboard

Bakeries

The Celtic Bakers
☎ 020 8452 4390
www.thecelticbakers.co.uk

Paul's Bakery
☎ 01664 560572
www.soyfoods.co.uk

The Village Bakery
☎ 01768 881811
www.village-bakery.com

Breakfast cereals

Alara
☎ 020 7387 9303
www.alara.co.uk

Doves Farm
☎ 01488 684880
www.dovesfarm.co.uk

Pertwood Organic
☎ 01747 820719
www.pertwood.co.uk

Herbs/spices

Essential
☎ 0845 458 0201
www.essential-trading.co.uk

Hambleden Herbs
☎ 0845 602 3447
www.hambledenherbs.co.uk

Suma
☎ 0845 458 2290
www.suma.co.uk

Pasta

Essential
brands: La Terra e Cielo

La Bio Idea
www.labioidea.com

Organico

Rice

Infinity Foods
☎ 01273 603563
www.infinityfoods.co.uk

RSPB (via Suma)

Traidcraft

Sugar

Co-op fair trade own brand
☎ 0800 068 6727
www.co-op.co.uk

Equal Exchange

Traidcraft

Cooking oil

Biona

Filippo Berio Organic
☎ 01494 463929
www.filippoberio.co.uk

Pertwood Organic

Suma

Zaytoun
☎ 0781 4477 188
www.zaytoun.co.uk

Health foods/wholefoods

Manufacturers

Goodlife
☎ 01925 837810
www.goodlife.co.uk

Plamil
☎ 01303 850588
www.plamilfoods.co.uk

Redwoods
☎ 01536 400 557
www.redwoodfoods.co.uk

Treats
Chocolate

Divine
☎ 020 7378 6550
www.divinechocolate.com

Dubble
☎ 020 7378 6550
www.dubble.co.uk

Green & Black's
☎ 020 7633 5900
www.greenandblacks.com

Plamil

Traidcraft

Ice cream (dairy)

Cream O'Galloway Organic
☎ 01557 814040
www.creamogalloway.co.uk

Green & Black's

Rocombe Farm
☎ 01626 834545
www.rocombefarm.co.uk

Ice cream (non-dairy)

Mother Hemp
☎ 01262 421100
www.motherhemp.com

Rocombe Farm

Crisps

Jonathan Crisp
☎ 0871 244 8510
www.jonathancrisp.co.uk

Kettle Chips Organic
☎ 0800 616996
www.kettlefoods.co.uk

Stour Valley
☎ 01206 397478

Tra'fo
☎ 0031 561 611 000
www.fzorganicfood.com

Dairy

Granovita
☎ 01933 273717
www.granovita.co.uk

Plamil

Provamel/Alpro Soya
☎ 08000 188180
www.alprosoya.co.uk

Sunrise
☎ 0161 924 2214
www.soya-group.com

Cheese

Biona

Loch Arthur Creamery
☎ 01387 760 296
www.locharthur.org.uk

Lye Cross Farm
☎ 01934 864 600
www.lyecrosscheese.co.uk

Butter

Biona

Yeo Valley
☎ 01278 652243
www.yeovalley.co.uk

Margarine

Biona

Suma

Yoghurt (dairy)

Woodlands organic sheep's yoghurt
☎ 01202 822687
www.woodlands-park.co.uk

Yeo Valley

Yoghurt (non-dairy)

Granovita

Provamel

Sojasun
www.sojasun.com

Supermarkets

Budgens
☎ 0870 050 0158
www.budgens.co.uk

The Co-op
☎ 0800 068 6727
www.co-op.co.uk

Sainsbury's
☎ 0800 636262
www.sainsburys.co.uk

to now-banned PCBs that have been shown to affect children's reading ages. The good news, though, is that the hundreds of different potential sources of toxins around our homes and gardens can be avoided, or their affect at the least minimised.

Waste

We have very little contact with the rubbish we create. We tie up a few bin bags a week, toss them into the wheelie bin or dustbin outside our home and that's the last most of us think about it. But some startling figures reveal the true extent of how wasteful we have become. In 2002 in the UK, we – a population of nearly 60 million – threw out six billion nappies, 468 million batteries, 24 million car tyres, two million mobile phones and 94,000 fridges. In total, we now throw away 434 million tonnes of rubbish each year, much of it emanating from our homes, with the majority of it ending up tossed into landfill sites, which are largely predicted to reach capacity by 2010.

Although up to 60 per cent of what we send to landfill or incinerators could be recycled, we currently recycle only about 12 per cent. But recycling should really be considered the last resort. Much more important is that we reduce the amount of stuff we throw away. From the plastic bags and food packaging we bring home from the supermarkets to the cardboard boxes our appliances come wrapped in, much of what we throw away is needlessly bought in the first place and could be reused or composted.

You might now feel that you don't want to step into your home and garden again, but there's plenty of things you can do to reduce your energy and water needs, lessen your exposure to toxins and cut back on what you put outside for the dustmen. This chapter will provide you with a range of ethical alternatives: how to apply for energy efficiency grants; supporting renewable energy; lessening your appliance reliance; replacing toxic cleaners with natural alternatives; encouraging wildlife back into your garden; growing your own organic vegetables and painting your walls safely. Welcome home.

Energy

Domestic energy has never been cheaper. Following a wave of privatisation throughout the energy industry during the 1980s and early 1990s, the domestic energy market has become a highly competitive environment. This has been great news for consumers as prices have fallen. Today, many of us hardly think about our energy costs. Bills can be paid via direct debit. Even better, we can earn Nectar points and Air Miles just by turning on a light switch. And for those who have been classified by the government as the 'fuel poor'– pensioners and families whose energy expenditure adds up to more than 10 per cent of their total outgoings – it has to be good news.

But in reality this new era of cheaper, more convenient energy has only distanced us from the truth about what our energy addiction is doing to the environment. The UK contributed around two per cent of global greenhouse gas emissions in 2001, a quarter of which was a result of the energy we consumed in our homes. And our appetite for domestic energy is rapidly growing. Between 1990 and 2001 energy consumption in British homes rose by 19 per cent.

It's easy to see what's been responsible for a large proportion of this rise when you break down how we typically use our energy. When the Department for Trade and Industry last analysed average domestic energy use in 2002, 60.8 per cent of energy was used for space heating, 23.4 per cent for water heating, 13.1 per cent for lighting and powering appliances, and 2.7 per cent for cooking. The rise in energy use starts to make sense when we learn that average temperatures inside our homes are estimated to have increased from 12.6C in 1970, to 16.9C in 1990 and 18.9C in 2001, helped by increased central heating ownership (up from 31 per cent in 1970 to 90 per cent in 2001).

Our use of appliances is also aggravating the problem. We now use £800 million worth of electricity a year just to run our washing machines, tumble dryers and dishwashers. And £1.2 billion worth of electricity a year is spent on running fridges and freezers. In fact, domestic refrigeration appliances use nearly as much electricity as all the offices in the UK.

We now want brighter homes, too. Electricity consumption by domestic lights and appliances has nearly doubled since 1970. And it's predicted to increase by 12 per cent by the end of the decade.

Making matters worse is the fact that our houses are woefully energy inefficient. Up to 75 per cent of all energy wasted in our homes is avoidable. According to the Energy Saving Trust, more than 40 per cent of all heat lost in the average home is through loft space and walls – something that is easily avoidable with extra insulation. In fact, the amount of heat lost annually through roofs and walls would be enough to heat three million homes for a year.

Health professionals despair at the number of unnecessary deaths caused each year due to poorly and inefficiently heated homes. According to the NHS, around a third of the 30,000 deaths each year caused by wintry weather are due to respiratory diseases or strokes that are exacerbated by poorly heated homes.

But where is all the energy we're using – and wasting – coming from? Should we be choosing some energy sources over others?

Electricity

In the UK, comparative pricing between different energy sources means that only a minority of homes are now heated using electricity. It is expensive compared to gas and produces about two and a half times as much CO_2 per unit of heat. Instead, we mainly use electricity to run appliances and light our rooms.

Baseload electricity – the electricity required to meet continuous user demand, but not peak-time surges – is mainly provided by the UK's nuclear power stations and CCGTs (combined cycle gas-fuelled turbines), with occasional contributions from the larger coal-fired stations and electricity imported from France (which is

1970 **12.6C**   1990 **16.9C**   2001 **18.9C**

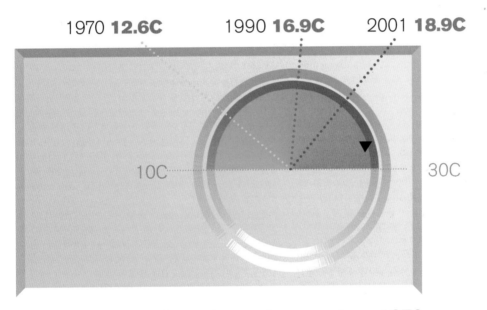

10C 30C

Average temperatures in our homes since 1970

mostly nuclear-generated). When demand spikes (typically between 6pm and 8pm on weekdays) more use is made of large coal-fired stations. Considering that coal is an extremely inefficient and polluting way to generate electricity (up to 47 per cent of coal's energy converts to electricity, meaning that over half of it is lost as wasted heat) it's certainly good news that the rise of natural gas and nuclear power over the past few decades has reduced our reliance on coal-fired power stations. However, global coal reserves are predicted

to last far longer than oil or gas and developing nations such as China and India are now heavily reliant on coal for generating their electricity. As the global demand for electricity increases so more and more coal will be burnt.

Our reliance on nuclear power is also highly controversial. Even the government seems at odds with itself as to what the best longterm strategy for the technology should be. The government's energy white paper, published in February 2003, set a headline target of reducing greenhouse emissions by 60 per cent by 2050. It stated that it would be preferable if energy efficiency and renewable energy sources were given priority over nuclear and fossil fuels. Nuclear energy was not ruled out but was put on hold for at least five years. Only a year later, Tony Blair said the UK may have to build a new generation of nuclear power stations to meet the challenge of climate change.

There are two problems with nuclear power: it's expensive, and it takes a decade or more for the industry to find sites and get planning permissions. Many environmentalists shun nuclear technology because it creates extremely dangerous waste that is notoriously hard to dispose of. But it does have high-profile fans. James Lovelock, the environmental guru and originator of the Gaia theory, has said that the world cannot hope to reduce CO_2 emissions without the help of nuclear power.

Far better for generating electricity than fossil fuels or nuclear technology are renewable sources, such as wind, solar, hydro and biomass. Domestic users of electricity can support these renewable sources in two ways; either by installing their own generation equipment at home (see page 90), or by supporting conventional power companies that offer their customers 'green tariffs' or 'green funds' (see page 130).

There is a subtle but important difference between these two terms. Since April 2002, all electricity supply companies have had to buy at least three per cent of their electricity from renewable power sources (the 'Renewables Obligation' set by the government says that all gas and electricity suppliers must provide 10 per cent of their energy from renewable sources by 2010). In order to meet this obligation, most electricity suppliers now offer a 'green tariff' to domestic customers. This means that for a small premium (although some companies don't charge extra), for every unit of electricity you use, your green-tariff supplier will buy renewable energy to match it – meaning that, in effect, every unit of electricity you use comes from a source of renewable, non-nuclear energy, such as wind and solar power projects.

Critics of green tariff schemes say that these companies are already obliged to meet renewable targets, so why pay a premium to help them? Instead they suggest directly investing in renewable technologies yourself by installing your own domestic solar panels or, depending on your circumstances,

a wind turbine. Alternatively, support a green fund-based supplier, such as Good Energy or Ecotricity, who, in addition to offering green-tariff electricity, invest money in funds used to directly finance new, often community-based, renewable energy projects.

Gas

In the UK, gas is by far the most popular way to heat water and central heating systems. Whether it's via a hot water storage tank, or through a gas-fired 'combi' boiler, in terms of heating rooms and water, gas is kinder to the environment and to your wallet. For cooking, particularly on the top of the stove, gas is also more efficient as it can be controlled with far greater accuracy.

Gas has a lower carbon content in relation to its energy content (14.6 kilograms per gigajoule) than oil (18.6 kilograms per gigajoule), which in turn contains less carbon than coal (24.1 kilograms per gigajoule). Therefore, both for domestic use, and for generating electricity, gas is preferable. But despite a few early flirtations with the concept by suppliers such as Amerada, no gas supplier currently offers green tariffs or green funds. Other than reducing your overall energy consumption, the best thing to do if you're relying on gas for heating space and water is to consider installing a condensing boiler. Even though modern boilers of other types, such as traditional gas-fired combi boilers, are now much more efficient than their predecessors, converting around 72 per cent of fuel into heat, condensing boilers manage around 88 per cent. They do, however, produce a plume of steam via the outside flue so it's best to site them away from your neighbour's view.

Oil

Oil-fired boilers are rather more efficient than traditional gas-fired heaters (with potentially a 95 per cent fuel-into-heat conversion rate). But oil is more polluting, and there are far fewer global reserves than of gas. It's also hard to sanction the use of oil if you believe it to be a catalyst of conflict, particularly in the Middle East, and it is a resource on which we are already far too reliant for our strategic and environmental interests.

Open fires

The comforting allure of a log fire is strong but open fires are an extremely inefficient way of heating a home. Up to 85 per cent of the heat they generate is wasted, largely up the chimney. Open fires, particularly ones fed on coal or anthracite, are also a major cause of household pollution. A far better option is to install a wood-burning stove. As most are made of cast iron, they are excellent at radiating heat efficiently, even after the fire has gone out. Some can also be used to heat water and radiators, or for cooking via a hot plate. (For the same reasons, Rayburns, Agas and kitchen ranges can – if using oil, gas or in some cases wood – provide efficient heating, for space and water, and cooking. However, models using electricity offer relatively poor efficiency in comparison.

Spotlight

Energy grants

Finding the most efficient fuel and system to heat your house is a major consideration, but just as important is keeping your home well insulated. Although the initial outlay costs may be offputting, the good news is that there are a surprisingly large number of grants available to help you increase the energy efficiency of your home, be it through government or local council schemes.

The government's principal grant for tackling fuel poverty is called Warm Front (also known variously as Warm Deal, Warm Home and Home Energy Efficiency Scheme grants, depending on where in the country you live). Grants of up to £1,500 are available to various groups: households on income-related benefits with children under 16; pregnant women on income-related benefits; and households receiving disability benefits. These can assist with the cost of installing cavity wall insulation, draught proofing, gas wall heaters, a dual element foam-insulated immersion tank, heating repairs and replacements.

Warm Front grants of up to £2,500 are also available to the over-60s and people receiving income-related benefits who do not have an existing heating system, or a central heating system for the main living areas of the house.

If you qualify for one of these grants, or you know anyone who would – a relative, neighbour or colleague – do apply, as they can make a huge difference to the thermal efficiency of a home.

For more information about applying for a Warm Front grant, visit www.defra.gov.uk/environment/energy/hees or telephone 0800 952 1555.

Many other grants are available that are not necessarily means tested but could be based simply on your postcode. By far the quickest way to find out what you may qualify for is to type your details into the grant-finder facility at the Energy Saving Trust website – www.saveenergy.co.uk/gid. Alternatively, ring 0845 727 7200.

Energy alternatives

A decade or so ago, most people would have laughed at the prospect of being able to generate much of the domestic energy they use themselves. They would have imagined bending over a spluttering generator with oily hands and a spanner, or standing under a lukewarm solar-fed shower willing the sun to come out. But renewable energy has made huge advances in recent years and is being adopted by more and more people across the UK.

While supporting the renewable sources that now increasingly supply the National Grid through green fund and tariff schemes, you can also greatly reduce the greenhouse-gas emissions you produce by generating power through renewable sources at home.

Don't be put off by the initial start-up costs: there are a range of grants now available, particularly through the government's Clear Skies initiative (up to 50 per cent of installation costs, www.clear-skies.org), and the greatly increased efficiency of much of today's equipment means that costs can normally be recouped within just a few years.

Solar

There are currently three ways to secure domestic power from the sun – passive, active or photovoltaic.

Passive solar energy is perhaps the most straightforward and is achieved through the careful planning and positioning of windows and glass doors during a home's construction. Few houses are currently built to maximise the heat created by the passing of the sun each day, but by having one side of the house largely faced with glass and positioned southward, the ambient temperature throughout the house can be greatly increased. Adding a conservatory to a home can also have the same effect. (Ground-source heat pumps are a way to heat your home and water using passive solar energy heat stored in the ground around your home, but are expensive and are at their most cost effective if fitted when a home is being built. See www.earthenergy.co.uk.)

Active solar panels (also known as solar collectors) are what most people associate with solar energy. In northerly countries such as the UK, active solar panels will not provide all your hot water needs, except in high summer (about 50 per cent on average), but they will greatly reduce the amount of conventional energy required to do so.

There are different types of solar panel but they all largely work on the same principle. Water is pumped through small pipes (an inexpensive process) positioned on a south-facing roof and heated by the sun's rays. A typical system will use a 3–4m² panel and feed a 150- to 200-litre tank. Costs vary but most systems cost between £2,500 and £4,000, less for a new-build home or if installed yourself. The energy pay-back period for active solar panels is 15–20 years for modern rooftop installations. There are many places to research this technology but www.solartradeassociation.org.uk is a good starting point.

Photovoltaic (PV) panels generate electricity through solar energy using technology largely developed for space exploration. PV panels can supply up to 50 per cent of a UK home's electricity needs, but they are currently very expensive (£8,000 to £18,000), almost to the point where they're not really competitive with conventional electricity prices (power generated by a PV system costs around 60p–70p/kWh once you've factored in the installation costs). At 20 per cent, their efficiency is also relatively low – on average, under UK skies, a 1m² PV panel will be able to generate 100W (300W in high summer). However, a PV panel could have many useful applications around the home, for example providing lighting for the garden. For more information visit the British Photovoltaic Association website at www.pv-uk.org.uk.

Wind

Whereas the use of solar power may not seem ideally suited to the UK, the use of wind power couldn't be more appropriate. It's a technology that, as a nation, we've already used in the past in the form of windmills, and today modern wind turbines are arguably the most promising renewable energy source: a third of the UK is classed as having sufficiently constant winds to make this technology viable. It's predicted that the whole of the UK's electricity supplies could theoretically be generated using wind. It has also been said that in the US, electricity provided by wind turbines in just three states – Kansas, North Dakota, and South Dakota – could provide all the electricity required by the entire country. Given how controversial many current wind farms have proved to be with local communities, this outcome seems unlikely. For example, in 2004 a protest against a proposed expansion of a wind farm in north Wales drew the support of the Snowdonia Society, the Campaign for the Protection of Rural Wales, the Conway valley civic society, North Wales tourism, the Ramblers, the National Trust, the local Labour MP and Welsh Assembly member, along with up to 1,800 individuals.

It's clearly a controversial technology, but one that the government and most energy companies are now committed to expanding. The 1,034 wind turbines already running in the UK produce about 700MW of electricity – about as much as one conventional power station – but over the next seven years more than 7,000MW of generating power will be installed on 73 new farms. This, despite almost 80 per cent of all wind-farm applications made in the past 14 years being turned down largely on aesthetic grounds.

One of the problems many people in the UK have with large-scale wind farms, besides the 'ruining' of rural sightlines, is that they do not believe wind farms meet the proportionate energy demands of the communities that host them. However, even a small wind turbine feeding a single home can illustrate how much energy can be harnessed from wind. Like solar panels, the initial outlay can put many people off, but seen as a longterm investment, a domestic wind turbine is an excellent source of renewable energy. Size is an issue though; to power a modern home on a good site, the blades would need to span about five metres from tip to tip. Therefore, wind is typically used as a supplementary domestic energy source. For example, a rotor diameter of two metres can yield about 500 kWh of electricity per year, compared with an average annual household consumption of about 4,500 kWh. For more information, contact the British Wind Energy Association (www.bwea.com), or visit the website of the UK's wind technology guru, Hugh Piggott, at www.scoraigwind.com.

Biomass

One of the best renewable sources of energy is the organic matter around us: trees, crops or manure, or, as it's collectively known, biomass.

The rest of the world is still largely reliant on this form of energy for heating and cooking, but the west is slowly reacquainting itself with the potential of biomass. Its beauty is that it can be used with existing infrastructure, be it coal-fired power stations or a wood stove at home. It is also carbon neutral in that the carbon emitted when burning the fuel is equal to that sequestered when the fuel was 'grown'. It's argued that our inefficient and heavily subsidised agricultural land should be turned over to 'energy crops' such as coppiced woods for use as fuel. The widespread reintroduction of coppicing (it was a large feature of the British countryside until the end of the 19th century), if carefully managed, could also benefit our much-depleted biodiversity.

In 2004, the UK made its first tentative steps into trialling the industrial use of biomass when Drax, Europe's biggest coal-fired power station, located in Yorkshire, tested the use of thousands of tonnes of coppiced willow pulped into biomass for burning. The trial aimed to displace 10,000 tonnes of coal – and 22,000 tonnes of carbon dioxide – from a power station that provides eight per cent of England and Wales's electricity. In the future, agricultural by-products and solid waste from sewage treatment plants could be used as fuel, too. (Energy is already commercially harvested by 'biodigestion' in the form of methane gas emitted from rotting rubbish buried in landfill sites.)

At home, though, biomass can also be a useful renewable technology either through a boiler or stove, both of which can be fed biomass fuel in the form of wood pellets or logs. Sustainably sourced ash, beech, hornbeam, hawthorn, crab apple and wild cherry are the most efficient woods to use as fuel. For more information about domestic biomass systems, contact British Biogen (www.britishbiogen.co.uk, tel: 020 7235 8474) or the Log Pile Project (www.logpile.co.uk, tel: 01908 665555).

For further advice about installing any renewable energy system at home, contact the National Energy Foundation (www.natenergy.org.uk, tel: 01908 665555) and the Centre for Alternative Technology (www.cat.org.uk, tel: 01654 705950).

Water conservation

Many people in the UK still find it hard to believe that we need to conserve water. We're an island surrounded by water and it seems to rain all the time, so surely we're excused on that count? But in certain parts of the country, it actually rains less than some may think. According to the Met Office, the driest part of the UK, along the Thames estuary, averages around 500mm from 150–200 'rain days' (those with rainfall of 0.2 mm or more). In comparison, the wettest parts of the country – the Lake District and the western Highlands of Scotland – receive about 5,000mm a year.

Water is a precious resource, one that takes much effort and energy to reach our taps. The UK water industry collects, treats and supplies about 18 billion litres of water per day. (It also collects and treats over 10 million tonnes of the resulting sewage water each day.) In the UK, two-thirds of water supplies are taken from surface sources – there are 666 reservoirs and 600 river water abstraction points across the country – and a third is taken from the 1,585 available boreholes. But our huge thirst for water still creates shortages, as summer hosepipe bans demonstrate.

To unthinkingly consume water also ignores how valuable and scarce a resource it is elsewhere around the world. About two billion people, approximately one-third of the world's population, depend on groundwater supplies, withdrawing about 20 per cent of global water (600–700 cubic kilometres) annually. Much of it is taken from shallow aquifers – vast, ancient underground stores of water that take centuries to replenish. These are fast becoming polluted with agrochemicals and heavy industry spillages.

Water scarcity is also leading to tension and conflict between states that border or share water sources. Much is made of future

wars being fought over water rather than oil, but Israel's prime minister, Ariel Sharon, has stated that he believes the Six Day War in 1967 really started because Syrian engineers were working on diverting part of the water flow away from Israel.

It is true that in the Middle East the problem is at its most acute. Israel's annual water use, for example, exceeds the renewable supply by 15 per cent. To partly resolve this problem, in 2004 Israel signed a deal with Turkey to pump 50 million cubic metres of water a year, for 20 years, from the Manavgat river in Anatolia – in return for arms.

There are, therefore, many reasons – and ways – to conserve water where you can.

- Wash dishes in a bowl rather than under a running tap.

- Only fill the kettle with the amount of water you need.

- Keep a bottle or jug of water in the fridge rather than waiting for the tap to run cold.

- Don't use the half-load programme on dishwashers and washing machines unless the machine is full. Despite their promise, they are rarely economical with water or energy when half full.

- Don't leave the tap running when you're brushing your teeth as you could be wasting as much as five litres of water a minute.

- Take a shower. A five-minute shower uses about a third of the water of a bath. However, modern power-showers can use more water than a bath in less than five minutes. Also, investigate using a low-flow showerhead that aerates the water, thereby reducing the volume of water used.

Toilet cisterns can use as much as nine litres of clean, drinkable water with every flush. Reduce this by placing ballast in the cistern in the form of a brick in a plastic bag. Alternatively, adjust the ballcock setting to force the cistern to refill to a lower level, or investigate buying a dual-flush toilet or even a waterless toilet. And think about whether you need to flush a toilet every time you use it.

Buy a 'flow restrictor' for your shower and taps. These switch between maintaining a six litres/minute flow and 20 litres/minute flow according to your needs.

'Bag it and bin it'. Cotton wool, disposable nappies, razors, women's tights, tampons, cotton buds and tissues should be put in a waste bin rather than flushed down the toilet. Thames Water estimates that over 100,000 cotton buds are disposed of in its sewer network each week, contributing to the 25,000 tonnes of debris removed from its sewers every year.

Fix leaking taps. Dripping taps can waste up to four litres of water a day.

Lag external pipes and taps. Burst water pipes during the winter can cause serious damage as well as waste huge amounts of water.

Report leaks to your water supplier and to WaterVoice (www.watervoice.org.uk), the consumer arm of the water regulator Ofwat. Leakages are a huge problem. In some cities around the world up to 40 per cent of all water is lost through leaks. Make water suppliers accountable for any lack of infrastructure maintenance.

Ask your water supplier to meter your water instead of charging you a fixed annual charge. In the UK, only 20 per cent of households are metered, yet studies have shown that water consumption — and bills — drop significantly when people know that they are paying for their water use.

Water your garden in the cool of the early morning or evening as it helps to reduce evaporation losses. Leave plants alone until they are showing the first signs of wilting.

Collect rain water in a water butt for watering your plants. Most councils now offer subsidised butts that can cost as little as £10–£15.

If you must use a hosepipe, fit a trigger nozzle to control the flow.

Consider planting flowers and shrubs that thrive in hot and dry conditions such as thyme, evening primrose, rock rose, lavender, and buddleia.

Make use of 'grey water' in the garden — any waste water that hasn't been mixed with waste water from a toilet. Water collected from the kitchen sink, bath, washing machine and dishwasher can be used to water plants as long as it has passed through a basic filter (tightly packed straw in a bucket, for example) to remove solid particles and grease, and you have used environmentally sensitive washing-up liquid and detergents. Better still, investigate systems that allow you to use grey water to flush your toilet.

Use mulches in the garden such as sustainably sourced wood chips or bark to help prevent water evaporation.

Lawns can survive long periods of dry weather if you let the grass grow longer. Even if the grass turns brown, it will quickly recover after a few days of rain. Better still, avoid having large areas of lawn.

Don't use garden sprinklers. They can use as much water in an hour — a staggering 300–650 litres — as a family of four uses in a day.

Use a bucket and sponge to wash your car instead of a hosepipe.

Saving energy around the home

There are dozens of things you can do to save energy (and money) around the home. As well as trying the suggestions listed below, always buy appliances labelled 'A-rated' for energy efficiency, and have a free energy audit carried out on your home by staff at one of the UK's many Energy Efficiency Advice Centres (www.saveenergy. co.uk, tel: 0800 512012). It will help you to ascertain your home's SAP (Standard Assessment Procedure) rating. SAP is the government's standard methodology for rating a home's energy efficiency. It also calculates a home's carbon emissions.

Kitchen

Cooker
Put a lid on a pan when boiling water – it will boil up to six per cent faster. Once the water is boiling, turn it down as most energy is used bringing water to the boil.

Match the size of the ring to the pan being used.

Think ahead and cook things in combination for two meals. For example, cook extra potatoes so that they are parboiled ahead of a roast the next day. Also use a multi-level steamer over one pan of shallow boiling water, or a pressure cooker for extra efficiency.

Resist the temptation to open the oven door during cooking for a quick peek. Over 20 per cent of the heat can be lost each time you open the door.

Turn the oven off a few minutes before you are due to take out the food – most modern ovens are well enough insulated to prevent any significant heat loss by doing this.

Ensure food is totally defrosted before cooking. Thawing food in the oven before it cooks requires up to 50 per cent more energy.

Most extractor fans above ovens are rarely effective, especially the ones that don't have an external flue. An open window is often just as good.

Buy a fan-assisted oven – they can heat up 30 per cent faster than conventional ovens.

Laundry

Coloured clothes rarely, if ever, need to be washed at anything higher than 40C. A wash at 60C uses more than 30 per cent more energy than washing at 40C and will fade the colours in your clothes faster too. White-wash settings use much more energy and water than other settings. Most whites wash well at 40C, especially if soaked in a sink or bath in advance.

Line-dry clothes – outdoors, or indoors on a clothes horse – whenever possible. If you must use a tumble dryer – one of the most energy-hungry domestic appliances – make sure all items are well spun beforehand.

Clean out the tumble dryer's lint tray regularly as lint reduces the machine's ability to expel damp air.

Use a hand water spray instead of the steam setting on an iron as energy is wasted heating the water. And turn the iron off with one item to go.

Fridges/Freezers
Regularly defrost your fridge and freezer to maintain efficiency. Internal frost should never be more than 6mm (a quarter-inch) thick. And keep the fridge temperature between 3C and 5C using a fridge thermometer.

Keep the condenser coils at the back clean and make sure they are not pushed up too close to a wall.

Never put hot food in the fridge or freezer. Until it has cooled, the appliance will require extra energy to maintain its base temperature.

Defrost things overnight in the fridge. The cooler temperature of the frozen food will allow the fridge to save energy.

Buy a SavaPlug (www.savawatt.com, tel: 01789 490340) for your fridge. It can save up to 20 per cent of a fridge's energy costs by better regulating its power use.

Fill any empty spaces in either a chest freezer or an upright freezer. Use empty cardboard boxes to minimise the airflow and save energy that would otherwise be spent fanning the air.

Dishwashers
Turn your machine off and open the

door just before it enters its drying setting. Air-drying dishes this way saves significant amounts of energy.

Don't needlessly use the largely superfluous 'rinse only' setting.

Wait for the dishwasher to be full before you use it. Avoid using the 'half-load' setting which uses more than half the amount of energy and water.

Bathroom
Using a shower (but not a power-shower) not only saves considerable amounts of water, it also saves on energy used to heat the water. Don't shave using a running hot-water tap. Equally, don't leave the tap running while you brush your teeth.

Lighting

Use energy-efficient compact fluorescent lightbulbs (CFLs) where possible. They save up to 80 per cent on lighting costs and last for years.

Don't over-light rooms needlessly.

Use sensor lighting outdoors to cut back on energy wasted by permanent security lighting.

Ignore the myth that fluorescent strip lights are more efficient if left on continuously. If you are leaving a room for more than a minute, turn them off.

Consider the effects of light pollution. For more information visit the Campaign for Dark Skies (www.dark-skies.org)

Central heating

Make sure your boiler is serviced at least every two years. Also, replacing a 15-year-old boiler could save you 20 per cent on your fuel bills (or 32 per cent if a condensing boiler is installed), and up to 40 per cent if you also install the right heating controls. To find out the most efficient boiler for your needs, visit the government-backed Boiler Efficiency Database at www.sedbuk.com.

Place aluminium foil (shiny side out) behind your radiators to help reflect heat inwards.

Don't overheat your home. Lowering the thermostat by just 1C can save up to 10 per cent on heating bills. A home should not need to be heated over 19C. In fact, if you have a baby, heating above this temperature is discouraged by health professionals.

When away from home for more than a few days during cold spells, remember to lower the thermostat and readjust

any timers to make your heating come on for just a few hours a day. Likewise, the heating should be set to go off when you are asleep.

Place your thermostat on an inside wall and away from draughts.

Regularly bleed radiators to rid them of inefficient air bubbles.

Lag water tanks and fit draught excluders where possible.

Turn the hot water temperature down – better to have hot water at the right temperature than cooling it down with extra cold water.

Living rooms

Don't rely on standby settings used by TVs, DVD players, VCRs, hi-fis, set-top boxes and PCs. It's estimated that up to 15 per cent of domestic electricity worldwide is wasted by people using standby unnecessarily.

Unplug mobile phone chargers when they are not in use. Likewise, when not in use, turn off any adapters that may be attached to your electrical appliances such as computers, answer phones etc.

Don't put sofas and chairs against outside walls where you will feel the cold and draughts the most.

Keep internal doors closed as much as possible.

Block up fireplaces that are not being used. Consider replacing open fires with wood-burning stoves.

Remember that smoking indoors can lead to a 50 per cent increase in heating costs because windows are left open for ventilation. Try to smoke outdoors, or in a room that is rarely used, with the door shut.

Loft, walls and floors

Make sure your loft and cavity walls are

well insulated. Instead of using modern mineral wool or blown cellulose fibre-based loft insulators, consider using the many natural alternatives now available, such as sheep's wool (www.secondnatureuk.com) or paper. By installing loft insulation to a depth of at least 250mm (10 inches), you can save around 25 per cent of your heating costs.

Filling cavity walls is also just as effective and should be considered for all houses built after the 1930s when cavity walls became the norm. Contact the Cavity Insulation Guarantee Agency (www.ciga.co.uk, tel: 01525 853300) for more details.

Fill gaps in floorboards and place newspaper beneath a carpet's underlay for extra insulation.

Windows

Small gaps in windows are responsible for up to 20 per cent of a home's heat loss. Consider investing in double glazing for your windows. Remember that double glazing requires good ventilation otherwise it can encourage damp. Ensure any window (or door) fitter is accredited by Fensa (www.fensa.co.uk, tel: 0870 780 2028). It ensures that fitters meet the best thermal performance standards. A much cheaper alternative to double glazing is to apply purposely designed plastic sheeting to the inside of each pane.

Close the curtains (well-lined curtains are always best) when a room is not in use during the daytime. It will keep the room cool in summer and warm in winter.

Home

The UK's annual spend on furnishings and DIY now stands at a record £23 billion. In fact, it seems as if the Englishman's proverbial castle is undergoing a perpetual makeover. The nation's weekends continue to be dedicated to home improvement. B&Q, the busiest DIY outlet, can expect to receive three million visits over an average bank holiday weekend, while every year, 26 million of us make at least one pilgrimage to Ikea, spending a collective £800 million on the company's 'democratic design'. Levels of mortgage equity withdrawals to free up money for house extensions and redecoration are also at record levels, despite equally high levels of consumer debt.

The nation's love affair with bricks and mortar also shows no signs of abating. By 2021, the number of new homes in England alone is projected to increase by 3.8 million. Although building will be centred on brownfield sites, one third of England's land area is still predicted to switch from rural to urban use by 2016. Up to 2.7 million of these new households will be single occupancy. Each new homeowner will inevitably buy more paint, wallpaper, appliances and tools. No wonder the home improvement industry is so buoyant.

But this huge appetite for cosmetically altering our homes – and keeping them clean – is fuelling a rapid rise in the amount of synthetic, harmful chemicals we are exposing ourselves to (see page 106). From paints to cleaning products, toxic ingredients have penetrated our domestic environments. The products that contain them may seem useful, but they can have negative health effects.

Research has shown that indoor air is almost 10 times more polluted than outdoor air. A Greenpeace report published in 2003, *Consuming Chemicals*, used dust as an indicator of exposure to toxic chemicals in the home and found 35 hazardous chemicals and a further 140 synthetic chemicals in dust, including flame retardants, solvents and petroleum additives.

Thousands of synthetic chemicals are now available to manufacturers to use in day-to-day products in our homes, ranging from furniture and textiles, to DIY products and conventional cleaners. However, a number of them have been linked to hypersensitivity, cancer, allergies, damage to the nervous system, reproductive disorders and disruption of the immune system. The full implications for human health – and that of the wider environment – are simply not known as research into their impact has hardly begun. What is clear, though, is that we should adopt a precautionary approach and attempt to minimise our exposure to such chemicals as far as possible.

Furnishings

Textiles

Fabric used in upholstery is treated to comply with fire regulations. This is good news if you happen to drop a cigarette but bad news if you are interested in avoiding brominated flame retardants, and their association with developmental defects and interference with thyroid hormones. More than 70 brominated flame retardants are routinely used for upholstery, carpets and other textiles, but many are persistent and bioaccumulative (see page 106) having been found in the tissues of wildlife and humans. Some are also suspected of being hormone disrupters. For those seeking safer alternatives, borax is a natural flame retardant used on organic and natural fibres.

Cotton

The common perception of 'pure' cotton is that it is an unadulterated, natural fabric, but, in truth, it is one of the most polluted and polluting crops in the world. Cotton production accounts for 25 per cent of all pesticides used over the world. Residues of cotton pesticides have been found to have entered the food chain and more than 76 per cent of conventional cotton production in the US is now from genetically modified crops.

However, organic cotton is growing in popularity and there are alternatives for most household items, from bath towels and pillow slips to laundry bags and duvets. Unbleached and naturally dyed, it offers a toxin-free alternative to conventionally produced products and synthetic alternatives.

Beds

As we spend around of a third of our lives in bed, it makes sense to ensure our bedroom is a relaxing sanctuary and not a place allergy sufferers should fear. However, mattresses are full of dust mites (gone are the days when beds were beaten weekly to remove dust), which affect 85 per cent of asthma sufferers and 90 per cent of eczema sufferers. However, vacuuming a square metre of bed mattress for two minutes can lift about one gramme of dust. As conventional mattresses often include brominated flame retardants, it's also best to opt for an organic latex version.

Curtains

As is the case with upholstery fabrics, brominated fire retardants, or similar compounds, are often used in curtain-weight fabrics. Use a natural fabric free of synthetic chemicals wherever possible. Blinds are a possible alternative – they absorb fewer toxins and dust than voluminous curtains – but, in comparison to curtains, are far less insulating.

Furniture

Amid the world of DIY makeovers and flat-pack MDF kits, it's easy to overlook Britain's more sustainable, ecologically minded traditions of furniture production. In the 1850s, the Arts and Crafts movement, led by designers such as William Morris, represented the antithesis of synthetic, mass-produced industrial design and production.

In common with the customers who bought those first Arts and Crafts pieces in the 1850s, today's consumers should pay attention to furniture's origins and materials and choose low-impact pieces where possible. This is particularly important in the case of wooden furniture. Around the world, old-growth forests, containing precious woods such as teak, mahogany and Brazilian rosewood, are fast disappearing, resulting in the loss of important wildlife habitats and resources for indigenous peoples. Friends of the Earth estimates that up to 50 per cent of tropical timber imports into the EU may be illegally sourced. In 2004, Greenpeace embarrassed the European Commission in Brussels by revealing that illegal hardwoods were being used to refurbish an EU building.

According to the Worldwatch Institute, a large proportion of furniture bears the 'invisible imprint of violence'. Illegal logging and deforestation in Liberia during the late 1990s, for example, raised an estimated $100 million per year, which went straight into the coffers of a warlord, thereby funding Liberia's brutal civil war.

Consequently, if you must buy new furniture, exotic hardwoods should always be avoided. Instead opt for sustainable wood options including birch, ash, sycamore and cherry woods. The Forestry Stewardship Council (www.fsc-uk.info) has certified more than 39 million hectares of forest and the FSC logo guarantees that timber is from a sustainably managed forest.

Fittings

Carpets and floorboards

On health and hygiene grounds, wooden floors seem to have the upper hand over carpets. Pure wool carpets might sound wonderfully natural and wholesome but they may have been treated with pyrethroids. Used to treat the wool, these act as nerve poisons and have been banned in the US for use in carpets for 15 years, but are still legal in the UK. Most carpets are usually backed with materials such as synthetic latex that can also emit toxins. Therefore, look for '100 per cent natural' carpets, as opposed to ones that are labelled '100 per cent wool'.

In their favour, carpets do prevent noise pollution and provide good insulation. Natural fibre products such as sea-grass, jute and coir are good, natural alternatives. Use traditional methods of fitting, such as tacking the carpet to the floor, instead of gluing, which can emit solvents.

Flooring

Tributyltin (TBT) is used in many synthetic floor coverings. A suspected endocrine disrupter, it prevents mould, mildew and bacteria in floor coverings and some fabrics, but contains organotin compounds that can find their way into the human body via the skin.

Vinyl floor coverings emerged during the second world war as a rubber substitute and went on to be a familiar feature in homes due to their warm-under-foot, wipe-clean qualities. Modified into Polyvinyl Chloride (PVC), it is now one of the world's most popular forms of plastic; global production rose from 12.8 million tonnes in 1988 to 22 million tonnes in 1996.

Unfortunately, it is also one of the most harmful plastics. Both its production and disposal create some of the planet's most damaging industrial pollutants in the form of dioxins and it continues to release toxins during every stage of its life cycle. Workers at PVC plants are routinely exposed to vinyl chlorine, a known human carcinogen. Therefore, PVC is certainly something to avoid in the home.

It may sound quaint nowadays, but linoleum, a 1950s standard, is a far more environmentally friendly alternative to vinyl. Its components include linseed oil, chalk, wood dust and pine resin.

DIY

Do-it-yourself culture has us firmly in its thrall. It's a rare home that doesn't possess a toolkit, electric drill or work bench. However, for every TV makeover show, there is an equivalent show featuring DIY disasters and half-finished jobs.

According to the Department of Trade and Industry, each year 250,000 serious injuries and 70 deaths are caused through carelessness and lack of knowledge when undertaking DIY. It's also wasteful and polluting. An estimated 12–25 per cent of the paint sold in the UK is never used, and many jobs use highly polluting, toxin-rich materials that pose risks to human health and the environment. Therefore, before starting any DIY project, ask yourself the following questions:

- **Is the job achievable and necessary?**

- **Are the materials the most low-impact available, both in terms of personal health and the environment?**

- **Are the materials from sustainable sources and, preferably, biodegradable?**

- **Do the materials need to be treated with toxic preservatives or sealants?**

- **How long will the completed work last before needing to be redone?**

Paint

Thousands of colours and finishes now jostle for our attention on the shelves of DIY retailers. You can even go off-chart and have colours specially mixed. Painting is seen as a relatively easy DIY job that can completely transform a space. However, while we tend to keep the windows open for as long as the 'wet paint' smell lingers, conventional paints are significant domestic pollutants. Solvents in some paints pass into the air for many weeks as they dry.

Most paints contain volatile organic compounds (VOCs, see page 106). Found in higher levels in gloss paint than in emulsion, they can cause nose and throat problems, headaches, allergic skin reactions, nausea, fatigue and dizziness. Paint manufacturers and paint outlets now put the VOC content of a paint on the tin's label. But some campaigners, such as Friends of the Earth, question how useful these ratings can be, as VOCs commonly include noxious gases, including known carcinogens such as toluene (which has been linked to longterm liver damage) and xylene (which has been linked to foetal damage).

Reacting to consumer anxiety, the big manufacturers have now come up with 'new generation' paints that claim to cut down on toxic vapours and harmful ingredients. However, in the case of 'low-VOC' paints, the organic compounds can still be converted into ozone pollutants. And while newer water-thinnable paints might be free from VOCs, campaigners claim that many contain more harmful chemicals than the traditional oil-based paints they replaced in the first place.

In contrast, 'natural' paints (see page 133) – which are made using biodegradable ingredients such as lime and chalk – are far more benign, as they tend to be alcohol- or water-based. Even so, look closely at the labels, as some natural paints can include ingredients such as synthetic alkyds or a small percentage of white spirit, which is a petroleum by-product sometimes labelled as 'aliphatic hydrocarbons'. The best paints avoid harsh chemicals and petrochemical by-products altogether. For example, look for 'd-limonene'. It is a natural solvent – a key component of paint – made from

12–25 per cent of the paint sold in the UK is **never used**

citrus fruits, produced by distilling the oil that's extracted after pressing the fruit peel. Similarly, turpentine is a natural solvent. Distilled from the pine tree, it is both renewable and biodegradable.

Paint strippers

Removing paint from walls and doors can be an arduous task. Unsurprisingly, we've got used to relying on aggressive substances to do the job. In the past, paint strippers contained extremely caustic chemicals such as sodium hydroxide and potassium hydroxide. These have now been largely replaced by methylene chloride and dichloromethane, which are still particularly toxic. In fact, when they first entered the market, recommended levels of exposure were quickly reduced from 500 parts per million to 50 and then to 25. Instead, buy the now available, and effective, water-based paint strippers (for example, try www.ecosolutions.co.uk).

Concrete

Environmentalists have something of a love/hate relationship with concrete. On the one hand, concrete is synonymous with ill-conceived post-war housing and pollution and is the single biggest manufacturing source of CO_2, responsible for seven per cent of manmade CO_2 emissions globally. On the other, concrete has found an unlikely calling as a valuable material in some eco-buildings. It possesses a high thermal mass and, in common with brick and stone, can help to conserve energy – particularly if used as a flooring or sub-flooring – or to create internal walls.

However, the global use of concrete looks increasingly unsustainable. Unbridled concreting has led to the creation of what geographers call 'impervious surface areas' (ISA), which can affect the water cycle and, by replacing heavily vegetated areas, reduce the depletion of carbon dioxide thereby speeding climate change (see page 152). Research by the US National Oceanic Atmospheric Administration has shown that the ISA of the contiguous states in the US is now larger than the wetland areas.

There are opportunities to cut back on concrete use. For example, buildings with lightweight or honeycombed concrete blocks have a higher insulation rate than those with solid concrete blocks. Fly ash, the waste from coal-fired power plants, can also be substituted for between 25 and 60 per cent of Portland cement.

A Tasmanian company, TecEco (www.tececo.com),

has developed a form of eco-cement. Made of magnesium carbonate rather than calcium carbonate, it aims to drastically reduce carbon dioxide emissions associated with cement production. Three to four times more waste products can also be used in its composition, including carbon-based organic waste. And once set, the concrete actually performs a 'carbon sink' function, attracting further CO_2 from the atmosphere, meaning that concrete has the potential to become part of the solution rather than the problem.

Plaster
You don't have to live in a straw-bale house to use a natural plaster. So-called earthen plasters and lime and gypsum-based plasters (see page 133) are a low-impact alternative to cement-based varieties. More permeable to heat and moisture, they allow houses to 'breathe' and help prevent the build-up of condensation. In contrast, synthetic stuccos or plasters have been shown to 'outgas', namely, emit potentially toxic gases over the long term.

Timber
In theory, timber should be one of the most eco-friendly and energy-efficient materials on the planet. Not only does timber have one of the lowest 'embodied energy values' (defined as the quantity of energy required by all of the activities associated with the production process) of any material, but it is naturally low in thermal conductivity and is an excellent insulator. In fact, a 2.5cm timber board has better thermal resistance than an 11.4cm brick wall. In construction terms, it is estimated that if all homes built in the UK since 1945 had been constructed to modern timber-frame standards, to date there would have been a reduction of more than 300 million tonnes of CO_2 emissions.

However, despite its ecological merits, sustainability and legitimate supplies are very real issues. Tropical rainforests are now being cleared at a rate of around 15 million hectares a year, a greater rate than that in 1992, when the world's leaders pledged to protect the world's forests at the Rio Earth summit. The global timber industry typically counters charges that it's helping to destroy the earth's great forests by highlighting the fact that it plants more trees than it fells. However, Friends of the Earth and other environmental organisations point out that old-growth

forests are being replaced by 'factory forests' full of quick-growing trees that do little to address the issue of the destruction of precious bio-diverse habitats.

The UK is one of the world's biggest timber consumers. Annual imports of timber for building, home improvements, furniture and paper are, according to Friends of the Earth, equivalent to over six million hectares of forest (about the size of Ireland). Despite an increase in native forestry land (around 20 per cent of the timber we use now comes from domestic trees), it's estimated that the UK needs to reduce wood consumption by 73 per cent by 2050 if it is to help reach sustainability. So it is up to us to use reclaimed and salvaged wood wherever possible.

If you are buying new timber, find out whether its origins are fully traceable. In common with diamonds and oil, timber is a precious global commodity and illegal logging and trafficking is hugely lucrative. According to the Worldwatch Institute, one quarter of the 49 wars and armed conflicts waged during 2000 were largely driven by the desire to control natural resources.

Many large corporations have been suspected of facilitating this illegal trade. To ensure that timber is legitimately sourced from sustainable forests it needs to be certified by a recognised international body such as the Forestry Stewardship Council.

Also watch out for conventional timber preservatives, most of which emit noxious gases and are toxic. Instead use natural preservatives, such as boron, where possible. Good-quality, certified native woods such as oak, chestnut or ash often don't require any preservatives at all.

Synthetic wood substitutes such as MDF (see right) have not proved to be the great guilt-free alternatives they set out to be. Look out for naturally based alternatives – flax and straw are now both being used to make low emission fibreboards.

PVC Windows
Billed as the low- or no-maintenance alternative to timber window frames, PVC windows became extremely popular during the 1970s and 1980s. Made from PVC-u, an unplasticised polyvinyl chloride, PVC windows are manufactured using a number of POPs (see page 106) – a group of chemicals so problematic that they are now being phased out from manufacturing. Creating PVC-u is one of the most

energy-intensive and polluting processes in plastics. Greenpeace describes PVC as 'an environmental poison throughout its life cycle'.

The National Housing Federation has also found PVC-u windows to be more expensive than timber ones in terms of outlay and now questions the 'no maintenance' claims. And contrary to popular belief, PVC-u windows do not last 'for ever', but degrade over 20–25 years, just like timber windows. Due to degradation, only a tiny part of a PVC window can be recycled and its eventual disposal, either at landfill or via

incineration, means that dioxins will continue to be released into the atmosphere. Well-maintained timber windows (double glazed, if possible, for more insulation) are a better option.

Finally, if you decide that DIY just isn't for you and you'd rather get the professionals in, investigate hiring a green-minded builder first by contacting the Association of Environmentally Conscious Builders (www.aecb.net, tel: 0845 456 9773). If you're feeling particularly ambitious and looking to self-build a home, visit www.newbuilder.co.uk for advice.

Spotlight

Our love affair with MDF

Although it was first produced in the 1960s, Medium Density Fibreboard (MDF) was virtually unknown until it became a TV star. An unglamorous product, it is simply made of wood dust bonded by formaldehyde-based glue. But during the 1990s it was to TV makeover shows such as *Changing Rooms* what sticky-back plastic had been to *Blue Peter*. Easy to cut and versatile, it made the perfect, warp-free cupboard doors, coffee tables or shelving units. The DIYing public put theory into practice and it flew off the shelves of DIY superstores. Growth was described by the Timber Research and Development Association as 'nothing short of spectacular'.

It seemed the perfect substitute for wood. But it wasn't long before health fears were raised; not only is MDF made using formaldehyde, which is itself a suspected carcinogen, but concern arose over the fine dust particles given off by MDF during cutting.

There are also energy and environmental considerations attached to its disposable nature. The production of fibreboard is a highly energy-intensive process and MDF is difficult to recycle. It's also estimated that one million tonnes of MDF waste is

generated each year by the furniture industry, creating a further environmental headache.

For now, MDF continues to be sold, though sales have slowed. B&Q now sells MDF with warning stickers and has begun stocking alternative low-formaldehyde fibreboard, too. Use a mask and make sure there is proper ventilation when cutting or sawing MDF.

Research conducted by the Health and Safety Executive produced no reason to ban MDF, though a hazard assessment did concede that there was 'some evidence for more frequent reporting of respiratory symptoms in workers receiving exposures rising from machining MDF, compared to other forms of wood'.

It remains to be seen whether the former DIY miracle material and successor to wood stays on the shelves or if it becomes as redundant a building material as asbestos.

Appliances

Our appliance reliance shows no sign of abating. In fact, sales of electrical appliances still have enormous potential for growth, particularly in developing countries. Sixty-five per cent of Chinese city dwellers now own a refrigerator and more than 90 per cent own a washing machine – both up from less than five per cent only two decades ago. In India, sales of frost-free fridges are currently projected to grow by 14 per cent annually.

Thankfully, contemporary appliances are substantially more energy-efficient than equivalent models manufactured at the end of the last century. The introduction of mandatory efficiency and rating labels has seen to that; by 2003, 43 countries in Europe and Asia had such labelling systems in place.

Yet the amount of energy used by household appliances continues to increase, largely negating the energy saved from their increased efficiency. Home appliances continue to be the world's fastest-growing consumers of energy, responsible for 30 per cent of energy consumption in industrial countries and 12 per cent of their greenhouse gas emissions.

Buying appliances

While people are generally familiar with the issue of sweatshops and child labour when it comes to clothes or carpets, they are less aware that components for washing machines and computers are often produced under similar sweatshop conditions. Some manufacturers may also use components or coatings containing brominated fire retardants (see page 106), which can have health implications for the worker and consumer alike. Equally, as a purchaser, you may unwittingly be buying appliances from multinationals who trade in arms, or have economic interests in countries governed by undemocratic regimes.

When buying white goods, first take note of the appliance's energy rating label

and then try to take the following points on board before buying:

- **How energy efficient is it?** Use the energy rating label. These are now mandatory in the EU, and energy ratings should even be displayed online, if you are buying online. For more information, visit www.energy-plus.org/english.
- **How much energy is likely to have been used in its manufacture and what was its impact on the environment?** Manufacturing a computer, for example, has been found to be more energy intensive than the manufacture of a car. Do you really need a new model, or can you extend the features of the one you have?
- **What is the potential lifespan of the machine?** Read consumer reports, such as *Which?*, to find out which brands are likely to last the longest and are the most reliable.
- **Where was it made, and what were the conditions of its manufacture?** Again, look at consumer reports, such as those carried out by Ethical Consumer (see page 9), which point out any manufacturers currently the subject of boycotts. Alternatively, do your own research by looking at company reports and finding out about a manufacturer's other business interests.

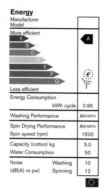

There is no doubt that appliances have brought us convenience and, in many cases, some degree of liberation: dishwashers on average save four hours of washing-up time per week. However, appliances need to be bought with longevity in mind. To keep energy-efficiency levels high and to prolong their lives, fridges need to be cleaned and defrosted, filters and vents to be kept clear in dishwashers, worn seals to be replaced in washing machines and dryers.

Do not leave the door open unnecessarily – ie avoid swinging on the fridge door trying to decide what to eat. The cold air will escape and the fridge will have to work harder to keep things cool

Try to keep it more than 5cm from the wall and leave space on either side to keep vents free and air flowing

Buy a fridge thermometer and keep the temperature at around 3°C

Keep it three-quarters full (at which maximum energy-efficiency is achieved)

Wait until cooked food has cooled before putting it into the fridge. Cooling warm food will require more energy from your fridge

Washing machines

Studying a washing machine's energy efficiency label is perhaps the most important thing you can do before buying. The European Energy+ Label, now mandatory for most large appliances, has featured on washing machines since 1996. 'A' is the top efficiency rating and 'G' the lowest. Also rated are washing performance, spin-drying performance, energy consumption per cycle (given in kWh) and water consumption in litres. Water consumption is a particularly important factor to be considered. Appliances tend to average at 53.5 litres each use – a typical bath requires 100 litres of water. Machines rated 'AA' are both energy-efficient and demonstrate excellent performance – proving that energy efficiency need not mean a drop in standards.

To minimise energy and water consumption, choose front-loading machines and use the lowest possible temperature settings for all but the most heavily soiled clothes. Pre-soak the washing by hand before putting it into the machine and resist the temptation to use harsh 'grime-busting' washing powder or specialist stain-shifting solutions (see page 110).

Refrigerators

Worth around £630 million a year, the refrigeration market has increasingly introduced 'status-related products', such as huge American fridges complete with drinks dispensers and icemakers. While expensive, their value lies in their design and they typically score 'F' and 'G' energy ratings, using almost double the amount of electricity consumed by a traditional fridge-freezer. Buy a fridge with a high energy-efficiency rating and position it well away from heat sources such as cookers, ovens and dishwashers – a fridge next to a heat source takes up to 15 per cent more energy to run. Fridges need to be well ventilated, so make sure there are a few centimetres at the rear and sides to allow the condenser coils to breathe. Don't over-chill a fridge or freezer as it uses an inefficient amount of energy.

Freezers

Unlike fridges – which should not be filled full of perishable goods, as it prevents air from circulating and makes them inefficient at cooling – freezers work best when they are tightly packed and don't have to work harder to freeze airspace. Chest freezers are usually considered preferable – densely packed, they use less power (see page 94). Freezers should also be kept in a cool environment, such as the basement or garage, or in an unheated room. Although 'frost-free' freezers are increasingly popular because they do not have to be defrosted, they can use up to 45 per cent more energy. A 'manual defrost' freezer is the most energy-efficient choice.

Cookers

There is a growing trend for large, new-style ranges that use a lot of power and are usually poorly insulated. Gas cookers and stoves use half the energy of electric ones but for those who prefer an electric cooker, ceramic hobs are more efficient than rings. Convection fan-assisted ovens use less energy than conventional ones. However, the most efficient cooker – if it is a non-electric model that also helps to heat the home and water – is an Aga or Rayburn, which, made of cast iron, are superbly insulated and combine to cook food as well as provide background heating.

Microwaves

Microwaves entered the domestic arena in the 1980s. Although the jury is still out on their longterm health effects, and recommended safety levels vary between countries, they are a feature of most homes. Microwave technology, which involves cooking 'from the inside out', uses less energy to cook food, in a fraction of the time of conventional cookers. However, the microwave culture also increases reliance on readymeals, a source of yet more packaging and described by the Consumer Association as 'a recipe for disaster' due to their high fat and salt content. Older microwaves are also thought more likely to leak radiation so in terms of personal health safety, it's best to update with a new, energy-rated model.

TVs/digital boxes/DVD players/VCRs

When the average Briton clocks up 3.5 hours of TV viewing per day and 98 per cent of households possess an average of 1.7 TV sets, it's not surprising that the UK spends £12 billion per year powering its TVs, VCRs, DVD players and set-top boxes. Unfortunately, to power them generates around seven million tonnes of CO_2 each year. The predicted change from analogue to digital (by 2010, insists the government) will render many older TVs that can't be retuned obsolete, and force other owners to buy yet another appliance in the form of a digital set-top box. Over the next decade, Britons will acquire more than 70 million set-top boxes, 63 million televisions and 14 million VCRs and DVD players.

To reduce energy consumption, switch the television off completely when you're not watching it. VCRs should also be turned off completely when not in use – about 85 per cent of the electricity used by your VCR is consumed while it is on 'standby'. When buying a new TV, DVD player or VCR, study the energy rating symbols (developed in 2004) and consider a flat-screen TV, which uses 14 per cent less energy than other models.

The home computer

Nearly 50 per cent of us now have access to a home computer. By 2002 the number of computers in existence globally had topped one billion and sales continue to rise at around 130 million every year. It is estimated that by 2005, in the US alone, 63 million computers will be 'retired', many of which will end up in landfill as consumers get used to a 2–3-year upgrade cycle.

This is particularly worrying when you consider that computer manufacturing is even more energy-intensive than car manufacturing. According to scientists at the University of Tokyo, a new computer uses at least 10 times its weight in fossil fuels and chemicals during manufacture. Much of the energy associated with making computers is consumed by the creation of high-tech components such as semiconductors, which cannot be recycled.

The price of computers and their associated hardware, such as printers and scanners, has fallen by 81 per cent since 1997. This is in part due to the advent of more powerful chips, but it is also due to the outsourcing of the manufacture of components to the developing nations. These countries typically have lower labour costs and poor standards of workers' rights, and the use of toxic chemicals puts the health of many of these workers at risk.

Ideally, the life of a computer should be extended by as much time as possible. Upgrade an existing machine rather than buy a new one. The second-hand market for computers was worth $2 billion in 2001 and continues to rise – many computer retailers now sell second-hand, reconditioned machines with warranties. Re-using a computer can

save up to 20 per cent more energy than recycling so if you don't want your old PC and accessories, donate them to a local organisation or charity.

In reality, computers should not be in the home at all; as a PC warms up it gives off potentially harmful, volatile organic compounds that later cool and find their way into household dust. Brominated flame retardants (see page 106) are also found in some computer monitors. Make sure replacement monitors use phosphorus-based alternatives.

Dilemma

Dishwasher versus washing-up

As only 27 per cent of British homes have a dishwasher, it's safe to assume that the remainder get by with the old-fashioned method of washing up by hand, unless we're all eating from paper plates that is. Is it the case then that dishwashers are just a non-essential, energy-hungry appliance?

According to recent research in both Europe and the US, dishwashers cannot be vilified quite so easily. They use substantially less water and equal or smaller amounts of energy than washing up by hand. One 2003 study by the University of Bonn monitored the washing-up habits and techniques of 75 people from seven countries. Although the British, along with the Germans, were found to use less water than other European washer-uppers, they still averaged 63 litres per set of dishes – the equivalent of more than two showers. This compares with the 20 litres required by an average dishwasher (high-grade, energy-efficient machines can lower this to just 15 litres), a figure that also allows for pre-soaking and rinsing. As it's common to wash up under running water – many people do this to rinse off suds – water use for a sink of dishes can, for a particularly high pile of washing-up, reach 150 litres. The dishwasher also proved to use less energy to heat the water than a typical gas

boiler. It is possible for washer-uppers to redress the balance slightly with good technique. Use a natural detergent, without potential toxins or pollutants, so that water can subsequently be used in the garden, avoid washing up using running water and remember that the water does not have to be very hot. Rinse dishes in a bowl of water on the side of the sink, not under a running tap.

There are a few caveats to using a dishwasher – some delicate items will always have to be washed by hand and it's important to remember that manufacturing a dishwasher is highly energy-consuming in the first place. The manufacturing process can also involve the use of toxic material, particularly for insulation materials or the metal casing around the machine. The machine must also be loaded properly, to full capacity, to be energy-efficient. Equally, it's important to buy the right size for your needs. A tabletop machine might be more energy-efficient for a single-person household, for example.

Toxic chemicals

What is a 'toxic' chemical?

From within the womb, to the day we die, we are exposed to toxic chemicals. Through the food we eat, the air we breathe, the water we drink, the toiletries we use, we can inhale, consume and absorb many different toxic chemicals every day.

But what is a 'toxic' chemical? Everything around us – and including us – is made up of chemicals of some description. But some chemicals contain a level of toxicity that can harm life-forms in varying degrees. Toxic chemicals are naturally produced all the time, as part of a plant's or animal's defences – snake poison, or deadly nightshade, for example – but what is of great concern is the amount of synthetic, that's to say 'man-made', toxic chemicals we are now exposed to.

Our heavily industrialised world now has at its disposal around 100,000 new and existing chemicals with which to make a varied range of goods and applications, such as medicines, food additives, agricultural pesticides, paints and shampoos. Hundreds more are invented, tested and registered every year.

A number of these synthetic chemicals are known to be toxic to the wider environment and to humans, especially if mishandled or carelessly discarded. The EU has identified 140 chemicals of 'high concern', but campaign groups such as Friends of the Earth, Greenpeace and WWF believe the environmental threat from synthetic toxic chemicals to be acute and have called for much tighter restrictions and even bans of certain synthetic chemicals.

There are two classes of chemicals that cause particular concern:

Persistent Organic Pollutants (POPs)

POPs are carbon-based chemical compounds that are primarily the products and by-products of heavy industry and chemical (particularly petrochemical) manufacturing. We are exposed to POPs in numerous ways – through many plastics, pesticides and paints, for example. But what makes them so potentially harmful is that they display two key negative characteristics: they are 'bio-accumulative' (ie, they can accumulate in body fat and can be passed on to the foetus and into the food chain) and 'persistent' (ie, they're very hard to break down, so can remain in the environment for decades). It has also been proved that POPs can 'downstream' (ie, travel huge distances through the air and water): traces of POPs have been found in polar bears in the Arctic and in the breastmilk of Inuit mothers.

In fact, the United Nations Environment Programme says that everyone in the world now has traces of POPs in their bodies – some even contain traces from POPs that were banned in the 1970s. The UNEP is particularly concerned by this, as POPs can cause cancer as well as damage the nervous, reproductive and immune systems of people and animals.

Endocrine-disrupting chemicals (EDCs)

Any chemical that can interfere with the endocrine system – the relatively little-understood systems of gland-secreted hormones that orchestrate much of the body's functions and growth – is classified as an EDC. Many POPs fall into this harmful class of chemicals.

EDCs can, even in minute concentrations, cause adverse effects, such as mutations, so can have a pivotal role in growth, development and reproduction. For this reason, babies and children are often cited as being most at risk. And, like POPs, EDCs can be found in many forms.

The following chemical groups are suspected EDCs:

Dioxins Chlorine-based toxins – which unwittingly formed the deadliest component of the notorious Agent Orange herbicide used in the Vietnam war – are typically emitted during the burning of commercial and domestic waste, cigarettes and even forest fires.

PCBs Now largely banned, but nonetheless persistent, polychlorinated biphenyls were used as coolants and lubricants in transformers, capacitors, and other electrical equipment.

Organophosphates A large group of chemicals – the most toxic of which are now banned – widely used as insecticides in agriculture and in homes.

Phthalates A group of esters that can be used to soften plastics – toys and vinyl flooring, for example – and are also used for their oily and solvent properties in, among other things, perfumes, hairsprays, and wood finishers.

Parabens Another group of esters, specifically of para-hydroxybenzoic acid, widely used for their preservative qualities in cosmetics and some foods.

VOCs Found in most homes in, among other things, paints, varnishes and plastics, some 'volatile organic compounds' can 'off-gas' (emit vapours after being applied).

How are we being protected?
While it is true that there is a swath of research, regulatory testing and legislation that aims to minimise our risk from these toxic chemicals, many of the most controversial ones are still being used in products all around us.

Some chemicals currently in use passed safety tests many years ago when some of the concerns now raised were not known about or suspected. But to re-test a chemical is very expensive and can take years. Companies reliant on such chemicals will clearly be reluctant to have to wait (and pay) for such testing to be completed. After all, the production of chemicals is big business – the Organisation for Economic Co-operation and Development (OECD) estimates that it accounts for seven per cent of global income – and any further restrictive regulation or testing will always face resistance.

But there have been some significant safety advances in recent years. In 2003, the European Commission adopted a new (much resisted, as well as much criticised) system known as REACH (Registration, Evaluation and Authorisation of Chemicals), to regulate the manufacture, import and use of substances. In an attempt to replace the current culture of 'no reasonable grounds for concern' with 'scientific certainty' when it comes to establishing the toxicity of a chemical, up to 30,000 chemicals will have to be registered on a new database and about 6,000 will have to be completely re-tested over the next decade (which is likely to mean a rise in animal testing, see page 180). The system aims to replace existing laws that have allowed as many as 99 per cent of chemical-based products to be sold without having passed through any environmental and health testing review processes.

Another significant advance came in 2004, when 50 countries (but not the US) ratified a UN pact called the '2001 Stockholm convention on POPs'. This bans the use of a number of pesticides, dioxins and PCBs, labelled by campaigners as the 'dirty dozen'. However, a number of controversial POPs were omitted, including brominated flame retardants (used in household items such as sofas, clothing and television sets) and lindane (an organochlorine pesticide banned in Europe but traces of which are still found in, for example, chocolate produced outside Europe).

Some retailers and manufacturers are now making their own efforts to protect consumers. In 2004, for example, the Co-op supermarket chain voluntarily removed chemicals such as phthalates and artificial musks (which give a perfume its 'staying power' but have been cited by groups such as Friends of the Earth as being persistent and bioaccumulative) from a range of its household products following customer consultation.

But despite these advances, there are still problems for consumers wishing to avoid certain chemicals. Current labelling laws rarely provide enough reassurance through detailed information. The catch-all term 'parfum', for example, is often used to describe a complex mixture of up to 100 synthetic chemicals used as a scenting agent within many cosmetic, toiletry and other household products and can be used as a blanket term for a range of chemicals including phthalates and artificial musks.

What is the 'cocktail effect'?
Whereas the toxicity of an individual chemical can be tested and monitored, it is much harder to predict – and

legislate against – the possible toxic effect two or more chemicals reacting together may have. This problem is commonly referred to as the 'cocktail effect' and is one of the least researched areas in product testing. The difficulty of understanding the full impact of the cocktail effect is best explained by Dr Vyvyan Howard, a foetal toxico-pathologist at Liverpool University. 'To test just the commonest 1,000 toxic chemicals in combinations of three would require at least 166 million different experiments,' he told the *Guardian* in 2004. 'We don't have the tools to analyse how mixtures of these chemicals work, and we probably never will.'

A high-profile reference to the cocktail effect in action is made by veterans of the 1991 Gulf war. An anti-nerve-gas drug and two different insecticides were used at the time of the conflict on a number of Allied soldiers and they believe the combined effect of these chemicals caused the debilitating condition known as 'Gulf war syndrome'. But, as Dr Howard suggests, the simple truth is that we will probably never know the full synergistic consequences of how all chemicals – toxic or otherwise – react with one another once allowed out of the laboratory and into the environment. As Professor Sir Tom Blundell, the chairman of the Royal Commission on Environmental Pollution, said upon the publication in 2003 of the RCEP's two-year study *Chemicals in Products: Safeguarding the Environment and Human Health*: 'Given our understanding of the way chemicals interact with the environment, you could say we are running a gigantic experiment with humans and all other living things as the subject. We [the RCEP] think that's unacceptable.'

What can I do to reduce my exposure?

General tips
● Seek natural alternatives to products laden with synthetic chemicals – food, paints, cosmetics, cleaners, toys, materials – whenever possible. Especially pertinent for children.

● Get into the habit of reading all product labels. Research the chemical names that keep reappearing and learn which ones to avoid. See Further Reading below, which suggests good websites for looking up current toxicity research data, as well as more general information about the threat of toxic chemicals.

● Urge companies to stop stocking products that use toxic chemicals. Use Friends of the Earth's easy-to-use 'email or fax a retailer' page on its website (www.foe.co.uk/campaigns/safer_chemicals/press_for_change/league_table).

Health and body care
● Clear out your bathroom cabinet and dump everything but the essentials.

● Avoid baby wipes, which can contain parabens and propylene glycol – a common ingredient in anti-freeze. A damp flannel will do the job just as well.

● Cut down on bubble baths, which can contain skin-irritating detergents.

● Splash your face with witch hazel or cold water instead of using over-the-counter toners.

● If you want to be sure a cosmetic product is organic, look for a Soil Association certification. Lax labelling laws ensure that words such as 'organic', 'natural' and 'hypoallergenic' generally mean little in the beauty industry (see page 188).

● Switch to organic tampons and sanitary towels. They're non-chlorine bleached, 100 per cent pure cotton and GM-free.

● Instead of heavy-duty hair dyes, use henna which is natural and less invasive.

● If you can't give up nail varnish, protect your cuticles with oil. Although the part of the nail you see is dead, it is still porous and can absorb the chemicals used in varnish and remover.

● A thick coating of aloe vera gel is a good alternative to shaving foams and gels.

● Greenpeace (greenpeace.org.uk) and the Women's Environmental Network (wen.org.uk) both provide useful lists of products to avoid, as well as listing companies with good track records.

Food

● Eat locally grown, organic produce. It is the single best way to reduce exposure to pesticides.

● Write to your MP and MEP demanding clearer and stricter UK and EU food labelling laws, especially with regard to additives. For more about what is tolerated under current labelling laws, visit www.foodstandards. gov.uk/foodlabelling.

● Increase the proportion of seasonal produce you eat. It will reduce your exposure to anti-fungal and anti-bacterial chemicals commonly used to extend shelf-life.

● When organic produce isn't available, remember that some items have lower levels of pesticide residues than others. Good candidates include aubergines, peppers, cabbages, frozen peas, garlic, leeks, marrow, radishes, swedes, sweetcorn and turnips. Conversely, high levels of pesticide residues have been found in spinach, apples, celery and salad leaves.

● Wash and peel all fresh fruit and veg to reduce exposure to pesticides – even if it claims to be 'ready-washed'. Also, discard outer leaves of leafy veg.

● Trim fat from meat and skin from poultry and fish – this is where pesticide residues can collect.

● Avoid clingfilm when storing foods. It contains plasticisers that can leach into food. The FSA says to avoid wrapping high-fat foods such as cheeses in clingfilm, and not to use it in contact with food in a microwave.

Around the home

● Be aware of the chemicals in the paints, solvents and cleaning products you buy. If possible, buy water-based, low-VOC paints and avoid using synthetic chemicals when there is a feasible natural alternative.

● Keep your house as dust-free as possible. Airborne toxins can build up in house dust then settle on upholstery, bed linen, carpets and curtains.

● Don't use air fresheners, open your windows instead. Use cedar blocks, dried flowers or fill a small mug with odour-absorbing bicarbonate of soda.

● Store all toxic chemicals outside or out of contact with you and your food. Petrol, paints, solvents and adhesives should be kept outdoors; kitchen cleaning products should not be kept in a cabinet next to your vegetables.

● Don't smoke indoors. The particles of smoke will stay lodged on furniture and soft furnishings inside your house and deteriorate the air quality.

● Take off your shoes at home, or at least buy a door mat, so that you don't tread any toxic chemicals from outside all over the house.

Further reading
www.guardian.co.uk/chemicalworld
www.greenpeace.org.uk/Products/Toxics
www.worldwildlife.org/toxics
www.foe.co.uk/campaigns/safer_chemicals
www.pan-uk.org
www.defra.gov.uk/environment/chemicals
www.rcep.org.uk/chemicals.htm
www.who.int/ipcs
www.oecd.org/ehs
www.chem.unep.ch
www.epa.gov/ebtpages/pollutants.html
www.scorecard.org
www.chemfinder.com
www.chemical-industry.org.uk
www.thebts.org
http://ecb.jrc.it/REACH
http://themes.eea.eu.int/Environmental_issues/
chemicals

Cleaning

If cleanliness is next to godliness, the UK can be pleased with itself. Worth a record £1.03 billion in 2002, the UK cleaning-product market continues to boom as we seek swift, low-effort solutions to the chores in our time-poor lives. Easy-to-use, convenient products such as antibacterial wipes and '3-in-1' solutions represent the biggest areas of growth.

But how do these products 'achieve quick, effective results'? In large part, by employing harsh, toxic chemicals.

The nation's favourite cleaning products don't just clean, they 'wage war', 'eradicate' and 'wipe out' those 'lurking' germs and bacteria. TV advertisements for these products leave us in no doubt that cleaning is not just a mundane domestic chore but an act of armed combat.

But what's the alternative? Obviously not to stop cleaning; better sanitation has played a major role in reducing incidence of infectious disease. But given the amount of potentially harmful chemicals within these products, it's preferable to seek out alternative means of keeping your home clean.

Good old-fashioned elbow grease and common-sense hygiene rules can largely cut down the need for products such as synthetic antibacterial solutions or potent air fresheners. Hygiene experts suggest:

● Frequent and thorough hand washing, using a simple soap under hot water for 30–40 seconds.

● Banning pets from the kitchen.

● Using separate hand and dish towels.

● Opening windows to keep air circulating.

When it comes to considering which cleaning products to use, instead of placing faith in solutions that 'kill' or 'exterminate' bacteria and germs, try using less aggressive cleaners more frequently. There are an increasing range of environmentally sensitive cleaning products on offer now (see page 134). But for a cheaper, more homespun approach, you'll find the most useful and versatile natural cleaning ingredients already in your kitchen…

Air fresheners

They may claim to make your home smell like a pine forest, but air fresheners contain nerve-deadening agents and oils that coat the nasal passages. In addition, they cover up odours with a potent synthetic scent.

In 2004, researchers at the University of Bristol linked the daily use of air fresheners (and other aerosols, such as polish, deodorant and hairspray) with diarrhoea and earache in infants and headaches and depression in mothers. Pregnant women and babies up to six months might be particularly susceptible, said the researchers, because they spend around 80 per cent of their time at home.

Plug-in air fresheners are particularly worrying. They provide unremitting exposure to a cocktail of harsh chemicals that can typically include formaldehyde and phenol, both substances that have been linked to a range of symptoms including shortness of breath and circulatory collapse.

Alternative: Place a cup of bicarbonate of soda, an inexpensive natural odour absorber, in the offending room. The king of natural cleaning, bicarbonate of soda (baking soda) can help with almost every cleaning chore. It can, however, be hard to source in large quantities as it's usually sold in tiny packets for use in baking. Ask a chemist to order in a larger pack. Lemon slices in a pan of boiling water are also an effective air freshener.

Multi-purpose cleaners

Typically, they contain a combination of detergents and grease-cutting agents, backed up by solvents and disinfectants. Ammonia, ethylene, sodium hypochlorite, trisodium phosphate and ethylene glycol monobutyl ether acetate also make regular appearances on labels. But studies have shown that repeated exposure to substances such as ethylene glycol monobutyl ether acetate can affect the central nervous system.

Alternative: Mix 125ml of pure vegetable-based soap (ideally in flake form) with four litres of hot water. Add 60ml of lemon juice to add a scent and to help break down grease. After cleaning, rinse surfaces with fresh water. For a stronger solution, double the amounts of soap and lemon juice. If you have trouble finding pure soap, try ordering it via the Soap Kitchen (www.thesoapkitchen.co.uk, tel: 01805 622944).

Anti-bacterial cleaners

Marketed as the ultimate weapon in the war on germs, antibacterial chemicals, such as Triclosan (see page 184), can be found in everything from cleaners to plastic kitchenware. Due to clever product marketing, 60 per cent of people surveyed by the Consumers' Association found the presence of antibacterial agents in household products 'reassuring'. However, antibacterials are believed to target the same enzymes as antibiotics and their overuse raises the same kinds of concern that some doctors have about the overuse of antibiotics leading to super-resistant bacteria. As a precautionary measure, it makes sense to restrict their use domestically.

Alternative: Tea tree oil is a natural antiseptic and disinfectant. Mix it with two cups of water then, using a spray bottle,, set it to work on mould and mildew, or kitchen surfaces. Leave for 30 minutes then rinse off with warm, soapy water. Tea-tree oil can also be used to deodorise musty fabrics and help disinfect nappy buckets.

Window cleaners

Interestingly, research shows that many householders believe 'blue' window cleaners to be more effective than 'clear' ones. In reality there is no difference. Both are made primarily of water, but ammonia is usually added to dissolve grease. Ammonia is corrosive, even in low concentrations, and can cause burns and irritation.

Alternative: Wash with pure soap and water, then rinse with a solution of one part white-wine vinegar to four parts water. Use crumpled newspaper to dry-shine the glass afterwards.

Drain and oven cleaners

There are few more arduous domestic chores than cleaning the oven or a drain. Consequently, we're accustomed to tackling them with the most aggressive chemicals we can find. Typically these cleaners contain sodium hydroxide (also known as 'lye') and sulphuric acid. Both are hazardous, highly corrosive substances.

Lye reacts dramatically with water, and has been shown to inhibit reflexes. Poured into the water system, these chemicals can cause huge damage to sensitive ecosystems. Drain cleaners also kill off beneficial bacteria in septic tanks, preventing them from working properly.

Alternative: For oven spills, immediately pour on salt and leave for an hour. Then scrub on neat baking soda, or combine it with the stronger version of the pure soap multi-purpose cleaner. For blocked sinkholes or drains, pour half a cup of baking soda down followed by half a cup of white-wine vinegar. It will cause a chemical reaction so remember to wear gloves and to ventilate the room.

Toilet cleaners

Received wisdom, again largely from TV advertisements, would suggest that the toilet bowl is one of the most hazardous places on earth. Heavy doses of aggressive cleaners and bleach are routinely tipped down the loo. These include sodium hypochlorite, which irritates and corrodes mucous membranes, and hydrochloric acid, a highly corrosive skin irritant. These chemicals are unnecessarily harsh for the task of cleaning toilets and are one of the principal causes of accidental childhood poisoning. In fact, the constant flush of clean water means that most toilets need little more than the attention of multi-purpose cleaners.

In-cistern and in-bowl fresheners give extra cause for concern. With every flush, they produce an extra dose of easily inhaled and potentially toxic chemicals.

Alternative: First use the stronger version of the all-purpose cleaner, mixed with some tea-tree oil. Then wipe the bowl with vinegar, or leave half a cup of vinegar in the bowl overnight.

Washing-up detergents

Surfactants, a form of detergent, feature in nearly all conventional washing-up products. Surfactants lower the surface tension of water, essentially making it 'wetter' and 'runnier'. Most solutions also include petroleum distillates.

Dry and irritable skin is a common side-effect of contact with detergents. Although dishwashers remove this initial contact, dishwasher tablets typically contain chlorine in a highly concentrated form. In the US, these tablets are the principal cause of accidental childhood poisonings.

Alternative: Use pure soap with hot water to wash dishes. To give glasses an extra shine, add white-wine vinegar to the rinse water. Less toxic dishwasher tablets and rinse aids are available from companies such as Ecover.

Floor cleaners

Most floor cleaners contain petroleum distillates and solvents. The majority also use pine oils that can, in extreme cases, cause convulsions and have been shown to induce comas if ingested. The potential impact of conventional floor cleaners on children of crawling age gives particular cause for concern.

Alternative: Use the multi-purpose cleaner. If the floors are wooden and they need to be polished, mix three parts olive oil and one part white-wine vinegar and rub on with a soft cloth. The same mixture can be used as an alternative furniture polish, but, as with any polish, test a small area first.

Laundry detergents

We demand a lot from our washing powder. 'Whiter than white', 'spring fresh' and 'soft enough for babies' are all claims used to sell us laundry powders and liquids. But highly corrosive substances such as sodium hypochlorite, calcium hypochlorite, linear alkylate sulphonate, and sodium tripolyphosphate are all common ingredients in washing powders and liquids. As well as 'optical brighteners' and bleaching agents, expect to find artificial musks in many laundry products. These give our laundry that 'super fresh' fragrance promised in the adverts, but many are suspected of being bioaccumulative.

Alternative: Companies such as Ecover make laundry detergents that use plant-based surfactants. Alternatively, try using Eco-balls (www.ecozone.co.uk) which, say the manufacturers, produce 'ionised oxygen' that activates the water molecules naturally, allowing them to penetrate deep into clothing fibres to lift dirt away. They are reusable for over 1,000 washes and cost about 3p per wash. For the ultimate natural replacement for optical whiteners and brighteners, mix a cup of lemon juice into half a bucket of water and soak items overnight before regular washing.

Other natural cleaning tips:

- Lemon juice is an excellent general cleaner. Use with salt to create a brass or copper polish, but be sure to rinse off well. The Good Housekeeping Institute also suggests using it to deodorise a microwave. Add a few slices to a bowl of water and microwave on high power.

- Olive oil can be lightly rubbed over stainless steel surfaces and utensils to get rid of fingerprints.

- White-wine vinegar works well as a descaler and can be used undiluted on shower heads, on taps, or left overnight in kettles (rinse the kettle thoroughly afterwards).

- Use baking soda dry to lift stains and odours from carpets.

- To polish sterling silver (not silver plate) items, mix in a pan one litre of water with one tablespoon of salt, one tablespoon of baking soda and a strip of aluminium foil. Bring the mixture to the boil then drop in the silver items, boil for three minutes then remove and polish with a soft cloth.

Dilemma

Should I employ a cleaner?

An Upstairs, Downstairs culture is still very much alive, according to recent statistics. Over two million people are now employed as domestic staff in the UK; the same number as in the 1930s. Across Europe, one in 10 households now uses domestic help.

Half of those surveyed by the Work Foundation claimed that they wouldn't be able to pursue their careers without domestic help. It seems that the 'lady who does' is increasingly a necessity rather than a luxury. And almost invariably your cleaner will be a 'lady'. Research by the National Office for Statistics confirms that cleaning is still a 'female-intensive industry', with one of the highest incidences of low pay. In fact, over a quarter of cleaners are paid below the minimum wage, and average pay currently stands at £6.50 an hour.

The industry is also notoriously informal. Three-fifths are recruited by word of mouth and the overwhelming majority are paid cash-in-hand. As this sector expands, this informality stores up problems for the future as women – already statistically poorer in retirement than men – continue to work without paying National Insurance contributions.

Many households communicate with their cleaner via a series of notes and instructions. There is often little personal contact, no holiday entitlement, no sickness or maternity pay and no pension rights. At the extreme end of the scale, Kalayaan, an advisory service for immigrant domestic workers, has collected testimonies from workers who have also suffered physical abuse.

It is difficult to justify the lack of formal rights that cleaners are given. However, many families genuinely need domestic help and at the moment the industry is largely unregulated. If you employ a cleaner, pay should be fair and ideally include holiday and sick pay. If you are using an agency, make sure that the cleaner is receiving an adequate proportion of the overall fee.

Finally, it might be your home but it's your cleaner's place of work. As such you should provide a safe environment. A Spanish study in 2003 found that female cleaners had twice the risk of women in other jobs of developing asthma and other breathing problems due to irritants in cleaning products. Health and safety standards should be adhered to and you should take into account the potentially harmful chemicals found in some cleaning brands and help to minimise a cleaner's exposure to these products.

Garden

For a 'nation of gardeners', we don't have too much to be proud of when considering the environmental legacy of our favourite pastime. While time spent in the garden is often the only time that many of us, particularly the urbanites, get to interact with nature in any meaningful way − nurturing plants, witnessing the changing seasons, getting close up to wildlife − our gardening habits, along with modern farming practices, have actually greatly helped to damage or destroy our native species and plant varieties.

To blame are modern gardening techniques and trends. Since the 1950s, the way we garden has changed dramatically, a change that largely parallels a shift in farming practices. Rather than 'working with nature', some gardeners see the forces and flows of nature as something to be killed and suppressed. At the first sight of a weed or a bug, out come the highly toxic pesticides and herbicides. Instead of replenishing the soil's nutrients with home-grown composts, we like to turn to 'miracle' feeds. We've lost patience with nature's cycles and want instant results. Whereas previous generations largely grew plants from seed and cuttings, we now pop down to the local garden centre in the car and buy bedding flowers in full bloom. And because the garden centres now offer us non-native plants, we can get the look we're after largely regardless of the time of year. Just as with the food we eat, the concept of seasonality is slowly being lost to a monoculture that now means that most of the nation's gardens are stocked with the few dozen plant varieties that the big-name garden centres are offering.

It is important to get a sense of how much of the UK's land is covered by gardens in order to show why it is so important that habits change. There are now about 16 million gardens in the UK (85 per cent of us have access to a garden) ranging from the humble rooftop or backyard with a few pots and window boxes, to the large country gardens spread over a couple of acres. In total, if you put all the gardens in the UK together they would cover roughly 1,214,000 hectares − an area five times the size of London. It is, therefore, crucial that we make every effort to change our habits in the garden − and it is through examining how our gardening habits have changed that it becomes clear where we have been going so wrong.

Perhaps the most significant shift is in the way that we use the garden. Before the second world war, domestic gardens were largely a functional place where we grew vegetables and fruit. Since then, the focus has moved more towards being a place to relax and socialise. Today, the mantra is that the garden is an 'extra room' or an 'extension of the living room'. An analysis by Focus Wickes of what people now have in their garden backs this up:

Lawns **86.7%**

Patio **66%**

Shed **54.5%**

Roses **51.7%**

Hosepipe **48.4%**

Garden furniture **34.4%**

Barbecue **26.2%**

Ponds **21.9%**

Tomatoes **19.5%**

Water feature **13.4%**

Compost heap **9.9%**

The desire to entertain outside has been one of the biggest drivers of garden centre sales over the past decade. A fifth of us now own garden lighting, one in 10 now has an area 'decked' (a phenomenon that was unheard of 10 years ago and has been created in large part by the plethora of 'lifestyle makeover' TV shows), and one in 10 has added a patio over the last two years. Other boom areas include garden furniture and garden heaters. In fact, garden furniture is now the most common purchase at garden centres, with the trend shifting from plastic and cast-iron furniture to hardwood items. In 2004, a national survey of gardeners asked respondents what they use their gardens for – the most popular answers were 'relaxing' and 'entertaining'. Many people added that they wanted 'minimal maintenance' and not to have to do anything 'too time-consuming'.

Their answers help to explain the rapid decline in the number of people growing their own vegetables and fruit. In 1983, four in ten gardeners grew vegetables. By 1988, this figure had fallen to just three in 10. But by 2002, the number stood at one in every seven, or 15 per cent. Likewise, one in three grew their own fruit in 1982 compared to just one in five by 2002.

The age of gardeners seems to be significant, too. Compost heaps, for example, are significantly more popular with those over the age of 55, where they are maintained by more than one in 10. This compares to just one in 100 gardeners aged 16–34. Greenhouse ownership follows a similar trend – they appear in three in 10 gardens owned by the over-55 age group, whereas only one in 10 gardeners aged 16–34 has one. Younger gardeners also favour growing herbs over vegetables, citing the fact that there is 'little reward' with the latter. Tomatoes now seem to be the sole plant that many people attempt to grow for food.

This attitude doesn't bode well for the future of the

allotment – a public amenity that has been in steady decline for decades. In the 19th and early 20th centuries, the allotment system supplied much of the fresh vegetables eaten by the poor. At the time of the first world war, there were around 1,500,000 allotments in the UK. By the late 1960s the number had fallen to 600,000, sparking the Thorpe inquiry, which investigated the decline and placed the blame on the reduction in available land, increasing prosperity and the growth of leisure activities. By 1997 the number of plots had plummeted to around 265,000, with over 44,000 plots vacant. It seems that within a generation, the joy of growing our own food could almost be lost if present trends continue.

But the shift in gardening habits hasn't just led to a decline in home-grown produce; more importantly, it has also put a huge strain on the environment, both locally and internationally. There are now four key areas of concern that are raised by modern gardening techniques – all of which are leading to the loss of native biodiversity:

● **The use of toxic chemicals**

● **The use of unsustainable materials**

● **The rise of a monoculture of plant varieties**

● **Water wastage**

The shelves of the average garden shed are probably the most toxic places in any home. Weedkiller, slug pellets, aphid deterrent, lawn feed, wood treatments – all of them can cause considerable damage to the environment. Friends of the Earth, for example, have called for an urgent review of two common weedkillers – 2,4-D and MCPA – after they were linked to human birth defects. Most slug pellets contain metaldehyde and methiocarb, which are dangerous to mammals, including humans.

While we may think that many of the products on offer 'help' the garden grow, many are only superficially assisting one plant while causing much harm elsewhere. A teaspoon of soil may contain more bacteria and fungi than there are people on the planet and these micro-organisms are vital for breaking down natural waste, such as dead leaves, into nutrients for the soil. But many garden products are killing these unseen micro-organisms, upsetting what should be the natural equilibrium of the garden.

The various items we now dress our gardens with – the furniture, the decking, the patios, the heaters – can also be extremely detrimental to the environment, particularly in the countries where the items were originally sourced and produced. Friends of the Earth believes that 66 per cent of tropical woods used in garden furniture are the product of illegal logging – a practice that destroys wildlife habitats and can leave indigenous populations homeless. In Indonesia, for example, illegal logging is threatening the Dayak tribe of central Borneo as well as the area's orang-utan population. More than two million hectares of the country's rainforest is now being logged every year and our appetite for hardwood garden furniture, unless we make sure the wood has been carefully sourced from sustainable forests, plays no small part. Equally worrying is that over 50 per cent of Indonesian-sourced barbecue charcoal comes from endangered mangrove swamps.

Patio heaters are also damaging. They are an extremely inefficient way to produce and consume heat. A standard 13kg canister of natural gas will warm an area outside of up to 25m^2 for 12 hours, whereas the same canister used in a gas fire could heat the same area indoors for 10 times longer. Patio heaters also emit, for every unit of heat, far more noxious fumes than most cars.

Elsewhere in the garden, the litany of environmental damage continues. Our appetite for limestone paving and limestone rockeries, for example, is in large part to blame for the fact that 97 per cent of the UK's 2,900 hectares of 'limestone pavement' has been damaged, particularly in Eaves Wood and Over Kellet in Lancashire. And despite the warnings, sales of peat-based compost and moss continue to rise. According to the RSPB, 65 per cent of growing media used by 'home' gardeners is peat-based. Every year, we buy 2.7million cubic metres of the stuff. However, less than six per cent of the UK's original lowland raised peat bog habitat now remains. In Northern Ireland more than 50 per cent of peat bogs have been destroyed. And in the Republic of Ireland, 2,000 hectares – an area 10 times the size of Monaco – of peat bog a year are destroyed to supply peat for UK horticulture.

Ironically, all this peat is largely helping non-native plants to grow. Garden centres are offering us more and more celebrity-endorsed, 'Plant of the Year' varieties in garden centres where the emphasis is on fashionable colours and low maintenance. But this often means that the plants are varieties that have been sourced abroad and vigorously modified and cultivated to resist disease and pests. In turn, this is leading much of our native wildlife to be starved of its natural habitat, a worrying trend when you consider that there are now 382 species listed as being of concern on the government's UK Biodiversity Action Plan.

Lastly, all life needs water but our gardens have a particularly burning thirst. We will typically use at least 10 litres of water a day on our garden, but on hot summer days this can increase to 50 per cent of our home's water use – on average, 150 litres a day. Much of our water use in the garden is wasteful and even needless, especially the use of mains-fed sprinklers and hosepipes. There are many ways to 'green' up your garden – as shown overleaf – and pouring dozens of litres of tap water on it each day isn't one of them.

Spotlight

Keep off the grass

'The sight is in no way so pleasantly refreshed as by fine and close grass kept short'
Albertus Magnus (1260)

Our nation's love affair with lawns is long and well-documented, although the ancient inhabitants of Greece, Rome and Persia could all lay claim to being the first to keep large patches of well-manicured grass. Even though the word 'lawn' comes from the French for an open space among woods, it has now become a classic icon of the British (well, English) summer – Wimbledon, garden parties at the palace, picnics on the grass, cricket, croquet... Annual expenditure in the UK on lawn-related equipment – mowers, grass seeds, fertiliser, sprinklers, etc – is now nearly £100 million. Of this, 24 per cent is spent over June and July.

But while a well-kept lawn may be easy on the eye, it is far from easy on the environment. From the moment the grass seed is first cultivated to when it's cut, a lawn requires vast amounts of energy and water as well as acting as a major source of pollution.

The sheer scale of landmass covered by lawn is staggering. In the US, for instance, the combined area of lawn – domestic, corporate, and government gardens, as well as roadside verges – is estimated to be about the same size as the state of Louisiana – more than for any other single agricultural group, such as wheat or maize. These lawns are fed more than 45 million kilos of fertilisers annually, which will ultimately find their way into the rivers and aquifers. To water this amount of lawn requires around 30 billion litres of water a day – about three-fifths of what the people of the UK use in total in a day.

To keep a lawn well-manicured it must also be regularly mown. But one lawnmower produces as much pollution in an hour as 40 cars. The grass-seed business, a multi-billion-dollar global industry, is unsurprisingly dominated by just a handful of corporate giants, mostly based in the Netherlands or Scandinavia: Barenbrug, DLF, Advanta and Cebeco. Ready-grown turf is so popular, for example, that Rolawn, Europe's largest turf-grower, has a 3,000-acre site in the Vale of York. This must rank as one of the largest lawns in the world: imagine having to mow that.

So rather than obsessing about achieving the 'perfect' lawn, let nature back into your garden by allowing your lawn to grow longer, sowing a few patches with wildflower seeds and watering and feeding it with less vigour. The grass will always be 'greener' this way.

The good garden

Whether you have only enough room for a few pots and containers or are lucky enough to own a few acres, there are dozens of things to do to 'green up' your garden. You will soon see how each action assists another, ultimately playing to nature's cycles at their best…

Encourage wildlife
- Install any or all of the following: batboxes, bumble-bee nests, nesting boxes for birds…
- Put out food (worms, nuts and feed) and fresh water for birds.
- Plant a patch of native wildflowers, such as Marsh Marigold, Purple Loosestrife and Creeping Jenny, to encourage insects, butterflies, dragonflies and bees.
- Design your garden so that it is inviting to frogs, hedgehogs, and even badgers. For advice, contact the Royal Society of Wildlife Trusts (www.wildlifetrusts.org, tel: 0870 0367711).

Pest control
- Stop using harsh chemicals to kill uninvited garden guests.
- There are many natural alternatives to slug pellets, ranging from beer traps and coffee grounds to egg shells and decoy plants such as comfrey.
- Ward off aphids with a fine spray of water left over from the washing up (as long as you've used an eco-friendly washing-up liquid).

- Grow 'companion' plants together that naturally deter each other's pests, for example carrots and onions, mint and beans, and garlic and roses.
- Let natural predators do the work. Frogs and toads love slugs, small birds savour aphids, bats devour mosquitoes…

Compost

- Build or buy a simple composting heap.
- Save all your kitchen waste (but not meat, fish or dairy waste) for composting.
- Add grass cuttings, comfrey, newspaper, cardboard, farmyard manure, seaweed – in fact, anything that will rot down.
- Inspect and turn your compost heap every few weeks to keep it aerated and to monitor moisture levels.
- Alternatively, if your garden isn't big enough to keep a compost heap, start a wormery instead. For more information, contact Wiggly Wigglers (www.wigglywigglers.co.uk, tel: 0800 216990).

Recycling
- Don't throw away any household item without considering whether it could be reused in the garden.
- Plastic bottles cut in half make perfect individual cloches for vulnerable seedlings.
- Plastic food trays are ideal for growing seedlings.
- Scraps of wood, glass, plastic

sheeting, carpet and string can all be reused when laying out new vegetable patches, building a compost heap or protecting seedlings.

Lawns

4cm

- Rather than turning on the sprinkler at the first sight of a brown patch, allow the grass to grow to at least 4cm in the summer months to help lessen the sun's impact.
- Leave cuttings on the lawn to help replenish the soil.
- If your lawn isn't too large, use a hand mower instead of a petrol mower.
- Use calcified seaweed to feed your lawn.
- Cut out dandelions and dock leaves with a knife rather than spraying them with weed killer.
- Use native grass seeds. They will produce lawns better suited to British conditions, and require less watering.
- Make a feature of large patches that grow 'wild'. It will encourage wildlife and mean less maintenance.

Weeds
- Firstly, are they all really so bad? And what is a 'weed' anyway? Could it just be a wild plant? If so, nurture and encourage it. Many wild-plant habitats have been destroyed over the past 50 years: 98 per cent of wildflower meadows, 75 per cent of open heaths, 96 per cent of open peat bogs, and 190,000 miles of hedgerows. For advice about how to use your garden to reverse this trend, contact Plantlife International (www.plantlife.org.uk, tel: 01722 342730).

- Use natural mulches such as bark chippings, leaf mould or grass clippings to suppress weeds without the need for toxic chemicals.
- Cut them back into the soil to add nutrients.
- Pull them out by hand, then add them to the compost heap or feed them to pets such as rabbits.

Boundaries

- Always consider planting a hedge rather than erecting a fence. It will encourage wildlife.
- Choose hedges that attract the largest amount of wildlife, for example, hawthorn, oak and blackthorn.
- Never use toxic wood preservatives such as creosote.

Water

- Always think ahead before watering your garden. Many of us now routinely water gardens each night – often with sprinklers. Only water the plants that need special attention.
- Install a water butt. Almost 100,000 litres of water falls on the average rooftop annually – collect this for your garden and avoid using tap water.
- Instead of light, daily waterings, drench shrubs and trees with a bucket of water in dry spells to encourage deeper roots.
- Build a pond to encourage insects, frogs and toads, but avoid controlling algae with harsh chemicals – apply barley straw to the pond instead. Or wait for snails to do the job for you.

- Water in early morning or early evening to minimise evaporation.
- Avoid water features that need electricity. Use a solar fountain or pump instead.
- Use 'trickle and drip' watering systems when you're away on holiday.

Vegetable patch

- Always have something growing in your garden that you can eat.
- Where possible, involve children in the maintenance and share any spare produce.
- Grow native varieties to help promote biodiversity.
- Put vegetable peelings and other kitchen waste into a shallow pit. Cover it over with earth then grow next season's vegetables on top.
- If space is limited, most vegetables can be grown in containers or pots.

Furniture

- Always look out for the Forestry Stewardship Council (FSC) symbol on wooden garden furniture to ensure it is sustainably sourced.
- Use linseed oil instead of toxic wood preservatives to maintain wooden furniture.
- Avoid plastic furniture unless it is made from recycled plastic.

Barbecue

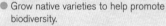

- Always use charcoal sourced from native coppiced woodland.
- Never use 'briquettes'. They invariably contain some kind of petroleum-based, flammable starter that will pollute your food and the environment.

Soil

- Aim to get as much humus (dark soil that is developed over time by the decomposition of organic matter) as possible into your ground to keep it rich with nutrients.
- Homemade compost, farmyard and poultry manure, seaweed, leaf-mould, nettles, hay, roadside cuttings, spent mushroom compost, prunings and straw are all good 'foods' for your soil.
- If you feel you still need to add a nitrogen fertiliser or alter the pH levels of the soil, use natural alternatives, such as bonemeal, organic potash or gypsum.
- Never use peat-based growing media.

Seating area

- As with garden furniture, carefully research the origins of any decking, patio stones or limestone that you may be considering. Make sure it has been sustainably sourced. Avoid concreting over an area.

Finally, learn from others then pass on your knowledge: join a local gardening club; sign up for an allotment; help out at the local community garden; share seeds, cuttings, produce and advice with neighbours; read as many gardening books as you can; and frequent gardening websites and message boards.

The best place to start is the Henry Doubleday Research Association (www.hdra.org.uk, tel: 024 7630 3517), the country's leading organic gardening organisation. Other good starting points are www.organicgarden.org.uk and www.goodgardeners.org.uk.

Rubbish

Every year in the UK we generate more than 434 million tonnes of waste. Around 26 million tonnes come straight from our homes – about 500kg per person. And linked to every tonne of physical rubbish you discard is 'hidden rubbish': an extra five tonnes of waste generated by manufacturing and 20 tonnes created at the point where the raw material is extracted.

This means UK homes are throwing away enough to fill the Royal Albert Hall every two hours. According to the Department for Environment, Food and Rural Affairs (Defra), in England (the only region for which such analysis currently exists) households in the north-east are the biggest offenders, generating more household waste per person than in any other area and possessing one of the lowest recycling rates. But the rest of England need not feel too smug; 75 per cent of all municipal waste goes straight to landfill, and around nine per cent is incinerated. The average household weighs in with 23.8kg of rubbish per week and with just 16 per cent of rubbish being recycled or composted, England languishes near the bottom of European recycling league tables.

These statistics are alarming enough, but the amount of waste we produce is rising by three per cent a year. By 2020, domestic rubbish could top 40 million tonnes a year. The most affluent households produce around 5kg more waste per week than poorer ones and urbanites in single households produce more per capita than other demographic groups. During holiday seasons, rubbish rates soar even further – Christmas sees an extra three million tonnes generated. In addition, there are an estimated 25 million tonnes of 'homeless rubbish' generated each year – waste that has been illegally fly-tipped or dropped as litter in entrances to buildings and on streets and grass verges.

As a result, landfills are filling up fast, and incineration – proposed by many as the main alternative – has failed to win the confidence of the public. All the while, recycling levels remain stubbornly low.

Britain's waste problem is extremely serious. But a solution remains elusive, especially when the majority of householders have an 'out of sight, out of mind' attitude. Furthermore, give us a bigger bin and it seems we'll rise to the challenge and fill it. With the introduction of wheelie bins in the early 1990s, many councils quickly noted a 30 per cent rise in rubbish. But what exactly are we putting in our bins?

In 1892, dust and cinders made up 80 per cent of the household dustbin. Today, it's packaging that takes the lion's share – responsible for 35 per cent of the weight and 50 per cent of the volume. Defra estimates that supermarkets alone generate 200,000 tonnes of extra waste every year through their use of plastic packaging and their food wastage. Equally, efforts on the part of the major food retailers to curb plastic packaging have been limited. Disposable nappies are another scourge of the waste stream (see page 212).

Traditionally, our waste has gone to landfill, a method of disposal with serious repercussions. Leachates, potentially toxic liquids from organic waste, can seep out of landfill sites and pollute nearby water resources, while the many thousands of synthetic chemicals (see page 106) used in modern-day manufacturing mean that some discarded items will continue to emit toxins and stubbornly refuse to biodegrade until well after we've biodegraded ourselves: some plastics will not degrade for around 450 years, long outlasting many natural materials such as wood.

As organic waste degrades in landfill it emits methane, one of the major greenhouse gases. Methane from the country's 400 or so landfill sites is now thought to be responsible for about 40 per cent of the UK's contribution to greenhouse-gas emissions – a costly problem when set against the fact that the 2003 UN conference on climate change put the cost of damage caused that year by climate change at $60 billion.

Despite the fact that it is neither a reliable nor risk-free means of waste disposal, landfilling waste is proving a hard habit to break. In the UK it is partly due to historical habit. While other countries were running

The most **affluent households** produce around 5kg more waste per week than poorer ones and **urbanites in single households** produce more per capita than other demographic groups

out of holes in which to bury their rubbish and so turned to incineration and recycling, the UK had plenty of former open-cast mines and quarries in which to dump its waste. However, this also means that communities who happen to live in these areas get a particularly raw deal – in many areas decommissioned steel works and slagheaps have just been swapped for huge landfills. The legacy for nearby communities can be profound beyond the stench. A 2001 study by the Small Area Health Statistics Unit, published in the *British Medical Journal*, showed an increased probability of birth defects and neural tube diseases, such as spina bifida, in children born within two kilometres of a landfill site.

The plastic problem

Global consumption of plastic materials has increased from five million tonnes a year in the 1950s to around 100 million tonnes today. In the UK, for example, we used 4.7 million tonnes of plastic in 2001, and yet only seven per cent was recycled; eight per cent was incinerated and the remainder went to landfill.

Typically derived from crude oil (a non-renewable source) or natural gas that is then processed into polymers using extensive chemical treatments, plastic is both energy-intensive and environmentally hazardous in its manufacture. Rather than being thought of as disposable, plastic should be considered a precious material. Instead, it is unceremoniously dumped around the world in places where it often adds to toxic emissions and can have a hugely detrimental effect on wildlife – stretches of coral reef in Jordan, for example, are being suffocated by drifting layers of plastic bags that block out sunlight.

About 17.5 billion plastic bags a year are handed out at checkouts in the UK alone. Their life expectancy is not known; estimates range from a conservative 100 years to the one million years suggested by Musgraves, an Irish grocery store that has introduced biodegradable bags. The Co-op was the first retailer in the UK to offer 100 per cent biodegradable carrier bags – 18 months after disposal, they 'melt away'. However, biodegradable plastic isn't the answer as it amounts to yet another product destined to 'waste away' rather than be reused. Biodegradables use the same amount of energy for production and transportation as well as 'contaminating' other recyclable plastics (one of the major costs of recycling is sorting types of plastic into different piles).

E-waste

The current norm of planned obsolescence – where products are designed to be quickly usurped by a 'bigger, better, faster' model – often means that we now would discard an appliance before ever thinking of donating or recycling it. Computers, appliances that are rarely 'broken' when discarded, are set to be the 'fridge mountains' of the not-too-distant future. By the year 2009, 250 million computers in the US are predicted to have become obsolete. In Europe, electronic and electrical waste – 'e-waste', as it's known – is growing three times faster than any other type of municipal waste. It now accounts for four per cent of all municipal waste.

Although the EU Waste Electrical and Electronic Equipment (WEEE) directive aims to bring e-waste under control over the coming years by placing a responsibility on manufacturers and retailers to provide 'take-back' facilities for all e-goods, it is likely to remain a considerable problem for some time. Made up of different materials and components, it is difficult to 'stream' into the recycling process. Many components can also be harmful – one cadmium battery, for example, has the potential to pollute 600,000 litres of water. When WEEE products are disposed of and not recycled, raw materials have to be processed to make replacement products. This is particularly pertinent when it comes to appliances, which are very energy-intensive.

At the moment two million TV sets are discarded every year in the UK. According to the Environment Agency, an estimated 500,000 of these TV sets then find their way to Africa and Asia as part of the annual £7 million illegal trade in e-waste, contravening EU law, and putting many poorly paid recycling workers at risk – many of whom recycle by hand without protective equipment.

The global dustbin

In common with the UK, the US has developed a similar dependency on landfill. In fact, the largest manmade structure in the world is a landfill – the Fresh Kill site on Staten Island, New York. Levels of household waste in the US continue to soar – 1.26 billion plastic bottles are discarded there every three weeks. In fact, US waste experts suggest there are only 18 more years of total landfill capacity left across the US.

Just as developing countries have begun to emulate the consumption habits of their wealthy neighbours, so their waste problems follow suit too. For example, 2.3 billion plastic bags are thrown away each year in Beijing alone, the majority of which seem to end up as 'white pollution' – the term used for the streams of bags that now blow along the streets.

But whereas the UK didn't begin to treat waste as a really serious issue until the 1990s, other EU countries have taken proactive and effective steps to reduce waste. In 1990 Austria introduced a Waste Management Act, tough legislation that put the country firmly on the road to 'zero waste'. Germany also introduced strict packaging laws in 1991 – a decade later, consumers were carrying home 17 per cent less packaging. And although the country experimented with diverting landfill waste into incineration during the 1990s, public pressure forced legislators to shift towards the intensive recycling route. The Netherlands has had a comprehensive kerbside 'wet and dry' (meaning compostable waste is collected too) recycling programme in place for a number of years, with householders who put rubbish out earlier than the designated rubbish day potentially facing a fine of up to €400. All three countries now boast recycling rates of over 45 per cent.

Swiss households manage to recycle 53 per cent of their waste due to strict policies – householders who contaminate a paper recycling bag with a bottle, for example, can expect to be fined around 100 Swiss francs (about £45). Since 2002, a tax has been collected from bottle manufacturers and importers and paid out to communities that recycle. While other European countries do not have such impressively high recycling rates, some have introduced initiatives to cut waste and divert disposal from dumping towards recycling. In 2002, Ireland levied a 15 per cent tax on plastic bags, cutting use by 95 per cent. South African authorities banned flimsy plastic bags in 2003 to halt a litter problem so endemic the bags had become known as 'South Africa's national flower'.

Courtesy of the 'trash-can economy', Brazil now recycles a higher percentage of aluminium cans than any other country. At the same time, street recyclers, known locally as catadores, are lobbying to become a recognised part of the labour force. Recent poster campaigns feature a recycler and the slogan, 'Don't treat me like trash'.

Waste legislation

Clearly the UK has been slow off the mark and has a lot of ground to make up. However, the government has set ambitious targets for rubbish recovery. In 2000, for example, it published its waste strategy for England and Wales in which targets for the recycling or composting of household waste were set at 25 per cent by 2005, 30 per cent by 2010, and 33 per cent by 2015. In 2002, the Prime Minister's Strategy Unit recommended that the targets be raised to 35 per cent by 2010 and 45 per cent by 2015. Those with the responsibility of achieving such targets – largely, local authorities – certainly have their work cut out.

A raft of tough EU regulations have been designed to tackle the main problem areas of rubbish: too much waste, too few mechanisms to convert rubbish to useful by-products, and too few markets for the new products. These mean that the UK has no choice but to mend its ways. For all waste producers, be they householders or big business, it seems that the stick rather than the carrot may be the best way to change old habits.

(Waste legislation is complex and constantly being amended and updated. For an overview, visit www.wasteonline.org.uk/resources/informationsheets/legislation.html).

Trash miles

Our rubbish is increasingly well-travelled. According to the Environment Agency, 42 per cent – around two million tonnes – crosses a regional boundary on its way to its final resting place, invariably a landfill site.

When it comes to dealing with our own rubbish, levels of regional self-containment vary hugely. Parts of Wales and the north-west handle 70 per cent of their own waste, but if you're throwing out a black sack of rubbish in London you can count on it travelling up to 50 miles to sites in the home counties – inner London's landfill sites closed many years ago.

Single objects are equally likely to clock up trash miles. In 2002, the UK found itself with a mounting fridge crisis when a new EU directive banned CFCs found in fridges from landfill. Consequently, container loads of unwanted fridges were driven across the country, contributing to pollution levels and traffic congestion, to a limited number of special closed units.

Other waste has racked up more miles than the average foreign correspondent. A proliferation in the number of redundant green glass wine bottles in the UK has led to them being shipped from the UK to South America, where they are broken down into cullet (glass fragments for melting) at low cost. This cullet is then shipped back to the UK for reuse.

This is all part of a gigantic waste swap. During the 1990s we exported on average 350,000 tonnes of waste a year but at the same time imported 131,450 tonnes.

Altogether 3.8 million tonnes of waste paper, glass cullet and iron-based scrap is exported. This may seem like a good solution for avoiding landfills, but there is a high environmental cost: each tonne of waste is responsible for 0.036kg of CO_2 emissions for every kilometre travelled by ship, rising to 0.248kg for every kilometre by road.

Hazardous waste is likely to be transported further than other materials. The record for the longest trip belongs to 2,500 tonnes of incinerator ash from Philadelphia that spent a staggering 16 years travelling the world. The initial 15,000-tonne cargo of ash had been destined for an island in the Bahamas. Over a dozen countries refused the cargo. Eventually the major part was dumped illegally in the sea, before the final 2,500 tonnes were dumped in Pennsylvania, 160 kilometres from where the cargo started out.

Rubbish solutions

The 4 Rs

In nature nothing is wasted. Every output is an input for something else. It is increasingly argued that our consumer society must find an equivalent system, and fast. That means embracing the 'four Rs': reducing, reusing, repairing and recycling. By changing the way we think about the lifespan of materials, many experts believe we can completely alter the way we manage rubbish. We can achieve a seismic shift from the consume-and-chuck-it impulses of contemporary life to finding new ways of extracting every last breath from each item, delaying the moment of final disposal as long as possible.

In fact, cutting our waste levels can be seen as an opportunity, not only to tackle unsightly rubbish heaps and prevent adverse health effects from landfill and incineration, but also to tackle climate change. A study of UK rubbish showed that diversion of waste from disposal by reusing and recycling 70 per cent of it could lead to savings of 14.8 million Metric Tonnes of Carbon Equivalent a year (MTCE is a unit of measurement, that allows the emissions of different greenhouse gases, such as CO_2, methane and nitrous oxide, to be added together) – a similar impact to taking 5.4 million cars off the road. Similarly, in the US, where half of municipal waste is made up of just five products – aluminium, paper, steel, glass and plastic – a quarter of greenhouse gas emissions could be cut by retaining the energy of these waste products by reusing or recycling.

Reduce

The most basic way to lighten both your dustbin and your waste 'footprint' is to buy less in the first place. In a consumer society, it is not usually viable to stop buying at all, but we can make different choices, such as buying products with the minimum of packaging, or protesting when we see excessive packaging. In Germany and Austria, consumers have long rebelled against irresponsible wrappings. It is not uncommon for them to rip plastic off products in supermarkets or post excess packaging back to retailers.

However, you don't have to be confrontational (unless you want to be) as there's still plenty of room to exercise consumer power. Purchase minimally wrapped goods, wherever possible substituting paper for plastics. There is no law that says that food must be carried in plastic bags. Refuse plastic shopping bags, instead using a bag made from natural fabrics, or at least reuse durable plastic bags.

There are other waste items over which we seem to have no control. Junk mail, for example, is not just a social irritant that stops you opening your front door properly, but is an environmental pest. Around a million tonnes of junk mail are binned in the UK every year. But simply by contacting the Mailing Preference Service (www.mpsonline.org.uk, tel: 020 7291 3310) householders can remove their name and address from 95 per cent of direct mailing lists for free.

Reuse

After making more effort to cut down and prevent rubbish from entering the home, the next step in the chain is reusing. This means buying products that are built to last, or can be adapted or added to, even in the case of appliances or gadgets. Furniture buys should be pieces with inherent longevity and value, preferably those that can be handed down the family tree. Try to avoid disposable goods wherever possible, from nappies and plastic cutlery to razors and cameras.

The US energy guru Dr Amory Lovins is one of the main proponents of the 'materials revolution': the rationale being that while labour shortages drove the first industrial revolution, a materials shortage (thanks in part to a decline in fossil fuels) will drive a second industrial revolution – one that requires resources to be used 10–100 times more productively.

While the onus is on the design fraternity to innovate products that can be reused and adapted to

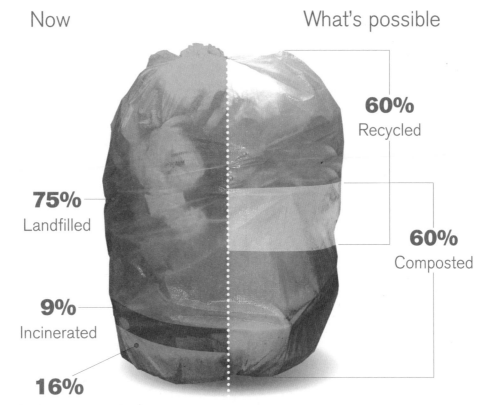

Now

What's possible

60%
Recycled

75%
Landfilled

60%
Composted

9%
Incinerated

16%
Recycled or composted

ensure their longevity, the consumer's role is vital. Visitors to developing nations are often struck by the level of inventiveness with which materials are reused, typically out of necessity. Consumers in the developed world can learn a lesson about the preciousness of materials and take note of the principle that everything has more than one use. For example, the environmental writer Nicky Scott suggests reinventing plastic drinks bottles as mini cloches to protect tender young plants from slugs.

If you can't reuse something yourself, try to find someone who can. Waste collectors are frequently incredulous at the perfectly good materials that get thrown away. Functional computers or appliances can nearly always be rehoused among neighbours, in the local community, or as part of a charitable scheme that donates technology or materials overseas. Broken equipment can be stripped for components.

Repair
It seems that when a possession breaks, repair is no longer our instinctive solution. Increasingly, we are faced with a fix-it-or-forget-it dilemma, where forgetting it often wins. In 2001, *Consumer Union* magazine in the

US repeated a 1997 survey among its readers to determine their feelings about repairing household appliances. It found that its current readers repaired 12 per cent fewer items than those who had taken part in 1997. VCRs and camcorders topped the list when it came to objects to be discarded. Small appliances such as shavers and toasters were shown to have 'decreased serviceability'. Thirty-four per cent cited cheap replacements as their reason for choosing to dump products and buy new ones, along with inconvenient repair times and a lack of repair facilities.

Despite the rapid turnover rate for the majority of goods, particularly electrical and electronic, the survey's respondents admitted to taking out more extended warranties than ever before, to insure against breakage and damage. Even so, some didn't seem to want to use them: 12 per cent chose to buy new instead of repairing, despite the fact that the item was still under warranty.

The WEEE directive (see page 121) aims to make manufacturers responsible for the disposal of appliances, by encouraging cost-effective recycling and reclamation of components and materials. But the repair stage still needs to be reintroduced to a product's lifetime, prolonging its usefulness. Make sure you get what you have paid for and use the repair facilities on warranties. If the repair service is not up to scratch, complain about it to the manufacturer and, if necessary, to consumer rights groups, such as the local Citizen's Advice Bureau (www.citizensadvice.org.uk) or the Consumers' Association (www.which.net, tel: 0845 307 4000).

Recycle

It is not surprising that many UK householders seem to have lost some motivation in the battle to divert waste from landfill. In comparison with recycling rates in other parts of Europe – Austria 64 per cent, Belgium 52 per cent and 47 per cent for the Netherlands – our own recycling rate of 12 per cent is dispiriting. Many householders have been dissuaded from recycling by poor local facilities and fragmented policies; a 2002 survey by the Environment Agency showed that nine out of 10 householders would recycle more waste if it were easier.

In 2003, 66 per cent of recycling relied on householders bringing waste to sites. Invariably this meant a car trip. In outer London, for example, trips to the tip account for one per cent of car traffic. But increased kerbside collections in most localities are now helping to improve the recycling infrastructure, giving householders the opportunity to recycle seriously.

However, it is still grassroots groups – the ones who make it their business to tackle waste on a local scale – who are the true trash heroes. They have helped to move the agenda away from incineration (protestors are thought to have prevented the building of more than 30 incinerators) and towards recycling. In 2002, according to the Shell Better Britain Campaign, 850 grassroots groups recycled rubbish from more than 4.5 million homes, and more than 300 furniture recycling projects distributed more than a million items of furniture to low-income households, second-hand stores and charity shops.

What can be recycled?

Over 60 per cent of our rubbish could be recycled. Just five different materials make up the bulk of the average dustbin: glass, cans, plastic bottles, textiles and paper account for about 50 per cent of weight and are all recyclable. Vegetable peelings and other organic material make up a further 20 per cent.

After garden and kitchen waste, paper and cardboard together are the second-biggest ingredient in most bins, making up around 18 per cent. Although, theoretically, the wood for papermaking is a renewable resource, producing just one tonne of top quality paper from virgin forest consumes over 98 tonnes of resources. It is crucial that waste paper is recycled to make more paper and cardboard in order to prevent deforestation and practices such as the carving of logging routes into remote forests and industrial harvesting. In addition, paper bleaching, along with plastics manufacturing, is among the biggest sources of global dioxin emissions (see page 106).

Plastics make up around seven per cent of the average bin, largely derived from packaging. Made almost exclusively from non-renewable fossil fuels, their recyclable value may well rise as fossil fuel supplies diminish. However, at the moment recycling rates are low, hampered by the fact that more facilities for dealing with mixed plastic are needed. Currently, most local authorities won't collect polystyrene, one of the most polluting plastics. Even so, 360 million plastic bottles were recovered and recycled in 2002. Made of PET or HDPE, the most valuable types of plastic, they are the most recyclable. The best way to see if a product is made of one of these two plastics is to look for the numbers '1' and '2' within a triangle symbol. There are five other plastic numbers, the full list of which can be found at www.wasteonline.org.uk/resources/informationsheets/plastics.html. (For more information about plastics recycling, visit www.recoup.org).

Since the 1970s, glass has been steadily superseded by plastic in the drive towards single-use disposable packaging. Consequently, it now makes up just seven per cent of household rubbish. The UK's glass recycling rate remains one of the lowest in Europe. But for every tonne of recycled glass used, 1.2 tonnes of raw materials are preserved. And recycled glass has many uses: the majority of wine bottles are made of green glass, and technologies have been developed to use recovered green glass in road surfaces and, as 'green sand', to help filter tap water.

The metal we discard – scrap metal, white goods, metal packaging, etc – makes up eight per cent of our overall rubbish. Two-thirds of it is either steel or aluminium. In 2000, we consumed five billion drinks from aluminium cans, of which just 42 per cent were recycled, despite aluminium being the most valuable used packaging material. But if all of the UK's aluminium cans were recycled there would be 12 million fewer full dustbins per year. Steel food cans are also equally recyclable, a fact that takes on heightened significance when you consider steel's energy-intensive and environmentally destructive manufacturing process.

See the Directory at the end of this chapter for a listing of organisations that can help you recycle more of your waste.

Closing the loop

Recycling culture is not just about recycling waste, but about buying recycled goods too. You can play a bigger

role, not only by providing materials courtesy of recycled household waste, but by demanding and using a range of recycled products, creating a closed-loop system where waste becomes obsolete. Buying recycled wherever possible helps to develop the market. Only when the business community sees recycled goods as a commercial opportunity will it increase its efforts to enter the market with better and more innovative products.

But recycled products are often viewed as substandard – a preconception that also needs to change if we are to successfully close the loop. Designers have a critical part to play in changing

Spotlight

Is 'zero waste' possible?

Zero waste means precisely that. In effect all rubbish is reused, recycled or composted by taking a 'whole system' approach. Surprisingly, the origins of this ecologically virtuous programme can be traced back to industry. An extension of the Japanese idea of Total Quality Management, it has direct links to the 'zero defects' policies adopted by Japanese car manufacturers, introducing rigorous criteria to attain the perfect score.

Restoring the Earth's carbon balance, through intensive recycling (which protects and conserves energy) and composting (which fulfils a sink function, see page 163) is central to the philosophy. However, it is not enough for products to be recycled – the energy used to reprocess them must also be renewable.

Nothing is worthless: products are designed to retain their value throughout their life cycle. When goods are recycled they typically lose their value, but in zero-waste world, smart design ensures they 'up-cycle' and hold their worth.

Waste is treated in alliance with manufacturing and consumption, and not as an isolated problem. If the source of the problem happens to be in manufacturing then manufacturing is tackled directly. A 'zero discharge' policy aims to remove all forms of toxicity during manufacture, and substitutes toxic ingredients

with non-toxic ones. The aim is clean production, which in turn facilitates clean recycling.

In addition, untreated biological waste cannot be landfilled as it would emit methane, a greenhouse gas contravening a zero-tolerance stance on atmospheric damage.

Although nobody has achieved the holy grail of zero waste yet, a number of communities are making good progress. In 1996, Canberra became the first city to adopt a zero-waste policy, hoping to achieve the target by 2010. This in turn inspired a zero-waste movement in New Zealand. Some parts of California, including San Francisco where a 50 per cent waste reduction rate has already been achieved, are also following the path. Pockets of the UK are now tentatively signing up too. Bath and North-East Somerset Council was the first local authority to sign up and others are following suit. But given the nature and size of the UK's waste problems, calls by some environmentalists for zero waste to be achieved by 2020 look over-hopeful. However, analysts have pointed to evidence that shows that after an initial slow growth, as in the case of the UK, the recycling rate can climb steeply to 50 or 60 per cent. Perhaps this is the start of a move towards intensive recycling, one of the major components of a zero-waste programme?

perceptions, creating products that both guarantee longevity and retain their value. In the case of electronic and electrical products, that means items that can be added to and be made more valuable, not just junked in favour of the most recent model. In this way they can continually circulate as high-quality products, leading to a process of 'upcycling' rather than just recycling.

Compost

After reducing, reusing, repairing and recycling, there's a strong case for adding a fifth 'R': rot. Three-fifths of our rubbish consists of material that could be composted, much of it paper and card. Although compost produced from household waste is not usually of sufficient quality to be used on farmland, there's plenty of call for second-grade compost in today's countryside. It can be used to restore old quarries, placed on top of old landfill sites to enable trees to grow, or on brownfield sites where houses can be built.

Home composting
'Waste not, want not', the government's 2002 strategy for tackling waste, proposed that 50 per cent of households should be carrying out home composting by 2006. Not only is it an efficient antidote to landfill but it's just about the only reprocessing everyone can do. Compost holds moisture in dry soil and 'opens up' clay soil. It can also be used to great effect in plant pots, window boxes, hanging baskets or troughs. In addition, it makes the household dustbin lighter and means that it won't smell so bad.

Paper and cardboard can also be composted, including windowless envelopes, toilet- and kitchen-roll centres, kitchen paper, cardboard boxes and paper packaging.

In common with nearly all life on earth, compost requires air, water, warmth and food. The food and water come courtesy of vegetable scraps, air pockets are created by scrunched-up paper and card, and the warmth is partly provided by the enormous explosion of micro-organisms and natural heat – small heaps work best from spring to autumn.

Small-scale cool composting takes from six months to a year to be ready. You can find out if it's ready by scooping the top layers off. The darker earth-like material is the finished compost.

Compost also provides a wildlife refuge. Flies and creepy crawlies are a normal part of composting, helping to increase biodiversity. You can even compost on concrete if necessary. Worms will crawl over huge distances of Tarmac and concrete to get into a heap. In fact, a wormery (a small bin that houses several thousand worms) is an excellent and compact way to manage a small amount of organic waste – perfect for small households without access to much outside space. For more information, visit www.wasteonline.org.uk/resources/InformationSheets/Compost.html.

Community composting
For those who live in a flat or don't have a garden, community composting still offers a chance to recycle household waste. In fact, many environmentalists think vibrant community composting schemes could hold the key to dealing with domestic organic waste. Despite this enthusiasm, there are still only around 125 centralised composting sites compared to more than 1,000 in Germany. Community-owned and run schemes are usually supported by the local authority. Some, as in the case of 'Proper Job' in Devon, one of the first successful community composting schemes, even receive 'recycling credits' – a system whereby local authorities pay out an amount equal to the saving they made by not having to dispose of the recyclable material collected by another agency, in this case a community composting scheme. For more information, visit www.communitycompost.org.

Vertical composting units
Targets requiring local councils to recycle or compost 25 per cent of household waste by 2005/06 have inevitably left boroughs looking for a solution. Considering that between 35 and 55 per cent of household waste is compostable, one solution is the Vertical Composting Unit (VCU). It's been a resounding success in New Zealand as part of the zero-waste drive and is now established in the UK in Sheffield, North Lincolnshire and Bromley. Developed by microbiologists in New Zealand, the units are modular and can alter capacity to fit any community or town. An average unit can process civic green waste into 25 tonnes of grade-A soil conditioner every week. For more information, contact your local authority, or visit the Composting Association website at www.compost.org.uk.

Incineration or landfill?

Seventy-three per cent of our rubbish has a one-way ticket to a landfill site. Once there, precious resource-rich technical materials and organic waste (that could have been diverted to compost to enrich soil) create a useless sludge. Worse still it's a sludge that poisons the surrounding environment.

But landfill regulations set in 2004, aimed at prohibiting the combined dumping of hazardous and non-hazardous waste in landfill sites, have led to waste that is, in effect, homeless. Is incineration, popular in countries such as Japan, Holland and Switzerland, where landfill is difficult, the answer to our trash prayers?

Not according to Greenpeace and Friends of the Earth. They point to studies showing that incineration releases toxic dioxins (see page 106) into the atmosphere. However, proponents of incineration say that new incinerators with cutting-edge technologies limit pollution and even recover energy from organic wastes, which could provide an alternative source of energy to fossil fuels. Furthermore, some metals can be recovered after incineration.

But detractors retaliate by pointing out that organic waste is low in energy, metals recovered after incineration are too low in quality to be of value and that cleaner chimney flues just transfer the toxicity into ash, which is dumped in landfill or spread on land, and contaminated water used for plant cleaning.

Incinerators are also so expensive to build that once a council decides on one for an area, in order to recoup the costs it typically has to commit its waste contracts for many years ahead. In short, once a community gets an incinerator, it's likely to be stuck with it for decades. Either way, it seems the general public are unconvinced: there has been only one new addition to the UK's small number of municipal incinerators in over a decade, largely thanks to public resistance. Using incinerators instead of landfills, it seems, is seen as little more than pushing a problem from one corner to another.

Effective micro-organisms

Another easy way to divert waste from landfill is by using a 'bokashi' system. In Japan, this natural method is commonplace in schools and homes. The bokashi system uses a solution – usually a wheat bran formula – containing 'effective micro-organisms' (EMs) that break down components naturally and efficiently. EMs are already being sprayed on landfill rubbish in other parts of Europe. In a 'local' bokashi system, such as a bucket container, the solution is layered between food waste, which breaks down over two weeks before it can be dug into a garden or window box. The liquid that collects in the bottom of the bucket even acts as a nature-enhancing drain cleaner (Japanese studies have shown this liquid to have a benign effect on rivers). Bokashi systems are now available in the UK: contact Living Soil (www.livingsoil.co.uk, tel: 01556 650116).

Directory

ENERGY

Advice

Whether you're looking for advice about energy-saving measures for your home, renewable technologies, or how to pick a green-energy tariff, these organisations will be able to help you.

Encraft
☎ 0845 602 2874
www.encraft.co.uk

Energy 21
☎ 01249 783415
www.energy21.org.uk

The Energy Saving Trust
☎ 0845 727 7200
www.est.org.uk/myhome

Energy Watch
(gas and electricity watchdog)
☎ 0845 906 0708
www.energywatch.org.uk

Friends of the Earth
(for green tariff ratings)
☎ 0808 800 1111
www.foe.co.uk/campaigns/climate/issues/green_energy

Green Electricity Marketplace
☎ 0117 980 9441
www.greenelectricity.org

Greenphase
www.greenphase.com

Green Prices
www.greenprices.co.uk

National Energy Foundation
☎ 01908 665555
www.nef.org.uk

Green electricity suppliers

National (except Northern Ireland)

Ecotricity
(not available in Scotland)
☎ 0800 032 6100
www.ecotricity.co.uk

Good Energy
(formerly called Unit[e])
☎ 0845 456 1640
www.good-energy.co.uk

Green Energy UK
☎ 0845 456 9550
www.greenenergy.uk.com

London Energy (Green Tariff)
☎ 0800 587 4433
www.london-energy.com

npower (Juice)
☎ 0800 316 2610
www.npower.com

Powergen (GreenPlan)
☎ 0800 363363
www.powergen.co.uk

RSPB Energy (available through Scottish Hydro Electric, Southern Electric and SWALEC)
☎ 0800 117116
www.southern-electric.co.uk

Scottish Power (Green Energy H2O and Green Energy Fund)
☎ 0141 568 2000
www.scottishpower.com

Seeboard Energy
(Green Fund Tariff and Greenlight)
☎ 0800 056 8888
www.seeboard-energy.com

SWEB Energy (Green Tariff)
☎ 0800 587 0266
www.sweb-energy.com

Northern Ireland
Northern Ireland Electricity
(Eco Energy)
☎ 0845 745 5455
www.nie.co.uk

Energy-saving equipment providers

Cavity Insulation Guarantee Agency
☎ 01525 853300
www.ciga.co.uk

Centre for Alternative Technology
☎ 01654 705993
www.cat.org.uk

Energy & Environment
☎ 0161 881 1383
www.energyenv.co.uk

Energy Saving World
☎ 01233 666000
www.lumin8.co.uk

Green Building Store
☎ 01484 854898
www.greenbuildingstore.co.uk

Sava Watt
☎ 01789 490340
www.savawatt.com

Thermafleece
☎ 01768 486285
www.secondnatureuk.com

Warmcel
☎ 01685 845200
www.excelfibre.com

RENEWABLE ENERGY SYSTEMS

Some of the following companies supply both solar water and wind systems – check their websites for details

Solar (water heating)

AES Solar Systems
☎ 01309 676911
www.aessolar.co.uk

Cel-F Solar Systems
☎ 0870 330 2202
www.cel-f-solar.com

Celtic Solar
☎ 01566 781509
www.celticsolar.co.uk

Eco-Exmoor
☎ 01598 763595
www.eco-exmoor.co.uk

Ecoheat
☎ 01422 843414
www.ecoheat.co.uk

Element Energies
☎ 01769 550555
www.elementenergies.co.uk

Filsol Solar
☎ 01269 860229
www.filsol.co.uk

Imagination Solar
☎ 0845 458 3168
www.imaginationsolar.com

ME Mechanical Services
☎ 01522 520146
www.memech.co.uk

Monaghan & Hornal
☎ 01786 822827
www.sun-harvester.co.uk

Powersun Solar Systems
☎ 0115 927 0880
www.powersun.co.uk

Powertech Solar
☎ 0870 730 0111
www.solar.co.uk

Rayotec
☎ 01932 784848
www.rayotec.com

Riomay
☎ 01323 648641
www.riomay.com

Solar Dawn
☎ 01588 680469
www.solardawn.co.uk

Solar Sense
☎ 0870 794 9620
www.solarsense.co.uk

Solar Trade Association
☎ 01908 442290
www.solartradeassociation.org.uk

Solartwin
☎ 0845 130 0137
www.solartwin.com

Solar UK
☎ 01892 667320
www.solaruk.net

Themba Technology
☎ 0800 083 0237
www.thembatech.com

The Very Efficient Heating Company
☎ 0151 606 0207
www.veryefficientheating.co.uk

Solar (photovoltaic)

B9nrg
☎ 0870 794 9621
www.b9nrg.co.uk

Becosolar
☎ 01803 833636
www.becosolar.com

British Photovoltaic Association
☎ 01908 442291
www.pv-uk.org.uk

Bull Electrical
☎ 01273 491490
www.bullnet.co.uk

PV Systems
☎ 029 2082 0910
www.pvsystems.com

Rainbow Solar Trading
☎ 01983 533129
www.rainbowtradingpost.co.uk

Select Solar
☎ 01793 752032
www.selectsolar.co.uk

Solarcentury
☎ 020 7803 0100
www.solarcentury.co.uk

Solar Energy Alliance
☎ 01502 515532
www.solarenergyalliance.com

SolarTech
☎ 01280 703607
www.solartech.plus.com

Southern Solar
☎ 0845 456 9474
www.southernsolar.co.uk

Spectrum Energy
☎ 01202 519825
www.spectrum-energy.co.uk

Sundog Energy
☎ 01768 482282
www.sundog-energy.co.uk

Sunseeker Solar Energy
☎ 0161 343 7077
www.sunseeker-solar.co.uk

Suntrader Solar Power Systems
☎ 01273 550225
www.suntrader.co.uk

Wind

Energy Development Co-operative
☎ 0870 745 1119
www.solar-wind.co.uk

Marlec Engineering Company
☎ 01536 201588
www.marlec.co.uk

NFP Ledbury
☎ 01531 631020
www.nfpledbury.co.uk

Proven Engineering Products
☎ 01560 485570
www.provenenergy.com

Shorepower
☎ 01823 666177
www.shorepoweruk.com

Turbine Services
☎ 01900 85616
www.turbineservices.co.uk

Wind and Sun
☎ 01568 760671
www.windandsun.co.uk

Windsave
☎ 0141 353 6841
www.windsave.com

Windsund International
☎ 01207 255365
www.winsund.com

Energy grants

Before considering investing in any energy-saving or renewable technology, check to see whether you qualify for any of the many grants now available

Clear Skies
(renewable-energy grants)
☎ 0870 243 0930
www.clear-skies.org

Energy Saving Trust *(solar grants)*
☎ 0800 298 3978
www.est.org.uk/solar

Scottish Community and Household
Renewables Initiative (SCHRI)
☎ 0800 138 8858
www.est.org.uk/schri

Warm Front Grants (England)
☎ 0800 316 2808
www.eaga.co.uk

Powergen Warm Front (East England)
☎ 0800 952 1555
www.powergen-warmfront.co.uk

Warm Deal/Central Heating
Programme (Scotland)
☎ 0800 072 0150
www.eaga.co.uk

Home Energy Efficiency Scheme
(Wales)
☎ 0800 316 2815
www.eaga.co.uk

Warm Homes Grant (Northern Ireland)
☎ 0800 181667
www.eaga.co.uk

WATER

Water-saving advice

Elemental Solutions
☎ 01981 540728
www.elementalsolutions.co.uk

Environment Agency
www.environment-agency.gov.uk/save-
water

Groundwork Wales
www.groundworkwales.org.uk/water

Thames 21
☎ 020 7248 2916
www.thames21.org.uk

Thames Water Wise
www.thameswateruk.co.uk/waterwise

WaterVoice
☎ 0121 625 3637
www.watervoice.org.uk

WaterWatch
☎ 01709 558561
www.waterwatch.org.uk

Water-saving equipment

**Includes suppliers of
greywater recycling
equipment**

Aqualogic
☎ 0151 638 6111
www.aqualogic-wc.com

Celtic Water Management
☎ 01239 811465
www.celticwater.co.uk

ech2o
☎ 020 8800 4157
www.ech2o.co.uk

ECO-Logic
☎ 0121 766 3016
www.ecologicuk.com

Envireau Rainwater Management
☎ 01296 633000
www.envireau.co.uk

Freerain
☎ 01636 894905
www.freerain.co.uk

Gramm Environmental
☎ 01273 844899
www.grammenvironmental.com

Green Building Store
☎ 01484 854898
www.greenbuildingstore.co.uk

Grey Water Central
www.oasisdesign.net/greywater

Hippo the Water Saver
☎ 01989 766667
www.hippo-the-watersaver.co.uk

Rainharvesting Systems
☎ 01452 772000
www.rainharvesting.co.uk

Save-a-flush
☎ 0161 610 8642
www.save-a-flush.co.uk

Variflush
☎ 01784 432449
www.peterton.co.uk

Waterless toilets

Barton Accessories
☎ 01604 411133
www.groundworkwales.org.uk/water/
barton.htm

Composting Toilet World
☎ 01765 650385
www.compostingtoilet.org

Eastwood Services
☎ 01502 478165
www.sun-mar.com

Maurice Moore
☎ 01932 254224

Wendage Pollution Control
☎ 01428 751296
www.wpc.uk.net

HOME

**Whether you're cleaning,
decorating or furnishing your
home, you should aim to
reduce your exposure to
harmful chemicals, as well
as being aware of a product's
environmental impact. The
following companies offer
healthier, more sustainable
alternatives to many
conventional suppliers**

General suppliers

Greenfibres
☎ 0845 330 3440
www.greenfibres.com

The Green Shop
☎ 01452 770629
www.greenshop.co.uk

Healthy House
☎ 01453 752216
www.healthy-house.co.uk

Medivac
☎ 0845 130 6164
www.medivac.co.uk

The World Wildlife Fund Shop
☎ 0870 750 7023
shop.wwf.org.uk

Building materials

**Includes reclamation
specialists**

Bygones Reclamation
☎ 0800 043 3012
www.bygones.net

Construction Resources
☎ 020 7450 2211
www.constructionresources.com

Ecomerchant
☎ 01795 530130
www.ecomerchant.co.uk

Forest Stewardship Council UK
www.fsc-uk.org
☎ 01686 413916

Friends of the Earth:
Good Wood Guide
www.goodwoodguide.com

Green Building Store
☎ 01484 854898
www.greenbuildingstore.co.uk

Old House Store
☎ 0118 969 7711
www.oldhousestore.co.uk

Ransfords
☎ 01327 705310
www.ransfords.com

Reclaimed Timber Specialists
☎ 020 8558 2811
www.reclaimed.uk.com

Salvo
☎ 020 8761 2316
www.salvo.co.uk

Source 4
☎ 01926 498444
www.source4you.co.uk

Ty-Mawr Lime (The Welsh Centre for
Traditional and Ecological Building)
☎ 01874 658249
www.lime.org.uk

Viking Reclamation
☎ 01302 835449
www.reclaimed.co.uk

Womersleys
☎ 01924 400651
www.womersleys.co.uk

Self-build advice

Association for Environment
Conscious Building
☎ 01559 370908
www.aecb.net

Building for a Future
☎ 01559 370798
www.newbuilder.co.uk

Build It Magazine
☎ 020 7772 8440
www.self-build.co.uk

Cob in Cornwall
☎ 01326 231773, 07789 780391
www.cobincornwall.com

ebuild
www.ebuild.co.uk

Ecological Building Design
☎ 07776 133396
www.ecologicalbuildingdesign.com

Forever Green
☎ 01892 614300
www.forevergreen.org.uk

Green Register of Construction
Professionals
☎ 020 7820 3159
www.greenregister.org

Green Street
www.greenstreet.org.uk

Homebuilding & Renovating
☎ 01527 834400
www.homebuilding.co.uk

Self Build ABC
www.selfbuildabc.co.uk

Sustainable Homes
☎ 020 8973 0429
www.sustainablehomes.co.uk

Walter Segal Self Build Trust
☎ 01668 213544
www.segalselfbuild.co.uk

Painting and decorating

Auro Organic Paints
☎ 01799 543077
www.auroorganic.co.uk

Cushini
☎ 020 7608 1104
www.cushini.com

EarthBorn Paints
☎ 01928 734171
www.earthbornpaints.co.uk

Ecoartisan
☎ 07939 973141
www.ecoartisan.org

Eco Solutions
☎ 01934 844484
www.strip-paint.com

Ecos Organic Paints
☎ 01524 852371
www.ecospaints.com

Georgina Barrow
☎ 01451 861040
www.naturalpaints.org.uk

Holkham Linseed Paints
☎ 01328 711348
www.holkhamlinseedpaints.co.uk

Keim Mineral Paints
☎ 01746 714543
www.keimpaints.co.uk

Mike Wye & Associates
☎ 01409 281644
www.mikewye.co.uk

Nutshell Natural Paints
☎ 01364 73801
www.nutshellpaints.com

Precious Earth
☎ 01584 878633
www.preciousearth.co.uk

Villa Natura
☎ 01273 685800
www.villanatura.co.uk

Beds and linen

Greenfibres
☎ 0845 330 3440
www.greenfibres.com

Mattress Doctor
☎ 0845 330 6607
www.matdoc.co.uk

Natural Collection
☎ 0870 331 3333
www.naturalcollection.com

The Sounder Sleep Company
☎ 0870 745 5002
www.soundersleep.co.uk

Textiles from Nature
☎ 020 7241 0990
www.textilesfromnature.com

Willey Winkle
www.willeywinkle.co.uk

Flooring

The Alternative Flooring Company
☎ 01264 335111
www.alternativeflooring.com

Ashcroft Reclaimed Timber Flooring
☎ 01243 554769
www.woodflooringuk.com

EC Forest Products
☎ 01825 872025

Forbo Nairn
☎ 01592 643777
www.forbo-linoleum.com

Kersaint Cobb
☎ 01675 430430
www.kersaintcobb.co.uk

The Natural Floor Company
☎ 020 8741 4451
www.natfloorco.com

Rugmark Foundation
(for fair trade carpets and rugs)
☎ 001 202 347 4205
www.rugmark.org

Treadplates
☎ 01608 685414
www.treadplates.co.uk

Treework Flooring
☎ 01275 464466
www.treeworkflooring.co.uk

Victorian Wood Works
☎ 020 8534 1000
www.victorianwoodworks.co.uk

Weston of Scandinavia (UK)
☎ 0845 644 9090
www.weston-carpets.co.uk

Yorkshire Reclaimed Flooring
☎ 01937 843532
www.yorkshirereclaimedflooring.co.uk

Furniture

Arbor Vetum
☎ 01386 840438
www.arborvetum.co.uk

LivingConcepts.co.uk
☎ 020 7043 8207
www.livingconcepts.co.uk

Pendlewood
☎ 0161 789 4441
www.pendlewood.com

Preston Door & Pine Stripping
☎ 01772 725943
www.oldpine-online.co.uk

Reclaimed Pine Online
☎ 01202 316434, 07876 770037
www.reclaimed-pine-online.co.uk

Reel Furniture
☎ 01603 629396
www.reelfurniture.co.uk

Re-Form Furniture
www.re-formfurniture.co.uk

Cleaning products

21st Century Health
☎ 020 7289 2121
www.21stcenturyhealth.co.uk

Bio-D
☎ 01482 229950
www.biodegradable.biz

The Caurnie Soaperie
☎ 0141 776 1218
www.caurnie.com

Clear Spring
☎ 0161 764 2555
www.faithinnature.co.uk

Ecover
☎ 01635 574553
www.ecover.com

Ecozone (UK)
☎ 0845 230 4200
www.ecozone.co.uk

Greenlands Environmental Care
☎ 01892 871285
www.greenlands-env.co.uk

Honesty Cosmetics
☎ 01629 814888
www.honestycosmetics.co.uk

Natural Eco Trading
☎ 01892 616871
www.greenbrands.co.uk

GARDEN

Gardening advice

The Garden Zone
www.gardenzone.info

Gardening Which?
☎ 0845 903 7000
www.which.net/gardeningwhich

Greenworks
☎ 01297 443659
www.greenworks.org.uk

HDRA
☎ 024 7630 3517
www.hdra.org.uk

Organic Gardening Magazine
www.organicgardening.com

Organic UK
www.organicgarden.org.uk

Vegan Organic Trust
www.veganorganic.net

Composting

Includes those offering advice as well as supplies

The Bin Company
☎ 0845 602 3630
www.thebincompany.com

Compost Technology
☎ 01938 570678

The Composting Association
☎ 0870 160 3270
www.compost.org.uk

Eco Composting
☎ 01202 593601
www.eco-composting.co.uk

Fertile Fibre
☎ 01584 781575
www.fertilefibre.co.uk

The Green Manure Page
www.kitchengardens.dial.pipex.com/
greenmanure.htm

Growganic
☎ 01380 871050
www.growganic.co.uk

Terra Eco•Systems
☎ 0118 373 8784
www.terraecosystems.com/graphics/
gardening_products

West Country Compost & Paignton Zoo Poo
☎ 01392 424846
www.ecosci.co.uk

Worm Hotel
☎ 01606 592145
www.thewormhotel.com

Gardening supplies

Butterworths' Organic Nursery
☎ 01290 551088
www.webage.co.uk/apples

Cottage Herbery
☎ 01584 781575
www.the-cottage-herbery.co.uk

GroWell Hydroponics
☎ 0800 328 1339
www.growell.co.uk

The Organic Gardening Catalogue
☎ 0845 130 1304
www.organiccatalog.com

Organic Seeds
☎ 01473 310118
www.organicseeds.co.uk

Original Organics
☎ 01884 841515
www.originalorganics.co.uk

The Soil Association
☎ 0117 929 0661
www.soilassociation.org

The Soil Association Scotland
☎ 0131 666 2474
www.sascotland.org

Straight Plc
☎ 0845 130 6090
www.evengreener.com

Suffolk Herbs
☎ 01376 572456
www.suffolkherbs.com

Tamar Organics
☎ 01822 834887
www.tamarorganics.co.uk

Wiggly Wigglers
☎ 0800 216990
www.wigglywigglers.co.uk

Garden furniture, wood and charcoal

See the Forest Stewardship Council's website, www.fsc-uk.org/products, for a list of FSC-certified products

BioRegional Charcoal Co
☎ 020 8404 2300
www.bioregional.com

B&Q
☎ 0845 609 6688
www.diy.com

British Eco
☎ 0191 209 4161
www.britisheco.com

The Dorset Charcoal Co
☎ 01258 818176
www.dorsetcharcoal.co.uk

EBC Woodfuels
☎ 01953 455854
www.ebc-ecofuel.co.uk

Focus
☎ 0800 436436
www.focusdiy.co.uk

Homebase
☎ 0845 077 8888
www.homebase.co.uk

Mercia Coppice Revival
☎ 01780 766745
www.merciacoppicerevival.org.uk

Woodman Services
☎ 01794 390182

Humane, pesticide-free pest control

Agralan
☎ 01285 860015
www.agralan.co.uk

Biowise
☎ 01798 867574
www.biowise-biocontrol.co.uk

The Flowerfortress
(slug and snail barrier)
☎ 01204 591717

GreenFingers Trading
☎ 0845 345 0728
www.greenfingers.com

Green Ways
☎ 01962 761600
www.green-ways.co.uk

Mike Long Garden Supplies
☎ 01566 783229
www.slugfence.com

Scarletts Plant Care
☎ 01206 242533
www.bio.scarletts.co.uk

Encouraging biodiversity

The Bat Conservation Trust
☎ 0845 130 0228
www.bats.org.uk

British Dragonfly Society
☎ 01743 282021
www.dragonflysoc.org.uk

British Hedgehog
Preservation Society
☎ 01584 890801
www.software-technics.com/bhps/

British Wildflower Plants
☎ 01603 716615
www.wildflowers.co.uk

Butterfly Conservation
☎ 0870 774 4309
www.butterfly-conservation.org

Ernest Charles
☎ 0800 731 6770
www.ernest-charles.com

Friends of the Red Squirrel
☎ 01539 816300
www.redsquirrel.org.uk

National Federation of Badger Groups
☎ 020 7228 6444
www.badger.org.uk

The Royal Society for the Protection of Birds
☎ 01767 680551
www.rspb.org.uk

WASTE

For information on material-specific local recycling centres, consult WasteConnect or Waste Watch's National Recycling Directory

Recycling advice

Environment Agency
☎ 0870 850 6506
www.environment-agency.gov.uk

Environmental Services Association
☎ 020 7824 8882
www.esauk.org

Envocare
☎ 020 8398 2333
www.envocare.co.uk/recycling.htm

letsrecycle.com
☎ 020 7823 6789
www.letsrecycle.com

National Community Wood Recycling Project
☎ 01273 696900
www.communitywoodrecycling.org.uk

Recycle for London
☎ 0845 331 3131
www.recycleforlondon.com

Recycle-more.co.uk
☎ 0845 068 2572
www.recycle-more.co.uk

Recycle Now
www.recyclenow.com

SWAP (Save Waste and Prosper)
☎ 0113 243 8777
www.swap-web.co.uk

Waste Aware Scotland
☎ 01786 468248
www.wascot.org.uk

The Waste Book
www.recycle.mcmail.com

WasteConnect
☎ 01743 343403
www.wasteconnect.co.uk

Waste Watch
☎ 0870 243 0136
www.wasteonline.org.uk

Women's Environmental Network
☎ 020 7481 9004
www.wen.org.uk

WRAP
☎ 0808 100 2040
www.wrap.org.uk

Products made from recycled waste

Many discarded items are now being refashioned into new goods as clothes, toys and gardening equipment

Recycle Now's Buying Recycled Guide
www.recyclenow.com/buying_recycled

WRAP's Recycled Products Guide
www.recycledproducts.org.uk

Furniture recycling schemes

Before throwing out old furniture items or appliances offer them to a furniture recycling scheme that will redistribute them to low-income families

Furniture Re-Use Network
☎ 01924 375252
www.frn.org.uk

Sofa Project
☎ 0117 954 3567
www.sofaproject.org.uk

Unless different for each product, company details are listed in first entry only.

Electricity suppliers

Eco Energy (Northern Ireland Electricity)

Ecotricity

Good Energy

Green Energy UK

RSPB Energy

Solar (photovoltaic)

Filsol Ltd
☎ 01269 860229
www.filsol.co.uk

Imagination Solar
☎ 0845 458 3168
www.imaginationsolar.com

Viessmann
☎ 01952 675000
www.viessmann.co.uk

Solar water heating

AES Solar Systems
☎ 01309 676911
www.aessolar.co.uk

Filsol Ltd

Imagination Solar

Solartwin
☎ 0845 130 0137
www.solartwin.com

Thermomax
☎ 028 9127 0411
www.thermomax-group.com

Wind power

Eoltec
☎ 01856 879086
www.eoltec.com

Iskra Wind
☎ 0115 841 3283
www.iskrawind.com

Marlec Engineering Company
☎ 01536 201588
www.marlec.co.uk

Proven Engineering Products
☎ 01560 485570
www.provenenergy.com

Gas

Equigas
☎ 0845 456 0170
www.ebico.co.uk/equipower.htm

RSPB Energy
☎ 0800 117116
www.southern-electric.co.uk

Scottish Hydro (Scotland)
☎ 0845 300 2141
www.hydro.co.uk

Scottish Power
☎ 0141 568 2000
www.scottishpower.co.uk

Southern Electric (England)
☎ 0845 7444 555
www.southern-electric.co.uk

SWALEC (Wales)
☎ 0800 052 5252
www.swalec.co.uk

Condensing boilers

Atmos
☎ 01327 871990
www.atmos.uk.com

Gas 210 Eco and Quinta
☎ 0118 978 3434
www.uk.remeha.com

Keston Boilers
☎ 020 8462 0262
www.keston.co.uk

Insulation

Thermafleece (sheep's wool)
☎ 01768 486285
www.secondnatureuk.com

Warmcel (100 per cent newsprint loose fill)
☎ 01685 845200
www.excelfibre.com

Household cleaners

Astonish
☎ 0113 236 0036
www.astonishcleaners.co.uk

Bio-D
☎ 01482 229950
www.biodegradable.biz

Ecover
☎ 01635 574553
www.ecover.com

Washing-up liquid

Bio D

The Caurnie Soaperie
☎ 0141 776 1218
www.caurnie.com

Clear Spring
☎ 0161 764 2555
www.faithinnature.co.uk

Ecover

Toilet cleaners

Ecover

Bio D

Vacuum cleaners

Dyson
☎ 01666 827200
www.dyson.co.uk

Goblin
☎ 08450 777700
www.goblin.ie

Hoover
☎ 01685 721222
www.hoover.co.uk

Medivac
☎ 0845 130 6164
www.medivac.co.uk

Morphy Richards
☎ 0870 060 2604
www.morphyrichards.co.uk

Sebo
☎ 01494 465533
www.sebo.co.uk

Vax
☎ 01905 795959
www.vax.co.uk

Laundry detergent

ACDO
☎ 01204 600 500
www.acdoco.co.uk

Bio-D

Clear Spring

Irons

Morphy Richards

Rowenta
☎ 0845 602 1454
www.rowenta.co.uk

Russell Hobbs
☎ 0845 658 9700
www.russellhobbs.com

Tefal
☎ 0845 602 1454
www.tefal.co.uk

Travel irons

Remington
☎ 0800 212438
www.remington.co.uk

Rowenta

Batteries

**All these companies make
rechargeable batteries.
Uniross only makes
rechargeables.**

Energizer
☎ 020 8882 8661
www.energizer-eu.com

Rayovac
☎ 01784 411411
www.rayovac.com

Uniross
☎ 0870 2206988
www.uniross.com

Varta
☎ 01784 411411
www.varta-consumer.co.uk

Cameras

Fuji
☎ 020 7586 5900
www.fujifilm.co.uk

Leica
www.leica-camera.com

Film

Fuji

Digital cameras

Casio
☎ 020 8208 7838
www.casio.co.uk

Fuji

Ricoh
☎ 020 8261 4000
www.ricoh-uk.com

Computers

Evesham
☎ 0870 160 9500
www.evesham.com

Mesh
☎ 0870 046 4747
www.meshcomputers.com

Viglen
☎ 020 8758 7000
www.viglen.co.uk

Cookers

Aga
☎ 01952 642000
www.aga-rayburn.co.uk

Baumatic
☎ 0118 933 6900
www.baumatic.co.uk

Belling
☎ 0870 458 9663
www.belling.co.uk

Candy
☎ 01685 721222
www.candy-domestic.co.uk

New World
☎ 0870 458 9663
www.newworldappliances.co.uk

Rosieres
☎ 0151 3342 781
www.rosieres.biz

Stoves
☎ 0870 458 9663
www.stoves.co.uk

Dishwashers

Asko
☎ 0121 568 8333 (via Servis)
www.antoniomerloni.it

Proline
☎ 08705 425425
www.comet.co.uk

Servis
☎ 0121 568 8333
www.servisuk.co.uk

DVD players

Bush
☎ 0870 873 0079
www.albaplc.com

Kenwood
☎ 01923 816444
www.kenwood-electronics.co.uk

Pioneer
☎ 01753 789500
www.pioneer.co.uk

Fridges and freezers
Brandt
☎ 01256 308000
www.brandt.fr

Candy

Hoover

Miele
☎ 01235 554455
www.miele.co.uk

Ocean
(via Brandt)

Servis

Hi-fis
Bang & Olufsen
☎ 0118 969 2288
www.bang-olufsen.com

Eltax
☎ 01327 860789
www.eltax.co.uk

Pioneer

Internet providers
Claranet
www.uk.clara.net
☎ 020 7685 8310

GreenNet
☎ 0845 055 4011
www.gn.apc.org

The Phone Co-op
☎ 0845 458 9000
www.thephone.coop

Kitchen appliances
Toasters
De'Longhi
☎ 0845 600 6845
www.delonghi.co.uk

Dualit
☎ 01293 652500
www.dualit.com

Kenwood
☎ 023 9247 6000
www.kenwood.co.uk

Rowenta

Russell Hobbs

Kettles
De'Longhi

Dualit

Kenwood

Krups
☎ 0845 602 1454
www.krups.co.uk

Rowenta

Russell Hobbs

Blenders
De'Longhi

Kenwood

Moulinex
☎ 0845 602 1454
www.moulinex.co.uk

Mixers
Moulinex

Sandwich toasters
De'Longhi

Food processors
Kenwood

Moulinex

Tefal

Deep fat fryers
De'Longhi

Kenwood

Moulinex

Tefal

Juicers
Moulinex

Russell Hobbs

Tefal

Light bulbs
Bell
☎ 01924 893380
www.belllighting.co.uk

Lumin8
☎ 01233 666000
www.lumin8.co.uk

Sylvania
☎ 01274 532552
www.sli-lighting.com

Microwaves
Hinari
☎ 020 8238 7650
www.hinari.co.uk

Whirlpool
☎ 0870 600 8989
www.whirlpool.co.uk

Carpets and floorcoverings
B&Q (for FSC-certified laminates, FSC
certified wood and CorkLOC cork
flooring)
www.diy.com

Interface (carpet tiles)
☎ 0870 530 4030
www.interface-europe.com

Marmoleum (lino)
☎ 01592 643 777
www.marmoleum.co.uk

Rugmark Foundation
(for fair-trade carpets and rugs)
☎ 001 202 347 4205
www.rugmark.org

Duvets
John Cotton
☎ 01924 496571
www.johncotton.co.uk

Northern Feather
☎ 01625 520255
www.northernfeather.ie

Slumberdown
☎ 01450 374 500

Trendsetter
☎ 0161 627 4458
www.the-fine-bedding-company.co.uk

Furniture

Buying second-hand or recycled furniture, or bespoke furniture from a local supplier using reclaimed or FSC-certified wood are the best environmental choices.

FSC-labelled items from B&Q and Argos are also good options. If you are buying soft furnishings, and second-hand isn't appropriate, the best environmental choice would be to buy from IKEA. Although it does not hold the highest company rating, it is the only company with a policy on potentially harmful chemicals and any soft furnishings – including mattresses and sofas – are guaranteed free of brominated flame retardants

Argos
www.argos.co.uk

B&Q
www.diy.com

Ikea
www.ikea.co.uk

Paint

Auro Organic Paints
☎ 01799 543077
www.auroorganic.co.uk

Biofa
☎ 01273 685800 (via Villa Natura)
☎ 01484 854898 (via Green Building Store)
www.biofa.com

Keim Mineral Paints
☎ 01746 714543
www.keimpaints.co.uk

Livos
☎ 01795 530130 (via Ecomerchant)
www.livos.co.uk

Nutshell Natural Paints
☎ 01364 73801
www.nutshellpaints.com

Power tools

Draper
☎ 023 8026 6355
www.draper.co.uk

Makita
☎ 01908 211678
www.makita.co.uk

Stanley
☎ 0114 276 4000
www.stanleyworks.com

Printers

Brother
☎ 0845 60 60 626
www.brother.co.uk

Epson
☎ 0870 241 6900
www.epson.co.uk

Olivetti
☎ 01908 525400
www.olivettitecnost.co.uk

Ricoh

Star (dot matrix)
☎ 01494 471111
www.starmicronicseurope.com

Televisions

Alba
☎ 020 8594 5533
www.albaplc.com

Bush

Goodmans
☎ 023 9239 1000
www.albaplc.com

Sanyo
☎ 01923 246363
www.sanyo-europe.com

VCRs

Alba

Bush

Goodmans

Sanyo

Washing machines

Asko
☎ 0121 568 6159
www.asko.se

Candy

Dyson

Hoover

Maytag
☎ 01737 231000
www.maytag.co.uk
brand: Admiral

Miele

Servis

Garden seeds

Tamar Organics
☎ 01822 834887
www.tamarorganics.co.uk

VidaVerde
☎ 01239 821107
www.realseeds.co.uk

Compost

Fertile Fibre
☎ 01584 781575
www.fertilefibre.co.uk

Natures Own
☎ 01484 609171
www.wrorganics.co.uk

Lawn mowers

Environmentally, hand-push machines are best, followed by electrical mowers, with petrol mowers the worst.

Alko
☎ 01926 818 500
www.alko.co.uk

Draper

Gardening tools

Draper

Travel

Introduction

It is said that to understand a problem, one must view it from a distance. Try 100 miles above the Earth's surface, says the British-born astronaut Piers Sellars.

In 2002, while aboard the international space station, Sellars was struggling to locate his homeland as he peered down from a window. Bad weather was obscuring much of Europe and there was just one way to visually pinpoint Britain down below. 'The only way I could find it was by all the jet contrails leading into Heathrow and Gatwick that made a big cross over the middle of the British Isles,' he explained when he got back to Earth. 'So that's how I knew somewhere down there was London.'

Such is our appetite for travel that we've now reached the point where our habit is scarring the view of our planet from space. Meanwhile, back on the ground, transport-related pollution – predominantly as a result of aviation and car use – is believed by many, including the government, to be playing a major part in global climate change. And it is getting worse each year: transport is predicted to become the largest source of greenhouse emissions by 2020 if current trends continue. It begs the question, both literally and metaphorically, where are we heading?

On a basic level, we are all travelling more than ever, and increasingly by car or plane. In the UK, half the population flies at least once a year. And on a daily level, we are travelling ever further and prefer our cars over public transport. A study conducted by the Department for Transport in 2001 analysed how far the average Briton travels each year within the UK. The distance was 6,815 miles – a rise of five per cent on the previous decade. Car travel made up four-fifths of the total distance travelled, an 11 per cent increase since the last such study in the early 1990s. Over the same period, the average distance travelled on shopping trips, daily commutes and school runs all increased by between 17 and 27 per cent – another indication of our growing reliance on cars. In contrast, walking distances fell by 20 per cent and local bus journeys outside London fell by 30 per cent. Only train travel increased alongside aviation and car use during this period.

The reasons for this can be largely pinned on two factors: basic economics and our perception of convenience. Despite drivers' concerns about high fuel costs and taxes, motoring is now cheaper by five per cent in real terms than it was 30 years ago, whereas over the same period rail fares have increased by over 80 per cent and bus fares by over 70 per cent. And as a result of the UK's long history of under-investment in public transport, many of us would still rather sit alone in a car in traffic jams (84 per cent of cars engaged in commuting or business trips have only one occupant) rather than jostle for a seat on late-running buses and trains.

In the skies the story is much the same. Aviation has been revolutionised by budget airlines that allow us to jet off to Europe and beyond on a whim, often for less than the price of a taxi journey to the airport. Holidaying abroad has never been cheaper or easier. The 1990s witnessed a transformation in the way we holiday, too. The traditional two-week package holiday has been joined by weekend 'minibreaks' and backpacker trips. As a result, our footprint is increasingly being felt – for good and bad – across the world.

For as long as we continue to rely on fossil fuels to move us from A to B, our unprecedented mobility will continue to have a profound impact on the environment. Transport is now responsible for 27 per cent of the UK's carbon dioxide emissions, a 50 per cent rise in just over a decade. To get a sense of how this problem could balloon even further we need only look at the scale of the problem in the US, a country that has about a third of the world's 776 million vehicles currently in use – almost, on average, a vehicle for every citizen. US cars alone now emit so much CO_2 that, if they were hypothetically considered a nation, they would be listed as the fifth most polluting nation in the world behind only the US, China, Russia and Japan (in order, the world's most polluting nations). And to power all its vehicles, the US needs vast amounts of oil. Of the 20 million barrels of oil the US uses a day, two-thirds are for transport. With over half of its oil imported from abroad, many claim that US demand for oil is causing tension and even conflict in oil-rich, but volatile regions of the world, such as the Middle East. It has been estimated by Dr Amory Lovins, the director of the Rocky Mountain Institute – a US sustainability thinktank – and co-author of *Natural Capitalism: The Next Industrial Revolution*, that this reliance on imports could be avoided by simply improving the average fuel efficiency of US vehicles by just 2.7 miles per gallon.

Where the US goes, others tend to follow. China, in contrast to the US, currently consumes just five million barrels of oil a day and has 18 million vehicles on its roads. But as its consumer class (see page 6) expands, what will be the oil demands of China's 1.3 billion people (as a comparison, the US population currently stands at 294 million) in 20 years' time? Such is the dominance of car culture in the west it is sometimes easy to forget that the car is the primary mode of transport for only six per cent of the world's population – a statistic that is surely set to rise.

However, climate change (see page 152) isn't the only negative consequence of our love affair with flying and driving. The list of other problems is long and far-reaching: localised air pollution leading to health problems such as asthma; road-related fatalities and injuries; social exclusion caused by busy roads; noise pollution; the impact of road-building on wildlife and rural environments; the rapid spread of disease through tourism…

So what's the answer? That everyone stop travelling? Now that we have a taste for super-mobility, it's unlikely that the distance we travel each year will ever be reduced. Instead, we must strive for two goals: an increased uptake of public transport, as well as more widespread use of greener fuels and forms of transport. Both strategies will require a huge shift in mindset for many of us and will largely hinge on our means and where we live. Relying on public transport in a remote rural area, for example, could be a challenge too far for many.

This chapter aims to show two things. First, why our car addiction needs to be tackled and how to meet that challenge. Second, how damaging our holiday habit can be and what the alternatives are.

Bon voyage.

On the road to where?

'The choice of vehicle you drive has a greater effect on the environment than any other choice you make as a consumer.' The Union of Concerned Scientists

They are one of the world's greatest sources of pollution, their presence blights much of our landscape, and they are responsible for thousands of deaths each year through accidents and air pollution. But for as long as cars continue to give us a sense of freedom and mobility, their allure will remain irresistible.

Despite repeated attempts by the government to drive us from our cars and onto public transport, the majority of us would still rather sit stubbornly behind the wheel, even if it means perpetuating the problems we all associate with driving – traffic congestion, escalating fuel prices, pollution, road taxation, parking, aggressive driving and so on.

We have become so accustomed to the convenience that a car offers – the ability to nip to the shops, drop the kids off at school, commute to work – that the thought of life without one is unthinkable for many. The problem is made worse by the fact that the alternatives – taking the bus or train, cycling or walking – are still not seen as equitable substitutes. So the government, which is committed to meeting strict transport pollution targets, has to turn to the stick as opposed to the carrot, using increasingly draconian methods – congestion charging, road tolls, high fuel tax – to reduce our car use.

Some of it works – the first year of congestion charging in London saw a 19 per cent reduction in carbon emissions within the congestion zone and a 38 per cent increase in bus use. But some of it is less successful – the M6 private toll road extension failed to attract the predicted number of users in its first year after opening in 2003, with many drivers preferring to avoid the tolls by sticking to the original congested motorway.

Meanwhile, car manufacturers and petrochemical giants continue to lobby hard for us to keep on the road. Adverts seduce us with images of cars as great liberators, speeding us with ease through empty, beautiful landscapes, all the while protecting us from danger as well as providing luxurious comfort. Driving a 'good' car has become one of the most overt symbols of one's wealth and status.

Behind the scenes, the mighty 'road lobby' – those with financial interests in car sales and use – pressure politicians to dilute any anti-car policy plans they may be considering. The economy would suffer, they say. Motorists – the vast majority of whom have a vote – would not be happy, they point out.

But something must be done to pour cold water on this love affair. It pays to point out in detail some of the facts and figures about how damaging to society our reliance on cars is proving to be:

- Of each 1,000 units of pollution in urban areas, 560 come from cars, and just seven from buses and coaches.
- Road congestion grew by 73 per cent between 1980 and 2002.
- According to the Department of Health, up to 24,000 early deaths a year result from poor air quality in our cities, much of it caused by exhaust fumes.
- In 2003, 3,508 people were killed on our roads – 171 of them children. Nearly 34,000 were gravely injured. Put another way, the people who die on our roads every year would fill 30 commercial airliners. In fact, deaths caused by cars in the UK since 1945 now

outnumber the deaths of British soldiers during the second world war. One in 17 of us will be killed or seriously injured in a road crash.

- A quarter of a car's lifetime environmental pollution and 20 per cent of its energy expenditure occur during its manufacture.
- The AA and RAC calculate that the true cost of keeping a car in the UK – tax, fuel, insurance, repairs, etc – is around 35p a mile. Public transport is typically far less costly – both in terms of wallet and pollution.
- Car ownership is increasing fast. Just 28 per cent of households in the UK did not have access to a car in 1999/2001, according to the Department for Transport, compared with 33 per cent in 1989/1991. This varied from 15 per cent in rural areas to 38 per cent in urban areas.
- Congestion and pollution are going to get worse as car use increases. There are already 31 million motorists and 50,000 commercial vehicle operators in the UK. Globally, the problem looks even bleaker with the appetite for cars expanding fast in economies such as China and India. In 1950, eight million cars were produced worldwide. In 1980 the figure stood at 28.6 million, whereas in 2002 the figure was 40.6 million (15.6 million of which were 'light trucks', see page 147).
- In 6,000 miles a car will produce roughly its own weight in CO_2 emissions.
- In Europe, about 75 per cent of a car is recycled through the scrap metal industry. The remaining 25 per cent – much of it made up of plastic and toxic components – is sent to landfill.
- Asthma rates in the UK have increased fourfold in the last 30 years, a problem that, in large part, is being blamed by the charity Asthma UK, as well as a growing consensus of scientists, on car fumes.
- Cars induce us to be lazier and so unhealthier. Over a third of car journeys are less than two miles in distance. Research in the US has shown that people who live in the suburbs, where car ownership tends to be at its highest, weigh six pounds (2.7kg) more than those living in the city centres, where the use of public transport, as well as cycling and walking, is much higher.

So what's the answer? Should cars be banned? Obviously, that idea would never even get out of first gear. As befits a complex problem, the answer appears to be multifaceted and requires urgent action from driver, manufacturer and government alike. All need to radically re-adjust their current mindsets and habits but, given the scale of damage that cars cause, it is the drivers who can make the most impact by:

- **Reducing car use wherever practicably possible**
- **Supporting emerging cleaner fuels and engines**
- **Supporting alternative forms of transport**
- **Using cars more efficiently and with greater consideration for others**

Naturally, this is always easier said than done but, amid the gloomy statistics listed above, there are signs that the problem is, at last, starting to be tackled.

Environmentalists have long dreamed that alternative fuel sources could be found to replace oil but it now appears that some car manufacturers are starting to make strides in building 'hybrid' engines, as well as engines that are powered with much cleaner fuels, such as hydrogen. Toyota and Honda now offer hybrid cars that combine two sources of power – petrol and electricity – and by doing so can achieve much improved fuel efficiency (currently, about twice that of conventionally powered cars). These cleaner cars entitle their drivers to receive road-tax concessions, congestion-charge exemptions and even government grants to help purchase these vehicles.

Alternative fuels are also starting to gain market acceptability. Hydrogen-powered travel has long been a fantasy – one that has always suffered from memories of the *Hindenburg* disaster in 1937 (mistakenly so, as it happens, because it was the zeppelin's highly flammable fabric that ignited, not the hydrogen) – but now the technology is starting to find its way onto our roads. Hydrogen-powered (or 'fuel cell', as the technology is more commonly known) cars and buses have already been manufactured, but the problem is that the 'green' hydrogen they run on almost always comes from mixing fossil fuels – such as natural gas – with high-temperature steam.

To break this chain, researchers are now looking for ways to generate hydrogen from the cheapest, greenest and least exhaustible source of energy of all – sunlight – principally through the production of ethanol (alcohol produced via the fermentation of plant matter).

Using ethanol as a biofuel is already big business in places such as Brazil, where fermented sugar cane is used to run cars, and in the US, where it is used as an additive in gasoline. In fact, some 2.8 billion gallons of ethanol are now produced each year for vehicles in the US from the fermentation of corn and other biomass. It costs about a dollar a gallon – roughly the same as for petrol in the US – but much of this cost comes from purifying rather than producing ethanol. The hope is that over the next decade this technology can be refined further and help replace more and more fossil fuels.

Beyond the adoption of these new technologies, many other simple efforts can help to reduce the impact of car use, as page 148 will show.

Spotlight

As cheap as chip oil

There's nothing like a financial incentive to change people's habits – even if it does mean breaking the law. In 2002, a small group of drivers from Llanelli in south Wales showed how quickly a viable market could be created for alternative fuels when they established a moonshine biofuel operation.

Suspicions were first aroused when the local Asda supermarket noticed that its extra-value cooking oil was selling in vastly greater quantities than at other stores around the country. A special 'frying squad' was set up by Dyfed-Powys police to investigate. Rationing was imposed and the frying squad – whose tactics included sniffing out the tell-tale chip-shop smell of the illegally powered cars – eventually discovered that hundreds of local drivers were running their diesel-powered cars on the cooking oil by mixing it with methanol at home. By doing so, they were creating a 32p-a-litre fuel supply compared with 73p at forecourt diesel pumps – thereby highlighting (and, of course, evading) the extensive levels of tax placed on fuels by the chancellor.

Dozens of motorists had their cars impounded and then were forced to pay £650 to Customs and Excise to get their vehicles back. The AA warned drivers that using cooking oil could severely damage their vehicles' engines, but drivers who were caught reported no ill-effects, maintaining that it had halved their motoring costs and resulted in much cleaner emissions.

The story illustrates how viable biofuels could be. Ironically, within a month of the operation's exposure, Asda announced it was trialling the use of waste from its kitchens' frying pans as fuel for its fleet of lorries. As Asda produces more than 50 million litres of used cooking oil and 138,000 litres of waste frying fat every year from its canteens, restaurants and rotisseries, it made sense. Unlike the moonshine fuel, this commercial biodiesel ('biodiesel', as seen in some garage forecourts, is typically a blend of five per cent biodiesel and 95 per cent ultra-low-sulphur diesel) was completely legal, but still undercut diesel prices by at least 10p a litre. Furthermore, the Asda trials showed that emissions were up to 40 per cent lower than from diesel.

Sadly, though, Asda later concluded that the duty levied on its biodiesel was still too high – by about 10p, it claimed – to make it economic in the long term and the scheme was abandoned. (Asda now sends much of its waste oil to be converted into 'technical oils' for use in industry.) But others are still striving to make more UK motorists consider the benefits of biofuels. For more information, visit www.biodiesel.co.uk.

Road hogs

In May 2004, London's mayor, Ken Livingstone, made headlines when he said that people who drove SUVs (Sports Utility Vehicles, but also known variously as 4x4s, 4WDs or 'off-roaders') were 'complete idiots' who deserved to pay double the city's normal congestion charge of £5. But as sales of SUVs in London grew by 51 per cent during 2004, it seems that we are not listening to the mounting evidence that these vehicles are a pernicious influence on both the environment and road safety.

● Only five per cent of SUVs are ever driven 'off-road'.

● SUVs are responsible for 43 per cent more greenhouse emissions and 47 per cent more air pollution than the average car.

● Driving a 13 miles-per-gallon (mpg) SUV rather than the average 22mpg car for one year wastes more energy than if you:

    Left a fridge door open for six years

    Left a TV on for 28 years

    Left a light on for 30 years

● The occupant death rate for a mid-sized SUV in a collision is six per cent higher than for a mid-sized car, according to US government studies.

● The occupants of a vehicle hit by an SUV are 27 times more likely to be killed than the occupants of a vehicle hit by a normal car. They also kill between two and three times as many pedestrians and cyclists than smaller cars.

● SUVs – which have been shown in some tests to be particularly unstable when turning tight corners at speed – roll over in 37 per cent of fatal crashes compared to a 15 per cent roll-over rate for normal cars. The world's largest SUV, the Ford Excursion, is 19 feet long (5.7m), six-and-a-half feet (2m) wide and weighs nearly four tonnes. It has safety bars to stop other vehicles sliding under it during an accident.

● Due to their elevated height, glare from SUV headlights can be 10 to 20 times worse than recommended levels.

● According to the manufacturers, the largest SUVs can travel 13mpg in urban areas. But US journalists recently found that the Ford Excursion, for example, achieves something more like 4mpg.

● Profit margins on SUVs are about 10 times that of smaller, more efficient cars. This helps to explain why they are so popular with manufacturers.

● 'Light trucks' is the government-sanctioned definition for SUVs in the US that allows them to escape fuel-efficiency laws applicable to cars. Light trucks now account for more than half of all new vehicles sold in the US. In comparison, the ten most fuel-efficient cars in the US make up just two per cent of annual sales.

Reducing the impact of cars

There are many ways to improve the fuel efficiency of your car. Below are some simple tips suggested by Transport Energy (www.transportenergy.org.uk), the transport arm of the Energy Saving Trust:

● Service your car regularly and check the pressure of your tyres, as this can make a huge difference when it comes to managing fuel consumption.

● Remove any unnecessary weight from the car, including roof racks when you're not using them.

● Drive smoothly and consistently using higher gears when you can.

● Switch off your engine if you're not moving.

● Share your car journeys with other people where possible.

● Use your air conditioning and other on-board electrical devices (for example, mobile phone chargers) sparingly.

● Don't rev your engine on cold starts. Modern engines now allow you to drive off as soon as possible after starting. Also remember that catalytic converters do not start their job of combusting harmful unburned hydrocarbons until a couple of miles into a journey.

● In the US, the Neighbourhood Pace Program urges members to act as 'mobile speed bumps' when driving to slow other drivers down to the speed limit. Drivers are also urged to take the 'Pledge to Slow Down' and place pledge bumper stickers on their cars. In the UK, Transport 2000 has now initiated a similar scheme.

● Attend a local speed awareness programme. For more information, visit www.slower-speeds.org.uk, www.brake.org.uk, and www.thinkroadsafety.gov.uk.

● Remember that driving at 50mph is 25 per cent more fuel-efficient than driving at 70mph.

● Urge your employer to set up a workplace travel plan to encourage more employees to travel car-free. In 2002, 70 per cent of people went to work by car (up from 59 per cent in 1986). Most travelled alone. For details on how to set up a travel plan, visit www.local-transport.dft.gov.uk/travelplans, or contact the Association for Commuter Transport (www.act-uk.com, tel: 020 7348 1987).

● Before buying a new car investigate whether joining a car-sharing scheme or car club could prove to be more time-efficient and cost-effective. Contact Carplus (www.carclubs.org.uk, tel: 0113 234 9299), www.liftshare.com and www.nationalcarshare.co.uk for more details.

● If you're buying a new car, consult the Environmental Transport Association's Car Buyer's Guide first for ratings of the cleanest cars on the market. However, co-ownership of a second-hand car is a better environmental option – if the car isn't too fuel-inefficient. ETA inspectors can advise on the enviro-credentials of used vehicles, looking for features such as a catalytic converter, low engine capacity and power, high miles per gallon and low top speed. Also, arrange your car insurance with ETA, which is not part of the road lobby and raises awareness about the various impacts of driving (www.eta.co.uk, tel: 01932 828882).

● Always primarily base any new car purchase on the vehicle's carbon emissions rating. For full emission listings on all new cars visit www.vcacarfueldata.org.uk.

● Always investigate using alternative fuels, such as electricity, biodiesel and LPG (liquid petroleum gas). Visit www.northwales.org.uk/bio-power, www.lpga.co.uk, www.biodiesel.co.uk, www.plugitin.co.uk, www.evuk.co.uk

and www.cleaner-drive.co.uk for more details. Grants now exist to help with the cost of adapting your current car, or with the purchase of a new cleaner car. In the first instance, apply for the PowerShift grant available through Transport Energy (www.transportenergy. org.uk, tel: 0845 602 1425).

● Don't believe the hype that diesel is necessarily 'cleaner' than petrol. Diesel engines are more fuel-efficient, but they emit more nitrogen oxides, sulphur dioxide and more particulates. Friends of the Earth recommend that the best option, if you must have a car, is to choose a petrol car with a catalytic converter.

● Never forget how much car ownership can cost you beyond the day-to-day costs of fuel. Most people pay between £2,500 and £3,800 a year to own a car, with the average car cost totalling £71.59 per week – more than food or housing on average. This includes depreciation, interest lost, insurance, breakdown cover, MOT, tax, spares, servicing, parking, fuel and fines.

● Pay attention to the way other people drive near your home. If you are irritated by their bad habits – speeding, revving of their engines, loud music, irresponsible parking – remember this when you're driving past other people's homes.

Leaving the car behind...

● One of the major complaints made by people using public transport is that the different services – bus, tram, train, tube – are not well integrated. To counter this, in 2004 the Department of Transport set up Transport Direct (www.transportdirect.info), the world's first door-to-door travel advice service.

● Join Sustrans (www.sustrans.org.uk, tel: 0845 113 0065). It is the UK's leading sustainable transport charity and has campaigned for the 10,000-mile-long National Cycle Network, as well as schemes such as Safe Routes to Schools, Safe Routes to Stations and Home Zones.

● Get a cycle map that shows you the safest road routes to use on a bike. The Sustrans website has a full listing, but most local councils and tourist offices also supply them free.

● Encourage children to walk or cycle to school. Since 1989/1991, the proportion of primary-aged children walking to school has declined from 62 to 54 per cent, with an increase from 27 to 39 per cent in the numbers being driven to school. Consider joining, or setting up, a 'walking bus' (see page 217).

● Lobby your local council for more cycle lanes. In 2003/4, cycling in London rose by 23 per cent, largely due to the city's increasingly cycle-friendly environment. The Netherlands has doubled the distance covered by its cycle lanes in the past 20 years and Germany has tripled its network. Cycling now accounts for some 12 per cent of all trips in Germany and some 27 per cent in the Netherlands, compared with less than one per cent in countries such as the US where the car is king. In addition, there are about four times as many cycling fatalities per kilometre travelled in the US as in Germany or the Netherlands.

● Campaign against ill-considered road-building. For a list of current anti-road-building campaigns around the UK visit www.roadalert.org.uk.

● Write to your local train operators to urge them to offer more cycle racks in stations and in carriages. There are 22 million bicycles in the UK and over 60 per cent of the population live within a 15-minute cycle ride of a railway station. Yet the proportion of rail journeys that start by bike is very low compared with many other comparable northern European countries: less than one per cent of the UK's rail journeys start by bike compared with 15 per cent in Germany, 35 per cent in Denmark, and 38 per cent by bike and scooter in the Netherlands.

● Support, or mimic, innovative 'healthy transport' ideas, such as the Walsall 'Groundmiles' scheme. The borough of Walsall has developed a loyalty scheme which rewards local citizens for attending 'healthy' guided walks through the area in exchange for loyalty vouchers redeemable as public transport tickets.

● Transport 2000, the national environmental transport body, campaigns for sustainable transport solutions and against excessive road building. Join its activists' email action group (www.transport2000.org.uk/takeaction/ JoinActionGroup.asp), which keeps activists and campaigners in touch with each other and encourages them to write letters of complaint to relevant organisations.

● Campaign for your residential street to become a HomeZone, where pedestrians and cyclists are given priority over car users. For more information, visit www.homezonenews.org.uk.

● Encourage confidence in your cycling by attending a cycling proficiency course (many courses are now free) as well as buying the right bike for your needs. Do your research and buy from a specialist bike shop. Look out for shops that belong to the Association of Cycle Traders (www.act-bicycles.com), and staff who are CyTech accredited — a national level of competence for mechanics accepted by all the major cycling organisations. To counter the threat of theft it is also a good idea to register your frame number with Bike Register (www.bikeregister.com), for added peace of mind.

● Join a local cycling club, or a national organisation such as the Cyclists' Touring Club (www.ctc.org.uk, tel: 0870 873 0060) and the British Cycling Federation (www.bcf.uk.com, tel: 0161 274 2000). Also, join a local walking club through the Ramblers Association (www.ramblers.org.uk, tel: 020 7339 8500).

● If you still have doubts about the merits of a bike over a car, remember that for an average journey of four miles in an urban area, cycling is the fastest mode of transport. Also, contrary to common perception, people in cars are, according to Transport for London, exposed to four times more air pollution than pedestrians or cyclists.

● Use the bus more. At least 87 per cent of households in the UK live within six minutes' walk of a bus stop.

● Remember that there are many local public transport user groups. All lobby for better services and you can use them to complain about poor standards if a service operator isn't responding to your needs or concerns. Full listings are available from the National Federation of Bus Users (www.nfbu.org) and the Rail Passengers Council (www.railpassengers.org.uk).

● Support any grassroots campaign in your area that aims to counter the impact of car culture on the local community. Good starting points include the Way To Go campaign (www.waytogo.org.uk) and the Living Streets initiative (www.livingstreets.org.uk).

● Do you even need to make a journey at all? Remember that innovations in home shopping, teleworking and teleconferencing are now making many mundane journeys redundant. Invest in broadband technology at home.

EXPLAINER Climate change

What is climate change?

In case you hadn't noticed, something is happening to our weather. Be it ever more severe droughts in sub-Saharan Africa, increased flooding in Bangladesh, or simply earlier springs in Britain, all these signs point to an overall rise in global temperature.

In fact, over the past century, there has been a 2C (3F) rise in the average global temperature – a similar rise to that which ended the last ice age. The knock-on effect of this rise has been marked: over the same period, there has been a 15 per cent retreat by the polar ice caps, a 25-centimetre rise in sea levels, and a recent run of record hot years – seven of the warmest years in recorded history globally occurred during the 1990s, with 1998 the hottest of all.

All climatologists accept that global temperatures have tended to rise and fall across the millennia, but what is causing concern is that this latest rise has happened so fast. The fact that it also coincides with a sharp spike in the amount of anthropogenic (man-made) carbon emissions released into the atmosphere is particularly unsettling as it heavily implies one thing: we are, in large part, to blame.

Although the detail is still fiercely debated, there is now little doubt among the world's climatologists that the planet's 'carbon cycle' – the balanced cyclical process by which carbon is repeatedly emitted (through, for example, forest fires) and then stored (plant photosynthesis) in our environment – has somehow been affected by anthropogenic emissions. Even though we have – in the past, at least – produced a relatively small percentage of the total amount of carbon dioxide (CO_2) released into the atmosphere (natural causes include decay by fungi and bacteria, respiration by other animals, forest fires and volcanoes), there is a growing body of evidence that suggests it has been enough to

'tip the balance' and, via the famous 'greenhouse effect', increase the average global temperature. But now that the tipping point has been passed, future rises could be much more rapid.

We have been releasing CO_2 into the atmosphere for thousands of years through the burning of wood, but it is only in the past 250 years – since the dawn of the industrial age – that evidence points to the carbon cycle being affected by our actions. Since 1750, for example, the overall atmospheric concentration of CO_2, anthropogenic or not, has increased by 31 per cent (and is still increasing at 0.4 per cent per year). It is believed that this rise is largely attributable to the burning of oil, coal and gas, and the large-scale felling of forests. This makes sense when you consider that anthropogenic CO_2 emissions have risen from 100 million tonnes per year in the 1700s to around 6.3 billion tonnes a year today – about twice what the biosphere (the sea and the atmosphere) can easily handle.

As a result of our ever burgeoning transport, heating, electrical and industrial needs, the atmospheric concentrations of CO_2, one of the principal greenhouse gases, are now probably higher than they have been for 20 million years. Quite some going for just 250 years' work.

What will be its effects?

Put simply, it is going to keep getting hotter.

The United Nations Intergovernmental Panel on Climate Change (IPCC), currently the most respected body of climate experts in the world, concedes that unless current emission trends are not just slowed, but reversed, global temperatures could rise by 4C (7F) by 2050 and 6C (10F) by 2100.

This won't simply mean that Britain enjoys a more Mediterranean-type climate. Future-gazing is a notoriously inaccurate business, but all predictions for the influence of climate change suggest the effects will be universally negative. For example, one study by Belgian and British scientists estimates that a 3C (5F) rise would be enough to see an increase of 80 million malaria cases a year and would allow the disease to spread to Australia, the US and southern Europe.

In 2004, researchers at the United Nations University announced that by 2050 two billion people — twice the present number — could be at risk from the type of devastating flooding that currently occurs once every 100 years or so. Also in 2004, a major study published in *Nature* magazine showed that climate change over the next 50 years is expected to drive a quarter of land animals and plants into extinction. Chris Thomas, a professor of conservation biology at Leeds University, and the lead author of the research from four continents, called the results 'terrifying', estimating that more than one million species will be lost by 2050.

But the effects are not just something for future generations to deal with; many argue that climate change is already having a devastating effect. In 2003, for example, 21,000 deaths in Europe — seven times the number killed in the September 11 terrorist attacks — were attributed to that summer's freak heatwave.

Are we really sure it is a man-made process?
'Two per cent of climatologists can't be wrong', goes the joke. Much is made of the fact that there is still doubt and rancour among scientists over whether climate change is being caused by human habits, or is simply a natural phenomenon. The truth, however — as the joke highlights — is that only a tiny percentage of scientists, most of whom are accused of having vested interests, doubt that climate change is linked to human activity. The prevailing concern is now over how extreme the effects of climate change will be in coming decades, and what the best strategies are to counter it.

Much of the public's uncertainty seems to have stemmed from a high-profile campaign in the late 1990s known as the 'Oregon Petition'. Eighteen thousand 'scientists' signed this, agreeing that they were sceptical of global warming theories linked to anthropogenic emissions. The campaign was later widely discredited as being the work of a fringe US institute that allowed a range of people, including Geri Halliwell, to be listed as 'scientists' on the petition. Even so, it achieved its intention of planting doubt in the public's mind.

As if to underline how far opinions have changed in the past few years, even oil chiefs are now agreeing we are to blame, as John Browne, the chief executive of BP, illustrated in 2004: '[Global warming] is undoubtedly due in large part to substantial increases in CO_2 emissions from human activity.'

How can it be stopped?
Not easily or immediately, and only with the combined will and co-operation of everyone on the planet.

To illustrate how acute the problem has become, even if we stabilised CO_2 emissions at today's levels, by 2100 the concentration of CO_2 in the atmosphere would be at 'dangerous' levels, according to the IPCC. In the 18th century, the atmosphere contained about 270 parts per million (ppm) of CO_2. Today the figure stands at 370ppm. Even by sticking at today's emission levels, concentrations would still rise by 1.5ppm a year, reaching 520ppm by 2100. However, most climatologists say levels would need to stabilise at 420ppm if we are to witness only what they describe as 'warming light', where climate change would be damaging, but sufferable.

In which case, we need to quickly reverse current

'Climate change is the most **severe problem** we are facing today, **more serious even** than the threat of terrorism'

Sir David King, the UK government's chief scientific adviser, January 2004

emissions trends. In simple terms, it is estimated that if we are to avoid reaching levels of 520ppm, each person on the planet would need to emit no more than 1.2 tonnes of carbon a year – which is about a third of average current per-capita emissions in industrialised nations, and one sixth of the per-capita emissions in the US, the world's largest polluter. A big task indeed. There are many ideas about how this could be achieved, but the overriding message is that our energy-intensive lifestyles must be curtailed, whether it's through self-discipline, technological advances, legislation or financial incentives.

International consensus over national emission targets is notoriously hard to achieve, as demonstrated by the diplomatically divisive Kyoto Protocol. (Russia finally signed up to the target-setting treaty in 2004, joining 29 other industrialised countries in doing so, and now, of the major industrialised countries, only the US and Australia still refuse to sign up.) Much hope is now pinned on the establishment of a market-based carbon-trading scheme in which every person on the planet would be given an annual quota of allowable emissions (the EU, and some states in the US, are currently trialling such schemes; for more information, visit www.pointcarbon.com). Richer, more polluting countries could then buy 'carbon credits' from poorer, less-polluting countries, creating a financial and equitable incentive to reduce emissions.

Others, especially the energy firms, are looking to sequestration as an answer – a way of 'locking away' carbon emissions by pumping them underground, typically into cavities left by oil and gas extraction. 'Sequestration is difficult, but if we don't have sequestration I see very little hope for the world…The timescale might be impossible. In which case I'm really very worried for the planet.' Not the alarmist words of an environmental campaigner, but, again, the view of an oil chief, this time Ron Oxburgh, the chairman of Shell. Even so, the logic behind such a move seems to be 'let's find a way to allow us to keep burning fossil fuels at the same rate as we do now'.

Ultimately, a meaningful reduction in emissions can't just be left to governments, multinationals and international agencies. Everyone must make their own individual effort to reduce the greenhouse gases being emitted as a result of their lifestyle. And with just 15 per cent of Americans associating global warming with fossil-fuel consumption, tackling apathy is perhaps the first battle.

Further reading
www.guardian.co.uk/climatechange
www.newscientist.com/hottopics/climate
www.bbc.co.uk/climate
www.tyndall.ac.uk
www.eci.ox.ac.uk
www.cru.uea.ac.uk
www.defra.gov.uk/environment/climatechange
www.rcep.org.uk
www.changingclimate.org
www.metoffice.com/research/hadleycentre
www.ukcip.org.uk
www.dtqs.org
www.climatescience.gov
www.ipcc.ch
www.risingtide.org.uk

Air travel

At any given moment, on average, 400,000 of us will be flying in 3,500 planes over Europe. Despite an illustrious, even glamorous history, aviation is now little more than a mundane, workhorse service.

Even so, we've developed quite a taste for it. Half the population of the UK now flies at least once a year and the industry is predicted to grow to three times its current size over the next 30 years. The distance flown by UK travellers has almost doubled between 1990 and 2000 from 125 billion kilometres to 260 billion kilometres a year. And three-quarters of this air traffic is classified as 'leisure' traffic, as opposed to business traffic. We're travelling more frequently and further than ever before in the pursuit of our holidays. By 2050 it is predicted that our airports will need to serve over one billion passengers a year which, according to campaign group Airport Watch, will necessitate the equivalent of five new Heathrows by 2030.

But as the capacity of current terminals and runways rapidly reaches saturation point, air congestion is already a very real problem. Some air traffic controllers have predicted that Europe's skies could be 'full' in just over a decade. To cope with booming numbers, the 'height separation' between aircraft has already been cut from 2,000ft to 1,000ft. With Swiss air traffic controllers reporting four near-misses in April 2004 alone, some experts, including the head of Eurocontrol, the agency that co-ordinates Europe's national air traffic control centres, are increasingly worried about the ability of current procedures to cope with the predicted growth in air traffic.

Budget flights

Compounding the problem is the take-off in popularity of the budget airlines over the past decade. The 20 or so different budget airlines currently operating within Europe now service around 500 routes across the continent, ferrying about 40 per cent of the UK's holidaymakers. Many domestic routes, such as the London to Newquay service introduced by Ryanair, offer previously unparalleled convenience and time-saving, while also routinely undercutting the price of rail services for the equivalent journey. Friends of the Earth points out that while bus fares rose by 42 per cent between 1984 and 1999, and rail fares by 35 per cent, air fares have dropped by 10 per cent over the past decade.

So should we praise budget flights for democratising air space, thereby providing everyone with membership to the 'jet set'? Not according to a MORI poll conducted in 2001. It found that just over half of all flights for that year were made by a mere 11.3 per cent of the population, comprised mostly of people earning over £30,000 per year.

Frequent fliers may think that dispensing with 'frills', such as a free sandwich, is what enables their flight to be so cheap. However, the truth lies closer to the industry's fierce competition and increased computerisation, added to the fact that aviation is one of the world's most subsidised industries, with aviation fuel still totally exempt from duty – an anomaly that remains from the days after the second world war when it was still a fledgling business. In addition, a substantial amount of EU and UK public money is directed into air traffic control systems and transport links to airports. Budget operators have also been shown to profit from 'incentivised landings', as local authorities lure them to airports in their area. Overall, the Heathrow Association for the Control of Aircraft Noise has calculated that a single person on a wage of £25,000 is paying an extra £557 a year in tax to subsidise the aviation industry.

Suddenly, budget flights don't seem so cheap.

Pollution

'Many airline customers have never thought of airports and flying as an environmental problem,' says Professor John Whitlegg, from the Stockholm Environment Institute at York University.

In fact, air travel is the world's fastest-growing source of greenhouse gas emissions. Aircraft emit vast quantities of CO_2 – one 4,428-mile flight from London to Miami, for example, produces emissions equivalent, per passenger, to 12,000 miles of car travel. To understand the full impact of one flight, now multiply this figure by the number of passengers on that flight – 350 on a Boeing 747 at full capacity.

The government has concluded that air travel already contributes 5.5 per cent of the UK's climate-changing emissions. However, because the harmful gases are released directly into one of the most sensitive parts of the atmosphere leading to 'radiative forcing', that's actually the equivalent of 11 per cent.

It is now estimated that at least one million people in the UK are affected directly by noise and air pollution due to aviation. Local pollution has been shown to have dramatic effects on areas up to 100 kilometres downwind of an airport. And noise pollution, claim people living under flight paths, can cause sleepless nights, increased blood pressure, and even impair learning capacity in children.

Innovations

Proponents of the aviation industry are putting their faith in technological improvements that minimise aircraft pollution. Aircraft designs with greater fuel efficiency can fly at lower cruise altitudes, limiting the more damaging effects of flight in the upper stratosphere.

However, while emissions have been substantially reduced for new aircraft over the past 40 years, by British Airways' own admission, these changes are 'unlikely to prevent global warming'. The Royal Commission on Environmental Pollution also warns that technological advances alone cannot take the strain, as the escalation in number of passengers outstrips the quantity and pace of any advances. The commission estimates that new models take a decade to design, plus a further decade in production, before reaching the market.

In common with runways and airports, the size of planes is expanding, too. The first A380, the world's largest passenger plane, is scheduled to fly out of Heathrow in 2006. At first glance, this seems like good news. With 558 seats, and a wingspan 15 metres larger than a Boeing 747, it could carry 10 million more passengers a year without having to increase the number of flights. But will these planes fly at full capacity? Currently, only 78 per cent of the total seats available on international flights out of the UK and 65 per cent of seats on domestic flights are filled.

As the industry continues to grow, the Institute for Public Policy Research, a UK thinktank, predicts that air travel will be responsible for one third of the UK's total greenhouse gas emissions by 2030, making 'flying by jet plane...the least environmentally sustainable way to travel'.

Far from adopting air travel as a routine part of life, we need to minimise air travel and begin to ask ourselves how necessary that plane trip is and whether there is another means of getting to our destination. The inevitable answer is to holiday more locally, use alternatives to business trips such as videoconferencing, and to use less polluting forms of transport, such as the train.

Tourism

In the summer of 2004, the number of visitors allowed to visit two popular islands off the French coast, Porquerolles and Port-Cros, was restricted to 5,000 and 1,500 a day respectively after the pressure from tourists was judged to be threatening the islands' ecosystem. Such measures could become increasingly common at the world's most popular sites, as the number of tourists continues to swell. In the 1950s there were around 25 million recorded tourist visits – defined as any leisure trip away from home, be it nationally or abroad – made globally each year; by 2002 there were 700 million. By 2020 an estimated 1.6 billion tourists will be on the move, in search of a getaway.

Overcrowding is not the only problem that tourist destinations must contend with. In Hawaii and Barbados, for example, one study found that each visiting tourist used between six and ten times as much water and electricity as a local. WWF, the environmental campaign group, has calculated that, such are the demands of the average Mediterranean holidaymaker on energy, water, food and other resources, they will use – assuming the world's citizens shared their resources equally – half of their annual 'share' of the earth's natural resources during their trip. Given that the Mediterranean receives 135 million visitors each year, that represents a significant strain.

Attempts to reduce the impact of tourism have largely met with limited success. For example, in 2002 the three million UK tourists who visited the Balearics were asked to pay an 'eco tax' of between one and two euros per night. The revenue was to be used to fund local environmental projects. But by 2003 the tax was so unpopular with the major tour operators it was scrapped by the new government. The onus, it seems, is on us, as individual tourists, to try to minimise our footprint abroad.

The country you choose to holiday in should also be a key consideration. The average UK family spends £1,830 on its annual holiday, according to research group Mintel, and package holidays are an ever-popular option with up to 20 million Britons taking them each year. But the origins of package holidays are actually political. Spain's former dictator General Francisco Franco encouraged the first UK package tourists to the sunny Costa Brava. It has been claimed that he wasn't so much seeking the company of holidaying Brits, as legitimising his regime and bringing in much-needed foreign currency. Legitimising a political regime through tourism is an idea that's existed ever since. Israel, the Philippines and Burma have each been accused in the past of doing the same thing. This leaves the tourist with the responsibility of reading between the lines of tourist brochures in order to ensure that the allure of sun and sand doesn't rise higher up their agenda than, for example, human rights issues.

The tour operators

Four out of 10 UK families who booked package tours in 2004 travelled with one of the UK's 'big five' – Thomson, Thomas Cook, First Choice, Mytravel and Cosmos. UK-based operators are known for securing some of the lowest prices in destination countries in the world. While this may sound good for those on the lookout for a bargain holiday, critics claim depressed prices paid to local hotels and associated trades, such as restaurants and day-trip firms, leave local economies completely dependent on a fickle, cut-throat market.

The long arm of multinational travel operators is not just confined to the Mediterranean region, of course. Up to 60 per cent of hotel beds in Kenya are owned by multinationals. This kind of dominance can lead to a loss of control by host countries over their tourism industry. It can also lead to a leakage of foreign currency (only 22 to 50 per cent of gross revenue, it is estimated, remains in destination countries) as well as the development of tourist enclaves that are completely isolated from local populations. This is the case with the Gambia's tourist areas, which are dominated by 17 large holiday villages, all owned by foreign companies.

Cruise ships

In 2003 revenue from British tourists taking cruises topped £1 billion for the first time. Globally, 250 cruise liners now carry 12 million passengers to some of the world's most unspoiled areas.

Superficially, at least, cruising seems like a clean and serene way to visit pristine marine ecosystems, but in reality these floating towns – the average ship carries 3,000 tourists and crew – can take a heavy environmental toll. For example, according to the Hawaii-based campaign group Earthjustice, every day the average cruise ship visiting Hawaii emits 30,000 gallons (136,500 litres) of sewage, 7,000 gallons (31,850 litres) of bilge water containing oil from engines, seven tonnes of rubbish, 255,000 gallons (1,160,000 litres) of 'grey' water, including residues of detergents, harmful dioxins and mercury from onboard incinerators, and the equivalent air pollution to 12,240 cars. The inhabitants of Molokai, the fifth largest island in Hawaii, who, say Earthjustice, receive no real financial benefits from the cruise ships that damage its natural reef system, have said they would

BANJUL INTERNATIONAL, GAMBIA

BIA

9 780091 901790 >

All of the Gambia's 17 'holiday villages' are owned by foreign companies

like to ban cruise ships from visiting.

Meanwhile, the environmental campaign group Oceana describes the cruise industry as having a 'sweet deal when it comes to environmental laws' because they are not strict enough. The global marine environment is currently protected from shipping pollution by the MARPOL Convention, which was initiated following the *Torrey Canyon* tanker spill off Cornwall in 1967. However, progress in ratifying and enforcing the convention has been slow. The current sewage discharge limits, for example, have only been enforced since 2003. A ship is now only allowed to discharge treated sewage no less than three nautical miles from the nearest land, or discharge untreated sewage no less than 12 nautical miles from the nearest land.

But the use of 'flags of convenience' can make a mockery of pollution legislation. With 72 per cent of all cruises now listed as 'fly-cruises', where passengers fly to a port before boarding their ship, many passengers may not realise that many cruise ships are, in fact, registered in places such as Panama, Liberia and the Bahamas, which can allow the owners to sidestep many international labour, environmental and safety laws.

If you are planning a cruise, thoroughly research the company you are considering travelling with. Ask to see details of what environmental standards it adheres to – in particular, evidence of your ship's track record on observing International Maritime Organisation regulations, such as the MARPOL Convention. Visit www.imo.org for more information. Also consult Oceana (www.stopcruisepollution.com) for more about the environmental impact some cruise ships can have on their destinations.

Paradise lost?

Paradise is not always what it seems. According to the campaign group Tourism Concern, nearly half of the population of the Maldives – an expensive holiday destination – now exist on less than one US dollar a day. A UN study also found 30 per cent of Maldivian children under five were suffering from malnutrition. Meanwhile, foreign tourists enjoy precious local fruit and vegetables within the confines of their tourist complexes, thereby, according to Tourism Concern, leading produce to 'bypass local people'.

Globally, jobs in tourism tend to be poorly paid and involve long, unsocial hours. Many indigenous people are becoming implicitly linked to the tourist economy, usually without any choice or benefit. In parts of eastern Africa, for example, tribes have been moved from ancestral homelands to make way for tourist resorts, giving up pastures where they have traditionally grown food. The charity Survival International says that Himalayan fields now lie uncultivated because the men who once farmed them have become porters to climbing expeditions.

The answer is not necessarily to boycott these destinations – many local people are now reliant on continued tourism – but to recognise that your holiday has consequences and to make choices accordingly.

Dilemma

Are second homes a selfish luxury or a harmless retreat?

More than one million Britons now possess a second home. Many argue that they bring extra economic benefits to their part-time community, providing custom for local businesses. This can be true, but equally, second homes can price local people out of the housing market, including many key workers such as school or medical staff.

Anger over the encroaching presence of 'second homers' isn't new. In the 1980s, Welsh extremists firebombed English-owned holiday cottages. More recently, in 2001, Exmoor National Park tried to ban second homers altogether – a move later declared to be illegal. Meanwhile, in Appledore, Devon, where four in ten homes are 'extra residences', council tax for weekenders has been increased from 50 to 90 per cent. Other councils have now followed suit.

But the second-home phenomenon is spreading its wings. British buyers now snap up thousands of foreign homes every year. Their dream of a place in the sun is increasingly realised by the expanding reach of low-cost airlines. By 2012, it is estimated that second homers will take 12 million flights a year to visit their properties, exacerbating the environmental impact of air travel.

In 2003, 40 per cent of all property sold in Spain went to non-nationals, while young Spaniards, unable to get on the property ladder, remain living with their parents in unprecedented numbers. By 2003, homes in the French region of Languedoc Roussillon cost 28 per cent more than the year before, a rise in large part attributable to second homes.

On the Istrian coast, 'for sale' signs are now displayed in English rather than Croatian, fuelling the inevitable language and cultural barriers between second homers and their part-time communities. The danger is that by living between two communities, second homers contribute fully to neither and can actually adversely affect the local community where the second home is located.

Ecotourism – is it the answer?

Over the past century, as the Grand Tour has given way to the Gap Year, tourism has emerged as one of the world's largest industries. Since it was originally seen by many as the ultimate 'smokeless' industry – and so a positive pathway to prosperity – governments all over the globe, particularly in developing nations, rushed to embrace it. Sadly, it has transpired that tourism is not as 'smokeless' as first thought.

Its negative effects were first voiced formally back in 1980 by the Ecumenical Coalition of Third World Tourism, now the world's largest travel NGO. It issued a statement arguing that tourism exploits indigenous people, pollutes fragile and important ecosystems, and rides roughshod over local cultures and communities.

Conventional tourism, it seems, is often guilty as charged, but it's clearly not possible to stop people from travelling wherever they please. However, to counter the negative impact of tourism, 'ecotourism' has emerged as a new solution. Its aim is to be a sustainable alternative, putting local people and the local environment before profit.

Despite the fact that the UN designated 2002 as the year of ecotourism, definitions of what the term precisely means remain hazy. The basic tenets of ecotourism are set out by the Washington-based International Ecotourism Society. Ecotourism, it says, should:

- **Minimise impact**
- **Build environmental and cultural awareness and respect**
- **Provide positive experiences for both visitors and hosts**
- **Provide direct financial benefits for conservation**
- **Provide financial benefits and empowerment for local people**
- **Raise sensitivity to a host country's political, environmental, and social climate**
- **Support international human rights and labour agreements**

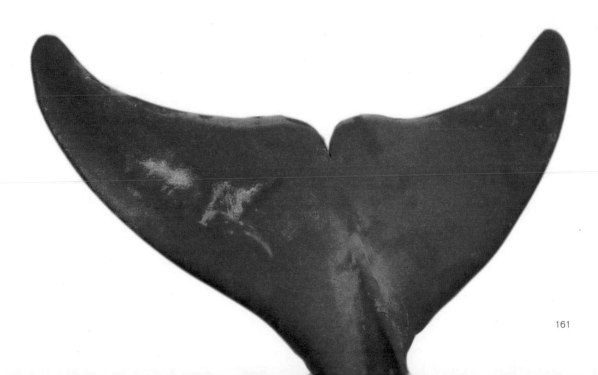

Jost Krippendorf, the late Swedish academic and author of *The Holiday Makers*, called for 'rebellious tourists and rebellious locals' to halt the march of negative mass tourism. At its best, that is what ecotourism offers. As opposed to passive holidays where holidaymakers, say, sit on the beach, the emphasis of ecotourism is on learning from an interaction with the local environment and its people. In the best-case scenarios, the local population will have an active stake in local tourist businesses, to take full advantage of the tourist dollar – as is the case, for example, for the Ese Eja Indian community, which jointly runs tourism ventures in the Tambopata National Park in Peru.

As with conventional tourism, ecotourism attracts travellers with differing views about how best to preserve and assist a destination. A 2001 study conducted by New York State's Cornell University defined 'hard end' and 'soft end' ecotourists. 'Hard end' ecotourists are environmentally aware holidaymakers who prefer long, specialised trips and maximum contact with nature via conservation projects. These travellers expect few or no luxuries on their trips. 'Soft end' ecotourists, on the other hand, expect a high level of comfort, such as, say, a luxurious hunting lodge while on safari in Kenya, but will visit national parks and game reserves. They are more concerned with leaving their destination in the same condition in which they found it, rather than actively conserving it.

Because of their appetite for seeing wildlife, ecotourists promote a 'wildlife pays, so wildlife stays' philosophy in host countries, helping to safeguard some of the world's most endangered animals. For example, tourists may pay $170 to spend an hour with gorillas in Rwanda. Overall, this generates $1 million a year to help conserve all of the gorillas in the region. Similarly, whale watching is now more lucrative globally than whale hunting and a Kenyan lion is worth an estimated $7,000 a year in tourist income.

However, ecotourism is not the perfect antidote to the ills of tourism. The environment writer David Nicholson-Lord once heard a casino in Laos being described as an example of ecotourism 'because it was positioned in untouched countryside'. Tourism Concern has highlighted the fact that many ecotourism destinations are places where native people have been excluded. The most famous example is that of the Masai communities in Kenya, evicted to make way for national parks, such as Amboseli. Equally, in Burma, thousands of people were forcibly relocated by the authorities to make room for tourist developments in Pagan.

Ecotourism is thought to account for around seven per cent of global tourism – and is predicted to grow. A poll by the World Travel Organisation showed that 85 per cent of German tourists wanted a more 'environmentally correct' holiday. This raises the question as to how sustainable ecotourism can remain as numbers swell. For instance, a cable car to carry 350,000 'ecotourists' to the world heritage site of Machu Picchu in Peru has long been under consideration – even though plans were suspended (but not abandoned) in 2001 following international protest, headed by UNESCO.

These issues serve as reminders that a backpacker can potentially do as much harm trampling to meet tribes in a rainforest as a busload of tourists visiting a popular site with an infrastructure for tourists. Consequently, the onus is on us, the potential tourists, to research our trips thoroughly, and take all the steps possible to ensure that ecotourism does not become a hollow phrase.

A **Kenyan lion** is worth an estimated **$7,000** a year in tourist income

Spotlight

'Carbon neutral'

The Day After Tomorrow, released in 2004, was the first Hollywood blockbuster to be centred on the issue of climate change. And, fittingly, it came with a 'carbon neutral' tag. To 'offset' the greenhouse-gas emissions associated with filmmaking, such as air travel and on-set generators, the studio behind the film funded a programme of tree planting in the US and Bhutan. The director, Richard Emmerich, said he got the idea from Coldplay, his favourite band, who had previously offset the emissions of a world tour by planting trees in Scotland.

The idea behind 'carbon neutralisation' is that you offset any carbon dioxide you may be responsible for by paying for enough trees to be planted to absorb the carbon released into the atmosphere as a result of your action, be it heating your home, flying to a holiday destination, or, if you're a band, going on a world tour.

Typically, this means offsetting transport emissions. A longhaul flight from London to Australia 'costs' five trees, whereas a car with a 1.8-litre engine, travelling an average of 12,000 miles per year, will set you back eight trees. Rather than getting your hands dirty, you can pay for a tree to be planted on your behalf – currently £8.50 a tree with Future Forests, the UK's leading carbon neutral company.

But there is increasing dissent as to whether this is the best way to atone for our carbon-emission sins. Some environmentalists believe that trees have a much more limited 'sink function' (the ability to absorb CO_2 then release oxygen whilst storing the carbon) than first thought. Critics such as Sinkswatch, a group that aims to 'track and scrutinise' carbon-sink projects, claim that for carbon neutrality to have any true effect on current UK emissions, trees would need to cover the whole country and not just small areas of Scotland. Of more concern to Sinkswatch, however, is that carbon-sink schemes only serve to legitimise wasteful behaviour. Leaving the carbon locked in fossil fuels would be a far more effective means of control, it says, than trying to soak up emissions afterwards.

It seems that while there can never be any harm in planting a tree, to rely on that alone as a strategy to appease the guilt associated with our energy-hungry lifestyles would be a mistake. Pre-emptive and preventative measures for cutting greenhouse emissions are always preferable.

For more information about 'carbon-neutral' schemes, visit www.futureforests.com, www.CO2.org, and www.sinkswatch.org.

To do

Way to go

According to the World Social Forum's Tourism Interventions Group, tourism should be 'equitable, people-centred, sustainable, ecologically sensible, child-friendly and gender-just'. That's a lot to consider before you've even worked out a destination, but there are simple steps you can take to reduce the impact of your holiday in both environmental and social terms…

● The least polluting holiday option by far is to explore your own 'green and pleasant land' by staying in the UK and arriving at your destination by train rather than by car or domestic flight. The mass summer holiday exodus to foreign climes is a relatively new phenomenon: 1998 was the first year that more Britons went abroad on holiday (29 million) than stayed in the UK (27 million). Try to reverse this trend.

● Venture out into new regions and spend money in local, independent hotels, restaurants and visitor attractions. Money brought into the UK by tourism tends to stay in the 'honey pots', such as Bath, York, Edinburgh and London.

● For those who like to be active, a volunteering holiday is perhaps the most community-minded way of spending your time off. UK-based Willing Workers on Organic Farms (www.wwoof.org) has placements all over the world on farms. But think hard about the method you use to get there…

● Many people find it hard to imagine going on holiday without catching a plane, but there are other ways. Train journeys, particularly across scenic routes, can become part of the holiday itself. By avoiding air transport, you'll also be bypassing the stress of airports, particularly during peak season. For inspiration, visit www.seat61.com.

● Ask yourself who will profit from your holiday. Who owns the hotel or airline? Who owns the tour agency? If you're travelling courtesy of a multinational operator and staying in a western-owned, all-inclusive resort then it's doubtful whether you'll end up contributing very much to the economy of your host destination. This is particularly true in the developing world where a significant proportion of the money you spend is likely to 'leak' out of the country to companies back in the developed world.

● Shun car hire in favour of alternative transport, such as buses, trains and bicycles. Studies have found that in the US, for example, damage to the Yosemite Valley and the southern rim of the Grand Canyon has been caused by cars.

● Stay in a locally run guesthouse, or small hotel, rather than one that's part of a large multinational chain. Not only does this ensure that money goes back to the local community, but you also get to interact more positively with the local people.

● If you're staying in a hotel, make sure it follows best environmental practice. Look for hotels that use renewable energy, such as solar power. Once there, use local resources, such as power and water, sparingly. The average tourist uses as much water in 24 hours as a villager in the developing world uses in 100 days. Reusing your hotel towel rather than sending it to the laundry every day saves precious water resources and reduces pollution caused by detergents.

● Be generous when tipping and patient with staff. Tourism is one of the most underpaid industries in the world. Staff routinely work unsocial hours for low wages, especially in hotels owned by the big multinationals.

● If considering a package holiday, remember that half-board is better than full-board. Full-board means that almost no money filters through to the local economy. The Gambian government tried banning all-inclusive holidays for this reason until it was overpowered by external commercial and political pressure.

- Eat and drink local produce. Further revenue 'leaks' out of host countries when tourists eat imported foods.

- Switch off your air conditioning when you are out for the day (only 18 per cent of holidaymakers do this). If just 50 per cent of people did, it is estimated that across the world five million tonnes of CO_2 emissions would be prevented each year.

- When visiting national parks and world heritage sites, stick to designated areas. The 700,000 annual visitors to South Africa's Kruger National Park are concentrated in just four per cent of the land, thereby financing, but not destroying, the rest of the wilderness.

- If you're booking through a tour operator, choose a member of the Association of Independent Tour Operators (www.aito.co.uk, tel: 020 8744 9280), which has formally adopted responsible tourism guidelines. They specify that member operators must protect the environment, respect local cultures, benefit local communities, conserve natural resources and minimise pollution.

- Look out for tour companies, such as ATG Oxford (www.atg-oxford.co.uk, tel: 01865 315678), that set aside part of their pre-tax profits for community projects in the host country.

- Visit greenglobe21.com to see which airlines, hotels and travel agents met the World Travel and Tourism Council's environmental standards. Likewise, for more hotel ideas, visit greenhotels.com.

- Follow Tourism Concern's traveller tips: haggle with humour and without aggression; put money into local hands by drinking local beer and fruit juice rather than imported brands; stay in locally owned accommodation; stick to footpaths, don't stand on coral, and don't buy products made from endangered animals or plants; wear respectful clothing; and always ask people if you may take their photograph. For more advice, buy a copy of Tourism Concern's *The Good Alternative Travel Guide* (www.tourismconcern.org.uk, tel: 020 7753 3330). Also buy a copy of *The Green Holiday Guide* for Great Britain and Ireland (Green Books, £9.95), which lists organic farms with B&Bs and other eco-friendly getaways.

Directory

TRANSPORT ORGANISATIONS, CHARITIES AND INFORMATION

Working towards a future with less transport-related pollution, and better public transport

A to B Magazine
☎ 01963 351649
www.atob.org.uk

Aviation Environment Federation
☎ 020 7248 2223
www.aef.org.uk

Choose Climate
www.chooseclimate.org/flying

HACAN ClearSkies
☎ 0207 737 6641
www.hacan.org.uk

The Man in Seat 61
www.seat61.com

National Federation of Bus Users
☎ 023 9281 4493
www.nfbu.org

National Rail Enquiries
☎ 08457 484950
www.nationalrail.co.uk

National Society for Clean Air
☎ 01273 878770
www.nsca.org.uk

National TravelWise Association
www.ntwa.org.uk

Rail Future
☎ 020 7249 5533
www.railfuture.org.uk

Rail Passengers Council
☎ 08453 022022
www.railpassengers.org.uk

Reclaim the Streets
www.reclaimthestreets.net

Road Alert
www.roadalert.org.uk

Roadrage
www.roadrage.org.uk

Royal Society for the Prevention of Accidents
☎ 0121 248 2000
www.rospa.com

The Slower Speeds Initiative
www.slower-speeds.org.uk

Sustainable Transport
☎ 020 7939 0781
www.sustainabletransport.org.uk

Sustrans
☎ 0845 113 0065
www.sustrans.org.uk

TRANSform Scotland
☎ 0131 467 7714
www.transformscotland.org.uk

Transport 2000
☎ 020 7613 0743
www.transport2000.org.uk

Transport Direct
www.transportdirect.info

Transport Impact Calculator
☎ 01273 878781
www.travelcalculator.org

Traveline
☎ 0870 608 2608
www.traveline.org.uk

UK Public Transport Information
www.pti.org.uk

Way to Go Campaign
www.waytogo.org.uk

Wiggly Bus
☎ 01249 460 600
www.wigglybus.com

Young TransNet
☎ 020 7843 6325
www.youngtransnet.org.uk

CARS

Information about road safety, reducing your reliance on cars, and reducing their environmental impact

Autoholics Anonymous
www.autoholics.org

Carfree Cities
www.carfree.com

Cutting Your Car Use
☎ 01904 654355
www.cuttingyourcaruse.co.uk

Department for Transport
☎ 020 7944 8300
www.dft.gov.uk

Environmental Transport Association
☎ 0800 212810
www.eta.co.uk

The Highways Agency
☎ 08457 504030
www.highways.gov.uk

In Town Without My Car
www.itwmc.gov.uk

RoadPeace
☎ 0845 4500 355
www.roadpeace.org

TransportEnergy
(for PowerShift grants)
☎ 0845 602 1425
www.transportenergy.org.uk

Vehicle Certification Agency's Car Fuel Data
☎ 0117 9515151
www.vcacarfueldata.org.uk

World Carfree Network
☎ 001 420 274 810849
www.worldcarfree.net

Alternative cars and fuels

A>>B Urban Vehicle Agency
www.agotob.com

Air Car
☎ 0034 93 362 3700
www.theaircar.com

Alternative Fuel Systems
☎ 01403 791116
www.afs.uk.com

Alternative Vehicles Technology
☎ 01823 480 196
www.avt.uk.com

The Battery Vehicle Society
☎ 020 8386 2348
www.bvs.org.uk

BioDiesel Filling Stations
www.biodieselfillingstations.co.uk

Biofuels for Sustainable Transport
www.biofuels.fsnet.co.uk

Bio-Power
☎ 01286 830312
www.bio-power.co.uk

Broadland Fuels
☎ 01493 748888
www.broadlandfuels.co.uk

Clean Vehicles
www.clean-vehicles.com

Drivelectric
☎ 0870 744 3006
www.drivelectric.com

Eco World UK
☎ 01379 652000
www.eco-world.co.uk

Electric Vehicles UK
www.evuk.co.uk

Goldenfuels
☎ 01865 423636
www.goldenfuels.com

Greenergy
☎ 020 7484 0500
www.greenergy.co.uk

Honda Civic and Insight
☎ 0845 200 8000
www.honda.co.uk

Lexus Hybrid
☎ 0845 278 8888
www.lexus-hybrid.com

Low Impact Living Initiative
(for biodiesel course)
☎ 01296 714184
www.lowimpact.org

The LP Gas Association
☎ 01425 461612
www.lpga.co.uk

Toyota Prius
☎ 0845 275 5555
www.toyota.co.uk

Vauxhall Dualfuel
☎ 01582 427200
www.vauxhall.co.uk

Veggiepower
www.veggiepower.org.uk

Lift sharing and car clubs

Carplus: the Car Club Network
☎ 0113 234 9299
www.carclubs.org.uk

Carshare (with North
London Transport)
www.northlondontransport.org

Freewheelers
www.freewheelers.co.uk

Liftshare.com
☎ 08700 111199
www.liftshare.com

MyLifts.com
www.mylifts.com

Schoolrun.org
www.school-run.org

Shareacar.com
☎ 0871 900 8201
www.shareacar.com

Shareajourney.com
☎ 01676 542901
www.shareajourney.com

Smart Moves
☎ 0845 330 1234
www.smartmoves.co.uk

VillageCarShare.com
www.villagecarshare.com

CYCLING

**Cycling retailers,
manufacturers, organisations
and advice. Also includes
electric bikes and scooters**

Bicycle Doctor
☎ 0161 224 1303
www.bicycledoctor.co.uk

Cycle Campaign Network
www.cyclenetwork.org.uk

Cycle 1st
☎ 0870 746 9557
www.cycle1st.co.uk

Cyclists', Touring Club
☎ 0870 873 0060
www.ctc.org.uk

ebikecentral
☎ 020 7727 6363
www.ebikecentral.co.uk

Eco-Lectric scooters
☎ 01246 431431
www.eco-lectric.com

The Folding Society
☎ 01384 256173
www.foldsoc.co.uk

Kinetics
☎ 0141 942 2552
www.kbikes.co.uk

London Cycling Campaign
☎ 020 7928 7220
www.lcc.org.uk

National Cycling Strategy
☎ 020 7944 2977
www.nationalcyclingstrategy.org.uk

Powabyke Electric Bikes
☎ 01225 44 3737
www.powabyke.com

ScootElectric
☎ 01206 233180
www.scootelectric.co.uk

Strida UK
☎ 0121 681 0964
www.strida.com

Velovision Magazine
☎ 01904 438224
www.velovision.co.uk

Workbike.org
www.workbike.org

Zero
☎ 020 7486 0379
www.zeroisbest.com

WALKING

**Information about achieving
a more pedestrian-friendly
environment**

Home Zone News
☎ 020 7843 6016
www.homezonenews.org.uk

Living Streets
☎ 020 7820 1010
www.livingstreets.org.uk

Oxford Pedestrians Association
☎ 01865 865070
www.oxpa.org.uk

The Ramblers Association
☎ 020 7339 8500
www.ramblers.org.uk

Sustrans: Safe Routes to Schools
☎ 0117 915 0100
www.saferoutestoschools.org.uk

Walking Bus
☎ 0870 420 3236
www.walkingbus.org

WalkingBus.com
☎ 01707 356269
www.walkingbus.com

Walk to School
www.walktoschool.org.uk

TOURISM

Ecotourism information

Including ecotourism campaign groups

Centre for Environmentally Responsible Tourism
☎ 01268 752827
www.c-e-r-t.org

Conservation International
☎ 001 202 912 1000
www.ecotour.org

Ecoturismo Latino
(for travel in South America)
www.ecoturismolatino.com

ECPAT UK
(campaigning to end child sex tourism)
☎ 0207 501 8927
www.ecpat.org.uk

Ethical Traveler
☎ 001 415 788 3666 (ext 207)
www.ethicaltraveler.com

Foreign & Commonwealth Office travel advice
☎ 0870 606 0290
www.fco.gov.uk/travel

Green Globe 21
☎ 0061 2 6257 9102
www.greenglobe21.com

The International Ecotourism Society
☎ 001 202 347 9203
www.ecotourism.org

ResponsibleTravel.com
www.responsibletravel.com

The Travel Foundation
☎ 0117 9273049
www.thetravelfoundation.org.uk

Tourism Concern
☎ 020 7133 3330
www.tourismconcern.org.uk

Holiday ideas and travel agents

Also see volunteering organisations in Community chapter

African Conservation Experience
☎ 0870 241 5816
www.conservationafrica.net

Alastair Sawday's Special Places to Stay
☎ 01275 464891
www.specialplacestostay.co.uk

ATG Oxford
☎ 01865 315678
www.atg-oxford.co.uk

Baobab
☎ 0870 382 5003
www.baobabtravel.com

Bicycle Beano
☎ 01982 560471
www.bicycle-beano.co.uk

BTCV Conservation Holidays
☎ 01302 572 200
www.btcv.org

The Cycle Holidays Directory
www.cycleholidays.co.uk

Discovery Initiatives
☎ 01285 643333
www.discoveryinitiatives.com

Dragoman
☎ 0870 499 4471
www.dragoman.com

Earthwatch Institute
☎ 01865 318838
www.earthwatch.org

Ecovolunteer
☎ 0117 965 8333
www.ecovolunteer.org.uk

Ethical Escape
☎ 01978 356273
www.ethicalescape.com

Exodus
☎ 0870 240 5550
www.exodus.co.uk

Frontier (The Society for Environmental Exploration)
☎ 020 7613 2422
www.frontier.ac.uk

Galapagos Adventure Tours
☎ 0207 407 1478
www.galapagos.co.uk

Guerba World Travel
☎ 01373 826611
www.guerba.co.uk

International Ecotourism Club
www.ecoclub.com

Little Earth Tours
☎ 01246 591155
www.little-earth.co.uk

Muir's Tours
☎ 0118 950 2281
www.nkf-mt.org.uk

Natural Discovery
☎ 0845 458 2799
www.naturaldiscovery.co.uk

Organic Holidays
☎ 01943 870791
www.organicholidays.com

Sabre Adventures
☎ 01753 585123
www.sabreadventures.co.uk

Simply Tanzania
☎ 020 8986 0615
www.simplytanzania.co.uk

Symbiosis Expedition Planning
☎ 0845 123 2844
www.symbiosis-travel.com

Tribes Travel
☎ 01728 685971
www.tribes.co.uk

Vegi Ventures
☎ 01760 755888
www.vegiventures.com

World Wide Opportunities on Organic Farms (WWOOF)
www.wwoof.org

ETHICALCONSUMER

Unless different for each product, company details are listed in first entry only.

Bicycles

Alex Moulton
☎ 01225 865895
www.alexmoulton.co.uk

Brompton
☎ 020 8232 8484
www.bromptonbicycle.co.uk

Burley Cycles
(via Fisher Outdoor Leisure)
☎ 01727 798 361
www.burley.com

Falcon Cycles
☎ 01652 656 000
brands: Claud Butler, British Eagle

Dawes
www.dawescycles.com

Orbit Cycles
☎ 0114 275 6567
www.orbit-cycles.co.uk

Pashley Cycles
☎ 01789 292 263
www.pashley.co.uk

Bus companies

For travel information, contact Traveline (www.traveline.org.uk, tel: 0870 608 2608)

First
www.firstgroup.com

Go-Ahead
www.go-ahead.com

Cars

If an alternative to a car is not possible, then:

Audi
☎ 0800 699888
www.audi.co.uk

Peugeot
☎ 0845 200 1234
www.peugeot.co.uk

Seat
☎ 0500 222222
www.seat.co.uk

Tyres

Cooper Avon Tyres
☎ 01225 703101
www.avontyres.com

Hankook
☎ 01327 304100
www.hankooktire-eu.com

Pirelli
☎ 01283 525252
www.pirelli.co.uk

Retread Manufacturers Association
☎ 01782 417777
www.greentyres.com

Petrol

Murco
☎ 01727 892400
www.murco.co.uk

Shell
☎ 0800 731 8888
www.shell.com

Motorbikes

Aprilia
www.aprilia.com

Harley Davidson
☎ 0870 904 1450
www.harley-davidson.com

Triumph
☎ 01455 251700
www.triumph.co.uk

Zap
www.zapworld.com

Car hire

Alamo
www.alamo.com

Enterprise Rent-a-Car
☎ 01252 353624
www.enterprise.com

Holiday Autos
☎ 0870 400 4447
www.holidayautos.co.uk

U-Drive
(south and south-west only)
☎ 0800 980 9966
www.u-drive.co.uk

Airlines

If an alternative to air travel is not possible, then:

Airtours
☎ 0870 238 7788
www.airtours.co.uk

bmi
www.flybmi.com

easyjet
www.easyjet.com

Holiday companies

Explore!
☎ 0870 333 4001
www.exploreworldwide.com

Responsibletravel.com
www.responsibletravel.com

Tribes Travel
☎ 01728 685971
www.tribes.co.uk

Ferries

Hoverspeed (Seacat)
☎ 0870 240 8070
www.hoverspeed.com

You

Introduction

We make a decision about the attractiveness of someone we meet in 150 milliseconds – about the same time it takes a sprinter to react to the starter gun in a 100-metre race. The snap judgement we reach will alter little beyond this point, even after we learn about the other attributes that we also associate with attraction, such as personality, sense of humour, education, wealth, status and occupation.

It's not surprising then that we spend so much time, energy and money making ourselves 'look good' – after all, attracting a mate is one of our most basic natural instincts. In both our personal and work relationships, appearance is everything. As a result, each year in the UK we spend billions on cosmetics, perfumes, gym memberships, designer clothes and toiletries. And in the past decade or so, there's been an explosion in demand for more costly or intensive services such as cosmetic surgery and luxury bodycare treatments.

In tandem with this increasing obsession with the 'body beautiful' is a booming interest in alternative medicines and treatments. In a world where 'wellbeing' is a buzzword, more and more of us are shunning the GP and instead seeking solace in non-conventional therapies that aim to cure us of the many ailments associated with our modern lifestyles, such as allergies, 'stress' (see page 264) and back pain.

An interesting reflector of this shift is the phone directory. In 2004, the Alternative Census report looked at changes in 108 key classifications in Yellow Pages directories between 1992 and 2002. The number of listings for many traditional businesses such as butchers, joiners and insurance brokers had dramatically declined. In contrast, businesses helping people to look and feel better had boomed. The section with the largest increase in entries was aromatherapy – up by 5,200 per cent. Other big growth areas included cosmetic surgery (up 1,780 per cent), diet and weight control schemes (up 1,445 per cent), make-up artists (up 1,007 per cent), reflexology (829 per cent), and saunas and sunbeds (up 299 per cent). In comparison, over the same period, greengrocers declined by 59 per cent, butchers by 40 per cent, and coppersmiths by 35 per cent.

Other research has thrown up similar findings. A report by Virgin Money in 2003 found that 'spiritual spending' (yoga, acupuncture, massage and other such therapies) had soared in Britain and was worth £670m a year. And, according to the Prince of Wales' Foundation for Integrated Health, about 20 per cent of Britons use one of the eight most popular alternative therapies (acupuncture, aromatherapy, chiropractic, homeopathy, hypnotherapy, medical herbalism, osteopathy and reflexology) between 2.8 and 5.3 times a year.

Will this interest in body improvement – whatever the method – continue to grow, or is it a passing fad? You only need to look at the US – where most of these trends originate – to see what an important part of our lives they can, and will continue to, play. In the past five years, for example, nail bars – previously almost unknown in the UK outside of the African-Caribbean community – have really taken off (with more than a little help from the aspiration- and fashion-forming TV series *Sex and the City*). In the US, the number of nail salons has increased by 374 per cent in the past decade. The industry is now worth over $6 billion a year and employs 300,000 people. Likewise, between 1997 and 2002, the number of cosmetic procedures carried out in the US more than doubled. In 2002 alone, almost 6.9 million procedures were performed, the top five being liposuction, breast augmentation, eyelid surgery, nose reshaping and breast reduction. On top of these came non-surgical procedures such as Botox, collagen injection and chemical peels.

Of more concern is that cosmetic surgery is becoming increasingly common among US teenagers. In 2002, 50,000 teenagers had chemical peels, 50,000 had laser hair-removal and 5,600 received Botox injections in the palms of their hands and under their arms to prevent sweating. A sign of things to come in the UK, perhaps?

So what do these trends say about us? That we are more self-obsessed and image-conscious than ever before? That we're now more affluent and so have the time and the means to spend on such things? The one certainty is that many of us have a complex, often troubled relationship with our body image. In 2003, an *Observer*/ICM survey provided a compelling snapshot of how we view our own bodies, as well as the bodies of those around us:

- 26 per cent thought their stomach was the least attractive part of their body
- 74 per cent believed body image affected their sex life
- 23 per cent supported genetic engineering to design 'attractive' children
- 77 per cent of men preferred women with suntans
- 41 per cent felt uncomfortable undressing in front of a new lover
- 82 per cent of women preferred clean-shaven men
- 3 per cent admitted to having had cosmetic surgery
- 59 per cent of men used at least one beauty product on a regular basis
- 16 per cent were currently members of a gym
- 41 per cent thought the media was the most important factor in dictating public perceptions of the ideal body shape
- 8 per cent said they had deliberately harmed them-selves physically

But what is the true cost of this obsession with self-image? Is all this preening, pampering, and self-medicating really 'healthy' for us? And are we happier as a result?

Most evidence suggests not. It helps to begin by looking at some of the causes. It's thought that we are living in an 'anxiety culture', where we battle – typically in vain – to meet the many expectations society sets us: to look as beautiful as a model; to have a fantastic job; to earn huge amounts of money; to be a social dynamo; to be a great lover. The reality is that striving for these goals leaves us tired, deflated, and full of self-loathing – all classic signs of depression.

The World Health Organisation (WHO) states that depression is now the second most common illness suffered by those between the ages of 15 and 44. Stress has now overtaken the common cold as the biggest cause of sick leave from work: more than five million days are lost in the UK each year due to stress. In fact, the problem is now so acute that 12 million people use antidepressant drugs in the UK, and five million people will, at any one time, be suffering some degree of depression. The future looks even bleaker with one in 10 teenagers now said to be suffering from depression.

But rather than looking to battle the causes, we still largely aim only to ease the symptoms. For example, in 2003 more than 500 under-16s were referred to plastic surgeons by their GPs, a rise of 50 per cent since 1999, with a growing number of surgeons now saying that children suffering from depression or other psychological problems can improve their self-confidence by changing their appearance.

But there's much more to be concerned about – as this chapter will show. The business of 'bettering ourselves' – be it through self-beautification, health regimes and therapies, or even fashion – can lead to many direct and indirect negative side-effects, all of which we should aim to minimise. The list of things to be aware of is long: increased exposure to the synthetic chemicals used in most cosmetics; addiction to faddy diets; obsession with a celebrity-led, image-conscious culture; over-dependence on antibiotics; rising consumer debt associated with 'keeping up appearances'; the increasing allure of self-diagnosis and self-medication; concerns about the working conditions of people making much of our high-street fashion. Here's looking at you.

Health

Wishing someone 'good health' is one of the most universal of gestures. Since time immemorial, humans have been striving to cure illness, ease pain and prolong life. Despite medical advances that have transformed, extended and saved many millions of lives, much of humankind's energy, time and intellectual capital is still spent tending the ill, seeking cures and improving medical treatments. While we have seen off or suppressed many of the diseases and illnesses, such as smallpox, that blighted previous generations, other ailments still cause much suffering around the world. Now that new health threats such as AIDS have arisen to mar lives, the wish for good health remains as potent and strong as it's ever been.

Within modern healthcare, there are three main fronts in the pursuit of understanding and then eradicating illness – environment, lifestyle and genetics. Each can be a threat to health, either in isolation or in unison. Environmental threats are arguably the most understood and most successfully countered. In the west, largely through the implementation of better hygiene and mass vaccination, many of the airborne, waterborne and contact diseases that killed so many people in past centuries have now been eradicated or are treatable. Much of the focus now lies in understanding how lifestyle (smoking, lack of exercise, poor diet etc) and genetic inheritance influence our health, particularly as these seem to be the root causes of the current big killers in the west – heart disease and cancer.

A better awareness of healthcare issues and rise in life expectancy among the developed nations in recent decades suggests we should collectively be feeling healthier. Yet we seem to be more obsessed and troubled by our state of health than ever before. As a population, we've been educated about what constitutes basic good health – eating regular healthy meals, drinking plenty of water, exercising regularly, getting plenty of sleep, avoiding stimulants such as alcohol, nicotine and caffeine and reducing stress. Even so, many of us seek alternative answers, particularly for modern, largely lifestyle-related ailments that conventional medicine has struggled to overcome, such as allergies, insomnia, back pain and depression.

Pill-popping has become the norm, whether prescription and over-the-counter drugs, multivitamins, supplements or herbal medicine. We're also increasingly shunning conventional medical advice and turning to self-diagnosis (largely fuelled by self-help medical books, publications and the internet) or alternative practitioners for help. This loss of confidence in conventional medicine may be explained by the now ubiquitous 'health scare', where a minor clinical report expressing some doubt about a treatment, drug or technique can be misinterpreted and then sensationally reported, causing many to avoid some courses of healthcare completely, as witnessed, for example, with the MMR jab.

Are we returning to something akin to the era of shamen and soothsayers, where many of us are putting our faith in treatments, diets and techniques that have yet to pass the conventional scientific scrutiny of peer review and extensive clinical trials? Have we become the 'worried well', a state of being where we are largely healthy – bar a few minor ailments that some alterations to our lifestyle could cure – yet seek solace by flitting between unconventional and conventional treatments and drugs, in the process becoming more and more discontent and, ultimately, unhealthy.

Healthcare throws up some of the most important ethical dilemmas that we face. So much so that there is a whole branch of healthcare devoted to discussing what's known as 'bioethics'. As the promotional literature for the MA course in medical ethics at King's College London states, it's 'for anyone wanting to think about and discuss some of the hardest human decisions'.

Bioethics

'I will maintain the utmost respect for human life from its beginning even under threat and I will not use my medical knowledge contrary to the laws of humanity.'
From the World Medical Association's 'Declaration of Geneva', the basis for the modern-day Hippocratic oath.

The 'laws of humanity' are currently being tested as never before. Medical advances in the past few decades have brought about organ transplants, test-tube babies, keyhole surgery and brain scans, but have also created previously unknown ethical dilemmas. Never has the phrase 'playing God' been more apt when applied to the medical profession. Here are just a handful of the more controversial issues and practices causing so much debate (and consternation) around the world today:

- **Animal testing (see page 180)**
- **Therapeutic and reproductive cloning (via stem-cell research)**
- **Euthanasia (assisted suicide)**
- **Xenotransplants (transplantation of organs between species)**
- **Prenatal screening**
- **Sale of organs**
- **Gender selection**
- **In vitro fertilisation**
- **Patenting the human genome**
- **Multi-dose vaccines**
- **Defining 'informed consent'**
- **Defining 'brain dead'**

Then there are a range of other more mundane, but nonetheless controversial ethical dilemmas facing the British medical care industry, such as the hiring of doctors and nurses from developing nations where their skills are invariably needed more, the over-use of antibiotics, and the 'postcode lottery' allocation of treatments and funds.

But how do we resolve such questions? Current practice is to defer these tough decisions to a committee of experts in which all sides of the debate should be represented. Wider public consultation will sometimes also be sought, but, ultimately, a relatively small number of people will decide on whether or not to proceed with the proposed technology.

A good example of this is stem-cell research. The decision on whether to use human embryo stem cells in research in the UK was backed by free votes in parliament, two rounds of public consultation and a commission of inquiry. In 2004, scientists were finally given permission to perform therapeutic cloning using stem cells. The Human Fertilisation and Embryology Authority – a non-departmental government body made up of 18 people including medical professors, a bishop, a law lecturer, and a philosopher among others – granted a licence to a team at the Newcastle Centre for Life investigating new treatments for conditions such as diabetes, Parkinson's and Alzheimer's disease.

However, deep public unease remains about the use of the technology and in many countries, including the US, the practice is banned. But all we can do, should we have ethical objections to such practices, is refuse to use them, and continue to lobby for their development or use to be outlawed. Wherever there is debate there will be campaign groups representing either side of the argument. There are dozens of such groups concerned with the broad issue of genetics, some of which are totally opposed to the technology, typically on religious or moral grounds. Some – such as GeneWatch UK – want to ensure that genetic technologies are developed and used, but only in an 'ethical and safe manner'. When forming your own opinion, whatever the issue, try to source as broad a range of views as possible and always be on guard for self-interested groups who stand to gain financially should the said technology proceed. This has been a big concern, for example, in the debate about genetics as vast 'biotech' firms jostle for market dominance and public acceptance.

Complementary medicine

Over a quarter of us in the UK now use some form of complementary or alternative medicine (commonly referred to as CAM), spending about £1.6 billion a year doing so. Around 400 different techniques fall under this umbrella, yet despite their popularity and increased use within the NHS, little solid research into CAM currently exists and at present it receives only about one per cent of UK medical research budgets.

So why do so many people place trust and hope in CAM if much of it remains far from proven? There is no doubt that there is growing public scepticism as to the safety of some conventional drugs following a run of high-profile scares about adverse side-effects. There is also a growing public belief that 'natural', often centuries-old treatments, such as herbal medicines and yoga, are better for achieving wellbeing than modern medicines – a trend that is, for good or bad, often fuelled by the trendsetting actions of celebrities. It is telling, too, that the most popular CAMs are ones that are used to treat the ailments associated with modern

Placebo

Placebo

For fast, effective relief
Take one a day

living such as allergies, sleep problems, back pain and stress – the ones that conventional medicine has had little joy in tackling.

But it is perhaps asthma – the chronic respiratory condition predominantly associated with allergies – that is the best example of why CAMs have achieved such widespread public acceptance. In the UK, 34 per cent of 13–14-year-olds now have active asthma, the highest prevalence in the world. Asthma rates (and other allergy-related conditions such as hay fever) have increased two- to threefold over the past two decades. Hospital admissions of anaphylaxis – a fatal form of allergy – have increased sevenfold in just 10 years. What's to blame? There is no definitive answer to date but most signs point to a combination of many features of modern lifestyles: centrally heated, sealed houses; a rise in ownership of furry pets; exposure to thousands of synthetic chemicals; lack of exposure to immunity-boosting bacteria and other micro-organisms during childhood; an overuse of antibiotics; and the fact that we spend over 80 per cent of our time sedentary, indoors. It is thought that by 2015 every second Briton will suffer from one or more allergies. Many people are now looking to CAM, saying that acupuncture, homeopathy, herbal medicine and controlled breathing, for example, have shown promise in treating asthma.

But others are also urging patience, keen not to see people suffering from asthma given false hope. Professor Edzard Ernst, Asthma UK's complementary medicine medical adviser as well as the UK's first professor of complementary medicine, has reacted to the allure of CAM to asthma sufferers by spelling out exactly what peer-reviewed, clinical research has so far

told us. Writing in the *Guardian* in 2004, he said:

'There is no convincing evidence that acupuncture or chiropractic are useful [in treating asthma]. In fact, the best evidence suggests that they are probably of no real value. For some therapies, including autogenic training (a self-help technique based on auto-hypnosis), homeopathy, relaxation and yoga, research is inconclusive. Encouraging, in some instances even compelling evidence, however, has been reported for biofeedback (a technique that aims to put normally unconscious information under our conscious control), breathing exercises (including the Butekyo technique, a new method for preventing hyperventilation), allergen avoidance diets, several herbal treatments, hypnotherapy, massage and meditation.'

Many believe that a vast majority of the perceived benefits of CAM are down to the 'placebo effect', either through the ingestion of a complementary medicine or via the therapeutic meeting between a patient and a practitioner. For example, a clinical trial recently showed arnica does nothing to reduce pain or accelerate healing, yet it is one of the most popular herbal medicines. Both echinacea and ginkgo biloba have enjoyed huge popularity and patronage in the past decade, yet little, if any, hard evidence suggests either actually 'works'. Is the placebo effect at play? Does it even matter, if people feel they are benefiting? Perhaps not, but should we be sold an expensive treatment or course of medicine if there's no evidence saying that it works?

Before considering any CAM, research its merits as thoroughly as possible, just as you would for any conventional treatment. For example, choose a therapist who belongs to a reputable professional body. Only two of the eight most popular therapies in the UK – chiropractic and osteopathy – are regulated by law in the same way dentists, doctors and nurses are. Similarly, if you are choosing herbal medicines or looking for a herbal practitioner, make sure they belong to a reputable body such as the National Institute of Medical Herbalists or the Professional Register of Traditional Chinese Medicine (see page 199). And always be on guard for the mismarketing of CAM. For instance, the herb Ma Huang (aka ephedra) is traditionally used in China to treat respiratory congestion, but in the US it was marketed as a dietary aid, where over-dosage led to at least a dozen deaths, heart attacks and strokes.

Good health

● Keep hydrated by drinking enough water – up to 1.5 litres a day.

● Think holistically. Is your lifestyle, environment or diet making you ill? Ask these questions before reaching for the pills.

● Avoid seeking solace in faddy diets. Instead, eat a healthy, balanced diet. Doing so should give you all the minerals and vitamins you need, but if you do take supplements keep up to date with the recommended daily allowances (RDAs) by regularly visiting www.food.gov.uk/healthiereating/vitaminsminerals.

● Think carefully before automatically buying toothpaste containing fluoride. Although fluoride's role in battling tooth decay is well documented, it is still a controversial chemical, with some critics claiming it can increase the likelihood of bone fractures. Can you fight tooth decay by simply reducing the sugar in your diet instead?

● To join the debate on whether tap water should contain fluoride, visit the websites of both the National Pure Water Association (www.npwa.freeserve.co.uk) and the British Fluoridation Society (www.bfsweb.org).

● Visit the Healthcare Without Harm campaign website (www.noharm.org). It is an international coalition of 435 organisations across 52 countries, trying to provide environmentally responsible healthcare, including bans on mercury use, commonplace toxic cleaners, and the careless disposal of medical waste, as well as a commitment to green purchasing. An essential read for anyone working in healthcare.

● Open your windows as much as possible to breathe in fresh air, as certain toxins and pollutants can build up in the home without ventilation. Better still, spend more time outdoors.

● Give blood regularly. Contact the National Blood Service (www.blood.co.uk, tel: 0845 7711711).

● Carry a donor card. For more information, contact the NHS Organ Donor Register(www.uktransplant.org.uk, tel: 0845 6060400).

● Healthcare throws up many complex and fiercely debated ethical issues. For an overview of what the WHO's view is on each matter, visit www.who.int/ethics.

For the Department of Health's view, visit www.dh.gov.uk/policyandguidance.

For information about the workings of the World Medical Association's 'Ethics Unit', visit www.wma.net/e/ethicsunit.

The Medical Research Council website (www.mrc.ac.uk) is also good for an introduction to the guidance and advice given to UK scientists when conducting controversial research.

For those interested in reading more about the dilemmas thrown up by bioethics, the *American Journal of Bioethics* website (www.bioethics.net) is an excellent resource, as is http://bioethicsweb.ac.uk

● The EU is currently attempting to bring herbal medicines and supplements into the same formal regulatory environment as conventional pharmaceutical drugs. However, many people are concerned that this broadbrush approach will outlaw many popular CAMs because the relatively small-scale manufacturers who produce the majority of CAMs will not be able to afford the extremely expensive clinical trials that would be mandatory to gain a licence. There are also fears that Big Pharma firms are keen to see off the 'challenge' of CAMs to their share of the marketplace and have put pressure on the EU to force through directives. For more information about the campaign, visit www.healthchoice.org.uk.

● If you feel concerned about a health-scare story and want to read more background information, visit www.quackwatch.org.

● Before considering a complementary medicine or alternative therapy, make sure you do your homework, in particular about the results of any clinical trials and whether that discipline is regulated by a respected authority. There are many good starting points but among the best are the following:

The US National Center for Complementary and Alternative Medicine (http://nccam.nih.gov)

BBC Online's Complementary Medicine homepage (www.bbc.co.uk/health/complementary)

The Foundation for Integrated Health (www.fihealth.org.uk)

Spotlight

'Big Pharma'

Business is booming for the multinational drug manufacturers. In 2002, total global drug sales reached $430 billion – a 20 per cent leap on from the previous year, a period that saw the stock market tumble after the September 11 terrorist attacks. Also in 2002, each of the top 10 drug firms recorded sales over $11.5 billion. No wonder shares in pharmaceuticals are among the most sought-after by traders.

But there's growing concern that the firms are simply getting too large and powerful for the common good, particularly that of the world's sick and needy. Many campaigners are troubled by the fact that, following a wave of mega-mergers over the past decade, the combined worth of the world's top five drug companies – known to pressure groups as 'Big Pharma' or 'Druggernauts' – now stands at more than twice the combined gross national product of all sub-Saharan Africa. This might be acceptable if the medicines being manufactured were principally aimed at curing the world's most pressing conditions, such as malaria and Aids, but the reality is that most of the firms' focus is on the health problems that generate the most profit, in short, the ones that trouble patients in the west.

It's no coincidence that of the 10 bestselling drugs of 2002, the top two (worth $13.5 billion in sales) were aimed at reducing cholesterol, and of the others, one tackled high blood pressure, one ulcers, and two were antidepressants. Although all valuable in alleviating conditions that blight us in the west, these conditions can hardly be claimed to be the world's most pressing health concerns. Globally, of the 1,393 new drugs approved for sale between 1975 and 1999, only 16 targeted tropical diseases and tuberculosis, which between them account for 11.4 per cent of the global disease burden. Similarly, only 10 per cent of the world's medical research budget is devoted to 90 per cent of the world's disease burden. Research funding into malaria, for example, a disease

that kills a child every 30 seconds around the world and affects up to 500 million people a year, is 20 times lower than for asthma.

While it could be argued that there should be an ethical imperative to prioritise research budgets towards the most pressing health concerns, in a fierce marketplace profits take precedence. Malaria once again provides a good example of 'Big Pharma' priorities. In 2000, Glaxo Wellcome (now GlaxoSmithKline, or GSK, after a mega-merger) launched the first new anti-malarial developed by a drug company for 40 years. But rather than expressly aiming it at those living in malaria-stricken areas, the drug was targeted at the estimated seven million tourists and visitors who venture into malarial regions, a much more lucrative market.

However, it's not only the priorities of the pharmaceutical giants that upset many, it's also their practices. These companies spend huge sums and expend vast amounts of energy making sure their products become market leaders. According to *Pharmaceutical Executive*, over $500 million was spent globally promoting each of the six top-selling drugs in 2002. But it's the promotional methods used that cause most concern. For example, in the past decade, the number of 'Big Pharma' sales reps has tripled to 90,000 in the US and 110,000 in Europe. The reps work hard to convince doctors and chemists to either prescribe or sell their drugs to patients. The reps' tactics differ around the world depending on local marketing and medical regulations. Whether it's in the form of being flown out to a nice location to attend one of the many sponsored 'continuing medical education' events where new products will be 'introduced' to attendees, or the paying of client referral bonuses, the incentives to use a firm's products can certainly be attractive. Sometimes the firms get punished for such practices – in 2004, Pfizer, the world's largest drug manufacturer, paid a £240 million fine for promoting a product with no

Of the **1,393** new drugs approved for sale globally between 1975 and 1999, **only 16** targeted tuberculosis and tropical diseases such as malaria

benefits, and GSK, according to the *Guardian* in 2004, was under investigation in Italy for giving an estimated £150 million worth of gifts to doctors. But when drug manufacturers make many billions a year such punishment must seem small beer. When necessary, they just seem to work harder to lever legislation in their favour. In the US election year of 2000, for example, the industry spent $92.3 million on 625 lobbyists – more than one for every member of Congress.

But perhaps the most pernicious and infamous practice of such firms, given how much profit they make, has been their dogged attempt to prevent the distribution of cheap generic versions of what the WHO calls 'essential medicines' in the poorest nations. The practice is known by campaigners as 'patents before patients' and even though there have been recent breakthroughs, with many governments pledging support and funding for the production of generic drugs, there is still opposition, most notably by the US (a country that, ironically, when faced by an anthrax scare in 2001, threatened the pharmaceutical giant Bayer that it would change the law and override the patent of Bayer's anthrax antibiotic drug Cipro if the price wasn't lowered).

If you want to help reduce the power and influence of the Big Pharma firms, support the Cut the Cost campaign headed by Oxfam and supported by other non-governmental organisations (www.oxfam.org/eng/campaigns_camp_cut cost.htm). You could also boycott their products as well as choosing not to invest in Big Pharma shares. For more information about the push to achieve universal, cheap access to 'essential medicines', visit www.accessmed-msf. org and www. who.int/health_topics/essential_medicines/en/. Other places to keep up with the actions of Big Pharma include www.nofreelunch.org, www.healthy skepticism.org, www.haiweb.org and www.corporate watch.org.uk.

EXPLAINER Animal testing

'It is morally acceptable for human beings to use other animals, but it is morally wrong to cause them unnecessary or avoidable suffering. There is at present a continued need for animal experiments both in applied research and in research aimed purely at extending knowledge.'

Report from the House of Lords select committee on animals in scientific procedures, July 2002

'Ethically speaking, to deliberately exploit, torture and kill another sentient creature, be they human or nonhuman, is an intrinsically evil abuse of power. Scientifically speaking, experimentation on animals is a fundamentally flawed approach to learning about human biology and disease.'

Statement by Uncaged, an anti-vivisection pressure group

How are animals used in testing?

For centuries, animals have been used to check the safety and efficacy of new products, medicines, medical procedures and toxic chemicals before testing moves on to human 'guinea pigs'. Today, animals are still used as 'models' to test a wide variety of drugs, chemicals and treatments, both for medical use and for non-medical applications ranging from household cleaners through to agrochemicals and chemical weapons.

According to the most recent Home Office statistics, 2.79 million animals were used in tests in 2003 in the UK, a 2.2 per cent increase on 2002, but part of a longterm decline since the 1970s, when about five million animals were used in tests each year. The animals now used are predominantly rodents; 85 per cent of testing in 2003 involved mice, rats and other rodents. The remaining tests in that year used a range of other animals including birds (four per cent) and fish (six per cent). Dogs, cats and non-human primates, such as macaques, marmosets and tamarins (the use of 'great apes' was banned in 1997), were collectively used in less than one per cent of tests. There are, incidentally, no laws covering the use of invertebrates, so there are no figures on how many worms and insects, for example, were used.

The British Union for the Abolition of Vivisection (BUAV) estimates that 100 million animals are used in testing each year worldwide, with between 10 million and 11 million used in the EU. The UK is the largest user in the EU. However, animals bred for research and then not used – which campaigners such as BUAV claim amount to many millions – are not included in Home Office figures. They are all killed as surplus. Advocates of animal testing have estimated that during our life, only 'two mice and half a rat' will be used for each of us for medical research.

The types of tests animals are subjected to vary hugely. They can range from simple blood tests through to much more traumatic procedures such as tumour-inducing treatments or the infamous Draize test that involves dripping toxic solutions into the eyes of rabbits. About 94 per cent of licences granted for animal testing in the UK allow procedures graded as 'mild' or 'moderate' in severity. Under two per cent are graded as being of 'substantial' severity. Overall, an anaesthetic is used in about 40 per cent of tests.

The majority of animal testing is performed within the medical sector, be it at hospitals, charities, universities or pharmaceutical companies. Under current UK law, all new medicines must be tested on animals. In fact, results must be presented to regulatory authorities from tests on two species – a rodent and one other – because different species can respond to medicine in different ways. In recent years, researchers have discovered huge advantages to testing on genetically modified animals and in 2003 these were used in 27 per cent of all tests. The Medical Research Council, the government-funded organisation that supports 'public interest' medical research, says that almost every drug and treatment in current use, including penicillin, insulin for diabetes, and polio vaccines, was developed or validated through animal testing – even before it become law to do so. Seen as a whole, though, less than 10 per cent of medical research uses animals and of all toxicity tests conducted on animals in 2003, 63 per cent were for pharmaceutical safety and efficiency.

What about for non-medical purposes?

The common public perception is that animal testing for cosmetics was finally banned in the late 1990s after much debate about the ethics of causing pain to animals in the name of human beautification. While it is true that laws were passed around this time, both in the UK and the EU, a total pan-European ban on testing cosmetics (both the ingredients and the final product) on animals will not actually come into force until 2009. Even then, exemptions will still exist until 2013 – products that may have adverse effects on fertility, for example – and some firms may simply use tests completed outside the EU, as many do now.

Equally controversial is the use of animal testing for household goods (cleaners, polishes, bleaches, washing liquid, weed killers, pest-control poisons etc) – products many campaigners point out exist solely to 'beautify' our homes. Why, they ask, ban animal testing on cosmetics and not testing on household goods? After all, none of them can really be classified as 'life-saving', often a justification for medical animal testing.

But the use of animal testing on household goods throws up an ethical dilemma: do we want to use animal testing to produce safer, more environmentally friendly chemicals for our everyday household products and so reduce our exposure to chemicals that are now linked to a range of health problems (see page 106)? Or do we want to stop animal testing on household products and, by doing so, leave ourselves, and the environment, exposed to potentially toxic chemicals? (It's a sad irony that our desire for safer chemicals is now predicted to lead to a rise in animal testing as tougher EU toxicity safety regulations are phased in over coming years.)

Animal testing also takes place in the development of military equipment and weapons. Although details are sketchy, the Ministry of Defence does publish sporadic statistics and information about how it uses animals. For example, in 2000, goats were used to test the effects of decompression when developing submarine escape equipment. Pigs were also used to develop personal protective equipment against blast injuries to the thorax. It doesn't take much imagination to think how much suffering those animals must have endured.

How is animal testing policed?

According to the Animal Procedures Act 1986, before any experiment can be performed on an animal, three Home Office licences must be granted. The test centre itself must be licensed, which ensures there is a vet in attendance at all times and that the premises are open to inspections by Home Office officials. The researchers themselves must also each have a

For

'The life of one human is worth more than the life of one other animal'

'Easing human suffering is worth the price'

'Many more millions of animals die each year to feed humans. Using animals in tests is far more morally justified'

'How else are we going to find cures for illnesses such as Alzheimer's, Aids, and cancer?'

Against

'Animals have as much right to life as us'

'Deaths through research are absolutely unnecessary and are morally no different from murder'

'Alternatives are available but the scientific community is too entrenched in animal testing to end it'

'Animal testing is of questionable scientific value. Testing on human volunteers is far more accurate'

personal licence to test on animals. Finally, before an experiment is allowed to proceed it must gain a 'project licence'. An independent committee will decide if the potential benefits outweigh any likely suffering, as well as investigating whether an alternative testing method could be sought. The degree of suffering will also be graded at this point.

Is there an alternative to using animals?

The subject of alternatives is extremely controversial. Views on animal testing fall largely into three camps: those that agree with animal testing; those that agree with it only if it genuinely benefits mankind and there is no alternative; and, lastly, the absolutists who believe there can never be any case for testing on animals and to do so amounts to 'speciesism', a crime equal to racism, sexism or even murder. The silent majority seem to agree with the central position, whereas there are vocal (and sometimes violent) advocates of the other views.

Achieving consensus on what alternatives should be used, or even whether they should be sought in the first place, is difficult. The law requires that scientists show that they have considered the 'Three Rs' — replacement, refinement and reduction — in order to keep animal suffering to a minimum. However, many claim the search for such alternatives is significantly hindered by poor funding and a widespread ambivalence among the research community to ending current practices. The government allocates about £300,000 a year to research into alternatives and is currently 'considering' establishing a Three Rs research centre. In contrast, of the £50 million or so spent each year on medical research by the British Heart Foundation — often a target of the anti-vivisectionists — not a penny is specifically aimed at developing alternatives to animal testing.

Those who want to speed up the adoption of the Three Rs point out that technological advance could be the answer, particularly with computer modelling and the further understanding of genetics. A US company, Xenogen, has created a GM mouse that incorporates the luciferase enzyme that makes some insects, jellyfish and bacteria glow. By planting a tumour in the mouse, the progress of the cancer can be monitored by watching the animal 'shine', meaning that 80 per cent fewer animals need to be killed to monitor its progress.

How can I avoid products developed using animal testing?

It's currently impossible to avoid conventional medicine that has been tested on animals, due to the fact that the law requires such testing. Complementary medicines are used by some as alternatives, but this option should only be considered after professional consultation, research and consideration.

Avoiding cosmetics and household items that have been tested on animals is significantly easier but still requires research and vigilance. Some organisations provide directories of companies that don't test their products on animals. For example, BUAV publishes its *Little Book of Cruelty-Free* which lists companies that are approved under the Humane Cosmetics Standard and the Humane Household Products Standard (available from www.buav.org/gocrueltyfree). Naturewatch's 80-page *Compassionate Shopping Guide* also provides similar information (£2.50 from www.naturewatch.org). Peta (People for the Ethical Treatment of Animals) has created a special website (www.caringconsumer.com) dedicated to listing companies that both do and don't test on animals. And the Vegan Society's book *The Animal-Free Shopper* (www.vegansociety.com) is also a comprehensive source.

What else can I do?

If you disagree with animal testing, or would like to see more effort put into seeking alternatives, there are a number of other things to do…

Write to your MP and the Home Secretary urging them to push for a Centre of Alternative Research. Also campaign for a Royal Commission inquiry into the merits and administration of animal experimentation in the UK – something previous governments have flirted with but, as yet, have never followed through.

Write to your MP, demanding a change to charity laws. Charities such as the RSPCA are currently not allowed to campaign against the use of animals for experiments because it may 'have a serious detrimental effect on humankind'.

Boycott airlines that transport primates from places such as Mauritius for testing in the UK. Email them to tell them why via BUAV's website, which also contains a list of target airlines (www.buav.org/campaigns/f_emailairline.html).

Donate to health charities that do not test on animals. Visit www.humaneseal.org for a list of over 200 charities that do not test on animals.

Further reading

www.advocatesforanimals.org.uk
www.abpi.org.uk/amric/amric.asp
www.apc.gov.uk
www.boyd-group.demon.co.uk
www.buav.org
www.curedisease.com
www.frame.org.uk
www.homeoffice.gov.uk/comrace/animals/faq.html
www.medicalprogress.org
www.mrc.ac.uk/public-cbpar

www.navs.org
www.newscientist.com/hottopics/animalexperiments
www.stopanimaltests.com
www.petersingerlinks.com
www.rspca.org.uk
www.simr.org.uk
www.uncaged.co.uk
www.ufaw.org.uk

Toiletries

Statistically, we are one of the 'cleanest' nations in Europe, coming just behind Germany and France. We spend nearly £6 billion on personal care every year, and by the time the average person is ready to leave the house in the morning, they will have used at least six products: typically soap, shampoo, conditioner, deodorant, toothpaste and moisturising cream.

This alone will bring the average person into contact with more than 100 different synthetic chemicals (see page 106) before they leave their home.

Research by the US National Research Council in 2002 showed that 85 per cent of petroleum introduced into North American oceans each year comes from the 'seemingly minuscule' actions of individuals, rather than the large oil spills or pipeline leakages of popular imagination. Similarly, most consumers do not relate the growing emergence of bioaccumulative chemicals in water sources, fish and shellfish to, in part, the products we put in the bathroom cabinet. But from mouthwashes to facial scrubs, our toiletries can contain resilient synthetic chemicals, able to survive the journey down the drain and through sewage treatment works until they reach rivers, lakes and eventually the sea.

The European Cosmetic Toiletry and Perfumery Association (COLIPA, a group that represents companies making such products) asserts that 'whatever the specific product, they all have one common aim: to promote the wellbeing of the person that uses them'. But the daily application of many different chemicals – synthetic and natural – makes those concerned about our overexposure to some chemicals, who include campaign groups and a growing number of toxicologists alike, uneasy. In fact, over 9,000 ingredients are now available to manufacturers of personal care and beauty products. However, according to Dr Gina Antczak and Dr Steve Antczak, authors of *Cosmetics Unmasked*, 1,000 of these are suspected of having harmful effects.

Given their possible effect on the environment as well as ourselves, it's vital that we ask ourselves some pertinent questions before we buy any product:

- **Do I need this product, or am I being driven by advertising?**
- **Does this product contain any ingredients that might damage my health or the environment?**
- **Is there a genuinely natural or organic alternative?**

Toothpaste

Advertising campaigns promote products that go further than just maintaining hygiene and preventing disease; they promise to make teeth whiter and breath fresher.

But toothpaste marketeers have a particularly difficult task: how do they get us to buy more of a product which most of us strictly use just twice a day? The answer seems to lie in advertising campaigns focusing on the horror of bad breath caused by bacteria. This has led to a rise in popularity of 'total' or 'complete' toothpastes. One ingredient commonly used is Triclosan. It is an antibacterial agent widely found in mouthwashes and toothpaste, as well as in household products such as washing-up liquids, dishcloths, chopping boards, bin liners, plastic kitchen utensils, scouring pads and toilet cleaners. It is even found in some clothing, such as socks and bicycle shorts. But, according to Friends of the Earth, Triclosan has been detected in human breastmilk and fish, which, the environmental campaigners say, suggests it is bioaccumulative.

Despite the widespread use of fluoride (see page 177) in toothpaste dental decay remains a largely social problem – the British Dental Foundation estimates that nationally 30 per cent of four-year-olds experience dental decay, concentrated in areas of deprivation. Dentists believe that the most effective way of fighting tooth decay is by preventative measures such as cutting down on sugar and implementing a routine of regular brushing and check-ups, and that this routine should begin in childhood. Abrasive whiteners and antibacterial pastes, therefore, will not put right damage done by years of bad oral health or, for example, smoking.

Soap and cleansing products

Triclosan is also regularly used in soaps, liquid handwashes and body washes. According to a joint statement from the Soap and Detergent Association, and the US Cosmetic, Toiletry and Fragrance Association, 'antibacterial hand soaps, when properly used, are effective at reducing the risk of infection by killing or controlling the growth of harmful transient microorganisms on the skin, as evidenced in their broad use in healthcare'. However, governmental environment agencies in Sweden, Denmark, Finland and Germany appear to disagree and have discouraged people from using products that contain such antibacterial agents.

In 2003, global consumer expenditure on disposable facial wipes passed the $2 billion mark for the first time. Many promise to exfoliate, moisturise and even add vitamins to your skin. This may be the case, but they also add extra synthetic chemicals to our morning ablutions. And they are typically made with viscose and rayon, both of which make disposable wipes much harder to biodegrade.

Fighting this trend means a return to the good old flannel-and-soap approach. And there's much to be said for it. Conventional soaps have a good track record in terms of safety and allergy – only 70 cases of soreness, irritation, itching and redness of the skin caused by 'pure' soap or detergent bars were reported to the US Food and Drug Administration in a major study between 1975 and 1977. Most soaps now include synthetic detergents, antibacterials and perfumes. Although traditional soap-making is hardly a glamorous business – vats of animal or vegetable fats (be sure to check the label if you're a vegetarian) are mixed with an alkali (traditionally, wood ash) – it does seem to produce a day-to-day product that is environmentally benign. Therefore, use as natural and unadulterated a soap as possible – many companies now produce organic versions. If you do want a soap with antibacterial qualities, try one containing tea tree oil.

Dilemma

Do we need to wash our hair?

In essence, most mainstream shampoos are glamorously packaged surfactants – chemicals that dislodge dirt and grease. As hair is naturally acidic, shampoos are also made to be acidic, hence the 'pH balanced' label popular in adverts. But is it possible to avoid the marketing hype of shampoos altogether and use plain old soap? As soap is alkaline, you'll need to rinse your hair in a weak acid such as lemon juice to restore smoothness.

Advertising also leaves many consumers under the impression that shampoos can transform hair for the better. Despite claims that products 'strengthen hair', no substance can miraculously transform limp hair into luscious locks. Products containing keratin, for example, will merely coat the hair, possibly making the hair appear thicker, but as nothing more than a temporary solution.

You'll find it hard to find a shampoo which doesn't specify its suitability for 'daily use' or 'frequent washing' despite the fact that most dermatologists warn that over-washing hair strips it of its natural oils. The scalp secretes sebum, which naturally lubricates and protects hair against dirt and bacteria. This poses the question; do we need to wash our hair at all? Left to their own devices, our own natural oils in effect wash our hair without water or extra products. Conversely, hair products have been shown to over-stimulate oil glands and attract dirt.

However, few of us are prepared to run the risk of possible social exclusion by leaving our hair unwashed. The first six weeks are said to be the most difficult, culminating in a very oily phase between weeks five and six. This first phase conforms to the popular perception of unwashed hair – uncomfortable and unhygienic. But after this period, non-hair washers report healthy, self-regulating hair that looks better than ever. So good in fact that many vow never to wash their hair again.

Shaving

With millions of disposable razors used every day, vast quantities of plastic and steel are required for their manufacture. Sadly, once disposed of, most end up in the local landfill. Therefore, follow the advice of North Lincolnshire Council's waste minimisation team: 'Use razor blades or an electric razor rather than disposable razors if you wet shave. By buying packs of disposable razors you are throwing out the plastic handle and pack as well as the worn out blade.'

In addition, many razors and shaving gels and lotions now incorporate moisturising lubricants (another extra helping of synthetic chemicals). The best option is to use an old-fashioned shaving brush, soap and reusable razor.

Deodorants

In 1999 thousands of people received a scare email claiming that 'the leading cause of breast cancer is antiperspirant'. It was suggested that aluminium compounds (particularly aluminium chlorohydrate), core ingredients in most antiperspirants, gained entry to the body via nicks caused by shaving, damaging DNA and causing cancer. This claim has never been substantiated, but it did highlight a number of concerns over the safety of some deodorants.

Studies by Reading University in 2003 suggested that chemicals in deodorants mimic oestrogen. In the course of this research, parabens (see page 106) were found in the tissue of cancerous breasts,

although no direct link was made to breast cancer. But as a precautionary measure it may be best to avoid such products until conclusive proof about the safety of their ingredients is established. Many natural and organic deodorants are available that mask body odour with naturally derived scents instead of inhibiting perspiration. Other options include using deodorising stones (that use potassium alum, a mineral salt, to inhibit odour-forming bacteria), or simply washing twice a day with soap and water.

Shampoos and conditioners

In adverts, hair products are imbued with miraculous restorative ingredients: amino acids, pro-vitamins and 'revitalising' minerals. While these substances may temporarily improve appearance, they are not a longterm fix for frazzled hair. In fact, all these highly nutritious ingredients, according to the authors of *Cosmetics Unmasked*, make hair products susceptible to microbial infection. To counteract this problem, some manufacturers add synthetic preservatives, typically parabens, which some suspect of being endocrine disrupters. However, there are now many alternative products on the market (see page 200). For example, nut oils act as effective conditioners. But always be wary of mainstream products using terms such as 'natural' and 'organic': unlike food labelling, the marketing of toiletries has no regulations guarding against their misuse.

Spotlight

Gym culture

Membership rates of gyms and health clubs continue to climb each year. Between 1993 and 2003, the number of people going to the gym in the UK doubled. But while figures from the Fitness Industry Association reveal that six million of us are now signed up to clubs and sports centres, obesity rates have grown by 400 per cent over the past 25 years, with levels continuing to rise.

According to recent government statistics, 70 per cent of British adults do not exercise enough. This inactivity means serious health problems, costing around £7.4 billion per year in obesity-related disease and illness. The average person now walks a total of 189 miles per year, a fall of 66 miles over 25 years, while most physically active jobs are typically poorly paid and therefore considered undesirable.

The continued growth in gym memberships should, therefore, be a fillip to those trying to raise the nation's collective health. But despite the keenness to join, a quarter of members drop out after six months, with 81 per cent carrying on paying direct debit payments for at least two months after they've stopped attending.

But are health clubs really that healthy? While we strive to reshape our bodies, the air conditioning is working overtime to keep the hermetically sealed room at optimum temperature, hundreds of fluffy towels are being boiled and dried in the laundry and the cardio gym is full of energy-guzzling equipment plugged permanently into MTV. (The energy demands of gyms have been recognised in Colorado in the US where energy shortages have already led to one-towel policies and the mandatory switching off of lights in unused rooms.) In the UK, 89 per cent of gym members drive to the gym. Arguably, our exercise regime should begin by cycling, walking or running to the gym in the first place.

But we can lessen the strain on the environment (and our wallets) by searching for more effective, less expensive workout facilities. This leads potential exercisers straight to the local park. Alfresco workouts range from a jog round the park, to formally organised circuits – British Military Fitness (www.britmilfit.com) is one of the best established, coordinating workouts on commons and parks around the UK.

Reclaiming your workout from neon-lit locker rooms and membership fees can also breathe life back into your fitness regime. Experts say that running on outdoor terrain gives muscles a better workout and a study conducted by the University of Queensland suggested that the great outdoors is also likely to keep us in a more balanced frame of mind – regular outdoor runners were found to be less anxious and depressed than those who used a treadmill. It also gives us a chance to indulge our natural 'biophilia', a term coined by the Pulitzer prize-winning author Edward O Wilson who asserted that we are naturally hard-wired to enjoy being outside.

The British Trust for Conservation Volunteers (BTCV) would agree. The charity pioneered 'Green Gyms' in which bicep curls and lateral raises are provided by building dry-stone walls, repairing footpaths or moving compost heaps. Not only does felling a tree burn up the same amount of calories as an advanced aerobics class, but it is claimed by BTCV that positive community involvement can form an important part of a person's overall wellbeing. For a full list of Green Gyms around the UK, contact BTCV (www.btcv.org/greengym, tel: 01302 572244).

Cosmetics

For the majority of women, and increasingly some men, cosmetics are as much a part of our everyday routine as toiletries. Ninety-three per cent of British women use cosmetics, on average using 20 different products every day.

It's a vast industry, employing over 150,000 people across the EU and is largely controlled by huge multinationals who own most of our favourite brands; Estée Lauder, for example, also owns, among others, Clinique, Origins, Prescriptives, Mac, Stila, Aveda and Jo Malone.

But it's also an industry frequently criticised for exploiting female insecurities over looks and youthfulness. For example, studies in the US at Stanford University and the University of Massachusetts showed that about 70 per cent of women at the colleges reported feeling worse about their own looks after reading women's magazines that typically contained many adverts for fashion and beauty products, such as cosmetics. But the industry cannot be wholly demonised. Whereas some users have been found to develop a psychological dependency on cosmetics, such products can also represent stress-busting, self-esteem-boosting breaks from the daily grind.

The Women's Environmental Network (www. wen.org.uk/cosmetics), a campaign group, advocates combining beauty with wisdom to take advantage of the positive aspects of the beauty industry, and to counteract negative aspects – which all too often include risking the environment and our own health. This should mean making informed purchases by shopping around, reading labels closely and sampling brands that demonstrate a sensitivity to the environmental impact of their products' ingredients.

Many cosmetics consumers are also under the false impression that the products they use were not tested on animals (see page 180), thinking that this kind of testing has already been phased out in the UK and EU. But this is not entirely the case; in 2001 the RSPCA estimated that 38,000 animals a year were still used to test cosmetics in the EU. What is now illegal is the testing of 'finished' products. The testing of various constituent parts of the 'finished' product is not due to be completely phased out until 2013. Companies such as the Body Shop and Beauty Without Cruelty began creating products free from animal testing in the 1980s and have continued to develop a market. Supporting these, and similar brands, sends a clear message to the industry as a whole.

Perceived as luxury goods, cosmetics are packaged accordingly, creating yet another landfill headache – as much as 50 per cent of the cost of a bottle of perfume can be attributed to packaging and advertising. Therefore, choose products that place an emphasis on recycling and minimal packaging. The Body Shop has long run a policy whereby customers can return bottles, and has also begun to use recycled plastic.

If no such scheme exists near you, buy glass bottles – they are more easily recycled and more valuable to recyclers. Where plastic is the only option, make sure it is PVC free (the recycling triangle on the bottom should display 1, 2, 4 or 5 in the middle) and resist free samples; small plastic bottles only add to the mountain of waste.

The average woman also gets through 2,000 cotton wool balls in a year. But cotton growers are some of the biggest users of agrochemicals in the world, and cotton is also often treated with chlorine, another major pollutant. Chose organic cotton wool, or reusable, washable pads.

We may now gasp at the 18th-century trend for arsenic-based face powder, but at the same time our own beauty products can contain many complex chemicals. While chemicals in shower gels and soaps will mostly be washed

The 'Adonis Complex'

It's not just women who are going in search of the body beautiful. Increasingly male products are vying for space in bathroom cabinets. In the UK alone, sales doubled from £200 million in 1995 to over £400 million by 2000.

Fifty-nine per cent of men surveyed for an *Observer* report in 2003 admitted to using at least one beauty product on a regular basis. This new interest in appearance and emphasis on grooming could be attributed to increased levels of disposable income and the desire to emulate well-groomed role models such as David Beckham.

However, men have also been hit by insecurities over body image, mirroring paranoia and anxieties that have traditionally affected women. In 1997 *Psychology Today* conducted a survey and found that 45 per cent of US men admitted to being dissatisfied with their body appearance. Meanwhile, in the UK, the incidence of anorexia and bulimia among boys and men has doubled since the mid-1970s. In 2001, the *Guardian* reported that males account for 10 per cent of all eating disorders.

Some men are consumed with the desire to get big muscles fast, regardless of their natural body shape or the cost to their health. This can be a symptom of muscle dysmorphia, nicknamed 'bigorexia', a syndrome first identified in 2002 by three US psychologists in *The Adonis Complex*.

Many turn to steroids. In November 2003, the *Guardian* reported a sharp increase in the numbers of British men who regularly use illegal anabolic steroids. The Home Office puts the number of users between 2001 and 2002 at 42,000, including children as young as 14.

The problem looks unlikely to disappear. In the UK, in some areas of the north-west, steroid users outnumber opiate users at needle exchanges. And in 2002, a British Medical Association survey found that one in three GPs had encountered patients who used anabolic steroids.

The irony is that steroid abusers flirt with common side-effects such as testicular atrophy, baldness and breast growth – the very antithesis of the body beautiful image they seek to create. Reported side-effects also include raised blood pressure, infertility, heart disease, as well as increased aggression and mood swings.

down the plughole, a regular lipstick wearer (81 per cent of women) actually ingests about 1kg of lipstick over the course of their life. Phthalates (see page 106), commonly used industrial compounds suspected of being endocrine disrupters, are also often found in cosmetics.

Hair dye is another area of concern. According to a survey conducted by L'Oréal, 60 per cent of US women colour their hair regularly. This is up from 40 per cent in 1976. Most use permanent dye, effective in disguising grey hair. Not only are permanents usually made from petroleum-based ingredients, but they typically contain arylamines, chemicals that in 2001 University of Southern California's researchers linked to bladder cancer. The researchers reported that women who use permanent dyes at least once a month for one year or longer have twice as much risk of bladder cancer as non-users.

So contemporary cosmetics are complicated. The Cosmetic, Toiletry and Perfumery Association, the UK industry's trade association, acknowledges that 'ultimately consumers do not expect to understand fully the science behind the products they consume every day; they want to be able to delegate choices to brands, manufacturers and retailers and to retain their trust in those choices'.

But how far can we trust the big brands, with their commensurately large advertising budgets (in the year up to March 2001, £32 million was spent in the UK on advertising make-up alone), to tell us everything about their products? Anita Roddick, co-founder and chair of the Body Shop, has commented that 'anything which says it can magically take away your wrinkles is a scandalous lie'. The majority of dermatologists, meanwhile, say that line-free skin is down to lucky genetics and staying out of the sun.

Where claims can be substantiated, it's not always good news either. Products may well, for instance, 'reveal younger-looking skin'. The alpha-hydroxy acids contained in some wrinkle creams and mild chemical peels do indeed remove the outer layer of skin, exposing newer skin below. What worries some people, however, is that this may also make the skin more susceptible to harmful UV rays – up to 18 per cent over a four-week period of use, according to research sponsored by the US Food and Drug Administration in 2000. Manufacturers have been obliged to list product ingredients since 2003. As reassuring as this is, especially for those prone to allergic reactions, it's questionable how much use these lists of complicated chemical names are to most consumers. Manufacturers can also apply to withhold 'secret' ingredients from listings where they are deemed to have the competitive advantage over another product. Nor do they have to declare the addition of preservative chemicals, despite the fact that after fragrances and colourants, these top the lists of common allergens.

Where labels single out specific ingredients and preface them with 'contains' or 'active ingredients include' then this could be because regulators consider it important for consumers to know about the presence of that specific substance. Also be aware of certain terms used on labels, such as the superficially comforting 'hypoallergenic'. Rather than guaranteeing that a product will not trigger an allergic reaction, it merely means that the manufacturer considers the product to be less likely to cause an allergic reaction than other cosmetic products; a subtle but crucial difference.

Because of such loopholes, rather than putting our trust in labels we should just simplify routines as much as possible. Patch test any new product first. Don't assume that just because ingredients are derived from plants they will not cause allergies. Plant extracts and natural ingredients, even organic ones, can cause allergies, too.

Perfumes and fragrances are estimated to be the biggest trigger of allergic reactions. As a result, many consumers may want to pick 'unscented' products. But confusingly this can mean 'no noticeable odour', and the product may contain fragrances,

A regular lipstick wearer (81 per cent of women) ingests about **1kg of lipstick** over the course of their life

including artificial musks (see page 106), in order to disguise other odours.

Watch out, too, for claims that the product is 'green' or 'natural'. Even those labelled 'organic' can be misleading – under present rules only one per cent of ingredients need be from an organic source for the product to qualify. Currently the Soil Association logo is the only accreditation guaranteeing that 95 per cent of a product's ingredients, excluding water, are derived from an organic source.

All the while, the cosmetics industry, operating in a fiercely competitive market, continues to develop new ingredients and techniques. And one new application in particular has raised eyebrows – nanotechnology. Some new sunscreens and face creams, for example, now include 'nanoparticles' that are 200–2,000 nanometres (one million nanometres = one millimetre) in size. These nanoparticles are used because they are small enough to penetrate deep into the skin, carrying with them a product's active ingredients. In sunscreens, for example, nanoparticles help boost the product's ability to block ultraviolet light. But the worry, according to some toxicologists, is that these particles are so small they will also pass into the bloodstream and then possibly be carried around the body where their effect is much harder to predict.

Fashion

'A fashion is nothing but an induced epidemic,' said George Bernard Shaw. And when every new season brings a different take on the length of skirts and trousers or the height of shoes, fuelling a fury of consumer spending in the process, it's not hard to find people who subscribe to his view.

Yesterday's fashion is history and, therefore, unappealing. The psychologist Oliver James believes the fashion industry to be just another facet of vacuous consumerism. 'Ever more precisely marketed products, and the power of the fashion industry, create a fetishistic concern to have this consumer good rather than that one, even though there is often no significant practical or aesthetic difference,' he said, writing in the *Ecologist* in 2004.

Whether you turn the spotlight on the use of teenage catwalk models, or the plight of sweatshop workers making apparel for our favourite clothing brands, it doesn't take much effort to expose the dark underbelly of this 'glamorous' industry. For example, fashion is frequently singled out as a key driver of anorexia among young women, and increasingly men.

But it is also claimed that dress is central to human culture; our relationships, aspirations and identity. Our personality, sexuality, social status and ethnicity are all bound up in what we choose to wear. Arguably, we have spent hundreds of years developing a complex relationship with our clothes. Surely it would be unfeasible to surrender that relationship now?

Yet deep down, most consumers know that all is not well in the global wardrobe. 'I've got nothing to wear' is a frequent lament, but in truth most of us in the developed world have got more to wear than ever before − much of which has been bought at low prices. But according to campaign groups such as Labour Behind the Label (www.behindthelabel.org) and the Clean Clothes Campaign (www.cleanclothes.org), this abundance of fashionable choice comes largely courtesy of starvation wages, bonded and child labour and the exploitation of both people and natural resources.

In the past decade the price of clothes and shoes has plummeted due to a cheap and expendable workforce, largely situated in the developing world. From 1999 onwards, the drop in prices was accelerated by the collapse of parts of the Asian economy, as labour became even cheaper and the workforce even more expendable. In addition, huge multinational companies with their formidable buying power are able to drive down prices even further.

In fact, garments are now so cheap they are almost disposable. According to the sociologist Juliet B Schor, writing in *Sustainable Planet: Solutions for the Twenty-First Century*, the wholesale price of used clothing has dropped 'precipitously' − by 80 per cent between 1997 and 2002 − as we discard clothes in ever-increasing quantities.

What happens to all these cast-offs? Most end up in landfill, but more and more is donated as 'humanitarian aid'. However, campaign groups such as Christian Aid and the International Textile Garment and Leather Workers Federation have highlighted the problems associated with flooding developing countries with unwanted clothes. So while we might donate clothes in good faith through a clothes bank, clearing some much needed wardrobe space for new items, only an estimated 10–20 per cent of charitable clothes donations actually find their way to charity shops in the UK. The rest are collected by private companies (who give charities a nominal sum) and sold in the developing world, undercutting local textile manufacturers. Second-hand cast-offs have all but destroyed the textile trade in Zambia, for example. In 1991, there were 140 textile manufacturers in Zambia, but by 2002 there were just eight.

To minimise this negative impact buy good quality pieces and wear them for more than one season. By being good quality, they should also have some resale value when you come to part with them and will therefore have more appeal to a local charity shop. Alternatively, donate clothes to Traid (www.traid.org.uk, tel: 020 8733 2580), which focuses on selling quality clothes, as well as 'vintage' clothes. It also aims to recycle every scrap via its 'Remade' label.

Swept up in the desire to keep up with trends, few of us think about the environmental impact of the fashion trade. Yet conventional cotton production accounts for 25 per cent of world pesticide use – even though it makes up just three per cent of global acreage. The WHO estimates that more than three million people worldwide are victims of pesticide poisoning each year, from which there are around 20,000 deaths.

From spinning and weaving to knitting and dyeing, cotton textile production requires huge amounts of water and energy. It has been estimated by WWF that 20,000 litres of water are needed to produce just one T-shirt. Meanwhile, synthetic fabrics come with their own set of environmental problems. For example, during production polyester fibres release a quarter of their weight as air pollution, which includes nitrogen and sulphur, hydrocarbons and carbon monoxide. Similarly, an estimated 50 per cent of all nitrous oxide emissions are derived from nylon production.

Then there's the dying process. Unlike in Germany, the Netherlands and Austria, azo dyes have not been banned in the UK, even though some of them have been declared carcinogenic by the European Commission. They remain the preferred choice of the majority of the world's textile manufacturers because they are cheap to produce.

The only solution in many cases is to fill as much of your wardrobe as possible with clothes made from natural fibres and organic cotton. In recent history, the idea of buying 'eco' clothes was enough to turn fashion-literate consumers visibly pale. Thankfully, 'eco' fashion is now moving on from tie-dye and chunky knits to embrace the world of fashion.

Currently, buying ethically usually involves stepping away from the high street. Spearheaded by designers such as Katherine Hamnett, who has made jackets from hemp and championed fair-trade T-shirts, other ethical fashion companies are beginning to set up shops, websites and mail-order businesses. American Apparel (www.americanpparel.net) is a good example of a company promoting 'clean' clothes with genuine fashion savvy.

Many consumers are understandably concerned about their clothes being produced under 'sweatshop' conditions. A sweatshop is defined by campaign group Sweatshop Watch as a workplace where workers are subject to 'extreme exploitation, including the absence of a living wage or benefits, poor working conditions, such as health and safety hazards, and arbitrary discipline'. First brought to the wider public's attention in the early 1990s when a number of well-known fashion companies were linked to sweatshop labour, the common perception is that they are restricted to developing nations. The truth is they also exist uncomfortably close to home: around 170,000 workers in the UK are estimated by No Sweat (www.nosweat.org.uk), a UK-based campaign group, to be working for less than the minimum wage, a substantial proportion of whom are likely to be working in the apparel trade.

In the 1990s, campaigners favoured boycotts as a means to pushing fashion towards a sweatshop-free future. However, boycotting a company is fraught with problems, largely due to complex, discrete supply chains. Oxfam, along with other aid organisations, now warns that boycotts can be counter-productive, resulting in the closure of factories altogether, leaving vulnerable workers destitute. It's best not to go down this route, it says, unless the workers themselves have called for a boycott.

But this doesn't mean that major brands and retailers should be let off the hook. Groups such as No Sweat suggest that consumers should develop a checklist of questions to present to clothing retailers before giving them your business:

- How does your company guarantee your clothes are produced under humane conditions?
- Do you have a list of all the factories that make your products around the world? Does it include the wages and working conditions in each factory? Can I see it?
- Do you have a code of conduct that protects human rights and forbids child labour and unsafe conditions in all the factories that make the clothes you sell? Can I see a copy?
- Is there an independent monitoring agency to ensure everybody lives up to the code?
- What do you do when you discover violations?

It may not be practical to do this every time you go clothes shopping so perhaps start with your favourite names first. For a real guarantee, consumers need detailed information about the origins of the product, but all we can currently derive from most garment labels is the optimum wash temperature. Many retailers do not even specify the country of origin of their apparel.

Following high-profile accusations of links to sweatshops, many companies responded by introducing a 'code of conduct', or signed up to be audited by organisations such as the Fair Labor Association (www.fairlabor.org). But critics argue that this often amounts to little more than a hollow public relations exercise. Without widespread independent monitoring of multinational clothing companies, it is virtually impossible for a consumer to dress 'sweat-free', certainly if you're shopping at mainstream stores. Therefore, the ethically minded consumer has to find alternatives. One way of bringing accountability back into fashion, and helping to foster a definable and transparent chain from the makers through to the retailers and consumers, is to use local, small-scale designers. Many smaller designers make their own clothes, or use subcontractors, who are paid and treated fairly.

Overall, despite fashion's notorious hunger for progression and revolution, the industry has been disappointingly slow to change. But the consumer is far from helpless. To create a sustainable, ethically minded industry, we need to push fashion towards a new aesthetic, where quality is prized over quantity and longevity over novelty. There are several ways in which we can help this agenda on:

- Spend more on each garment, but buy fewer pieces. A willingness by the consumer to spend more on well-made and timeless pieces helps to alter the current 'more is more' attitude.
- Get your fashion news, not just from glossy magazines, but from organisations such as Labour Behind the Label, No Sweat and Oxfam's Clean Clothing campaign.
- Wherever possible support organic cotton production and fair-trade clothing. Convert your basics – underwear, vests and T-shirts – first. For a full list of mail-order companies and shops in the UK selling certified organic clothes and household textiles, contact the Soil Association (www.soil association.org/textiles, tel: 0117 929 0661).
- Organise a clothes-swapping party (no, not that kind of party). Invite some friends round and tell them to bring all their unwanted clothes. Sort them into piles according to the type of garment, then invite everyone to move – in an orderly manner – between the piles looking for anything they may want. Give any clothes left over to a local charity shop.
- Ask yourself whether the fur of an animal should ever be used in fashion products. For more information about why animal welfare groups such as Peta believe the answer is no, visit www.furisdead.com. To find out why the fur industry believes yes, visit the International Fur Trade Federation's website at www.iftf.com.

20,000 litres of water are needed to produce just one T-shirt

Jewellery's hidden cost

We know that 'diamonds are for ever' because the advertising agency NW Ayer told us so, on behalf of diamond cartel De Beers, 60 years ago. It became one of the most famous advertising campaigns ever.

However, what we also now know, thanks to campaigns by Amnesty International, the UN, Global Action and Action Aid, is that sparkle comes at a price. The illegal mining and contraband selling of diamonds (and gold, in some cases) has been the foundation stone of some recent brutal wars across Africa – from Sierra Leone and Angola to Liberia and the Democratic Republic of Congo (formerly Zaire). According to Action Aid (one of the UK's largest development agencies), over three million people have died as a result of the wars largely funded by so-called 'conflict diamonds'.

Throughout the 1990s, consumers around the world spent an average of $125 million every year on conflict diamonds (or 'blood diamonds', as they are also known) from Sierra Leone alone. This money helped to supply guns to child soldiers, provided arms to fight UN peacekeeping forces and ensured that Sierra Leone remained a 'murderous sinkhole of death and torture', as described by Amnesty International.

Easy to smuggle, hard to detect and facilitated by 'legitimate' European and US diamond dealers, rough gems are cleaned up and polished into respectability. Over half of the world's diamonds are processed in India, where many of the cutters and polishers are children. Furthermore, the mining of gems, silver and gold – where cyanide is used to separate the metal from the ore – is environmentally hazardous and puts the lives of poorly paid workers at risk.

In 2003 the diamond industry attempted to clean up its act by launching the Kimberley Process certification scheme (www.kimberleyprocess.com) in cooperation with international governmental representatives and several NGOs. However, the scheme hinges on self-regulation by the gem industry and research by Global Action has concluded there is still no reliable way for consumers to be sure they are not purchasing conflict diamonds. For instance, the UN has criticised Switzerland, not a diamond-producing nation but a diamond free-trade area, for its role as a transit point for almost half the rough diamonds entering the UK. Antwerp, the 'diamond capital of the world', has also been criticised for facilitating the trade in conflict diamonds. Against this backdrop, a certificate of origin means very little.

Scientists are working on ways to trace the origins of diamonds, but so far there have been few breakthroughs. Until the jewellery trade allows an independent regulatory body to monitor its actions, there is only one way of tracing jewels from the mine to the point of sale: buying ethically sourced and mined jewellery. Choco Gold, mined by an indigenous cooperative in Colombia without using environmentally damaging chemicals, is available from Green Karat (www.greenkarat.com). Silverchilli (www.silverchilli.com) sells fair-trade silver jewellery made in Mexico. There's even local bling – scoring high on the traceability front – in the form of Welsh Gold (www.welshgoldplc.co.uk).

Mobile phones

In 1992, less than one per cent of the world's population had access to a mobile phone and only one-third of countries had a mobile phone network. However, just a decade later, there were more mobile phones in the world – 1.14 billion – than landlines. Today, there are over 50 million mobiles in the UK alone and, if we are to believe predictions made by Nokia, the world's largest handset manufacturer, by 2015 some four billion people – well over half the world's predicted population of 7.2 billion – will have a mobile.

But whereas there are some advantages to be gained from such global omnipresence – faster responses to emergencies, increased crime detection through tracking, reduced pollution through a suppressed need to travel – in their short history, mobile phones have thrown up a number of concerns for users that suggest they should be used sparingly and with consideration for others...

Health concerns

The simple fact that mobile phones emit microwave radiation has been enough to cause over a decade's worth of consumer angst and, as a result, a considerable amount of research into whether mobiles pose a health risk. To date, no compelling evidence has been published that proves conclusively that mobile phones directly harm the user. A government report published in 2000 found no evidence that mobiles were a health hazard but suggested more research was needed and that, as a precaution, children should be discouraged from using them regularly. (In 2002, the WHO also cautioned against children using mobiles for too long.) Subsequent research has proved to be contradictory. Some findings suggest there are no harmful effects whereas others suggest, for example, that microwaves (from handsets and/or phone masts) can confuse and stress animals such as pigeons. In 2004, Hungarian researchers produced a study that suggested men who carry mobiles in their pockets may be at risk of reducing their sperm count by as much as 30 per cent. However, other scientists said these findings were not conclusive.

Equally, many have concerns about the health effect of living close to mobile phone masts – or base stations, as they are known. Action groups such as MastSanity.org and MastAction.co.uk are campaigning for the erection of base stations to be under the control of full planning regulations, as well as for further research into the potential health risks they pose, especially when placed near schools, homes and hospitals. The debate continues.

But there are other more tangential health concerns, too. Mobile technology can blur the lines between work and play – the user can, in theory, be 'on call' 24/7, leading to increased stress levels. For example, people now actively seek sanctuary from mobiles – witness the establishment of 'phone-free' carriages on trains.

There's also concern that the craze for 'texting' can, in extreme cases, cause symptoms similar to those experienced by sufferers of RSI (Repetitive Strain Injury; for more information contact the RSI Association at www.rsi.org.uk, tel: 023 8058 4314).

Waste

Mobile phones create considerable amounts of waste at both ends of their life cycle. As is the case with all electronic consumables, mobiles are made up of a number of components – plastic casing, electronic circuitry, battery, liquid crystal display – all of which typically involve a highly polluting manufacturing process.

Given that they are seen as a status symbol for many, once in use, mobiles also have a short life – they are typically discarded after just 18 months. The US-based environmental research group INFORM estimates that by 2005 the stockpile of unused mobile phones in the US alone (a country that per head uses far fewer mobiles than the UK) will total 500 million. In the EU we will be discarding 100 million phones a year by 2005, most of which will end up in landfills where they could leach toxic chemicals such as arsenic, lead, mercury and brominated flame retardants (see page 106).

Thankfully, the market for reconditioned phones is growing. A number of charities now gain from various high-street phone recycling schemes. Greener Solutions (www.greenersolutions.co.uk, tel: 020 8274 4040), who facilitate most of the phone recycling schemes in the UK, can provide a list of places to

The average monthly bill in 2004 for those using a contract phone was **£44.18**

recycle your old phone via a freepost envelope. Most of these phones end up being reconditioned then reused in developing nations.

Legislation is also getting much tougher on the need for recycling. By June, 2006, electronics manufacturers will be required to finance the collection, treatment, recovery and disposal of their products, according to the EU's WEEE (Waste Electrical and Electronic Equipment) directive (see page 121).

Car safety

In 2003, after much public debate, the government finally banned the use of hand-held mobile phones while driving. But the enforcement of the £30 fine has proved to be patchy, with one in 10 drivers admitting that they still drive using hand-held mobiles, despite the ban. As was the case with drink-driving, it may take a number of years before it becomes socially accepted by the vast majority of drivers that using a hand-held is highly dangerous.

New research, though, is suggesting that driving while using a hands-free phone is also dangerous. The US National Highway Traffic Safety Administration has said that it adds to the risk of accident, and a study in 2004 by the University of Utah of 48 adults in a driving simulator found that those on a hands-free phone missed four times as many road exits as those talking to another passenger. An earlier study at the same university found that mobile phone users were twice as likely to miss red lights as those who were not using a phone (with no difference between hands-on and hands-free). The message is simple: never drive while talking on the phone, be it on a hand-held or hands-free.

Children

According to the mobile phone consultancy Mobile Youth, children under the age of 10 are 'the fastest-growing segment of mobile phone ownership within Britain'. In fact, at least 20 per cent of primary school children now own mobiles and by 2006 it is predicted that a third of all 5–9-year-olds will own mobiles. While some parents may claim that they welcome the comfort this form of permanent contact with their child brings, the trend does raise some concerns beyond those connected to the potential impact on health.

Mugging people for their phones is a growing crime and children are five times more likely to be targeted than adults. Children are also, like adults, spending more and more money on their mobile phones; buying ring tones and sending text messages are particularly popular. But using a mobile can be costly – in 2004, for example, the average monthly bill for those using a contract phone was £44.18; 'pay-as-you-go' phone users spent on average about £24.

With video and picture messaging now widely available, there are concerns that children could access the growing number of adult-orientated services, such as gambling and pornography, offered by phone companies.

While these firms have voluntarily adopted an 'opt in' policy for such services to prevent them inadvertently being marketed at, or used by, children – as well as using moderators for chat services – the fear remains that such measures can never be 100 per cent foolproof.

Coltan

Inside most mobile phones (and other electrical goods such as laptops) is a heat-conducting mineral called coltan (short for columbite-tantalite). When refined, coltan becomes a heat-resistant powder that can hold a high electrical charge, a very useful attribute when making capacitors. The problem is that 80 per cent of the world's coltan is found in the war-torn Democratic Republic of Congo (DRC). During the tech stock boom of the late 1990s, the price for coltan rocketed from $65 to $600 a kilogram and, as a result, a number of human rights campaigners claimed that warlords in the DRC were using profits from coltan mining to fund the fighting.

To compound this, the coltan-rich areas of the DRC also include areas where the country's endangered gorilla population lives. Both the Dian Fossey Gorilla Fund (www.dianfossey.org) and the Born Free Foundation (www.bornfree.org.uk) have campaigned for coltan mining to be banned from the gorilla reserves in eastern DRC and the world's largest coltan purchasers, such as the leading handset manufacturers, have agreed to stop buying illegally mined coltan from the region. But despite peace efforts in recent years, the country remains extremely volatile and there are still concerns that coltan from the area is finding its way into the international market.

The only practical action you can take while waiting for a credible coltan certification system to be established is to lobby your phone manufacturer to use alternatives, or to at least source coltan elsewhere – for example from Australia, Japan, or the US. You can also support charities, such as the Dian Fossey Gorilla Fund and the Born Free Foundation, which aim to secure the gorilla reserves of DRC, as well as helping the local communities make a living other than through the mining of coltan.

Directory

HEALTH

Advice and information

The following organisations are listed for research purposes only. If you are unwell, always consult your doctor or NHS Direct in the first instance

The British Complementary Medicine Association
☎ 0845 345 5977
www.bcma.co.uk

The British Dental Association
☎ 020 7935 0875
www.bda.org

The British Fluoridation Society
☎ 0161 220 5223
www.bfsweb.org

The British Homeopathic Association
☎ 0870 444 3950
www.trusthomeopathy.org

The British Medical Acupuncture Society
☎ 01606 786782
www.medical-acupuncture.co.uk

Centre for Complementary and Integrated Medicine
☎ 023 8033 4752
www.complemed.co.uk

Corporate Watch (on the pharmaceutical industry)
☎ 01865 791391
www.corporatewatch.org/profiles/
pharmaceuticals/pharmaceuticals.html

Department of Health
☎ 020 7210 4850
www.dh.gov.uk

The General Council and Register of Naturopaths
☎ 0870 745 6984
www.naturopathy.org.uk

General Chiropractic Council
☎ 020 7713 5155
www.gcc-uk.org

General Osteopathic Council
☎ 020 7357 6655
www.osteopathy.org.uk

Health Care Without Harm
www.noharm.org

Health Watch
☎ 020 8789 7813
www.healthwatch-uk.org

Institute for Complementary Medicine
☎ 020 7237 5165
www.icmedicine.co.uk

Medical Research Council
☎ 020 7636 5422
www.mrc.ac.uk

National Institute of Medical Herbalists
☎ 01392 426022
www.nimh.org.uk

National Pure Water Association
☎ 01226 360909
www.npwa.freeserve.co.uk

Natural Health Advisory Service (for women)
☎ 01273 487366
www.naturalhealthas.com

Natural Healthcare Today
☎ 01322 290821
www.naturalhealthcaretoday.com

NHS Direct Online
☎ 0845 4647 (England and Wales)
☎ 0845 424 2424 (Scotland)
www.nhsdirect.nhs.uk

NHS Gateway
www.nhs.uk

Oxfam's Cut the Cost campaign
www.oxfam.org/eng/campaigns_
camp_cutcost.htm

Professional Register of Traditional Chinese Medicine
☎ 00353 1855 9000
www.chinesemedicine.ie

Research Council for Complementary Medicine
www.rccm.org.uk

Wholistic Research Company
☎ 01438 833100
www.wholisticresearch.com

World Health Organisation
☎ 0045 39 171717
www.euro.who.int

WorldWideHealthCenter.net
☎ 0870 321 0099
www.worldwidehealthcenter.net

COSMETICS, BODYCARE AND TOILETRIES

General suppliers

Beauty Naturals
☎ 0800 980 6662
www.beautynaturals.com

CrueltyFreeShop.com
☎ 01462 436819
www.crueltyfreeshop.com

Farmacia
☎ 0870 111 8123
www.farmacia123.com

Fresh & Wild
☎ 020 7254 2332
www.freshandwild.com

The Green Shop
☎ 01452 770629
www.greenshop.co.uk

Honesty Cosmetics
☎ 01629 814888
www.honestycosmetics.co.uk

Natural Collection
☎ 0870 331 3333
www.naturalcollection.com

The Organic Pharmacy
☎ 020 7351 2232
www.theorganicpharmacy.com

ThinkNatural
☎ 0845 601 1948
www.thinknatural.com

Tree of Life UK
☎ 01782 567100
www.treeoflifeuk.com

Products and stores

Absolute Aromas
☎ 01420 540400
www.absolute-aromas.com

Aesop
☎ 020 7487 4479
www.aesop.net.au

Akamuti (The Little Tree)
☎ 0845 458 9242
www.akamuti.co.uk

Aubrey Organics
☎ 001 800 282 7394
www.aubrey-organics.com

Avalon
www.avalonnaturalproducts.com

Avea Organic
☎ 0870 199 3818
www.avea.co.uk

Aveda
☎ 01730 232380
www.aveda.com

Barefoot Botanicals
☎ 0870 220 2273
www.barefoot-botanicals.com

Beauty and the Bees
www.beebeauty.com

Beauty Without Cruelty
☎ 01206 752722

Body & Face
☎ 01561 378811
www.bodyandface.co.uk

Body Organic
☎ 0870 870 8586
www.bodyorganic.co.uk

The Body Shop
☎ 01903 844554
www.thebodyshop.com

Burt's Bees
www.burtsbees.com

Circaroma
☎ 020 7359 1135
www.circaroma.com

Comfort and Joy
☎ 01367 850278
www.comfortandjoy.co.uk

Culpeper
☎ 0870 950 9001
www.culpeper.co.uk

Doux Me
☎ 020 7221 8627
www.douxme.com

Earthbound Organics
☎ 01597 851157
www.earthbound.co.uk

Essential Care
☎ 01284 728416
www.essential-care.co.uk

Faith in Nature
☎ 0161 764 2555
www.faithinnature.co.uk

Green People
☎ 0870 240 1444
www.greenpeople.co.uk

Dr Hauschka
☎ 01386 792622
www.drhauschka.co.uk

HealthQuest
☎ 020 8424 8844
www.healthquest.co.uk

Jason Natural Cosmetics
☎ 020 7435 5911
www.jason-natural.com

Janet Carter Enterprises
☎ 01738 630259
www.janetcarter.co.uk

Jurlique
☎ 0870 770 0980
www.jurlique.com.au

The Keeper
www.menses.co.uk

Lavera
☎ 01557 870203
www.lavera.co.uk

Light of Nature
☎ 0151 281 6390
www.lightofnature.co.uk

Living Nature
☎ 01794 323222
www.livingnature.com

Liz Earle
☎ 01983 813913
www.lizearle.com

Lush
☎ 01202 668545
www.lush.co.uk

Mariposa Alternative Bodycare
☎ 01273 242925
www.mariposa.co.uk

Modern Organic Products
☎ 01282 613413
www.moppproducts.com

Mother Earth
☎ 01229 885266
www.motherearth.co.uk

Natracare
☎ 01275 371764
www.natracare.com

Naturisimo.com
☎ 020 7584 7815
www.naturisimo.com

Neal's Yard Remedies
☎ 020 7627 1949
www.nealsyardremedies.com

NHR Organic Oils
☎ 0845 310 8066
www.nhrorganicoils.co.uk

Nirvana Natural
☎ 01494 880885
www.nirvananatural.co.uk

Organic Botanics
☎ 01273 773182
www.organicbotanics.com

Pure 'Nuff Stuff
☎ 01736 366008
www.purenuffstuff.co.uk

Ren
☎ 0845 225 5600
www.renskincare.com

Scent Systems
☎ 020 7434 1166
www.scent-systems.com

Simply Gentle
☎ 0161 624 5641
www.simplygentle.com

Simply Soaps
☎ 01603 720869
www.simplysoaps.com

Spiezia
☎ 01326 231600
www.spieziaorganics.com

Verde
☎ 020 7720 1100
www.verde.co.uk

Weleda
☎ 0115 944 8200
www.weleda.co.uk

You're Gorgeous
☎ 01492 585460
www.youre-gorgeous.co.uk

CLOTHING

Retailers and labels

American Apparel
☎ 0207 837 6767
www.americanapparel.co.uk

Bishopston Trading Company
☎ 0117 924 5598
www.bishopstontrading.co.uk

Chandni Chowk
☎ 01823 327377
www.chandnichowk.co.uk

Clothworks
☎ 01225 309218
www.clothworks.co.uk

Dress Organic
☎ 020 7503 0279
www.dressorganic.co.nr

Easyhemp
☎ 01752 775124
www.easyhemp.com

Ecoclothing.co.uk
☎ 01604 621531
www.ecoclothing.co.uk

Epona
☎ 0191 415 1201
www.eponasport.com

Equop
☎ 0117 953 9991
www.equop.com

Ethical Threads
☎ 020 8682 4224
www.ethicalthreads.co.uk

Ford Barton
☎ 01398 351139
www.fordbarton.co.uk

FunkyGandhi.com
www.funkygandhi.com

FunkyWare
☎ 01274 566247
www.funky-ware.com

Ganesha
☎ 020 7928 3444
www.ganesha.co.uk

Garthenor Organic Pure Wool
☎ 0845 408 2437
www.organicpurewool.co.uk

Get Ethical
☎ 020 7419 7258
www.getethical.com

Gossypium.co.uk
☎ 0800 085 6549
www.gossypium.co.uk

Greenfibres
0845 330 3440
www.greenfibres.com

The Hebridean Woolhouse
☎ 01932 254855
www.hebrideanwoolhouse.com

The Hemp Store
☎ 01223 309993
www.thehempstore.co.uk

The Hemp Trading Company
☎ 020 8630 9347
www.thtc.co.uk

The House of Hemp
☎ 01288 381638
www.thehouseofhemp.co.uk

Howies
☎ 01239 614122
www.howies.co.uk

Hug.co.uk
☎ 0845 130 1525
www.hug.co.uk

Isle of Mull Weavers
☎ 01681 700265
www.isleofmullweavers.co.uk

Marlo
☎ 01736 755928
www.marlo.co.uk

Natural Collection
☎ 0870 331 3333
www.naturalcollection.com

One World is Enough
☎ 0845 166 1212
www.one-world-is-enough.net

Organic Attire
☎ 020 7924 3345
www.organicattire.co.uk

Patagonia
☎ 0800 0000 0041
www.patagonia.com

People Tree
☎ 0845 450 4595
www.peopletree.co.uk

Siesta
☎ 01227 786066
www.siestacrafts.co.uk

Tonic T-Shirts
☎ 07838 250749
www.tonictshirts.com

Traid
☎ 020 8733 2580
www.traid.org.uk

Traidcraft
☎ 0870 443 1017
www.traidcraftshop.co.uk

Shoes

Beyond Skin
☎ 01494 871655
www.beyondskin.co.uk

Fair Deal Trading
(for No Sweat trainers)
☎ 0870 766 5196
www.fairdealtrading.com

Green Shoes
☎ 01803 864997
www.greenshoes.co.uk

Vegetarian Shoes
☎ 01273 691913
www.vegetarian-shoes.co.uk

Jewellery

Bolly Bazaar
☎ 0870 011 5077
www.bollybazaar.com

Ethical Wares
☎ 01570 471155
www.ethicalwares.com

Fair Trade South Africa
☎ 01903 218901
www.fairtradesouthafrica.com

Silverchilli.com
www.silverchilli.com

Tearcraft
☎ 0870 240 4896
www.tearcraft.org

World Source Jewellery
☎ 0700 253 9355
www.worldsourcejewellery.co.uk

Unless different for each product, company details are listed in first entry only.

Healthcare

Antiseptics

Amphora Aromatics
☎ 0117 904 7212
www.amphora-retail.com

Avasafab
☎ 0115 963 4237
www.veganvillage.co.uk/dolma

Tea Tree Antiseptic Oil
☎ 01274 488511
www.thursdayplantation.com

Tisserand
☎ 01273 325666
www.tisserand.com

Painkillers

Aspar
☎ 020 8205 9846
www.aspar.co.uk

Lloyds Pharmacy
☎ 01494 874656
www.lloydspharmacy.com

Cold remedies

Aspar

Coldenza
☎ 020 8780 4200
www.nelsonshomoeopathy.co.uk

Olbas Oil and Sinotar
☎ 01452 524012
www.laneshealth.com

Tisserand (Clear Breathe)

Contact lens solutions

Sauflon Pharmaceuticals
☎ 020 8322 4200
www.sauflon.co.uk

Opticians

Independent, local opticians are a good option, but also:

Dollond and Aitchison
☎ 0800 052 8000
www.danda.co.uk

Specsavers
☎ 01481 236000
www.specsavers.co.uk

Vision Express
☎ 0115 986 5225
www.visionexpress.com

Indigestion remedies

In the first instance, try milk, tea (peppermint, ginger or chamomile) or a pinch of bicarbonate of soda in water. For a commercial product:

Asilone Windcheaters
☎ 01484 842217
www.thorntonross.co.uk

Birley's Antacid and Moorlands Indigestion Tablets
☎ 01603 735200
www.typharm.com

Lane's Indigestion Tablets
☎ 01452 524012
www.laneshealth.com

Numark
☎ 01827 841200
www.numarkpharmacists.com

Remegel
☎ 01565 624000
www.ssl-international.com

Vitamin pills

Nature's Own
☎ 01684 310022
www.natures-own.co.uk

Sage Organic
☎ 01672 811777
www.sageorganic.com

Viridian
☎ 01327 878050
www.viridian-nutrition.com

Cosmetics and toiletries

Cosmetics

Barry M
☎ 020 8349 2992
www.barrym.co.uk

Beauty Without Cruelty
☎ 01206 752722

Body Shop
☎ 01903 844554
www.thebodyshop.com

Deodorants

The Deodorant Stone
☎ 01559 384856
www.deodorant-stone.co.uk

Pit Rok
☎ 020 8563 1120
www.pitrok.co.uk

Tawas Crystal Deodorant
☎ 0800 074 9645
www.crystaldeodorant.com

Tisserand

Weleda
☎ 0115 944 8200
www.weleda.co.uk

Perfume

Dolma
☎ 0115 963 4237
www.veganvillage.co.uk/dolma

Lush
☎ 01202 668544
www.lush.co.uk

Neal's Yard Remedies
☎ 020 7627 1949
www.nealsyardremedies.com

Weleda (aftershave)

Razors and electric shavers

Remington
☎ 0800 212438
www.remingtontitanium.co.uk

Reuseable
Wilkinson Sword
☎ 01494 533300
www.wilkinson-sword.co.uk

Shaving gel

Body Shop (Sugaring)

Green People
☎ 0870 240 1444
www.greenpeople.co.uk

King of Shaves
☎ 0800 083 8416
www.shave.com

Weleda

Recycled toilet paper

Essential
☎ 0117 958 3550
www.essential-trading.co.uk

Suma
☎ 0845 458 2290
www.suma.co.uk

Sanitary protection

Mooncup
☎ 01273 673845
www.mooncup.co.uk

Moontime Alternatives
☎ 01428 685661
www.beinggirls.co.uk

Natracare
☎ 01275 371764
www.natracare.com

Shampoo

Faith In Nature
☎ 0161 764 2555
www.faithinnature.co.uk

Honesty Cosmetics
☎ 01629 814888
www.honestycosmetics.co.uk

Weleda

Skincare

Green People

Honesty Cosmetics

Weleda

Soap

Bio D
☎ 01482 229950
www.biodegradeable.co.uk

Caurnie Soaperie
☎ 0141 776 1218
www.caurnie.com

Faith In Nature

Honesty Cosmetics

Natural Organic Soap
☎ 020 8488 2469
www.organicsoap.net

Suntan lotion

Banana Boat
☎ 01954 719899
www.bananaboat.co.uk

Honesty Cosmetics

Malibu
☎ 020 8758 0055
www.malibusun.com

Weleda

Toothpaste

Green People

Kingfisher
☎ 01603 630484
www.kingfishertoothpaste.com

Sarakan
☎ 01420 544424
www.sarakan.com

Weleda

Clothing

Clothes shops

No high-street clothing chains currently meet the demands of campaigners for systematic protection of workers' rights. Specialist ethical clothing suppliers include:

Bishopston Trading Company
☎ 0117 924 5598
www.bishopstontrading.co.uk

Chandni Chowk
☎ 01823 327377
www.chandnichowk.co.uk

Greenfibres
☎ 0845 330 3440
www.greenfibres.com

Natural Collection
☎ 0870 331 3333
www.naturalcollection.com

People Tree
☎ 0845 450 4595
www.peopletree.co.uk

Directories of 'green clothing' companies

Ethical Consumer
☎ 0161 226 2929
www.ethicalconsumer.org

Green Guide
☎ 020 7354 2709
www.greenguideonline.com

Jeans

Greenfibres

Lee Cooper and Falmer
☎ 01695 552400
www.matalan.com

Jewellery

Ethical Wares
☎ 01570 471155
www.ethicalwares.com

Get Ethical
☎ 020 7419 7258
www.getethical.com

People Tree

Traidcraft
☎ 0870 443 1017
www.traidcraftshop.co.uk

Shirts

Bishopston Trading

Chandni Chowk

Greenfibres

Natural Collection

People Tree

Sports shoes

Cheatah
☎ 01273 691913
www.vegetarian-shoes.co.uk

New Balance
☎ 01925 423000
www.newbalance.com

Walsh Sports (fell-running shoes)
☎ 01204 370374
www.walshsports.co.uk

Tights

Greenfibres

Natural Collection

Spirit of Nature
☎ 0870 725 9885
www.spiritofnature.co.uk

Shoe shops

* exclusively non-leather footwear

Clarks
☎ 01458 443131
www.clarks.co.uk

Ecco
☎ 0870 777 7323
www.ecco.com/uk

Ethical Wares

Freerangers*
☎ 01207 565957
www.freerangers.co.uk

Green Shoes
☎ 01803 864997
www.greenshoes.co.uk

Veganline*
☎ 0800 458 4442
www.veganline.com

Vegetarian Shoes*
☎ 01273 691 913
www.vegetarian-shoes.co.uk

Family

Introduction

'Happiness is having a large, loving, caring, close-knit family – in another city.'

George Burns (1896–1996)

Today, the family is a beleaguered institution. It is fashionable to blame many of our current social ills – youth delinquency, illiteracy, lack of respect for the environment, depression, social intolerance, etc – on the 'breakdown' of the family unit. While these points may be vigorously debated, what is certainly clear is that the changing shape, make-up and mechanics of the typical family have huge implications for our consumption habits, if not our overall emotional wellbeing. The rise of single households, increasing sums spent by parents on children, the shrinking of the extended family, a rise in life expectancy – these are all going to greatly influence patterns of consumption over coming years and decades.

It pays to look closely at how the family has changed over the past few decades. The post-war dominance (some say myth) of the 'nuclear family' – a household consisting solely of two parents and their legal children in which the father is the sole breadwinner and the mother oversees the domestic spending, chores and childcare – has now largely faded. In fact, in 2000, research showed that 37 per cent of Europe's population lived as part of a nuclear family, but that by 2005 the figure was predicted to have decreased to 34 per cent. In Britain, over the same period, there would be 1.7 million fewer people living in a home with other family members. There would be one million more people aged over 50 than there were in 2000.

The current trend across all of Europe is for couples to delay marriage and childbirth. Tied into this trend is the fact that the percentage of youths is shrinking and the percentage of pensioners increasing. This is creating a new market: people who live alone and whose purchases reflect different values from those of people who live as part of a family or household. For example, research has shown that those living on their own are more likely to buy services and products to avoid chores, to choose convenience foods, and to look for products with health benefits or 'added value'.

But there are many other social trends that point to a significant shift in a typical family's consumer and service demands:

● According to Census 2001, there are 21,660,475 households in England and Wales, of which 30 per cent are one-person households – up from 26.3 per cent in 1991.

● Half of these one-person households are occupied by pensioners, with three-quarters of one-person households occupied by women.

● The average number of people living in a household in the UK is shrinking. In 2002 it stood at 2.31 persons, down from 2.91 in 1971.

● The proportion of households containing a married or co-habiting couple with dependent children declined from 31 per cent in 1979 to just 21 per cent in 2002.

● Lone-parent families have grown from eight per cent of families in 1971 to 27 per cent in 2002.

● Two-thirds of mothers are now returning to work after maternity leave, up 50 per cent from 1988, when under half returned to work.

● The average age of first marriage is rising. In 1999, it stood at 28 years for women and 30.1 years for men. In 1971, it stood at 22.6 years for women and 24.6 for men.

● Real incomes have quadrupled since the 1950s.

● The average life expectancy is rising. However, the amount of time we remain in good health is failing to keep up. In 2001, 'healthy' life expectancy at birth was 67 years for men, but total life expectancy was 75.7 years, leaving 8.7 years of expected poor health. For women, total life expectancy was 80.4 years, but healthy life expectancy was 68.8 years, a gap of 11.6 years.

- In 2001, children made up 20 per cent of the population, compared with 23 per cent in 1961. By 2011, the percentage will fall to 18 per cent. There were 9.4 million people aged 65 or over in 2001, an increase of 51 per cent since 1961. Government projections suggest the number of people aged 65 and over will exceed the number aged under 16 by 2014.
- Largely due to rising rates of divorce and childlessness, the number of 'lonely and isolated' older people (as described by the thinktank Demos) in the UK will grow by a third to 2.2 million by 2021.

These trends are already having a profound effect on how family members interact with one another, as well as how families behave as a whole. The demand for care for the elderly is booming as people live longer and households decrease in size. Likewise, the demand for childcare is increasing as more parents, particularly mothers, choose to work. The allure of convenience products and services is also on the rise as families become more 'time-poor' due to work commitments, and choose increasingly to seek 'down time' as opposed to tackling mundane chores such as cleaning and cooking. This in turn is leading to a rise in the use of disposable nappies, readymeals, time-saving appliances and 'miracle' cleaning products.

It's no surprise then that the nuclear family is being replaced by what government statisticians are calling 'beanpole' families – those made up of fewer children and multiple generations of older people. Fewer brothers and sisters in one generation leads to fewer aunts and uncles in the next. So, instead of a 'bushy' family tree with lots of lateral branches, we now have longer, thinner patterns of family relationships.

How these families operate at home is also interesting, particularly the relationship between the mother and father figures. Sociologists have noticed that families are less dictatorial nowadays and increasingly 'negotiative'. Where the father may have 'laid down the law' before, families are now 'debating' issues and, in theory, life is more equitable for all. However, such democratic tendencies, say sociologists, are inevitably increasing conflict and tension as compromise and consensus are often unsuccessfully sought.

The small amount of time couples are now spending with one another is also noteworthy. The average British couple, according to the Office for National Statistics, spend just 126 minutes awake in each other's company during a working day – and that includes 51 minutes in front of the television. For those with children, time together falls to 78 minutes. In fact, across the week as a whole, many significant activities are spent apart, including 61 per cent of television watching, 65 per cent of the time spent eating, 73 per cent of sports and 79 per cent of socialising with friends or family. About 90 per cent of housework is done alone, too.

With the increasing number of children who have computers and televisions in their rooms, families as a whole are spending less and less time in each other's presence. In fact, 77 per cent of children aged 11–14 have a television in their bedroom, and 64 per cent have their own DVD player or video recorder. One in four also has a computer in their room. In a particularly telling survey conducted in 2004, three out of five 11–14-year-olds agreed with the statement that 'everyone at home is free to get on with their lives and interests', with 53 per cent agreeing with the statement, 'as long as they do well at school, they can do what they like'. Just over half said they preferred spending time on their own to time with their family.

The atomisation of the family inevitably leads to an increase in the use of domestic energy (think of all those appliances concurrently switched on), as well as consumption of food and other household products with 'everyone doing their own thing'. For example, the average household now has three different types of shampoo and three types of breakfast cereal as everyone's tastes and needs are met. But these trends also suggest we are all leading more 'lonely' lives – even within the confines of the family unit.

Even so, there are plenty of ways to counter this shift. From the cradle to the grave, this chapter aims to show how all aspects of family life – raising children, looking after the elderly, tending the family pet, even organising funerals – can be considerate to the environment, less wasteful, but perhaps most important, more inclusive for all involved.

Children

Who'd be a parent? Actually, about 70 per cent of us will be a parent at some point in our lives. But amid the joy, what angst it can bring. Whether it's trying to persuade your child to eat anything other than crisps and cola, getting them not to answer back or deciding whether to give your toddler the MMR jab, facing up to constant worries and dilemmas is a fundamental and inescapable part of parenting.

Despite popular perception, we are arguably more conscientious as parents now than we were a generation ago. Parents in the 1990s spent an average of 85 'face-to-face' minutes a day per child, compared to 25 minutes a day in the mid-1970s. Of course, many socio-economic factors are likely to explain this rise, such as less time spent cooking and doing domestic chores, but there is certainly a sense – just look at the number of parenting guides in bookshops – that we worry more now about our parental duties.

But are we worrying about the right things? It's no surprise to learn of the three things that concern today's parents the most – education, health and safety. Certainly on the last two points concerns are possibly misplaced: children are statistically now both healthier (with regard to life-threatening diseases and basic nutrition) and safer from danger (with regard to both accidents and abduction) than ever before, yet we tend to keep our children under much tighter rein than our parents did. Surveys repeatedly show that many parents, if given the chance, would like their children to be electronically tagged. Likewise, parents now consult a doctor on average 24 times in the first four years of a child's life – a high figure, perhaps, given that children are healthier than ever before.

There's no doubt that we now live in more of a 'scare' culture, in which one screaming headline can move a million mothers and fathers to doubt their parenting skills. Further fuelling this anxiety, the current manner of parenting is more aspirational and competitive than ever before – we live in a world of school league tables and 'must-have' children's designer accessories and toys. It is only natural and right that parents want the best for their child, but all this pressure is creating a generation of what the sociologist Frank Furedi calls 'paranoid parents', whose perspectives are being skewed by external influences: advertisers, politicians and the media.

What may be being lost on many parents are some of the other, more hidden but worrying trends: that children are being exposed to increasing amounts of synthetic chemicals; that children watch many thousands of adverts a year; that families are being isolated from each other within their own homes by computers, mobile phones and televisions; that companies are able to advertise their goods to children within schools. . .

Pregnancy and birth

The birth rate is falling in the UK. The time when people had 2.4 children has long gone. In 2003 the average stood at 1.73: higher than in Spain, but a long way short of Gaza, Niger and Angola where women, on average, have just over seven children in their lifetime.

Every pregnancy and baby is special, but as the birth rate drops in the UK, more inevitably gets invested in each child. It may be good news for global population rates, but it doesn't automatically equate to a reduction in overall consumption. That's because 'serving' new parents are the many companies with their 'must-have' baby accessories – pushchairs, moses baskets, feeding bottles, car seats, rocking chairs, musical mobiles, changing stations, nappy bags, and all manner of lotions and potions. Again, clever marketing sows subtle seeds of doubt into the minds of new parents: 'are you sure you could do without this product?'; 'will your baby be safe without this item?'

It's obviously a successful strategy as parents now spend, on average, £2,382 on equipment during a baby's first 12 months. And whereas previous generations would give 'hand-me-downs' to friends and family, or save items for later children, the current trend, especially for first-time parents, is to buy everything new.

To reverse this trend where possible, try to source second-hand baby items (although this isn't recommended for car seats unless you can be absolutely sure of their provenance). There's a healthy market for such goods online (try eBay or parenting websites such as Mumsnet.com, particularly their message boards) and in local papers. You can also try local 'mothers' groups'. Equally, try to pass on any items that you may have finished with to people you know or to a charity, or even to the local maternity or children's ward.

The pressure to consume starts well before a baby is even born. From the moment parents first discover they are expecting, our culture expects them to 'prepare'. A natural 'nesting' instinct is inevitable – a desire to make the home as comfortable, safe and inviting to a newborn as possible. But there is also a tendency to establish an hyper-hygienic environment. Although this inclination is only natural, there is a danger that both the mother-to-be and the unborn child can be exposed to potentially harmful chemicals. For example, many parents will freshly decorate a spare room, but paint fumes can be potentially dangerous to both a pregnant woman and her unborn child. Likewise, pregnant women should be careful to avoid harsh household cleaners and foods likely to contain synthetic additives and pesticide residues. Some doctors now advise pregnant women to completely avoid suncreams due to the active compounds they contain. A team at the University of Zurich looked at the active compounds in common suncreams and, of 10 tested, found nine mimicked the female hormone oestrogen.

Another chemical high on the list to be wary of is vitamin A, often called retinol in cosmetics. Professor Nigel Brown from St George's Hospital, London, explained to the *Guardian* that 'vitamin A derivatives are used by the embryo in the development of many areas of the body, including the heart, the limbs and the central nervous system. Anything that interferes with that can cause serious malformations'. Retinol is used in small amounts in anti-ageing creams, but in such low concentrations that it is unlikely to cause problems. More damaging, Brown said, is taking too much vitamin A as a supplement while pregnant.

One of the most enduring concerns is the effect of hair dye and perming solution on pregnant women. Studies have found that hairdressers who regularly handle bleaches, dyes and other hair chemicals over many years with no protection can have a higher risk of miscarriage.

Questions have also been raised about some essential oils. Aromatherapists suggest that, as a precaution, pregnant women may want to avoid birch and wintergreen because the main chemical in them (methyl salicylate) is absorbed easily into the skin. Women with a record of early miscarriage might also want to avoid clary sage (which is drunk as a tea or used as an essential oil).

If you ever have any concerns about the possible effects of a 'teratogen' (a chemical that is known to cause birth defects, or increase the risk of miscarriage) then contact the NHS-funded National Teratology Information Service (www.ncl.ac.uk/pharmsc/entis.htm, tel: 0191 232 1525) for advice.

Understandably, the majority of pregnant women focus most of their attention and anxieties on the actual birth itself. There has been a huge surge of interest in recent years in the 'natural birth' movement, fuelled in large part by growing concerns – misplaced or otherwise – about the impact on both baby and mother of commonplace medical procedures such as epidurals, caesarean sections and forced induction. The decision how best to 'manage' labour should be a personal decision that only the mother can make. The choice of what pain relief to use is one of the biggest considerations and there are myriad options, which partly explains the anxiety.

The choices largely fall into two camps – drug-based and 'natural'. The norm across many NHS maternity units – although there are some noticeable exceptions – is to, in the first instance, offer drug-based pain relief, namely, entonox ('gas and air'), pethidine (a drug similar to morphine) and epidural (an anaesthetic that is administered through the spine). More and more hospitals are now also offering the use of a large bath

Family celebrations

Are birthdays, weddings and religious festivals such as Christmas joyous family occasions, or examples of excessive and wanton consumption at their worst? The most accurate answer is probably both. Whereas these occasions are the few times that many families will get together throughout the year, they also often act as catalysts for huge spikes in spending – much of which can send people into debt. The average wedding, for example, now costs about £16,000 – and that doesn't even include the money spent on gifts for the bride and groom. Over the Christmas period, 1.7 billion cards are sent, six million turkeys eaten and 7.5 million Christmas trees bought.

Part of the problem is that many people feel huge social pressure to spend 'like for like' or not to 'seem cheap' which only acts to further escalate spending. But there are many ways to reduce the impact of consumption and still more than live up to the maxim that 'it's the thought that counts'. Rather than filling their homes with extra toasters and salad bowls, some newlyweds are now asking their guests to make an offering to charity (see www.thealternativeweddinglist.co.uk), plant a tree or choose from a list of fair-trade gifts. Some are also making an effort to reduce the environmental impact of the big day itself. In Hereford, for example, the 'Green Wedding Hotel' offers 'the only venue entirely dedicated to organic and environmentally friendly weddings in the UK' (bookings via www.responsibletravel.com).

Equally, for birthdays or Christmas you could make your own cards. Wrapping paper is another excess when you consider that over Christmas as much as 83 square kilometres of wrapping paper will be thrown in the bin – enough to cover an area the size of Guernsey. Would recycling newspaper, or using a piece of material, make such a difference? Also be wary of buying massmarket flowers that are typically grown thousands of miles away using pesticides and harvested with cheap labour. (Fairtrade roses are now available from retailers such as Tesco.) And when it comes to giving gifts there are many alternatives to the CDs, toys and high-street vouchers that we usually plump for. Here are the Environment Agency's top ideas:

- Give plants, especially drought-resistant plants – great for the environment.

- Give fountain pens (that refill from a bottle of ink, as opposed to cartridges) to replace disposable pens.

- Buy Fairtrade food and drink that benefit the growers and farmers of the Third World.

- Help to conserve natural resources by giving presents made of recycled materials.

- Avoid presents that rely on disposable parts, such as batteries, but if they do, make sure they can use rechargeable ones.

- Keep waste to a minimum by choosing presents without layers of packaging.

- Buy gifts that are durable – especially toys.

- Give gifts of experiences, such as theatre and sports tickets, and gift certificates for restaurants.

- Consider giving items that save energy such as low-flowing shower heads and fluorescent light bulbs that use much less energy than candescent bulbs.

The World Health Organisation recommends that **babies are breastfed** for at least two years

known as a birthing pool (although few women actually give birth in such a pool, instead the pool's sense of weightlessness acts as a way to relieve pain during labour). Usually, the onus falls on the mother to provide any other forms of relief such as a TENS machine (a 'Transcutaneous Electrical Nerve Stimulation' machine that administers small electric pulses to relax muscles) or a 'birthing ball' (a large inflatable ball that helps to ease the pressure placed on the back during labour). Some women will also have learned breathing and exercise techniques aimed at reducing pain.

There is no 'best' way to minimise pain through labour, but it certainly pays to research all the options available as thoroughly as you can and, where possible, reduce the use of drug-based relief to help maintain control of the labour, as well as to minimise any possible side-effects suffered by mother and baby. Most midwives will be able to talk you through the different options and associated risks, but it is also useful to attend antenatal classes, join a local mothers' group and read up at home.

It pays, too, to be aware that there are two very distinct schools of thought with regard to the management of labour. The medical mainstream, typified by the attitude of much of the NHS, is that 'midwife, not mother, knows best', which, given a midwife's training and daily experience, should be correct. But there is a growing movement of parents that believes some maternity ward professionals can be too keen to favour intervention which, they claim, can lead to a so-called 'cascade of management': one interventional procedure inevitably leads to another and soon the parents have 'lost control'. This is currently a hot topic of debate in the health industry and with

parenting campaign groups, but knowledge is power in this situation, and both parents (and any birth partners) should be aware of all the options and make sure they're fully briefed at every stage of labour.

A home birth is another option (and right) of all parents, but again it should be thoroughly researched, assessed and debated. The local branch of the National Childbirth Trust (www.nctpregnancyandbabycare.com, tel: 0870 7703236) is a good starting point to discuss any of the above issues, as are local antenatal classes.

Another key decision prior to the birth is whether or not to breastfeed. And for once, the advice is simple and clear: breast is best. Only two-thirds of UK mothers breastfeed, with just two-fifths of them still breastfeeding when the baby is four months old. (It's important to stress, though, that it's not always a choice; in some rare cases, mothers are not physically able to breastfeed, or simply find it too painful.) The World Health Organisation recommends that babies are breastfed for at least two years. The advantages of breastfeeding to both baby and mother are overwhelming, but social stigma, an incorrect perception that it's inconvenient, and a belief that it's difficult to maintain all combine to put many mothers off. Thankfully, there are many organisations offering help, encouragement and advice on topics ranging from expressing milk at work through to easing mastitis:

NHS National Breastfeeding Awareness Week (www.breastfeeding.nhs.uk); Association of Breastfeeding Mothers (www.abm.me.uk, tel: 0870 401 7711); Breastfeeding Network (www.breastfeedingnetwork. org.uk, tel: 0870 900 8787); La Leche League (www.laleche.org.uk, tel: 0845 120 2918); and NCT's breastfeeding advice line (tel: 0870 4448708).

On the subject of breastfeeding, there is also widespread concern about the way that infant formula milk is being marketed to mothers around the world, particularly in developing nations. For detailed information, contact Babymilk Action (www.babymilkaction.org, tel: 01223 464420).

Nappies

Nappies deserve special attention because they are a particularly nasty blight on the environment. The figures are simply staggering:

• Eight million disposable nappies are discarded every day in the UK, the vast majority ending up in landfill.

• The average baby using disposable nappies produces one tonne of nappy waste during its two-and-a-half years in nappies.

• Depending on the area, between two and eight per cent of landfill sites are filled with nappies.

• Nappy disposal costs each local authority, and therefore taxpayers, many hundreds of thousands of pounds a year. For every pound we spend on disposable nappies, taxpayers spend 10p disposing of them.

The answer from most local authorities, under pressure from Landfill Directive targets, has been to try to encourage as many parents as possible to use washable nappies. But the fact remains that a large percentage of parents – up to 90 per cent, say manufacturers – still prefer the convenience of disposable nappies.

What is the better option: washable or disposable? It's still very much up for debate. The manufacturers of disposable nappies have spent much time and energy trying to prove that, over the entire life cycle of a nappy, there is little to choose between disposables and washables in terms of water and energy used. A survey commissioned by the Women's Environmental Network (WEN), a campaign group that urges parents to use washable 'real' nappies, concluded that disposable nappies have twice the impact on the environment as home-laundered nappies and two-and-a-half times the impact of service-washed nappies (which use energy and water more efficiently due to the economies of scale involved).

Simply in terms of cost, washable nappies hold the advantage: WEN estimates that they can save parents up to £500 per child. Buying a set of 20 washable nappies, wraps and liners will cost between £70 and £200 depending on the brand and whether you choose

Eight million disposable nappies are discarded every day in the UK, the vast majority ending up in landfill

organic cotton or not. Disposables, on average, cost about 13 pence each, so it's easy to see how the cost can add up when you consider that babies, particularly newborns, get through up to eight nappies a day.

The other important advantage that washables hold over disposables is the materials from which they are made. Disposables tend to be made from plastics, wood pulp and super-absorbent gels. Some also contain bleaching agents and chlorine. You may want to question whether you want these types of material sitting next to your baby's skin, but there's also the serious issue of how biodegradable these materials are. Manufacturers claim that up to 80 per cent of a modern nappy is biodegradable but WEN points out that disposable nappies could take hundreds of years to fully break down. If you do need to buy disposable nappies, search for brands that aim to use as much recycled or biodegradable material and as few potentially toxic chemicals as possible, such as Tushies, Moltex Öko and Nature Boy & Girl (now available at many supermarkets and chemists).

Many parents still hold on to the myth that washable nappies are extremely hard work. Certainly a generation ago, when it was commonly perceived that terry nappies needed to be boiled on a stove for hours then air dried throughout the house, washable nappies were quite labour intensive. But modern washing machines and contemporary nappy designs (most washable nappies are now ergonomically shaped and have convenient poppers or Velcro side straps replacing the nappy pins of old) mean that washable nappies are much less of a chore than most believe.

Why not buy a sample washable nappy and see how you get on? They are increasingly easy to get hold of via mothers' groups or mail-order/internet catalogues, but if you are having trouble finding a local supplier, contact the Real Nappy Association (www.realnappy.com, tel: 01656 783405). Also try the Women's Environmental Network (www.wen.org.uk, tel: 020 7481 9004) and the Nappy Lady (www.thenappylady.co.uk). All will answer questions on what nappy type is best suited to your baby's needs.

And if you don't want to wash your own nappies, try a nappy-laundering service. Most are limited to cities and larger towns but check for local services by contacting the National Association of Nappy Washing Services (www.changeanappy.co.uk, tel: 0121 693 4949).

Remote controlled

As children get older so they increasingly become the target of advertisers. It makes sense: children are big business. Research in the US has shown that American children now influence more than $600 billion of consumer spending each year. As a result of this, spending on marketing directed at children has increased 2.5 times in the past decade in the US to $15 billion a year.

Advertising can come in many forms – cereal packets, school vending machines, T-shirts – but by far the biggest conduit of advertising is television. The average child in the UK now watches the equivalent of 217 adverts a week (11,284 a year), according to figures from the Food Standards Agency. Of these, 41 per cent are for food products, with 70 per cent of this total for sweets, fast food, breakfast cereals with added sugar, savoury snacks and soft drinks. Parents aren't ignorant of this fact, with many expressing in surveys that they feel television is putting too much pressure on their children to consume. But the pressure of our 'time-poor' lives leads to the strong temptation to let children watch many hours of television a week.

The majority of children now have a television set in their bedrooms, meaning that not only is viewing further encouraged but that it is unregulated by parents. It explains why research has shown that children are being exposed to more and more violent and sexual imagery at a younger age through a range of 'screen-based' sources – music videos, computer games, movies, and the internet.

Unsurprisingly, most evidence points to television being a negative influence on children. A report in the *Lancet* in 2004 warned parents of a link between children's excessive viewing habits and longterm health problems such as poor fitness and raised cholesterol. It also claimed that youthful television addicts were more likely to smoke. One study has linked television viewing to obesity and another to aggressiveness. But most research has taken place in the US – a country where

each child, on average, sees 40,000 adverts a year – and is therefore possibly the best place to catch a glimpse of where we could be heading.

A US survey in 2004 claimed to have found an association between television viewing among toddlers and attention deficit and hyperactivity disorder (ADHD) at school age. The problem is perceived to be so acute that the American Academy of Pediatrics now gives the following advice to parents in the US: 'Too much television can negatively affect early brain development. This is especially true at younger ages, when learning to talk and play with others is so important. Until more research is done about the effects of television on very young children, the AAP does not recommend television for children age two or younger.'

Others go further. Some suggest that children under two shouldn't even see their parents watching television. Robert Shaw, an American family psychiatrist and author of bestselling *The Epidemic: The Rot of American Culture, Absentee and Permissive Parenting, and the Resultant Plague of Joyless, Selfish Children*, believes that under-fives should be allowed to watch television only in moderation and never unattended.

The trouble with exposure to adverts, claim many, is that children, particularly under-fives, have trouble differentiating between adverts and programmes. Research has shown that, until the age of eight, children cannot understand the persuasive intent of advertising. Whether children 'understand' adverts or not, the result is invariably the same: they want what they're being shown and they won't give in until they get it. Internal research within the US marketing industry (ie, research the marketeers don't want parents to know about) has shown that up to 46 per cent of sales of products aimed at children are generated by the so-called 'nag factor' (or what we call in the UK 'pester power'). Part of the research involved 150 mothers keeping a 'nag diary' for their children aged three to eight for two weeks. On average, the results showed a mother received 66 nags over this period – or 4.7 nags a day. Another US study found that between the ages of 12 and 17, children would nag on average nine times before they gave up.

Compounding the problem of watching too much television is that fewer and fewer children are being encouraged, or even allowed, outside to play. This is largely down to today's 'worry' culture, but is also due to a perception by many adults that children will only end up getting up to no good when allowed out. In 2003, a National Playday survey of children aged 7–16 found that two-thirds said they liked to play outside daily. However, four out of five said they had been regularly 'told off' for doing so. Among those under 11, almost half said the main person who told them off was a parent. In another example, in 2003 children in Cumbria raised £100,000 and got 1,500 people to sign a petition for a skateboard park, yet planning was refused. The Children's Society also reports that by-laws are increasingly inhibiting children's play. For example, 115 'No Ball Games' signs were counted on one housing estate in the north-west of England in which four out of five playgrounds had also been shut down.

With parents seeking absolute safety for their children, it's perhaps inevitable that they are increasingly keeping their children indoors, but by doing so we may also be raising increasingly unfit and overweight children who spend much of their time in front of a screen absorbing messages from advertisers. It seems that the only answer is to get children up and outside more, be it by supporting local youth clubs and play groups, going on nature trails together, playing in the park, visiting a city farm, teaching them how to grow vegetables, walking to school, going to the local swimming pool, joining a sports club, encouraging them to stay on for an after-school activity... The list is endless. As a classic children's television show once said with self-effacing irony in its opening titles: 'Why don't you just switch off your television set and go out and do something less boring instead?'

Dilemma

What should I think about during sex?

Whether it's for pleasure or procreation (or even both!), sex throws up many thorny dilemmas, most of which are fraught with emotional, psychological, moral, religious and even environmental overtones.

Contraception is one such dilemma. Some believe – typically on religious grounds – that contraception itself is fundamentally wrong as it denies potential life. Or that it has led to a 'permissive society'. Others believe passionately that contraception has emancipated and empowered millions of women by handing them both control and choice, has reduced unwanted births and greatly helped to further minimise the spread of sexually transmitted diseases.

Then there are those concerned about the impact of certain forms of contraception on the environment. In 2002, Environment Agency researchers said that the steady drop in male fertility in Britain may be caused by men ingesting female hormones in drinking water drawn from rivers containing recycled sewage. Millions of oral contraceptive pills containing synthetic oestrogen (known as ethanol oestradiol) are consumed every day and this compound is ultimately discharged into the sewage system and then flushed into rivers and the sea where it remains active for up to a month. Research showed that in some rivers from which drinking water is taken, all the male fish of some species had become 'feminised'.

There are also concerns about some spermicides commonly used on condoms and caps. One in particular – nonoxynol-9 – has been the focus of much debate in recent years, with some studies suggesting that, as its high toxicity can cause genital lesions, it may increase the risk of HIV infection among women already at high risk of infection. (The official WHO stance is that nonoxynol-9 is no more effective than silicone-based spermicides and should not be promoted due to these concerns.)

But condoms themselves can also be harmful to the environment. The Environment Agency estimates that in the UK, 61 million to 100 million condoms a year are thrown away, with many of the ones flushed down toilets being found in rivers, on beaches and in the sea. And often they're not even 'our' condoms – according to the Tidy Britain Group, more than a third of rubbish found in the sea off the west coast of Britain has crossed the Atlantic.

Choosing a method of contraception is clearly a personal decision based on individual needs (for more information, visit www.fpa.org.uk and www.nhsdirect.nhs.uk/selfhelp/info/advice/contraception.asp) but it's important not only to research all your options but also to consider the wider environmental impact of your choice. For example, if you use condoms, wrap them up and put them in a bin rather than flushing them away.

On a broader level, it could be argued that procreation itself needs to be carefully considered. With concerns about global overpopulation and the resultant pressure on resources, adding another 'mouth to feed' to the six billion-odd people on the planet clearly carries with it a considerable responsibility.

Could adopting or fostering a child be an option? The charity Fostering Network found in 2004 that the shortage of foster carers in the UK had reached more than 8,000, a 35 per cent rise since the last survey in 2002. It's a considerable problem. In England, for example, there are over 41,000 children and young people living with 32,000 foster families on any given day. But the shortfall in foster carers means that many children are being housed away from their home town, and with carers who don't share their religion or first language. For a list of organisations that can provide advice and support should you ever consider adopting or fostering, see the directory at the end of this chapter. For more general information about adopting and fostering, visit http://society.guardian.co.uk/adoption.

Bringing up baby

• Get involved at your children's school. Be on guard for companies 'sponsoring' events, coursework, books or facilities there. What are their motives, other than raising awareness of their brand? Urge the school to consider how it can save energy and materials such as paper. For inspiration visit www.eco-schools.org.uk and www.est.org.uk/schools. Suggest it apply for further advice from the Energy Saving Trust's SchoolEnergy programme (www.schoolenergy.org.uk). Encourage a school trip to a local landfill site to show children the impact of our waste problem. Become a school governor. Get the school to start up a pupil-managed vegetable plot. Finally, push for the school to raise awareness among children about sustainability and the environment – get the head teacher to contact the Council for Environmental Education (www.cee.org.uk, tel: 0118 950 2550).

• Where possible, teach your child how precious resources such as energy and water are by getting them to do the small but important things – turning off lights as they leave rooms, brushing teeth without the tap running, etc.

• Buy second-hand toys, repair broken ones, and improvise games (good old dressing up, for example). Or borrow toys from the National Toy Library (www.natl.org.uk).

• Make every effort not to add to the pollution and congestion caused by the school run. Lobby your local school to start a 'walking bus' (www.walkingbus.com).

• Subscribe to *Juno* magazine, the quarterly that provides 'a natural approach to parenting' (www.juno magazine.com, tel: 01444 891460).

• Donate any outgrown toys to your local children's wards, GP and dentist waiting rooms and charity shops.

• Look out for toys made under the Fairtrade scheme (see page 60) which guarantees that the people in developing nations employed to make them work in safe conditions and earn a fair wage. For details visit www.traidcraft.co.uk, or call 0191 491 0591.

• If you see a 'bounty pack' being offered to new mothers in a maternity ward complain to the hospital staff. Companies will give away trial samples of nappies, baby wipes, vouchers etc in the hope of securing the longterm custom of a parent. Campaigners are now calling for the practice to end.

• Buy a copy of *The Organic Baby Book* by Tania Maxted-Frost (Green Books, £7.95). It lists and reviews hundreds of organic baby products.

• If parenting is leaving you feeling depressed, or with financial concerns, there is plenty of advice out there. Parentline (www.parentline.co.uk, tel: 0808 800 2222) is an excellent resource for all parenting queries. Gingerbread (www.gingerbread.org.uk, tel: 0800 018 4318) offers support for lone parents; and Fathers Direct (www.fathersdirect.com, tel: 0845 634 1328) offers help to fathers.

• Children are particularly vulnerable to toxic chemicals (see page 106) so it's wise to make every effort to reduce their exposure to them. Avoid baby wipes, which can contain parabens and propylene glycol – a common ingredient in anti-freeze. A damp flannel will do the job just as well. Try to choose clothing and bedding made with organic cotton. Use natural soaps and don't use a shampoo on a child every day. In fact, all a baby really needs to keep clean is a small tub or sink full of warm water. Try to use chlorine-free swimming pools. Keep children away from the fumes emitted by household cleaners and solvents. Soft plastic toys can also expose children to phthalates. For more about how toxic chemicals are affecting the health of children visit the WWF website's special section on children and chemicals at www.wwf.org.uk/chemicals.

• There are, of course, many additional subjects that trouble parents – childcare, methods of discipline, child abuse, child poverty, the effects of divorce, to name a few. For an overview of all these issues, visit http://society.guardian.co.uk/children.

Who cares?

It is often said that a society can be judged by how it cares for its most vulnerable members. In the UK we have traditionally cared for the elderly, sick and disabled members of our society by either paying for carers and nurses to do so – a luxury afforded only to the world's most affluent nations – or relying on the goodwill of unpaid spouses, relatives or close friends. But it is predicted that our society will undergo some hugely significant changes in coming decades that will provide a telling test of our collective character.

The principal change is that the population in the UK is getting older. A declining birth rate combined with a rise in life expectancy is pushing the average age up and up: in 2002 it stood at 39.3 but in 2031 it is predicted to be 43.6. As this trend continues it is predicted that the number of octogenarians in the UK will treble over the next half-century and reach nearly seven million in the early 2050s. Two huge questions are now looming for the UK: who is going to care for the elderly, and how is that care going to be paid for?

A care deficit is already starting to emerge as women – who have traditionally provided most of the informal, unpaid caring in the UK – continue to enter the salaried workplace. This means that, increasingly, caring will need to take place in formal care environments, such as private hospices and homes. And this will cost huge amounts of money.

It is estimated that by 2050 the UK will be three million short of the number of 'informal' carers needed to deal with the predicted increase in demand. The Scottish Executive – the only region in the UK to accept the recommendations of a recent Royal Commission into longterm care policy that all nursing care such as bathing, washing and dressing should be met by the taxpayer – says it is costing its constituents £1 billion a year to implement its care-for-all policy. Considering this, the annual bill to offer formal care is going to balloon.

The cost burden is going to have a significant impact on the taxpayer, but is also likely to considerably change the way people organise their finances and retirement plans (something that is already very much highlighted due to the financial impact of pension shortfalls; see www.pensions.gov.uk). And then there's the question of who is actually going to do all this caring – traditionally,

a low-paid, largely undervalued job in the UK. Do we invite people from other countries who will be tempted by the poor pay, as we are already doing in our hospitals? Or do we better incentivise family members and friends to care for the elderly and disabled with higher state benefits? In 2004, for example, a carer's allowance for a minimum 35-hour week stood at just £44.35 – the lowest of all income-replacement benefits and scant recognition for the fact that informal carers, who perform 70 per cent of all longterm care in the UK, actually save society an estimated £57 billion a year.

What is certain is that if we are to face up to this challenge, our 'care ethic' is going to have to go some way to matching our 'work ethic'. Current attitudes towards caring for the needy are telling. Surveys indicate that 63 per cent of people in the UK believe that the responsibility lies with the government, rather than the family, to provide for and care for the elderly. The popular perception of caring for someone else is that it is unrewarding, mundane and even demeaning. Without the career advancement, financial reward and social prestige that most people seek from their jobs, caring simply doesn't appeal. The increasing dislocation and mobility of families serves to cement these attitudes as people spend more and more time at work as well as living further and further apart.

The demise of the 'extended family' – the large network of close-by family members who would share and assist with care – may be over-exaggerated but it is true that for many families, the days when an aunt 'popped by to help' are fading into history, in contrast to the 1950s when people could, according to research at the time, count between 37 and 246 blood relatives living close by.

So what are we to do? As a society we certainly need to be better prepared for an older population. This means more public funds diverted into care, increased public discussion about how we should care for one another, and better tolerance and understanding of what caring for another person entails.

On a more personal, familial level there are many things that can be done:
● As a family, make detailed plans about how everyone is to be looked after in the event of illness, disability or dementia. A sudden change of circumstance is what

Informal carers perform 70 per cent of all longterm care in the UK, saving society an estimated £57 **billion** a year

trips many families up so advance preparation is key. Openly discuss everyone's pension provision.

• Carers need to be cared for, too. Morale is often low among the seven million carers in the UK as they feel that society largely undervalues them. Pitiful benefits mean that finance worries many carers. All support is welcome – from a phone call or visit, to help with shopping or provision of meals. For more information about the typical needs and concerns of informal carers, visit www.carersinformation.org.uk.

• Lobby for your workplace to be more tolerant and understanding of employees who may need to time off to care for someone they know. For more information visit www.employersforcarers.org.uk.

• Help battle the threat of the 'digital divide'. There are fears that the underprivileged and more vulnerable members of society are unable to gain access to information available on the internet and digital television that may make a difference to them, such as researching benefit entitlements, sourcing local services, contacting distant friends etc. If you have access to such facilities, offer them to others where possible.

• Volunteer to help out in a local hospice or home, particularly if you have a useful skill that can either entertain or assist residents, such as being able to play an instrument, helping with administrative chores or just being good company.

• If anyone you know is facing the prospect of having to find a home or hospice to move into, offer to research the establishment on their behalf. This is a particularly vulnerable time for many. The Office of Fair Trading was so concerned about exploitation that in 2004 it launched an investigation into the practices of the £9 billion care-home market after complaints were made about unfair, confusing and excessive contracts and fees. Help The Aged (www.helptheaged.org.uk/ AdviceInfo, tel: 0808 800 6565) has a huge amount of advice and information about this subject, as well as advice about other matters, such as home security, money worries and choosing the best form of care.

• For further information on the issue of how society provides longterm care, visit http://society.guardian.co.uk/longtermcare.

Pets

As a supposed nation of animal lovers, it's no surprise to learn that almost half of British households have a dog or a cat. Overall, we have 30 million pets, ranging from rabbits and caged birds, through to exotic species and ornamental fish.

Increasingly, we see our pets as fully fledged members of the family, with the same rights as the human members. Dogs in particular seem to have had a successful upward trajectory, finding their way from the backyard to the bedroom and, in many cases, onto the bed.

By attaching more value to our pets and their place in the family, are humans finally conceding that some animals are sentient beings and not just commodities? Some people are now replacing the word 'pet' with the less pejorative term 'companion animal', denoting the real role that many animals play in our lives.

But the tendency to anthropomorphise our pets (ascribe to them human characteristics) can also lead to problems. Some overly pampered and groomed dogs have developed detrimental skin conditions due to excessive visits to the 'doggy spa'. Poor discipline and training, particularly of dogs, can lead to irritating and possibly dangerous behavioural problems. And once the novelty and cuteness of a new pet recedes, a huge number of pets are abandoned as owners seek a way out of the duty of care that comes with looking after an animal.

Owning a pet requires a great deal of commitment, not least financial commitment. The RSPCA estimates that the average dog costs £9,996 over an average 12-year lifespan, or £833 every year. At £9,450 over a 14-year average lifespan, the cost of keeping a cat is significant, too. Those who own more exotic creatures can expect, for example, to spend around £500 for a plastic snake enclosure and £1.40 for every dead rat to feed it.

Many new pets are soon abandoned. The Royal Society for the Prevention of Cruelty to Animals (RSPCA) picks up around 150,000 discarded pets a year. In 2004, the Dogs Trust said 105,349 stray dogs had been collected in the UK that year by local authorities – a slight decline on the previous year. Of those dogs, 9,989 were destroyed (thousands of other healthy dogs are also destroyed due to the lack of a home by other welfare groups, vets etc), with the rest ending up in refuges. Only a small percentage of stray dogs are ever re-homed. It's the main reason why groups such as the RSPCA urge owners to consider neutering their pet.

Another simple measure to reduce the number of strays is to get your dog (or other pets) microchipped – something that is compulsory under the Pet Travel Scheme, which allows pets to travel from the UK to certain countries, and back again, without quarantine. Despite some concern over the migration of chips round the animal's body, the British Small Animal Veterinary Association has concluded that microchipping 'represents a safe and reliable method of pet identification'.

But things are arguably looking up for the welfare of companion animals. In 2005, the Department for Environment, Food and Rural Affairs (Defra) contributed to the funding of the Companion Animal Welfare Council for the first time. Meanwhile, in 2004, a draft animal welfare bill was launched, representing the most significant overhaul of animal laws since 1911, when the Protection of Animals Act became law. Under the bill, animals can no longer be given as prizes – marking an end to goldfish being given away at fairs. It also places a duty of care on pet owners and defines what constitutes cruelty.

The end bill, it is hoped, will also phase out tail docking, the practice of shortening an animal's tail by partial or total amputation, particularly in the case of pedigree dogs. Although the Royal College of Veterinary Surgeons has, since the early 1990s, instructed vets not to dock tails, some have continued. A seven-year study by Edinburgh University's Veterinary School found insufficient evidence to back up a claim by practitioners that tail docking is desirable because it 'prevents future tail injuries'.

Mongrel vs pedigree

It is often commented that owning a pet is an excellent, drug-free way of coping with stress, as contact with pets can reduce the heart rate and lower blood pressure. In fact, doctors often allow dogs and cats to visit patients in hospital. But this is dependent on having the right animal – a mismatch can lead to increased stress.

Many people choose to buy a pedigree puppy, for example, thinking that opting for a certain breed with specific traits will ensure that the dog will fit in with a particular lifestyle or domestic set-up. However, purebred dogs (and other animals) can be beset with problems such as hereditary disease and defects caused by closed gene pools, gene pool fragmentation and genetic drifting. 'Inbreeding was once a valuable tool in shaping today's breeds,' according to Dr Hellmuth Wachtel, a canine genetic-diversity expert. 'As these have now reached a high degree of homogeneity, it has lost its importance and turned into a fatal and disastrous habit.'

There is also a certain amount of snobbery, together with an emphasis on physical perfection and purity, attached to the ownership of a pedigree dog. But according to James Lamb Free, the author of *Training Your Retriever*, 'many pedigrees, if you know how to read them, virtually guarantee qualities that are just the reverse – stupidity, stubbornness and a generally ornery nature'. Rehoming a dog – whether mongrel, cross-breed or pedigree – could be a much better option than buying a pedigree puppy.

Sourcing a pet
(NB This advice is, in large part, for sourcing a dog, but is pertinent for most other animals.)

Before committing to owning a pet, ask yourself the following question: am I a suitable owner? Each member of a household must be consulted, irrespective of age (never surprise someone, especially a child, with a pet as a gift) and you must all decide whether you are prepared to care for a pet. Discuss who would have what duties. If you live alone, can you care for all the pet's needs? Are you only ever at home at night and at weekends?

If you do decide to proceed, the RSPCA unites with most animal welfare groups in advising that you always try to source a pet via an animal rescue centre before considering breeders or pet shops. The RSPCA also advises against buying an animal out of pity alone or ever buying a kitten or puppy from a pet shop, as they are often taken away from their mothers at an early age and mixed with other litters, where they may catch diseases.

There are dozens of rescue centres around the UK and you should have no problem finding one local to you. Many also have regularly updated websites that allow you to browse and research suitable pets before suffering the heartache of visiting a centre in person.

If you do decide on visiting a pet shop, investigate its reputation for animal welfare. In the first instance, look for members of the Pet Care Trust (www.petcare.org.uk, tel: 08700 624400). Member shops display the trust's logo, abide by its code of practice, and hold local authority pet sellers' licences. The trust also maintains the Puppy Index, a list of reputable breeders.

Try to avoid buying pets via newspaper advertisements or from 'the man in the pub' – sadly, still a very common route. Unless you can guarantee via references that the vendor is reputable and has the animal's interests at heart, it is best avoided.

If you decide to buy from a breeder (bearing in mind the information above about pedigrees), it is important to spend as much energy as possible in tracking down someone responsible. Get as many referrals as you can: ask friends, ask local vets, phone breed clubs and associations, or speak to your local rescue centre (assuming you can't find an animal there). Once you have a shortlist, ask the breeder if you can visit them before making any decisions. Ask to look around the premises and be wary of a breeder who is not keen to show you all their facilities. What are they hiding? Also ask to see the animal's parents. You want to see puppies with their mothers and, ideally, their fathers, raised in comfort with the whole litter. And ask the breeder if they would take back the animal should you find life with a pet too testing; quality breeders, if they are true animal-lovers rather than business people, should be willing to take back an animal for any reason.

More broadly, People for the Ethical Treatment of Animals

(Peta), the international animal welfare campaign group, urge those who are buying a companion animal to remember the following points:

• 'Puppy mills' breed thousands of dogs every year in deplorable conditions to supply disreputable pet stores, compounding the overpopulation crisis. There are far too many homeless animals in shelters waiting for a loving family.

• Fragile tropical fish suffer miserably when forced to spend their lives enclosed in glass. Robbed of their natural habitat and denied the space to roam, they must swim and reswim the same boring cubic inches. Many of these delicate animals die in transit.

• It takes patience, love and time to train animals – and even this is not always enough. Declawing cats is cruel, so make sure there are scratch posts available and that energetic dogs get plenty of playtime.

• Be prepared to keep cats indoors unless you are taking them out on a leash (with a harness – much more comfortable for the cat). Outside, cats are vulnerable to cruel people, cars, disease, and may get lost or stolen. Cats, acting on their natural instinct, may also kill birds, rabbits and other wildlife when outside. Therefore, fit a bell on their collar.

• Never buy a bird from a pet shop. Birds have complicated needs that are rarely met in a home environment. Exotic birds can live for 20–70 years and the stress of confinement can lead to neurotic behaviour and self-mutilation. If you are adopting birds, do you have an area where they can fly freely? Furthermore, birds should always be kept with at least one other member of their own species. For more information, contact Peta (www.peta.org.uk, tel: 020 8870 3966).

Feeding pets

It seems our companion animals are succumbing to the same problems of spiralling obesity as their human owners. Hill's Pet Nutrition, a pet-food manufacturer, conducted a survey of 672 pet owners and found that 60 per cent of cat owners were unclear about how much to feed their pets, 89 per cent regularly supplemented their pets' diet with treats, and only 30 per cent checked the weight of their pets on a regular basis.

Obesity is estimated to occur in 25 per cent of dogs and cats in westernised societies, and has been linked to a rise in feline diabetes – it now affects one in 300 cats – as well as kidney disease, arthritis and heart conditions in dogs. Obesity in rabbits results in breathing problems and strokes, while overweight horses are more likely to suffer from laminitis, a painful hoof condition.

Many owners have tried to alleviate a pet's weight problem by using low-calorie, low-carbohydrate food – as they might to counter their own weight problems. But by so doing, they are arguably playing straight into the hands of the multinationals behind the new era of pet foods. In addition, animal-welfare groups, such as Peta, have alleged that some manufacturers, looking for an edge in a fiercely competitive market, are using animal testing to help refine their products' attributes. They also believe that many nutritional claims made by pet-food manufacturers are little more than marketing puff.

If you're worried about whether the manufacturer of your preferred brand of pet food has been linked to

animal testing, both Peta and the British Union for the Abolition of Vivisection (www.buav.org) have lists of companies that guarantee they do not use animal experimentation. For the pet-food industry's view on what constitutes best practice with regard to pet nutrition, contact the Pet Food Manufacturers' Association (www.pfma.com).

Like their owners, many pets lead a sedentary lifestyle – certainly compared to the lives of their counterparts in the wild. Giving your pet access to regular exercise is clearly an excellent way to help it beat obesity. It's also worth looking at the ingredients of any pet food and using the same caution as you would for your own food. Ask, for example, if it is really necessary for the food to contain added extras, such as artificial colourings and preservatives. Many pet-food manufacturers (see page 229) now shun such ingredients. The RSPCA can offer advice about the dietary requirements for different species of pet.

Dilemma

Dwarf crocodile or Doberman?

Changes to the Dangerous Wild Animals Act 1976 could soon make it easier for householders to keep a porcupine, emu or racoon, but harder to own an anaconda or dwarf crocodile. But why are some species considered acceptable pets and some not?

More than 1,000 species of non-domesticated animals are kept by private owners in the UK, but the RSPCA continues to hold its position that 'exotic animals do not make suitable pets', stating in its 'Policies on Animal Welfare', revised in 2003, that 'exotic animals such as snakes, lizards and terrapins often carry disease, are difficult to look after, and are rarely provided with adequate facilities. Such animals are unsuitable as companion animals.'

But the Federation of British Herpetologists has accused the RSPCA of demonising reptiles. Some reptile owners claim that public health is at far greater risk from domestic pets than so-called 'exotic' species, citing a research paper that showed that, out of over 17,250 cases of salmonella infection reported in 1999, only seven cases were confirmed as contracted from a reptile source.

And how realistic is the portrayal of the cute domestic cat when the average feline can have such a negative impact on local wildlife? According to the Mammal Society, the average cat leaves a yearly trail of death and destruction consisting of nine mice, eight whole birds, five voles, three rabbits, two-and-a-half shrews, half a mole, half a rat, half a toad, one and a half frogs and half a snake.

A report in 2003 by the Companion Animal Welfare Council made the case for the more exotic pet, stating: 'It may be easier to keep some non-domesticated species to high welfare standards than some that are domesticated. Thus, meeting all the requirements – space, dietary, social, thermal, and so on – of a small, hardy reptile may be more readily achievable for many people than adequately fulfilling all the needs of some breeds of dog.' Indeed, you don't have to go very far to find a large, aggressive dog kept in a small space with limited opportunities for exercise.

But even if dog and cat owners can't automatically claim the pet-owning high ground, arguably the biggest sticking point is getting hold of an exotic animal in the first place. The trade in wild animals has grave implications for many fragile ecosystems and the transportation of exotic species can be alarmingly cruel. It's a sad irony that there are an estimated 10,000 privately owned tigers in the US, more than now exist in the wild.

Green goodbyes

In 2001, the *Guardian* reported that the business of green funerals was the fastest-growing 'green enterprise' in the UK. And in 2003 an eco-friendly vicar hit the headlines when he implored his congregation to think green when it came to their own demise and to begin planning an ecologically friendly funeral.

When it comes to death there is still a reticence to consider the practicalities. Death remains one of the last taboos. Its certainty is often quoted, but, when it comes to our last breath, we often have trouble thinking outside of the box – typically a faux-wood coffin made of chipboard. Every year in the UK, 600,000 coffins are made from chipboard, wood or MDF. Of all coffins sold, 89 per cent are of the chipboard variety. But chipboard degrades slowly, leaking formaldehyde and glues into ground water. When burned through cremation, it can emit toxic gases into the air. Meanwhile, the handles are usually made from plastic, which can take hundreds of years to degrade.

Many people are just not aware that there are other, more eco-friendly options. When a death occurs, the vast majority of us unquestioningly ring a conventional undertaking firm and go through the usual procedure.

While the conventional funeral service offers choice and dignity – we can choose the price of the funeral package, type of coffin, service, flowers and make the all-important choice between cremation and burial – in reality most funerals follow the same pattern. It's also an expensive process.

The Natural Death Centre in north London, which acts as a funeral industry watchdog as well as dispensing advice, has investigated the sharp increase in funeral prices in the past decade. Research for the 2003 *Natural Death Handbook* found that the average funeral cost £753, a 28.8 per cent increase on the £585 average for 2000. This was despite the fact that the price of coffins had only increased by nine per cent over the same period. So is the funeral industry withholding information from consumers when they could be opting for a funeral that is both greener and cheaper?

Biodegradable cardboard coffins can be as cheap as £35. And what many people don't realise is that some burial sites and crematoria don't require coffins at all – a biodegradable shroud is often acceptable if the body is supported on wood. If this doesn't provide the dignity many of us associate with death, there are other options. The sustainable coffin cover is one, (sold through www.memorialcentre.co.uk, tel: 0800 731 4972). Here, the decorative outer shell is made of wood, but this is returned to the undertakers to be reused, while the biodegradable coffin inside is buried or cremated.

If you're uncomfortable breaking with funerary tradition completely, then you can choose coffins made from wood certfied by the Forest Stewardship Council (www.fsc-uk.info). The coffin-maker JC Atkinson & Son (www.jcatkinson.co.uk, tel: 0191 385 2599), which produces around 60,000 coffins every year, offers a full range of certified coffins. Increasingly, beautifully designed and hand-crafted eco-coffins are becoming available. The Mawdsley coffin (also available at www.memorialcentre.co.uk) is a wicker coffin made by traditional basket weavers in Lancashire. One of the most successful designs is the 'Ecopod' (produced by Arka, www.eco-funerals.com). Based on ancient Egyptian caskets, it uses reclaimed materials and natural varnishes, and is overlaid with handmade paper. It is 100 per cent biodegradable and a favourite for woodland burials. Ironically, the Ecopod has achieved a degree of immortality: in 2004 London's Design Museum bought one for permanent exhibition.

In the absence of any pre-determined instructions from the deceased, once relatives or friends have chosen the casket, they then have to decide between burial and cremation. About 70 per cent of funerals in the UK now end in cremation. Many people opt for cremation in the belief that it is a more sustainable solution, not wanting to take up precious space in cemeteries. Indeed, cremation was revived in the UK in the late 1800s as a solution to an environmental problem, because, according to Queen Victoria's physician Sir Henry Thompson, it was 'the necessary sanitary precaution against the propagation of disease among a population daily growing larger in relation to the area it occupied'.

But is cremation really a green choice? It is now estimated that crematoria release up to 16 per cent of the UK's total mercury emissions, in addition to hydrogen chloride, carbon monoxide, nitrogen oxide, volatile organic compounds and dioxins (see page 106).

But conventional burials also bring their own set of environmental problems. In essence, death is a process rather than event, and as it degrades a body has a changing impact on the environment. Conventional funerary practice dictates that bodies are embalmed, and embalming fluid includes formaldehyde. Once buried, formaldehyde can pollute the ground and nearby water sources. In woodland burial sites, embalming is usually prohibited.

However, cemeteries can encourage biodiversity, not least because they are usually safe from the march of urban development. They are particularly effective at promoting lichens on gravestones and fostering communities of bats. But the conventional graveyard must also be kept neat and tidy, as a sign of respect, and this can be at odds with biodiversity – grass is frequently mown and weedkiller is typically used.

By contrast, 'green' or 'natural' burial sites actively promote biodiversity. There are now 200 such sites in the UK, ranging from designated woodlands and meadows, to wooded areas next to conventional cemeteries. Natural burial sites specify the use of biodegradable coffins or shrouds and prohibit the use of toxic embalming fluids. Bodies are sealed naturally within the earth and degrade quickly. Instead of granite headstones, trees mark the burial spot (or some relatives choose to chart the grave on a map for future visits).

Green burials can link land conservation with ritual and people in a fundamental way. If their relatives are buried there, people have a vested interest in preserving the habitat. By drawing up a green funeral plan, we can make sure that our last breaths denote a responsible goodbye.

For further information about organising a green funeral, contact the Natural Death Centre (www.naturaldeath.org.uk, tel: 0871 288 2098), or buy a copy of its *Natural Death Handbook* (£15.50).

Directory

CHILDREN

Advice and information

For parents seeking more information about environmentally friendly and ethical baby products and services

BabyG.R.O.E.
☎ 0131 555 5065
www.babygroe.co.uk

The Green Parent Magazine
☎ 01273 424802
www.thegreenparent.co.uk

Juno Magazine
☎ 01444 891460
www.junomagazine.com

Retailers

The following companies offer a range of baby and children's products

The Baby Catalogue
☎ 0870 120 2018
www.thebabycatalogue.com

Baby-O
☎ 0870 7606564
www.baby-o.co.uk

Beaming Baby
☎ 0800 0345 672
www.beamingbaby.com

Birth and Baby
☎ 01323 722777
www.birthandbaby.co.uk

Born
☎ 01225 334434
www.borndirect.com

The Bottom Line
☎ 01543 250810
www.thebottomlinenappies.co.uk

Eco-Babes
☎ 01366 387851
www.eco-babes.co.uk

Ecobaby Basics
☎ 01223 811633
www.ecobabybasics.com

Free Range Kids
☎ 01253 896290
www.freerangekids.co.uk

Green Baby
☎ 0870 240 6894
www.greenbaby.co.uk

Little Earthlings
☎ 028 2954 1214
www.littleearthlings.com

Little Green Earthlets
☎ 08701 624462
www.earthlets.co.uk

MulaDula
☎ 01453 768549
www.muladula.com

Natural Child
☎ 01242 620445
www.naturalchild.co.uk

Nature's Fibres
☎ 01622 853517
www.naturesfibres.com

Planet Organic
☎ 020 7221 1345
www.planetorganic.com

Smile Child
☎ 0800 1956 982
www.smilechild.co.uk

Spirit of Nature
☎ 0870 725 9885
www.spiritofnature.co.uk

Tiny Sprout
☎ 01892 863646
www.tinysprout.co.uk

Clothing and bedding

Clothworks
☎ 01225 309218
www.clothworks.co.uk

Cut4Cloth
☎ 01326 340956
www.cut4cloth.co.uk

Eczemaclothing.com from Cotton Comfort
☎ 01524 730093
www.eczemaclothing.com

Garthenor Organic Pure Wool
☎ 0845 408 2437
www.organicpurewool.co.uk

Greenfibres
☎ 0845 330 3440
www.greenfibres.com

Greensleeves Clothing
☎ 0208 455 2809
www.greensleevesclothing.com

Schmidt Natural Clothing
☎ 0845 345 0498
www.naturalclothing.co.uk

Nappies

Includes washable and eco-disposable nappy suppliers, as well as nappy washing services

Bambino Mio
☎ 01604 88 3777
www.bambinomio.com

Cotton Bottoms
☎ 0870 777 8899
www.cottonbottoms.co.uk

CuddleBabes
☎ 01430 425257
www.cuddlebabes.co.uk

Easy Peasy Nappies
☎ 01865 841359
www.easypeasynappies.co.uk

Ecobaby
☎ 00353 1620 5050
www.ecobaby.ie

Eco Nappy Trials
☎ 01833 640400
www.econappytrials.co.uk

Kittykins
☎ 01986 798939
www.kittykins.co.uk

Little Lams
☎ 01233 637447
www.littlelams.co.uk

Lollipop Children's Products
☎ 01736 799512
www.teamlollipop.co.uk

Nappy Baby
☎ 01795 599519
www.nappybaby.co.uk

National Association of
Nappy Services
☎ 0121 693 4949
www.changeanappy.co.uk

The Natural Baby Company
☎ 01983 810925
www.naturalbabycompany.com

Naturally Nappies
☎ 0845 1664716
www.naturallynappies.com

Naturebotts Ltd (suppliers of Moltex
Öko eco-disposable nappies)
☎ 0845 226 2186
www.naturebotts.co.uk

The Nice Nappy Company
www.nicenappy.co.uk

Plush Pants Cloth Nappies
☎ 01865 408040
www.plushpants.com

The Scottish Nappy Company
☎ 0800 0155570
www.scottishnappy.co.uk

Snazzy Pants
☎ 01522 778440
www.snazzypants.co.uk

Tots Bots
☎ 0141 550 1514
www.totsbots.com

Twinkle Twinkle
☎ 0118 934 2120
www.twinkleontheweb.co.uk

Women's Environmental Network
☎ 020 7481 9004
www.wen.org.uk/nappies

WRAP Real Nappy Helpline
☎ 0845 850 0606

Zayoodee Organics
www.zayoodee.com

Toiletries

Akamuti
☎ 0845 4589242
www.akamuti.co.uk/babycare.htm

Beauty and the Bees
www.beebeauty.com

Calmia
☎ 0845 009 2450
www.calmia.com

Earthbound Organics
☎ 01597 851157
www.earthbound.co.uk

Erbaviva (available from Calmia)
www.erbaviva.com

Green People
☎ 08702 401444
www.greenpeople.co.uk

HealthQuest (suppliers of
Earth Friendly baby products)
☎ 020 8424 8844
www.healthquest.co.uk

Little Me Baby Organics
☎ 020 8614 4700
www.littlemebabyorganics.co.uk

Mother Earth
☎ 01229 885266
www.motherearth.co.uk

Neal's Yard Remedies
☎ 020 7627 1949
www.nealsyardremedies.com

OrganicChildren (available from Green
People)
www.organicchildren.com

Spiezia Baby
☎ 01326 231 600
www.spieziaorganics.com

Toys

Arujo
☎ 01295 271218
www.arujo.co.uk

Gaia Distribution
☎ 0117 942 0165
www.gaiadistribution.com

Good to be Wood
☎ 01494 723360
www.goodtobewood.com

The Green Board Game Company
☎ 01494 538999
www.greenboardgames.com

In 2 Play
www.in2play.co.uk

Lanka Kade
☎ 01536 461188
www.lankakade.co.uk

Mulberry Bush
☎ 01403 754400
www.mulberrybush.co.uk

Myriad
☎ 01725 517085
www.myriadonline.co.uk

Adoption and fostering

Adoption & Fostering Information Line
☎ 0800 783 4086
www.adoption.org.uk
www.fostering.org.uk

Adoption-net.co.uk (incorporating
Foster-net.co.uk)
☎ 0116 227 3136
www.adoption-net.co.uk

Adoption UK
☎ 0870 7700 450
www.adoptionuk.org.uk

British Association for Adoption
and Fostering
☎ 020 7593 2000
www.baaf.org.uk

Department for Education and Skills:
Adoption
www.dfes.gov.uk/adoption

The Fostering Network
☎ 020 7620 6400 (England)
☎ 028 9067 3441 (Northern Ireland)
☎ 0141 204 1400 (Scotland)
☎ 029 2044 0940 (Wales)
www.fostering.net

LondonKIDS
www.londonkids.org.uk

NORCAP
☎ 01865 875000
www.norcap.org.uk

TALKadoption
☎ 0808 808 1234
www.talkadoption.org.uk

UKkids
www.ukkids.info

CARING FOR OTHERS

General information and advice

Barton Hill Advice Service
www.bhas.org.uk

Benefits Now
www.benefitsnow.co.uk

Benefits Now Shop
☎ 01983 539954
www.benefitsnowshop.co.uk

British Geriatrics Society
☎ 0207 608 1369
www.bgs.org.uk

Care Direct
www.caredirect.gov.uk

Carers UK
☎ 0808 808 7777
www.carersuk.org.uk

Caring About Carers
www.carers.gov.uk

Centre for Policy on Ageing
☎ 020 7553 6500
www.cpa.org.uk

Contact a Family
☎ 0808 808 3555
www.cafamily.org.uk

Counsel and Care
☎ 0845 300 7585
www.counselandcare.org.uk

Direct.gov's Caring For Someone
www.direct.gov.uk/Audiences/

The Pension Service
www.thepensionservice.gov.uk

The Princess Royal Trust for Carers
☎ 020 7480 7788
www.carers.org

Rethink
☎ 020 8974 6814
www.rethink.org

SAGA
☎ 0800 414525
www.saga.co.uk

Seniors Network
www.seniorsnetwork.co.uk

Silverhairs
www.silverhairs.co.uk

ukcare.net
www.ukcare.net

Winged Fellowship Trust
☎ 020 7833 2594
www.wft.org.uk

Care homes and supported housing

The Abbeyfield Society
☎ 01727 857536
www.abbeyfield.com

The Almshouse Association
☎ 01344 452922
www.almshouses.org

Anchor Trust
☎ 01274 381666 (residential care homes)
☎ 08457 758595 (housing)
www.anchor.org.uk

A-Z Care Homes Guide
☎ 01488 684321
www.carehome.co.uk

Bettercaring.co.uk (database of care homes)
☎ 0845 644 1701
www.bettercaring.co.uk

ERoSH (The national consortium for sheltered housing providers)
☎ 01249 654249
www.shelteredhousing.org

Hanover Housing Association
☎ 01784 446000
www.hanover.org.uk

HousingCare.org (from the Elderly Accommodation Counsel)
www.housingcare.org

Charities, campaign groups and organisations specialising in helping the elderly

Action on Elder Abuse
☎ 0808 808 8141
www.elderabuse.org.uk

Active for Life
☎ 01179 406409
www.active-for-life.com

Age Concern
☎ 0800 009966
www.ageconcern.org.uk

Alzheimer's Society
☎ 020 7306 0606
www.alzheimers.org.uk

Contact the Elderly
☎ 0800 716543
www.contact-the-elderly.org

Dementia Care Trust
☎ 0870 443 5325
www.dct.org.uk

Help the Aged
☎ 0808 800 6565 (England)
☎ 0131 551 6331 (Scotland)
☎ 02920 346 550 (Wales)
☎ 0808 808 7575 (Northern Ireland)
www.helptheaged.org.uk

Low Incomes Tax Reform Group
www.litrg.org.uk

The Relatives & Residents Association
☎ 020 7359 8136
www.relres.org

Rukba
☎ 08457 585680
www.rukba.org.uk

PETS

Information and advice

Animal Health Trust
☎ 08700 502424
www.aht.org.uk

The Blue Cross
☎ 01993 825500
www.bluecross.org.uk

The British Bird Council
☎ 0121 476 5999
www.britishbirdcouncil.com

The British Horse Society
☎ 08701 202244
www.bhs.org.uk

The British Rabbit Council
☎ 01636 676042
www.thebrc.org

British Union for the Abolition of Vivisection
☎ 020 7700 4888
www.buav.org

Feline Advisory Bureau
☎ 0870 742 2278
www.fabcats.org

The Guide Dogs for the Blind Association
☎ 0870 600 2323
www.guidedogs.org.uk

The International Herpetological
Society
www.international-herp-society.co.uk

The Kennel Club
☎ 0870 606 6750
www.the-kennel-club.org.uk

National Fancy Rat Society
www.nfrs.org

National Gerbil Society
www.gerbils.co.uk

National Hamster Council
www.hamsters-uk.org

People for the Ethical Treatment
of Animals (Peta)
☎ 0207 357 9229
www.peta.org.uk

Pet Care Trust
☎ 08700 624400
www.petcare.org.uk

RSPB
☎ 01767 680551
www.rspb.org.uk

RSPCA
☎ 0870 3335 999
www.rspca.org.uk

Support Dogs
☎ 0114 2577997
www.support-dogs.org.uk

UK Pets
www.ukpets.co.uk

WWF
☎ 01483 426444
www.wwf.org.uk

Rescue centres

Battersea Dogs Home
☎ 020 7622 3626 (London)
☎ 01474 874994 (Brands Hatch)
☎ 01784 432929 (Old Windsor)
www.dogshome.org

The Blue Cross (see above)

Cats Protection
☎ 08702 099099
www.cats.org.uk

Dogs Trust
☎ 020 7837 0006
www.dogstrust.org.uk

The Index of Animal Rescue Centres
www.animalsanctuaries.co.uk

The Mayhew Animal Home
☎ 020 8969 0178
www.mayhewanimalhome.org

RSPCA (see above)

UK Animal Rescuers
www.animalrescuers.co.uk

Bedding

Includes cat litter

100 Per Cent Green
☎ 01366 387978
www.100percentgreen.co.uk

Friendship Estates
☎ 01302 700220
www.friendshipestates.co.uk

Snowflake Pet Products
☎ 01205 311 332
www.snowflakepets.co.uk

Pet food

Bluepet
☎ 0845 3306451
www.bluepet.co.uk

Graig Farm Organics
☎ 01597 851655
www.graigfarm.co.uk/pets.htm

James Wellbeloved
☎ 01935 410600
www.wellbeloved.co.uk

Pascoe's
☎ 01377 252571
www.pascoes.co.uk

Pero Organic
☎ 0800 9179697
www.pero-petfood.co.uk

VeggiePets.com
☎ 02392 699859
www.veggiepets.com

Wafcol
☎ 0870 906 8090
www.wafcol.co.uk

Yarrah Organic Pet Foods
☎ 02392 699859
www.yarrah.com

Pet foods approved under BUAV's 'No Animal Testing' standard

Arden Grange
☎ 01273 833390
www.ardengrange.com

Burns Pet Nutrition
☎ 0800 018 1890
www.burns-pet-nutrition.co.uk

Europa Pet Foods
☎ 0845 658 0987
www.europa-pet-food.co.uk

Happidog
☎ 0800 0182955
www.happidog.co.uk

Nature Diet Pet Foods Ltd
☎ 08700 132960
www.naturediet.net

Postal Pets Products (suppliers of
Fromm Family pet foods)
☎ 01531 633985
www.postalpets.co.uk

Trophy Pet Foods
☎ 01367 240333
www.trophypetfoods.co.uk

The Vegan Society (suppliers of
VegeKit and VegeCat)
☎ 0845 4588244
www.vegansociety.com/shop

Pet health

Aloe Vera UK
www.aloevera-shop.co.uk/pets.htm

Armitage Pet Care
☎ 0115 938 1200
www.armitages.co.uk

Denes Natural Pet Care
☎ 01273 325364
www.denes.com

PAN UK Flea Control
www.pan-uk.org/pestnews/home-
pest/flea.htm

PEThealthcare.co.uk
www.pethealthcare.co.uk

GREEN FUNERALS

Directories and general information

iGreens: Woodland Burial Sites
www.igreens.org.uk/woodland_burial_
sites_uk.htm

The Natural Death Centre
☎ 0871 288 2098
www.naturaldeath.org.uk

UK Funerals Online: Green Funerals
& Woodland Burials
www.uk-funerals.co.uk/
green-funerals.html

Funeral companies and woodland burial sites

Arka Original Funerals
☎ 01273 766620
www.eco-funerals.com

Bidwell Woodland Burial
☎ 07973 459065
www.bidwellwoodland.co.uk

Birdsong Green Burial Site
☎ 01507 466644
www.greenburialsite.co.uk

Breach Farm Woodland Burial
Ground
☎ 01264 738279
www.breach-farm.co.uk

Brocklands Woodland Burial
☎ 01729 840102
www.brocklands.co.uk

Colney Woodland Burial Park
☎ 01603 811556
www.woodlandburialparks.co.uk

Countryside Burials (Brinkley
Woodland Cemetery)
☎ 01638 600693
www.countryside-burials.co.uk

Craufurdland Woods
☎ 01560 600760
www.craufurdland.co.uk

Crossways Woodland Burials
☎ 01647 24382
www.crosswayswoodlandburials.co.uk

Friends of Nature Burial Ground
☎ 0161 432 2131
www.burialswithnature.co.uk

The Funeral Company: Green Burials
☎ 01908 225 222
www.thefuneralcompanyltd.com

The Green Burial Company
☎ 01234 241808
www.thegreenburialcompany.plc.uk

Green Endings
☎ 020 7424 0345
www.greenendings.co.uk

Green Lane Burial Field
☎ 01686 630331
www.greenlaneburialfield.co.uk

Hamdown Green Burial
☎ 01258 860284
www.hamdown-greenburial.co.uk

Hinton Park Woodland Burial Ground
☎ 01425 278 910
www.woodlandburial.com

Memorial Woodlands
Funeral Directors
☎ 01454 414 999
www.memorialwoodlands.com

Peace Funerals
☎ 0800 093 0505
www.peacefunerals.co.uk

Springwood Woodland Burials
☎ 01983 868688
www.springwood-cemetery.com

Tarn Moor Memorial Woodland
☎ 01756 701688
www.tarnmoor.co.uk

The Woodland and Wildlife
Conservation Company
☎ 01992 814909
www.green-burial.co.uk

Woodland Burial Place
☎ 01736 731310
www.woodlandburialplace.co.uk

Biodegradable coffins

The Coffin Cover
☎ 0800 7832225
www.coffincovers.co.uk

Eco-coffins.com
☎ 01303 850856
www.eco-coffins.com

Ecopod
☎ 01273 746011
www.ecopod.co.uk

Greenfield Coffins
☎ 01440 788886
www.greenfieldcoffins.com

Heaven on Earth
☎ 0117 926 4999
www.heavenonearthbristol.co.uk

Memorial trees

Cashel: Dedicate a Tree
☎ 01360 870450
www.cashel.org.uk

The Family Tree Scheme
☎ 0870 7744269
www.internationaltreefoundation.org

The National Memorial Arboretum
☎ 01283 792333

Road Peace Wood
☎ 0845 4500 355
www.roadpeace.org/contact/
rpeawood.html

Trees for Cities
☎ 020 7587 1320
www.treesforcities.org

Trees for Life
☎ 01309 691292
www.treesforlife.org.uk

Woodland Creation
☎ 01208 873618
www.woodlandcreation.co.uk

World Land Trust: Green Memorials
☎ 0845 054 4422
www.worldlandtrust.org/supporting/
greenfunerals.htm

Unless different for each product, company details are listed in first entry only.

Baby/child seats

Bébé Confort
☎ 020 8236 0707
www.dorel.com

Jané
☎ 0034 93 703 1800
www.jane.es

Maxi-Cosi
☎ 020 8236 0707
www.dorel.com

Pushchairs

Baby Dan
☎ 0045 8695 1155
www.babydan.com

Bugaboo
☎ 0800 587 8265
www.bugaboo.nl

Cosatto
☎ 0870 050 5900
www.cosatto.com

Baby slings

BabyBjörn
☎ 0870 1200 543
www.babybjorn.com

Huggababy
☎ 0870 046 4844
www.huggababy.co.uk

Wilkinet
☎ 0800 1383 400
www.wilkinet.co.uk

Condoms

Condomi Animal-Free
www.vegansociety.com

Durex
☎ 020 7367 5760
www.durex.co.uk

Femidom
☎ 020 8965 2813
www.femalehealth.com

Mates
☎ 0800 2673 5555
www.mates.co.uk

Washable nappies

Cotton Bottoms
☎ 0870 777 8899
www.cottonbottoms.co.uk

Modern Baby
☎ 0800 093 1500
www.modernbaby.co.uk

Sam I Am
☎ 01522 778926
www.sam-i-am.co.uk

Disposable nappies

Moltex Öko
☎ 01536 269744
www.ontex.be

Nature Boy & Girl
☎ 0046 86 44 9696
www.naty.com

Tushies (via Green Baby)
☎ 0870 241 7661
www.tushies.com

Pet food

Happidog (vegetarian)
☎ 0800 0182955
www.happidog.co.uk

Pascoe's
☎ 01377 252571
www.pascoes.co.uk

WackiDog (vegetarian)
www.veggiepets.com

Yarrah Organic Pet Foods
www.yarrah.com

Flea treatments for pets

Armitage Pet Care
☎ 0115 938 1200
www.armitages.co.uk

Bob Martin
☎ 0800 0850113
www.bobmartin.co.uk

Johnson's
☎ 0121 378 1684
www.johnsons-vet.com

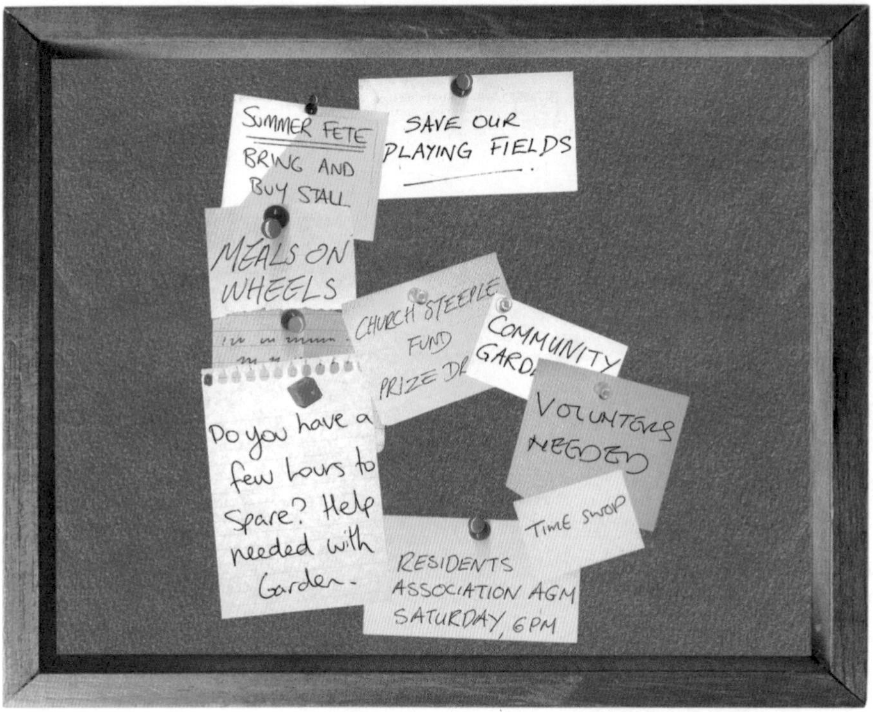
SUMMER FETE
BRING AND BUY STALL
SAVE OUR PLAYING FIELDS
MEALS ON WHEELS
CHURCH STEEPLE FUND
COMMUNITY
VOLUNTEERS NEEDED
Do you have a few hours to Spare? Help needed with Garden.
TIME SWOP
RESIDENTS ASSOCIATION AGM SATURDAY, 6PM

Community

Introduction

Did you have a hand in the regeneration of the local canal? Have you worked on a cultural project with sufferers of mental health problems? When you walk by the new community hall, do you feel a glow of pride because you helped secure funding for a new roof or donated some unwanted paint?

If you answered 'yes' to any of the above, you are one of the 22 million people who make up the UK's army of volunteers – contributing to either local or global community life. According to many psychologists, you're also likely to be happier and have a better quality of life, attributable to the network of connections you've made in the community.

But despite the impressive number of volunteers in the UK, it seems we have a rather narrow idea of who can and should get involved in not-for-profit community projects, and why they do it. The concept of being 'active in the community' is equated by some people with being a 'do-gooder'. This is one of the reasons why, according to the We Are What We Do initiative (www.wearewhatwedo.org), an offshoot of the Community Links charity, our parents were eight times more likely to join a community association than we are today.

We could of course ignore this and put it down to some sort of evolution. After all, many of now us live independent, anonymous lives. Friends, it is often said, are the 21st century family, and who wants to spend time hanging out with the neighbours? It is also often commented that many of the institutions that once knit communities together – the church, the mine or factory, the town hall, the weekly market – are in decline.

But by shrugging our shoulders, we could be storing up problems for ourselves and the society in which we live. Better associations within the community can help to ward off social isolation, defined as 'living alone and having no weekly contact with neighbours, friends or relatives'. We inhabit a world increasingly devoid of deep social connections. Every day in the UK, 32 elderly people die unnoticed, at home, alone. Failure to connect with the local community, allied with falling birth rates and soaring divorce figures, threatens to exacerbate the situation. Currently, 17 per cent, some 1.62 million, of those over 65 can be classified as socially isolated. By 2021, if current trends continue, this will rise to some 2.5 million.

The US political scientist Robert Lane believes 'there is a kind of famine of warm interpersonal relations, of easy-to-reach neighbours, of encircling, inclusive memberships, and of solidary family life'. A survey of English households conducted by the Office of the Deputy Prime Minister in 1997–1998 (the last of its kind) found that only 46 per cent of respondents thought their area had 'a lot of community spirit'. This mirrored findings in 1992 and 1994.

Nurturing a rise in community spirit begins by taking personal responsibility for our local area. In his book *The Fifth Discipline*, Peter Senge defines our often ambivalent approach to collective, community action. 'When things are going poorly, we blame the situation on incompetent leaders, thereby avoiding any personal responsibility. When things become desperate, we can easily find ourselves waiting for a great leader to rescue us. Through all of this, we totally miss the bigger question: "What are we, collectively, able to create?"'

Opting out of community life means disengaging

from and abdicating responsibility for important decisions – in effect, handing over our power. The website www.antiapathy.com attempts to address the issue head on, calling on us to wake up and become a source for positive social change. Research shows that well-run, inclusive community projects are powerful tools, capable of re-energising neighbourhoods, and encouraging cooperative initiatives and behaviour. This in turn enhances the quality of residents' lives. At the Rio Earth Summit in 1992 the UK government signed up to a series of sustainability targets to protect growth of both the economy and the environment. These ranged from waste reduction and land regeneration to dealing with social exclusion. If the UK is to achieve these targets, the involvement of grassroots organisations is critical. Proving that community engagement doesn't just attract sock-and-sandal-wearing stereotypes, even the World Bank has time for it: according to the World Bank's overview of social capital, 'increasing evidence shows that social cohesion is critical for societies to prosper economically and for development to be sustainable'.

But perhaps the biggest barrier to a successful community is that of social exclusion. In *Faiths, Hope and Participation*, a combined report by the New Economics Foundation, the Church Urban Fund and the Department for Transport, the authors Julie Lewis and Elizabeth Randolph-Horn make the point that 'building a community is very like weaving. In every neighbourhood we can easily name the threads – such as the local authority, statutory and voluntary agencies, faith groups, civic and residents' associations – but if even one person is considered unimportant and dropped, then the whole fabric of a community begins to unravel.'

Many different and disparate social groups make up our communities, including those who have traditionally been excluded from the local government decision-making process. In 2001/2002, 2.5 million British people were reported as living below the poverty threshold. People without qualifications are three times less likely to receive job-related training compared with those with some qualifications. Ten thousand pupils were permanently excluded from school in 2001/2002. All these groups could benefit from community initiatives and programmes.

In fact, if we fail to embrace community living, we can actually end up missing out, not only on the opportunity to help to improve life for others, but on the opportunity to increase our own happiness and wellbeing. In 2004, the Economic & Social Research Council revealed the results of its research programme into participation and volunteering. It compiled a happiness league of UK cities and found that it was topped by Bristol, Chester and Aberdeen. These cities were also the areas that recorded high levels of informal voluntary activity. As a result of greater levels of community participation and volunteering, the research found that citizens enjoyed better health, students received higher GCSE grades and there were fewer burglaries.

Proponents say that community action is enormously empowering. In an age when power is often gradually lost or handed over to governments, local authorities or even to multinational companies, re-engaging with the local community provides a real chance to take control over our lives and the issues that affect us on a day-to-day basis – whether it be access to local, fresh produce through a community gardening scheme, lobbying for environmentally sound transport, or dealing with issues such as social exclusion through a mentoring scheme (see page 240).

There is no single best way of engaging with or enhancing your community, but the following pages give some ideas. Some of the most successful and innovative schemes come from relatively simple concepts. For instance, the Black Environmental Network (www.ben-network.org) addresses ethnic environmental participation and transport and recycling issues by reconditioning unwanted police bicycles and passing them on to asylum seekers. Among many benefits, community participation helps resolve collective problems more easily, makes everyday business easier and encourages us to be more tolerant and empathetic. It can also help us to build a vital network of personal contacts, friends and supporters. This makes us feel less isolated, exposed and, in a sense, shares the burden of responsibility. As the old adage says, a problem shared is a problem halved.

A community for all

If a successful, flourishing community depends on greater levels of participation, it is vital that everyone in the community gets involved. Increasingly, successful communities not only depend on diversifying the target audience for community projects, but also on making sure that the people doing the volunteering themselves are from diverse groups.

Many are following the lead set by the local Bedfordshire community organisation, Luton Lives. In 2001, when Luton Lives wanted to attract new volunteers, existing members decided to actively seek out members of the community who do not traditionally volunteer. And so posters reading 'volunteering is for everyone – volunteering is for you' were put up in gay and lesbian bars. The project director commented afterwards that these had led to a 'huge increase in the number of lesbians and gay men coming through our doors'. The poster was later translated into five Asian languages to catch the eye of Luton's multicultural population.

Thankfully, it seems that community projects are experiencing something of a renaissance, driven in part by the government, which sees active citizenship as a key element in its domestic policy. ChangeUp (www.homeoffice.gov.uk/comrace/active/developing), established by the government in 2004, aims to promote community participation and volunteering in the public services. Detractors claim that this is a way of blurring lines between public services and volunteering, and of getting public services on the cheap. Those in favour see it as a positive move towards making community groups and services more effective by providing a real, and effective, infrastructure. By 2014 the £80 million project aims to have set up community and volunteering 'hubs' all over the UK, which will provide centres and resources for all forms of community engagement. In addition, the National Mentoring Network and Volunteering England were awarded £800,000 in 2004 to develop a national mentoring and befriending body, while the Women's Royal Volunteering Service (www.wrvs.org.uk) – a network of volunteers providing services such as meals on wheels, particularly for older members of the community – was awarded £600,000 to promote the involvement of older volunteers.

Community and conservation

There is a very special relationship between community projects and the safeguarding of the natural world. Continued community involvement in conservation zones helps to protect these precious areas from development and keep them flourishing as wild habitats and centres for education and leisure. Community involvement in nature conservation has also been proved to be a cost-effective method of regenerating derelict land, as well as promoting and increasing biodiversity.

In 1990, the local Groundwork Trust in St Helens (www.groundwork.org.uk) purchased Bold Moss, a large colliery spoil heap, for just £1. Within a few years the unappealing site had been transformed into a diverse range of habitats, from scrub and heathland to wetlands formed from former coal-washing lagoons and fostering a spectacular array of wildlife.

The US conservationist Peter Forbes defines the connection between people and the land as a symbiotic relationship. 'Unlike conservation biology, this work of protecting ways of life, or habitats for people, has no highly defined project selection criteria. But it includes growing healthy food, having safe parks and clean rivers accessible to people, building relationships with the land that inspire our sense of ethics and art, maintaining a culture of mutual aid and an appreciation of local beauty, defining our limits as responsible creatures, protecting our cultural and ethnic diversity – all of which contribute immeasurably to the health and wellbeing of all species on this planet.'

In fact, there are plenty of examples of the positive impact community groups and volunteers can have on the natural environment. For example, in 2003 alone, across the UK 323 hectares of land (equivalent in area to Hyde Park in London) and 70km of bridleways and pathways were improved, litter weighing as much as two double-decker buses was recycled, and 20,000 wildflowers and 14,000 trees were planted, all by members of Community Service Volunteering (www.csv.org.uk).

Volunteering

The year 2005 is the UK Year of the Volunteer, as promoted by the Home Office to recognise the fact that volunteers are true pillars of the community. In fact, the value of volunteering to the UK economy is estimated to be around £40 billion a year.

If you want to volunteer, the first thing to ask yourself is how much time you can give. This will help you decide what type of scheme to get involved with.

Some schemes are formal, such as the yearly placements offered by Voluntary Service Overseas (VSO, as it's more commonly known), where volunteers offer their skills to the 'global community' while simultaneously learning from their host community. If you have limited time, but, for example, would like to spend more time outdoors, you might consider a one-off commitment such as a day clearing an overgrown footpath with British Trust for Conservation Volunteers (BTCV), the UK's oldest conservation charity. Some schemes such as mentoring programmes (see page 240) require sustained commitment, or need volunteers to commit to a rota, as with delivering meals on wheels.

Many people are now choosing to volunteer during the course of the working day, usually sacrificing their lunch hours. In 2002, David Blunkett, the home secretary, urged employers to give staff more time off to let them volunteer for local charities and play a greater part in civic life. He urged employers 'to consider releasing their employees more often and giving them paid leave to work, for example, as a special constable'.

In 2004, around 1.5 million employees participated in employer-supported volunteering schemes, each contributing on average 68 hours per year. The rewards for employers can be substantial. Volunteering can promote feelings of self-worth which in turn increases staff morale. Staff can expand their organisational and interpersonal skills-base. Research by the National Centre for Volunteering found that six out of 10 volunteers said volunteering had given them the chance to learn new skills. Research consistently shows that it is one of the best ways to increase employability. The VSO, for example, places emphasis on the reciprocal nature of volunteering – their volunteers get paid a local wage and live in the local community providing a sense of equality which the VSO believes adds to the likelihood of a successful project.

Notions of altruism are sometimes considered outmoded and offputting. Increasingly, however, volunteering is a symbiotic relationship. Now that time is at a premium for so many, people will choose a certain volunteering project for what they hope to get back from it. A stressed office worker, for example, might want to donate time to an outdoor project run by the BTCV, in order to get a chance to connect with the natural world.

How to start a voluntary project

Most voluntary organisations are born out of a need to resolve a local problem. For example, you might have a child of pre-school age and notice that playgroup facilities are few and far between in your area so get together with other people in a similar position and try to set up a playgroup yourselves. Or, as is increasingly the case, you might feel strongly that a particular waterway or building needs to be conserved. In either case, community projects, by definition, are bigger than one person.

The first step in setting up a community or volunteering project is to identify the project and then to set up a committee of like-minded volunteers. Most experienced voluntary managers and community leaders suggest applying a 'who, what, why, where and when' approach:

Who is the project for? Any fledgling project needs to canvass support from the local community, by persuading people that the project is important and that addressing the issue will have a positive effect on their lives. Remember that funding bodies will want to measure how effective their money may be. The project will also have to prove that its effects will be wide-reaching and above all inclusive, involving a range of ethnic, age and income groups.

What is the project? This sounds obvious, but it is critical to pin down the aims of a community project from the very start and to get everyone to agree to them. This ensures that as the project proceeds (in the case of a restoration or conservation project this could take a number of years) everyone can be sure it's moving successfully in the right direction. It is also important to remember that the project will need a continual supply of motivated volunteers.

Why is the project needed? To secure funding you will have to identify a 'need' for the project, rather than a 'want'. Needs are usually:

'Felt' – for example, local residents might 'feel' angry about a local park that has been allowed to go to seed.

'Expressed' – your project might be responding to petitions to save a city farm which has educational value.

'Comparative' – a next-door village might have substantially more sports facilities.

'Legislative' – your area may need to start a community recycling project to help the council reach waste minimisation targets.

Where will the project be centred and how far will it reach? Carefully define the physical scope of the project and decide where its base is. Everyone needs an HQ of some sort.

When is the project needed? You will need to draft a synopsis of the project for funding purposes so it's important to draw up a timeframe. For instance, is a community project focusing on a day centre for elderly people needed before the winter sets in?

Who should be involved? As many members of the community as possible, is the obvious answer. Feeling useful, according to the New Economics Foundation, is a basic human need. It's also one that many people in society are denied. Some sections of society are statistically less likely to volunteer than others. Disabled and ethnic-minority people, as well as those with criminal records or with learning difficulties, are all less likely to volunteer than other members of the community, largely because these groups have traditionally felt alienated from mainstream society.

The Commission for Racial Equality, for example, is looking at ways to engage people from ethnic-minority communities in wider community action by making initiatives more overt and high-profile. In 2004, a survey by TimeBank (see right) and the Ethnic Media Group (which specialises in publications for ethnic-minority groups) found that 62 per cent of ethnic-minority citizens thought their local area needed improving and more than half wanted to help improve it but didn't know how to get started.

Disabled people often want to be seen as active proponents rather than passive recipients of voluntary work. Similarly, people with learning difficulties are often viewed by society as passive recipients. Statistically, this group is more likely to suffer from unemployment, lack of confidence, feelings of isolation and inability to make or sustain friendships – all of which volunteering and community projects can help to redress.

Therefore, do all you can to engage and involve as many people from the local community as possible.

Any other issues? Remember that police checks will need to be run on anyone working with children. Insurance can also be an issue for some projects. In 2002, BTCV was forced to suspend two-thirds of the work by its 2,600 groups across the UK after its insurer pulled cover on conservation projects that involved some volunteers working at height or underwater. Work was able to resume after a new insurer was found, but it does serve to illustrate that anybody setting up a conservation or restoration project using unpaid volunteers should take comprehensive insurance cover into account.

Funding Once the basis of the project and support from the community (and, hopefully, larger agencies such as the local authority) has been established, it's time to apply for funding.

The simplest form of community grants are the lottery grants available from Awards For All (www.awardsforall. org.uk). These usually range from £500 to £5,000. The application process is relatively straightforward.

In June 2004, the Community Fund and the New Opportunities Fund merged to become the Big Lottery Fund (www.biglotteryfund.org.uk), the organisation that hands out the majority of large-scale community funding.

Anybody setting up a new volunteering project

should investigate the resources available from Volunteering England (www.nvab.org.uk), the umbrella group for the majority of the UK's volunteer organisations. The site also contains links to funding bodies, including corporate sources of funding. Regional volunteer advice organisations also exist, such as Volunteer Development Scotland (www.vds.org.uk), Wales Council for Voluntary Action (www.wcva.org.uk) and Volunteer Development Agency Northern Ireland (www.volunteering-ni.org).

In 2004, the government launched initiatives such as ChangeUp and Future Builders (www.futurebuilder. org.uk), to help fund, promote and increase the effectiveness of voluntary organisations. For an oversight of such schemes, look at the Home Office website (www.homeoffice.gov.uk/comrace/active).

Once a project is up and running, nascent organisations can attract additional volunteers by advertising on www.do-it.org.uk, the UK's only national database of volunteering.

Spotlight

Bartering your time

One way of fighting social exclusion is to create a local currency exchange where the 'currency' is people's time and skills.

Local Exchange Trading Schemes (LETS) are a good example of how this can be achieved. Communities using LETS – in essence a collective barter system – in different regions have come up with their own currencies, be it 'reekies' in Edinburgh, 'merlins' in Camarthen or 'acorns' in Totnes. The specifics of LETS vary from place to place, but there are some common factors. For instance, each scheme is run by a small core group of people who create a currency and compile a directory listing the goods and services that members can offer (for example, one member might be a teacher, another a plumber). Then a record is kept of all transactions made. While trade is encouraged, members are dissuaded from going too far into credit or debt. Operating in this way, LETS can be very inclusive.

Another advantage of LETS is that they separate opportunity from cold hard currency, allowing people who are traditionally disenfranchised from society (such as the longterm unemployed) to keep in touch

with the labour market. Some schemes prefer members' time to be of equal value (a lawyer's time is equal to, say, that of a gardener); others prefer a more free-market approach, where certain skills are afforded a particular 'cost'. Either way, wages tend to be closer to one another than in the sterling economy.

In many ways, TimeBanks (www.timebank.co.uk) are an updated form of LETS. Billed as the 'easy way to volunteer, share your time and interests with the local community', TimeBanks, like LETS, involve an alternative currency, in this case specifically time. An hour spent helping a fellow TimeBank account holder means a credit in the bank and entitlement to an hour's help when it's needed in the future. Help could mean a practical skill, such as assistance with building work, or it could mean an hour spent reading to someone with learning difficulties. TimeBank co-ordinators broker deals through national volunteer centres. This kind of sharing of skills and reciprocal exchange of labour and support has proved attractive to younger people. Encouragingly, more than half of TimeBank's 18,000 volunteers are under 25, and 80 per cent are volunteering for the first time.

Mentoring

Public awareness of mentoring is growing – in August 2004 the Home Office awarded £800,000 to the National Mentoring Network (www.nmn.org.uk) and Volunteering England to help develop a designated national mentoring and befriending body – but the concept is not new.

In Homer's *Odyssey*, for example, when King Odysseus left to fight in the Trojan war who did he entrust his son, Telemachus, to? None other than Mentor of course, the older individual who played a pivotal, positive and supportive role in Telemachus' upbringing.

Though not exactly in loco parentis, the contemporary mentor is usually a knowledgeable and often older person who can listen, provide practical and objective advice, and help a mentee to realise their potential.

Mentoring schemes facilitate meetings (usually once a week for an hour) between the mentor and the mentee, and can be informal or formal. A formal structure is usual for school programmes, for example, as clearly defined roles and boundaries are necessary. Whether formal or informal, it's important that meetings take place in 'safe' and reassuring surroundings, and that anything discussed remains totally confidential.

Mentors have a quite specific role. They are there to tackle issues and 'blockages', whether practical, emotional or professional, identified in conjunction with the mentee. Mentors commonly describe the experience in positive terms, even as a privilege.

The volunteering directory www.do-it.org.uk has lately been extended to include mentoring. Increasingly, mentoring plays an important part in the UK's schools. Older mentors can work with students during the run-up to GCSEs and help them talk through career and study choices for the future. Alternatively, a scheme may guide mentees through a specific period of change: for example, schemes working with newly released prisoners, new parents, asylum seekers or refugees (TimeBank (www.timebank.co.uk) runs a service called Time Together to enable members of the community to mentor refugees).

But should prospective mentors worry about possessing the right skills? Formal schemes normally provide a small amount of initial training, but mentoring does require certain personal skills, whether innate or learned. According to Professor David Clutterbuck, author of *Developing Mentor Competencies*, the ability to listen, self-awareness, behavioural awareness, a sense of proportion and communication competence are key qualities that a mentor must possess, along with a sense of humour. He makes the point that 'enthusiasm is far more closely associated with learning than boredom'.

The most important consideration, however, is undoubtedly the question, what do mentees get from it? And results seem encouraging. In 2000, the National Foundation for Educational Research undertook a survey of mentoring across 40 schemes where young people aged 7–19 had been matched with older mentors, largely from the business community. The results showed that mentoring was said to have 'supported inclusion' by reducing the incidence of exclusion and truanting, raising confidence levels, and making mentees more positive about future options. One programme co-ordinator also noted a reduction in anticipated court appearances among a group of young offenders.

To do

Ways to donate your time

● If you want to become more active in your community and are now galvanised into committing yourself to volunteering, the next step is to decide exactly what to do. Seasoned volunteers suggest you should be realistic about the amount of time you have to offer. If you over-commit you could end up letting people down. Also think about what sort of scheme you might enjoy most, as some organisations are more formal than others. Do you have a specialist skill you can offer or a desire to expand on a hobby? Or are you more interested in expanding your skill base?

● Visit www.antiapathy.org. Apathy is the enemy of volunteering and community schemes.

● To find your nearest volunteer centre (formerly called volunteer bureau) visit www.vde.org.uk.

● www.do-it.org.uk has links to hundreds of UK volunteering programmes. You can also find out a little of what to expect through the Do-It weblog, an online diary compiled by all sorts of volunteers, from the novice to the very experienced.

● Give your local neighbourhood a makeover and organise a community litter-clearing day. Not only is it unsightly, litter is also dangerous to wildlife. ENCAMS (www.encams.org), the charity behind the Keep Britain Tidy campaign, advises on how to organise a campaign from scratch. Order its designated booklet by post or online. This will help you decide whether to tackle a local landmark or a well-known 'grot spot'. It also gives advice on how to liaise with the local council over collection of the rubbish.

● Gain valuable work experience as a volunteer. Increasingly, charities and community organisations are trying to woo gap year students away from the delights of backpacking and get them volunteering. It could work in their favour: a 2001 survey of more than 200 top businesses conducted by recruitment group Reed Executive for TimeBank showed that three-quarters of employers prefer applicants with voluntary work and over half thought this experience was actually more valuable than that gained in paid employment. Any students who are tempted should contact Student Volunteering (www.studentvolunteering.org.uk).

● Connect with a diverse group. Volunteering represents an important opportunity to engage with members of the community who you ordinarily might not meet or get the opportunity to understand better.

● Consider less obvious or immediately glamorous types of volunteering that sometimes get overlooked, along with issues that are sometimes stigmatised. For example, in 2004 the BBC reported that a Lincolnshire support group working with people with learning difficulties was suffering from a volunteer drought. Mind (www.mind.org.uk), the leading mental health charity in the UK, can help direct you to a voluntary project involved in this area.

● Sign up for VSO (www.vso.org.uk) and volunteer in one of 30 countries in Africa and Asia where it has a presence. The organisation has 40 years' experience in fighting global poverty and disadvantage.

● TimeBank (www.timebank.org.uk) (see page 239) is striving to get each of us to donate two hours a week to voluntary projects in the local community or overseas. It offers opportunities for all ages, with all levels and variety of skills.

● Join national initiatives such as Big Arts Week (www.bigartsweek.com). It claims that 80 per cent of teachers say they don't have the time or resources to concentrate on the creative arts so your help could make a big difference.

● Watch the Community Channel (www.communitychannel.org). Sitting in front of the television is usually regarded as the antithesis to community activity, but in this case watching the community channel might actually inspire you or at least open up your mind to the potential of community projects and the range of issues that can be addressed. The digital channel is available on Sky, Telewest, NTL and Freeview, and is funded by the Home Office's Active Community Unit.

● Work with your community to improve access to affordable healthy, fresh (and often organic) food by getting involved in community gardens. Visit www.foodshare.net for inspiration.

● During retirement, put your skills to good use. REACH, the Retired Executives Action Clearing House (www.volwork.org.uk), matches up those with high skill levels with community organisations and charities.

● Join the community composting network (www.communitycompost.org). Around 60 per cent of our food waste, currently deposited in our bins and taken to landfill, could be composted (see page 128). At the last count there were 230 community composting schemes around the UK.

● Paint a community building. Giving the village hall or youth centre a lick of paint can be completely free if you team up with Re>Paint (www.communityrepaint.org.uk). It encourages donations from householders and businesses – 100 million litres of unused paint are estimated to be languishing around the UK's homes.

● Become a mentor (see page 240). For inspiration visit www.chanceuk.org or www.friendsunitednetwork uk.com. For example, spend a couple of hours each week with a child or young adult who may have behavioural problems, focusing on that child's capabilities to set realistic behavioural goals.

● Be a virtual volunteer. Thanks to the internet, you don't even have to leave your home to volunteer. Community groups, charities and volunteering organisations need an online profile, and are often grateful for volunteers with web skills or just general computer literacy to design a website, construct a database, carry out research and data analysis, to monitor online discussion groups, or to co-ordinate an online campaign.

● Join the Media Trust (www.mediatrust.org). Media professionals can join this not-for-profit organisation and volunteer their time and skills across PR, press and marketing, online media and video communications. This is a particularly useful service for small charities and community groups without the funds for a designated press officer, but with a need to communicate their work to the media in order to gain coverage.

● Nominate a local community group or charity for an award. For example, the Environment Agency's Action Earth campaign (www.environment-agency.gov.uk) in conjunction with Community Service Volunteering (CSV) presents annual awards to the most unusual location or type of environmental project; best project involving improving waterways; best urban project; the project involving the highest number of volunteers over the age of 16; and the project involving the highest number of volunteers under the age of 16.

● Start a tenants' or residents' association to improve communication between neighbours and improve the place where you live. A residents' association is an independent and voluntary group that represents the views and interests of people who all live in a certain area or estate, or all have the same landlord. People normally start a residents' association because they want to improve the area they live in and the services they receive. An association will usually have a committee, a code of practice and a sense of purpose. Many associations have proved to be enormously empowering, allowing residents to develop a strong community, fight against negative external factors and influence landlords in their favour. The local authority's volunteer centre or your local community volunteer service can advise on how to go about setting up an association. Sometimes funding or facilities to enable meetings may also be available from the local authority.

● Try 'easy' volunteering by signing up to We Are What We Do (www.wearewhatwedo.org.uk). Although this organisation is all about promoting community actions, and the power of working as a team, all you need do is access the website then carry out individual actions and report back.

● Work in a charity shop. Charity shops have experienced something of a resurgence in recent years, alongside trends for vintage clothes and second-hand chic. Most charities have shops all round the UK. For a full list, contact the Association of Charity Shops (www.charityshops.plus.com, tel: 020 7255 4470).

● Finally, do the little things that can mean a lot: give blood; help someone in need of help cross the road; offer to do the grocery shopping for someone less mobile than you; pick up litter; defend someone who is being bullied; offer a lift to someone without a car; give some food to a homeless person...

Directory

VOLUNTEERING

National

The following organisations offer advice about how best to donate your time

Big Lottery Fund
☎ 0845 410 2030
www.biglotteryfund.org.uk

British Trust for
Conservation Volunteers
☎ 01302 572244
www.btcv.org

CharityCareers.co.uk
☎ 0870 013 1200
www.charitycareers.co.uk

Charity Choice
☎ 020 7549 8646
www.charitychoice.co.uk

Charity Commission
☎ 0870 333 0123
www.charitycommission.gov.uk

Charity People
www.charitypeople.com

Community Action Network
☎ 0845 456 2537
www.can-online.org.uk

Community Service
Volunteering (CSV)
☎ 020 7278 6601
www.csv.org.uk

Directory of Social Change
☎ 020 7391 4800
www.dsc.org.uk

Do-it!
☎ 020 7226 8008
www.do-it.org.uk

Ethical Careers
☎ 01865 245678
www.ethicalcareers.org

GovernmentFunding.org.uk
www.governmentfunding.org.uk

Jobs in Charities
☎ 0870 141 7029
www.jobsincharities.co.uk

National Association of Councils
for Voluntary Service (England)
☎ 0114 278 6636
www.nacvs.org.uk

National Council for
Voluntary Organisations
☎ 020 7713 6161
www.ncvo-vol.org.uk

National Neighbourhood
Watch Association
☎ 020 7963 0160
www.neighbourhoodwatch.net

Neighbourhood Renewal Unit
☎ 0845 082 8383
www.neighbourhood.gov.uk

People & Planet
☎ 01865 245678
www.peopleandplanet.org

PrimeTimers
☎ 0845 456 2537
www.primetimers.org.uk

REACH
☎ 020 7582 6543
www.reach-online.org.uk

Student Volunteering England
☎ 0800 018 2146
www.studentvolunteering.org.uk

Third Sector Magazine
☎ 020 8267 4955
www.thirdsector.co.uk

Voluntary Sector National
Training Organisation
☎ 020 7520 2494
www.voluntarysectorskills.org.uk

Volunteering England
☎ 0845 305 6979
www.volunteering.org.uk

Volunteers Week
www.volunteersweek.org.uk

Working For A Charity
www.workingforacharity.org.uk

Regional

The Charities Information Bureau
(West Yorkshire)
☎ 01924 239063
www.cibfunding.org.uk

CSV Scotland
☎ 0131 622 7766
www.csv.org.uk/Scotland

CSV Wales
☎ 029 2041 5717
www.csv.org.uk/Wales

Cultivating Communities –
Community Supported Agriculture
☎ 0117 914 2425
www.cuco.org.uk

The Experience Corps
☎ 020 7921 0565
www.experiencecorps.co.uk

London 21 – Sustainability Network
☎ 020 7359 8228
www.london21.org

London Voluntary Service Council
(running Action Link)
☎ 020 7700 8107
www.actionlink.org.uk

Millennium Volunteers
www.mvonline.gov.uk

Northern Ireland Council
for Voluntary Action
☎ 028 9087 7777
www.nicva.org

Social Enterprise London
☎ 020 7704 7490
www.sel.org.uk

Volunteer Development Scotland
☎ 01786 479593
www.vds.org.uk

Wales Council for Voluntary Action
☎ 0870 607 1666
www.wcva.org.uk

WorkWithUs.org
(for Scotland's voluntary sector)
www.workwithus.org

Worldwide

Anti-Apathy
www.antiapathy.org

Green Volunteers
☎ 01767 262481
www.greenvol.com

United Nations Volunteers
☎ 00 49 228 815 2000
www.unvolunteers.org

UNV Online Volunteering Service
www.onlinevolunteering.org

VolunteerGuru (from NetAid)
☎ 001 212 537 0500
www.netaid.org/volunteer/abroad

World Service Enquiry
☎ 0870 770 3274
www.wse.org.uk

World Volunteer Web
www.worldvolunteerweb.org

CHARITIES AND CONSERVATION GROUPS

The following organisations are all actively seeking volunteers

UK-based

British Red Cross
www.redcross.org.uk

Childline
☎ 020 7650 3267
www.childline.org.uk/Volunteering.asp

The Conservation Foundation
☎ 020 7591 3111
www.conservationfoundation.co.uk

Groundwork Trust
☎ 0121 236 8565
www.groundwork.org.uk

The National Association
of Citizens Advice Bureaux
☎ 0845 126 4264
www.citizensadvice.org.uk

RSPCA
☎ 0870 333 5999
www.rspca.org.uk

Samaritans
☎ 0870 562 7282
www.samaritans.org/support/
volunteer.shtm

Save the Children UK
☎ 020 7012 6400
www.savethechildren.org.uk

WEA Northern Ireland
☎ 028 9032 9718
www.wea-ni.com

WEA Scotland
☎ 0131 226 3456
www.weascotland.org.uk

WEA South Wales
☎ 029 2023 5277
www.swales.wea.org.uk

Workers' Educational Association
☎ 020 7375 3092
www.wea.org.uk

WRVS
☎ 01235 442900
www.wrvs.org.uk

Worldwide

AidCamps International
☎ 020 8291 6181
www.aidcamps.org

Amnesty International UK
☎ 020 7814 6200 (England)
☎ 028 9064 3000 (Northern Ireland)
☎ 0131 466 6200 (Scotland)
☎ 029 2037 5610 (Wales)
www.amnesty.org.uk/amnesty/
volunteer

Blue Ventures
☎ 020 8341 9819
www.blueventures.org

Campaign for Nuclear Disarmament
☎ 020 7700 2393
www.cnduk.org

Coral Cay Conservation
☎ 0870 750 0668
www.coralcay.org

Friends of the Earth
☎ 020 7490 1555
www.foe.co.uk/press_for_change/
volunteer

Global Vision International
☎ 0870 608 8898
www.gvi.co.uk

Greenforce
☎ 0870 770 2646
www.greenforce.org

Greenpeace
☎ 020 7865 8100
www.greenpeace.org.uk

International Service
☎ 01904 647799
www.internationalservice.org.uk

OneWorld International
☎ 020 7239 1400
www.oneworld.net

Oxfam
☎ 0870 333 2700
www.oxfam.org.uk/what_you_can_do/
volunteer

Refugee Council
☎ Volunteering: 020 7820 3112
www.refugeecouncil.org.uk

Students Partnership Worldwide
☎ 020 7222 0138
www.spw.org

Survival International
☎ 020 7687 8700
www.survival-international.org/help.htm

Trekforce Expeditions
☎ 020 7828 2275
www.trekforce.org.uk

UNICEF
☎ 020 7405 5592
www.unicef.org.uk/gettinginvolved

World Wide Opportunities
on Organic Farms
www.wwoof.org

The Young Apprentices' Association
www.aja.org.br

COMMUNITY SKILLS EXCHANGES

Includes Local Exchange Trading Schemes (LETS), TimeBanks and other skills-sharing organisations

UK-based

Community Exchange Network
☎ 01309 676128
www.cxn.org.uk

Fair Shares
☎ 01452 541337
www.fairshares.org.uk

LetsLink Scotland
☎ 01337 870406
www.letslinkscotland.org.uk

LetsLink UK
www.letslinkuk.net

Open Money
☎ 020 8365 2010
www.openmoney.org

Near 2
www.near2.org

SchooLets
☎ 020 7470 6100
www.ippr.org/schoolets

TimeBank
☎ 0845 601 4008
www.timebank.org.uk

TimeBanks UK
☎ 01452 541439
www.timebanks.co.uk

Worldwide

*The ACCESS (Alliance of
Complementary Currencies Enabling
Sustainable Societies) Foundation*
www.accessfoundation.org

*Community Exchange System
from SANE*
www.ces.org.za

*International Journal of
Community Currency Research*
www.le.ac.uk/ulmc/ijccr

LetsEurope.info
www.letseurope.info

LETS-Linkup
www.lets-linkup.com

*Local Exchange Systems
in the Global South*
www.appropriate-economics.org

New Economics Foundation
☎ 020 7820 6300
www.neweconomics.org

ReinventingMoney.com
www.reinventingmoney.com

Skillshare International
☎ 0116 254 1862
www.skillshare.org

VSO UK
☎ 020 8780 7500
www.vso.org.uk

MENTORING

The Coaching & Mentoring Network
☎ 0870 733 3313
www.coachingnetwork.org.uk

MentorsForum
☎ 01727 813747
www.mentorsforum.co.uk

National Mentoring Network
☎ 0161 787 8600
www.nmn.org.uk

Rainer
☎ 01959 578200
www.raineronline.org

*Youth Justice Board
(England & Wales)*
☎ 020 7271 3033
www.youth-justice-board.gov.uk/
youthjusticeboard/prevention/mentoring

GIVING BLOOD

The National Blood Service
☎ 0845 771 1711
www.blood.co.uk

*Northern Ireland
Blood Transfusion Service*
☎ 0500 534666
www.nibts.org

*Scottish National
Blood Transfusion Service*
☎ 0845 909 0999
www.scotblood.co.uk

The Welsh Blood Service
☎ 0800 252266
www.welsh-blood.org.uk

PRISONER SUPPORT

Bridging the Gap
☎ 0870 855 4095
www.btguk.org

*Earth Liberation Prisoners
Support Network*
www.spiritoffreedom.org.uk

Prisoners Abroad
☎ 020 7561 6820
www.prisonersabroad.org.uk

Money

Introduction

What did you spend your money on today? A sandwich at lunchtime? A bus fare? A pint at your local? A newspaper?

The sad truth is that 'your' money was also possibly spent on a range of other less mundane, but certainly more nefarious items such as military hardware, illegally felled tropical hardwoods, and pornography – all without you knowing a thing about it. This is because nearly all of us have money other than the cash in our pocket (even if at times it may not feel that way). Whether it's in the form of a share certificate, pension, or bank account, there are now a range of ways for you to hold your money other than in crumpled notes and loose change.

But because we want our money to be working hard in our absence, much of it is under the daily control of an authority other than ourselves – a bank, a pension fund manager, a stockbroker. And in order for us to be paid interest or a dividend, the people managing our money will search high and low for profitable investments, even if that sometimes means investing in less-than-palatable products or practices.

Money may not necessarily be the root of all evil but it certainly acts as a temptress. It's the one thing our capitalist society can't do without; and in an affluent country such as the UK there's an awful lot of it about (even if it isn't dispersed as equitably as some might like). There's about £35 billion of cash in circulation at any one time, enabling many millions of cash transactions to take place every day. Then there are all the financial assets – equivalent to roughly £2 trillion – held on our behalf in the form of stocks, shares and pensions. Much of this vast wealth is fluid and will be traded regularly in the search for profit – in fact, it is the legal imperative on directors of a public company to make as much profit as they can for shareholders.

Of course, all of this spending carries with it huge power and influence. Money moves markets, after all. Unfortunately, the urge to please shareholders and to make profits can inevitably lead some companies to cut corners, bend rules and exploit the weak. But in recent years there's been a growing awareness that money can be used to much more positive effect if it is funnelled into ring-fenced accounts and funds that are managed 'ethically'.

When used in relation to finance, the term 'ethical' can mean many different things to many different people, but the present-day concept of 'ethical investment' requires money to be invested responsibly with regard to issues such as the environment, social welfare and animal rights. This allows the investor to know that their money isn't being used to fund something that may run counter to their principles.

In fact, investing 'ethically' has a longer tradition than many might think. For centuries, Muslims have screened out certain businesses and chosen not to invest with them on ethical grounds. Under Sharia law, it is prohibited to earn pre-determined interest on one's money (wealth creation must be the result of a relationship between investor and investee in which risks and rewards are shared) or to invest in anything that is deemed 'haram' (unlawful) such as alcohol, pork, gambling or pornography. In broader terms, Islam forbids any investment that is deemed morally or socially injurious. The 1970s saw a widespread revival of institutional Islamic banking and now a number of banks offer services that adhere to these principles.

Other religions have also encouraged similar investment conditions. In the 1800s the Quakers refused to invest in companies involved in the slave trade. In the early 1900s the Methodist church, which preaches temperance, started to consciously avoid investing in companies involved in alcohol and gambling. The first example of ideological and politically motivated investment was in 1971 with the establishment of the Pax World Fund, which forbade investments linked to the Vietnam war. This continued into the 1980s when opposition to the apartheid regime in South Africa helped kickstart the current wave of interest in ethical investment.

In the UK, ethical investments were valued at £4.2 billion at the end of 2003, a figure that Ethical Investment Research Services (EIRIS) – a not-for-profit organisation that researches the social, environmental and ethical performance of 2,600 companies around the world for ethical investors – estimates was ten times higher than just a decade earlier. Surveys suggest that the appetite for such funds is likely to keep growing, too. One conducted in 2004 found that two-thirds of people polled wanted their investments to be more socially responsible.

But using your money more responsibly extends beyond investing it in ethically managed funds, pensions or savings accounts. Charitable giving is another important way people choose to be more philanthropic with their money. About 70 per cent of us regularly give to charity, but the UK average is £12.93 a month – not that much, perhaps, when you consider that the average weekly salary rose above £400 for the first time in 2004. In fact, over 60 per cent of total annual donations in the UK (which stood at £7.3 billion in 2002, down a quarter over the past decade) are given by just 7.6 per cent of donors, who on average give around £50 a month. The most popular way to give to charity is via a collection box or through charity shops. But, as this chapter will show, there are increasingly sophisticated ways to donate money – and in ways that can escape the clutches of the chancellor.

Being 'good' with money doesn't just mean buying shares in a wind farm, or donating large sums to charity. It is equally important to be responsible with how you manage your own money in everyday living. British consumers, constantly enticed by 'cheap money', are now among the most indebted in the world. In fact, we currently borrow far more than the UK government, which itself owes a sum that exceeds the external debt of the whole of Africa and South America combined. In 2004, UK consumer debt passed the symbolic £1 trillion mark for the first time. This is principally down to the fact that we are a nation of homeowners and our mortgages account for about 80 per cent of this sum. But we are also a nation in love with credit cards, store cards, personal loans

and the like – and suffer all the associated stress that consumer debt brings with it.

Debt entrapment is becoming an increasing problem – just witness the number of adverts for consolidated loan services on television. It raises an important quandary: is it ethical to loan to people who cannot afford a debt burden? Equally, is it ethical not to loan to people who need it for basic essentials? To get a sense of the problem, it is sobering to learn that, seen as a percentage of annual income, total personal debt (mortgage, personal loans, store cards etc) increased on average from 54 per cent in 1993 to more than 70 per cent in 2003. No wonder we're a nation that lives in fear of a fall in house prices.

Compounding the problem is the fact that we are not a nation that is historically particularly prudent when it comes to saving for the future. Instead we have relied on the positive equity of our homes to see us through – with mixed (and cyclical) success. In fact, saving levels are relatively low at the moment, representing 6.1 per cent of earnings – down from 8 per cent in the 1960s. As a result, with an ageing population, we are facing an ever-growing pensions crisis, a problem that is only worsened by the fact that a significant proportion of our income is spent servicing loan repayments. In other words, we are largely paying for our past actions rather than our future actions.

What makes an investment 'ethical'?

There are now over 50 investment funds in the UK listed as being, in one way or another, 'ethical'. But what does this term mean?

There are three different strategies ethical fund managers can employ when looking for companies in which to invest: 'engagement', 'preference' and 'screening'.

Engagement means that, instead of excluding any company on the grounds of its activities, fund managers try to 'engage' with the companies in which they choose to invest, in an attempt to get them to 'change their ways'. Some see this as the least effective form of ethical investment. Others argue that engagement is actually the most likely way to encourage a firm to alter its unsavoury habits and practices because its directors are persuaded through dialogue – ie the 'language they speak' – rather than by exclusion or boycott.

Preference means that a list of ethical guidelines – labour rights record, attitude to environment, etc – is drawn up by fund managers. Prospective companies are then compared with one another. The one that adheres to the most guidelines will then be 'preferred' over the others. However, this method still means that funds may be invested in sectors that others would perhaps balk at.

Screening is often seen as the purest form of ethical investment, in that companies are completely avoided if they trade in a blacklisted industry or service. Typically, an 'acceptable list' of companies will be drawn up and funds can be invested only with companies on the list. However, there are two important further distinctions involved with screening, namely whether to adopt 'positive' or 'negative' screening.

Positive screening

Also known as 'light green' investments, funds that are chosen using positive screening restrict themselves to companies that trade only in a 'positive' industry, or, more controversially, are judged to be 'best of class' in an industry that is working to improve its practices. For example, a firm will be accepted if it is involved in a trade such as healthcare, reusable energy or public transport, as these are seen as being 'positive' to society. This form of positive screening is sometimes referred to as 'thematic' investment. With 'best of class' positive screening, firms are judged to be acceptable if for example they have a much improved environmental record even though they may be an oil company.

Negative screening

Also known as 'dark green' investments, funds that are chosen using negative screening exclude any companies that trade in blacklisted 'negative' sectors. For example, any company that trades in military hardware would be excluded. It is up to the investors themselves, in dialogue with a fund manager or independent financial adviser, to establish which sectors they believe should be blacklisted. Some sectors may seem obvious contenders but others will be down to personal choice. For instance, pharmaceutical firms that use animal testing may be deemed 'ethical' by some and 'unethical' by others.

As a guide to what ethical fund managers typically consider before deciding to invest in a company, below is a list of some of the areas EIRIS investigates on behalf of its clients:

Governance issues
- Board practice (disclosure of corporate activities, director salaries and bonuses, proportion of women on the board, etc)
- Codes of ethics
- Social, environmental and ethical risk management

Environmental issues
- Standard of environmental management, policy, performance and reporting
- Record on using chemicals of concern, felling tropical hardwood and causing water pollution
- History of pollution convictions

Social issues
- Links to controversial industries, such as gambling, pornography, tobacco and military production
- Levels of community involvement
- Equal opportunities for staff
- Record towards health and safety
- Attitude to human rights/oppressive regimes
- Relationship with supply chains
- Attitude to trade unions and employee participation
- Levels of staff training

Other issues

- Attitude to animal testing, fur, and genetic engineering
- Involvement in intensive farming and/or meat production
- Involvement in socially and environmentally 'positive' products and services

(For more detailed information, visit www.eiris.org, or call 020 7840 5700)

The most popular areas of concern that investors want to avoid, using negative screening, include nuclear technology, military hardware, animal testing, GM technology, tobacco, oil and mining. Interestingly, in 2004 the Co-operative Insurance Society asked its five million policyholders to vote on what it should prioritise when setting its ethical policy for 2005. After initial consultation, the highest rated area of concern was the environment, followed by human rights and animal welfare.

Similarly, the FTSE4Good Index, which is one of the best-known ethical investment services and acts as a tool for investors to identify companies that meet 'globally recognised' standards of corporate responsibility, will only include companies that meet the following criteria: 'working towards environmental sustainability'; 'developing positive relationships with stakeholders'; and 'upholding and supporting universal human rights'. It also excludes companies with interests in the following industries: tobacco; the manufacturing of parts for nuclear weapons systems; the manufacturing of whole weapons systems; nuclear power stations; and the extraction or processing of uranium.

However, the search for 'profit with principles' is not just confined to ethical investment funds. Similar considerations can also be applied to other forms of finance. Some investors choose to put money into an individual cause or company that they believe in, for example a charity or sustainable home-building development. This is usually called cause-based investment and is typified by the services offered by the Triodos Bank and the Ecology Building Society. Other examples include credit unions that allow investors to fund low-interest loans to under-privileged people within the local community who might not qualify for normal high-street banking services. It therefore pays to closely examine precisely what 'ethical' means when you see it applied to a financial service.

Dilemma

Do I have to forgo profit for ethics?

A question that is often, and understandably, asked of ethical investments is whether they will ever offer a return for your money. Are they, some ask, little more than an act of conscience for investors that will ultimately leave them out of pocket?

When the first ethical investment fund was launched two decades ago in the UK there was much scepticism that any fund that willingly left out oil, tobacco and pharmaceuticals stocks could ever make any money. However, 20 years on that first fund, the Stewardship Growth Fund, is proving its doubters wrong. It was calculated in 2004 that an investment in 1984 of £100 would have matured into £769.80. This compared with £714 for the whole market over the same period. Furthermore, the fund had displayed a particularly precious trait: consistency. At its first,

third, fifth and tenth birthdays, it had been ahead of the fund market average – even though it excluded nine of the 10 largest companies from its portfolio.

In fact, ethical funds outperformed mainstream funds by almost 10 per cent from 1999 to 2004 – a period that saw the dotcom bubble burst and the stock market fallout from the September 11 attacks – with the ethical market returning, according to Lipper Analytical Services, -4.03 per cent compared with the FTSE All Share's return of -13.77 per cent.

According to another analysis by Lipper, if an investor had saved £50 a month, with net income reinvested, in the average ethical fund in the 15 years up to 2003, they would have been sitting on a sum of £13,794.90. Over the same period, the average global growth fund would have returned →

...£12,570.83 and the average UK all-companies fund would have returned £14,343.35. Not much in it, but certainly not as poor an investment as some consider ethical funds to be.

On the contrary, there now appears to be a growing consensus that ethical funds could actually be a particularly savvy investment, purely in terms of growth. In 2004, the Association of British Insurers produced research showing that companies with a culture of corporate responsibility were likely to offer sound longterm prospects for investors because firms that could keep a clean bill of ethical health would see their stock rise.

This was the result of a hard-nosed assessment of the effect of tightening environmental regulations worldwide: any firm that continued to pollute would be heavily fined or restricted and hence its stock market value would be hit. With the same logic, if any company continued with a poor record on health and safety, investors would be scared off. And with the issue of corporate social responsibility sweeping through boardrooms, as has been the case in the past few years (see page 266), so the trend for disclosure will continue to mean that companies find it harder and harder to obscure unethical practices from investors.

But in case you take this to mean that ethical investments are a sure-fire money-making machine, please heed the warning that is, by law, in the small print of all funds: 'Warning. You should remember that the value of investments and the income from them may go down as well as up.'

How to make your money more 'ethical'

Current accounts

For handling money on a day-to-day basis, most people rely on the convenience of current accounts offered by high street banks. Each one will typically offer a debit card, cheque book, limited overdraft facility, very low interest rates, as well as free services such as direct debit and standing orders. There will usually be a few 'hooks' to seal your business such as a period of free travel insurance and the like.

Currently, for the ethically minded, there's not much choice on the market, with the two leading ethical current accounts both being offered by the same bank: the Co-operative Bank. One account (though it actually has four subtly different incarnations) is the 'bricks and mortar' version offered by the bank itself and the other is offered by Smile, its successful and highly rated online sister.

Switching current accounts is made especially easy these days – the new bank does virtually all the paperwork. However, remember to tell a bank why you are considering switching to an ethical alternative, otherwise it will never learn why you chose to do so. Ask them what efforts they are making that could persuade you to stay with them. Equally, once you have switched, take an active role in how your bank sets its ethical

policy – there will always be the opportunity for customer consultation, such as policyholder votes or even feedback forms.

Savings and investments

Considering that we're a nation of poor savers, we have an awful lot of choice when it comes to choosing a method of building a nest egg. Those that do put a lot of effort into saving often take advantage of this fact and will have their money spread across a number of different investments – savings accounts, tax-free ISAs (Individual Savings Account), premium bonds, credit unions, shares, funds – the list is a long one.

Thankfully, for the ethical investor the options for saving are good too. In fact, most forms of saving or investment now have an ethical equivalent. Unless you are very confident and knowledgeable about the best strategies for organising your personal finances, the safest option before you part with any cash is to seek the advice of an IFA (independent financial adviser). With one important caveat: only choose one that is accredited by a recognised body that specialises in ethical investments, such as EIRIS or the Ethical Investment Association (www.ethicalinvestment.org.uk). EIRIS, for example, has compiled a nationwide list of

IFAs who have experience of how to help investors understand and then invest in ethical investments. The easiest way to find an EIRIS-accredited IFA is to go to www.eiris.org/pages/PersonalFinance/Search.htm and type in your postcode. It will then give you five local IFAs. And unless you know the difference between with-profit bonds, gilts and unit trusts, it's also wise to contact the Financial Services Authority's consumer information service for additional background advice about the types of personal finance services on offer (www.fsa.gov.uk/consumer, tel: 0845 606 1234).

An IFA will be able to help and advise you in a number of areas, but first they must perform a 'factfind' on you. This will involve a series of questions about your financial needs, aspirations and circumstances. A good IFA should ask you detailed questions about exactly what you are seeking from an ethical investment – whether you want to screen companies negatively or positively, what sectors you are most keen to avoid, what sectors you actively want to encourage etc.

You should also ask the IFA a number of questions, too. How many clients does the IFA have (400–500 clients per IFA would be normal) and how many of them invest ethically? How is the IFA paid – by wage or commission (less preferable as the IFA is more likely to 'push' fee-earning products first)? Are they truly independent, or tied to a larger firm (and, therefore, will earn commission to offer their products)? Are they a member of an ethical investment body, such as the Ethical Investment Association or the UK Social Investment Forum (www.uksif.org)?

Once through the introductory round of questioning, the IFA will present you with a range of investment options. This may include advice about which of the 50 or so ethical funds now available is best suited to your needs. It is also likely to include advice about the best-suited ethical ISAs (the government-initiated Individual Savings Account that offers the opportunity to invest up to £5,000 tax-free each year), of which 30 or more now exist. It may also include advice about investing in a particular company or share offering. In the past two decades there has been increased interest in

Alternative Public Offerings (APOs), a take on the conventional stock market terminology of Initial Public Offerings (IPOs), best popularised during the dotcom boom of the late 1990s. Successful ethical share issues have included Traidcraft (the first such issue in 1984) and the Ethical Property Company. In 2004, Cafédirect, the fair-trade coffee company, raised £5 million in a fully subscribed share issue. Some of the above stocks are now listed on Ethex (www.triodos.co.uk, tel: 0845 600 9662), Triodos's ethical stock exchange that acts to introduce traders to each other to allow them to buy and sell exclusively ethical shares.

Beyond the intricacies of stocks, shares, ISAs, funds and the like, there are a number of far more routine savings options. A number of banks now offer standard ethical savings accounts. Triodos, for example, offers more than 15 variations of its standard savings accounts to meet the different ethical considerations of its customers. In 2002, an interesting new savings account entered the market with the launch of the Charity Bank. Charity Bank (www.charitybank.org, tel: 01732 520029) uses the funds deposited by its savers to provide loans – over £7 million since its launch – to charitable organisations whose loan requests have been turned down by high street banks, or who have been offered loans on terms they cannot afford. The interest earned on the savings account can either be kept by the depositor, or donated to the bank or to a charity of your choice. While the interest earned is not, at first glance, as competitive as at some other banks, customers of the Charity Bank benefit from the Community Investment Tax Relief scheme, introduced by the government in 2002, allowing the bank to offer a gross return for savers. Unlike ISAs, which are capped at £5,000 a year, there is no limit on the amount you can save, but the deposit must be kept in the account for five years to receive full tax relief.

Credit unions work on a similar principle. They typically allow community members to build funds with the express purpose of offering loans to those in that community who might not otherwise qualify for one from a high-street bank or building society. The objectives of a credit union – technically defined as a mutually owned financial co-operative – are laid down in law, as stated in the Credit Union Act 1979:

- The promotion of thrift among the members of the society by the accumulation of their savings
- The creation of sources of credit for the benefit of the members at a fair and reasonable rate of interest
- The use and control of members' savings for their mutual benefit
- The training and education of the members in the wise use of money and in the management of their financial affairs

Most areas, particularly urban areas, have a local credit union – just ask your local council or citizen's advice bureau for details, or search online. Members save by subscribing for non-transferable shares. Members may then take out loans, at a maximum rate of interest of one per cent per month and up to £5,000 in excess of their shareholding. Credit unions aim to pay a dividend once a year to all their members. This can be as much as eight per cent of total savings, but is typically more like two or three per cent. For more information about credit unions contact the Association of British Credit Unions (ww.abcul.org, tel: 0161 832 3694), the National Association of Credit Union Workers (www.nacuw.org.uk) and the Financial Services Authority (www.fsa.gov.uk/credit_union), which regulates credit unions. The FSA also produces the Credit Union Sourcebook for people running, or thinking about establishing, a credit union.

National Savings and Investment (NS&I) premium bonds and savings accounts both remain a popular form of saving for many. The ethos behind their conception was certainly worthy enough: the Palmerston government established the 'Post Office Savings Bank' in 1861 to encourage workers 'to provide for themselves against adversity and ill health'. One of the founding principles, which still remains today, was to

provide a completely secure savings environment backed by the government. Even so, the enterprise wasn't entirely altruistic – one of the other founding principles was that the bank should provide the Exchequer with a steady source of funding. As is the case with tax, there is no real way of determining exactly how your money is being spent by the government. It could be on the NHS, but it could also be on the armed forces. For example, the savings certificates issued during the first world war helped to finance the war effort, so buying premium bonds or opening a NS&I savings account may not be quite as benign as you may think. It's really down to you whether you want to invest – any more than you are already doing with your taxes, that is – in what the government of the day sees fit to fund from 'its' coffers.

Lastly, EIRIS produces a quarterly publication called the *Ethical Investor*. It covers the latest developments in ethical investments and is worth reading before committing to any investment. It is available to view for free on the EIRIS website, or hard copies can be posted to you for £15 a year.

Pensions

Pensions deserve special mention because of the vast sums now held in pension funds. In fact, a significant proportion of the stock market – a sum estimated to be well in excess of £1 trillion – is controlled by pension funds. A pension fund manager can therefore have considerable leverage when it comes to getting companies to change their less savoury ways.

The potential of this power was recognised in 2000 when the Pensions Act was amended. Those controlling occupational pension funds – but not personal pensions – must now disclose the extent to which they take into account ethical, social and environmental considerations when investing. So if you are fortunate to have an occupational pension (firms employing five or more staff must now offer at least a company stakeholder pension

plan), the onus is on you to find out where your money is being invested. In fact, influencing the manner in which your pension is invested is arguably the most significant ethical gesture you can make with your money given the sums involved.

Ask the fund managers how they ensure they act responsibly. Ask what ethical strategies, if any, the trustees are adopting and why. Request a copy of the Statement of Investment Principles. Finally, ask whether they are aware of Just Pensions (www.justpensions.org, tel: 020 7440 9712), the UK Social Investment Forum's programme for educating pension fund managers about the principles of socially responsible investment.

You may also want to do your own research into what investments are held under the aegis of your pension. For example, the Campaign Against Arms Trade has identified many company pensions, including those held by local authorities, universities, health authorities and charities, as holding shares in arms-exporting companies − information unknown to the majority of pension members. Its 'Clean Investments' campaign (www.caat.org.uk, tel: 020 7281 0297) helps people identify if their pension holds such investments. The campaign group War on Want has also teamed up with Just Pensions to form the Invest in Freedom campaign (www.globalworkplace.org), which also aims to raise awareness about how pension fund managers can invest ethically.

If you hold a standard personal or stakeholder pension, or are thinking of investing in one, speak to the pension manager about what ethical considerations are taken into account when investing funds. If you are not happy with the answer, consult an IFA who is a specialist in ethical investments (see above) about alternatives.

Mortgages
As is the case with current accounts, there is at present a paucity of choice on offer when it comes to ethical mortgages. Again, what constitutes 'ethical' is subtly different from other types of financial services. When used in relation to mortgages, 'ethical' generally means that the mortgage lender will lend only to borrowers buying or building a home that meets strict environmental standards, such as high energy-efficiency ratings. The Ecology Building Society, for example, lends only on properties that give what it calls 'an ecological payback' − new homes built from recycled, energy-efficient or sustainable materials, or old houses in need of renovation.

Norwich & Peterborough offers its 'green' mortgage only to homes with very strict energy-efficiency standards. For the first five years of the mortgage it also plants eight trees to 'carbon neutralise' the property (see page 163). Likewise, the mortgage offered by the Co-operative Bank incorporates an annual donation to Climate Care, an organisation dedicated to helping solve global warming. It also provides a free 'home energy report' with the valuation. In addition, the Co-operative Bank adopts a strict ethical policy that bars it from investing in, for example, oppressive regimes, animal testing or companies making military hardware.

It's also worth bearing in mind the difference between 'mutual' building societies and banks when it comes to choosing a mortgage. The majority of building societies lend money only to fund mortgages and are prohibited from lending money to companies. More significantly, a building society has no shareholders; its 'owners' are its customers. Profits are typically used to offer better rates to the 'mutual' benefit − hence the name − of members. In contrast, a bank will invariably invest profits elsewhere, such as the stock market.

Insurance
Again, only a handful of companies offer ethical insurance services. For buildings and contents insurance the choice is currently limited to a small group

Spotlight

The rise of 'unethical' investments

Just as interest grows in ethical funds, so, perhaps predictably, people also choose to invest in so-called 'unethical' funds. These are funds that exclusively invest in sectors such as tobacco, military hardware, gambling and alcohol. It says a lot about the human condition that such funds are among the most lucrative.

The US-based 'Vice Fund', which requires a minimum investment of $2,500, has provided a 19 per cent annual average return for its investors since it was launched in August 2002. In the financial year 2003/2004, it returned an impressive 57 per cent compared with the Dow Jones Industrial Average rise of 33 per cent over the same period. In fact, the fund was ranked by Lipper Analytical Services, a recognised industry standard-bearer, in the top two per cent of US funds in that year.

It may be shocking to think that people are actively investing their money in sectors that can cause misery and suffering, but it's legal, and profitable, so is it any surprise that some investors are attracted? An extract from the Vice Fund prospectus illustrates how investors are persuaded: 'It is the [fund] adviser's philosophy that, although often considered politically incorrect, [tobacco, aerospace and defence, gambling and alcohol] and similar industries and products...

will continue to experience significant capital appreciation during good and bad markets. The adviser considers these industries to be nearly "recession-proof". Interest in the success of the fund spawned a book in 2004. Its title says it all: *Investing in Vice: The Recession-Proof Portfolio of Booze, Bets, Bombs, and Butts.*

The US is not the only country where interest in 'unethical' funds is growing. Since 2001, *Money Observer* magazine in the UK has tracked the performance of the 25 FTSE 100 stocks excluded from the group of 75 stocks that make up the FTSE4Good UK index. It calls the excluded group the 'Sindex' and in its first year it outperformed the FTSE4Good index by 13 per cent. And in 2004, Money Portal, a UK-based independent financial advising firm, was reported to be looking at starting its own 'vice fund', one that invested exclusively in tobacco, alcohol, gambling, pornography and sex shops. It held discussions with the Financial Services Authority but said at the time that it was at least two years away from launch.

But the question is: could your conscience bear making such an investment?

of firms that includes Naturesave and the Co-operative Insurance Society (CIS). Naturesave places 10 per cent of premiums into the Naturesave Trust, which funds a range of environmental and conservation initiatives. CIS, launched in 1867 and the only co-operative insurance company in the UK, is a sister company of the Co-operative Bank and holds similar principles. Beyond offering insurance for the home, it also offers life assurance, health insurance, and motor insurance, as well as mortgages, pensions, with-profits bonds and ISAs.

It is also worth considering the Environmental Transport Association (ETA). By offering a range of insurance — motor, home, travel, bicycle — to its members, it funds efforts to 'raise awareness of the impact of excessive car use'. However, you must first be a member in order to receive a quote for anything other than motoring insurance.

For those with pets, Animal Friends (www.animalfriends.co.uk, tel: 0870 40 30 300) dedicates its net profits from its dog and cat insurance products to the care of animals and their environment.

Giving to charity

Donating money to a cause, group or person in need has a long tradition. All the world's major religions, for example, encourage their faithful regularly to offer a percentage of their earnings and wealth to others. Indeed, the Christian practice of 'tithing' (from the Old English word 'teotha' meaning a tenth), in which a tenth of annual produce or income is donated to support the church, has many parallels.

Muslims give 'zakat' (meaning both 'purification' and 'growth') at 2.5 per cent a year on all income, and after Ramadan give an amount roughly equal to the price of a meal. Jews practise 'tzedakah' (charitable giving), part of which advocates the voluntary giving of 'maaser' (like tithe, meaning a tenth part). The Sikh 'Code of Conduct' advocates 'vand chakna', the sharing of wealth with others, which again is typically 10 per cent. The Vedic tradition guides Hindus to give according to their ability and position – which for a family man can be up to 50 per cent – and the *Bhagavad Gita* instructs Hindus to 'give without expectation of return'. Buddhists practise 'right livelihood' and 'right action' in accordance with the 'Noble Eightfold Path'.

Of course, the act of donating to charity isn't solely restricted to followers of the world's religions. About 70 per cent of people in the UK give regularly to charity. However, on average we give roughly one per cent of our monthly wage; the richest 20 per cent give 0.7 per cent of their household expenditure to charity, while the poorest 20 per cent give three per cent. (Interestingly, a survey by the British Heart Foundation in 2003 showed that the Scottish are the most generous in the UK, whereas Londoners tend to be the least likely to donate.)

The way that we tend to donate is significant, too. Collection boxes are still the most popular way to give money, with people giving about twice as much over the Christmas period. We also tend to give disproportionately to the largest charities – unsurprisingly perhaps, given their marketing budgets. One fifth of the total income from donations to the top 500 charities in 2002–03 was generated by the top 10 charities alone, which received £1.6 billion between them. In 2003, the five most popular charities with donors were, in order, Cancer Research UK, Oxfam, The National Trust, the Royal National Lifeboat Institution and the British Heart Foundation.

But many smaller charities stress that we're not spreading our charity around equally, and that we're also not donating as effectively or efficiently as possible. For example, in 2004 it was revealed that charities in the UK were losing out on £395 million a year because many of us donate money without taking advantage of new charitable tax breaks. There are a number of ways that can help your money go further. There are also many ways to research which causes are out there for you to donate your money to…

● Firstly, you can always give more. In 2001, the government backed a three-year initiative called the Giving Campaign to persuade the British to give more to charity, in part inspired by the culture and methodology of giving seen in the US. A major aspect of the campaign was to get more employees to donate money via their payroll; 35 per cent of US employees give to charity this way, compared with two per cent in the UK. As a result of the campaign there's been a recent surge in interest in Payroll Giving, which allows a gift to be deducted from your pay or pension before your tax is worked out. For example, if you have £10 a month donated from your pay and your income tax rate is 22 per cent, the net cost to you is actually £7.80 (the 22 per cent tax valued at £2.20 is deducted from the £10 pledge). The Charities Aid Foundation (www.cafonline.org.uk), an international non-governmental organisation that provides specialist financial services to charities, operates Give As You Earn (www.giveasyouearn.org, tel: 01732 520055), the largest payroll-giving scheme in the UK. For more information about payroll giving, ask your employer or contact Inland Revenue (www.inlandrevenue.gov.uk/payrollgiving, tel: 08453 020203).

● The tax breaks don't stop there though. The Giving Campaign left a legacy of other tax-efficient ways to donate money; some new, some improved. The best known is Gift Aid which allows a charity to claim tax relief on your donation – an extra 28p for every £1 you give. You must, however, complete a Gift Aid declaration for every charity that you donate money to. For more information, speak to the charity direct or contact the Inland Revenue Gift Aid help line on 0151 472 6038.

● Share Giving is a way of donating unwanted shares to charity and thereby gaining tax relief from income and capital gains tax. The system was actually set up to solve a problem: there are millions of pounds tied up in tiny holdings of shares that would cost more to sell than they are worth. Share Giving facilitates the shares to be handed to a charity without the donor suffering any tax implications. For more information, contact ShareGift (www.sharegift.org, tel: 020 7337 0501).

● If you're feeling particularly generous, you could donate some land or property. Since 2002, donors who give land or property to charity are eligible for full tax relief from income and capital gains tax. It's a system that David Gilmour from Pink Floyd famously employed in 2003 when he sold his London home to Earl Spencer to raise over £3 million for the charity Crisis. Contact a charity or the Inland Revenue for more details.

● Some people choose to set up a charitable trust because it allows the trustees to set out the aims and priorities for the trust, as well as establishing the criteria for how people apply for funds. For help in setting up a charitable trust contact the Association of Charitable Foundations (www.acf.org.uk, tel: 020 7255 4499).

● Fewer than one in 20 people leave money to a charity in their will despite the fact that it is one of the most traditional forms of donating money. Over 125 charities have established Remember a Charity (www. rememberacharity. org. uk, tel: 0808 180 20 80) to help people make a bequest in their will to charity.

● Before donating any money, research a range of charities that work in fields that match your concerns. There are a number of organisations that offer charity search facilities but good places to begin include www.allaboutgiving.org, www.charity-commission.gov.uk and www.charitychoice.co.uk (remember with this site, though, that charities can pay to be listed above others). It is also interesting to see what new issues, particularly humanitarian disasters around the world, are currently concerning fundraisers and charities by visiting www.fundraising.co.uk and www.alertnet.org.

● Think twice before donating money via charity Christmas cards, charity-affiliated credit cards or 'chuggers' (the 'charity muggers', as they've been nicknamed, who approach you in the street with a clipboard). While the intention behind these methods is perfectly honourable, they are not the most cost-effective way to give money to a charity. All of them require an administrative overhead (chuggers are usually also paid a commission – for more information contact the Public Fundraising Regulatory Association [www.pfra.org.uk, tel: 020 7401 8452]) that could be cut out if you donated via the methods listed above. Furthermore, a number of charities complain that the National Lottery is an inefficient way of distributing money and, worse, diverts people away from giving direct.

● Get children aged 11 to 16 to visit the G-Nation website (www.g-nation.co.uk). It's a government-sponsored campaign aimed at encouraging children to give more of their time and money to charity.

● Lastly, it's far better to set up a direct debit or give via your payroll than giving small amounts here and there to a number of different charities. Doing so only acts to raise a charity's administrative overheads, reduces the impact of your giving and can lead to an increase in the amount of 'chunk' (charity junk mail) pushed through your letter box as your details find their way on to more and more mailing lists.

Directory

GENERAL INFORMATION AND ADVICE

Includes independent financial advisers specialising in ethical investment

Barchester Green Investment
Barchester House, 45/49 Catherine Street, Salisbury, Wiltshire SP1 2DH
☎ 01722 331241
www.barchestergreen.co.uk

Best to Invest
71 London Road, Leicester LE2 0PE
☎ 0800 542 4255
www.best-to-invest.com

Ethical Investments
272 Ringinglow Road, Sheffield, South Yorkshire S11 7PX
☎ 0800 018 0881
www.ethicalinvestments.co.uk

Ethical Investment Association
☎ 01242 539848
www.ethicalinvestment.org.uk

The Ethical Investment Co-operative
12 St Nicholas Drive, Richmond, North Yorkshire DL10 7DY
☎ 0845 458 3127
www.ethicalmoney.org

Ethical Investment Research Services
80–84 Bondway, London SW8 1SF
☎ 020 7840 5700
www.eiris.org

Ethical Investors Group
Montpellier House, 47 Rodney Road, Cheltenham GL50 1HX
☎ 01242 539848
www.ethicalinvestors.co.uk

Ethical Money
83–85 Mansell Street, London, E1 8AN
☎ 0870 871 6594
www.ethicalmoneyonline.com

The Ethical Partnership
146 Bournemouth Road, Chandler's Ford, Eastleigh, Hampshire SO53 3AL
☎ 023 80361361
www.the-ethical-partnership.co.uk

Ethical Screening
Montpellier House, 47 Rodney Road, Cheltenham GL50 1HX
☎ 01242 539850
www.ethicalscreening.co.uk

FTSE4Good Index
15th Floor, St Alphage House, 2 Fore Street, London EC2Y 5DA
☎ 020 7448 1810
www.ftse4good.com

The Gaeia Partnership
1 The Arcade, 829 Wilmslow Road, Manchester M20 5WD
☎ 0161 434 4681
www.gaeia.co.uk

Impax Group
Broughton House, 6/8 Sackville Street, London W1S 3DG
☎ 020 7434 1122
www.impax.co.uk

Investing Ethically
Freepost ANG 20449, Norwich NR3 1BR
☎ 01603 661121
www.investing-ethically.co.uk

Kanuq Money
160 Drakefell Road, London SE4 2DS
☎ 020 7277 8566
www.kanuq.com

Profit with Principle
St. Walburge's Centre, St. Walburge's Gardens, Preston, Lancashire PR2 2QJ
☎ 01772 733338
www.profitwithprinciple.co.uk

UK Social Investment Forum
Unit 203, Hatton Square Business Centre, London EC1N 7RJ
☎ 020 7405 0040
www.uksif.org

BANKS, BUILDING AND LENDING SOCIETIES

The following organisations offer products guided by an ethical policy

Co-operative Bank
☎ 0845 721 2212
www.co-operativebank.co.uk

Ecology Building Society
☎ 0845 674 5566
www.ecology.co.uk

Shared Interest Society
☎ 0191 233 9100
www.shared-interest.com

Smile
☎ 0870 843 2265
www.smile.co.uk

Triodos Bank
Customer Services: ☎ 0500 008720
www.triodos.co.uk

Unity Trust Bank
☎ 0121 631 2743
www.unity.uk.com

CHARITABLE GIVING

The following organisations provide directories of UK charities and/or general information about the different ways to donate. Be aware that some organisations allow charities to pay a fee to be placed above others in their directories

All About Giving
☎ 01732 520055
www.allaboutgiving.org

Charities Aid Foundation
☎ 01732 520000
www.cafonline.org

CharitiesDirect.com
☎ 020 7566 8210
www.charitiesdirect.com

Charity Choice
☎ 020 7549 8646
www.charitychoice.co.uk

The Charity Commission
☎ 0870 333 0123
www.charitycommission.gov.uk

GiveNow.org
www.givenow.org

National Giving Week
☎ 01732 520088
www.nationalgivingweek.org

UK Charities
www.ukcharities.org

VeggieGlobal
www.veggieglobal.com/directory

Will to Charity
☎ 01483 898967
www.willtocharity.co.uk

INSURANCE

**The following organisations
are guided by an ethical
policy. Alternatively, a number
of mutual building societies
offer insurance services.
A list is available at
www.ukinsurancedirectory.
com/links/buildingsocieties.
html, but be aware that not all
building societies are mutual**

Animal Friends Insurance
☎ 0870 4030300 or ☎ 0870 7772677
www.animalfriends.co.uk

Co-operative Insurance Society
☎ 08457 464646
www.cis.co.uk

Ecclesiastical Insurance
☎ 01452 384848
www.ecclesiastical.co.uk

Environmental Transport Association
☎ 0800 212810 or ☎ 01932 828882
www.eta.co.uk

Naturesave
☎ 01803 864390
www.naturesave.co.uk

CREDIT UNIONS

Association of British Credit Unions
(for a comprehensive list of local credit
unions)
☎ 0161 832 3694
www.abcul.coop

Financial Services Authority's credit
unions department
☎ 0845 606 1234
www.fsa.gov.uk/credit_union

National Association of Credit Union
Workers
www.nacuw.org.uk

ETHICAL FUNDS

**The various ethical/green
funds are listed below for
reference. However, before
making any investments, it is
recommended you contact an
independent financial adviser,
as well as obtain full product
information from each fund's
manager. Also see 'fund
supermarkets', such as
www.fidelity.co.uk and
www.cofunds.co.uk, for
more information**

Abbey 'Ethical'
www.abbey.com

Aberdeen 'Ethical World'
☎ 0845 300 2890
www.aberdeen-asset.co.uk

AEGON 'Ethical' and 'Ethical Income'
☎ 0800 454422
www.abetterway.co.uk

Allchurches 'Amity'
☎ 01452 419221
www.ecclesiastical.co.uk

AXA 'Ethical'
☎ 0845 300 0480
www.axa.co.uk

Banner 'Real Life'
☎ 01342 717917
www.bannergroup.com

Capita Financial 'Berkeley
Socially Responsible'
☎ 020 7556 8800
www.capitafinancial.co.uk

Charities Aid Foundation
'Socially Responsible'
☎ 0870 264 3296
www.cafonline.org

Clerical Medical 'Ethical Life'
(see Insight)
www.clericalmedical.co.uk

Co-operative Insurance Society
'Environ'
☎ 08457 464646
www.cis.co.uk

Credit Suisse 'Global Sustainability'
☎ 00 352 436 1611
www.csam.com

Family Assurance 'Family Charities
Ethical Trust', 'Family Ethical ISA' and
'Ethical Bond'
☎ 01273 724570
www.family.co.uk

Friends Provident 'Stewardship'
☎ 0845 757 3036
www.friendsprovident.co.uk

Halifax 'Ethical'
☎ 01904 611110
www.halifax.co.uk/investments/funds_
ethical.shtml

Henderson 'Ethical', 'Global Care'
and 'Socially Responsible'
☎ 0800 832832
www.henderson.com

Homeowners Friendly Society
'Green Chip'
☎ 01423 855 000
www.homeowners.co.uk

Insight 'European Ethical'
and 'Evergreen'
☎ 0845 850 0861
www.insightinvestment.com

ISIS 'Stewardship'
☎ 0845 600 6166
www.isisam.com

Jupiter 'Ecology', 'Environmental
Opportunities' and 'Global Green
Investment Trust'
☎ 020 7314 7699
www.jupiteronline.co.uk/greens

Legal & General 'Ethical Trust'
☎ 0800 096 6959
www.landg.com

Lincoln 'Green'
☎ 0845 605 2323
www.lal.lincolnuk.co.uk

Merchant Investors 'Ethical Cautious'
☎ 0117 926 6366
www.merchant-investors.co.uk

Minerva Fund Managers
'Green Portfolios'
☎ 01225 872 300
www.minfm.com

Norwich Union 'UK Ethical' and
'Sustainable Future'
☎ 01904 688444
www.norwichunion.com/sri

Old Mutual 'Ethical'
☎ 0808 100 8808
www.oldmutualfunds.co.uk

Prudential 'Ethical Pension'
☎ 0800 000000
www.pru.co.uk

QUADRIS 'GoodWood'
☎ 01483 756800
www.quadris.co.uk

Rathbone 'Ethical Bond'
☎ 020 7399 0399
www.rathboneunittrusts.com

Scottish Amicable 'Ethical Trust'
☎ 0870 234 0007
www.pruifa.co.uk

Scottish Equitable 'Ethical Funds'
Contact AEGON

Scottish Mutual 'Ethical'
☎ 0845 600 0436
www.scottish-mutual.co.uk

Scottish Widows
'Environmental Investor'
☎ 0845 767 8910
www.scottishwidows.co.uk

Skandia Life 'Skandia Ethical'
☎ 023 8033 4411
www.skandia.co.uk

Standard Life 'UK Ethical'
☎ 0800 333353
www.standardlifeinvestments.com

St James's Place 'Ethical'
☎ 0800 0138 137
www.sjp.co.uk

Teachers 'Sovereign Ethical'
☎ 08080 133133
www.teachers-group.co.uk

Best Buys
ETHICALCONSUMER

Banks and building societies

Current accounts

The Co-operative Bank
☎ 08457 212212
www.co-operativebank.co.uk

Nationwide
☎ 08457 302010
www.nationwide.co.uk

Norwich & Peterborough
☎ 0845 300 6727
www.npbs.co.uk

Savings accounts

Coventry Building Society
☎ 0845 766 5522
www.coventrybuildingsociety.co.uk

Ecology Building Society
☎ 0845 674 5566
www.ecology.co.uk

Leeds & Holbeck
☎ 08450 505075
www.leeds-holbeck.co.uk

Portman
☎ 0845 609 0600
www.portman.co.uk

Triodos Bank
☎ 0500 008720
www.triodos.co.uk

Yorkshire Building Society
☎ 0845 120 0100
www.ybs.co.uk

Charity credit cards

The Co-operative Bank
☎ 0845 600 6000
www.co-operativebank.co.uk

Ethical investments

Alternative investments

Industrial Common
Ownership Finance
☎ 020 7251 6181
www.icof.co.uk

Radical Routes
☎ 0870 458 1132
www.rootstock.org.uk

Shared Interest
☎ 0191 233 9100
www.shared-interest.com

Triodos Bank

Screened funds

AEGON 'Ethical'
☎ 0800 454422
www.abetterway.co.uk

Friends Provident 'Stewardship'
☎ 0845 7573 036
www.friendsprovident.co.uk

Henderson 'Ethical'
☎ 0800 832832
www.henderson.com

Legal & General 'Ethical Trust'
☎ 0800 096 6959
www.landg.com

Standard Life 'UK Ethical'
☎ 0800 333353
www.standardlifeinvestments.co.uk

Insurance

Ecclesiastical
☎ 01452 384848
www.ecclesiastical.co.uk

Northern Rock
☎ 0845 799 3322
www.northernrock.co.uk

Royal London
☎ 0800 195 1000
www.royal-london.co.uk

Mortgages

The Co-operative Bank
☎ 0800 028 8288
www.co-operativebank.co.uk

Ecology

Norwich & Peterborough

Pensions

Ethical fund-based pensions

Ecclesiastical

Friends Provident
☎ 0870 240 6920
www.friendsprovident.co.uk

Scottish Equitable
☎ 08456 100010
www.scottishequitable.co.uk

Standard Life

Ethical fund-based
stakeholder pensions

Friends Provident

Scottish Equitable

Scottish Mutual
☎ 0141 275 8000
www.scottishmutual.co.uk/main.html

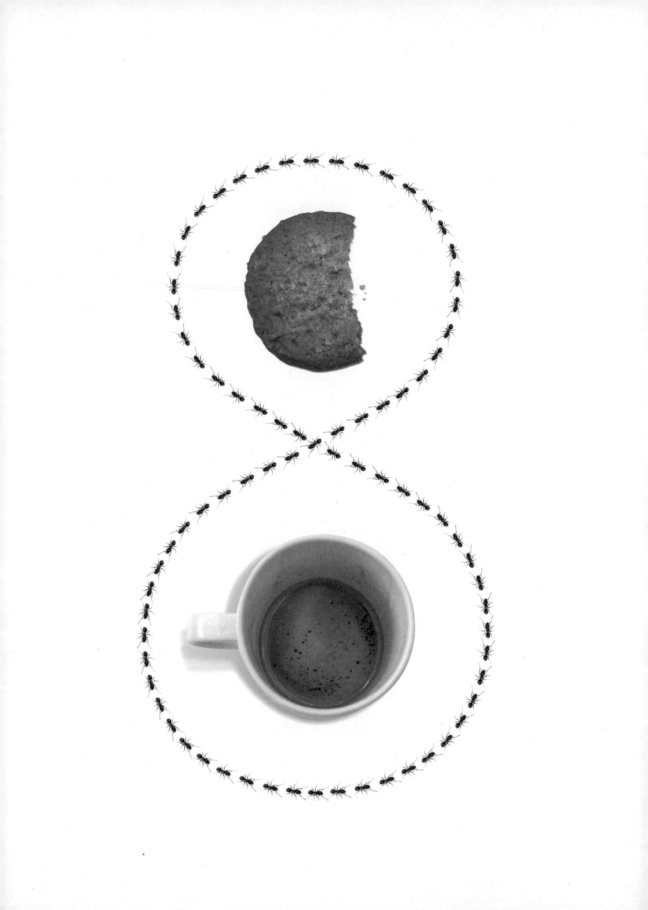

Work

Introduction

We've come a long way from the days

of the workhouse, mine and mill.

In theory, the appeal of 'going to work' in Britain today should be the highest it's ever been: health and safety legislation ensures we are safer at work than ever before; unemployment rates are at a historic low; today's workers are more 'skilled' and qualified than their predecessors; we're guaranteed a minimum wage; and annual holiday allowance and flexible working rights for parents are now enshrined in law. So why are more and more of us 'stressed', pulling 'sickies' and expressing a desire to 'downshift'?

'Stress' is a controversial term and a number of health professionals and academics refuse to believe in the notion of modern workplace stress. After all, who's to say that a coal miner or factory worker 100 years ago wasn't more 'stressed' than today's office worker? Instead, they say that where we once worried about 'real' concerns such as 'putting enough food on the table' and 'making ends meet', today most of us have the 'luxury' of worrying about whether we have the best car or job title. This may be a 'we've never had it so good' take on life, but it does appear that workplace anxieties and pressures are on the increase.

But let's first dispel a common myth about our current working practice – do we really toil for longer hours than ever before? While this is certainly the case for the poorest paid at one end of the scale and senior managers and executives at the other, the average number of hours a week we now work is at an all-time low. In fact, for the second quarter of 2004, the length of the average working week – including both full-time and part-time work – was the lowest on record, at 31.8 hours. For full-time workers, the average over this period stood at 37.1 hours, down from 38.9 hours a decade earlier. For part-time workers, the average stood at 15.5

hours a week. And this trend is likely to continue as the effects of new EU working-time regulations are felt across the continent with the average full-time working week in France and Germany now at about 35 hours.

But there are a number of reasons why we might feel that we are working harder than ever before. Being 'multi-skilled', for example, is seen as an asset, but being so can mean we are constantly 'juggling' work that may have been done by more than one person in the past.

This is part of the ceaseless drive to make the workplace ever more efficient, which includes the use of pressure-inducing factors such as targets, bonus incentives and worker assessment. And the rapid advance in telecommunications and technology in the past decade – email, laptops and mobile phones (meant to 'free us up' from being 'chained to the desk') – means that we are always 'on call' and under the gaze of our bosses. It seems there is always something work-related that we can be worrying about, even away from the workplace. How poignant that a common workplace clarion call should be for us to 'Live the Brand'.

But there are other trends to consider. We are, anecdotally at least, becoming more and more frustrated by our daily commute to work, with news about road congestion and public transport delays forever making headlines. We spend, on average, 25 minutes getting to work (56 minutes if you travel into central London) – then there's the trip home.

We also tend to work through, or compress, our lunch hour, which now lasts, on average, 27 minutes. And this applies only to those who actually leave their workplace at lunchtime; 20 per cent of workers in a 2004 survey said that they never take a break at all. This compares with just seven per cent when the same survey was first conducted in 1990.

So are we experiencing a rise in workload? The signs about how we will work in the future don't offer much comfort. A report in 2004 by the thinktank Future

Foundation presented a vision of British society in 2020. It predicted that a quarter of the UK population – 13 million people – would be 'economically active' between the hours of 6pm and 9am, compared to seven million now. In other words, we are moving towards a 24/7 culture where banks, pubs, cinemas, restaurants and call centres will be open around the clock to serve our new leisure-time demands. More and more people working 'unsocial' hours, especially in the service industries, will further aggravate common problems such as organising quality childcare and finding time to eat healthily and exercise regularly. According to the Joseph Rowntree Foundation, in the majority of two-parent families, one or both parents now frequently work 'atypical' hours (defined as before 8.30am and after 5.30pm on weekdays and anytime at the weekend), and 54 per cent of employed single mothers fell into this category, too.

An obvious question to ask is why aren't we protesting? Rather than act collectively for change, we seem to shrug with resignation, fantasise about 'giving it all up', or just call in 'sick'. The number of days lost to 'stress' in the UK rose from 18 million in 1995 to 33 million in 2002 and there are now 60 times more days a year lost to stress than, for example, to industrial action in the UK. With union membership in longterm decline (in 2004, TUC-affiliated unions had 6,492,389 members compared to the record high of 12,172,508 in 1980, the year after Margaret Thatcher become prime minister), the traditional 'voice of the worker' is in danger of being drowned out. The decline of the unions doesn't bode well for those wanting more equitable pay, better working conditions, or even a 'work-life balance'. After all, who else currently represents our interests at work?

However, there is better news when it comes to reintroducing the 'ethics' back into the term 'work ethic'. First, over the past few years there has been a boom in interest by companies in 'corporate social responsibility' (CSR) – the examination by a firm of its impact, both positive and negative, on its employees, suppliers, customers and even the environment. But second, there is greater interest among employees, partly as a result of CSR, in putting some 'meaning' and 'pride' back into their work through informal initiatives such as office recycling schemes, 'green purchasing', and workplace volunteering schemes.

Ultimately, it boils down to establishing our own priorities as well as gaining a sense of perspective about what kind of life we want to lead. As Madeleine Bunting, *Guardian* columnist and author of *Willing Slaves: How the Overwork Culture is Ruling our Lives*, has said: 'We want a life, not just an escalator of higher living standards paid for with exhaustion and stress. What's the point of that new kitchen if you only ever get to use the microwave? What's the point of the wonderful holidays if you spend them sleeping?'

265

Working towards a better future

On average, we can expect to spend more than 70,000 hours of our life at work. Given this investment of time, it comes as little surprise that we increasingly want our working lives to reflect the values and beliefs we hold outside of work hours. In 2003, a survey by online recruitment agency Totaljobs.com found that 43 per cent of jobseekers would not work for a company that did not have environmental or ethical policies. Further research in 2004 by the global accounting firm Ernst & Young showed 89 per cent of graduates considered high ethical standards to be 'imperative' when deciding whether to join a company.

Whether you work for a huge corporation or a small business, it is easy to forget that we can make meaningful contributions to the way the firm we work for operates. This can take many forms, depending on an employee's particular passion, area of knowledge or interest, or even their prejudices. For instance, you might see a colleague's bin overflowing with recyclable rubbish and feel moved to initiate a recycling programme. Or your journey to work might bring you through a noticeably deprived and run-down estate, and you might persuade your firm to become more active in the wider community, perhaps through a volunteering or mentoring programme (see page 240). There are multiple ways of ensuring that your work life is as indicative of your ethical beliefs as your home life.

Employee-led initiatives really work. Much is made of the potential power wielded over businesses by external bodies – such as non-governmental organisations and campaigning groups – which can help to push organisations down the path towards greater transparency and responsibility. Far less celebrated, however, is our own individual power to effect change, making our company more socially and environmentally accountable, by working from the inside out. In 2002, the Industrial Society found that 65 per cent of businesses would change their policies if pushed by employees, which shows how much power you have.

Decreasing the corporate footprint

In contemporary business, there is considerable emphasis placed on corporate social responsibility (see page 276) as companies try to move on from negative associations of corporate excess. To a certain extent this could be seen as businesses growing up: those that remain 'immature' – ie, corporations who are profligate with resources and continue to exploit and degrade the environment – will increasingly appear unattractive. The first people to notice that a company is irresponsible will be the employees – it stands to reason that those who try to reduce, reuse, rethink and recycle at home will be looking to follow the same principles at work.

Many companies are still spectacularly wasteful. Manufacturing, by definition, uses more resources than other sectors. It also wastes more. According to Envirowise (www.envirowise.gov.uk) – the government organisation that advises on minimising waste at work – 93 per cent of the resources used to produce goods – plastic moulds, coal, corrosive chemicals, etc – are never used in the final product and 80 per cent of products are discarded after a single use. Envirowise can help you set up a dedicated 'waste minimisation club' that will tackle issues such as cleaner design processes, reacting to legislation and the reduction of overall environmental impact. Don't be surprised if your employer is receptive to this idea; Envirowise claims that £1,000 per employee can be saved through the effective use of raw materials.

The Waste Action Resource Programme (WRAP, www.wrap.co.uk) is a government-funded organisation that deals with all aspects of waste minimisation. In October 2004, WRAP launched Recycle Now, a £10 million, celebrity-led campaign to encourage domestic householders to recycle. It also has a designated department to advise business and industry. If you're starting a recycling scheme from scratch, WRAP should be your first port of call. Removing individual bins under desks and replacing them with designated recycling points around a building can significantly reduce the amount of waste going to landfill.

Take the tea break, for example; these days, the reusable mug has largely been replaced by plastic or polystyrene cups. Save A Cup (www.save-a-cup.co.uk) collects 180 million vending-machine cups a year, from workplaces and schools across the UK, and Remarkable Recycling (www.remarkable.co.uk) turns them into useful stationery items to be bought back by offices, creating a market for recycled items.

The great paper chase
Of all of the materials used by UK businesses, paper is still the resource most typically taken for granted and unthinkingly squandered. UK office and printing paper (also known as graphics paper) has the lowest recycling rate of all paper grades: 86 per cent is sent to landfill (where it adds methane to the atmosphere as it decomposes), or incinerated (releasing potentially toxic chemicals used in paper production into the atmosphere).

At current levels of consumption, paper production accounts for 43 per cent of industrial forest use. Meanwhile, demand grows faster than for any other kind of wood product and worldwide consumption is predicted to double by 2020. In the UK we get through 4.8 million tonnes of printing paper every year – almost double the 2.6 million tonnes of newsprint we use over the same period. We may assume that our paper comes from a sustainable source, but as recently as May 2001 Friends of the Earth found that some of the largest and most widely used paper merchants were still importing paper from Indonesian paper mills that were supplied by timber from ancient forests.

Encourage your office not only to sign up to a scheme to recycle paper, but to use recycled paper as well, preferably from as local a source as possible. Office paper is the highest quality paper in circulation, meaning that it can be successfully recycled up to five or six times, working its way down

the paper chain until it is converted into toilet or kitchen paper. The Bioregional Development Group (www.bioregional.com), an independent environmental organisation, runs 'The Laundry', a paper recycling scheme for central London, as well as a local, sustainable paper project for Surrey businesses. The schemes collect office paper, recycle it and sell it back to local firms. The BioRegional initiatives provide a useful blueprint of a successful and sustainable local paper chain. A life-cycle assessment of the London scheme showed the ecological footprint of Bioregional's local paper loop to be just 14 per cent of an imported paper loop. Recycled paper, re-supplied to local business, uses less than half of the energy required to produce virgin paper, saves trees and is far preferable to either incineration or landfill.

Supporting local paper initiatives rather than buying from the huge, multinational mills that comprise the bulk of the paper trade also helps to promote smaller operations, known as 'mini mills'. In turn, mini mills are able to lessen the environmental impact of conventional paper production by sourcing wood from sustainably managed, smaller woodlands (also providing income for local farmers and foresters who use less industrial and more sustainable forestry techniques, such as coppicing) and using a greater variety of raw materials. For example, four million tonnes of straw goes to waste in the UK each year – straw that could be used to make your office paper.

Whether or not you can sign up to a greener, more sustainable supplier, you can minimise paper use in your office in a number of different ways:

● Use email instead of paper and read emails on screen. Although email presents a great opportunity to cut down on paper use, electronic mail has actually increased paper consumption by 40 per cent, so dissuade colleagues from following up email with hard copies of documents and printing emails out.

● Collect scrap paper to make notepads.

● Adjust the margins on documents to fit more text on each page.

● Use both sides of paper, particularly when using fax machines or printers. Although we pay for a two-sided product when we buy paper, how often do we use more than 50 per cent of it? On laser printers, change the 'features' setting to print double-sided.

● Reuse envelopes, particularly for internal mail.

Paper is not the only stationery used wastefully in offices. Opportunities to reduce, reuse, rethink and recycle lurk in every drawer. Staples, for example, are made from steel, the manufacturing of which is a resource-rich and highly polluting process. It is estimated that if each one of the UK's ten million office workers used one less staple every day, 120 tonnes of steel would be saved each year. Use reusable mini bulldog clips instead.

If each one of the UK's ten million office workers used one less staple every day, **120 tonnes** of steel would be saved each year

Green purchasing

Green purchasing is a concept that has grown in stature over the past decade. Its roots are in public services. Following the Rio Earth Summit in 1992, local authorities in the UK signed up to green purchasing as part of Agenda 21 – a comprehensive plan of action to protect the environment and promote sustainable development. Since then, the procurement of 'green' or 'sustainable' goods and services in order to ensure high environmental and social values across supply chains has become a core part of public-service purchasing. Over £1 billion is now spent on green procurement for public services across the EU. Increasingly, the corporate world too has adopted green purchasing as central to corporate social responsibility charters, since company culture has been able to learn from the way public service procurement has influenced a dynamic new marketplace. If you want to shift to green purchasing, there are plenty of best-practice examples to be found in the public services. Businesses within the Thames Gateway, for instance, can get the benefit from London Remade (www.londonremade.co.uk), an organisation launched by Ken Livingstone in 2002 to provide advice and entry points into the local green-purchasing network.

Wherever a company is based, establishing the best 'green buys' for a workplace requires a similar approach to ethical purchasing at home. Before buying, or signing contracts, an ethical purchaser should:

● Ask whether their organisation needs the product/service in the first place.

● Find out whether the product has the maximum recycled or re-used content possible.

● Consider the amount of packaging used on a product.

● Consider the life cycle of a product – how long is it likely to last? If a new photocopier is an expensive model, will it save money in the long run because it is more energy efficient? Is the product easy to recycle?

● How will a product be disposed of? The Environment Agency guidelines on green procurement give paint as an example of a green purchasing decision. Because water-based paints are safer and cheaper to dispose of, they are preferable to solvent-based paints.

Green purchasing should also cover the ethical treatment of suppliers – swift payment of invoices to improve cashflow for smaller businesses for example – and fairness of contracts. For more information, visit www.sustainable-development.gov.uk.

Donations in kind

Making more ethical purchasing decisions at work is part of the equation, but not the whole picture. A large amount of corporate 'waste' has the potential to contribute in a very meaningful way to society. Take toner cartridges, for example. In the UK over two million non-biodegradable toner cartridges are thrown away every year. These could have been sent to companies such as Accutecc UK, Europe's largest cartridge refilling firm, on behalf of designated charities. They would then have been sold on to companies (perhaps through a green-purchasing scheme) with a proportion of the resale value going back to charity. As it takes 0.7 litres of oil to make a new cartridge, to throw them away also represents a serious waste of non-renewable resources. Encourage your workplace to collect spent cartridges. It just requires one person to take responsibility for collecting a number (10 is a good amount) before sending them on (many charities operate a freepost scheme). Contact an organisation such as Cartridges4charity.co.uk or Oxfam's LaserXchange initiative (www.oxfam.org.uk) for details.

To close the loop – and help to perpetuate a market for remanufactured printer cartridges – don't just donate, but also buy them from firms such as Office Green Technologies (www.officegreen.co.uk). An Office of Fair Trading study found that 78 per cent of printer users had not switched to refilled cartridges because the manufacturer's guidelines (unsurprisingly) specified the use of new, own-brand cartridges. However, a 2002 *Which?* report by the Consumers' Association found that the performance difference between refilled and new branded cartridges was negligible, and that in some cases refilled cartridges came out on top.

You should also look out for discarded products that could be donated in kind. In Kind Direct (www.inkinddirect.org) co-ordinates this type of charitable aid. Products could be seconds, samples or end-of-line stock, which, because they are branded, manufacturers often send to landfill to prevent brand names from becoming devalued. In Kind Direct brokers deals between suppliers and charities, carefully protecting brand image while enabling charities to receive new products for a fraction of the cost. In 2003, the charity redistributed more than £6 million worth of surplus, including toys, toiletries, tools, household appliances, cleaning products, office equipment, clothes, books and bedding, from more than 550 companies direct to charities. And, as a result, away from landfill.

The office environment

When George Orwell was looking for a room to house his protagonist Winston Smith's worst nightmares in his novel *1984*, he just imagined his old office at the BBC, Room 101. Many of us, it seems, can relate to this. Badly designed workspaces feature long, depressing corridors, isolating rooms, cramped areas and noisy open-plan spaces. A survey by *Management Today* found that 50 per cent of managers would willingly exchange a week's holiday for better offices. Clearly, many employers and employees alike would benefit from a more holistic and better-designed workspace – positive office environments can substantially boost productivity and staff retention. For tips on how to improve your work environment, take a look at www.enjoywork.com.

It is estimated that 80 per cent of people will experience back pain lasting more than a single day at some point. The charity Back Care (www.backcare.org.uk) promotes better back care and offers advice to those already suffering from back pain. Overall, muscular skeletal disorders represent the leading cause of absence from work. More than 1.1 million people in the UK suffer from RSI (repetitive strain injury). Prevention is obviously preferable to chasing cures, so make sure your employer provides expert health advice (such as an ergonomic expert to assess your work station) to ensure that you're not at risk. The Health and Safety Executive publishes a number of books on RSI prevention and best practice, including *The Law on VDUs: an easy guide* (£8.50, HSE Books, www.hsebooks.com, 2003) and *Work with Display Screen Equipment* (£8.95, HSE books, www.hsebooks.com, 2003), as well as a free leaflet, *Aching Arms (or RSI) in Small Businesses*, which can be downloaded from www.hse.gov.uk.

Being happier and healthier

Work-life balance

It is not easy to effect change, instigate recycling schemes, nurture charitable donations and investigate green purchasing if you're struggling to keep up with your workload in the first place. While the average number of hours we work a week is at an all-time low, the Work Foundation's 2004 UK at Work survey still found around 4.5 million workers (18 per cent of the UK workforce) regularly toiling for over 48 hours a week. Meanwhile, the TUC claims that we work £23 billion worth of unpaid overtime every year. This is equivalent to each employed person in the UK donating £4,500 of free time to their employer every year.

This sector of the workforce can no doubt identify with the 62 per cent of US employees surveyed by *The New York Times* in 2004 who reported an increase in workload in the six months to September 2004. Fifty-three per cent said that work left them feeling 'tired and overwhelmed'.

In this situation it can be difficult to ensure that you actually *have* a life, never mind any quality of life. The concept of work-life balance seeks to redress the problems caused by a live-to-work culture. Initially,

work-life balance focused on easing the burden on parents and those with other caring responsibilities, but now the concept has widened to encompass all types of life outside work; whatever our domestic or personal arrangements, every single worker has a right to a life outside of their job. In 2000, the UK government launched its definition of work-life balance, advising that employees should be:

● **Given some flexibility of working hours**

● **Allowed to work from home where possible**

● **Granted leave arrangements that enable them to meet non-work commitments and realise non-work goals**

Clearly, these points cover a broad range of issues. Work-life balance can include leaving the office at a reasonable hour, having whole weekends off and using up all your holiday (annual leave) entitlement. But it can also include the promotion of equal opportunities:

The TUC claims that we work **£23 billion** worth of unpaid overtime every year. This is equivalent to each employed person in the UK donating **£4,500** of free time to their employer every year

flexible working patterns, for example, have been shown to encourage the retention of female staff, since working mothers are better able to find viable childcare solutions. In fact, the nine-to-five working regime may soon be more of an anomaly than the norm. According to the Institute of Directors, three-quarters of its member firms now offer some kind of flexible working arrangements. This type of arrangement tends to be of an informal nature so trade unions advise that agreements, however informal, should be written down. It's not necessary to draw up a formal document – an email will provide a useful record of agreement should any dispute occur. This way, if you've based your childcare arrangements around flexible working times agreed informally with a line manager, the agreement will be protected, even if that line manager leaves the company or changes their mind.

In order to try and secure greater work-life balance some employees might like to take a more direct approach:

● Take all holidays owed and campaign for more holidays or the right to a sabbatical; the Netherlands and Denmark have both introduced systems of 'voluntary unemployment' whereby every worker has the right to one year's leave from their working life subsidised by state payments at 60–70 per cent of their original wage.

● Support parental leave and campaign for higher rates of paternity pay. For the first time in 2003, new fathers in the UK became eligible for a fortnight's paid paternity leave. The Department of Trade and Industry (DTI) forecast that in the first year 80 per cent of the 400,000 eligible fathers would take up this entitlement. But in reality, a disappointing one in five actually took the time off. Many were seemingly deterred by the low rate of paternity pay – at £103 per week – choosing to take annual leave instead.

Working from home

Flexible working patterns will see more of us working from the comfort and convenience of our own homes. But enticing as it may seem, working from home presents a whole new range of issues. To begin with, most home office setups leave a lot to be desired in ergonomic terms, making workers vulnerable to

conditions such as RSI. Home workers can also suffer from a lack of contact with other people, leading to a sense of isolation. And without the physical act of leaving the office, it can often be hard for home workers to limit their hours and switch off from work. So while 'teleworking' – defined as the use of technology to work away from the traditional office environment – has liberated more than two million workers from the traditional office environment, it's important to bear the DTI's guide to teleworking in mind: 'Staff who are using their homes for working have a right to privacy out-of-hours, and to be able to separate their working and home lives.' Specific guidelines can be found at www.dti.gov.uk/er/individual/telework.pdf.

Inequality

Issues over inequality have dogged the workplace for the past century and, somewhat dishearteningly, the same issues seem to crop up time and time again. So when a 2004 report from the Chartered Management Institute excitedly trumpeted the news that female heads of departments earned more than their male counterparts, it didn't take long for *Guardian* columnist Polly Toynbee to ask 'what's the catch?' Neither did it take very long for her to find out. The women cited in the study were still anomalies, leading Toynbee to conclude that 'only a quarter of department heads are women. There are more women managers than five years ago, but women still make up only one in seven of company directors.' She also pointed out that although the 'cards are stacked against even [the] high fliers,' the real inequalities and injustice over women's employment could be traced to low-paid workers. On average, women working full-time still receive 18 per cent less than men, while 43 per cent of all working women earn less than £5 per hour, falling below the Council of Europe's 'decency threshold' figure for 2004 of £6.31. For more information, visit the Equal Opportunities Commission's campaign for equal pay at www.eoc.org.uk.

Nobody should have to put up with discrimination and there are laws to this effect. The new Disability Discrimination Act, for example, which came into effect in October 2004, means that no company, even those with fewer than 15 members of staff, can get away with discriminating against disabled job applicants on the basis of their disability. The act covers around 9.8 million adults.

Ageism in the workplace is also a worry, despite the fact that older workers have been shown to achieve the same levels of performance as younger workers and are more likely to stay in their jobs – an important factor when you consider that the cost of replacing the average employee is £3,500. One in five people have been discouraged from applying for a job because it contained an age restriction, according to research in 2004 by the Chartered Institute of Personnel and Development. For more information, visit the Age Positive Campaign (www.agepositive.gov.uk).

Keeping sick days at bay

It stands to reason that workers under pressure, who feel they can never get on top of their workload and who are juggling the pressures of everyday life, such as childcare, will sometimes fall prey to illness. Time off due to stress-related illness has increased by 500 per cent since the 1950s. (Bear in mind, though, that the concept of 'stress' has only been developed since the 1950s.)

Whether or not you believe in the concept of workplace stress, three million Britons are estimated to be on longterm sickness benefits, and the number of claimants citing stress-related illness, anxiety and depression has risen by more than a third since 1997. Rhondda in South Wales was dubbed the 'sickness capital of Europe' when statistics revealed that one in three adults of working age were on incapacity benefit. In the UK as a whole, women now make up two-fifths of those claiming incapacity benefit, rising from 32 per cent of claimants in 1995 to 40 per cent in 2004. In part, this rise could be due to the fact that a greater number of women have joined the workforce overall, but some of the reason could also be attributed to the strain placed on women as they juggle workloads, and in some cases, long working hours, with the responsibilities of family life.

If you believe your health is suffering because of your workload, hours and responsibilities, your employer has a responsibility to tackle work-related stress. This responsibility has been legally enshrined by amendments to the Health & Safety at Work Act in 2004. Employers failing to tackle workplace stress could, in theory, face criminal prosecution and unlimited fines. For more information, visit www.hse.gov.uk.

To increase your overall health, try to do the following:

- Stop smoking. Contact www.quit.org.uk for advice or find out if your employer runs a scheme to help employees quit, or is prepared to help with the cost of treatment. According to the charity Action on Smoking and Health, 34 million days a year are lost to British industry through smoking so it's small wonder that employers are increasingly keen to help.

- Take regular exercise. Many gyms offer corporate rates – or, better still, join a 'green gym' (see page 187).

- Prioritise sleep. It's important. Lack of sleep can age the immune system and lead to illness. For advice, visit www.sleepcouncil.com.

- Eat sensibly. Research has found that night workers in particular are susceptible to diabetes and obesity, as they may often 'load up' on sugar-rich snacks.

When the training body City & Guilds compiled a recent 'Happiness' index, 91 per cent of survey respondents, taken from a cross-section of the workforce, revealed they felt some degree of unhappiness at work. Although there are many contributing factors to 'happiness', feeling valued and appreciated has consistently been shown to increase the chances of contentment at work. Training and the development of skills is a crucial way to achieve this. The Campaign for Learning (www.campaign-for-learning.org.uk) runs an annual Learning at Work Day encouraging employers to 'dig for the wealth that lies buried and invisible in your people'. The organisation also offers year-round support to promote learning in the workplace.

Time off due to stress-related illness has increased by **500 per cent** since the 1950s

Dilemma

If we worked less, wouldn't we achieve more?

In a pan-European poll conducted in 2000, 37 per cent of Britons said they worked on Sundays, compared to 18 per cent in Ireland and France, 16 per cent in Germany and 14 per cent in Spain. A *Guardian*/ICM survey in 2004 found that 61 per cent of respondents thought they spent too much time at work.

The social commentator and writer Pat Kane wants our flawed work ethic to be replaced by a 'play ethic' (www.theplayethic.com). He maintains that our non-work lives are not sufficiently valued and that play has nothing in common with idling or loafing, but is 'as the great philosophers understood it: the experience of being an active, creative and fully autonomous person'. This involves making time and space for activities that are voluntary and separating the concept of 'play' from 'leisure and entertainment', making it part of the creative process. In turn, by working less, and taking time out, we will have the freedom to be 'inventive, nurturing and modern', qualities valued by employers, and qualities that would also benefit the economy.

In *How to be Idle*, his manifesto on idleness, writer Tom Hodgkinson dismisses the proverb 'early to bed, early to rise, makes a man healthy, wealthy and wise' and advocates lying in bed half-awake in a 'hypnagogic' state as it is 'positively beneficial to health and happiness'.

Anybody using the 'hypnagogic' theory as a 'sorry-I'm-late' excuse might expect short shrift from their boss. Perhaps, then, their employer should be referred to evidence that suggests cutting down on work can in fact boost productivity, not just happiness. When an EU directive commanded that junior doctors work shorter hours, the Royal Liverpool NHS Trust reported that 'this must be beneficial for patient care…response times to night calls are quicker…The initiative has raised morale not only among doctors but also nursing staff.'

In fact, by making employees work harder, we may be barking up the wrong tree entirely. Despite longer hours, UK productivity lags behind that of the US, France and Germany by 15–25 per cent. A Treasury calculation has priced this variation as making everyone in the country £6,000 worse off. Meanwhile, a study of UK productivity by the Work Foundation concluded that 'having exhausted the market reforms of the 1980s, too many companies are still trying to improve performance by making people work harder, rather than smarter, with swiftly diminishing returns'.

The ethical career

There is a growing wave of job hunters specifically on the lookout for an 'ethical career'. A survey in 2004 by graduate careers publisher Axiom Software found that more than 50 per cent of all graduates surveyed would take a job which fitted their ethical principles above a higher-paying job – even though many had student debts to pay off.

Ethical employment opportunities are mostly found in the charitable sector, environmental and regeneration agencies, and public-sector jobs for local authorities. However, ethical job hunters should also look out for opportunities in new markets: an ethical fashion designer with knowledge of fair-trade cotton producers might soon be in demand over someone with knowledge of the conventional fashion trade, for example.

According to the Chartered Institution of Water and Environment Management, the environment sector in the UK has a £16 billion turnover and employs about 170,000 people. The main employers continue to be major government agencies, such as English Nature and the Environment Agency, which, along with local authorities, recruit personnel to deal with recycling, conservation, countryside management, environmental health, planning, pollution control, transport and waste management. But as the environmental market develops and business (driven largely by legislation) becomes more environmentally minded, expect more jobs to appear in renewable energies and technologies. In addition, as more companies sign up to environmental management systems to help to increase resource productivity, as well as to minimise waste and environmental degradation, they are increasingly employing their own in-house environmental officers. The Centre for Alternative Technology (www.cat.org.uk) publishes *The Sustainable Careers Handbook*, while www.ciwen.com/publications/careers provides an inside guide to environmental careers.

Traditionally, jobs in the public sector have suffered an image problem. Many have become associated with low remuneration and heavy workloads. However, a survey conducted by the NHS in 2003 found that three-quarters of staff are satisfied with their jobs and many said they had a good work/life balance, flexible working patterns and good opportunities to take advantage of training. Meanwhile, in January 2004, there had been a 7.5 per cent rise in the preceding 12 months in the number of applicants to take a Post Graduate Certificate of Education (PGCE). In fact, UCAS figures for 2004 showed a surprising surge in the number of university applicants for degrees in the caring professions. Applications for social work rose by 94.6 per cent, while figures for nursing were up by 23 per cent and pre-clinical medicine by 21.7 per cent.

But now social enterprise is challenging the charity, environmental and public sectors for the ethical employment crown. If running a business that trades for social purpose used to be rare, highly publicised businesses such as Jamie Oliver's restaurant Fifteen (where young unemployed adults were trained to be chefs) have helped to bring social enterprise initiatives into the mainstream. Such enterprises put social change, rather than profit, at their core, but do not ask for charitable donations. Instead, they provide a particular product or service, bridging the gap between social projects and corporate successes. The scheme might be a recycling service or remanufacturing venture, but it will be run with the same energy and commitment one would expect to find in the mainstream corporate world and marketed as innovatively and aggressively as a conventional product. The bulk of the profits will be reinvested in the scheme. The Social Edge chatroom explains in further detail (www.socialedge.org) and is hosted by the Skoll Foundation (Jeff Skoll is a former president of the online auction site eBay and set up the Saïd Business School at Oxford University, the centre for social entrepreneurship). Also visit the Cat's Pyjamas website at www.the-cats-pyjamas.com.

If you are looking for an ethical career, the first question you need to ask is how much a company genuinely fulfils your ethical criteria. This is a very personal decision and will involve looking behind any glossy CSR report (see page 276), sometimes referred to as 'PR fig leaves'. Delving a little deeper may mean finding out if a company is listed on the FTSE4Good index (see page 251) or researching what campaigning groups or NGOs that you respect think of an organisation. Visit the EU's European Pollutant Emission Register at www.eper.cec.eu.int to see how a company is rated. In the first set of results in 2004, several UK-based corporations were named and shamed as top industrial polluters. Also, use People and Planet's ethical careers service (www.peopleandplanet.org/ethicalcareers) and find out how *Ethical Consumer* (www.ethicalconsumer.org) rates the company you want to work for.

Ultimately, nobody can tell you who to work for. Even if you disagree vehemently with a company's perceived values, arguably it's possible to change a corporation from the inside out. And no employee should be barred from finding an ethical dimension to their job, whatever sector they choose. The organisation Scientists for Global Responsibility (www.sgr.org.uk/ethics.html), for example, demonstrates that scientific and ethical careers are not mutually exclusive. Alternatively, you may only be able to give a proportion of your time to ethical work. A solicitor, for example, might become involved in some pro bono work (www.barprobono.co.uk).

Spotlight

Working in union

The fortunes of unions have fluctuated since the Trades Union Congress (www.tuc.org.uk) came into being in 1868. At its peak, the TUC, now the umbrella organisation for 70 unions, represented the most powerful body of working people in the world.

In the 1970s union behaviour was characterised by the type of mass walkouts, lightning strikes and work-to-rule directives that still linger on in the public memory. This memory has dogged the union movement ever since, and led to reforms of trade union laws. Throughout the 1990s union membership slumped. With the focus on increasing economic prosperity, to many workers joining a union seemed anachronistic, and possibly irrelevant.

In 2003 there were 7.42 million union members in the UK. Membership profiles continue to follow a traditional regional pattern with the highest membership rates in the north-east and Wales and the lowest in the south-east. With more women joining the labour market, the number of women who are union members is now almost equal to male membership.

But even if unions are unlikely to recapture their popularity of old, some have demonstrated that they are able to change with the times, shaking off the belligerent image of the 1970s and offering solutions to contemporary employment issues such as gender pay gaps, pensions and working hours.

But a union should not just be used for times of trouble and mass unemployment. Sweden is one country that has demonstrated successfully that unions can play an important role in times of relative prosperity, by maintaining record levels of employment and trade union membership, simultaneously.

All workers should seriously consider signing up to a trade union, as an effective means of safeguarding employment, and achieving high levels of health and safety, as well as good employment conditions. In recent years a decline in union membership has coincided with an increase in accidents at work, particularly in the construction industry. By becoming a member of a trade union you are less likely to be sacked or injured at work, and more likely to earn more money – according to DTI figures, in 2003 earnings of union members averaged at £11.06 per hour, 17.7 per cent higher than the non-union average. Unions also protect against discrimination: on average black and Asian trade union members earn 32 per cent more than their non-unionised colleagues. In the light of these benefits we should be less inclined to question how relevant unions are in this day and age, and quicker to ask ourselves what's kept us from joining.

EXPLAINER Corporate social responsibility

What is CSR?

As an idea, corporate social responsibility (CSR) has been around for more than 20 years. It surfaced in the UK as early as 1981, when, after riots in Toxteth, Liverpool, the Business in the Community initiative was set up to create links between business and society. But it is only in the last few years that CSR has developed from a buzz phrase to an integral part of business strategy.

CSR is a broad term, and interpretations vary from company to company, but in essence, CSR acknowledges that business has an impact on society and the environment in various, not always positive, ways and so must be responsible for its actions, giving equal weight to social, environmental and financial considerations.

Fifty per cent of FTSE100 companies now produce an annual CSR-related report, with 21 per cent of large companies producing a full CSR report. In the not too distant future, the presentation of the annual CSR report could be as much of a fixture in the business calendar as the annual financial report.

Also referred to as the 'triple bottom line' approach, CSR is frequently seen as the business contribution to sustainable development. The government defines the role of CSR as:

- **Maintaining economic growth and employment**

- **Recognising the needs of everyone through social progress**

- **Ensuring effective protection of the environment**

- **Using natural resources prudently**

Business is about increasing profit and cutting costs, so why would any corporation be interested in CSR?

In a world dogged by social and environmental problems, CSR argues that business must become more sustainable in order to ensure longevity and continued prosperity. According to the re-insurance group Munich Re, the dramatic trajectory of climatic disasters attributable to climate change means that by 2065 insuring the world against human-induced disasters could bankrupt the global economy. In short, 'business as usual' is not an option.

CSR concerns itself with risk management. Contemporary risks to the business community include: potential damage to reputation — corporate legend has it that reputation accounts for 60 per cent of a company's value; risks to the environment and the health of local and wider communities that may result in litigation and/or negative publicity; and the risks to sustainability posed by the depletion of non-renewable resources such as oil.

Many analysts argue that rather than being a wholly altruistic process, adopting CSR policies can actually increase a corporation's value. Both the Dow Jones Sustainability Index (DJSI) and the FTSE4Good index (see page 251) have been set up to track 'good' companies. And those DJSI companies with high levels of 'stakeholder engagement' — those who work with NGOs to produce CSR reports — have been found to have higher share prices than conventionally listed companies.

Some companies have also found that embracing CSR provides a new niche market. David Grayson and Adrian Hodges, business experts specialising in CSR, cite Cemex, a Mexican cement company, which has made cement available at affordable prices to hospitals and people on low incomes. The car rental company Avis has modified vehicles and facilities for people with disabilities, creating an £8 billion market in the process.

So CSR is just a way of helping big business to 'greenwash' itself?

It's not hard to find flaws in the arguments for CSR and many sceptics would hold with Mark Twain's view that 'the secret of success is honesty and fair dealing. If you can fake these you've got it made.' So just how far can we trust CSR reports?

It is precisely CSR's broadness of scope and lack of

concrete definition that provokes criticism. At times it can seem an uneasy mix between business and virtue. And because it embraces a wide spectrum of best practices and policies, from engaging with local communities to adequate provisions for health and safety, it can seem to be confusingly wide-reaching.

It is true that some CSR reports have been found to be lacking in probity and transparency, precisely the things they are supposedly designed to promote. Friends of the Earth even goes so far as to run a spoof annual Xpose awards ceremony which 'congratulates big businesses and their lobby groups for ruining the planet' and includes an award for the 'best omission from a CSR report'.

As the old adage says, the road to hell is paved with good intentions, and CSR can seem similar. 'Researchers have found no correlation between company ethics codes and ethical policies,' insists Kirk Hanson, a US CSR expert. Recent research suggests that CSR mission statements and reports mean little unless there is an organised structure to put intentions into action, backed up by legislation.

Why does society now demand that corporations be more accountable and transparent?

Increasingly, we are demanding an improvement in quality of life, a redressing of social inequalities and a cleaner, healthier environment. And so we increasingly expect business to conform to these values too.

According to the business research organisation GlobeScan, almost half of British consumers now expect a company to demonstrate a commitment to social progress. In 2002, 44 per cent of the British public said that when buying a company's product they thought it was very important that the company demonstrated a high degree of social responsibility – almost double the amount of people in 1998 who attached importance to a company's reputation for social progress.

Globescan research has also found that consumers in North America, Europe and Australia pay much more attention to CSR reports than previously thought. Over 50 per cent of those polled in those countries had either read a CSR report, briefly looked at one, or heard about the contents of one. For the UK the figure was around 41 per cent. Opinion leaders – those who are most likely to speak out on corporate issues – are twice as likely to say they have read a report.

But there are other drivers for CSR. The past decade has witnessed a dramatic rise in both influence and stature of NGOs. Arguably, many are now the unofficial watchdogs of business, attracting major support and, increasingly, the ear of policy makers. Similarly, many NGOs have a good relationship with the media. A company that does not operate under a strict CSR code, and is found to be acting unethically or irresponsibly, will find that bad news travels very fast.

Legislation, such as the EU Directive on Waste Electrical and Electronic Equipment (WEEE, see page 121), has also helped to manoeuvre companies towards CSR. Neither should we underestimate the effect of supply chain pressure: as larger companies sign up to CSR, they will require their suppliers to mirror their commitments.

Further reading
www.csr.gov.uk
www.guardian.co.uk/society/givinglist
www.societyandbusiness.gov.uk
www.csrwire.com
www.csrforum.com
www.nottingham.ac.uk/business/ICCSR
www.mallenbaker.net
www.christian-aid.org.uk/indepth/0401csr
www.corporatewatch.org.uk

Directory

ADVICE

Organisations that can help make your office kinder to the environment

Best Foot Forward
☎ 01865 250818
www.bestfootforward.com

Bioregional
(paper for London/Surrey area)
☎ 020 8404 4886
www.bioregional.com

Envirowise
☎ 0800 585794
www.envirowise.gov.uk

The Green Compass
☎ 01752 217733
www.pepper.co.uk/gwt/index.html

Green Office Action Plan & Green Office Supplier's Directory
(Friends of the Earth Scotland)
☎ 0131 554 9977
www.foe-scotland.org.uk

The Green Office Manual
☎ 020 7387 8558
www.earthscan.co.uk

Groundwork Environmental Business Services
www.groundwork.org.uk/business

National Centre for Business and Sustainability
☎ 0161 834 8842
www.thencbs.co.uk

New Academy of Business
☎ 01225 388648
www.new-academy.ac.uk

RECYCLING

Also see Waste listings in Chapter 2's directory

Biffa Waste Services
☎ 0800 307307
www.biffa.co.uk

Industry Council for Electronic Equipment Recycling
☎ 020 7729 4766
www.icer.org.uk

Office Green Technologies
☎ 08700 502050
www.officegreen.co.uk

SalvoMIE
www.salvomie.co.uk

Save A Cup
☎ 01494 510167
www.save-a-cup.co.uk

Shred-it
☎ 020 8232 6333 or
☎ 0800 028 1164
www.shredit.com

WasteConnect
☎ 01743 343403
www.wasteconnect.co.uk

Wastetraders
(online waste exchange)
www.wastetraders.com

Waste Watch
☎ 0870 243 0136
www.wasteonline.org.uk

Office supplies

Beacon Press
☎ 01825 768611
www.beaconpress.co.uk

The Cartridge Family
☎ 0800 980 9399
www.thecartridgefamily.co.uk

Cartridge World
☎ 0800 183 3800
www.cartridgeworld.org

The Conscious Designer
☎ 0161 226 0875
www.theconsciousdesigner.co.uk

Eco Display
☎ 01348 837762
www.ecodisplay.com

Ecographic
☎ 01273 201361
☎ 07786 365999
www.ecographic.co.uk

European Furniture Group
☎ 01744 813671
www.efgmatthews.co.uk

Eurotek Office Furniture
☎ 01243 868686
www.eof.co.uk

Forest Stewardship Council
☎ 01686 413916
www.fsc-uk.org/products.asp

Green ISP
☎ 07974 002048
www.greenisp.net

The Green Stationery Company
☎ 01225 480556
www.greenstat.co.uk

Hands of Wycombe
☎ 01494 524222
www.hands.co.uk

Inveresk
☎ 01324 827280
www.inveresk.co.uk

Paperback
☎ 020 8980 5580
www.paperback.coop

Recycled Paper Supplies
☎ 01676 533832
www.recycled-paper.co.uk

Remarkable
☎ 020 8741 1234
www.remarkable.co.uk

Retone
☎ 0161 839 0500
www.retone.co.uk

Roc Office Furniture
☎ 0870 757 7600
www.roc-office.co.uk

Sussed Design
www.susseddesign.com

Workspace Office Solutions
☎ 0800 581516
www.workspace-os.co.uk

Yo-Promotions (recycled products)
☎ 01252 620593
www.recycled-products.co.uk

ETHICAL JOBS

Includes recruitment agencies and directories

Countryside Jobs Link
www.countrysidejobslink.co.uk

Countryside Jobs Service
☎ 01947 810220
www.countryside-jobs.com

Eden Recruitment
☎ 0870 787 7630
www.edenrecruitment.com

ENDS (Environmental Job Search)
www.ends.co.uk/jobs

EnvironmentJob.co.uk
www.environmentjob.co.uk

Evergreen Resources
☎ 01256 314620
www.evergreen.org.uk

The Green Directory: Jobs
☎ 01268 468000
www.greendirectory.net/jobs

Growing-careers.com
☎ 01245 424200
www.growing-careers.com

Index Environmental
☎ 01252 811333
www.index-environmental.co.uk

People & Planet: Ethical Careers
☎ 01865 245678
www.ethicalcareers.org

Further reading and resources

GENERAL INFORMATION AND ADVICE

Earth Day Network
☎ 001 202 518 0044
www.earthday.net

eekos
www.eekos.com

Energy Saving Trust
www.est.org.uk

Environment Agency
☎ 08708 506506
www.environment-agency.gov.uk

Envocare
www.envocare.co.uk

Ethical Junction
☎ 0161 224 0749
www.ethical-junction.org

Ethical Matters
☎ 020 7419 7258
www.ethicalmatters.co.uk

Ethics Resource Centre
☎ 001 202 737 2258
www.ethics.org

Friends of the Earth
☎ 0808 800 1111
www.foe.co.uk

Green Choices
www.greenchoices.org

Green Consumer Guide
www.greenconsumerguide.com

Green Guide
☎ 020 7502 1089
www.greenguide.co.uk

Green Matters
www.greenmatters.com

Greenpeace
☎ 0207 865 8100
www.greenpeace.org.uk

Greenphase
www.greenphase.com

Low-Impact Living Initiative
☎ 01296 714184
www.lowimpact.org

People and Planet
☎ 01865 245678
www.peopleandplanet.org

Scottish Environmental Protection Agency
☎ 01786 457700
www.sepa.org.uk

The Soil Association
☎ 0117 929 0661
www.soilassociation.org

The Soil Association Scotland
☎ 0131 666 2474
www.sascotland.org

Sustain
☎ 020 7837 1228
www.sustainweb.org

US Environmental Protection Agency
www.epa.gov

The Vegetarian Society
☎ 0161 925 2000
www.vegsoc.org

The Vegan Society
☎ 0845 4588244
www.vegansociety.com

Women's Environmental Network
☎ 020 7481 9004
www.wen.org.uk

Worldwatch Institute
☎ 001 202 452 1999
www.worldwatch.org

WWF
☎ 01483 426444
www.wwf.org.uk

GENERAL RETAILERS

Includes shopping directories

A Lot of Organics
www.alotoforganics.co.uk

Animal Free Shopper
www.animalfreeshopper.com

Ecomania
☎ 01453 752345
www.ecomania.co.uk

Ecozone
☎ 0845 230 4200
www.ecozone.co.uk

EIY Online (database of UK environment companies)
☎ 020 7566 8262
www.eiy.co.uk

Ethical Exchange
www.ethicalexchange.co.uk

Get Ethical
☎ 020 7419 7258
www.getethical.com

Go Green
☎ 0121 472 2903
www.gogreen.cellande.co.uk

Go Holistic
www.goholistic.co.uk

Gooshing
☎ 0207 229 2115
www.gooshing.co.uk

The Green Directory
☎ 01268 468000
www.greendirectory.net

Greenlands Environmental Care
☎ 01892 871285
www.greenlands-env.co.uk

The Green Shop
☎ 01452 770629
www.greenshop.co.uk

Healthy House
☎ 01453 752216
www.healthy-house.co.uk

Naturewatch Compassionate
Shopping Guide
www.naturewatch.org/shoppingguide

Natural Collection
☎ 08703 313333
www.naturalcollection.com

Planet Organic
☎ 020 7221 1345
www.planetorganic.com

WWF Earthly Goods
☎ 0870 750 7023
http://shop.wwf.org.uk

PUBLICATIONS

A to B
☎ 01963 351649
www.atob.org.uk

Adbusters
☎ 001 604 736 9401
www.adbusters.org

The Big Issue
☎ 020 7526 3200
www.bigissue.com

Building for a Future
☎ 01559 370798
www.newbuilder.co.uk

Car Busters
☎ 001 420 274 810849
www.carbusters.org

Clean Slate
☎ 01654 705950
www.cat.org.uk

Corporate Watch
☎ 01865 791391
www.corporatewatch.org

E – The Environmental Magazine
☎ 001 203 854 5559
www.emagazine.com

Eco-logic Books
☎ 01225 484472
www.eco-logicbooks.co.uk

The Ecologist
☎ 01795 414963
www.theecologist.org

Ergo
☎ 020 7405 5633
www.ergo-living.com

Ethical Consumer
☎ 0161 226 2929
www.ethicalconsumer.org

Ethical Corporation
☎ 0207 375 7561
www.ethicalcorp.com

Food Magazine
☎ 020 7837 2250
www.foodcomm.org.uk

Green Books
☎ 01803 863260
www.greenbooks.co.uk

Green Events
☎ 020 7424 9100
www.greenevents.fsnet.co.uk

Green Futures
☎ 01223 564334
www.greenfutures.org.uk

Green Guides and Pure Magazine
☎ 020 7502 1089
www.greenguide.co.uk

The Green Parent
☎ 01273 424802
www.thegreenparent.co.uk

Living Earth (from the Soil
Association)
☎ 0117 314 5000
www.soilassociation.org

Mother Jones
☎ 001 415 665 6637
www.motherjones.com

New Internationalist
☎ 01858 438896
www.newint.org

Peace News
☎ 0207 278 3344
www.peacenews.info

Permaculture
☎ 0845 458 4150
www.permaculture.co.uk

Positive Health
☎ 023 9265 3266
www.positivehealth.com

Positive News
☎ 01588 640022
www.positivenews.org.uk

Radical Economics
☎ 020 7820 6300
www.neweconomics.org

Red Pepper
☎ 0207 281 7024
www.redpepper.org.uk

Resurgence
☎ 01208 841824
www.resurgence.gn.apc.org

SchNEWS
☎ 01273 685913
www.schnews.co.uk

Velo Vision
☎ 01904 438224
www.velovision.co.uk

yOUR Future
☎ 01865 245678
www.ethicalcareers.org

World Watch Magazine
☎ 001 202 452 1999
www.worldwatch.org

Sources

What is ethical living?

...'happiness' levels have not risen in the past 50 years. 'Money and happiness', The Guardian, March 7, 2003

...in 2001 humanity's ecological footprint exceeded global biocapacity by 21 per cent. 'Living Planet Report 2004', WWF, www.wwf.org.uk/filelibrary/pdf/lpr2004.pdf

...if the whole world lived as Americans do we would need six Earths. 'Ecological footprint analysis', Redefining Progress website, www.redefiningprogress.org/footprint

...a significant rise in the world's 'consumer class' has been detected. State of the World 2004, The Worldwatch Institute, WW Norton & Co, 2004, www.worldwatch.org

...Professor Lord Layard has identified seven key factors that most affect our emotional wellbeing. 'We can't get no satisfaction', The Guardian, March 5, 2003; also see http://cep.lse.ac.uk/layard

...proposes a new indicator, the Measure of Domestic Progress. 'Social progression stagnant as GDP soars', New Economics Foundation press release, March 16, 2004, www.neweconomics.org/gen/news_mdp.aspx

...the total value of ethical consumption in the UK in 2003 was £24.7 billion. 'The Ethical Consumerism Report 2004', The Co-operative Bank, www.co-operativebank.co.uk/epi

...two-thirds of respondents saw themselves as 'green' or 'ethical' consumers. 'How green is your trolley', Spark supplement, The Guardian, February 12, 2004

Chapter 1: Food and Drink

...farming subsidies make up about half the entire EU budget. 'Britain to fight Brussels to keep rebate', EU Business Ltd, July 14, 2004, www.eubusiness.com/afp/040714155056.94arfyj5

...40 per cent of haulage on our roads is food related. 'Greening the farms', The Guardian, January 28, 2002

...a third didn't know that eggs are produced by chickens. 'Bid to crack egg ignorance', BBC News Online, May 2, 2002, http://news.bbc.co.uk/1/hi/scotland/1963435.stm

...over 2.5 million tonnes of pesticides. 'Pesticide policies, practices and initiatives – can the UK's know-how be transferred to Chile?', Central Science Laboratory, September 23, 2004, www.csl.gov.uk/science/organ/pvm/puskm/costa2.cfm

...worth over $30 billion. 'Stark facts revealed', Pesticide Action Network, June 2001, www.pan-uk.org/pestnews/ pn52/pn52p22.htm

...pesticides in Europe, pouring twice the average amount on to crops. 'UK progress towards a pesticide reduction plan', Pesticide News, number 59, March 2003, www.pan-uk.org/pestnews/pn59/pn59p3.htm

...220,000 deaths a year are directly caused by pesticide poisoning. 'Chemicals, Trade and Public Health: An Overview', World Health Organisation, www.who.int/trade/en/S.Bjorkquist.pdf

...pesticides, directly or indirectly, kill 67 million birds a year. 'When it Comes to Pesticides, Birds are Sitting Ducks', Smithsonian Migratory Bird Centre, http://nationalzoo.si.edu/ConservationAndScience/MigratoryBirds/Fact_Sheets/default.cfm?fxsht=8

...pesticide residues are found in human breastmilk. 'Government urged to tackle "hand-me-down" poisons', World Wildlife Fund, July 12, 1999, www.wwf.org.uk/news/n_0000000183.asp

...about 51 billion animals were slaughtered in 2003. 'Statistical Databases', UN Food and Agriculture Organisation, 2003, http://faostat.fao.org/faostat/collections?subset=agriculture

...837 million chickens killed in the UK alone (1,592 a minute). ibid

...70 per cent of the world's agricultural land – 80 per cent in the UK. McCarthy D, Saving the Planet Without Costing the Earth, Fusion Press, 2004

...one third of the world's grain crop, is used to rear livestock. ibid

...50,000–100,000 litres of water needed to produce one kilo of meat. 'Why vegans were right all along', The Guardian, December 24, 2002

...(compared with 900 litres to produce one kilo of wheat). 'What's the problem?', Vegan Society Online, 2003, www.vegansociety.com/html/environment/water/

...24 acres (9.7 hectares) of land to sustain an American. 'The objective of Sustainable Development: Are we coming closer?', European Commission Directorate General For Research, 2002, www.cepii.fr/anglaisgraph/communications/pdf/2002/siap1102/vonschomberg.pdf

...nine acres (3.6 hectares) an Italian. ibid

...(0.4 hectares) for an Indian. 'Cropland Footprint', Living Planet Report: WWF, 2002, www.wwf.org.uk/filelibrary/pdf/livingplanet2002.pdf

...grew by 400 per cent in the 1990s. 'Maintaining their hold: market for meat products', Convenience Store, March 27, 1998

...obese people are now found in the developing world. Williams J, 50 Facts That Should Change the World, Icon Books, 2004

...45 per cent of our food in the UK is imported from abroad. Sams C, The Little Food Book, Alistair Sawday, 2003

...56 per cent of the organic produce we buy is also imported. 'Organic Food: facts and figures 2003', Soil Association, 2003, www.soilassociation.org/web/sa/saweb.nsf/0/97a734e738f9766080256dd500383c91?OpenDocument

...leads to five times its own weight in greenhouse gas emissions. Buckman G, Globalization: Tame It or Scrap It?, Zed Books, 2004

...one sixth of what we pay in the UK for food goes on packaging. 'Loaded! Why supermarkets are getting richer and richer', The Observer, January 25, 2004

...£470 per household per year. ibid

...classify 'local' food as that grown in the UK. 'Local Food in Supermarkets in Nottingham', Friends of the Earth, June 2002, http://nottfoe.gn.apc.org/locfdrep.htm

...costs 13p to grow one, but the farmer will earn only 11p. 'Bitter harvest', The Guardian, March 26, 2001

...pay 47p for it at the supermarket. ibid

...that's more than the daily income of 75 per cent of Africans. Williams J, 50 Facts That Should Change the World, Icon Books, 2004

...£120 million is spent annually removing pesticide residues from our drinking water. 'Climate change and flooding: Did you know?', Environment Agency, www.environment-agency.gov.uk/commondata/103599/new_years_factfiles_632414.doc

...the whole pesticide market is worth £500 million. 'Why is organic food more expensive, and when will it change?', Organic Food, www.organicfood.co.uk/sense/tooexpensive.html

...despite receiving £3 billion worth of subsidies a year. 'New Farming for Britain', The Fabian Society, May 9, 2001, www.fabian-society.org.uk/documents/ViewADocument.asp?ID=39&CatID=52#pretty

...pound spent on food at supermarkets, just 9p makes it back. ibid

...this was nearer 50–60p. ibid

...30 per cent of cancers in the west linked to dietary factors. 'Cancer: diet and physical activity's impact', World Health Organisation, 2004, www.who.int/dietphysicalactivity/publications/facts/cancer/en/

...325,000 deaths a year are attributed to obesity. 'Annual deaths attributable to obesity in the United States', Obesity Research Center, October 27, 1999, www.ncbi.nlm.nih.gov/entrez/query.fcgi?cmd=Retrieve&db=PubMed&list_uids=10546692&dopt=Abstract

...McDonald's is 11 minutes. Honore C, In Praise of Slow, Orion, 2004

...spends more than $1 billion a year globally on advertising. 'Hearing on the role of government in combating obesity', US House of Representatives, June 3, 2004, http://reform.house.gov/UploadedFiles/CSPI%20-%20Silverglade%20Testimony.pdf

...Coca-Cola $800 million. 'Riding high on its Coke win, the 7-year-old shop proves it's the real thing', Adweek, January 12, 2004

...food advertising on children's prime-time television. 'The Food Commission Guide to Children's Food', The Food Commission, April 30, 2004

...eat five portions of fruit and vegetables a day – equal

to 400g. 'Where did the recommendation to eat at least five portions of fruit and veg a day come from?', Food Standards Agency, www.foodstandards.gov.uk/healthiereating/asktheexpert/fruitandveg/fivebackground

...actually be eating nine portions a day. 'Are You Being Served?', The Guardian, May 15, 2004

...we ate over 341g of fresh green vegetables a week. 'Family Food in 2002/03', Defra, 2004, http://statistics.defra.gov.uk/esg/publications/efs/2003/default.asp

...in 2002/03 the figure stood at just 231g. ibid

...just 228g of fruit 'products' a week. ibid

...in 2002/03 that weekly figure had risen to 413g. ibid

...spend on fresh fruit and vegetables each week was £5.40. 'Family Spending', National Statistics Online, revised June 17, 2004, www.statistics.gov.uk/downloads/theme_social/Family_Spending_2002-03/Family_Spending_2002-03_revised.pdf

...£5.50 was spent on buns, cakes, biscuits, chocolate and soft drinks. ibid

...much of it being rejected during the dreaded 'grade out'. Lawrence F, Not on the Label, Penguin, 2004

...still detectable in our blood today. 'We have become allergic to our western way of life', The Guardian, February 28, 2004

...nerve agents during the second world war. Sams C, The Little Food Book, Alastair Sawday, 2003

...a 40–120 per cent increased risk of miscarriage or birth defects. 'A Case-Control Study of Pesticides and Fetal Death Due to Congenital Anomalies', Epidemiology, 12(2), March 2001, www.ncbi.nlm.nih.gov/entrez/query.fcgi?cmd=Retrieve&db=PubMed&list_uids=11246574&dopt=Abstract

...US family $7 million in damages. 'Eyeless children championed by Observer win $7m test case', The Observer, December 21, 2003

...could expect the amount to rise to £25 or more over the next five years. 'Nitrate pollution raises water bills', The Guardian, August 11, 2003

...Dilemma: Should I eat the NZ organic apple, the Kent non-organic apple, or the Fairtrade apple from South Africa. 'Home Grown Apples in Short Supply in Big Supermarkets', Friends of the Earth, November 18, 2003, www.foe.co.uk/resource/briefings/apples_short_supply.pdf; 'Tests spark pesticide concerns', BBC News Online, September 20, 2000, http://news.bbc.co.uk/1/hi/health/933141.stm

...the contents of the basket was a staggering 100,943 miles. 'Miles and miles and miles', The Guardian, May 10, 2003

...more than 40,000 different products available to us at some larger stores. 'Wise Moves: exploring the relationship between food, transport and carbon dioxide', Transport 2000 Trust, November 6, 2003, www.transport2000.org.uk/campaigns/WiseMoves.htm

...is at least 20 per cent. 'Forging links for a sustainable, local food system in the East of England', East Anglia Food Link, www.eafl.org.uk/default.asp?topic=ByTheme&topic=Carbontopic=ByTheme&topic=Carbon&topic=Carbonplus

...boasting an incredible 80 per cent share. 'Food Miles – Still on the Road to Ruin', Sustain, October 1999, www.sustainweb.org/publications/downloads/foodmiles_ruin.pdf

...flown in from South Africa, 66 calories of fuel will be expended. 'Eating Oil', Sustain, December 10, 2001, www.sustainweb.org/pdf/eatoil_pr.PDF

...only five will have been grown in the UK. ibid

...over 10kg of carbon dioxide (CO2) will be emitted. ibid

...one per cent of food moved by train. 'Wise Moves: Exploring the relationship between food, transport and carbon dioxide', Transport 2000 Trust, November 6, 2003, www.transport2000.org.uk/campaigns/WiseMoves.htm

...80 per cent of the nation's fruit and vegetable sales. 'Strange Fruit', The Guardian, September 7, 2002

...90 per cent of fresh produce in the UK was sold. ibid

...90 per cent of its vitamin C in the 24 hours after harvest. 'Miles and miles and miles', The Guardian, May 10, 2003

...now have to differentiate produce grown in 'Gaza' and 'Israel'. 'Israel: Produce Grown in the Occupied Territories', Defra, August 15, 2002, www.defra.gov.uk/foodrin/impreg/not01.htm

...pretty much got an arm-lock on you at the moment. 'Store accuses Blair of "scapegoating"', BBC News Online, March 2, 2001, http://news.bbc.co.uk/1/hi/uk/1198146.stm

...to pay much attention to what Tony Blair said. ibid

...fell beneath £10,000 a year. 'Farming crisis as young desert industry', BBC News Online, January 7, 2003, http://news.bbc.co.uk/1/hi/england/2634423.stm

...worked wonders in solving the post-war food shortages. 'To them that have', The Guardian, January 22, 2004

...had deducted 'rent and transport costs'. 'Gangmasters paid migrant workers 78p a week', The Guardian, February 26, 2004

...given up buying pricey items such as plums. Blythman J, Shopped: The Shocking Powers of British Supermarkets, Fourth Estate, 2004

...since 1999, over 2,000 hectares. 'Pastures of plastic', The Guardian, May 3, 2004

...now grown under plastic for up to six months of the year. ibid

...turned down following complaints from locals. 'Strawberry fields forever? Not in Herefordshire', The Guardian, May 13, 2004

...calendar of British seasonal produce. 'British season', The Guardian, May 24, 2003

...sales of organic food topped £1 billion for the first time. 'Sales of organic food top £1 billion', Soil Association, August 27, 2004, www.soilassociation.org/web/sa/saweb.nsf/0/f212e22509087efd80256dd5003ceeae?OpenDocument

...soil life, plants, animals and people. 'UNFAO/WHO Codex Alimentarius Commission Guidelines for the Production, Processing, Labelling and Marketing of Organically Produced Foods', UN Food and Agricultural Organisation, 1999, www.fao.org/organicag/welco-e.htm

...minimise damage to the environment and wildlife. 'Organic food and farming', Defra, November 26, 2003, www.defra.gov.uk/farm/organic/introduction

...there are now more than 4,000 [organic producers]. 'Is organic food better for you?', FSA speech by Sir John Krebs, Cheltenham Science Festival, June 4, 2003, www.food.gov.uk/news/newsarchive/2003/jun/cheltenham

...450 pesticides have been passed for use. 'Organic Food and Farming: Myth and Reality', Soil Association and Sustain, 2001, www.soilassociation.org/web/sa/saweb.nsf/0/915aa86cf16fd77f80256e45005cdcb3/$FILE/Myth&Reality.pdf

...soft soap and sulphur. ibid

...found on over 70 per cent of organic products in the UK. Litchfield C, The Organic Directory, Green Books, 2004

...supports organic methods. 'A Better Way', Compassion In World Farming Online, www.ciwf.org.uk/littleredtractor/A_Better_Way.htm

...cite taste and health benefits as their reasons for trying organic fruit or vegetables. 'Desire for better health and quality drive growth in the market, but high cost is still the main deterrent', The Guardian, November 6, 2003

...'the current scientific evidence does not show that organic food is any safer or more nutritious than conventionally produced food.' 'Is organic food better for you?' FSA speech by Sir John Krebs, Cheltenham Science Festival, June 4, 2003, www.food.gov.uk/news/newsarchive/2003/jun/cheltenham

...main debate focuses on the comparative use of pesticides, additives and antibiotics. 'Is organic food always better for you?' The Guardian, July 15, 2003

...only six organic samples contained residues. 'Bite the dust', The Guardian, May 10, 2003

...a US study published in Food Additives and Contaminants. 'Pesticide residues in conventional, IPM-grown and organic foods: Insights from three US data sets', Food Additives and Contaminants, volume 19, number 5, May 2002

...a comparison of soups made with organic and non-organic vegetables. Baxter GJ et al, 'Salicylic acid in soups prepared from organically and non-organically grown vegetables', European Journal of Nutrition, 6/40, 2001

...the percentage is now about half (56 per cent). 'Food and Farming Report – Executive Summary', Soil Association, 2003, www.soilassociation.org/web/sa/saweb.nsf/0/97a734e738f9766080256dd500383c91?OpenDocument

...Which? report in 2003 found organic food to be up to 40 per cent more expensive. 'Is organic food always better for you?', The Guardian, July 15, 2003

...Spotlight: A life in the day of a potato. Pesticides Action Network, www.pan-uk.org; British Potato Council, www.potato.org.uk; Defra, www.defra.gov.uk

...more than 60 arrests were made after over 30 crop destructions. 'Melchett refused bail on GM crop charges', The Guardian, July 31, 1999

...allowing crops to grow in inhospitable soils. 'Breakthrough may bring life to barren earth', The Guardian, May 21, 2004

...will hamper the UK's ability to trade globally in the future. 'Starved of the truth', The Guardian, March 18, 2004

...only two per cent would eat GM foods. 'GM crops to get go ahead', The Guardian, February 19, 2004

...the potential health effects of GM entering the food chain. 'You reap what you sow', The Guardian, April 7, 2004

...biotech firms would have control over the global larder. 'Starved of the truth', The Guardian, March 18, 2004

...stabilise by 2050 so no urgent increase in production of food is required. 'Farming is not like any old business', The Guardian, May 12, 2004

...could potentially kill other crops and require huge amounts of polluting herbicides and pesticides to control. 'World Agriculture Towards 2015/30', UN Food and Agriculture Organisation, 2003, www.fao.org/docrep/005/y4252e/y4252e00.htm

...driven off the land as big growers dedicated more than 11 million hectares. 'Superweed warning as GM soya miracle in Argentina turns sour', The Guardian, April 22, 2004

...damaged soil bacteria and allowed herbicide-resistant weeds to grow out of control. 'Argentina's bitter harvest', New Scientist, volume 182, issue 2443, April 17, 2004

...granted a controversial US patent for three basmati rice varieties. 'Of Rice and Men', Science, volume 290, number 5493, November 3, 2000, www.sciencemag.org; 'Basmati Rice Update', Biotech Online, January 4, 2000, www.biotech-info.net/basmati_rice.html; 'India outraged as USA company wins patents on rice', The Guardian, August 23, 2001

...159 applications from biotech firms to start field trials in the UK. 'Despairing GM firms halt crop trials', The Guardian, April 22, 2004

...But by 2004 only one crop, a herbicide-resistant pea. ibid

...interpreted by industry watchers as despair at ever getting the technology accepted in the UK. ibid

...announced that it was withdrawing from the UK. 'Six UK GM seed applications withdrawn by Bayer', Friends of the Earth, December 19, 2003, www.foe.co.uk/resource/press_releases/six_uk_gm_seed_application.html

...confined to four countries – the US, Argentina, Canada and China. 'You Reap What You Sow', The Guardian, April 7, 2004

...end of a five-year hiatus that had kept all new GM products out of Europe since 1998. 'Farming ministers get caught in the maize', The Guardian, April 27, 2004

...dozens of products still awaiting EU approval. ibid

...vitamins to be bred directly into plants, or to create allergen-free soya beans. 'World Agriculture Towards 2015/30', UN Food and Agriculture Organisation, 2003, www.fao.org/docrep/005/y4252e/y4252e00.htm

...five per cent of the population claim to be vegetarian. 'World turned upside down!', Vegetarians International Voice for Animals, www.viva.org.uk/guides/vhfk01.html

...860 million animals are reared in the UK for food every year. 'Local Food – The Connections', Devon Food Links, www.devonfoodlinks.org.uk/Docs/FoodHealth.pdf

...95 per cent of food poisoning incidents are attributable to meat. 'Bad Habits Are Hard to Quit', Vegetarian and Vegan Foundation, www.vegetarian.org.uk/campaignsbadhabits.htm

...760 chickens, 20 pigs, 29 sheep, five cows and half a trawler net of fish in a lifetime. '10 things we didn't know last week', BBC News Online, May 23, 2003, http://news.bbc.co.uk/1/hi/uk/3050821.stm

...obesity is linked to at least five per cent of cancers. 'Obesity and alcohol – key causes of cancer', Cancer Research UK, August 2004, www.cancerresearchuk.org/aboutus/ourresearch/researchnews/obesityalcohol_cancer

...Since 1950, worldwide production of meat has increased fivefold. 'The United States and China: The Soybean Connection', Worldwatch Institute Online, November 9, 1999, www.worldwatch.org/press/news/1999/11/09/

...account for 10 per cent of greenhouse gases. 'Reducing Meat Consumption: The Case for Urgent Reform', Compassion In World Farming Trust, 2004, www.ciwf.org.uk/publications/reports/Global_benefits_summary.pdf

...high levels of damaging chemicals such as ammonia nitrate, polluting land, water and air. 'The Global Benefits of Eating Less Meat', Compassion in World Farming, 2004, www.ciwf.org.uk/publications/reports/The_Global_Benefits_of_Eating_Less_Meat.pdf

...one billion people in the world manage to exist as vegetarians or vegans. Cannon G, Feeding the World a Healthy Diet, Earthscan, 1999

...21 per cent of UK men and 24 per cent of UK women are clinically obese. 'A Deadly Slice of American Pie', The Observer, September 21, 2003

...as opposed to the 35 per cent we paid in the 1930s. Lawrence F, Not On The Label, Penguin, 2004

...was £7.90, with a further £1.60 on fish. 'Family Spending', National Statistics Online, June 17, 2004, www.statistics.gov.uk/StatBase/Product.asp?vlnk=361

...around £4 billion and still counting. 'How cheap is organic food?', Living Earth – the Soil Association magazine, April 2002

...around £5 billion in lost tourism revenue. 'The impact of the foot and mouth crisis on rural farms', The Centre for Rural Economy report, 2001

...excessive meat consumption as one of the top threats to the stability of human kind. 'The Global Benefits of Eating Less Meat', Compassion in World Farming Trust, 2004, www.ciwf.org.uk/publications/reports/The_Global_Benefits_of_Eating_Less_Meat.pdf

...per capita consumption of meat globally has more than doubled. 'United States Leads World Meat Stampede', Worldwatch Institute Online, July 2, 1998, www.worldwatch.org/press/news/1998/07/02/

...(consuming half of the world's grain supplies in the process). 'The Poor Get Stuffed', The Guardian, December 24, 2002

...one third of the world's arable land. ibid

...one billion pigs, 1.3 billion cows, 1.8 billion sheep and goats and 15.4 billion chickens. 'Eat less meat and you'll help save the planet', The Guardian, March 14, 2004

...Dilemma: Should meat substitutes be an option? 'What's in those nuggets?', The New York Times, May 14, 2002; 'Victims Urge "Whole Foods" Supermarkets Not To Sell Quorn', Center for Science in the Public Interest, December 9, 2003, www.cspinet.org/new/200312091.html; 'Asthma Attack Blamed on Quorn', The Guardian, May 30, 2005; 'Foods that cause allergy', Food Standards Agency, www.food.gov.uk/healthiereating/allergyintol/foodall/; 'Soya', Institute of Food Research, June 2000, www.ifr.bbsrc.ac.uk/public/FoodInfo Sheets/soya.html

...the equivalent amount of land and water as four billion people. 'The Global Benefits of Eating Less Meat', Compassion in World Farming Trust, 2004, www.ciwf.org.uk/publications/reports/The_Global_Benefits_of_Eating_Less_Meat.pdf

...there could be as many as 9.3 billion people on the planet by 2050. 'Nine billion people by 2050', BBC News Online, February 28, 2001, http://news.bbc.co.uk/1/hi/world/1194030.stm

...first insight into the world of intensive meat and dairy production. Harrison R, Animal Machines: The new factory farming, Vincent Stuart, 1964

...1997 that the EU even recognised livestock as 'sentient beings'. 'Animals are moral beings', BBC News Online, May 9, 2003, http://news.bbc.co.uk/2/hi/science/nature/3014747.stm

...23,000 high street butchers, whereas in 2000 there were just 9,721. 'Lord of the aisles', The Guardian, May 17, 2003

...both 'reasonably anticipated to be a human carcinogen'. 'Overall Evaluations of Carcinogenicity to Humans', International Agency for Research on Cancer, July 22, 2004, www-cie.iarc.fr/monoeval/crthall.html

...modified atmosphere processing or been washed in chlorine. 'Are Scientists Putting You Off Your Dinner?', Observer Food Monthly, May 14, 2004

...pig farmers in the UK no longer use tethers in sow stalls. 'Report on the Welfare of Laying Hens', Farm Animal Welfare Council, July 24, 1997, www.fawc.org.uk/newsrel/fawc2.htm

...sow stalls will not be outlawed until 2013. ibid

...an increase from 450cm^2 to 600cm^2. 'From Shell to Hell: the modern egg industry', Animal Aid, August 2004, www.animalaid.org.uk/farming/shell.htm

...stocking density of birds per cage is also reduced – from five to four. ibid

...Spotlight: Meat delicacies. 'Animal groups call for foie gras to be kept off menus', World Society for the Protection of Animals, June 1, 2000, www.wspa.org.uk/index.php?page=461; 'The Pain Behind Foie Gras', People for the Ethical Treatment of Animals, www.peta.org.uk/factsheet/files/FactsheetDisplay.asp?ID=119; 'Marketwatch: Global round-up', Datamonitor, February 19, 2004, www.datamonitor.com/~3c8901b0acdd433f95a4a6eb37661f1b~/Products/Free/Brief/BFAU0138/020BFAU0138.htm; 'Beluga sturgeon stock overestimated', The Guardian, September 29, 2003; 'The Shark Fin Trade: Mindless Slaughter For a Bowl of Soup', The Shark Protection League, www.eurosolve.com/charity/spl/fin_trade.html

...pigs wear nose rings...they don't meet the standards of animal husbandry. 'Memorandum submitted by the Provision Trade Federation (F 33)', Select Committee on Agriculture, June 13, 2000, www.parliament.the-stationeryoffice.co.uk/pa/cm200001/cmselect/cmagric/149/149ap30.htm

...less than one quarter of organic pork on sale in Asda was from UK farms. 'Supermarkets "undermining" organic farmers', The Guardian, April 19, 2004

...'crowded, unhealthy and likely to lead to the spread of infections'. 'Antibiotics in Farm Animals', Compassion In World Farming, January 2004, www.ciwf.org.uk/publications/Factsheets/Fact%20sheet%20-%20Antibiotics.pdf

...the ramifications are 'still not well understood'. 'Antibiotics in Farm Animals', American Society for Microbiology, 2002, www.microbeworld.org/htm/cissues/resist/resist_3.htm

...contained bacteria, such as E coli, resistant to the broad-spectrum antibiotic chloramphenicol. 'If Max eats up all of his chicken, he'll grow up to be a big, strong boy. Unless it kills him first', Observer Food Monthly, August 10, 2003

...a link between variant CJD in humans and BSE in cattle was finally confirmed. 'Transmissible spongiform encephalopathy agents: safe working and the prevention of infection', Department of Health, June 2003, www.advisorybodies.doh.gov.uk/acdp/tseguidance

...3,800 Britons could be harbouring CJD. 'Young "more susceptible to CJD"', BBC News Online, August 10, 2004, http://news.bbc.co.uk/1/hi/health/3549396.stm

...cows were allowed into the food chain without being tested. 'BSE testing oversights lead to full FSA investigation', The New Farm Online, June 7, 2004, www.newfarm.org/international/news/060104/060904/mad_tests.shtml

...converted to organic farming practices and none in established organic herds. 'Keeping the Organic Herd

Free of BSE', Soil Association, 2001, www.soilassociation.org/web/sa/saweb.nsf/0/80256a d80055454980256745 0053dd05?OpenDocument

...eat 820 million chickens every year in the UK. 'UK Judge Backs Factory Farmers', Grace Factory Farm Project, November 2003, www.factoryfarm.org/news/ archives/2003-11.php

...five times more than we ate in the 1980s. 'Too hard to swallow', Soil Association, June 19, 2001, www.soilassociation.org/web/sa/saweb.nsf/0/ ef999544438cd73380256ae500390dd6/$FILE/ SAtoohardtoswallow.pdf

...the fastest growing form of intensive farming in the world. 'Welfare of Broiler Chickens in the EU', Compassion in World Farming, 2003, www.ciwf.org.uk/publications/reports/Welfare_of_Broiler_ Chickens_in_the_EU.pdf

...stuffed into crates and taken to rearing sheds, each one holding 30,000–50,000 birds. ibid

...bred to reach slaughter weight in just 41 days. ibid

...being hung upside down and shackled for as long as three minutes. 'Nociceptors in the legs of poultry: implications for potential pain in pre-slaughter shackling', Roslin Institute, 2000, www.ufaw.org.uk/ journal/Volume.9%20abstracts.htm#abs931

...gassed instead of electrocuted as it claims this is the more humane option. 'Peta launches worldwide KFC campaign', Ananova, 2004, www.ananova.com/ news/story/sm_736636.html

...unearthed Dutch and German additive suppliers and protein manufacturers. 'Scandal of beef waste in chicken', The Guardian, May 21, 2003

...is actually cheaper than it was 20 years ago. Lawrence F, Not on the Label, Penguin, 2004

...frozen chicken breasts from a Dutch company were found to contain 40 per cent water. 'Dutch Chicken was 40% Water', The Food Magazine, issue 50, July/September 2000

...limited to 400 per acre by the EU. 'Sustainable Poultry: production overview – part II', The Poultry Site, February 2002, www.thepoultrysite.com/ FeaturedArticle/FATopic.asp?AREA=ProductionMgmt& Display=113

...free-range chickens be killed before they are 56 days old. 'Marketing standards for eggs and poultrymeat', Defra, June 12, 2003, www.defra.gov.uk/foodrin/poultry/epfaq.htm

...at least 50 per cent of a bird's feed is maize or corn. ibid

...Dilemma: Vegetarian, vegan or fruitarian? 'Consumer Attitudes to Food Standards', Food Standards Agency, February 2004, www.food.gov.uk/multimedia/pdfs/cas2003.pdf; 'Food, nutrition, and the prevention of cancer', The World Cancer Research Fund, 1997, www.wcrf- uk.org/report/index.lasso?WCRFS=C2C8FDFD02ee4 18DBDiWr1C9CFDC; 'Food for all our futures', The International Vegetarian Congress, July 2002, www.ivu.org/congress/2002/texts/bowler-thursday.html

...2,000 pig farmers have gone out of business since 2001. Lawrence F, Not on the Label, Penguin, 2004

...breeding sows in the British pig herd has fallen from 800,000 to 500,000. ibid

...routinely injected or fed with up to 10 different types of antibiotics. 'Antibiotics – Use and Mis-use', Soil Association, October 10, 2001, www.soilassociation.org/web/sa/saweb.nsf/printable_ library/NT00002732

...demand for year-round 'spring' lamb led supermarket buyers to instruct producers 'to alter the

seasonal output'. 'MAFF and the meat industry', The Food Magazine, issue 37, April/June1997

...drugs help to speed up ovulation, allowing the 'spring' lamb to be born around Christmas and ready to slaughter at Easter. 'The shepherd's calendar revised', The Guardian, May 10, 1995

...around four million lambs die each year from exposure, hypothermia, starvation and disease. 'Foot and Mouth: The suffering of sheep didn't start here', Animal Aid, March 22, 2001, www.animalaid.org.uk/press/0103foo3.htm

...35,000 orphaned lambs to be sent to market each year. ibid

...increasing flock sizes have led to environmental problems. 'The Silence of the Lambs', New Renaissance Magazine, volume 5, number 2, 1995, www.ru.org/artlambs.html

...between one million and one-and-a-half million lambs are still exported for slaughter abroad. 'The Economics of the Transport of Live Farm Animals Over Long Distances', Compassion in World Farming, PS/MJ/BR8046, June 2001, www.ciwf.org.uk/publications/Briefings/BR8046.pdf

...70,000 tonnes of lamb (half of which is produced in the UK) is exported to France and Belgium every year. ibid

...one sixth of these exports will travel 'live'. ibid

...live transport should be avoided whenever possible. ibid

...almost 80,000 tonnes of New Zealand lamb is imported to the UK each year. 'NZ Meat Exports Rise', Meat News, volume 4, issue 6, February 6, 2002, www.meatnews.com/index.cfm?fuseaction=Article&art Num=2628&Status=Archive

...have dropped by 90 per cent in the past 50 years. McCarthy D, Saving the Planet Without Costing the Earth, Fusion Press, 2004; 'Fall in fish stocks hits crisis point', The Guardian, May 15, 2003

...a 70 per cent drop in the last 30 years. 'Cods walloped', The Guardian, May 19, 2004

...of the world's commercially important marine fish stocks, 25 per cent are under-exploited. 'Fish Facts', Marine Stewardship Council, 2002, http://eng.msc.org/html/content_528.htm

...with harsh chemicals and fertilisers seeping into local water sources. 'Factory Farms of the Sea', Worldwatch Institute Online, August 18, 2003, www.worldwatch.org/press/news/2003/08/18/

...contains traces of mercury, dioxins and PCBs. 'Food for thought', The Guardian, February 23, 2003

...a third of us already exceed the recommended maximum for ingesting contaminants? 'Scientists weigh up risks and benefits of eating fish', The Guardian, August 12, 2002

...recommending that we eat two portions per week, one of which should be oily fish. 'Advice on fish consumption: benefits and risks', Food Standards Agency, June 24, 2004, www.food.gov.uk/news/ newsarchive/2004/jun/fishreport2004

...girls and women who may become pregnant at some point in their lives. ibid

...over 40 per cent of fish is sold internationally. 'Report World Fisheries: Chapter 7, World Agriculture Towards 2015/30', UN Food and Agriculture Organisation, 2003, www.fao.org/docrep/005/y4252e/y4252e00.htm

...natural sea cod are in danger of extinction by 2020. 'Cods Walloped', The Guardian, May 19 2004

...just 12,000 fishermen in the UK, 33 per cent fewer

than in 1995. 'Fishermen are tough, but this may be the final straw', The Guardian, March 26, 2004

...just under 1,000 boats are now in pursuit of the last remaining cod, haddock, sole and plaice stocks. ibid

...the national fleet needs to be cut to 801 boats by 2013. ibid

...negotiated deals with other nations to fish their waters via 'transfer agreements'. 'Report World Fisheries: Chapter 7, World Agriculture Towards 2015/30', UN Food and Agriculture Organisation, 2003, www.fao.org/docrep/005/y4252e/y4252e00.htm

...over 40 per cent of the salmon in the ocean are now thought to have escaped from fish farms. 'International News', The Salmon Farm Monitor, April 2003, www.salmonfarmmonitor.org/documents/ intlnewsapril2003.html

...contained the highest levels of cancer-causing chemicals anywhere in the world. 'Scare over farmed salmon safety', BBC News Online, January 8, 2004, http://news.bbc.co.uk/1/hi/health/3380735.stm

...who said the benefits of eating salmon outweighed the risks. ibid

...more than 25 different chemical treatments, including antibiotics, disinfectants and antimicrobial drugs. 'The One That Got Away – Marine Salmon Farming in Scotland', Friends of the Earth, 2001, www.foe-scotland.org.uk

...fed dyes, usually canthaxanthin or astaxanthin, to make them pink. ibid

...traces of a toxic antiparasitic chemical called malachite green were found in farmed trout and salmon. 'Annual Report for Surveillance of Veterinary Residues 2002', Veterinary Residues Committee, www.vet-residuescommittee.gov.uk/reports/ vrcresrep02.pdf

...the temptation to use powerful antiparasitic drugs to protect fish from possible infections could be too much. 'Are You Being Served?' The Guardian, May 15, 2004

...spent over £254 million on cod in 2003. 'Fish facts', Seafish, www.seafish.org/plate/facts.asp?p=gi

...90 per cent of the catch from the North Sea was less than two years old and had not yet had a chance to breed. 'Ban fishing in third of all seas, scientists say', The Independent, August 31, 2003

...by 53 per cent in 2004 due to restored stock levels. 'How to buy fish', The Guardian, March 27, 2004

...proposed new legislation to allow the killing of whales to 'protect' its fish stocks. 'Iceland's whaling comeback', Whale & Dolphin Conservation Society, May 2003, www.wdcs.org/dan/publishing.nsf/ c525f7df6cbf01ef802569d600573108/b2460680b c28d8f480256d4a0040d97b/$FILE/Iceland-report-english.pdf

...species of tuna are now endangered, according to the Marine Conservation Society. 'For cod's sake stick to salmon, scampi and sprats', The Telegraph, August 8, 2004

...dubbed it 'the new foie gras'. 'Tuna farming threatens wild tuna populations in the Mediterranean', World Wildlife Fund, February 14, 2002

...according to research carried out by the hydrodynamics expert Daniel Weihs at the Israel Institute of Technology. 'Friendly fishing still kills dolphins', The Guardian, May 4, 2004

...during the canning process the tuna's fats are reduced to levels similar to white fish. 'Oily fish advice: your questions answered', The Food Standards Agency, June 24, 2004, www.food.gov.uk/ news/newsarchive/2004/jun/oilyfishfaq

...caught by boats dragging huge nets across many of the world's estuaries and bays. 'Factory Farms of the Sea', Worldwatch Institute Online, August 18, 2003, www.worldwatch.org/press/news/2003/08/18/

...prawn farms are found in Asia in developing areas. 'Report World Fisheries: Chapter 7, World Agriculture Towards 2015/30', UN Food and Agriculture Organisation, 2003, www.fao.org/docrep/005/y4252e/y4252e00.htm

...prawn fisheries routinely use child labour and many workers are very poorly paid. 'Did our taste for prawns do this?', The Guardian, June 19, 2003

...almost one third of all children in the UK now obese or overweight – a rise of 50 per cent since 1990. 'Crunch time for crisps', The Guardian, May 19, 2004

...half of all British children could be obese by 2020. ibid

...99 per cent of children between four and 11 now regularly buy and eat snacks. 'Carrots or Chemistry?' Organix, March 2004, www.babyorganix.co.uk/report/default.asp

...61 per cent of four- to five-year-olds actually buying their own snacks – some spending up to £1.50 a day. ibid

...30 times more soft drinks and 25 times more confectionery than they did 50 years ago. ibid

...75 per cent of children, whereas just 68 per cent regularly eat any fresh fruit. ibid

...when licensing its Tweenies, Fimbles, Bill & Ben and Teletubbies characters to food manufacturers. 'Parent Power Works', The Food Magazine, issue 65, April/June 2004

...from eating all the chocolate that would need to be bought. 'Cadbury's targets school children by using sport to encourage chocolate consumption', The Food Magazine, issue 61, April 2003

...in a way never done before', and managed to 'not let mum in on the act'. 'How firms target children', The Guardian, May 27, 2004

...sales of an extra 114 million packets of crisps over a two-year period. ibid

...a 330ml bottle of Coca-Cola contains 35g sugar, equivalent to one and a quarter packs of Rowntrees Fruit Gums. 'Soft Drinks – Liquid or Candy?', The Food Magazine, issue 64, January/March 2004

...with the RDA of sugar for a 10 year-old being 60g. ibid

...up to 80 additives a day – 50 of which come from snack foods. 'Carrots or Chemistry?' Organix, March 2004, www.babyorganix.co.uk/report/default.asp

...spent on snacks by children at school each day is 73p. ibid

...less than half this amount is spent by the school's meal provider on the ingredients for the main meal at lunch. ibid

...with 60 per cent of them eating a packet of crisps. 'Crunch time for crisps', The Guardian, May 19, 2004

...putting the world's first 'TV dinner' on the market. 'Clever inventions that came out of the cold', The Christian Science Monitor, January 8, 2002, www.csmonitor.com/2002/0108/p18s1-hfks.html

...the UK accounted for almost half of all sales. 'The European Ready Meals Market', Ready Meals Info, www.readymealsinfo.com/articles/eurmm.htm

...over 40 per cent a year, while a quarter of the country remains undernourished. 'The global spread of food uniformity', Worldwatch Institute, 2004, www.worldwatch.org/pubs/goodstuff/fastfood/

...in China, there are now 800 KFCs and 100 Pizza Huts. ibid

...more than 10 billion bags of crisps a year. 'Fat profits: Crunch Time for Crisps', March 9, 2004, BBC News Online, http://news.bbc.co.uk/1/hi/business/3547601.stm

...more than 150 packs per person per year and more than the rest of Europe put together. ibid

...Americans drank 189 billion fizzy drinks. 'Good Stuff: Beverages, the price of quenching our thirst', Worldwatch Institute, 2004, www.worldwatch.org/pubs/goodstuff/beverages

...that's 650 per person a year, or nearly two cans or bottles a day. ibid

...now recognise the golden arches of McDonald's than the Christian cross. Williams J, 50 Facts That Should Change the World, Icon Books, 2004

...we were hunter-gatherers for 100,000 generations, farmers for 500 generations. 'New Farming for Britain', The Fabian Society, May 9, 2001, www.fabian-society.org.uk/documents/ViewADocument.asp?ID=39&CatID=52#pretty

...consumers of processed, highly industrialised food for just two generations. ibid

...weighed 73.7kg and woman 62.2kg. 'Obesity's huge challenge for humans', BBC News Online, September 9, 2002, http://news.bbc.co.uk/1/hi/in_depth/sci_tech/2002/leicester_2002/2246450.stm

...81.6kg and 68.8kg respectively. ibid

...nearly half of Britons eat their evening meal in front of the TV. Honore C, In Praise of Slow, Orion, 2004

...6p to sweeten a litre of soft drink with sugar. 'Guide to Food Additives', The Food Commission, 2001, www.foodcomm.org.uk

...2p to sweeten it with aspartame (E951) or 0.2p with saccharin (E954). ibid

...each of the 540 food additives currently available to food manufacturers. 'Food Chained', The Guardian, May 15, 2004

...doubts remain for about 200 of them. ibid

...eat between six and seven kilos of food additives each year. Millstone E & Lang T, The Atlas of Food, Earthscan, 2003

...spend 10 per cent of their income on mobile phones versus 12 per cent on what they eat. Honore C, In Praise of Slow, Orion, 2004

...costing £1.36 would actually cost £4.10. Sams C, The Little Food Book, Alastair Sawday, 2003

...purchase 80 per cent of our food from them. Blythman J, Shopped: The Shocking Power of British Supermarkets, Fourth Estate, 2004

...£8 spent by UK consumers, £1 goes to Tesco. 'For good or ill we're in thrall to our lords of the aisles', The Independent on Sunday, April 25, 2004

...the UK's £100 billion grocery market. 'UK Market Overview', Interbrew UK, 2003, www.interbrewmarketreport.co.uk/2003/ukmarket02.html

...21 per cent of us are said to have picked up 'copycat' versions of our favourite brands. Dobson PW, 'The Competition Effects of Look-Alike Products', University of Nottingham discussion paper, 1998:VI, 1998

...one of the most advanced own-label programmes in the world. 'Supermarkets Own Label Assessment', Research & Markets, January 2000, www.researchandmarkets.com/reportinfo.asp?cat_id=0&report_id=3855

...50 per cent of our shopping baskets are filled with them. 'Leaving the big names on the shelf', The Scotsman, April 19, 2004

...subject to constant price squeezes and forced to

compromise on quality. Blythman J, Shopped: The Shocking Power of British Supermarkets, Fourth Estate, 2004

...as the animals may have been pastured in that area for only two weeks. 'Sins of the Superstores Visited on Us', The Guardian, March 1, 2001

...60 per cent of us have a loyalty card. 'UK consumers failing to take advantage of loyalty card schemes to the tune of £413 million', Argos survey, August 27, 2003, www.gusplc.com/gus/news/argosarchive/argos2003/2003-08-27/

...11 million of us now holders of a Nectar combination reward card. 'The cost of Nectar loyalty', BBC News Online, February 17, 2003, http://news.bbc.co.uk/1/hi/business/2770689.stm

...buys one McDonald's Medium Value Extra Meal or a movie rental from Blockbuster. Blythman J, Shopped: The Shocking Power of British Supermarkets, Fourth Estate, 2004

...causing us to spend an extra 1–4 per cent. 'The card up their sleeve', The Guardian, July 19, 2003

...57 per cent of a store's profits come from just 30 per cent of customers. Blythman J, Shopped: The Shocking Power of British Supermarkets, Fourth Estate, 2004

...100 buyers hold the key to the 250 million consumers in Europe. ibid

...35 per cent of fruit and vegetables are routinely rejected during the 'grade out'. ibid

...identified RFIDs as a major concern. 'Calling in the Chips: Findings from the first summit exploring the future of RFID technology in retail', The National Consumer Council, 2004, www.ncc.org.uk/technology/calling_in_chips.pdf

...purchases could also in theory be scanned in subsequent stores, enabling sophisticated spending profiling. 'Ruhr tries out razorblade radio', The Guardian, May 17

...an extra £52 million each year would find its way into the local economy. 'Plugging the Leaks: A briefing by the Centre for Participation', New Economics Foundation, 2001, www.pluggingtheleaks.org

...in the five years up to 2002, 50 specialist stores closed every week. 'Ghost Town Britain parts I and II', New Economics Foundation, 2002/2003, www.neweconomics.org/gen/local_ghost.aspx

...typically employing between two and 15 people. 'Rural services in 2000', Countryside Agency, 2001, www.epolitix.com/NR/rdonlyres/3011E570-40F8-4AAF-BD16-C81622F890BC/0/PBRuralServices.pdf

...supplies fresh food to around 3,000 households and sources from 36 organic farmers. 'Some benefits and drawbacks of local food systems', Sustain AgriFood Network, November 2, 2001, www.sustainweb.org/pdf/afn_m1_p2.pdf

...there are now at least 450 markets with a combined annual turnover of more than £160 million. 'Farmers' Markets – A Business Survey', National Farmers' Union, September 2002, www.nfu.org.uk/stellentdev/groups/public/documents/farming_facts/farmersmarkets-ab_ia412f45c7-1.hcsp

...10 per cent or so they could expect to receive from the supermarket buyers. 'Taking back the middle for local economies', University of Essex, 2000, www2.essex.ac.uk/ces/ConfsVisitsEvsGrps/Local FoodSystems/localfoodjp.htm

...60,000 households across the UK are supplied by 400 box schemes. 'Some benefits and drawbacks of local food systems', Sustain AgriFood Network, November 2, 2001, www.sustainweb.org/pdf/afn_m1_p2.pdf

286

…300 of which are certified organic by the Soil Association. 'Organic vegetable box schemes briefing paper for consumers', Soil Association, May 23, 2001, www.soilassociation.org.uk/web/sa/saweb.nsf/librarytitles/briefing_sheets27072001

…more than 1,000 schemes with 77,000 members. 'Some benefits and drawbacks of local food systems', Sustain AgriFood Network, November 2, 2001, www.sustainweb.org/pdf/afn_m1_p2.pdf

…the scheme also guarantees farmers a steady income. ibid

…as they incorporate their freshly grown produce into their diets. ibid

…a cow called Marissa broke milk records in the UK. 'From farm to plate – a sick industry', The Guardian, February 28, 2001

…from 4,000 litres a few decades ago to 5,800 litres today. ibid

…male calves are usually killed within two weeks. 'Dairy monsters', The Guardian, December 13, 2003

…up to 20 per cent of the UK dairy herd has a 'physiological abnormality causing them to be lame'. 'Letter to Defra regarding the proposed Animal Health and Welfare Strategy', Farm Animal Welfare Council, December 15, 2003, www.fawc.org.uk/pdf/let_defra_ahws.pdf

…decreased and now lasts on average only three or four 'lactations'. 'Report on the welfare of dairy cattle', Farm Animal Welfare Council, 1997, www.fawc.org.uk/reports/dairycow/dcowrtoc.htm

…a quarter are culled before they are 39 months old. ibid

…a synthetic version of a cow's growth hormone called recombinant bovine somatotropin (rBST). 'Dairy monsters', The Guardian, December 13, 2003

…18-23p on average to produce a litre of milk. 'Milk pricing in the United Kingdom', Commons Environment, Food and Rural Affairs Committee, September 8, 2004, www.parliament.the-stationery-office.co.uk/pa/cm200304/cmselect/cmenvfru/1036/1036.pdf

…seven times more subsidies than dairy farmers. 'Land of Milk and Money?' Sustain, May 2003, www.sustainweb.org/pub_type.asp?iType=1077&view=Go

…between 1961 and 1999, milk exports increased by 500 per cent. Millstone E & Lang T, The Atlas of Food, Earthscan, 2003

…149,000 tonnes of milk (mostly to non-EU countries). 'Statistical Databases', UN Food and Agriculture Organisation, 2003, http://faostat.fao.org/faostat/collections?subset=agriculture

…imported 110,000 tonnes of fresh milk (mostly from the EU). ibid

…a hypothetical truck travelled over 1,000 kilometres using 400 litres of diesel. 'Road transport of goods and the effects on the spatial environment', Living Earth magazine, October 27, 1994

…six per cent of animal feed in the UK is now GM. 'Dairy monsters', The Guardian, December 13, 2003

…just under 1p per litre of milk. 'GM and Dairy Cow Feed: Steps to a GM-free Future for the UK Dairy Industry'. Greenpeace, May 2004, www.greenpeace.org/international_en/multimedia/download/1/475869/0/gp_lupins_final.pdf

…a diet rich in rapeseed yields healthier milk. 'Butter that spreads straight from a cow', The Guardian, March 18, 2004

…one fifth of regular, full-fat butter is subsidised. 'Land of Milk and Money?' Sustain, June 19, 2003

…22 per cent of Britons are obese and three-quarters are deemed overweight. 'Hot topics: Obesity', BBC Science Online, www.bbc.co.uk/science/hottopics/obesity/index.shtml

…increased consumption of processed fatty, salty and sugary foods. 'The World Health Report: Message from the Director General', The World Health Organisation, 2004, www.who.int/whr/2002/message_from_the__director_general/en/

…10 per cent of six-year-olds are obese, rising to 17 per cent of 15-year-olds. 'Hot topics: Obesity', BBC Science Online, September 7, 2004, www.bbc.co.uk/science/hottopics/obesity/index.shtml

…a quarter of EU butter enters our food in this way. 'Dairy monsters', The Guardian, December 13, 2003

…school and hospital caterers to use butter instead of vegetable oils. ibid

…Dilemma: Why cow's milk? Why not donkey milk? '3-A-Day: Why 3-A-Day', The Dairy Council, 2002, www.milk.co.uk/content/3aday; 'Dairy monsters', The Guardian, December 13, 2003; 'Food Pyramid Scheme', Alternet, July 5, 2000, www.alternet.org/story/9412; 'Goat's milk unsafe for infants with cow's milk allergy', Journal of Allergy and Clinical Immunology, June, 1999

…now 'lays' 8,940 million eggs a year. 'Egg statistics', International Institute for Environment and Development, 2002, www.racetothetop.org/case/case3.htm#stats

…'go to work on an egg' slogan in the 1960s and sent egg sales soaring. '1968: Egg Board "should be scrapped"', BBC On This Day, http://news.bbc.co.uk/onthisday/hi/dates/stories/june/21/newsid_2988000/2988175.stm

…one hen must lay over 300 eggs in a year. 'Report on the welfare of laying hens', Farm Animal Welfare Council, 1997, www.fawc.org.uk/reports/layhens/lhgretoc.htm

…leads to broken bones and extensive feather and foot damage. ibid

…hens are typically sold to processors for as little as 2p. ibid

…sales fell by 10 per cent and over 5,000 producers went out of business. 'Medical notes: Salmonella', BBC News Online, May 19, 1998, http://news.bbc.co.uk/1/hi/health/medical_notes/84481.stm

…a link between eggs and salmonella. ibid

…two million chickens were slaughtered as a precaution. ibid

…risk of salmonella had been halved through vaccination. 'FSA survey shows very low level of salmonella contamination of eggs', Food Standards Agency, Ref: 2004/0475, March 19, 2004, www.food.gov.uk/news/pressreleases/2004/mar/salmonellaeggs

…only one in every 290 boxes of six eggs was found to have any salmonella contamination. ibid

…high levels of use of drugs in the poultry industry. 'Are you being served?', The Guardian, May 15, 2004

…nearly one in 10 chickens tested breached limits for the drug nicarbazin. ibid

…three million eggs eaten each day in the UK were contaminated with another such drug, lasalocid. 'Too hard to crack? The problem of drug residues in eggs', Soil Association, April 14, 2004, www.soilassociation.org/web/sa/saweb.nsf/0/e67b81eb27eca66980256e760030af48?

…'disappointed by the failure of industry to take effective action'. 'FSA response to lasalocid report from the Soil Association', Food Standards Authority, April 14, 2004, www.food.gov.uk/news/newsarchive/2004/apr/lasalocidreport

…announced that battery cages would be phased out by 2006. 'Campaigns – Egg-laying hens', RSPCA Online, 2004, www.rspca.org.uk/servlet/ContentServer?pagename=RSPCA/Campaigns/Egglayinghens

…follow Germany's lead and ban all cages. ibid

…free-range eggs already cost around 50p more than eggs from caged hens. 'Egg Production', British Egg Information Service, www.britegg.co.uk/beissection/beis_eggp.html

…15 per cent of the chickens even poked their heads outside. 'Free Range Better? Not if you're a Chicken!', World Farming Union, July 14, 2003, www.wfu.org.uk/news_old7.htm

…which help egg yolks to score 8/9 on the Roche scale, the official egg yolk colouring chart. 'The critical questions on egg yolk colour', The British Free Range Egg Producers Association, www.theranger.co.uk/husbandry/hus17.htm

…82 million Freedom Food eggs are now sold every month. 'Campaigns – Egg-laying hens', RSPCA Online, 2004, www.rspca.org.uk/servlet/ContentServer?pagename=RSPCA/Campaigns/Egglayinghens

…broken through the £100 million-a-year barrier. '10 years of fairtrade: sales reach £100 million per year', Fairtrade Foundation, March 1, 2004, www.fairtrade.org

…choose from more than 250 products from more than 100 companies. ibid

…world trade has grown sixfold since the early 1990s. 'Retail therapy: Consumer's awareness of how and where goods are produced has soared – and so, as a result, has the fair trade movement', The Guardian, April 24, 2003

…a price to producers that covers the costs of sustainable production and living. 'Fairtrade Standards', Fairtrade Foundation, www.fairtrade.org.uk/about_standards.htm

…Since 2004, FLO standards have existed for coffee. ibid

…seven billion bananas are shipped to the UK each year. 'Behind the Price Tag', Fairtrade Foundation, 2003, www.fairtrade.org.uk/downloads/doc/Bananas%20-%20behind%20the%20price%20tag.doc

…a million Fairtrade bananas. ibid

…100 different fair trade ranges. 'Why do only some Traidcraft products carry the Fairtrade mark?', Traidcraft, April 2002, www.traidcraft.co.uk/template2.asp?pageID=1674&fromID=1652

…in March 2004 the Office of Government Commerce issued guidelines on how government. '10 years of fair trade: sales reach £100 million per year', Fairtrade Foundation, August 2004, www.fairtrade.org.uk/pr010304.htm

…$1 billion a day on agricultural subsidies. 'Rigged rules & double standards: trade, globalisation, and the fight against poverty', Oxfam, 2002, www.maketradefair.com/en/index.php?file=03042002121618.htm

…'if Africa, East Asia, South Asia, and Latin America'. ibid

…one way or another, unfair free trade is now on trial. Ransom, David, The No-Nonsense Guide to Fair Trade, New Internationalist/Verso, 2003

…rice is the world's most common crop, covering about one per cent of the Earth's land surface. 'Study Determines Levels Of Ozone-Depleting Gases Emitted By Rice Paddies Into Atmosphere', Science Daily, November 2000, www.sciencedaily.com/releases/2000/11/001103071346.htm

...the primary food source for billions of people. ibid

...one per cent of the total methyl bromide and five per cent of the methyl iodide emissions. ibid

...first certified crop of organic rice at their Riet Vell nature reserve in Spain's Ebro Delta. 'RSPB Rice scoops award', Royal Society for the Protection of Birds, April 15, 2004 www.rspb.org.uk/supporting/shopping/food/rice/award.asp

...bread sold in the UK is the sliced, plastic-wrapped product of the ubiquitous 'Chorleywood Bread Process'. 'Bread Street: The British Baking Bloomer?', Sustain, 2004, www.sustainweb.org/publications/pubinfo/pubinfo_bread.asp

...81 per cent of the UK's bread is made by just 12 companies. ibid

...accounting for 55 per cent of sales. ibid

...in terms of omega-3 content. 'Fat of the Land', Sustain, 2000, www.sustainweb.org/publications/downloads/ff_fat.pdf

...has been the focus of campaigns by Friends of the Earth and WWF. 'Can it', Ethical Consumer, 81, February/March 2003

...the equivalent of 132 Eiffel Towers, or 4,000 jumbo jets. ibid

...which accounts for 82 per cent of the world's production. 'Sweet and Sour', Sustain, 2000, www.sustainweb.org/publications/downloads/ff_sweet.pdf

...an extra five million litres of water per hectare can raise yields by three tonnes per hectare. ibid

...up to 13 different pesticides in some cases in the UK. ibid

...The US is the largest consumer of orange juice by far, drinking about half of all the world's juice. 'Taking the Pith', Sustain, 2000, www.sustainweb.org/publications/downloads/ff_pith.pdf

...now the largest in the world and a producer of a third of the world's oranges – 95 per cent of which are juiced. ibid

...requires 22 glasses of water for processing and over 1,000 glasses of water for irrigation. ibid

...oranges from a range of countries including Israel, Morocco, South Africa, Spain and Zimbabwe. ibid

...links to child labour are also of major concern. ibid

...it could cost them up to £34.67 for a litre. 'Pure juice for children that costs parents £34 a litre', The Guardian, April 30, 2004

...50 or so countries located near the equator and provides a living for more than 20 million farmers. 'Spilling the beans on the coffee trade', Fairtrade Foundation, March 2002, www.fairtrade.org.uk/downloads/pdf/spilling.pdf

...coffee trade has doubled to reach $60 billion a year. ibid

...30 per cent of that revenue, now they keep only 10 per cent. ibid

...13 per cent of the world's coffee beans. Lawrence F, Not on the Label, HarperCollins, 2004

...50 per cent of total export revenues. In Burundi, the figure is 80 per cent. ibid

...other additives, including volatile oils, are added to make it smell of fresh coffee. ibid

...61 per cent of organic and 87 per cent of conventional wines. 'Are you being served?', The Guardian, May 15, 2004

...a second study found that while lead contamination of wine. ibid

...more than double the maximum amount of lead allowed. ibid

...lowering the permissible blood alcohol level for drivers as a drink-driving strategy. 'That's the Spirit', Ethical Consumer, February/March 2004

...Spotlight: Dasani's watery grave. 'Busted brands', The Guardian, March 20, 2004; Sams C, The Little Food Book, Alastair Sawday, 2003; 'Water Wars Part III: Bottled water', BBC News Online, Friday, 17 March, 2000, http://news.bbc.co.uk/1/hi/world/europe/679838.stm

...supporting sanctions against Cuba while using images of Cuban heritage in its marketing campaigns. ibid

...hired rightwing death squads to intimidate unions at the plants. 'Coca-Cola faces down shareholder revolt and ejects protester', The Guardian, April 22, 2004

...'are false and outrageous'. ibid

...depleting water supplies in local communities and causing pollution with discharged materials. 'Coke on trial as Indian villagers accuse plant of sucking them dry', The Guardian, November 19, 2003

Chapter 2: Home and Garden

...thermometers hit 100F. 'Bookies lose shirts as record tumbles', The Guardian, August 11, 2003

...one quarter of all CO2 emissions come from the energy we use to heat and light our homes. 'Global warming and climate change', Sustainable Wales, October 2002, www.sustainablewales.org.uk/documents/energydocs/Globalwarmingandenergyfull.doc

...we will purchase more than 70 million set-top boxes. 'Ethical living: Hell's kitchen', The Observer, September 12, 2004

...to make a single 32-megabyte microchip for a computer. 'The 1.7 Kilogram Microchip: Energy and Material Use in the Production of Semiconductor Devices', Environmental Science and Technology, Vol. 36, Issue 24, December 15, 2002

...new-build houses were 38 per cent bigger. 'Good Stuff? A Behind-the-scenes Guide to the Things We Buy', Worldwatch Institute, 2004, www.worldwatch.org

...US homes now average 210 square metres. ibid

...we are building about 170,000 homes a year. 'More cash pledged as house building plunges to new low', The Guardian, June 20, 2002

...when in 2003 there were 718,720 empty homes in England alone. 'National Statistics 2003', Empty Homes Agency, www.emptyhomes.com/statspages/nstats.htm

...world's richest people use about 25 times more energy than the poorest. 'Executive Summary, The Energy Challenge', World Energy Council, www.worldenergy.org/wec-geis/publications/reports/etwan/exec_summary/sum_energy_challenge.asp

...almost a third of the world's population have no access to electricity at all. 'The quest to grow without grime', The Guardian, August 22, 2002

...we each use around 150 litres of water a day domestically. 'Security of supply, leakage and the efficient use of water 2002–2003 report', OFWAT, The economic regulator for the water and sewerage industry in England and Wales, 2003, www.ofwat.gov.uk/aptrix/ofwat/publish.nsf/AttachmentsByTitle/leakage_02-03.pdf/$FILE/leakage_02-03.pdf

...more than three times the amount of water a Kenyan would use. 'Changing Levels of Domestic Water Use', International Institute for Environment and Development, 2003 www.iied.org/sarl/dow/summary/chapter3.html

...In the Thames Water region alone, 25,000 tonnes of debris is removed from sewage water every year. 'Bag It And Bin It', Thames Water, www.thameswater.co.uk

...up to ten times as much pollution inside the home as outside. 'Sources of Indoor Air Pollution – Organic Gases (Volatile Organic Compounds – VOCs)', US Environmental Protection Agency, www.epa.gov/iaq/voc.html

...Over the past decade, the market has grown from an annual turnover of £8.7 billion in 1993 to £16 billion in 2003. 'Latest Verdict DIY monitor predicts further £5bn growth for DIY retail sector by 2008' press release, Focus Wickes, January 12, 2004, www.focusdiy.co.uk/stry/120104

...10 per cent of a two-year-old pillow's weight. 'How Clean is Your House?', Discovery Home and Leisure, www.homeandleisure.co.uk/howclean/how_clean2.shtml

...burnt toast can expose you to carcinogens such as benzopyrene. 'Close Encounters', The Guardian, May 22, 2004

...threw out six billion nappies, 468 million batteries, 24 million car tyres, two million mobile phones and 94,000 fridges. 'Evidence of Norman Baker, House of Commons Hansard Debates: Waste Management, Department For Environment, Food And Rural Affairs', June 19, 2003, www.publications.parliament.uk/pa/cm200203/cmhansrd/vo030619/debtext/30619-27.htm

...we now throw away 434 million tonnes of rubbish each year. 'Wacky waste facts', Waste Online, www.wasteonline.org.uk/topic.aspx?id=19

...up to 60 per cent of what we send to landfill or incinerators could be recycled. 'Glossary', Capital Waste Facts.com, www.capitalwastefacts.com/glossary/glossary.php4

...we currently recycle only about 12 per cent. 'Waste At Home', Waste Online, www.wasteonline.org.uk/topic.aspx?id=21

...the UK contributed around two per cent of global greenhouse gas emissions in 2001. 'Global warming "biggest threat"', BBC News Online, January 9, 2004

...between 1990 and 2001 energy consumption in British homes rose by 19 per cent. 'Energy Consumption in the UK', Department of Trade and Industry, July 2002, www.dti.gov.uk/energy/inform/energy_consumption/ecuk.pdf

...When the Department for Trade and Industry last analysed average domestic energy use in 2002. 'Table 3.7: Domestic energy consumption by end use and fuel, 1990 to 2002', Department for Trade and Industry website, www.dti.gov.uk/energy/inform/energy_consumption/table.shtml

...temperatures inside our homes are estimated to have increased. 'Table 3.16: Internal and external temperatures', Department for Trade and Industry website, www.dti.gov.uk/energy/inform/energy_consumption/table.shtml

...£800 million worth of electricity a year just to run our washing machines, tumble dryers and dishwashers. 'Factsheet: Energy Efficiency Facts and Figures', Energy Saving Trust, September 2002, www.saveenergy.co.uk/downloads/ee_factsfigures.doc

...domestic refrigeration appliances use nearly as much electricity as all the offices in the UK. 'Did You Know? Energy Facts & Figures', DEFRA Market Transformation Programme, www.mtprog.com/approvedbriefingnotes/Didyouknow EnergyFactsAndFigures.aspx?kintUniqueID=335

...electricity consumption by domestic lights and appliances has nearly doubled since 1970. 'Home Energy Use', Energy Saving Trust, www.est.org.uk/myhome/climatechange/stats/homeenergy/

...Up to 75 per cent of all energy wasted in our homes is avoidable. ibid

...enough to heat three million homes for a year. ibid

...around a third of the 30,000 deaths. 'Do try this at home', The Guardian, September 23, 2004

...two and a half times as much CO2 per unit of heat. 'Energy Efficiency – The Basics', Energy Saving Trust, www.practicalhelp.org.uk/housing/information/energyefficiency/co2/index.cfm

...up to 47 per cent of coal's energy converts to electricity. 'Materials In Electricity', Institute of Materials, Minerals and Mining, www.materials-careers.org.uk/careers/electric.htm

...60 per cent by 2050. 'Our energy future – creating a low carbon economy', Department of Trade and Industry, February 2003, www.dti.gov.uk/energy/whitepaper/ourenergyfuture.pdf

...'Renewables Obligation' set by the government. 'Complying with the Obligation', Department of Trade and Industry, www.dti.gov.uk/energy/renewables/policy/complying.shtml

...Gas has a lower carbon content in relation to its energy content. Salomon T & Bedel S, The Energy Saving House, Centre for Alternative Technology Publications, 2003

...condensing boilers manage around 88 per cent [of fuel into heat]. 'What is a high efficiency condensing boiler?', Energy Saving Trust, www.est.org.uk/myhome/efficientproducts/boilers/what/

...with a potentially 95 per cent fuel-into-heat efficiency rate. 'Oil central heating systems', National Energy Foundation, www.natenergy.org.uk/oil-ch.htm

...up to 85 per cent of the heat they generate is wasted. Salomon T & Bedel S, The Energy Saving House, Centre for Alternative Technology Publications, 2003

...about 50 per cent on average. 'Solar Hot Water', Energy Saving Trust, www.practicalhelp.org.uk/housing/information/renewableenergy/hotwater/index.cfm

...energy pay-back period for active solar panels is 15–20 years. 'Clear skies from local renewables', Renew newsletter, The Network for Alternative Technology and Technology Assessment, March/April 2003, www-tec.open.ac.uk/eeru/natta/renewonline/rol42/2.htm

...costs around 60p-70p/kWh. 'Press & Events: Questions About Solar Power', Department for Trade and Industry, www.dti.gov.uk/renewable/solar_qa.html

...UK's electricity supplies could theoretically be generated using wind. 'The Royal Commission on Environmental Pollution's 22nd Report: Energy – The Changing Climate', The Royal Commission on Environmental Pollution, June 2000, www.rcep.org.uk/pdf/chp7.pdf

...Kansas, North Dakota, and South Dakota. Sawin J, Mainstreaming Renewable Energy in the 21st Century, Worldwatch Paper 169, May 2004, www.worldwatch.org

...in 2004 a protest against a proposed expansion of a wind farm in north Wales drew the support. 'An Ill Wind?', The Guardian, May 7, 2004

...1,034 wind turbines already running in the UK produce about 700MW of electricity. ibid

...almost 80 per cent of all wind-farm applications made in the past 14 years. ibid

...the blades would need to span about five metres from tip to tip. 'Build Your Own Wind Turbine', The British Wind Energy Association, www.bwea.com/you/byo.html

...In 2004, the UK made its first tentative steps into

trialling the industrial use of biomass. 'Drax goes green with willow', The Guardian, March 19, 2004

...averages around 500mm from 150–200 'rain days'. 'Climate of the British Isles', Met Office, www.metoffice.com/education/curriculum/leaflets/bi_climate.html

...receive about 5,000mm a year. ibid

...UK water industry collects, treats and supplies about 18 billion litres of water per day. 'Towards Sustainability – Moving Ahead Sustainability Indicators 2001/2002', Water UK, www.water.org.uk/static/files_archive/1FinalReport0102.PDF

...two billion people, approximately one-third of the world's population, depend on groundwater supplies. 'Groundwater depletion and pollution', People and Planet, July 14, 2003, www.peopleandplanet.net/doc.php?id=627

...Ariel Sharon has stated that he believes the Six Day War in 1967. 'Analysis: Middle East water wars', BBC News Online, May 30, 2003 http://news.bbc.co.uk/1/hi/world/middle_east/2949768.stm

...Israel's annual water use exceeds the renewable supply by 15 per cent. 'Freshwater: lifeblood of the planet', People and Planet, June 17, 2004, www.peopleandplanet.net/doc.php?id=671&section=14

...Israel signed a deal with Turkey to pump 50 million cubic metres of water. ibid

...over 100,000 cotton buds are disposed. 'Bag It And Bin It', Thames Water website, www.thameswater.co.uk

...up to 15 per cent of domestic electricity worldwide is wasted .'What is Energy Star?', The Australian Greenhouse Office, April 27, 2003, www.energystar.gov.au/why.html

...annual spend on furnishings and DIY now stands at a record £23 billion. 'DIY boom set to continue', The Guardian, September 18, 2002

...B&Q can expect to receive three million visits over an average bank holiday weekend. 'The jobs about the house to DIY for – and some to avoid', The Guardian, March 30, 2002

...26 million of us make at least one pilgrimage to Ikea. 'Ikea remains king of hearts and purses', Cabinet Maker, February 22, 2002, www.cm1st.com/pdfs/cm220202.pdf

...number of new homes in England alone is projected to increase by 3.8 million. 'Households', Environment Agency website, www.environment-agency.gov.uk/yourenv/eff/people_lifestyles/househol/?version=1&lang=_e

...one third of England's land area is still predicted to switch from rural to urban use by 2016. ibid

...Greenpeace report published in 2003. 'Consuming Chemicals 2: Hazardous chemicals in house dusts as indicators of chemical exposure in the home', Greenpeace Research Laboratories, December 2003, http://eu.greenpeace.org/downloads/chem/ConsumingChemicalsReportNo2.pdf

...cotton production accounts for 25 per cent of all pesticides used over the world. 'Environmental impacts of clothing', Ethical Consumer, EC50, December 1997, www.ethicalconsumer.org/magazine/buyers/clothes97/clothingenvironment.htm

...more than 76 per cent of conventional cotton production in the US is now from genetically modified crops. 'Genetically Modified Crops in the United States', Pew Initiative on Food and Biotechnology, August 2004, http://pewagbiotech.org/resources/factsheets/display.php3?FactsheetID=2

...dust mites affect 85 per cent of asthma sufferers and 90 per cent of eczema sufferers. 'The big list', The Guardian, May 22, 2004

...about one gramme of dust. 'A Sharp Intake Of Breath', The Guardian, May 22, 2004

...up to 50 per cent of tropical timber imports into the EU may be illegally sourced. 'European League Table of Imports of Illegal Tropical Timber', Friends of the Earth, August 2001, www.foe.co.uk/resource/briefings/euro_league_illegal_timber.pdf

...illegal hardwoods were being used to refurbish an EU building. 'EC building "used illegal wood"', The Guardian, May 12, 2004

...'invisible imprint of violence'. 'From War Zones to Shopping Malls', Worldwatch Institute press release, October 17, 2002, www.worldwatch.org/press/news/2002/10/17/

...raised an estimated $100 million per year. 'Liberia breaches UN Sanctions – whilst its logging industry funds arms imports and RUF rebels', Global Witness press release, September 6, 2001, www.globalwitness.org/press_releases/display2.php?id=114

...Tributyltin...contains organotin compounds that can find their way into the human body via the skin. 'Poisons underfoot – carpets and vinyl linked to indoor pollution', Greenpeace UK press release, October 10, 2001, www.greenpeace.org.uk

...global production rose from 12.8 million tonnes in 1988 to 22 million tonnes in 1996. 'Dioxin Elimination: A Global Imperative', Greenpeace International, March 8, 2000, http://archive.greenpeace.org/toxics/reports/dioxelim.pdf

...250,000 serious injuries and 70 deaths. 'DIY Accidents: Introduction', Department of Trade and Industry, August 27, 2004, www.dti.gov.uk/homesafetynetwork/dy_intro.htm

...an estimated 12 to 25 per cent of the paint sold in the UK is never used. 'Paint Policy', B&Q Social Responsibility report, October 1997 www.diy.com/diy/jsp/aboutbandq/social_responsibility/BQSRPAIN.PDF

...from 500 parts per million to 50 and then to 25. 'Things To Do Before You DIY', The Guardian, May 22, 2004

...[concrete] is the single biggest manufacturing source of CO2. 'Evidence Received for Renewable Energy in Scotland inquiry', Scottish Parliament, February 10, 2004, www.scottish.parliament.uk/business/committees/enterprise/inquiries-04/rei/ec04-reis-davenport,aj.htm

...research by the US National Oceanic Atmospheric Administration has showed that ISA of the contiguous states. 'US concrete "would cover Ohio"', BBC News Online, June 15, 2004, http://news.bbc.co.uk/1/hi/sci/tech/3808765.stm

...a 2.5cm timber board has better thermal resistance than an 11.4cm brick wall. 'Timber Factfile', Howarth Timber, www.howarth-timber.co.uk/about_fact.php

...it is estimated that if all homes built in the UK since 1945 had been constructed to modern timber-frame standards. ibid

...tropical rainforests are now being cleared at a rate of around 15 million hectares a year. 'Deforestation Continues At A High Rate In Tropical Areas; FAO Calls Upon Countries To Fight Forest Crime And Corruption', United Nations Food and Agriculture Organisation press release, October 3, 2001, www.fao.org/waicent/ois/press_ne/presseng/2001/pren0161.htm

...equivalent to over six million hectares of forest.

'Wood and environmental space', Friends of the Earth briefing sheet, April 20, 1999, www.foe.co.uk/pdf/ sustainable_development/tworld/wood.pdf

...around 20 per cent of the timber we use now comes from domestic trees. 'Timber Factfile', Howarth Timber, www.howarth-timber.co.uk/about_fact.php

...73 per cent by 2050 if it is to help reach sustainability. 'Wood and environmental space', Friends of the Earth briefing sheet, April 20, 1999, www.foe.co.uk/pdf/sustainable_development/tworld/ wood.pdf

...one quarter of the 49 wars and armed conflicts waged during 2000. 'State of the World 2002', Worldwatch Institute, February 2002, www.worldwatch.org/pubs/sow/2002/

...'an environmental poison throughout its life cycle'. 'Why PVC is bad news', Greenpeace PVC Alternative database, http://archive.greenpeace.org/toxics/ pvcdatabase/bad.html

...the National Housing Federation has also found PVC-u windows to be more expensive than timber ones. 'PVC Alternatives Database', Greenpeace International, http://archive.greenpeace.org/toxics/ pvcdatabase/productalt.html

...Spotlight: Our love affair with MDF. 'Medium Density Fibreboard', Timber Research and Development Association press release, www.trada.co.uk; 'A good life: DIY', The Guardian, September 9, 2004; 'Wood panel recycling', Timber Research and Development Association www.trada.co.uk/techinfo/research/EnviroFibre.htm; 'Frequently Asked Questions', British Woodworking Federation, www.bwf.org.uk/faq/faqhome.html

....Sixty-five per cent of Chinese city dwellers. 'Appliances: Boosting Efficiency, Saving Energy', Worldwatch Institute website, 2004, www.worldwatch.org/pubs/goodstuff/appliances/

...90 per cent own a washing machine. ibid

...grow by 14 per cent annually. ibid

...43 countries in Europe and Asia. Ibid

...30 per cent of energy consumption in industrial countries. ibid

...found to be more energy intensive than the manufacture of a car. 'Computers must be greener', People and Planet website, March 10, 2004, www.peopleandplanet.net/doc.php?id=2162

...average at 53.5 litres each use. 'Wash your whites greener, Ethical Consumer, EC82, April/May 2003, www.ethicalconsumer.org/magazine/buyers/82/washin g%20machines.html

...around £630 million a year. 'A Bite of the Big Apple: American influence bites into lower and middle refrigerator market', ER Magazine, February 1, 2003

...increasingly introduced 'status-related products'. ibid

...15 per cent more energy to run. Wilhide E, Eco, Quadrille Publishing, 2002

...can use up to 45 per cent more energy. 'DECADE: Domestic Equipment and Carbon Dioxide Emissions: Transforming the UK Cold Market', University of Oxford Environmental Change Institute, 1997, www.eci.ox.ac.uk/pdfdownload/transforming.pdf

...'a recipe for disaster'. 'Ready meals are recipe for ill health', The Guardian, May 29, 2004

...3.5 hours of TV viewing per day. 'The Drug of the Nation?', Ethical Consumer, EC 78, August/September, 2002

...98 per cent of households possess an average of 1.7 TVs. ibid

...UK spends £12 billion. ibid

...seven million tonnes of CO2 each year. 'UK Urged to Save Energy at Home for World Environment Day', Energy Savings Trust press release, June 3, 2004, www.est.org.uk/aboutest/news/press/index.cfm?mode =view&category_id=25&press_id=206

...85 per cent of the electricity. ibid

...50 per cent of us now have access. 'Living In Britain – the General Household Survey', Office for National Statistics, December 17, 2002, www.statistics.gov.uk/lib2001/index.html

...topped one billion and sales continue to rise at around 130 million. 'PCs: the latest waste mountain?', The Guardian, March 8, 2004

...63 million computers will be 'retired'. 'Ewaste: The Problem', Computer Recyclers of America website, www.crasd.com/ewasteproblem.html

...ten times its weight in fossil fuels and chemicals during manufacture. 'PCs: the latest waste mountain?', The Guardian, March 8, 2004

...fallen by 81 per cent since 1997. 'Printing Matters', Ethical Consumer, EC88, May/June 2004

...worth $2 billion in 2001. Kluwer R & Williams E, 'Computers and the environment: Understanding and managing their impacts', Kluwer Academic Publishers and the United Nations University, 2004, www.neutrino.co.jp/abi_ecoe/1-4020-1679-4.PDF

...Dilemma: Dishwasher versus washing-up. 'A comparison of washing up by hand with a domestic dishwasher', Market Transformation Programme report, www.mtprog.com/approvedbriefingnotes/Dishwashing Acomparisonofwashingupbyhandwithadishwasher appliance.aspx?kintUniqueID=286

...has at its disposal around 100,000 new and existing chemicals. 'Chemicals', European Environment Agency, http://themes.eea.eu.int/Environmental_issues/chemicals

...the EU has identified 140 chemicals of 'high concern'. 'Future EU Chemicals Policy', Defra, December 4, 2002, www.defra.gov.uk/environment/chemicals/eufuture.htm

...traces of POPs have been found in polar bears in the Arctic and in the breastmilk of Inuit mothers. 'Arctic Life Threatened by Toxic Chemicals, Groups Say', National Geographic, October 8, 2002, http://news.nationalgeographic.com/news/2002/ 10/1008_021008_arctic.html

...UNEP says that everyone in the world now has traces of POPs in their bodies. '"Dirty dozen" toxins are banned by UN pact', The Guardian, May 17, 2004

...OECD estimates that it accounts for seven per cent of global income. 'OECD Environmental Outlook for the Chemicals Industry', OECD report, 2001, www.oecd.org/ehs

...up to 30,000 chemicals will have to be registered. 'EU Chemicals Policy', Parliamentary Office of Science and Technology: Postnote, Number 229, September 2004, www.parliament.uk/documents/ upload/POSTpn229.pdf

...99 per cent of chemical-based products to be sold. 'Analysis: A precautionary tale', The Guardian, May 12, 2004

...Lindane traces found in chocolate. 'Is organic food always better for you?', The Guardian, July 15, 2003

...'To test just the commonest 1,000 toxic chemicals in combinations of three'. 'Food chained', The Guardian, May 15, 2004

...a high-profile reference to the cocktail effect in action is made by veterans of the 1991 Gulf war. 'Veteran death linked to Gulf War', BBC News Online, November 24, 2003, http://news.bbc.co.uk/1/hi/health/3234908.stm

...'Given our understanding of the way chemicals interact with the environment'. 'Chemicals in Products: Safeguarding the Environment and Human Health', Royal Commission on Environmental Pollution news release, June 26, 2003, www.rcep.org.uk/news/03-02.htm

...What can I do to reduce my exposure? Tips from the Guardian's 'Chemical World' series of supplements, May 8, 22 & 15, 2004, www.guardian.co.uk/chemicalworld

...worth a record £1.03 billion in 2002. 'Household Cleaning Products in the UK', Euromonitor report, Reference MMPUK325, http://worldofinformation.safeshopper.com/30/ 1382.htm?547

...antibacterial wipes and '3-in-1' solutions. 'Household cleaning superpanel survey', Taylor Nelson Sofres, 2003, www.tutor2u.net/business/marketing/ casestudy_%20products_household_cleaning.asp

...diarrhoea and earache in infants and headaches and depression in mothers. The Avon Longitudinal Study of Parents and Children (ALSPAC), University of Bristol, October 19, 2004, www.alspac.bris.ac.uk/press/air_fresheners.shtml

...typically include formaldehyde and phenol. 'Agent Lemon', The Observer, August 22, 2004

...ethylene glycol monobutyl ether acetate can affect the central nervous system. 'Kitchen confidential', The Guardian, May 22, 2004

...60 per cent of people surveyed. 'Chemical Household', Consumers' Association Which? Report, August 2002

...more effective than 'clear' ones. Thomas P, Cleaning Yourself to Death, Newleaf, 2001

...one of the principal causes of accidental childhood poisoning. 'Children can open pill bottles', BBC News Online, June 20, 2004, http://news.bbc.co.uk/1/hi/health/3816279.stm

...these tablets are the principal cause of accidental childhood poisonings. 'Home Sickness', The Ecologist, April 22, 2001, www.theecologist.org/ archive_article.html?article=126&category=35

...pine oils that can, in extreme cases, cause convulsions. Thomas P, Cleaning Yourself to Death, Newleaf, 2001

...Dilemma: Should I employ a cleaner? 'Domestics: UK Domestic Workers and their reluctant employers', The Work Foundation, June 2004, www.theworkfoundation.com/pdf/Domestics.pdf; 'Personal Accounts', Kalayaan: Justice for Overseas Domestic Workers', http://ourworld.compuserve.com/homepages/ kalayaan/lh_news_3.htm; 'Cleaners' increased asthma risk', BBC News Online, October 28, 2003, http://news.bbc.co.uk/1/hi/health/3218785.stm

...85 per cent of us have access to a garden. 'Opportunities and constraints on the use of peat alternatives as growing media', Department of the Environment, Transport and the Regions seminar record, October 2000, www.odpm.gov.uk/stellent/ groups/odpm_planning/documents/source/ odpm_plan_source_606564.doc

...an area five times the size of London. 'Wild in your Garden: How to garden for wildlife', BBC Online, www.bbc.co.uk/nature/animals/wildbritain/wildinyourg arden/gardens/fswg_garden.shtml

...what people now have in their garden. 'The Focus Wickes Gardening Monitor', Focus Wickes, April 2004, http://media.venda.com/focus/ebiz/focus/images/ gardeningmonitor2004.pdf

...asked respondents what they use their gardens for. ibid

...four in ten gardeners grew vegetables. ibid

...more popular with those over the age of 55. ibid

...called for an urgent review of two common weedkillers. 'Garden Pesticides Health Warning', Friends of the Earth press release, July 14, 2003, www.foe.co.uk/resource/press_releases/garden_pesticides_health_w.html

...teaspoon of soil. 'Organic Tales of the Country: Awaiting an agricultural revolution', The Independent, October 3, 2003

...66 per cent of tropical woods. 'Why garden centres are killing the planet', The Daily Mirror, May 26, 2004

...50 per cent of Indonesian-sourced barbecue charcoal. 'BBQ at B&Q'. Ethical Consumer, EC 84, August/September 2003, www.ethicalconsumer.org/magazine/news/newsarchive.htm#84

...13kg canister of natural gas will warm an area outside of up to 25m² for 12 hours. 'Why Garden Centres Are Killing The Planet', The Daily Mirror, May 26, 2004

...97 per cent of the UK's 2,900 hectares of 'limestone pavement' has been damaged. 'Rock Gardens Based on Nature', Royal Horticultural Society, November 2003, www.rhs.org.uk/publications/pubs/garden1103/newsrhs.asp

...65 per cent of growing media used by 'home' gardeners is peat-based. 'Peatering Out – towards a sustainable UK growing media industry', RSPB, www.rspb.org.uk/Images/peateringout_tcm5-31088.pdf

...we buy 2.7million cubic metres of the stuff. 'Waste Not Want Not', The Garden, Royal Horticultural Society Magazine, February 2000, www.rhs.org.uk/publications/pubs/garden_98-00/pubs_journals_garden_0200_compost.asp

...less than six per cent of the UK's original lowland raised peat bog habitat now remains. 'Destruction of Peat Bogs', RSPB, www.rspb.org.uk/policy/waterwetlands/peat_bogs/index.asp

...in the Republic of Ireland, 2,000 hectares of peat bog a year are destroyed. 'Eco-Trashing Peat Plant to Shatter Village Quiet', Friends of the Earth press release, August 14, 2003, www.foe.co.uk/resource/press_releases/ecotrashing_peat_plant_to.html

...382 species listed as being of concern on the government's UK Biodiversity Action Plan. 'Species Action Plans', UK Biodiversity Action Plan, www.ukbap.org.uk/GenPageText.aspx?id=94

...use at least 10 litres of water a day on our garden. 'Environmental Facts and Figures', Cambridge Water, www.cambridge-water.co.uk/saving/envfacts.htm

...'The sight is in no way so pleasantly refreshed as by fine and close grass kept short.' Albertus Magnus, De Vegetabilis et Plantis [On Vegetables and Plants], 1260

...annual expenditure in the UK on lawn-related equipment is now nearly £100 million. 'Turf Love', The Guardian, June 29, 2004

...the combined area of lawn is estimated to be about the same size as the state of Louisiana. Starke L (ed), State of the World 2004, WW Norton and Company, 2004

...lawns are fed more than 45 million kilos of fertilisers annually. ibid

...30 billion litres of water a day. ibid

...about three-fifths of what the people of the UK use in a day. 'Wetland wonderland', WWF, www.wwf.org.uk

...one lawnmower produces as much pollution in an hour as 40 cars. 'Quick Facts', Clean Air Foundation, www.cleanairfoundation.org/mow_down/md_eng/html/mowdown_facts.asp

...more than 434 million tonnes of waste. 'Wacky Waste Facts', Waste online, 2004, www.wasteonline.org.uk/topic.aspx

...26 million tonnes come straight from our homes. 'Recycling is coming home', Recycle Now website, 2004, www.recyclenow.com/at_home/index.html).

...about 500kg per person. 'Wacky Waste Facts', Waste online, 2004, www.wasteonline.org.uk/topic.aspx

...five tonnes of waste generated by manufacturing. 'Waste Prevention', Waste Online, 2004, www.wasteonline.org.uk/resources/InformationSheets/WastePrevention.htm

...20 tonnes created at the point where the raw material is extracted. ibid

...fill the Royal Albert Hall every two hours. 'Wacky Waste Facts', Waste online, 2004, www.wasteonline.org.uk/topic.aspx

...north-east are the biggest offenders. 'Municipal Waste Management Survey 2002/03', Defra, www.defra.gov.uk/environment/statistics/wastats/mwb0203/wbch03.htm

...75 per cent of all municipal waste goes straight to landfill. ibid

...nine per cent is incinerated. ibid

...23.8kg of rubbish per week. ibid

...just 12 per cent being recycled or composted. ibid

...the UK languishes near the bottom of European recycling league tables. ibid

...rising by three per cent a year. ibid

...40 million tonnes a year. 'The big clear up', The Guardian, July 17, 2002

...5kg more waste per week than poorer ones. 'On the bins', The Guardian, May 20, 2002

...more per capita than other demographic groups. ibid

...three million tonnes generated. 'Cutting Down on Christmas Waste', Waste Online, www.wasteonline.org.uk/resources/informationsheets/christmasrecycling.htm)

...25 million tonnes of 'homeless rubbish' generated each year. 'ENCAMS: Clean up competition', Warden – The Neighbourhood Warden Team Newsletter, Office of the Deputy Prime Minister, Summer 2003, www.cleansafeworldwide.org/upload/public/attachments/3/warden_newsletter_summer03.pdf

...30 per cent rise in rubbish. 'On the bins', The Guardian, May 20, 2002

...In 1892, dust and cinders made up 80 per cent. ibid

...35 per cent of the weight and 50 per cent of the volume. ibid

...200,000 tonnes of extra waste. 'Farming & Food – a sustainable future', Policy Commission on the Future of Farming and Food Report, January 2002, www.soilassociation.org/web/sa/saweb.nsf/printable_library/NT00006536

...not degrade for around 450 years. 'Plastics Information Sheet', Waste Online, updated September 2004, www.wasteonline.org.uk/resources/InformationSheets/Plastics.htm

...about 40 per cent of the UK's contribution. 'Landfill gas bio-oxidation in active biofilters', Enviros Research, www.landfill-gas.com/html/research.html

...by climate change at $60 billion. '2003 climate havoc "cost $60bn"', BBC News Online, December 11, 2003, http://news.bbc.co.uk/1/hi/world/americas/3308959.stm

...within two kilometres of a landfill site. 'Study by the Small Area Health Statistics Unit on the health outcomes in populations living around landfill sites',

Department of Health, August 2001, www.advisorybodies.doh.gov.uk/cotnonfood/landfill.htm

...five million tonnes in the 1950s to around 100 million tonnes today. 'Plastics Information Sheet', Waste Online, updated September 2004, www.wasteonline.org.uk/resources/InformationSheets/Plastics.htm

...4.7million tonnes of plastic in 2001. ibid

...seven per cent was recycled. ibid

...eight per cent was incinerated and the remainder went to landfill. ibid

...stretches of coral reef in Jordan. 'Plastic Planet: The world has a big bag problem', The Guardian, October 17, 2002

...17.5 billion plastic bags a year. 'Wacky Waste Facts', Waste Online, 2004, www.wasteonline.org.uk/topic.aspx

...100 years to the one million years. 'Plastic Planet: The world has a big bag problem', The Guardian, October 17, 2002

...the Co-op was the first retailer. ibid

...250 million computers in the US. 'eCycling', US Environmental Protection Agency website, May 18, 2004, www.epa.gov/epaoswer/hazwaste/recycle/ecycling/

...three times faster. 'Electrical and Electronic Equipment', Waste online, September 2003, www.wasteonline.org.uk/resources/InformationSheets/ElectricalElectronic.htm

...four per cent of all municipal waste. ibid

...pollute 600,000 litres of water. 'Mobile industry to set up phone recycling system', The Guardian, September 25, 2002

...two million TV sets. 'Electrical and Electronic Equipment', Waste online, September 2003, www.wasteonline.org.uk/resources/InformationSheets/ElectricalElectronic.htm

...an estimated 500,000 of these TV sets. 'Dumped computers and TV sets sold illegally to developing world', The Guardian, June 30, 2004

...Fresh Kill site on Staten Island, New York. Woo R, 'Fresher Kills?', Metropolis Magazine, March 2002, www.metropolismag.com/html/content_0302/ob/ob03.html

...1.26 billion plastic bottles are discarded there every three weeks. Williams, J, Fifty Facts That Should Change the World, Icon Books, 2004

...18 more years of total landfill capacity left. ibid

...2.3 billion plastic bags. 'Putting an end to a plastic plague', Asia Times, August 17, 1999

...17 per cent less packaging. 'Rubbish Free by 2020', A Greenparty local elections briefing, April 2003, www.greenparty.org.uk/files/reports/2003/waste.htm

...facing a fine of up to   400. 'Down in the dumps', The Observer, January 25, 2004

...rates of over 45 per cent. ibid

...53 per cent of their waste due to strict policies. 'Scottish Green Party Manifesto', 2003, www.scottishgreens.org/policies/2003/waste.htm

...fined around 100 Swiss francs. ibid

...cutting use by 95 per cent. 'The wearing of the green', The Guardian, September 21, 2002

...'South Africa's national flower'. 'South Africa bans plastic bags', BBC News Online, May 9, 2003, http://news.bbc.co.uk/1/hi/world/africa/3013419.stm

...higher percentage of aluminium cans than any other country. 'Brazil pushes recycling to record level', Beverage World, July 7, 2004, www.beverageretailingsummit.com/beverageworld/headlines/article_display.jsp?vnu_content_id=1000564388

...25 per cent by 2005. 'Guidance on Municipal Waste Management Strategies', Department of the Environment, Transport and the Regions, March 2001, www.defra.gov.uk/environment/waste/management/guidance/mwms/pdf/mwms.pdf

...30 per cent by 2010. ibid

...33 per cent by 2015. ibid

...35 per cent by 2010. 'Legislation Affecting Waste', Waste Online, 2004, www.wasteonline.org.uk/resources/InformationSheets/Legislation.htm

...45 per cent by 2015. ibid

...Spotlight: Trash miles. 'Waste Movements', The Environment Agency, 2002, www.environment-agency.gov.uk; 'Row over £40m fridge "mountain"', BBC News Online, June 20, 2002, http://news.bbc.co.uk/1/hi/uk_politics/2055285.stm; 'Glass Recycling – Choose Your Colour', Sustainable Epsom website, www.sustainable-epsom.fsnet.co.uk/waste/glass.htm; 'Green Capital', Greater London Assembly, May 2003, www.london.gov.uk/gla/publications/environment/green_capital.rtf; 'Ashes to ashes: cruising rubbish is home after 16 years', The Guardian, July 18, 2002

...reusing and recyling 70 per cent. 'Creating Wealth from Waste', DEMOS report, 1999, www.demos.co.uk/creatingwealthfromwaste_pdf_media_public.aspx

...14.8 million Metric Tonnes of Carbon Equivalent a year. ibid

...a similar impact to taking 5.4 million cars off the road. ibid

...half of municipal waste is made up of just five products. 'Greenhouse Gas Emissions from Management of Selected Materials in Municipal Solid Waste', Environmental Protection Agency report, September 1998, http://yosemite.epa.gov/oar/globalwarming.nsf/uniquekeylookup/shsu5bumgj/$file/greengas.pdf

...quarter of greenhouse gas emissions could be cut. ibid

...rip plastic off products in supermarkets or post excess packaging back to retailers. 'Down in the Dumps', The Observer, January 25, 2003

...million tonnes of junk mail are binned in the UK every year. 'Junk the Junk Mail', Recycle Now, 2004, www.recyclenow.com/at_home/junk_mail.html:

...Amory Lovins is one of the main proponents of the 'materials revolution'. 'Natural Capitalism', Rocky Mountain Institute, 2003, www.natcap.org

...one that requires resources to be used 10–100 times more productively. ibid

...plastic drinks bottles as mini cloches to protect tender young plants from slugs. Scott N, Reduce, Reuse and Recycle, Green Books, 2004

...In 2001, Consumer Union magazine in the US repeated a 1997 survey. 'Fix It or Forget It', Consumer Union, October 2001, www.consumer.org

...Austria 64 per cent, Belgium at 52 per cent and 47 per cent for the Netherlands. 'EU recycling league table', European Environment Agency, 2002, www.eea.eu.int

...nine out of 10 householders would recycle more. 'Dismal Record Leaves Britain with a Rubbish Reputation', The Guardian, July 12, 2002

...66 per cent of recycling relied on householders. 'Household Waste Recycling', Municipal Waste Management Survey 2002/03, Defra, August 11,

2004, www.defra.gov.uk/environment/statistics/wastats/mwb0203/wbch02.htm

...850 grassroots groups recycled rubbish from more than 4.5 million homes. 'Cinderella army's green revolution', The Guardian, August 15, 2002

...over 60 per cent of our rubbish can be recycled. 'Bring Recycled Rubbish to Exeter High Street!', Recycle Devon online, June 25, 2003, www.recycledevon.org/pages/news_detail.asp?ID=12

...second-biggest ingredient in most bins. 'Analysis of household waste composition and factors driving waste increases', Waste Resources Action Programme, December 2002, www.wrap.org.uk

...over 98 tonnes of resources. Imhoff D, 'Thinking outside of the box', Whole Earth magazine, Winter 2002, www.wholeearthmag.com

...seven per cent of the average bin, largely derived from packaging. 'Analysis of household waste composition and factors driving waste increases', Waste Resources Action Programme, December 2002, www.wrap.org.uk

...360 million plastic bottles were recovered and recycled in 2002. Scott N, Reduce, Reuse and Recycle, Green Books, 2004

...drive towards single-use disposable packaging. 'Glass Recycling Information Sheet', Waste Online, October 2004, www.wasteonline.org.uk/resources/InformationSheets/Glass.htm

...glass recycling rate remains one of the lowest in Europe. 'Reduce, Reuse and Recycle', Friends of the earth, www.foe.co.uk/campaigns/waste/issues/reduce_reuse_recycle/index.html

...1.2 tonnes of raw materials are preserved. 'Glass Recycling Information Sheet', Waste Online, October 2004, www.wasteonline.org.uk/resources/InformationSheets/Glass.htm

...in road surfaces and, as 'green sand', to help filter tap water. 'Green virtues of sand', The Guardian, 23 October, 2003

...five billion drinks from aluminium cans. 'Aluminium Recycling', Waste Watch online, www.wasteonline.org.uk/resources/InformationSheets/Aluminum.htm

...42 per cent were recycled. ibid

...aluminium being the most valuable used packaging material. ibid

...12 million fewer full dustbins per year. ibid

...Spotlight: Is 'zero waste' possible? Scott N, Reduce, Reuse and Recycle, Green Books, 2004; 'Down in the dumps', The Observer, January 25, 2004; 'Measure your treasure', Community Recycling Network, 2004, www.crn.org.uk/myt/Infoforall/Formatted%20Measure%20Your%20Treasur1WEB.htm; 'Zero Waste', Greenpeace Environmental Trust, February 2002, www.greenpeace.org.uk/trust; 'Guidance on Municipal Waste Management Strategies', Department of the Environment, Transport and the Regions, March 2001, www.defra.gov.uk/environment/waste/management/guidance/mwms/pdf/mwms.pdf

...'upcycling' rather than just recycling. McDonough B & Braungart M, 'The Extravagant Gesture', Solutions for a Sustainable Planet, Beacon Press, 2002

...Dilemma: Incineration or Landfill? '2002/03 Municipal Waste Management Survey', Defra, August 17, 2004, www.defra.gov.uk/news/2004/040811d.htm; 'Tipping ban set to create toxic waste mountain', The Guardian, May 26, 2003; 'Beyond Recycling: Zero Waste', No-Incinerator website, www.no-incinerator.org.uk/Beyond%20Recycling.htm; 'Incineration Campaign Homepage', Greenpeace, 2002,

www.greenpeace.org.uk; 'FOE calls for pollution cuts and no new incinerators', Friends of the Earth press release, November 16, 2001, www.foe.co.uk/resource/press_releases/20011116111918.html; 'The Problem With Incineration', Greenpeace, May 14, 2002, www.greenpeace.org.uk

Chapter 3: Travel

...jet contrails leading into Heathrow and Gatwick. 'British astronaut spots homeland from space', BBC News Online, October 14, 2002, http://news.bbc.co.uk/1/hi/sci/tech/2326349.stm

...largest source of greenhouse emissions by 2020. McCarthy D, Saving the Planet Without Costing the Earth, Fusion Press, 2004

...half the population flies at least once a year. 'The Future of Transport – White Paper CM 6234', Department for Transport, July 2004, www.dft.gov.uk/stellent/groups/dft_about/documents/divisionhomepage/031259.hcsp

...how far the average Briton travels each year. 'Revised National Travel Survey Data for Urban and Rural Areas: Key Points', Department for Transport, December 2002, www.dft.gov.uk/stellent/groups/dft_transstats/documents/page/dft_transstats_507678.pdf

...motoring is actually now cheaper. 'Road-User Charging', Friends of the Earth, July 2004, www.foe.co.uk/resource/media_briefing/road_user_charging.pdf

...over 80 per cent and bus fares over 70 per cent. 'Oil prices, fuel tax and climate change', Friends of the Earth, June 2004, www.foe.co.uk/resource/briefings/oil_prices_fuel_tax.pdf

...84 per cent of cars engaged in commuting. 'Revised National Travel Survey Data for Urban and Rural Areas: Key Points', Department for Transport, December 2002, www.dft.gov.uk/stellent/groups/dft_transstats/documents/page/dft_transstats_507678.pdf

...27 per cent of UK carbon dioxide emissions. 'Oil prices, fuel tax and climate change', Friends of the Earth, June 2004, www.foe.co.uk/resource/briefings/oil_prices_fuel_tax.pdf

...a 50 per cent rise in just over a decade. 'Driving into the abyss', The Guardian, July 6, 2004

...a third of the world's 776 million vehicles. McCarthy D, Saving the Planet Without Costing the Earth, Fusion Press, 2004

...now emit so much CO2. 'Driving Up the Heat: SUVs and Global Warming', Sierra Club, www.sierraclub.org/globalwarming/suvreport/pollution.asp

...20 million barrels of oil the US uses a day. 'Evolution of a hydrogen revolution', The Guardian, May 10, 2004

...efficiency of US vehicles by just 2.7 miles per gallon. 'How to Get Real Security', Whole Earth, 109, Fall 2002, www.wholeearth.com; also see Lovins A et al, Natural Capitalism: The Next Industrial Revolution, Earthscan, 2000

...consumes just five million barrels of oil a day. 'Evolution of a hydrogen revolution', The Guardian, May 10, 2004

...the US population currently stands at 294 million. 'US and World Population Clocks', US Census Bureau, October 4, 2004, www.census.gov/main/www/popclock.html

...six per cent of the world's population. 'A good life: Transport', The Guardian, April 15, 2004

...greater effect on the environment than any other

choice. 'Buying a Greener Vehicle: Electric, Hybrids, and Fuel Cells', Union of Concerned Scientists, June 30, 2003, www.ucsusa.org/clean_vehicles/advanced_vehicles/page.cfm?pageID=213

...19 per cent reduction in carbon emissions. 'Oil prices, fuel tax and climate change', Friends of the Earth, June 2004, www.foe.co.uk/resource/briefings/oil_prices_fuel_tax.pdf

...failed to attract the predicted number of users. 'Calls to reduce M6 toll road fee', BBC News Online, May 9, 2004, http://news.bbc.co.uk/1/hi/england/west_midlands/3696979.stm

...560 come from cars, and just seven from buses and coaches. 'A good life: Transport', The Guardian, April 15, 2004

...road congestion grew by 73 per cent. ibid

...up to 24,000 early deaths a year. 'Reducing the environmental impacts of road and air transport: Position Statement', Environment Agency, www.environment-agency.gov.uk/aboutus/512398/289428/655143/?version=1&lang=_e

...3,508 people were killed on our roads. 'Think inside the box', The Guardian, July 27, 2004

...a quarter of the environmental pollution. 'A good life: Transport', The Guardian, April 15, 2004

...the true cost of keeping a car in the UK. ibid

...28 per cent of households in the UK. 'Revised National Travel Survey Data for Urban and Rural Areas: Key Points', Department for Transport, December 2002, www.dft.gov.uk/stellent/groups/dft_transstats/documents/page/dft_transstats_507678.pdf

...31 million motorists and 50,000 commercial vehicle operators. 'Take two: Making the car a star', The Guardian, May 29, 2004

...eight million cars were produced worldwide. The Worldwatch Institute, Vital Signs 2003, NW Norton

...a car will produce roughly its own weight in CO2 emissions. 'Driven to Destruction', Ethical Consumer, EC83, June/July 2003, www.ethicalconsumer.org

...about 75 per cent of a car is recycled. ibid

...Asthma rates in the UK have increased fourfold. McCarthy D, Saving the Planet Without Costing the Earth, Fusion Press, 2004

...over a third of car journeys are less than two miles in distance. ibid

...weigh six pounds (2.7kg) more than those living in the city centres. Honore C, In Praise of Slow, Orion, 2004

...some 2.8 billion gallons of ethanol are now produced each year. 'Green grows the future fuel', The Guardian, February 19, 2004

...Spotlight: As cheap as chip oil. 'Chicken fat to power lorries', The Guardian, October 29, 2002; 'Police impound cars run on cooking oil', BBC News Online, http://news.bbc.co.uk/1/hi/wales/2312521.stm; author conversation with Asda's environmental manager, October 2004

...Road hogs. 'Driven to Destruction', Ethical Consumer, EC83, June/July 2003; 'SUVs: Danger on the Road', The SUV info link, www.suv.org/newsarticle.html; 'Driving Up the Heat: SUVs and Global Warming', Sierra Club, www.sierraclub.org/globalwarming/suvreport/pollution.asp; 'Driving into the abyss', The Guardian, July 6, 2004; Roberts P, The End of Oil, Bloomsbury, 2004

...70 per cent of people went to work by car. 'Driven to Destruction', Ethical Consumer, EC83, June/July 2003, www.ethicalconsumer.org

...average car cost totalling £71.59 per week. 'How to Cut Your Car Use', Semlyen Net, www.semlyen.net/transport/carfree.htm

...walking to school has declined from 62 to 54 per cent. 'Revised National Travel Survey Data for Urban and Rural Areas: Key Points', Department for Transport, December 2002, www.dft.gov.uk/stellent/groups/dft_transstats/documents/page/dft_transstats_507678.pdf

...cycling in London rose by 23 per cent. 'Cyclist numbers soar to record high', Transport for London, July 22, 2004, www.transportforlondon.gov.uk/tfl/press-releases/2004/july/press-PN1117.shtml

...22 million bicycles in the UK. 'Bikes and trains: Good practice in Britain and abroad', Transport 2000, www.transport2000.org.uk/goodpractice/BikesTrains.htm

...cycling is the fastest mode of transport. 'Cyclist numbers soar to record high', Transport for London, July 22, 2004, www.transportforlondon.gov.uk/tfl/press-releases/2004/july/press-PN1117.shtml

...four times more air pollution than pedestrians or cyclists. 'On your bikes, get set, go!', Transport for London, June 8, 2004, www.transportforlondon.gov.uk/tfl/press-releases/2004/june/press-1051.shtml

...live within six minutes' walk of a bus stop. 'Revised National Travel Survey Data for Urban and Rural Areas: Key Points', Department for Transport, December 2002, www.dft.gov.uk/stellent/groups/dft_transstats/documents/page/dft_transstats_507678.pdf

...(3F) rise in the average global temperature. Roberts P, The End of Oil, Bloomsbury, 2004

...has increased by 31 per cent. 'Activists' briefings: Climate change', Transport 2000, www.transport2000.org.uk/activistbriefings/ClimateChange.htm

...CO2 emissions have risen from 100 million tons. Roberts P, The End of Oil, Bloomsbury, 2004

...higher than they have been for 20 million years. 'Activists' briefings: Climate change', Transport 2000, www.transport2000.org.uk/activistbriefings/ClimateChange.htm

...4C (7F) by 2050 and 6C (10F) by 2100. Roberts P, The End of Oil, Bloomsbury, 2004

...80 million malaria cases a year. ibid

...by 2050 two billion people. 'Flood risk to 2bn by 2050, says study', The Guardian, June 14, 2004

...a quarter of land animals and plants into extinction. 'Under threat: An unnatural disaster', The Guardian, January 8, 2004

...21,000 deaths in Europe. 'Never mind the weather overkill', The Guardian, May 13, 2004

...known as the 'Oregon Petition'. 'Activists' briefings: Climate change', Transport 2000, www.transport2000.org.uk/activistbriefings/ClimateChange.htm

...[Global warming] is undoubtedly due in large part. 'Beyond Kyoto', Foreign Affairs, 83:4, July/August, 2004, www.foreignaffairs.org

...at 'dangerous' levels. Roberts P, The End of Oil, Bloomsbury, 2004

...270 parts per million (ppm) of CO2. ibid

...climate change is the most severe problem. 'Top scientist attacks US over global warming', The Guardian, January 9, 2004

...1.2 tonnes of carbon a year. Roberts P, The End of Oil, Bloomsbury, 2004

...'Sequestration is difficult'. 'I'm really very worried for the planet', The Guardian, June 17, 2004

...15 per cent of Americans. 'Careful with that planet, Mr President', The Guardian, February 19, 2004

...400,000 of us will be flying in 3,500 planes. 'Safety warning as Europe's skies come close to saturation point', The Guardian, May 17, 2004

...half the population of the UK. 'The Future of Transport – White Paper CM 6234', Department of Transport, July 2004, www.dft.gov.uk/stellent/groups/dft_about/documents/divisionhomepage/031259.hcsp

...three-quarters of this air traffic. 'The sky's the limit: policies for sustainable aviation', Institute for Public Policy Research report, 2003, www.ippr.org

...by 2050 it is predicted that our airports will need to serve. 'The Environmental Effects of Civil Aircraft in Flight', Royal Commission on Environmental Pollution report, November 29, 2002, www.rcep.org.uk/aviation.htm

...five new Heathrows by 2030. 'Parliamentary Briefing No. 1', Airport Watch, Autumn 2002, www.airportwatch.org.uk/publications/mpbriefingb.pdf

...skies could be 'full' in just over a decade. 'Safety warning as Europe's skies come close to saturation point', The Guardian, May 17, 2004

...four near misses in April 2004. ibid

...500 routes across the continent. 'Market Analysis of Europe's Low Cost Airlines', Air Transport Group, Cranfield University, Report 9, January 2004 (second edition), www.cranfield.ac.uk/soe/airtransport

...half of all flights for that year were made by a mere 11.3 per cent. 'Parliamentary Briefing No. 1', Airport Watch, Autumn 2002, www.airportwatch.org.uk/publications/mpbriefingb.pdf

...people earning over £30,000 per year. 'Attitudes Towards Air Travel', Mori (on behalf of the Freedom to Fly Coalition), January 12, 2001, www.mori.com/polls/2001/freedomtofly.shtml

...EU and UK public money. 'Aviation: the social, economic and environmental impact of flying', Ashden Trust, 2000, www.scan-uk.mmu.ac.uk/whitelegg.pdf

...is paying an extra £557 a year. 'It's the economy, stupid!', HACAN ClearSkies, February 2003, www.hacan.org.uk/learn/HACANfulleconomicsreport.htm

...flight from London to Miami. 'Landing us in it', The Guardian, December 6, 2003

...5.5 per cent of the UK's climate-changing emissions. 'The Future of Transport – White Paper CM 6234', Department of Transport, July 20, 2004, www.dft.gov.uk/stellent/groups/dft_about/documents/divisionhomepage/031259.hcsp

...actually the equivalent of 11 per cent. ibid

...one million people in the UK. 'The Hidden Cost of Flying', Aviation Environment Federation, February 2003, www.airportwatch.org.uk/publications/Hidden%20Cost%20Final.pdf

...with 558 seats, and a wingspan 15 metres larger. 'Airbus sings £3.7 billion deal', The Guardian, July 20, 2004

...in the 1950s there were around 25 million. 'Green Tragedy', Resurgence, 212, May/June 2002, http://resurgence.gn.apc.org/issues/lord212.htm

...in Hawaii and Barbados, for example, one study found. 'The Politics of Travel', The Nation, October 8, 1997, www.thenation.com; or full article: www.emily.net/~schiller/pol_trvl.html

...half of their annual 'share' of the earth's natural resources. 'Holidays abroad needn't cost the Earth', WWF, March 27, 2002, www.wwf-uk.org/news/n_0000000538.asp

...by 2003 the tax was so unpopular. 'Balearics defend scrapping eco tax', The Guardian, July 19, 2003; 'Tourist tax spreads its wings', The Guardian, May 11, 2003

...the average UK family spends £1,830. 'British Family Holidays', Daily Research News Online, July 14, 2004, www.mrweb.com/drno/frmemail/article3262.htm

...20 million Britons taking them each year. 'Real Lives: 14 nts fully inc £219. Free bar, sunburn, foam parties. Sex: optional extra', Observer Magazine, July 25, 2004

...Four out of 10 UK families. 'Check out supermarkets', Travel Trade Gazette, June 18, 2004, www.ttglive.com/NArticleDetails.asp?aid=1030

...critics claim depressed prices. Shaw G & Williams A M, Critical Issues in Tourism: A Geographical Perspective, Blackwell, 2001

...only 22 to 50 per cent of gross revenue. ibid

...in 2003 revenue from British tourists. 'Annual Cruise Review 2003', Cruise Information Service, 2004, www.discover-cruises.co.uk/pdf/acr2003.pdf

...250 cruise liners now carry 12 million passengers. 'Cruise ships must clean up their act', The Observer, March 28, 2004

...emits 30,000 gallons (136,500 litres) of sewage. 'Cruise Ships: Impacts on the Island of Molokai', Earthjustice, www.earthjustice.org/factsheets/Cruiseships_041803.pdf

...no less than three nautical miles. 'International Convention for the Prevention of Pollution from Ships, 1973, as modified by the Protocol of 1978 relating thereto (MARPOL 73/78)', International Maritime Organisation, www.imo.org/Conventions/contents.asp?doc_id=678&topic_id=258

...72 per cent of all cruises. 'Annual Cruise Review 2003', Cruise Information Service, 2004, www.discover-cruises.co.uk/pdf/acr2003.pdf

...less than one US dollar a day. 'The Maldives: Lost in Paradise', Tourism Concern, www.tourismconcern.org.uk/campaigns/the-maldives.html

...30 per cent of Maldivian children under five. ibid

...Dilemma: Are second homes a selfish luxury or a harmless retreat? 'One million Britons own second homes', The Guardian, February 3, 2001; 'Second homes market doubles in six years', The Guardian, March 8, 2004; 'Second home ban "illegal"', BBC News Online, September 6, 2001, http://news.bbc.co.uk/1/hi/uk/1528320.stm; 'Anger grows over second homes', BBC News Online, October 27, 2003, http://news.bbc.co.uk/1/hi/england/cornwall/3216823.stm; 'Holiday homes causing resentment', BBC News Online feature, December 23, 2003, www.bbc.co.uk/devon/news_features/2003/housing_second_homes.shtml; 'A Poor Deal', HACAN ClearSkies pamphlet, April 26, 2003, www.stopstanstedexpansion.com/documents/Aviation_Equity.doc; 'Britons swamp Spanish property market' The Guardian, July 14, 2004

...basic tenets of ecotourism. 'What is Ecotourism', The International Ecotourism Society, www.ecotourism.org/index2.php?what-is-ecotourism

...called for 'rebellious tourists and rebellious locals'. Krippendorf J, The Holiday Makers, Butterworth-Heinemann, 1999

...'hard end' and 'soft end' ecotourists. 'Ecotourism as Mass Tourism: Contradiction or Reality?', Center for Hospitality Research, Cornell University, 2001, www.hotelschool.cornell.edu/chr/pdf/showpdf/publications/hraq/feature/pdf/420401a.pdf

...$170 to spend an hour with gorillas in Rwanda. 'Eco-tourism: Encouraging Conservation or Adding to Exploitation?', Population Reference Bureau, April 2001, www.prb.org/Template.cfm?Section=PRB&template=/ContentManagement/ContentDisplay.cfm&ContentID=5948

...Kenyan lion is worth an estimated $7,000. 'The Politics of Travel', The Nation, October 8, 1997, www.thenation.com; or full article: www.emily.net/~schiller/pol_trvl.html

...David Nicholson-Lord once heard a casino in Laos. 'Green Tragedy', Resurgence, 212, May/June 2002, http://resurgence.gn.apc.org/issues/lord212.htm

...in Burma, thousands of people were forcibly relocated. Mann M, The Good Alternative Travel Guide, Earthscan, 2002

...seven per cent of global tourism. 'Eco-tourism: Encouraging Conservation or Adding to Exploitation?', Population Reference Bureau, April 2001, www.prb.org/Template.cfm?Section=PRB&template=/ContentManagement/ContentDisplay.cfm&ContentID=5948

...85 per cent of German tourists. 'The Politics of Travel', The Nation, October 8, 1997, www.thenation.com; or full article: www.emily.net/~schiller/pol_trvl.html

...cable car to carry 350,00 'ecotourists'. 'Green Tragedy', Resurgence, 212, May/June 2002, http://resurgence.gn.apc.org/issues/lord212.htm

...Spotlight: 'Carbon Neutral'. 'Flying with cleaner air in mind', CNN.com, June 4, 2004, www.cnn.com/2004/TRAVEL/06/03/bt.clean.travel/; www.sinkswatch.org; www.futureforests.com

...1998 was the first year that more Britons went abroad. Mann M, The Good Alternative Travel Guide, Earthscan, 2002

...stay in the 'honey pots'. 'Parliamentary Briefing No. 1', Airport Watch, Autumn 2002, www.airportwatch.org.uk/publications/mpbriefingb.pdf

...average tourist uses as much water in 24 hours. 'A good life: Holidays', The Guardian, March 11, 2004

...five million tonnes of CO2 emissions. ibid

...the 700,000 annual visitors to South Africa's. 'Ecotourism as Mass Tourism: Contradiction or Reality?', Center for Hospitality Research, Cornell University, 2001, www.hotelschool.cornell.edu/chr/pdf/showpdf/publications/hraq/feature/pdf/420401a.pdf

...follow Tourism Concern's traveller tips. 'A good life: Holidays', The Guardian, March 11, 2004

Chapter 4: You

...in 150 milliseconds. 'The skin we're in', The Observer, October 26, 2004

...the Alternative Census report. 'The new Yellow Pages', The Guardian, August 3, 2004

...a report by Virgin Money. 'When there's no real alternative', The Guardian, December 16, 2003

...about 20 per cent of Britons. ibid

...in the past five years, for example, nail bars. 'Flight from reality', The Guardian, August 16, 2003

...the number of cosmetic procedures carried out in the US. ibid

...increasingly common among US teenagers. 'Ops are on the up for children of the plastic generation', The Daily Mail, April 19, 2004

...an Observer/ICM survey. 'The uncovered poll', The Observer, October 26, 2003 (Part of 'Body Uncovered', http://observer.guardian.co.uk/bodyuncovered)

...second most common illness. 'Health Awareness Campaigns', BBC Online, www.bbc.co.uk/health/awareness/herbal.shtml

...more than 500 under-16s. 'Ops are on the up for children of the plastic generation', The Daily Mail, April 19, 2004

...MA course in medical ethics. 'Postgraduate Prospectus 2005 Entry: MA Medical Ethics & Law', King's College London, www.kcl.ac.uk/pgp04/programme/149

...'I will maintain the utmost respect for human life'. 'World Medical Association International Code of Medical Ethics', World Medical Association, www.wma.net/e/policy/c8.htm

...in 2004, scientists were finally given permission. 'HFEA grants the first therapeutic cloning licence for research', Human Fertilisation and Embryology Authority, August 11, 2004, www.hfea.gov.uk/PressOffice/Archive/1092233888

...government body made up of 18 people. 'HFEA Members', Human Fertilisation and Embryology Authority, www.hfea.gov.uk/AboutHFEA/HFEAMembers

...over a quarter of us in the UK. 'If the drugs don't work...', The Guardian, March 2, 2004

...400 different techniques fall under this umbrella. ibid

...one per cent of UK medical research budgets. ibid

...34 per cent of 13-14-year-olds. 'We have become allergic to our western way of life', The Guardian, February 28, 2004

...increased two- to threefold. ibid

...80 per cent of our time sedentary. ibid

...by 2015 every second Briton will suffer. ibid

...'There is no convincing evidence that acupuncture'. 'If the drugs don't work...', The Guardian, March 2, 2004

...a clinical trial recently showed arnica does nothing. 'If the arnica pills don't work: do any other homeopathic remedies work?', The Guardian, February 4, 2003

...only two of the eight most popular therapies. 'When there's no real alternative', The Guardian, December 16, 2003

...the herb Ma Huang. 'Traditional Medicine', World Health Organisation, revised May 2003, www.who.int/mediacentre/factsheets/fs134/en/

...Spotlight: 'Big Pharma'. 'Big Pharma: The Facts', New Internationalist, 362, November 2003, www.newint.org/issue362/facts.htm; 'Drug industry stalks the US corridors of power', The Guardian, February 13, 2001; 'The great health grab', New Internationalist, 362, November 2003, www.newint.org/issue362/keynote.htm; 'Bad medicine', The Guardian, June 12, 2004

...'It is morally acceptable for human beings to use other animals'. 'Animals in Scientific Procedures Committee Report', House of Lords, July 16, 2002, www.publications.parliament.uk/pa/ld200102/ldselect/ldanimal/150/15001.htm

...to deliberately exploit, torture and kill another sentient creature. 'End Vivisection', Uncaged Campaigns, www.uncaged.co.uk

...according to the most recent Home Office statistics. 'Annual Statistics, Animals in Scientific Procedures, version 1.4.2', Home Office, September 7, 2004, www.homeoffice.gov.uk/docs/animalstats.html

...100 million animals are used in testing. 'Animal testing – the facts and the figures', The Independent, July 30, 2004

...two mice and half a rat. 'Research Using Animals', Coalition for Medical Progress, www.medicalprogress.org

...94 per cent of licences granted for animal testing. 'Mice and Medicine: Animal experiments, medical advances and the MRC', Medical Research Council, www.mrc.ac.uk/pdf-mice_and_medicine.pdf

...an anaesthetic is used in about 40 per cent of tests. 'Annual Statistics, Animals in Scientific Procedures, version 1.4.2', Home Office, September 7, 2004, www.homeoffice.gov.uk/docs/animalstats.html

...27 per cent of all tests. ibid

...less than 10 per cent of medical research uses animals. 'Animal testing – the facts and the figures', The Independent, July 30, 2004

...goats were used to test the effects of decompression. 'Sixth Report of the Animal Welfare Advisory Committee', Ministry of Defence, February 2002, www.mod.uk/linked_files/awac_6th_rpt.pdf

...The government allocates about £300,000. 'The hunt for another way', The Guardian, 26 February, 2004

...£50 million or so spent each year. ibid

...Xenogen, has created a GM mouse. ibid

...£6 billion on personal care. 'Particles of Faith', The Guardian, May 8, 2004

...used at least six products. 'The European Cosmetic Toiletry and Perfumery Association', Colipa, www.colipa.com/home.html

...100 different synthetic chemicals. 'Chemical World Part 1: Health and Beauty', supplement front cover, The Guardian, May 8, 2004

...85 per cent of petroleum. 'Cradle-to-Cradle Stewardship of Drugs for Minimizing Their Environmental Disposition While Promoting Human Health – Part I: Rationale for and Avenues toward a Green Pharmacy', Environmental Health Perspectives, volume 111, number 5, May 2003, http://ehp.niehs.nih.gov/members/2003/5947/5947.html

...over 9,000 ingredients are now available. 'Lip service', The Guardian, May 8, 2004

...1,000 of these are suspected. Antczak S & Antczak G, Cosmetics Unmasked, Thorsons, HarperCollins, 2001

...Triclosan has been detected in human breastmilk and fish. 'New Warning on Triclosan Threat', Friends of the Earth, September 23, 2003, www.foe.co.uk/resource/press_releases/new_warning_on_triclosan_t.html

...dental decay remains a largely social problem. 'Tooth decay worst among children in the north', The Guardian, August 31, 2001

...'antibacterial hand soaps, when properly used'. 'Proper Perspective Needed on Antibacterial Studies', Joint Statement – The Soap and Detergent Association and the Cosmetic, Toiletry, and Fragrance Association, October 23, 2002, www.ctfa.org/Template.cfm?Section=Antibacterials&template=/ContentManagement/ContentDisplay.cfm&ContentID=447

...agencies in Sweden, Denmark, Finland and Germany. 'New Warning on Triclosan Threat', Friends of the Earth, September 23, 2003, www.foe.co.uk/resource/press_releases/new_warning_on_triclosan_t.html

...disposable facial wipes passed the $2 billion mark. 'Wipes make a clean sweep', Euromonitor International, March 11, 2004, www.euromonitor.com/article.asp?id=2768

...'Use razor blades or an electric razor'. 'Shopping for Household Items (Waste Minimisation)', North Lincolnshire Council, www.northlincs.gov.uk/NorthLincs/Environment/waste/WasteMinimisation/Shoppingforhouseholditems.htm

...In 1999 thousands of people received a scare email. 'Under arm tactics', The Guardian, May 8, 2004

...Studies by Reading University in 2003. ibid

...In the course of this research, parabens. ibid

...all these highly nutritious ingredients. Antczak S & Antczak G, Cosmetics Unmasked, Thorsons, HarperCollins, 2001

...Spotlight: Gym Culture. 'Gym goers on the increase', The Mirror, June 4, 2003; 'Mixed Fortunes Re-Shape the Fitness Industry', Fitness Industry Association, March 2004, www.fia.org.uk/FIA_Trade_Releases-89.htm; 'Health – Third Report', Select Committee on Health: House of Commons, May 10, 2004, www.parliament.the-stationery-office.co.uk/pa/cm200304/cmselect/cmhealth/23/2302.htm; 'Work it out', The Observer, August 1, 2004; 'Back to Nature', The Guardian, September 22, 2001; 'Well-Being Comes Naturally... Evaluation of the Portslade Green Gym', Oxford Centre for Health Care Research and Development, Oxford Brookes University, 2001, www.btcv.org/greengym/health/psresearch.html

...Ninety-three per cent of British women use cosmetics. 'Ending the Cosmetics Cover-Up: Cosmetics facts', Women's Environmental Network, www.wen.org.uk/cosmetics/facts.htm

...studies in the US at Stanford University. Kilbourne J, Deadly Persuasion: Why Women and Girls Must Fight the Addictive Power of Advertising, Simon & Schuster Adult Publishing Group, 1999

...the RSPCA estimated that 38,000 animals. 'Getting Lippy: Cosmetics, toiletries and the environment', Women's Environmental Network, December 2003, www.wen.org.uk/cosmetics/reports/cosmetics_norefs.pdf

...not due to be completely phased out until 2013. 'Cosmetics tested on animals to be banned', The Guardian, November 8, 2002

...50 per cent of the cost of a bottle. 'Ending the Cosmetics Cover-Up: Cosmetics facts', Women's Environmental Network, www.wen.org.uk/cosmetics/facts.htm

...average woman also gets through 2,000 cotton wool balls. 'Why is it important to use environmentally friendly cosmetic products?', WorldwideHealth.com, www.worldwidehealth.com/Library/article.php/ltp20040705.html

...Spotlight: The 'Adonis Complex'. 'Muscle mania', The Guardian, July 21, 2001; 'The uncovered poll', The Observer, October 26, 2001; Pope HG, Phillips K & Olivardia R, The Adonis Complex: The Secret Crisis of Male Body Obsession, Simon & Schuster, 2002; 'From gym to club to school: the shock spread of steroid abuse', The Guardian, November 14, 2003

...(81 per cent of women) actually ingests about 1kg of lipstick. 'Getting Lippy: Cosmetics, toiletries and the environment', Women's Environmental Network, December 2003, www.wen.org.uk/cosmetics/reports/cosmetics_norefs.pdf

...60 per cent of US women. 'Daily ritual is going down the drain', The Wall Street Journal, January 6, 2003

...arylamines. 'Genetic connection in link between permanent hair dye use and bladder cancer risk', University of Southern California, April 9, 2002, www.eurekalert.org/pub_releases/2002-04/uosc-gci040802.php

...'ultimately consumers do not expect to understand'. 'Making Sense of Risk', The Cosmetic Toiletry and Perfumery Association, March 2004, www.cosmeticweb.co.za/pebble.asp?relid=8102

...£32 million was spent in the UK on advertising. 'Getting Lippy: Cosmetics, toiletries and the environment', Women's Environmental Network, December 2003, www.wen.org.uk/cosmetics/reports/cosmetics_norefs.pdf

...'anything which says it can magically take away your wrinkles'. 'The Truth about Cosmetics', Cosmetics Unmasked, January 3, 2002, www.gina.antczak.btinternet.co.uk/CU/COSMET.HTM

...18 per cent over a four-week period. 'AHAs and UV Sensitivity: Results of New FDA-Sponsored Studies',

Center for Food Safety and Applied Nutrition, March 7, 2000, www.cfsan.fda.gov/~dms/cosahauv.html

...these nanoparticles are used. 'Particles of Faith', The Guardian, May 8, 2004

...but the worry, according to some toxicologists. ibid

...'Ever more precisely marketed products'. James O, 'Consuming Misery', The Ecologist, May 2004, www.theecologist.org/archive_article.html?article=196&category=46

...the price of clothes and shoes has plummeted. Schor J B & Taylor B (eds), Sustainable Planet: Solutions for the Twenty-First Century, Beacon Press, 2002

...from 1999 onwards the drop in prices. ibid

...according to the sociologist Juliet B Schor. Schor J B & Taylor B (eds), Sustainable Planet: Solutions for the Twenty-First Century, Beacon Press, 2002

...10–20 per cent of charitable clothes donations. 'Clothes line', The Guardian, February 25, 2004

...140 textile manufacturers in Zambia. 'Cast-off UK clothes make Zambia poor', The Observer, May 23, 2004

....25 per cent of world pesticide use. 'Environmental impacts of clothing', Ethical Consumer, EC50, December 1997, www.ethicalconsumer.org/magazine/buyers/clothes97/clothingenvironment.htm

...more than three million people worldwide are victims of pesticide poisoning. Walker MJ, 'Home Sickness', The Ecologist, May 2001, www.theecologist.org/archive_article.html?article=126

...20,000 litres of water are needed to produce just one T-shirt. 'The Aral Sea in Central Asia is Drying Out', WWF, www.wwf.ch/images/progneut/upload/ARAL_SEA.pdf

...a quarter of their weight as air pollution. Schor J B & Taylor B (eds) Sustainable Planet: Solutions for the Twenty-First Century, Beacon Press, 2002

...estimated 50 per cent of all nitrous oxide emissions. 'Environmental impacts of clothing', Ethical Consumer, EC50, December 1997, www.ethicalconsumer.org/magazine/buyers/clothes97/clothingenvironment.htm

...azo dyes have not been banned in the UK. 'Still Dirty: A Review of Action Against Toxic Products in Europe', WWF-UK, March 2004, www.wwf.org.uk/filelibrary/pdf/stilldirty.pdf

...declared carcinogenic by the European Commission. 'Commission bans dangerous textile colourings to protect the aquatic environment', Europa, January 7, 2003, http://europa.eu.int/rapid/pressReleasesAction.do?reference=IP/03/11&format=HTML&aged=0&language=EN&guiLanguage=en

...a sweatshop is defined. 'The Garment Industry', Sweatshop Watch, www.sweatshopwatch.org/swatch/industry

...170,000 workers in the UK. 'Who we are', No Sweat, www.nosweat.org.uk/files/leaflets/No_Sweat_leaflet.pdf

...Spotlight: Jewellery's hidden cost. 'Economic causes of civil war and their implications for policy', World Bank, June 15, 2000, www-wds.worldbank.org/servlet/WDS_IBank_Servlet?pcont=details&eid=000265513_20040310161100; 'Diamonds in the Rough', New Internationalist, 367, May 2004, www.newint.org/issue367/diamonds.htm; Roberts J, Glitter & Greed: The Secret World of the Diamond Cartel, The Disinformation Company Ltd, 2003; 'Dying for De Beers', The Ecologist, volume 33, number 7, September 2003

...In 1992, less than one per cent of the world's population. 'Good Stuff? A Behind-the-Scenes Guide to the Things We Buy: Cell Phones', Worldwatch Institute online guide, 2004, www.worldwatch.org/pubs/goodstuff/cellphones

...over 50 million mobiles in the UK. 'The Green consumer: mobile phones', The Guardian, August 28, 2004

...by 2015 some four billion people. 'Dialling the globe', The Guardian, February 26, 2004

...no compelling evidence has been published. 'Mobile phones safety fears', The Guardian, January 25, 2002

...of reducing their sperm count by as much as 30 per cent. 'Mobiles cut sperm count, says report', The Guardian, June 28, 2004

...typically discarded after just 18 months. 'Good Stuff? A Behind-the-Scenes Guide to the Things We Buy: Cell Phones', Worldwatch Institute online guide, 2004, www.worldwatch.org/pubs/goodstuff/cellphones

...will total 500 million. ibid

...discarding 100 million phones a year by 2005. 'Why recycle your old mobile phone?', Greener Solutions website, www.greenersolutions.de/fs_e.html

...by August 13, 2005, electronics manufacturers will be required. Environment Agency website, www.environment-agency.gov.uk/netregs/legislation/380525/473094/?lang=_e

...one in 10 drivers admitting. 'Drivers flout mobile phone law', The Guardian, March 8, 2004

...the US National Highway Traffic Safety Administration said. 'Drive, don't phone', The Guardian, July 26, 2004

...a study in 2004 by the University of Utah. ibid

...According to the mobile phone consultancy Mobile Youth. 'Generation text', The Guardian, June 24, 2004

...at least 20 per cent of primary school children. ibid

...a third of all 5–9-year-olds. ibid

...children are five times more likely to be targeted than adults. 'Mugging victims in battle on crime', Transport for London website, http://tube.tfl.gov.uk/content/metro/02/0206/27/

...the average monthly bill of an adult using a contract phone. 'Mobile users ring up rising bills', The Guardian, May 27, 2004

...80 per cent of the world's coltan. 'Mobile phones "fuel gorillas" plight', BBC News Online, June 11, 2002, http://news.bbc.co.uk/1/hi/sci/tech/2036217.stm

...coltan rocketed from $65 to $600 a kilogram. ibid

Chapter 5: Family

...37 per cent of Europe's population lived as part of a nuclear family. 'Single households set to soar', The Guardian, November 27, 2002

...there are 21,660,475 households in England and Wales. 'Census 2001: Households Report', National Statistics Online, May 7, 2003, www.statistics.gov.uk/cci/nugget.asp?id=350

...Half of these one-person households are occupied by pensioners. ibid

...number of people living in a household in the UK is shrinking. 'Living in Britain: Results from the 2002 General Household Survey', Office of National Statistics, April 2004, www.statistics.gov.uk/downloads/theme_compendia/lib2002.pdf

...declined from 31 per cent in 1979. ibid

...Lone-parent families have grown. ibid

...Two-thirds of mothers are now returning to work. 'Facts & Figures on Family Life', Parentline Plus, December 2001, www.parentlineplus.org.uk/fileadmin/parentline/downloads/Publications/family-life/facts-and-figures.pdf

...average age of first marriage is rising. ibid; 'Average age at marriage and divorce: Social Trends 34', Table 2.12, National Statistics Online, www.statistics.gov.uk/STATBASE/ssdataset.asp?vlnk=7264

...Real incomes have quadrupled. 'Bringing reality to the dream – the myth of decline', The Future Foundation, March 2004, www.futurefoundation.net

...average life expectancy is rising. 'Better home care urged for terminally ill', The Guardian, July 23, 2004

...children made up 20 per cent of the population. 'Beanpole families sprout social change', The Guardian, January 30, 2003

...number of 'lonely and isolated' older people in the UK will grow. 'Older people face a lonely future, thinktank warns', The Guardian, June 30, 2004

...what government statisticians are calling 'beanpole' families. 'Beanpole families sprout social change', The Guardian, January 30, 2003

...spend just 126 minutes awake in each other's company. 'Couples spend just two hours together a day', The Guardian, July 16, 2004

...77 per cent of children. 'Keep out: TV, DVD and computers rule', The Daily Telegraph, August 13, 2004

...three out of five 11–14-year-olds. ibid

...the average household now has three different types of shampoo. Willmott M & Nelson W, Complicated Lives, John Wiley & Sons, 2003

...about 70 per cent of us will be a parent. ibid

...an average of 85 'face-to-face' minutes a day. ibid

...like their children to be electronically tagged. ibid

...parents now consult a doctor on average 24 times. ibid

...what the sociologist Frank Furedi calls 'paranoid parents'. Furedi F, Paranoid Parenting, Allen Lane, 2001

...the average stood at 1.73. 'Live Births', Office for National Statistics, May 13, 2004, www.statistics.gov.uk/CCI/nugget.asp?ID=369&Pos=3&ColRank=1&Rank=374

...where woman, on average, have just over seven children. 'Data Finder', Population Reference Bureau, www.prb.org/datafind/prjprbdata/wcprbdata4.asp?DW=DR&SL=&SA=1

...parents now spend, on average, £2,382 on equipment. 'Parents spend £2,000 on baby's first year', The Scotsman, January 6, 2004

...looked at the active compounds in common suncreams. 'Throw out the bath water?', The Guardian, May 8, 2004

...Professor Nigel Brown from St George's Hospital, London, explained to the Guardian. ibid

...hairdressers who regularly handle bleaches. ibid

...pregnant women may want to avoid birch and wintergreen. ibid

...Spotlight: Family celebrations. 'Average cost of wedding tops £15,000', The Guardian, February 12, 2004; The Ecologist, Go M-A-D: Go Make a Difference – 365 Daily Ways to Save the Planet, Think Publishing, 2001; 'Christmas is coming…', The Ecologist, www.theecologist.org/article.html?article=217; 'Dreaming of a white Christmas?', Environment Agency press release, December 5, 2003, www.environment-agency.gov.uk/news/610962

...only two-thirds of UK mothers breastfeed. 'Do try this at home', The Guardian, August 12, 2004

...recommends that babies are breastfed for at least two years. 'Global Strategy on Infant and Young Child Feeding', World Health Organisation, 2001, www.who.int/nut/inf.htm

...eight million disposable nappies are discarded every day in the UK. 'Nappy Facts', Women's Environmental Network, 2004, www.wen.org.uk/rnw/nappy_facts.htm

...using disposable nappies produces one tonne of nappy waste. 'Nappies', The Guardian, February 16, 2004

...eight per cent of landfill sites are filled with nappies. Oral evidence given by Ray Georgeson, director of policy and communications of the Waste & Resources Action Programme, to the House of Commons Select Committee on Environment, Food and Rural Affairs, January 29, 2003, www.publications.parliament.uk/pa/cm200203/cmselect/cmenvfru/385-i/3012910.htm

...taxpayers spend 10p disposing of them. 'Do try this at home', The Guardian, August 12, 2004

...still prefer the convenience of disposable nappies. 'Nine out of ten mothers prefer disposable nappies', Absorbent Hygiene Products Manufacturers Association press release (AHPMA), March 04, www.nappyinformationservice.co.uk/AHPMA_press_statement_04mar04.htm

...twice the impact on the environment as home-laundered nappies. 'Nappy Facts', Women's Environmental Network, 2004, www.wen.org.uk/rnw/nappy_facts.htm

...washable nappies...can save parents up to £500 per child. ibid

...up to 80 per cent of a modern nappy is biodegradable. 'Environment', Nappy Information Service, www.nappyinformationservice.co.uk/environment.htm

...$600 billion of consumer spending each year. Linn S, Consuming Kids: The Hostile Takeover of Childhood, The New Press, 2004

...now watches the equivalent of 217 adverts a week. 'Stars should fight child obesity, says FSA', The Guardian, March 9, 2004

...a report in the Lancet in 2004. 'Is television destroying our children's minds?', The Guardian, July 21, 2004

...sees 40,000 television adverts a year. Linn S, Consuming Kids: The Hostile Takeover of Childhood, The New Press, 2004

...television viewing among toddlers and attention deficit and hyperactivity disorder. 'Is television destroying our children's minds?', The Guardian, July 21, 2004

...the American Academy of Pediatrics now gives the following advice. 'Television and the Family', American Academy of Pediatrics, www.aap.org/family/tv1.htm

...be allowed to watch television only in moderation. 'Is television destroying our children's minds?', The Guardian, July 21, 2004

...cannot understand the persuasive intent of advertising. Linn S, Consuming Kids: The Hostile Takeover of Childhood, The New Press, 2004

...Internal research within the US marketing industry. ibid

...children would nag on average nine times before they gave up. ibid

...a National Playday survey. 'We can't go to the park because parents have a go at us', The Guardian, August 6, 2003

...children in Cumbria raised £100,000. ibid

...115 'No Ball Games' signs. ibid

...Dilemma: What should I think about during sex? 'Water changes may force sewage works to clear birth pill hormone', The Guardian, March 18, 2002; 'Safety of Nonoxynol-9 when used for contraception', WHO, October 2001, www.who.int/reproductive-health/rtis/nonoxynol9.html; 'Clean Sex, Wasteful Computers and Dangerous Mascara', E: The Environmental Magazine, March–April 2003, www.emagazine.com; 'Foster carer shortage hits "critical" level', The Guardian, August 24, 2004

...in 2002 it stood at 39.3. 'Octogenarians set to treble in 50 years', The Guardian, July 29, 2004

...will treble over the next half century. ibid

...by 2050 the UK will be three million short of the number of "informal" carers. 'Elderly care costs "to increase"', The Guardian, May 7, 2004

...it is costing its constituents £1 billion a year. 'Long-term care: the issue explained', The Guardian, February 6, 2004

...who perform 70 per cent of all longterm care. 'Elderly care costs "to increase"', The Guardian, May 7, 2004

...save society an estimated £57 billion a year. 'Carers are missing millions', Carers UK press release, December 14, 2003, www.carersuk.org/Newsandcampaigns/ Newsreleases/Carersaremissingmillions

...63 per cent of people in the UK. 'Beanpole families sprout social change', The Guardian, January 30, 2003

...count between 37 and 246 blood relatives living close by. 'Home alone? No, planning a party', The Observer, July 4, 2004

...launched an investigation into the practices of the £9 billion care-home market. 'OFT to examine price transparency in the care homes sector', Office of Fair Trading, March 3, 2004, www.oft.gov.uk/news/ press+releases/2004/35-04.htm

...estimates that the average dog costs £9,996. 'Expensive things fur coats', The Observer, May 2, 2004

...[RSPCA] picks up around 150,000 discarded pets a year. 'How to buy: Pets', The Guardian, April 23, 2002

...105,349 stray dogs. 'Facts and Figures', Dogs Trust, www.dogstrust.org.uk/main.asp?structureid=607

...'represents a safe and reliable method of pet identification'. Journal of Small Animal Practices, Vol 41, May 2000

...'prevents future tail injuries'. 'Information on dog tail docking provided for the Animal Welfare Division: A review of the scientific aspects and veterinary opinions relating to tail docking in dogs', Department for Environment, Food and Rural Affairs, October 2002, www.defra.gov.uk/animalh/welfare/domestic/ awbillconsulttaildocking.pdf

...according to Dr Hellmuth Wachtel. 'Evangelizing Canine Genetic Diversity', Working Dogs Cyberzine, November 1998, www.workingdogs.com/doc0192.htm

...'many pedigrees, if you know how to read them'. Lamb Free J, Training Your Retriever, Putnam, 1991

...a pet-food manufacturer, conducted a survey of 672 pet owners. 'UK Cats Face Diabetes Epidemic', UK Pets, August 12, 2004, www.ukpets.co.uk/? section=Home&sub=News&method=fetch&item=784

...is estimated to occur in 25 per cent of dogs. 'New Dietary Guidelines Issued for Cats and Dogs', The National Academies' National Research Council, September 8, 2003, www4.nationalacademies.org/ news.nsf/isbn/0309086280?OpenDocument

...and has been linked to a rise in feline diabetes. 'UK cats face diabetes epidemic', UK Pets, August 12, 2004, www.ukpets.co.uk/?section=Home&sub =News&method=fetch&item=784

Dilemma: Dwarf crocodile or Doberman? 'Consultation launched on dangerous exotic pets', Defra, June 29, 2004, www.defra.gov.uk/news/latest/ 2004/290604wildanimal.htm; 'For the love of a llama', The Guardian, August 14, 2004; RSPCA Policies on Animal Welfare, RSPCA, revised 2003; 'Cash Strapped Charity Squanders Over a Million Pounds on a Witch Hunt', Federation of British Herpetologists, January 24, 2003, www.f-b-h.co.uk/fbhprsquander.htm; 'Salmonella Information', Proteus Reptile Trust,

www.proteus.uk.net/info.php?id=41&cat=7; Author conversation with Mammal Society press officer, October 2004; 'Report on the Welfare of Non-Domesticated Animals Kept for Companionship', The Companion Animal Welfare Council, June 12, 2003, www.cawc.org.uk/CAWCNDAreport.pdf

...In 2001, the Guardian reported. 'Green revolution waged after death', The Guardian, April 17, 2000

...an eco-friendly vicar hit the headlines. 'Vicar's plea for green funerals', BBC News Online, June 1, 2003, news.bbc.co.uk/1/hi/england/lancashire/2953798.stm

...Every year in the UK 600,000 coffins are made from chipboard, wood or MDF. 'First Forest Stewardship Council Certified Coffins Produced', Forest Stewardship Council, March 14, 2002, www.fsc-uk.info/news_item.asp?news_id=25

...89 per cent are of the chipboard variety. 'Good buy: The Ecopod', The Observer, August 22, 2004

...investigated the sharp increase in funeral prices in the past decade. 'The Natural Death Handbook 4th edition', Natural Death Centre, www.ac026.dial.pipex.com/ naturaldeath/funeraltradesurvey2003.htm

...coffin maker JC Atkinson & Son, which produces around 60,000 coffins. 'First Forest Stewardship Council Certified Coffins Produced', Forest Stewardship Council, March 14, 2002, www.fsc-uk.info/news_item.asp?news_id=25

...about 70 per cent of funerals in the UK. 'National Cremation Statistics 1960–2003', Cremation Society of Great Britain, www.srgw.demon.co.uk/CremSoc4/ Stats/National/2003/StatsNat.htm

...cremation was revived in the UK in the late 1800s. 'History of Modern Cremation in Great Britain from 1874: The First Hundred Years', Cremation Society of Great Britain, www.srgw.demon.co.uk/CremSoc/ History/HistSocy.html#introduction

...crematoria release up to 16 per cent of the UK's total mercury emissions. 'Action on Crematoria Mercury', BBC New Online, May 9, 2003, http://news.bbc.co.uk/1/hi/health/3013049.stm

Chapter 6: Community

...to join a community association than we are today. 'Why do we do this?', We Are What We Do, 2004, www.wearewhatwedo.org/page.aspx?page=whyarewe

...'living alone and have no weekly contact with neighbours, friends or relatives'. 'Home Alone', Demos, 2004, www.demos.co.uk/catalogue/homealonebook

...32 elderly people die unnoticed, at home, alone. 'Generation of Swinging Singles Growing Old – And Lonely', Global Action on Aging, July 20, 2004, www.globalaging.org/elderrights/world/2004/ swinging.htm

...17 per cent...of those over 65 can be classified as socially isolated. 'Independent lives lead to loneliness', WRVS, June 30, 2004, www.wrvs.presscentre.com/corp/releases/release.asp? releaseid=1758&NID=Press%20Releases

...'a kind of famine of warm interpersonal relations'. 'The politics of happiness', New Economics Foundation Report, 2002, www.neweconomics.org/gen/uploads/ 4bnnmjil4o4jbn45fbqbtgi219112003184915.pdf

...46 per cent of respondents thought their area had 'a lot of community spirit'. 'Creating Sustainable Communities', Office of the Deputy Prime Minister, 1997/98, www.odpm.gov.uk/stellent/groups/odpm_ housing/documents/page/odpm_house_604674.hcsp

...in his book The Fifth Discipline. Senge P, The Fifth Discipline, Currency, 1994

...'critical for societies to prosper economically and for development to be sustainable'. 'What is social

capital?', The World Bank, March 29, 2004, www.worldbank.org

...'building a community is very like weaving'. Lewis J & Randolph-Horn E, 'Faiths, Hope and Participation: Celebrating Faith Groups' Role in Neighbourhood Renewal', New Economics Foundation, September 2001, www.neweconomics.org

...2.5 million British people were reported. 'Monitoring Poverty and Social Exclusion', Joseph Rowntree Foundation Report, 2001/2002; Gordon D, Poverty and Social Exclusion in Britain, York Publishing Services Ltd, 2002

...people without qualifications are three times less likely. ibid

...permanently excluded from school in 2001/2000. ibid

...the Economic & Social Research Council revealed the results of its research programme. 'The art of happiness – Is volunteering the blueprint for bliss?', The Economic & Social Research Council, September 20, 2004, www.esrc.ac.uk

...were put up in gay and lesbian bars. 'A call to all', The Guardian, October 10, 2001

...the National Mentoring Network and Volunteering England were awarded £800,000 in 2004. 'Volunteering Grants Will Boost Individuals' Impact in Communities', Home Office, 276/2004, August 25, 2004, www.homeoffice.gov.uk/n_story.asp?item_id=1059

...in 1990 the local Groundwork Trust in St Helens. 'Rebuilding the post-industrial landscape: interaction between landscape and biodiversity on derelict land', University of Manchester Centre for Urban and Regional Ecology, October 2000

...defines the connection between people and the land as a symbiotic relationship. 'Another Way of Being Human', The Trust for Public Land, 2002, www.tpl.org/tier3_cd.cfm?content_item_id=5482& folder_id=831

...in 2003 alone, across the UK 323 hectares of land. 'Environment Agency Action Earth', The Environment Agency, 2004, www.environment-agency.gov.uk/wed/677450/?lang=_e

...litter weighing as much as two double-decker buses was recycled. ibid

...20,000 wildflowers and 14,000 trees were planted. ibid

...estimated to be around £40 billion a year. 'Economic Value of Volunteering', Institute for Volunteering Research, 2004, www.ivr.org.uk/economic.htm

...time off to let them volunteer for local charities. 'Bosses told to encourage volunteering army', The Guardian, May 14, 2002

...1.5 million employees participated in employer-supported volunteering schemes. 'Business plays vital role in active community', Home Office, 308/2004, October 5, 2004, www.homeoffice.gov.uk/n_story.asp?item_id=1094

...the National Centre for Volunteering found that six out of 10 volunteers. 'Volunteering: the issue explained', The Guardian, June 5, 2002

...one of the best ways to increase employability. 'The Role of Volunteers in International Development', VSO, www.vso.org.uk/Images/position_papers_role_of_ volunteers_tcm8-1604.pdf

...feeling useful, according to the New Economics Foundation, is a basic human need. 'Time Banking: A Briefing', New Economics Foundation, March 2001, www.neweconomics.org/gen/uploads/doc_ 93200102134_Timebank.pdf

...a survey by TimeBank and the Ethnic Media Group. 'Step forward and step up', The Guardian, January 17, 2004

...BTCV was forced to suspend two-thirds of the work. 'Rise in insurance costs hits conservation charity's work', The Guardian, June 5, 2002

...Spotlight: Bartering your time. 'The changing face of volunteering', The Guardian, June 17, 2001

...Spotlight: Mentoring. 'The changing face of volunteering', The Guardian, June 17, 2001; Clutterbuck, D Developing Mentor Competencies, Clutterbuck Consultancy, 2003; 'The Impact and Outcomes of Mentoring', National Foundation for Educational Research, November 2000, http://nmn.org.uk/uploads/media/p_impact.pdf

Chapter 7: Money

...there's about £35 billion of cash in circulation. 'Bank return figures', Bank of England, October 13, 2004, www.bankofengland.co.uk/bankreturn/041013.pdf

...£2 trillion. 'Is the UK in debt danger?', BBC News Online, July 29, 2004, http://news.bbc.co.uk/1/hi/business/3932509.stm

...a widespread revival of institutional Islamic banking. For more information about Islamic banking visit www.islamic-banking.com

...ethical investments were valued at £4.2billion. 'Be charitable – all the way to the bank', The Guardian, June 26, 2004

...ten times higher than just a decade earlier. ibid

...two-thirds of people polled. ibid

...70 per cent of us regularly give to charity. 'Are we a nation of Scrooges?', The Guardian, November 22, 2003

...£12.93 a month. 'Why the widow's mite is an example to us all', The Observer, October 5, 2003

...average weekly salary passed £400. 'Pay in all regions tops £400 per week', Office of National Statistics, October 16, 2003, www.statistics.gov.uk/CCI/nugget.asp?ID=285&Pos=&ColRank=2&Rank=224

...60 per cent of total annual donations. 'The smart donor's guide to giving this Christmas ... and beyond', The Guardian, December 18, 2003

...£7.3 billion in 2002. 'Are we a nation of Scrooges?', The Guardian, November 22, 2003

...most popular way to give to charity. ibid

...we currently borrow far more than the UK government. 'Is the UK in debt danger?', BBC News Online, July 29, 2004, http://news.bbc.co.uk/1/hi/business/3932509.stm

...exceeds the external debt of the whole of Africa and South America combined. ibid

...consumer debt passed the symbolic £1 trillion mark. ibid

...mortgages account for about 80 per cent of this sum. ibid

...total debt increased from 54 per cent. 'How I kicked the debt habit', BBC News Online, September 8, 2003, http://news.bbc.co.uk/1/hi/business/3167407.stm

...6.1 per cent of earnings. 'Is the UK in debt danger?', BBC News Online, July 29, 2004, http://news.bbc.co.uk/1/hi/business/3932509.stm

...areas Ethical Information Research Services investigates. Author conversation with EIRIS press office, October 2004. For more information about how it researches companies, contact EIRIS (www.eiris.org, tel: 020 7840 5700)

...the highest rated area of concern was the environment. 'CIS launches door-to-door ethics', CIS press release, September 28, 2004, www.cis.co.uk/servlet/Satellite?cid=1053329505221&pagename=Smile%2FNCView&cpid=1096960542119&c=Page

...FTSE4Good Index. 'FTSE4Good index series', FTSE4Good, www.ftse.com/ftse4good

...an investment in 1984 of £100 would have matured into £769.80. 'A fund of goodwill and great growth', The Observer, May 9, 2004

...outperformed mainstream funds by almost 10 per cent from 1999 to 2004. 'Ethical investment "gains momentum"', The Guardian, June 2, 2004

...if an investor had saved £50 a month. 'Rake in the rewards and keep your conscience clear', The Observer, November 2, 2003

...the Association of British Insurers produced research. 'Going green is proving to be the best policy', The Guardian, March 6, 2004

...Cafédirect...raised £5 million. 'The Cafédirect share issue is now fully subscribed', Cafédirect, May 28, 2004, www.cafedirect.co.uk/news.php/000087

...over £7 million since its launch. 'Be charitable – all the way to the bank', The Guardian, June 26, 2004

...as stated in the Credit Union Act 1979. Financial Services Authority, www.fsa.gov.uk/credit_union

...'to provide for themselves against adversity and ill health'. 'Our story', National Savings & Investments, www.nsandi.com/about

...a sum estimated to be well in excess of £1 trillion. 'Retirement cash gets the green light', The Guardian, June 7, 2003

...the US-based 'Vice Fund'. All fund performance information taken from www.vicefund.com

...extract from the Vice Fund prospectus. Vice Fund Prospectus, July 30, 2004, www.vicefund.com/docs/ViceProspectus.pdf

...spawned a book. Ahrens D, Investing in Vice: The Recession-Proof Portfolio of Booze, Bets, Bombs, and Butts, St Martin's Press, 2004

...outperformed the FTSE4Good index by 13 per cent. 'Sinners set to feel the heat', The Guardian, May 28, 2002. Further 'Sindex' analysis is available from Money Observer (www.moneyobserver.com, tel: 0870 870 1324)

...Money Portal was reported to be looking at started its own 'vice fund'. 'Advisers urged to pass on the green message', The Guardian, July 3, 2004

...all the world's major religions encourage their faithful regularly to offer. 'Why the widow's mite is an example to us all', The Observer, October 5, 2003

...70 per cent of people in the UK give regularly to charity. 'Are we a nation of Scrooges?', The Guardian, November 22, 2003

...the richest 20 per cent give 0.7 per cent. 'Campaign Review 2001–04', Giving Campaign, May 2004, www.givingcampaign.org.uk/images/uploaded/campaign_review.pdf

...a survey by the British Heart Foundation. 'Are we a nation of Scrooges?', The Guardian, November 22, 2003

...twice as much over the Christmas period. ibid

...one fifth of the total income. 'CAF launches Charity Trends 2004', Charities Aid Foundation press release, June 30, 2004, www.cafonline.org/news/default.cfm

...the most popular charities with donors. 'Britain's favourite charities announced', Charities Aid Foundation press release, June 18, 2003, www.cafonline.org/news/pr/2003/pr20030625%5F21.cfm

...losing out on £395 million. 'Charities lose £395m in tax perks', The Guardian, February 11, 2004

...35 per cent of US employees. 'Campaign Review 2001–04', Giving Campaign report, May 2004, www.givingcampaign.org.uk/images/uploaded/campaign_review.pdf

...David Gilmour from Pink Floyd famously employed. 'Rock star gives £3m to homeless', The Guardian, May 21, 2003

...Fewer than one in 20 people leave money. 'Everyone can leave the world a better place', Remember a Charity, www.rememberacharity.org.uk

Chapter 8: Work

...the average number of hours a week that we now work is at an all-time low. 'Britons working shorter weeks', The Guardian, September 16, 2004

...at about 35 hours. ibid

...25 minutes getting to work. 'Usual time taken to travel to work: by gender', Social Trends 31, Office for National Statistics, Autumn 1999, www.statistics.gov.uk/STATBASE/ssdataset.asp?vlnk=3482

...lunch hour which now lasts, on average, 27 minutes. 'Lunch is for wimps, survey finds', The Guardian, July 15, 2004

...a report in 2004 by the thinktank Future Foundation. 'The Shape of Things to Come', The Future Foundation, September 2004, www.futurefoundation.net/Mint_pressrelease_Sep04.html

...one or both parents now work 'atypical' hours. 'The influence of atypical working hours on family life', The Joseph Rowntree Foundation, September 2002, www.jrf.org.uk/knowledge/findings/socialpolicy/982.asp

...the number of days lost to 'stress' in the UK rose. 'New year, same grind', The Guardian, January 6, 2003

...now 60 times more days a year lost to stress than industrial action. ibid

...TUC-affiliated unions had 6,492,389 members. 'Details of Past Congresses', TUC website, www.tuc.org.uk/extras/Congresspresidents.pdf; author correspondence with TUC press office, September 23, 2004

...'We want a life, not just an escalator of higher living standards'. 'New year, same grind', The Guardian, January 6, 2003

...more than 70,000 hours of our life at work. 'Do the right thing', The Guardian, May 19, 2004

...43 per cent of jobseekers. ibid

...65 per cent of businesses would change. 'A map through the moral maze', The Guardian, January 24, 2004

...86 per cent is sent to landfill. 'Facts & Statistics', Bioregional,www.bioregional.com/programme_projects/pap_fibres_prog/lp4london/lpaper_facts.htm

...43 per cent of industrial forest use. ibid

...Worldwide consumption is predicted to double by 2020. ibid

...4.8 million tonnes of printing paper every year. ibid

...the 2.6 million tonnes of newsprint we use. 'A capacity for improvement', British Printer, December 2000, www.dotprint.com/fpaper/newsp00.htm

...some of the largest, and most widely used paper merchants. 'Paper Tiger, Hidden Dragon', Friends of the Earth, May 2001, www.foe.co.uk/resource/reports/paper_tiger_hidden_dragons.pdf

...it can be successfully recycled up to five or six times. Desai P, Bioregional solutions for living on one planet, Green Books for the Schumacher Society, 2002

...just 14 per cent of an imported paper loop. 'Facts & Statistics', Bioregional, www.bioregional.com/programme_projects/pap_fibre_prog/lp4london/lpaper_facts.htm

...four million tonnes of straw goes to waste in the UK each year. ibid

...increased paper consumption by 40 per cent. 'The bane and boon of information technology', State of the World, The Worldwatch Institute, 2004

...120 tonnes of steel would be saved each year. Scott, N, Reduce, Reuse, Recycle, Green Books, 2004

...Over 1 billion is now spent on green procurement. 'Green Public Procurement', European Commission website, May 17, 2004, http://europa.eu.int/comm/environment/gpp

...two million non-biodegradable toner cartridges are thrown away every year. 'Recycling directory', Cambridge Sustainable City, www.cambridge.gov.uk/sustainablecity/rt_next_7.html

...It takes 0.7 litres of oil to make a new cartridge. 'Recycle your printer cartridges: Trash for cash', Multiple Sclerosis Trust website, 2004, www.mstrust.org.uk/fundraising/recycling.jsp

...78 per cent of printer users. 'The great ink jet cartridge scandal', IT Week, March 6, 2003

...the performance difference between refilled and new branded cartridges was negligible. 'The Money of Colour', Which? Report, The Consumers' Association, September 2002

...redistributed more than £6 million worth of surplus. In Kind Direct website, August 3, 2004, www.inkinddirect.org/med_001_pres.htm

...50 per cent of managers would willingly exchange a week's holiday for better offices. 'Fun in the park', The Guardian, August 2, 2004

...80 per cent of people will experience back pain. 'BackFacts: Back pain affects most of us', Back Care website, 2000, www.backcare.org.uk/pages/f_pages/facts2000.php

...muscular skeletal disorders represent the leading cause of absence from work. 'Back in work', Health & Safety Executive, June 7, 2004, www.hse.gov.uk/msd/backpain/index.htm

...more than 1.1 million people in the UK suffer from RSI. 'Health and Safety Targets: how are we doing?', Supplement to the HSC Annual Report & HSC Accounts, Health & Safety Executive, 2001/2, www.hse.gov.uk/aboutus/reports/anrsupp.pdf

...UK at Work survey still found around 4.5 million workers. 'UK slogs around the clock', The Observer, September 12, 2004

...we work £23 billion worth of unpaid overtime. 'Fathers failing to take up paid paternity leave', The Guardian, July 27, 2004

...62 per cent of US employees. 'Always on the job, employees pay with health', New York Times, September 5, 2004

...53 per cent said that work left them feeling 'tired and overwhelmed'. ibid

...three-quarters of its member firms now offer some kind of flexible working arrangements. 'Do your home work', The Guardian, August 28, 2004

...the Netherlands and Denmark have both introduced systems of 'voluntary unemployment'. 'For centuries, the work ethic has kept us chained to our jobs and routines. But the play ethic will change all that', The Observer, October 22, 2000; Kane P, The Play Ethic, Macmillan, 2004

...80 per cent of the 400,000 eligible fathers would take up this entitlement. 'Fathers failing to take up paid paternity leave', The Guardian, July 27, 2004

...'teleworking' has liberated more than two million workers from the traditional office environment. 'Beyond the office', The Guardian, September 14, 2002

...female heads of departments earned more than their male counterparts. 'A new Deal', The Guardian, September 24, 2004

...18 per cent less than men. ibid

...Ageism in the workplace is also a worry. 'Diversity at work: when People mean business', The Guardian, June 21, 2004

...cost of replacing the average employee is £3,500. 'The costs of losing employees', BBC, October 25, 2000, http://news.bbc.co.uk/1/hi/business/989848.stm

..One in five people have been discouraged from applying for a job. ibid

...Time off due to stress-related illness has increased by 500 per cent since the 1950s. 'Micawber was right: Money doesn't buy happiness but poverty makes you miserable', The Guardian, October 25, 1998

...three million Britons are estimated to be on longterm sickness benefits. 'Benefit figures reveal stress on women workers', The Observer, September 12, 2004

...one in three adults of working age were on incapacity benefit. ibid

...rising from 32 per cent of claimants in 1995 to 40 per cent in 2004. ibid

...34 million days are lost to British industry through smoking. 'No wonder you want out!', No Smoking Day, 2004. www.nosmokingday.org.uk/downloads/photocopykit.pdf

...night workers in particular are susceptible to diabetes and obesity 'Tips for shift workers: How to eat, sleep and stay fit when you work unusual hours', CNN, June 18, 2004. www.cnn.com/HEALTH/library/HQ/01388.html

...91 per cent of survey respondents. 'Relax – it's only work: Longer working hours. Shorter lunch breaks. More stress. Is therapy the answer to the pressures of modern life?', The Guardian, April 19, 2004

...Dilemma: If we worked less, wouldn't we achieve more? 'Pay and conditions: what we get and what we want', The Observer, October 22, 2000; 'Britain's family revolution', The Guardian, August 17, 2004; 'For centuries, the work ethic has kept us chained to our jobs and routines. But the Play Ethic will change all that'. The Observer, October 22, 2000; Hodgkinson T, How to be Idle, Hamish Hamilton, 2004; 'NHS survey: hit squads move in as hospitals prepare to deal with limits on working hours', The Guardian, July 30, 2004; 'Management: work smarter, not harder', The Guardian, November 16, 2003

...50 per cent of all graduates surveyed. 'A map through the moral maze: students and graduates shouldn't underestimate their power to effect change by choosing an ethical employer', The Guardian, January 24, 2004

...£16 billion turnover and employs about 170,000 people. 'Do the Right Thing', The Guardian, May 19, 2004

...three-quarters of staff are satisfied with their jobs. ibid

...7.5 per cent in the preceding 12 months. ibid

...a surprising surge in the number of university applicants for degrees in the caring professions. ibid

...Applications for social work rose by 94.6 per cent. ibid

...UK-based corporations were named and shamed as top industrial polluters. 'EC names and shames worst industrial polluters', The Guardian, October 9, 2004

...Spotlight: Working in union. 'Trade Union Membership: estimates from the autumn 2003 Labour Force Survey', Department of Trade and Industry, 2003, www.statistics.gov.uk/articles/labour_market_trends/Trade_union_membership.pdf; 'Women see rise in union density', Labour Research Department, Sep 2003, www.lrd.org.uk/object.php3?pagid=4&objectid=21900; 'The 35 hour week is now a problem', The Guardian, August 9, 2004; 'The killer that lurks beneath: Asbestos in buildings poses the UK's biggest occupational health threat', The Guardian, October 16, 2004; 'Trade Union Membership 2003', Department of Trade and Industry, 2003. www.dti.gov.uk/er/emar/tum2003.pdf; '10 good reasons to join a union', UNISON, www.unison.org.uk/young/tengoodreasons.asp

Explainer: CSR

...Fifty per cent of FTSE100 companies now produce an annual CSR-related report. 'Push or pull for CSR reporting', Environcorp, www.environcorp.com/img/media/sustain_-_pushpull%5B1%5D.pdf

...21 per cent of large companies producing a full CSR report. ibid

...the government defines the role of CSR as. 'The Government's Sustainable Development Strategy: What does it mean for UK business?', Sustainable Development factsheets, April 26, 2004, www.sustainable-development.gov.uk/uk_strategy/factsheets/ukbus/index.htm

...by 2065 insuring the world against human-induced disasters could bankrupt the global economy. 'Facing up to the storm', Christian Aid, 2003, www.christianaid.org.uk/indepth/0307stor/facinguptothestorm.pdf

...DJSI companies with high levels of 'stakeholder engagement'. 'Statistics on...Stakeholder Engagement', Dow Jones Sustainability Indexes Newsletter, 1/2004, www.sustainability-index.com/djsi_pdf/news/QuarterlyNewsletter/DJSI_Newsletter_0401.pdf

...creating an £8 billion market in the process. 'Forget responsibilities, think opportunities', The Observer, July 4, 2004

...Friends of the Earth, even goes so far as to run a spoof. 'Friends of the Earth to give spoof award to 'planet ruiners' and voluntary groups', Ethical Corporation website, September 14, 2004, www.ethicalcorp.com/content_list.asp?m=s

...'Researchers have found no correlation between'. 'Corporate Codes of Conduct', BWZ Editorial, Better World website, www.betterworld.com/BWZ/9608/editor.htm

...almost half of British consumers now expect a company to demonstrate a commitment to social progress. 'Guess what? People do read CSR reports', Globescan CSR Montior Survey, April 22, 2004, www.globescan.com/news_archives/csr04_gri_PR.html

...44 per cent of the British public said that when buying a company's product. 'The Business Case for Corporate Responsibility', Arthur D Little, 2003, www.bitc.org.uk/docs/aurr_A4__The_Business_Case_2003.pdf

...over 50 per cent of those polled. 'Guess what? People do read CSR reports', Globescan CSR Montior Survey, April 22, 2004, www.globescan.com/news_archives/csr04_gri_PR.html

INDEX

Main references are indicated in bold type.